MW01068815

Volume 9

The Broadman Bible Commentary

EDITORIAL BOARD

BROADMAN PRESS · Nashville, Tennessee

The
Broadman
Bible
Commentary

Volume 9

Luke - John

Dewey Decimal classification: 220.7
Library of Congress catalog card number: 78–93918
Printed in the United States of America

Preface

THE BROADMAN BIBLE COMMENTARY presents current biblical study within the context of strong faith in the authority, adequacy, and reliability of the Bible as the Word of God. It seeks to offer help and guidance to the Christian who is willing to undertake Bible study as a serious, rewarding pursuit. The publisher thus has defined the scope and purpose of the COMMENTARY to produce a work suited to the Bible study needs of both ministers and laymen. The findings of biblical scholarship are presented so that readers without formal theological education can use them in their own Bible study. Footnotes and technical words are limited to essential information.

Writers have been carefully selected for their reverent Christian faith and their knowledge of Bible truth. Keeping in mind the needs of a general readership, the writers present special information about language and history where it helps to clarify the meaning of the text. They face Bible problems—not only in language but in doctrine and ethics—but avoid fine points that have little bearing on how we should understand and apply the Bible. They express their own views and convictions. At the same time, they present alternative views when such are advocated by other serious, well-informed students of the Bible. The views presented, therefore, cannot be regarded as the official position of the publisher.

This COMMENTARY is the result of many years' planning and preparation. Broadman Press began in 1958 to explore needs and possibilities for the present work. In this year and again in 1959, Christian leaders—particularly pastors and seminary professors—were brought together to consider whether a new commentary was needed and what shape it might take. Growing out

of these deliberations in 1961, the board of trustees governing the Press authorized the publication of a multivolume commentary. Further planning led in 1966 to the selection of a general editor and an Advisory Board. This board of pastors, professors, and denominational leaders met in September, 1966, reviewing preliminary plans and making definite recommendations which have been carried out as the COMMENTARY has been developed.

Early in 1967, four consulting editors were selected, two for the Old Testament and two for the New. Under the leadership of the general editor, these men have worked with the Broadman Press personnel to plan the COMMENTARY in detail. They have participated fully in the selection of the writers and the evaluation of manuscripts. They have given generously of time and effort, earning the highest esteem and gratitude of Press employees who have worked with them.

The selection of the Revised Standard Version of the Bible text for the COMMENTARY was made in 1967 also. This grew out of careful consideration of possible alternatives, which were fully discussed in the meeting of the Advisory Board. The adoption of an English version as a standard text was recognized as desirable, meaning that only the King James, American Standard, and Revised Standard Versions were available for consideration.

The King James Version was recognized as holding first place in the hearts of many Christians but as suffering from inaccuracies in translation and obscurities in phrasing. The American Standard was seen as free from these two problems but deficient in an attractive English style and wide current use. The Revised Standard retains the accuracy and clarity of the American Standard and has a pleasing style and a growing use. It thus enjoys a strong advantage over each of the others, making it by far the most desirable choice.

Throughout the COMMENTARY the treatment of the biblical text aims at a balanced combination of exegesis and exposition, admittedly recognizing that the nature of the various books and the space assigned will properly modify the application of this approach.

The general articles appearing in Volumes 1, 8, and 12 are designed to provide background material to enrich one's understanding of the nature of the Bible and the distinctive aspects of each Testament. Those in Volume 12 focus on the implications of biblical teaching in the areas of worship, ethical duty, and the world mission of the church.

The COMMENTARY avoids current theological fads and changing theories. It concerns itself with the deep realities of God's dealings with men, his revelation in Christ, his eternal gospel, and his purpose for the redemption of the world. It seeks to relate the word of God in Scripture and in the living Word to the deep needs of persons and to mankind in God's world.

Through faithful interpretation of God's message in the Scriptures, therefore, the COMMENTARY seeks to reflect the inseparable relation of truth to life, of meaning to experience. Its aim is to breathe the atmosphere of life-relatedness. It seeks to express the dynamic relation between redemptive truth and living persons. May it serve as a means whereby God's children hear with greater clarity what God the Father is saying to them.

Abbreviations

BBC – *Broadman Bible Commentary*
fn. – footnote
Gr. – Greek
IDB – *Interpreter's Dictionary of the Bible*
LXX – Septuagint
marg. – marginal reading in RSV
NEB – New English Bible
RSV – Revised Standard Version
TDNT – *Theological Dictionary of the New Testament*
TEV – Today's English Version

Contents

Luke

MALCOLM O. TOLBERT

Introduction

I. The Literary Unity of Luke and Acts

Luke and Acts were written by the same man. This opinion is so widely held and is so incontrovertible that it is unnecessary to defend it here. Style, vocabulary, characteristic motifs, and development according to a unifying plan are signs of a common authorship to be detected in every section of both books. Together, they set forth the two phases of redemptive history outlined in Luke 24:46–47, one fulfilled in the life of Jesus and the other in the mission of the church. By the use of established literary devices the author indicated that Luke and Acts were two parts of the same work. These include the reference in Acts 1:1 to the preceding volume, the address of both to Theophilus, and the overlapping sections at the end of the third Gospel and the beginning of Acts.

The nature of the relationship between Luke and Acts must be taken into consideration in any study of either volume. Both arise out of the same life situation and are shaped from the same theological perspective. The purpose or purposes of each must be defined in the context of the total work. Characteristic motifs are common to both volumes. The Gospel presents the story of what "Jesus began to do and teach" (Acts 1:1), whereas Acts describes the evolution of the elements inherent in that beginning. Thus, themes that might otherwise seem minor or even go undetected in the Gospel are given their full significance in Acts.

II. The Author

Although a tag identifying the author was probably attached to the original manuscript, the third Gospel is anonymous in the form which has come down to us. The superscription is representative of the tradition which unanimously ascribes both the Gospel and Acts to Luke, the physician and associate of Paul. We can begin to document this tradition definitely from the time of Irenaeus (*ca.* A.D. 180), who says that Luke composed his work after the death of Paul. The Muratorian Canon, representing the opinion of the church in Rome toward the end of the second century, also witnesses to Lukan authorship. The "anti-Marcionite" prologue to the Gospel gives some interesting additional details about Luke. Although its historical value is subject to question, some of the information may be rooted in fact. According to this witness, Luke was a Syrian of Antioch, a physician by profession, and a companion of Paul, after having been first a follower of the apostles. The prologue also states that he lived unmarried until his death, composed the Gospel in Achaia, and died at the age of 84 in Boeotia.

The only unquestionably reliable data about Luke are the notices found in the New Testament itself (Col. 4:14; Philemon 24; 2 Tim. 4:11). Three facts about him emerge from the meager material. (1) He was a Gentile. This conclusion is based on Colossians 4:10–11, where Luke's name is not included among the "men of the circumcision" who were companions of Paul in his imprisonment. (2) He was a physician. (3) He was an associate of Paul. These three items of information should be corroborated by the internal evidence of Luke-Acts if the traditional attribution of the work to Luke is correct.

1. Was the author a Gentile? The evidence has led the great majority of scholars to believe that he was. The preface to the Gospel indicates that his self-identification is with Hellenistic litterateurs. His command of the Greek language puts him with the author to the Hebrews at the forefront of New Testament writers in this regard. With the exception of a few uses of "amen" he avoids the Semitic words completely. The Evangelist betrays his non-Palestinian, Hellenistic background at many points as, for example, in 6:47 f.; 8:16; 11:33; 12:54; 13:19. The tendency to omit references to conflicts over matters of Jewish law also points to a Gentile author.

Of course, his selection of materials and writing style are influenced to some extent by the background of the Hellenistic Gentiles for whom the work is intended. But one gets the general impression that he is addressing people whose racial and cultural heritage he shares.

2. Was the author of Luke-Acts a physician? The time was when respected New Testament scholars were convinced that they had established an indisputably affirmative answer to this question. W. K. Hobart [1] concluded from his investigations that the case for the medical vocation of the author was clearly proven. He based his conclusions on studies of parallels between the medical terminology of the Lukan writings and that of Greek physicians, such as Galen, Hippocrates, Discorides, and Aretaeus. To prove the case, however, it is also necessary to show that Greek physicians employed a terminology distinctly different from that of nonmedical writers, which Hobart failed to take into consideration. H. J. Cadbury [2] exposed this fallacy in Hobart's methodology when he demonstrated that Lukan medical expressions were also found in the LXX, Josephus, Plutarch, and Lucian. The truth is that no specifically technical medical vocabulary existed in the ancient world, the use of which would sharply distinguish the specialist from the knowledgeable layman.

Nevertheless, it is unfair to dismiss peremptorily the third Evangelist's apparent interest in and knowledge of medicine. He does make accurate use of terminology employed by physicians in a number of passages (4:38; 5:18,31; 7:10; 8:44; 21:34; Acts 5:5,10; 9:40). Moreover, Luke's omission of Mark's damaging reference to the medical profession (cf. Mark 5:26 and Luke 8:43) may be an especially significant clue to the author's bias.

In conclusion, while internal evidence of Luke-Acts does not prove anything definitely about the author's profession, a number of references are congenial to the tradition that he was a physician.

3. Was the author a companion of Paul? This is the crucial question and the one over which scholarly opinions diverge most widely. Supporters of the traditional position call attention to the affinity between certain characteristic Lukan features in the third Gospel and important Pauline emphases. Among these are the universal note (4:27; 24:47), the emphasis on joy (1:14; 2:10; 10:17,20; etc.), the concern for sinners (15:1 ff.), and the use of some words and expressions found elsewhere in the New Testament only in Paul.[3]

On the other hand, it has been maintained that Luke's concept of the meaning of Jesus' death differs so markedly from Paul's as to rule out the possibility of a close relationship between the two. In the

---

[1] *The Medical Language of St. Luke* (Dublin: Hodges, Figgis and Co., 1882).

[2] *The Beginnings of Christianity*, ed. E. J. Foakes-Jackson and Kirsopp Lake (London: Macmillan, 1942), II, 349–55.

[3] Sir John Hawkins, in *Horae Synopticae* (Oxford: Clarendon, 1899), gives a list of 101 words from Pauline epistles found elsewhere in the NT only in Luke-Acts (p. 198 f.).

third Gospel the crucifixion is presented as a divine necessity, prerequisite to Jesus' exaltation (9:22; 24:26), and is not given the redemptive significance that Paul accords to it. Also we note two particularly important omissions: Mark 10:45 is not found in Luke; neither are the words "which is poured out for many" (Mark 14:24; Luke 22:17 f.). Nevertheless, the view that Luke-Acts was written by an associate of Paul is not seriously threatened by arguments based on evidence from the Gospel. The major problems arise with reference to the book of Acts.

An inquiry into the authorship of Luke-Acts revolves around two basic questions: (1) Who wrote the diary sections of Acts? And, (2) did the same man write the rest of Luke-Acts? The diary or so-called "we" sections of Acts (16:10–17; 20:5—21:18; 27:1—28:16) are marked by two distinctive characteristics: the narrative begins abruptly to be told in the first person plural, and it is characterized by an unusual precision of detail. The first-person quality of the account leaves little doubt that these sections are based on the personal experiences of a companion of Paul. The meager available evidence points to Luke as a likely author of these passages. That is, it can be demonstrated that Luke was probably with Paul during the periods referred to in the "we" sections, whereas some of Paul's other associates must be ruled out.

Furthermore, the "we" sections are marked by the style and characteristic vocabulary of the other portions of Luke-Acts. The same man put all of it in final form. Now, if that man were not the author of the diary sections, we are faced with an unusual phenomenon. He worked this material over so carefully as to make it his own, marked in every part by his distinctive literary style. At the same time, he committed the most unusual oversight of failing to change the personal pronoun— not once, but several times.

Nor can we solve the problem by the conjecture that "we" is a deliberate device, adopted by the author to give a more authentic ring to his narrative. "We" appears in such an artless fashion that it can hardly have been a contrived ploy. A more natural assumption is that the author of the diary sections is also the author of Luke-Acts, who unconsciously retained the "we" at the points where he was a personal participant in the events. In this case, the author could well have been Luke.

Add to this the fact that Luke is one of those minor, almost faceless figures of the New Testament. He would go unnoticed if he were not named by tradition as the author of a considerable portion of the New Testament. Such a person would hardly have been chosen for this role if there had not been some basis in fact for connecting his name to Luke and Acts.[4]

Nevertheless, many scholars argue that Luke could not have written Luke-Acts because of the wide divergence in theological viewpoint between Acts and the Pauline epistles on such crucial matters as soteriology, Christology, eschatology, and the law. They also see in Acts a changed and later concept of the church, the portrait of a Paul subservient to the Jewish Christian community and its leaders, and a failure to emphasize Paul's apostolic authority.

More serious than any of these, however, are the differences in data which can be seen by comparing the Acts account of Paul's experiences from conversion through the Jerusalem Conference (Acts 9:1 ff.; 15:1 ff.) with the autobiographical data of the letters, especially Galatians 1:11— 2:10. A special problem attaches to the resolution of the Jerusalem Conference reported in Acts 15:19–21. This is often held to be inadmissible in the light of Paul's statement at Galatians 2:9–10.

Much of the criticism levelled against Lukan authorship is unconvincing because it is based on presuppositions that are not

4 A different point of view has been suggested by Cadbury. He conjectures that the attribution of Luke-Acts to Luke, a companion of Paul, arose as a logical conclusion based on the available data in Acts and the Epistles and that it began to be circulated in the second century (*Op. cit.*, II, 260 ff.; cf. *The Making of Luke-Acts*, pp. 351 ff.).

necessarily true. They require us to believe that Luke was a longtime associate of Paul, completely dominated by his point of view, fully equipped to appreciate his struggles and as emotionally involved in the fight against Jewish legalism.

So far as we can determine, Luke was not with Paul during the great crises reflected in the Galatian and Corinthian correspondence. He probably did not even know Paul until some time after the Jerusalem Conference, and, as a Gentile, was hardly as sensitive to the meaning of its decisions. The most serious problems for the traditional position occur in connection with events of this period when we suppose that Luke was not with Paul.

Also we should ask: What changes might have been wrought by the passing of three decades? The different political and social environment of the church, the contemporary exigencies of Christian discipleship, and the difficulty of working at a distance with events known through oral reports are some of the factors that could have entered into the creation of the problems with which scholars struggle. Furthermore, we are working with bits of evidence that do not tell the whole story.

We conclude, therefore, that the most satisfactory working hypothesis is that the author of the third Gospel was Luke the physician, one of Paul's associates during the latter part of his known ministry.

III. Sources

Luke was not a participant in the events described in the third Gospel (1:1–4). Because of this he was dependent for his information on sources. These may be divided conveniently into four categories: (1) Mark, (2) Q, (3) L, and (4) the birth and infancy narratives.

1. Mark. A widely accepted conclusion of New Testament critical studies is that Luke had access to and used extensively a copy of Mark substantially equivalent to the text that we possess. Approximately 300–350 verses of Luke's total of 1,119 or about 28 percent of the Gospel was derived from this source.

About 70 percent of the substance of Mark appears in Luke, mostly in large blocks, in keeping with Luke's tendency to use one source at a time. By way of contrast, Matthew conflated passages from his sources, weaving them together to form more or less homogeneous sections related to certain major themes.

Luke used considerably less of Mark than did Matthew. The controlling determinant in his failure to use all the material may have been lack of space. Nevertheless, in each case we must ask: Why this passage rather than another? In a number of instances the answer is apparently the fact that Luke had a similar passage which he preferred. Thus, Mark's account of the call of the first disciples (1:16–20) is replaced by the story found in Luke 5:1–11. The Beelzebul controversy (Mark 3:22–30) is not used because Luke possessed a version from Q (11:14–22). The same is true of the parable of the mustard seed (Mark 4:30 f.; cf. Luke 13:18–19), whose companion, the parable of the mysterious growth of the seed (Mark 4:26–29), is also missing. Other omitted Markan passages to which there are at least partial Lukan parallels are: Mark 6:1–6—Luke 4:16 ff.; Mark 10:1–12—Luke 16:18; Mark 11:12–14,20–25—Luke 13:6–9; Mark 12:28–34—Luke 10:25–28.

The request of the sons of Zebedee (Mark 10:35 ff.) is omitted because Luke tends to suppress material that shows the disciples in an unfavorable light. The failure to record the execution of John the Baptist (Mark 6:17 ff.) must be considered in connection with Luke's singular treatment of other Baptist passages (cf. Conzelmann, pp. 22 ff.).

The so-called "great omission" (Mark 6:45—8:26) constitutes a special case. Various explanations have been offered for the fact that Luke used nothing at all from this long passage. It has been argued that the section was missing from Luke's copy of Mark (Streeter, pp. 172 ff.), but this idea has not gained wide acceptance. The omission was most likely deliberate, resulting from a variety of motives: (1) Mark

6:45–52 is very similar to the story at Luke 8:22–25 (Mark 4:35 ff.). (2) Mark 6:53–56 is not used, probably (cf. Vincent Taylor, p. 91), because Luke thinks of Gennesaret as a lake rather than as a region. (3) Mark 7:1–23 tells of hostility between Jesus and Jewish leaders over points of Jewish law, the kind of passage avoided by Luke. (4) Mark 7:24–37 tells of a journey to Gentile lands and is, therefore, not in keeping with Luke's principle of confining Jesus' ministry to Jewish territory (Taylor, p. 91). (5) Mark 8:1–21 may be considered a doublet of Mark 6:35 ff. (Luke 9:12 ff.). (6) Mark 8:22–26 describes the cure of a blind man in such a way that it may have been thought to impugn Jesus' power to heal immediately and completely.

The Markan material determines the basic structure of the third Gospel. With the exception of four dislocations, Luke respects the Markan order.

Luke follows his source with a marked degree of fidelity, using as high as 68 percent of Mark's actual words in some passages. A large proportion of the alterations of Mark by Luke have little or no theological significance. He makes many changes in Markan passages with the intent of improving the language and style. All Aramaisms with the exception of *amēn* (six times) are rejected; a number of Latin barbarisms are translated into Greek terms; the historic present is eliminated except for one instance; more sophisticated expressions replace some of Mark's repetitious style; participles substitute for the first element of compound verbs connected by *kai* (and); connective particles are added in keeping with good Greek style; and variations are introduced which are designed to make the text clearer to Gentile readers. On the other hand, there is a paradox in Luke's style in that he often uses grammatical constructions and expressions which one would expect a Greek writer to avoid.[5]

---

[5] See Xavier Léon-Dufour, "The Synoptic Gospels," *Introduction to the New Testament*, ed. André Robert and André Feuillet (New York: Desclee, 1954), pp. 223 ff.

As noted above, some changes are the result of Luke's admiration for the earliest disciples (see, e.g., Mark 4:13—Luke 8:11; Mark 4:40—Luke 8:25; Mark 9:28 f. —Luke 9:43; etc.). Also, Luke's reverence for Jesus causes him to make certain alterations. For example, strong human emotions are not attributed to Jesus (e.g., Mark 1:41—Luke 5:13; Mark 3:5—Luke 6:10; Mark 6:34—Luke 9:11). He does not use Mark 3:19–21 where Jesus is said by his family to be "beside himself." Neither does he have the cry of desolation (Mark 15:34; cf. Luke 23:46).

2. Q. Many non-Markan passages in Luke are parallel to sections of Matthew. These are derived from another common source to which the designation Q has been given. Luke is indebted to Q for some 220–230 verses, or about 20 percent of the material of the third Gospel. Numerous Q passages in Luke are very similar to their parallels in Matthew—in some instances, verbatim. Also, there are places where the same order of passages is followed. This indicates that Q was a written Greek document of which both writers possessed a copy. Behind it lies an Aramaic original either written or oral. Q contained very few parables and no miracle stories, insofar as we can determine. (Luke 7:1 ff. is not classified usually as a miracle story.) There are also only one or two references to exorcisms in this material. Q consisted primarily of sayings of Jesus, preserved because they were relevant to the needs and problems faced by the Christian community. The original setting of many of these sayings was lost, and no attempt was made to supply the lack. For this reason the interpreter confronts special problems when he encounters in the text a series of sayings of Jesus with no real inner connection.

The exact extent of Q cannot be defined precisely. Both Matthew and Luke are thought to contain passages from Q without parallels in the other. Also, some of Q may not be found in either, although it is very unlikely that this would be a significant amount. Reverence for the sayings of Jesus worked against the omission of this kind of material.

Although such generalizations are misleading and dangerous, it is usually conceded that Luke tends to preserve the original order of Q and to reproduce the text in its more primitive form.

The following Lukan passages may be derived from Q: 3:7–9,16–17; 4:1–13; 6:20–49; 7:1–10,18–34; 9:57–60; 10:2–16, 21–24; and others.

3. Luke's Special Material. The bulk of the third Gospel is based on sources used by Luke alone. Some 530–580 verses, representing in excess of 50 percent of his total work, find no parallels in either Mark or Matthew. The symbol L is usually given to Luke's special material outside the first two chapters.

A glance at the following passages included in L will indicate how much poorer the Christian community would be without the third Gospel: 3:1–2,5–6,10–14,23–38; 4:14–30; 5:1–11; 6:24–26; 7:11–17,36–50; 8:1–3; 9:51–56,61–62; and others. When we discuss characteristic Lukan ideas we shall draw heavily from these passages. The interest in tax collectors, Samaritans, sinners, and women, as well as the Lukan concern for subjects like prayer and wealth, finds ample illustration in the L material.

Here also one finds the most numerous traces of the style and vocabulary of the editor-writer of the third Gospel. For this reason and because of the absence of any well-defined scheme of organization, we may conclude that the materials came to Luke piecemeal in oral form. They probably represent the results of his own personal investigations (cf. 1:3). These passages bear the mark of a Jerusalem tradition. If we can assume that Luke, the companion of Paul, was the author of the third Gospel, we may conclude that he acquired most of this special material during his stay in Caesarea after Paul's imprisonment. As a person with literary inclinations, he may have accumulated them in some sort of personal notebook against the day when they would be useful.

4. The birth and infancy narratives. The stories about the birth and childhood of John the Baptist and Jesus belong to Luke's special material, but their singular character demands that they be considered in a separate category.

The language in which these narratives are cast is very similar to that of the LXX (Greek translation of the O.T.). Because of the ease with which they can be translated into Hebrew, some scholars have advocated the thesis that the narratives are Greek translations of a Hebrew original. Still others have concluded that they were cast in their present form by Luke, who consciously produced them in the style of the LXX in order to emphasize the Hebrew environment in which they are set. This argument cannot be settled by the available evidence. What can be affirmed is that the unmistakable evidence of Lukan style is present in this section as it is in the rest of Luke-Acts. In other words, he put them into final form.

The material is presented as a series of connected narratives, which is in itself an unusual phenomenon in the Gospels. For the most part—the story of the passion being a significant exception—the sayings, stories, parables, etc., out of which the Gospels were formed circulated independently in small units, which scholars call pericopes, during the period of oral transmission.

The birth and infancy stories of Luke are centered in Jerusalem and probably came to him from the Jerusalem Christian community. They coincide with their Matthean counterparts with reference to the description of the parents of Jesus, the affirmation of the virgin birth, and the designation of Bethlehem as the place of the nativity and of Nazareth as the place where Jesus was reared.

IV. The Composition of Luke

One of the interesting questions about the third Gospel relates to the procedure used by the author in putting the materials from his various sources together. The main facts are as follows:

1. There are two opening chapters which are set apart from the rest of Luke by content, language, and style. If by some accident of history these chapters had been lost, no one could detect that anything was missing from the third Gospel.

2. Luke 3:1 ff. makes a very plausible beginning for the Gospel from a literary point of view. And, since the crucial events of the Gospel begin with the baptism of John (Acts 1:21–22), this is also a good beginning from the perspective of the early church's understanding of salvation-history.

3. The genealogy in Luke 3:23–38, is in a very unusual context if we are to suppose that chapters 1—2 belong to Luke from the very beginning. It would more naturally go with the account of the birth of Jesus, as in Matthew.

4. Mark is used primarily in large blocks. One long section of the second Gospel is not used at all.

5. Luke's story of the Last Supper and the passion (22:14 ff.) shows marked differences from Mark's account and appears to depend heavily on a different source.

6. Luke has his own source for the resurrection narratives which are set in Jerusalem and its environs. Mark, on the other hand, leads us to expect resurrection appearances in Galilee (16:7; cf. Luke 24:6–7), which is what we find in Matthew (28:16).

A number of outstanding scholars, notably B. H. Streeter (*The Four Gospels*) and Vincent Taylor (*Behind the Third Gospel*), have concluded that these phenomena are best explained by the hypothesis that an earlier, shorter gospel lies behind the present Gospel of Luke. To this they have given the name Proto-Luke. According to this theory, Proto-Luke was composed of the materials assigned to Q and L. It began with the historical notice of 3:1 f., followed by an account of the Baptist's ministry, Jesus' baptism, the genealogy, the temptation, and the rejection in Nazareth. It concluded with Luke's version of the passion and resurrection. Later, Luke ac-

quired a copy of Mark, which he inserted, primarily in blocks, into the Gospel already written. To this the birth and infancy narratives were prefixed. The Gospel was completed by the composition of a preface to serve as an introduction to the whole.

To begin with, no one has demonstrated satisfactorily that a document composed of Q plus L can be considered a viable composition intended for an independent existence. Furthermore, the structure of the Gospel indicates that we are not dealing with a secondary literary composition superimposed on an earlier work. For example, the references to the cessation of temptations by the devil in 4:13 and to his renewed activity in 22:3 have been shown to indicate the author's concept of the beginning and ending of Jesus' public ministry (Conzelmann, pp. 16, 28, 80.). In other words, these are key references, essential to the whole plan of Luke-Acts and fundamental clues to the author's understanding of salvation-history. Luke 4:13 is connected with a Q passage, while 22:3 is found in a Markan context.

The journey motif gives Luke the occasion for inserting the considerable section of rather heterogeneous Q and L passages (found in 9:51—19:27) into the framework of the ministry of Jesus. And it is to Mark's outline of Jesus' activities that Luke is indebted for this motif (Mark 10:1; 11:1).

The Nazareth episode, again a key passage in Luke-Acts, presupposes mighty works to be done in Capernaum (4:23). It is precisely the Markan narratives of miracles in Capernaum (Luke 4:31 ff.) which illustrate this reference. The preface to Acts describes the Gospel as an account of "all that Jesus began to *do* and teach." The third Gospel does in fact begin its presentation of Jesus' activities with a program of miracles in Capernaum and its environs (Mark). Only then does Luke, in contrast to Matthew, tell of the teaching ministry of Jesus in 6:12–49, a passage from Q.

These considerations justify the conclusion that Luke-Acts was constructed on a plan whose execution brought together the materials from Luke's sources in a kind of literary unity that virtually rules out the possibility of an earlier gospel.

V. The Date and Place of Writing

Luke must be placed between Mark and Acts, the first being a source and the second a later volume written by the same author (Acts 1:1). This means that the outside limits for dating the third Gospel are determined by the dating of Mark and Acts.

An early date, prior to A.D. 67, has been urged. Some would even place it before the Neronian persecution (A.D. 64). The arguments used to support an early date are based on what is considered to be the abrupt ending of Acts, the lack of references to the persecution under Nero, the failure to tell about the outcome of Paul's trial, and an unawareness of the destruction of Jerusalem.

These arguments are not convincing. A good case can be made for the position that Acts does not end abruptly but that it is brought to a dramatically appropriate and satisfactory conclusion.[6] Nor does Luke end his treatment of Paul any more abruptly than he does the account of Peter's activities, about whom we are also left with unanswered questions. There are also good arguments for maintaining that certain aspects of Luke are understandable only if it was written after the Neronian persecution and the Jewish-Roman War of A.D. 66-70.

On the other end of the spectrum Luke-Acts has been dated well into the second century. The most telling argument against a date much later than A.D. 90, however, is the writer's apparent unawareness of the Pauline epistles, which were becoming widely circulated by the end of the century.

A number of factors seem to require a date between A.D. 70 and 90. Among them are the following:

1. Mark is dated by most scholars at

[6] Cf. Frank Stagg, *The Book of Acts* (Nashville: Broadman, 1955), pp. 3 f.

about the time of the Neronian persecution, A.D. 64, which, if true, precludes an extremely early date for Luke.

2. Two passages in Luke can best be explained if the Gospel was written after the Jewish-Roman War. The description of the siege of Jerusalem in Luke 19:43-44 gives an accurate picture of that disastrous event as reported by contemporaries. It can also be argued on the other side that such a paragraph written after the war might be expected to contain more specific details. The more important passage is Luke 21:20 where Mark's apocalyptic reference to "the desolating sacrilege" is transformed into a statement about the siege of Jerusalem. Streeter's comment about this sums up the situation: "Seeing that in A.D. 70 the appearance of the Anti-Christ did *not* take place, but the things which Luke mentions *did*, the alteration is most reasonably explained as due to the author's knowledge of these facts" (p. 540).

3. Enough time needs to have elapsed to make Luke's treatment of the Parousia necessary (see below). This would seem to call for a time after the death of the first generation of Christian witnesses.

4. The polemic against the Jews is more logical if we assign Luke-Acts to a period after the gulf between Christianity and Judaism had widened to such an extent that a definitive breach had been established. The Jewish-Roman War was the point of no return in Jewish-Christian relations, because Jewish Christians refused to support the nationalistic messianism of their countrymen.

5. The political apologetic of Luke-Acts seems to come out of a period after the Christian movement had already experienced persecution due to a misunderstanding of its nature and motives. Nevertheless, there was still hope that the Roman government, rightly informed, could continue to be the kind of protective power that it is shown to be on various occasions in the book of Acts. The Neronian persecution fits these prerequisites.

On the other hand, the persecution during the time of Domitian probably effectively killed any hopes that the government would be the protector of the Christian movement. We would, therefore, date Luke between the persecutions under Nero and Domitian, or around A.D. 80–85.

The "anti-Marcionite" prologue to the Gospel states that it was written in Achaia, but this is probably no more than a guess. Various suggestions have been offered in more recent times—Rome, Caesarea, and Achaia—none of which can be supported adequately. It is both fruitless and pointless to speculate about the place of composition.

VI. The Purpose

Luke-Acts is similar to a symphony in that we can detect in it various themes which emerge again and again. One of these, it is true, may be the dominant one. Thus, writers have contended that the work must be understood, e.g., as a political polemic, an explanation of the Gentile mission, a defense against Gnosticism, or a definitive solution to the problem of a delayed Parousia. Perhaps the best that can be done in an introduction to the Gospel is to list some of the major concerns that apparently influenced the writer in his choice and adaptation of the materials which constitute the third Gospel.

1. The author wanted to tell a story that would faithfully present the events upon which the Gospel was based. Probably the multiplicity of sources then extant, both written and oral, were a challenge to him. His effort, as it appears, was to put the materials which he had encountered into logical sequence, encompassed in the scope of one volume. He also wished to add the indispensable sequel to the deeds and words of Jesus. This would then constitute a full record of what had been "accomplished" (1:1).

We think of the third Evangelist as a historian, but we must be careful not to judge him by the criteria of modern historiography. His affinity is with the writers of two millenia past, e.g., Polybius, Tacitus, and Josephus, and not with those of a more recent era. Furthermore, he writes as a Christian passionately committed to his point of view, rather than as a dispassionate, objective scientific observer. He, along with the other Evangelists, wrote "from faith for faith."

One of the fruits of modern scholarship has been a recovery of the proper perspective from which to approach the Gospels. They are theological documents and not "lives of Jesus." Nevertheless, this is theology rooted in history and for which the truth about what took place is extremely important. We can believe that it was no less important for Luke. The supreme truth for him was not, however, an objectively verifiable phenomenon. It was his conviction that Jesus of Nazareth was the exalted Lord of the church. From this perspective he approached his task as the recorder of a supremely significant chain of events.

2. He was interested in delineating the relationship between Christianity and Judaism. His treatment of the subject is determined by the wide gulf which separated the two at the time of his writing. This called for him (1) to establish the continuity between Christianity and Jewish redemptive history and (2) to show how the alienation between the two movements occurred.

In the Gospel it is made clear that Christianity began in the matrix of orthodox Judaism and that Jesus was the Messiah of Jewish expectation. The Temple in Jerusalem is the setting for the first episode of the Gospel; the people involved in it are described as impeccably orthodox and pious Jews. Zechariah was performing one of the most important rituals of Temple worship when the heavenly messenger appeared to him.

The stories of Jesus' infancy and childhood serve to link him with Judaism: (1) he is circumcised (2:21); (2) he is presented in the Temple (2:22–24); (3) Simeon and Anna, representatives of genuinely pious Jews, recognize Jesus as the expected Messiah (2:25–38); (4) Jesus is taken to Jerusalem at the age of twelve and, when discovered missing, is found talking to the rabbis in the Temple (2:41–50). Nothing is told of the early years in Nazareth, which may represent a limitation imposed on Luke by the lack of a source for such accounts. Nevertheless, it seems correct to conclude that the stories preserved for us are integral to the purpose of the writer.

In the body of the Gospel the continuity between Jesus and the promises of the Scriptures is affirmed (3:4–6). At the very outset it is made clear that the program of his ministry fulfills the prophetic requirement (4:18–19). At the conclusion of the Gospel the risen Lord tells his disciples that his experience should be understood as a fulfillment of all that had been written about him in the Scriptures (24:44–46).

Luke makes an effort to establish the fact that the gulf which existed in his day between Judaism and Christianity had not been created by Jesus and his followers. Indeed the opposite was really the case, according to the third Evangelist.

In the third Gospel Jesus begins his ministry by presenting himself to the inhabitants of his own hometown, i.e., to his own people, but they reject him. Luke is the only writer who portrays Jesus as weeping over Jerusalem (Luke 19:41–44). Jesus' words on that occasion are a poignant witness to his own desire for acceptance by his people. Thus, Jesus' attitude toward the nation is set in contrast to the rejection which he experienced.

Acts continues this theme, making it much more explicit, as Paul's efforts to win his countrymen continue to the very last. The rejection which he encounters is similar to that which Jesus experienced in Nazareth.

The Jews did not understand the Scriptures and reacted, therefore, against those developments which fulfilled them. Because of this, the Judaism of Luke's day had forfeited its heritage. The Christian community was the true Israel. In contrast to contemporary Judaism, it understood the Old Testament and was, in fact, the fulfillment of it. Luke seems to cast the Jews primarily in the role of troublemakers, responsible for the misunderstanding that others had of the Christian movement. They had contrived through their specious charges and the pressure exerted on Pilate to bring about the death of Jesus. This hostility was also directed against early Christians, especially the apostle Paul. Most of his difficulties with authorities were caused by false charges brought against him by his own people.

3. Luke wrote to prove that Christianity was no threat to the political authority of the Empire. If, as is very likely, Theophilus was a Roman official with a distorted concept of the political character of the Christian movement (see on 1:3), we shall understand the preface to Luke as an introduction to the political apologetic that runs throughout Luke-Acts. The recognition by Luke that the church might continue to exist in the context of the Empire for some time made it necessary for him to come to grips with the problem of the relationship between Christianity and the state (Conzelmann, p. 138).

The nonpolitical and even congenial nature of the church's message is expressed first of all in the admonitions of John the Baptist to servants of the Empire in the persons of tax collectors and soldiers (3:12–14). In both cases there is no suggestion that service to the state is wrong in itself.

Jesus sets forth his messianic program in terms which are easily seen to be apolitical. Throughout Luke-Acts the kingship of Jesus is defined in a way that does not constitute a threat to the Roman ruler.

The story of Zacchaeus the tax collector (19:1–10) also has political implications. Upon responding to the demands of the person of Jesus, Zacchaeus does not repudiate his profession; rather, he voices the intention of using his wealth for charity and of making amends for any exploitation of others.

The third illustration of the attitude expressed in Luke toward the payment of taxes is found in 20:19–26, where the question of tribute is raised. The editorial comment (20:19; cf. Mark 12:13) shows that the intention of the Jewish leaders is to find some excuse to charge Jesus with subversion. It is also shown that the plot was foiled (v. 26) and that Jesus, contrary to the hopes of his enemies, sanctioned the payment of taxes.

These passages constitute the background for Luke's description of the trial of Jesus in which the apologetic motif comes to the fore. The Jewish leaders themselves frame the charges against Jesus (23:2). These charges are patently specious in the light of such passages as the ones referred to above. Three times Pilate affirms Jesus' innocence of the crimes of which he is accused (23:4,14,22). To this is added also the testimony of Herod Antipas, tetrarch of Galilee (23:15). Finally, the centurion at the crucifixion, the third representative of the imperial government mentioned in the account declares: "Certainly this man was innocent!" (23:47; cf. Mark 15:39). The responsibility for the death of Jesus is placed completely on the shoulders of the Jewish leaders and their followers. They pressed the charges, and one could infer that they supervised the crucifixion (23:25–26—the antecedent of "they" is found in 22:66). Their own attitude toward the imperial government is demonstrated by their insistence on the release of Barabbas, a genuine insurrectionist (23:25; cf. Mark 15:15).

4. Luke wrote to give a solution to problems arising out of wrong views of the Parousia, or so-called second coming. This may be detected both in the editing of his Markan source and in the special material that he introduces.

First of all, there is the effort to guard against the idea that the Parousia should *necessarily* take place soon. We do not find Mark 1:15: "The time is fulfilled, and the kingdom of God is at hand." Rather, Luke emphasizes the proclamation of the good news of the kingdom, i.e., the nature of the kingdom rather than its imminence (cf. 4:17–21,43; 16:16; also the Greek text of Acts 1:3). The kingdom of God is a future, transcendent, eschatological reality that is placed beyond the context of history. One cannot speak, therefore, of signs nor of the time of its coming (17:20–21; 21:8; Acts 1:6–7). The coming of the kingdom is separated from such events as messianic wars (21:9; cf. Mark 13:7), the persecution of Christians (21:12), and the destruction of Jerusalem (21:20–24). These are events in history, not to be considered as portents of the end.

In Luke 19:11–27 an experience of the disciples is related to give the kind of warning Luke would issue to his contemporaries. The error of the disciples was their expectation of an imminent coming of the kingdom, which resulted from their relating it to the appearance of Jesus in Jerusalem. To Mark's warning against messianic pretenders (Mark 13:6), Luke also adds the admonition against being misled by apocalyptists who proclaim: "The time is at hand" (21:8). The question of the disciples about the time of the kingdom is rejected as inappropriate (Acts 1:6–7). They are also chided for gazing into the heavens (Acts 1:10–11). They are to go about their tasks undergirded by the confidence that Jesus would return as he had been taken up.

Hans Conzelmann has worked out in detail what he understands to be Luke's solution to the problem caused by the delay of the Parousia (p. 16). He detects a conception of salvation-history that falls into three parts: (1) the period of Israel, (2) the period of Jesus' ministry, and (3) the period of the church. In this way the ministry of Jesus is removed from its position as the decisive eschatological event, the immediate prelude to the end of history. The ministry becomes instead the midpoint of salvation-history. The time of Jesus is separated from the Parousia by the time of the church. In this way Luke has given a definitive solution to the problem of eschatology no matter how long the delay until the end. The Lukan solution is considered to be a substitute for the expectation of an imminent Parousia which had prevailed until then.

It is possible, however, to exaggerate the difference between Luke and his predecessors. There is a difference in emphasis rather than a totally new and different understanding of redemptive history. Luke's affinity with his predecessors is shown by the presence in the Gospel of texts like 3:9,17; 10:9,11; 18:7 f.; 21:32. All these are also susceptible to an interpretation which would support the expectation of an imminent Parousia.

Moreover, we find that Mark also allows for a mission to the Gentiles (13:10), however brief this may have been thought to last. And in Romans 9—11 Paul develops a view of salvation-history in which the mission to the Gentiles plays a crucial role, not incompatible with the Lukan framework. Paul seems to have been more dominated by an awareness of the end of the age and by a sense of its nearness than was Luke. To go further than this seems to be unwarranted.

Luke was careful to guard against the excesses of an exaggerated apocalypticism, but he also wanted to prevent the problems caused by the disappointments and disillusionments that the passing of the years could bring to Christians who had lived in the expectation of the victorious coming of their Lord (e.g., 12:35–40; 17:22–37; 18:1–8). His unique contribution to the New Testament was made possible because he recognized the role of the church in salvation-history. It is possible to hold with many interpreters that this concept is the correct response to the ministry of Jesus. It is based on the conviction that Jesus' intention was to create a community that would give continuity in history to the work that he had set in motion.

VII. Characteristic Lukan Motifs

A comparison of Luke with the other Gospels shows that it treats a number of themes in a special manner.

1. The Holy Spirit. There are 17 references to the Holy Spirit in Luke and 57 in Acts. In contrast, Mark contains only 6 and Matthew, 12. These references occur with unusual frequency in the first two chapters of the Gospel, primarily to show that the gift of prophecy had been revived under the inspiration of the Holy Spirit (1:41,67; 2:25–27). This was a sign that the long-awaited age of the Messiah had dawned. Jesus is said to be "full of the Holy Spirit" (4:1), and by the Spirit's power he works miracles (4:14) and heals the sick (5:17). The Holy Spirit is God's good gift to his children (11:13). During times of persecution the disciples will be ministered to by the Spirit (12:12). The disciples are not to be concerned about the time of the Parousia (Acts 1:6–8) but instead are to expect the "promise of the Father," i.e., the Spirit (24:49; Acts 1:8). The church is to live in the power of the Spirit until the Parousia.

2. Prayer. Luke stands alone in relating prayer to a number of crucial events in Jesus' ministry. These include the baptism (3:21), the calling of the twelve (6:12), the confession (9:18), and the transfiguration (9:28 ff.). He alone tells that the Lord's Prayer was a response to a request inspired by Jesus' experience in prayer (11:1). In Luke, Jesus utters a prayer of rejoicing over the success of the disciples' mission (10:21), intercedes for Peter (22:32), and prays on the cross (23:34,46). The parables of the insistent friend (11:5–8), the importunate widow (18:1–8), and the Pharisee and tax collector (18:9–14) are examples of Jesus' teaching on prayer.

3. Social Concern. Special attention is given to people who stood outside the pale of religious and social responsibility. The parable of the good Samaritan is given by Luke alone (10:25–37). Of ten lepers who were healed, a Samaritan is held up as the example of genuine gratitude (17:11–19).

Jesus' sympathy for tax collectors is attested especially by Luke. The tax collectors who came to John for baptism

(3:12–13), the parable of the Pharisee and the tax collector (18:9–14), and Zacchaeus (19:1–10) all appear in Luke's special material.

The contrast between the attitude of Jesus and that of the religious leaders toward sinners is illustrated in the story of the penitent woman (7:36–50), the parables of the fifteenth chapter, and the encounter with Zacchaeus (19:1–9). Only Luke tells of the penitent thief (23:39–43).

The Gospel stresses that the humble poor are the recipients of the kingdom of God (1:48,51–53; 4:18). Jesus is born in poor surroundings (2:7), while lowly shepherds are the first to receive news of his birth (2:8–14). Blessings are pronounced on the poor (6:20); woes, on the rich (6:24–26).

4. Women. Luke gives a significant place to women in his writings. Mary and Elizabeth figure prominently in the birth narratives. In Luke's special material are found stories like the raising of the widow's son (7:11–17), the penitent woman (7:36–50), the visit with Mary and Martha (10:38–42), and the healing of the crippled woman (13:10–17). We also find the interesting detail that a number of women provided support for Jesus and his disciples (8:1–3).

5. Wealth. A characteristic attitude toward wealth runs through the third Gospel. Generally suspect, it is called "unrighteous mammon" (16:9), although possession of wealth is not in itself condemned. Two of the most vivid parables, the foolish farmer (12:13–21) and the rich man and Lazarus (16:19–31) point out the folly of a secular approach to life. The sin of the two men is that they used their wealth solely for personal gratification, whereas it should be shared with those who are deprived (3:11; 12:33). Zacchaeus' conversion is signaled by this proper attitude toward his possessions (19:8).

The gospel as presented by Luke was pertinent to the great social issues of his day. It is colored throughout by a compassion for the exploited and despised. The third Gospel is a reminder that violence is done to the message of Jesus Christ when it is severed from a concern for man's social problems.

Outline of the Gospel

Preface (1:1–4)
I. Birth and childhood narratives (1:5—2:52)
  1. The births of John and Jesus (1:5—2:20)
    (1) The annunciation to Zechariah (1:5–25)
    (2) The annunciation to Mary (1:26–38)
    (3) Mary's visit to Elizabeth (1:39–56)
    (4) The birth of John (1:57–80)
    (5) The birth of Jesus (2:1–20)
  2. The early childhood of Jesus (2:21–52)
    (1) Circumcision and presentation (2:21–40)
    (2) The boy Jesus in the Temple (2:41–52)
II. Introduction to Jesus' ministry (3:1—4:13)
  1. The ministry of John (3:1–20)
    (1) John's call (3:1–6)
    (2) John's preaching (3:7–14)
    (3) John and the Coming One (3:15–17)
    (4) John's imprisonment (3:18–20)
  2. The preparation of Jesus (3:21—4:13)
    (1) The baptism (3:21–22)
    (2) The genealogy (3:23–38)
    (3) The temptation (4:1–13)
III. The ministry in Galilee (4:14—9:50)
  1. Teaching in the synagogues (4:14–30)
    (1) Acceptance in Galilee (4:14–15)
    (2) Rejection in Nazareth (4:16–30)
  2. The mighty works of Jesus (4:31—5:16)
    (1) The demon-possessed man (4:31–37)
    (2) Healings outside the synagogue (4:38–41)
    (3) Departure from Capernaum (4:42–44)
    (4) The first disciples (5:1–11)
    (5) The cure of a leper (5:12–16)
  3. Conflicts with religious leaders (5:17—6:11)
    (1) The healing of a paralytic (5:17–26)
    (2) Association with outcasts (5:27–32)
    (3) The question of fasting (5:33–39)

Selected Bibliography

BARRETT, C. K. *The Holy Spirit and the Gospel Tradition.* London: S.P.C.K., 1966.

CADBURY, HENRY J. *The Making of Luke-Acts.* London: S.P.C.K., 1958.

CAIRD, G. B. *The Gospel of St. Luke.* "The Pelican Gospel Commentaries," ed. D. E. NINEHAM. Baltimore: Penguin Books Inc., 1963.

CONZELMANN, HANS. *The Theology of St. Luke.* Tr. GEOFFREY BUSWELL. New York: Harper and Row, 1960.

CREED, JOHN MARTIN. *The Gospel According to St. Luke.* New York: Macmillan and Co., 1965.

ELLIS, E. EARLE. *The Gospel of Luke.* "The Century Bible." London: Thomas Nelson and Sons Ltd., 1966.

GILMOUR, S. MACLEAN. "The Gospel According to St. Luke," *The Interpreter's Bible,* ed. GEORGE ARTHUR BUTTRICK, Vol. VIII. New York: Abingdon Press, 1951.

GRUNDMANN, WALTER. *Das Evangelium nach Lukas.* Berlin: Evangelische Verlagsanstalt, p. 141.

JEREMIAS, JOACHIM. *The Parables of Jesus.* Tr. S. H. HOOKE. New York: Charles Scribner's Sons, 1963.

KITTEL, GERHARD (ed.). BROMILEY, GEOFFREY W. (trans.). *Theological Dictionary of the New Testament.* Grand Rapids: William B. Eerdmans Publishing Co.

LEANEY, A. R. C. *The Gospel According to St. Luke.* "Black's New Testament Commentaries," 2nd ed. London: Adam and Charles Black, 1966.

MANSON, WILLIAM, *The Gospel of Luke.* "The Moffatt New Testament Commentary" ed. JAMES MOFFATT. New York: Harper & Bros., n.d.

PLUMMER, ALFRED. *The Gospel According to St. Luke.* "The International Critical Commentary," 5th ed. Edinburgh: T. and T. Clark, 1964.

RICHARDSON, ALAN. *The Miracle Stories of the Gospels.* London: SCM Press Ltd., 1959.

STAGG, FRANK. *New Testament Theology.* Nashville, Tenn.: Broadman Press, 1962.

STRACK, HERMANN L. and BILLERBECK, PAUL, *Kommentar zum Neun Testament aus Talmud und Midrasch.* Munich: C. H. Beck'sche Verlagsbuchhandlung, 1924.

STREETER, BURNETT HILLMAN. *The Four Gospels.* London: MacMillan and Co., 1956.

TAYLOR, VINCENT. *Behind the Third Gospel.* Oxford: Clarendon Press, 1926.

Commentary on the Text

The use of a preface was common among Hellenistic writers. Its presence at the beginning of the third Gospel indicates that Luke, more than any other New Testament writer, considered his work to be a contribution to the wider literary world of the age. Apparently he was writing not only for the church but also with the hope of making an impact on educated, influential classes of non-Christians.

The preface to the third Gospel consists of a single, well-constructed sentence, composed of carefully chosen words. By common judgment it approximates classical Greek style to a greater extent than any other passage of the New Testament. The preface is similar to others of its kind in scope: therein are references to the work of predecessors, to the author's own preparation for writing, and to the purpose of his work. Also Luke follows common practice in putting the name of the addressee at this place.

Preface (1:1–4)

¹ Inasmuch as many have undertaken to compile a narrative of the things which have been accomplished among us, ² just as they were delivered to us by those who from the beginning were eyewitnesses and ministers of the word, ³ it seemed good to me also, having followed all things closely for some time past, to write an orderly account for you, most excellent Theophilus, ⁴ that you may know the truth concerning the things of which you have been informed.

The author makes it clear that he is not an innovator in his attempts to preserve the Christian tradition in written form. Many others have preceded him, giving him both the incentive and, although he does not say it directly, the sources for his writing.

Which have been accomplished among us expresses the writer's conviction that the events which he is to narrate were neither aimless nor fortuitous. The phrase is better rendered "which have been fulfilled among us." These *things*, including both the Gospel narrative and the book of Acts, fulfilled God's purpose as seen in the Old Testament, when properly interpreted (cf. 24:45–47). The story that follows, therefore, tells what God had done.

The author was not a member of the earliest Christian community. Thus, he was dependent on others who were *eyewitnesses and ministers of the word.* He claims for the church's knowledge about Jesus the firm foundation of the apostolic witness. By Luke's definition, an apostle, in the sense of one of the twelve, was one who had been with Jesus *from the beginning*, i.e., from "the baptism of John until the day when he was taken up" (Acts 1:22). During those early, formative years of the Christian movement, the guarantee for the fidelity of the reports to the actual events of Jesus' ministry were the people who could say: "We know the facts, because we heard what he said and saw what he did." Luke's intention was to pass on information *just as* it had been reported by first generation witnesses. The third Gospel, therefore, was designed to perform the function for later generations that the eyewitnesses had performed for theirs.

Verses 3–4 furnish a valuable insight into Luke's concept of his own work. Any adequate concept of inspiration of the biblical record must come to grips with this the sole autobiographical statement of a Gospel writer about his method. He is no automaton whose only role is to transcribe a verbatim revelation which he has received in some magical, otherworldly way. He is a Christian scholar, motivated by a conviction about the redemptive significance of certain events, using the sources at his disposal, and the resources of intellect, energy, and time in careful investigation and faithful reporting. Because of his qualifications and purposes, this kind of person could be the unique instrument used by the Holy Spirit to preserve the gospel story in writing for subsequent generations.

Luke proposes to write *an orderly account;* yet his method is to insert other materials into the basic Markan framework with the result that his outline of Jesus' ministry is really Mark's. Perhaps *orderly account (kathexés)* should be understood with reference to Luke's disparate sources (see Intro.). He has gathered the existing information about the ministry of Jesus, which he now proposes to put together in a logical sequence encompassed in the scope of one volume.

The title *most excellent* probably marks out *Theophilus* as a Roman official of some importance and influence, of procuratorial rank or above. Theophilus means "friend of God" and possibly was a pseudonym used to hide the person's real identity. Due to the lack of concrete data about him, any suggestion as to his identity is a mere guess.

There are two options in the interpretation of the reference to Theophilus. The traditional and more common idea is that he had been *informed* about Christianity by people who were trying to win him to faith. From this point of view he was either an adherent or was on the verge of becoming one.

A totally different possibility has been raised by another suggestion. According to it Theophilus was a Roman official who had a distorted notion about Christianity due to erroneous information which he had received.[7] His concept of Christianity had come from its enemies, whose reports had contributed to a misunderstanding of its political character and purposes. This means that his notion probably represented a common attitude in government circles where the Christian movement had been viewed with varying degrees of hostility and suspicion since the time of Nero. The hope of the author was to set the record

straight, initiating thereby a process that would reverse the general attitude toward Christianity. The *truth* can have a meaning similar to the popular phrase "the real facts."

Whatever the case, we may assume that Luke intended his work for more than one man. The patronage of Theophilus probably could secure a wider reading for the work among a more influential and cultured class.

I. Birth and Childhood Narratives (1:5— 2:52)

1. The Births of John and Jesus (1:5— 2:20)

Three major motifs give unity to the material in the first two chapters: (1) the relationship between John and Jesus; (2) the close relationship between Judaism and Christianity at the moment when the latter began; (3) the gift of the Holy Spirit and the revival of prophecy as a sign that the messianic age was dawning.

The evidence indicates that the Christian movement faced a significant challenge from followers of John the Baptist in its early history. It appears that a Baptist sect taught that John was the Messiah and, consequently, was superior to Jesus whom he baptized (see on 3:21). The birth stories in Luke's Gospel are designed to counter this claim. They are presented as a series of five episodes or tableaux, rather loosely connected by editorial comment. The distinctive roles of John and Jesus are set forth in them in such a way as to emphasize the significance of each but, at the same time, to maintain the superiority of Jesus.

More important to Luke's purpose, however, is the affirmation in this section that Jesus is Israel's Messiah, the long-awaited King and Deliverer. Although the fulfillment motif takes a somewhat different turn in Luke than in Matthew, it is just as significant. Possibly it answers to the threat of Gnostic ideas that would have severed Christianity from its historical foundations

[7] Cf. Cadbury, *op. cit.,* II, 510.

in the Old Testament and Judaism (see p. 21, fn. 8).

(1) The Annunciation to Zechariah (1:5–25)

5 In the days of Herod, king of Judea, there was a priest named Zechariah, of the division of Abijah; and he had a wife of the daughters of Aaron, and her name was Elizabeth. 6 And they were both righteous before God, walking in all the commandments and ordinances of the Lord blameless. 7 But they had no child, because Elizabeth was barren, and both were advanced in years.

8 Now while he was serving as priest before God when his division was on duty, 9 according to the custom of the priesthood, it fell to him by lot to enter the temple of the Lord and burn incense. 10 And the whole multitude of the people were praying outside at the hour of incense. 11 And there appeared to him an angel of the Lord standing on the right side of the altar of incense. 12 And Zechariah was troubled when he saw him, and fear fell upon him. 13 But the angel said to him, "Do not be afraid, Zechariah, for your prayer is heard, and your wife Elizabeth will bear you a son, and you shall call his name John.

14 And you will have joy and gladness, and many will rejoice at his birth;

15 for he will be great before the Lord, and he shall drink no wine nor strong drink, and he will be filled with the Holy Spirit, even from his mother's womb.

16 And he will turn many of the sons of Israel to the Lord their God,

17 and he will go before him in the spirit and power of Elijah, to turn the hearts of the fathers to the children, and the disobedient to the wisdom of the just, to make ready for the Lord a people prepared."

18 And Zechariah said to the angel, "How shall I know this? For I am an old man, and my wife is advanced in years." 19 And the angel answered him, "I am Gabriel, who stand in the presence of God; and I was sent to speak to you, and to bring you this good news. 20 And behold, you will be silent and unable to speak until the day that these things come to pass, because you did not believe my words, which will be fulfilled in their time." 21 And the people were waiting for Zechariah, and they wondered at his delay in the temple. 22 And when he came out, he could not speak to them, and they perceived that he had seen a vision in the temple; and he made signs to them and remained dumb. 23 And when his time of service was ended, he went to his home.

24 After these days his wife Elizabeth conceived, and for five months she hid herself, saying, 25 "Thus the Lord has done to me in the days when he looked on me, to take away my reproach among men."

Herod the Great, who was named the *king of Judea* (Palestine) by the Roman Senate in 40 B.C., died in 4 B.C. According to the evidence of the Gospel records, John and Jesus were born prior to his death (Matt. 2:1). These were difficult and troubled times for the Jewish people, most of whom resented deeply the Roman rule that Herod represented. In fact many believed that they were living in the days just prior to God's expected intervention on behalf of his beleaguered and oppressed people.

Priests in Palestine were divided into 24 *divisions, Abijah's* being the eighth of these (1 Chron. 24:10). In the introductory comments about *Zechariah* and *Elizabeth* the emphasis is on their impeccable religious credentials. To be a priest and to be married to a woman of priestly lineage was a double honor.

Zechariah and Elizabeth were outstanding representatives of orthodox Jewish piety. In spite of their irreproachable conduct, however, God had not blessed the couple with children. Nor was there any reasonable hope that this lamentable situation could be changed since the couple had passed the age of childbearing. In this way the author underlines the miraculous character of the events which he is about to describe.

According to some estimates, there were approximately 20,000 priests in Palestine at this time. Each of the 24 divisions ministered in the Temple for one week twice during the year. Since there were hundreds of priests in a division, they were chosen by lot to officiate at certain rituals. Such a privilege as the burning of *incense,* which took place daily morning and evening, would fall to the lot of a given priest no more than once during his lifetime. The *multitude,* consisting of male Israelites, were assembled in the Court of Israel while the priest inside the sanctuary proper performed the ritual. The *temple* was an appropriate place for God to reveal to a genuine Israelite that a significant moment had arrived in his life and in his peoples' history.

Both the Hebrew and Greek words for *angel* mean messenger. In the earlier Old Testament books the angel of Yahweh is God's intermediary in dealing with men. The angel offered a way of thinking and speaking about the presence of God who could not himself be seen by men. The references witness to a belief in a holy God who is exalted above man and his universe. They also express the conviction that this transcendent God is able to communicate with men and to become involved in the historical process. The angel is God's envoy to man; his message is God's message.

Whatever modern man does with the references to angels in the biblical record, he must come to grips with the two basic questions involved in them. Is there a God who transcends man's world? Is this God able to become involved in the lives of those who must play their roles in the context of space, time, and history? With these matters rather than with the nature of angelic visitations must faith ultimately concern itself.

To what *prayer* does the angel refer? For an heir? Or for the birth of Messiah? The latter would be more intelligible in the circumstances, but the context seems to require the former. *John,* the name to be given to the promised son, means "God is gracious."

The heavenly messenger describes the effect of John's anticipated ministry (v. 14), his qualifications for it (v. 15), and its nature (vv. 16–17). The experience of *joy* will be the natural response of those who become aware of God's mighty act of salvation in the series of events that begins to unfold with the birth of John the Baptist.

By the world's standards the great men of the day were the Caesars and the Herods. By God's standards true greatness belonged to an obscure, self-effacing wilderness prophet. A mark of John's special consecration to God will be his abstention from *wine* or *strong drink.* This is one aspect of the Nazirite's consecrated status (cf. Num. 6: 1–8). The positive aspect of his consecration is that he will be *filled with the Holy Spirit* from birth, which marks him out for a prophetic role of unusual significance. Here we find the first mention of the Holy Spirit in Luke. In rabbinic literature the Spirit of God is primarily the Spirit of prophecy, associated especially with the renewal expected during the messianic age when men will hear the voice of God directly again.

John is to call Israel to repentance so that the people will be *prepared* for God's long-awaited visitation. According to Malachi 4:5–6, on which this passage is based, Elijah the prophet will appear prior to the arrival of the "great and terrible day of the Lord." The Christian community believed that John was to be identified with Elijah of Jewish messianic expectation, being endued with the prophet's *spirit and power.* As the forerunner to Jesus, John had fulfilled the role anticipated in Malachi.

Zechariah finds the idea that he is to have a son at his age unbelievable, the unsupported word of the unknown messenger being insufficient to overcome his incredulity. In response to Zechariah's unbelief the angel identifies himself. He is *Gabriel,* one of the angels of the Presence who appear in later Jewish writings (cf. Dan. 10:13; 12:1; Enoch 9:1; 10:11). Furthermore, Zechariah is given a sign which is at the same time punishment for his doubt. He will be *unable to speak* until the angel's words are fulfilled.

Any *delay in the temple* would be the cause of general uneasiness among the waiting people. There were possible dangers attendant upon the performance of so sacred a rite as offering incense (cf. Num. 16; Lev. 10: 1–2; 2 Chron. 26:16–21). Upon emerging, Zechariah could not pronounce the customary benediction on the people, which was interpreted to mean *that he had seen a vision.* The sabbath brought to an end *his time of service.*

A childless woman was thought to be inferior to those who had children (cf. Gen. 16:4). The stigma which Elizabeth had borne for so many years was about to be removed. Her report of this fact would hardly be believed, however, until unmistakable physical evidence of her pregnancy appeared. At the end of *five months* it would be clear to all that Elizabeth was indeed to become a mother.

(2) The Annunciation to Mary (1:26–38)

26 In the sixth month the angel Gabriel was sent from God to a city of Galilee named Nazareth, 27 to a virgin betrothed to a man whose name was Joseph, of the house of David; and the virgin's name was Mary. 28 And he came to her and said, "Hail, O favored one, the Lord is with you!" 29 But she was greatly troubled at the saying, and considered in her mind what sort of greeting this might be. 30 And the angel said to her, "Do not be afraid, Mary, for you have found favor with God. 31 And behold, you will conceive in your womb and bear a son, and you shall call his name Jesus.
32 He will be great, and will be called the Son of the Most High;
and the Lord God will give to him the throne of his father David,
33 and he will reign over the house of Jacob for ever;
and of his kingdom there will be no end."
34 And Mary said to the angel, "How can this be, since I have no husband?" 35 And the angel said to her,
"The Holy Spirit will come upon you,
and the power of the Most High will overshadow you;
therefore the child to be born will be called holy,
the Son of God.
36 And behold, your kinswoman Elizabeth in her old age has also conceived a son; and this is the sixth month with her who was called barren. 37 For with God nothing will be impossible." 38 And Mary said, "Behold, I am the handmaid of the Lord; let it be to me according to your word." And the angel departed from her.

Two passages of Scripture furnish the evidence that the early church believed in the supernatural conception of Jesus. They are Matthew 1:18–25 and Luke 1:34–37.

Some scholars think that the idea was interpolated into Luke's original text and that it represented a later development. There is no substantial reason for rejecting the conclusion that belief in the virgin birth antedated both Matthew and Luke and was a general conviction held by early Christians.

There is no reference, however, to the virgin birth in any other New Testament writing. Furthermore, neither in Matthew nor Luke is it used to support claims about the person of Christ. Clearly this concept of Jesus' birth did not figure prominently in the earliest Christian apologetic of which Luke-Acts is a prime example. Claims for Christ are based primarily on his resurrection. Yet the conviction that the resurrected Christ was also the incarnate and preexistent Christ underlies the theology of every writer in the New Testament.

The question then arises: What purpose does the story of the virgin birth serve in Matthew and Luke? There are various possible answers. It was an affirmation of the uniqueness of Jesus. His followers believed that Jesus was God's Son in an ultimate sense, different from any person who had ever lived or who would appear. The story of the virgin birth traced this uniqueness back to the beginning, showing that God and God alone was responsible for his birth.

The story also showed that God's Son had actually been born of a human mother and had entered the world as a real human being. The emphasis on divine genesis does not detract from the fact that from the moment of his conception Jesus developed as any other child and that he entered the world through completely normal human processes. In this way the story of Jesus' birth served to counter the influence of teachers who argued that the divine Christ had no real identity as a human being. That Jesus was not the Christ was an axiom of later Gnostic Christology.[8] The story of

---

[8] Gnosticism, a movement which posed a radical challenge to Christianity, is first encountered in literature of the second century. Already in the first century, however, Gnostic ideas were prevalent in the Greco-

the virgin birth said in unmistakable terms that the human Jesus and the divine Christ were the same.

The annunciation to *Mary* is parallel to the annunciation to Zechariah, a device that enables the writer to set forth the superiority of Jesus to John. There is, of course, no attempt to denigrate John, but there is the clear affirmation that Jesus is the son of *David*, i.e., the Messiah. It was also essential to show, as Luke does in chapters 1—2, that Jesus and John did not represent divergent, opposing movements. The unity between them is the unity that also embraces the prophets and the church in an ongoing stream of divine action and revelation. But there can be no rival for the central position in this drama of redemption, for this belongs to Jesus alone.

The annunciation to Mary is made in the sixth month of Elizabeth's pregnancy, for reasons that become clear as the story unfolds. The instrument of divine revelation is *Gabriel* in this instance also. The information that *Nazareth* is a *city of Galilee* is a reminder that Luke is writing for a Gentile audience unacquainted with the geography of Palestine.

In Matthew the story of the virgin birth revolves around Joseph and his problem. In the Lukan story Mary is the center of attention. The description of Mary is intended to bring out two ideas: Mary was still a *virgin*, and she was *betrothed* to *Joseph*. Betrothal was much more serious than modern engagements, for the woman was considered to be the legal wife of the man to whom she was betrothed. A period of time commonly elapsed between betrothal and the actual celebration of the marriage, when the couple would begin to live together as husband and wife. The Messiah was expected to be a descendant of *David*, which accounts for the identifica-

tion of Joseph.

There is no basis in the text for the idea that Mary was "full of grace" in the sense that she thereby became a source of grace. The passive participle translated *favored one* declared that Mary was the object of God's grace or unmerited favor. The greatest favor that a Jewish maiden could anticipate was the privilege of being Messiah's mother. When the event finally takes place, God chooses as the instrument of his miracle a simple Galilean maiden. Herein lies the wonder! This is but another example of the surprising ways of God who "chose what is foolish in the world to shame the wise" and "what is weak in the world to shame the strong" (1 Cor. 1:27).

Mary's troubled reaction to the angel's greeting brings additional reassurance. She has nothing to fear from this heavenly visitation, for the messenger comes to bring joyous news that God has selected her for the honor for which so many Jewish women had prayed. *Jesus* is the Greek translation of the Hebrew Joshua which means "Yahweh is salvation." The name is not defined in the Lukan account, but the whole Gospel is an unfolding of its meaning.

In vv. 32–33 the future Son is described in such a way as to let Mary know that she is to give birth to Israel's Messiah. *Son of the most high* is a messianic title. The rest of the statement is phrased so as to declare that the birth of Jesus is the fulfillment of such prophecies as 2 Samuel 7:13–16 and Isaiah 9:6–7. In other passages the universal outlook of Luke will emerge, but for the moment the author is content to let the story make its point. Jesus is the fulfillment of the hopes and expectations of his own people, the Messiah of Old Testament prophecy. Yet he goes beyond the popular messianic conception in the affirmation of his eternal sovereignty.

An old Latin manuscript omits v. 34. Some scholars believe that this verse is an interpolation and that the story as originally written did not teach the supernatural conception of Jesus. The manuscript evidence as well as the natural interpretation of v. 27

Roman world. One of the characteristic dogmas was the equation of matter with evil, which led to the denial of the reality of the incarnation. This idea also resulted in the teaching that the God who created the world, Judaism's Yahweh, was an inferior, evil being, not to be identified with the God of Christ who was absolute Spirit.

indicate that the generally accepted text is original. The way Mary phrases her problem shows that she understands that conception is to take place prior to the consummation of her marriage.

In v. 35 is the answer to Mary's question: *How can this be* (v. 34). It is not an explanation but rather an affirmation. Mary's unique Son is to come into the world as a result of the creative power of God's Spirit. *Spirit* in Greek is neuter; the corresponding Hebrew noun *ruah* is usually feminine. There is no basis in Old Testament thought for the idea that the Spirit is the male principle. The verb *come upon* "denotes non-material action, and so, according to frequent usage in the LXX, does [*will*] *overshadow*, which is never used of sexual intercourse" (Barrett, p. 7). God's Spirit is active in bringing into being a new creation, a new humanity or a new Adam in Pauline terminology, in whom will be embodied the new Israel. What takes place, therefore, is creation rather than conception as generally understood. *Son of God* goes beyond the description in vv. 32–33. Son of David is not adequate to describe the One who is about to enter the world. The title *Son of God* marks Jesus off from all other men, for it ascribes to him a relationship to deity that is claimed for no other human being.

Elizabeth's pregnancy is cited to Mary as a sign of the power of God who is not frustrated by the natural factors that limit men. The God who has worked a miracle in the life of Elizabeth can accomplish what he has spoken to Mary. Unlike Zechariah, Mary does not seem to require any sign but humbly submits to the will of God for her life. She conceives of herself as a *handmaid* or, literally, "slave" of the Lord.

(3) Mary's Visit to Elizabeth (1:39–56)

39 In those days Mary arose and went with haste into the hill country to a city of Judah, 40 and she entered the house of Zechariah and greeted Elizabeth. 41 And when Elizabeth heard the greeting of Mary, the babe leaped in her womb; and Elizabeth was filled with the Holy Spirit 42 and she exclaimed with a loud cry, "Blessed are you among women, and blessed is the fruit of your womb! 43 And why is this granted me, that the mother of my Lord should come to me? 44 For behold, when the voice of your greeting came to my ears, the babe in my womb leaped for joy. 45 And blessed is she who believed that there would be a fulfilment of what was spoken to her from the Lord." 46 And Mary said,
"My soul magnifies the Lord,
47 and my spirit rejoices in God my Savior,
48 for he has regarded the low estate of his
      handmaiden.
   For behold, henceforth all generations will
      call me blessed;
49 for he who is mighty has done great things
      for me,
   and holy is his name.
50 And his mercy is on those who fear him
   from generation to generation.
51 He has shown strength with his arm,
   he has scattered the proud in the imagina-
      tion of their hearts,
52 he has put down the mighty from their
      thrones,
   and exalted those of low degree;
53 he has filled the hungry with good things,
   and the rich he has sent empty away.
54 He has helped his servant Israel,
   in remembrance of his mercy,
55 as he spoke to our fathers,
   to Abraham and to his posterity for ever."
56 And Mary remained with her about three months, and returned to her home.

The visit of Mary to Elizabeth serves to bring the two threads of the story together in such a way as to illustrate dramatically the relationship between the sons which the two women are to bear.

Mary responds to the angel's revelation by going hurriedly to visit Elizabeth, ostensibly to verify the sign given to her. It is impossible to identify the *city* referred to as Elizabeth's home. *Hill country* is the name of the topography of Jerusalem given by both Josephus and Pliny. A trip from Nazareth to a Judean city in the vicinity of Jerusalem would involve a distance of some 80 miles, a long journey for a young woman.

The purpose of the visit, personal verification of Elizabeth's pregnancy, is lost sight of in the story. At the sound of Mary's voice the unborn child moves in Elizabeth's womb. The verb translated *leaped* signifies a movement motivated by joy. The statement that Elizabeth was *filled with the Holy Spirit* marks her out as a prophetess of the new age (see on v. 15).

The point in the story is the superiority of Mary's child over Elizabeth's. Elizabeth blesses Mary because she is the *mother* of her *Lord*, that is, Messiah's mother. *Why is this granted to me* translates a Semitic phrase meaning "How could this happen to one so unworthy?"

Elizabeth explains how she had come to the recognition of Mary's significant role as Messiah's mother. Perhaps the reader is to understand that Mary had already conceived. In this case the idea may be that John had *leaped for joy* because he was in the presence of Jesus.

The RSV indicates the two possibilities of translating the last clause of v. 45, depending on how one understands the underlying Greek conjunction. In the marginal reading a clause beginning with *for* states the reason for Mary's blessedness. Mary represents the genuine Israelite who believes the promises of God. Such a one is *blessed* or happy because God fulfills his word.

Magnificat, the first word of Mary's song in the Vulgate, serves as its title. A question is raised about the attribution of the Magnificat to Mary. In a few old Latin manuscripts Elizabeth is the speaker, a reading supported by evidence from a limited number of Church Fathers.

Some internal evidence also supports the ascription to Elizabeth. The Magnificat is patterned after Hannah's song of rejoicing and praise in 1 Samuel 2:1–10. Elizabeth's experience of prolonged childlessness, ended by God's special mercy, bears a great similarity to Hannah's. Furthermore, v. 48 would more naturally refer to Elizabeth. *Low estate* most often describes a humiliation suffered as the result of a distressing experience, such as the stigma of Elizabeth's barrenness. Also, v. 56 would be clearer grammatically if Elizabeth were the speaker of the Magnificat. The pronoun *her* would then have a logical antecedent, and the repetition of Mary's name would be less awkward.

Some interpreters have concluded that the Magnificat originated among followers of John the Baptist and was attributed by them to Elizabeth. Nevertheless, the overwhelming weight of textual evidence, including all Greek manuscripts, supports the ascription of the song to Mary. It is a hymn of messianic rejoicing which in the Lukan context expounds the significance of Jesus' birth more appropriately than it does John's.

The fabric of the Magnificat is composed by weaving together phrases and ideas taken from different parts of the Old Testament. Following the pattern of Hannah's song it falls into two parts. The first (46b–50) is an expression of praise for personal blessings. The second (51–55) describes the significance for Israel of God's great act. The interpreter makes a mistake if he understands this and other references to Mary in Luke 1—2 in an exaggerated personal sense. Mary in her lowliness represents a humble and oppressed people. It is the Jewish nation that, in the person of Mary, gives birth to Jesus. What God has done for her he has done for Israel.

Soul and *spirit* are parallel terms for which the personal pronoun "I" can be substituted. Soul (*psuche*) corresponds to the Hebrew *nephesh* and describes man as an animate being. The popular concept of soul as a kind of disembodied spirit is totally inappropriate for understanding the biblical use of the term (cf. Stagg, pp. 28–32). *Magnifies* means to praise God by declaring his greatness. God's demonstration of power on behalf of his *handmaiden* is a manifestation of his character as *Savior* or Deliverer.

Interpreters have often pointed out that there is nothing specifically Christian in the Magnificat itself. Only with reference to the context can one understand that the hymn of praise to God's power and mercy is inspired by the promised birth of Jesus. This event is the evidence of God's faithfulness to his own character in that he pours out his mercy *on those who fear him from generation to generation,* i.e., always and without exception.

The prophets' assurance that God will be faithful to his word is often shown by casting into the past tense events which are yet to be realized in the future. In this spirit, the hymn talks about what God will do as though it had already taken place.

The *proud,* the *mighty,* and the *rich* describe people who use their position and power to exploit and oppress. On the other hand, the humble and the poor are the people who have placed their trust in God alone and wait confidently on him for their deliverance. The terminology used, therefore, has religious and moral overtones that modify the class descriptions. The coming of Messiah is seen as God's challenge to the unjust power structures of society. God acts to overthrow the oppressor and to deliver the oppressed.

It is clear that the passage refers to the dawn of the long-awaited messianic age. God's purpose is the redemption of Israel. He is responding to the helplessness and oppression of his *servant* in fulfillment of the promise which is centuries old.

Three months in addition to the six of v. 36 brings the narrative to the time for the termination of Elizabeth's pregnancy. Apparently the reader is to understand that Mary ended her visit prior to the birth of John, which is described in the subsequent episode. The modern reader raises a question that the writer does not answer: Was it to her parents' home or Joseph's that Mary returned?

(4) The Birth of John (1:57–80)

a. Circumcised and Named (1:57–66)

57 Now the time came for Elizabeth to be delivered, and she gave birth to a son. 58 And her neighbors and kinsfolk heard that the Lord had shown great mercy to her, and they rejoiced with her. 59 And on the eighth day they came to circumcise the child; and they would have named him Zechariah after his father, 60 but his mother said, "Not so; he shall be called John." 61 And they said to her, "None of your kindred is called by this name." 62 And they made signs to his father, inquiring what he would have him called. 63 And he asked for a writing tablet, and wrote, "His name is John." And they all marveled. 64 And immediately his mouth was opened and his tongue loosed, and he spoke, blessing God. 65 And fear came on all their neighbors. And all these things were talked about through all the hill country of Judea; 66 and all who heard them laid them up in their hearts, saying, "What then will this child be?" For the hand of the Lord was with him.

The birth of a child to a barren woman was considered a signal mark of divine mercy. Especially was this true in Elizabeth's case, where advanced age made childbearing impossible apart from God's miraculous intervention. Circumcision, the sign of the covenant between God and his people (Gen. 17:11), made the individual a member of the covenant community. It took place *on the eighth day,* i.e., one week, after birth. All pre-Christian references indicate that the name was given to Hebrew children at birth. The earliest evidence outside the New Testament for giving names at circumcision comes from the eighth century. Nevertheless, it is difficult to believe that the author would have affirmed that John and Jesus (2:21) were named at circumcision if this had been inconsonant with recognized contemporary custom.

Giving a child a name was a serious business, for the name represented the essential character or personality of the one who bore it. The suggestion that the child be named Zechariah after his father presumably came from relatives and friends who had gathered for the occasion. The objection to Elizabeth's choice of a name is based on the argument that no relative had borne the name John. They failed to understand that this child had been chosen by God for a role that set him apart from all other members of the family. His name, therefore, is not selected by men but determined by God (cf. Gen. 17:5; 32:28).

The punishment for Zechariah's doubt was aphasia or dumbness (v. 20). Here he is pictured as being deaf also, since people have to employ *signs* to communicate with him. The *tablet* was the kind made of wood and covered with wax. Zechariah corroborated in writing Elizabeth's choice of a name for their child, indicating thereby his conviction that John was the son of the angel's promise. This brought the time of his punishment to an end, and his speech returned.

The unusual events surrounding the birth and naming of John inspired an attitude of *fear* or reverential awe appropriate to those who recognized that God was doing strange and wonderful things in their midst. Upon hearing reports of witnesses about the extraordinary happenings, inhabitants of the region *laid them up in their hearts,* i.e., stored them in their memory, against the day when the mystery of it all would be revealed. The narrative ends on a note of heightened expectancy as people anticipate an extraordinary destiny for one marked by such arresting signs of God's involvement in his life.

b. Zechariah's Prophecy (1:67–80)

67 And his father Zechariah was filled with the Holy Spirit, and prophesied, saying,
68 "Blessed be the Lord God of Israel,
    for he has visited and redeemed his people,
69 and has raised up a horn of salvation for us
    in the house of his servant David,
70 as he spoke by the mouth of his holy prophets from of old,
71 that we should be saved from our enemies,
    and from the hand of all who hate us;
72 to perform the mercy promised to our fathers,
    and to remember his holy covenant,
73 the oath which he swore to our father Abraham, 74 to grant us
    that we, being delivered from the hand of our enemies,
    might serve him without fear,
75 in holiness and righteousness before him all the days of our life.
76 And you, child, will be called the prophet of the Most High;
    for you will go before the Lord to prepare his ways,
77 to give knowledge of salvation to his people
    in the forgiveness of their sins,
78 through the tender mercy of our God,
    when the day shall dawn upon us from on high
79 to give light to those who sit in darkness
    and in the shadow of death,

to guide our feet into the way of peace."
80 And the child grew and became strong in spirit, and he was in the wilderness till the day of his manifestation to Israel.

Zechariah is the second person who becomes a prophet of the new age as the result of being filled with the *Holy Spirit* (cf. vv. 41–42). Benedictus, the first word in the Latin version of his hymn, is the name that has been given to it. The Benedictus is divided into two parts. The first (vv. 68–75) describes the role played by Israel's Deliverer, God's Messiah. The second (vv. 76–79) describes the role of the Forerunner. To a great extent the hymn pictures the work of the Messiah in terms of the nationalistic hope for liberation. But there are some significant modifications to this theme in the last part.

Two basic beliefs determined the approach to the Old Testament seen in the earliest Christian writings. The first was the conviction that the God who revealed himself in Jesus Christ was also the God of the Old Testament and that there was coherence between his revelation in Jesus and his activity in Israel's history. Second, early Christians believed that Jesus Christ was the eschatological or ultimate revelation of God in history and, therefore, was the key to interpreting what God had already done. Furthermore, Luke regarded the church as the true Israel of God and would understand passages such as those in the Benedictus from this perspective.

In the opening verses of the Benedictus the messianic hope is expressed in the narrowest of nationalistic terms based on various Old Testament sources. God is closely identified with Israel which in turn is called *his people.* The redemption anticipated by Jews since 63 B.C. had been primarily liberation from the power of Rome. The *horn* is the weapon of certain animals and, for this reason, is a symbol of power. *Horn of salvation* means powerful deliverer. The Jewish people anticipated that their mighty Liberator would reestablish the Davidic dynasty. An unknown Jew of this period expressed the aspirations of many of his people when he prayed: "Lord, look down and raise up for them their king, the son of David, at the time which thou hast seen, O God, that he shall rule over thy servant Israel" (Psalms of Solomon XVII. 23). Jesus reinterpreted this hope and redirected it toward spiritual and universal goals.

The Messiah acts in accordance with the word of God's promise to the *prophets* (v. 70), redeeming the pledge made to *Abraham* (v. 73; cf. Gen. 22:16–18). Liberation is to bring a condition of religious freedom in which God's people will be able to express their religious life without *fear* of hostility and persecution (vv. 74–75).

Prophet of the Most High is to be contrasted with *Son of the Most High* (v. 32). In this way the role of John the Baptist is delineated so as to show the greater significance of Jesus. Here as in v. 17 John is identified with Elijah, an identification which Luke avoids in the body of his Gospel. At this point the Benedictus moves to a new level as salvation is spoken of in more spiritual and universal terms.

John is to give *knowledge of salvation.* This knowledge is not the gnosis or esoteric wisdom extolled in Gnostic thought. It is rather that knowledge which rises from an experience, namely, the *forgiveness . . . of sins.*

Day (dayspring-KJV) *. . . from on high* is difficult to translate. There is a possibility that it is to be equated with the Hebrew word for branch, since it is used to translate this messianic title in the LXX. In this case it means "Messiah of God." According to some manuscripts the verb *shall dawn* should be put in the past tense (see marg.). The text is probably correct, however, since the whole section beginning with v. 76 is cast in the future tense.

The universal note so prominent in the main body of the Gospel first surfaces at this juncture. Luke identified *those who sit in darkness* with Gentiles. The Messiah is to guide his people *into the way of peace* rather than into a war of national liberation.

The wilderness is usually identified as the Judean wilderness west of the Dead Sea. There is a strong possibility that John, who both in his youth and in his ministry is placed *in the wilderness,* had sustained some kind of association with the Qumran sect. This is the region in which this ascetic Jewish group had reestablished their community subsequent to the death of Herod the Great. But geographic proximity is not the only clue to a relationship between John and Qumran. His asceticism, eschatology, divergence from orthodox Judaism, and practice of baptism may also manifest links with the sect.[9] On the other hand, John is clearly different in that he was not seeking to form an isolated, monastic community. Neither did he sympathize with the emphasis on religious ritual, such as purificatory ablutions, so important to the Dead Sea community.

Manifestation can be understood as the public installation of John in his divinely appointed office. It emphasizes the view held by all the Gospel writers that the crucial phase of redemptive history begins with the history of John the Baptist. The close relation between 1:80 and 3:2 is a point in the argument for the original unity of Luke's Gospel as it now stands.

(5) The Birth of Jesus (2:1–20)

The purpose of Luke's reference to a census is to show why Mary and Joseph happened to be in Bethlehem when Jesus was born. Various questions, some of a relatively minor nature, have been raised about the historical accuracy of the account. Any event connected with the birth of Jesus must be dated shortly before the death of Herod the Great, which occurred in 4 B.C. The governors, more properly legates, of Syria for the crucial period were Sentius Saturninus, 9–6 B.C., and Quintilius Varus, 6–4 B.C. It is a known fact, therefore, that *Quirinius* does not fit into the succession of legates at the appropriate time.

Moreover, Josephus is silent about a cen-

---

9 Cf. Charles Scobie, *John the Baptist* (London: SCM, 1964), pp. 37–40, 46, 58–59, 102 ff.

sus during the reign of Herod the Great. He does write of one conducted by Quirinius in A.D. 6. This census, ordered for the purpose of composing tax rolls, was an infuriating expression to the Jews of their subjugation to Rome. It fanned a deep resentment which burst into the abortive revolt led by a certain Judas of Galilee.

Many scholars believe that this is the event described by Luke. They hold that he made the mistake of pushing the census back several years and used it erroneously to account for the circumstances of Jesus' birth.

The most forceful defense of the historical accuracy of the Lukan account was presented many years ago by Sir William Ramsay.[10] His case is built on the possibility that Quirinius was in Syria in charge of military operations against rebels during at least part of Saturninus' term of office. Ramsay suggests that Quirinius and Saturninus filled dual administrative roles in Syria at the time of the census, the former for military matters and the latter for internal affairs. The term *governor* is susceptible to a broad interpretation and could well apply to a position of military authority. Ramsay concludes that the census of Herod was "tribal and Hebraic, not antinational" and that "it was wholly and utterly unconnected with any scheme of Roman taxation" (p. 108). Because it aroused little popular reaction, it passed unnoticed by Josephus. According to this reconstruction of the situation, the birth of Jesus would have occurred in approximately 8 B.C.

a. Born in Bethlehem (2:1-7)

¹ In those days a decree went out from Caesar Augustus that all the world should be enrolled. ² This was the first enrollment, when Quirinius was governor of Syria. ³ And all went to be enrolled, each to his own city. ⁴ And Joseph also went up from Galilee, from the city of Nazareth, to Judea, to the city of David, which is called Bethlehem, because he was of the house and lineage of David, ⁵ to be enrolled with Mary, his betrothed, who was with child. ⁶ And while they were there, the time came for her to be delivered. ⁷ And she gave

birth to her first-born son and wrapped him in swaddling cloths, and laid him in a manger, because there was no place for them in the inn.

Jesus was born during the reign of *Caesar Augustus*, the great administrative genius who ruled the Roman Empire 27 B.C. to A.D. 14. There is no evidence outside this Gospel to connect Augustus with a census of the Empire, but an argument from silence is not conclusive. Some have also contended that Herod as a semi-independent sovereign would hardly have allowed such meddling in the internal affairs of his kingdom. Once again it must be said that in the absence of evidence the interpreter cannot affirm dogmatically what Herod would or would not have done. *All the world* is hyperbole for the Roman Empire. But a simultaneous, empire-wide census seems ruled out by extant historical notices, which show that censuses of different regions were conducted at different times. *All the world* could be a mistaken translation of an Aramaic phrase meaning "all the folk," i.e., all the Jewish people (Manson, p. 16).

Because censuses of the kind that began in Egypt in A.D. 20 were used to compute tax rolls, inhabitants were required to register where they lived and owned property. As has been suggested, the requirement for Jews to return to their ancestral home, as specified by the Lukan account, may have been designed to secure a less resentful compliance with a distasteful measure by giving it a nationalistic form.[11] Joseph, a descendant of David, went to the *city of David* (cf. 1 Sam. 17:12). According to Micah 5:2, Bethlehem was the city from which would come the one destined to be "ruler of Israel."

His betrothed is the reading supported by the best witnesses to the text. A few manuscripts have the reading "his wife," which is preferable on intrinsic grounds. The tendency which culminated in the doctrine of perpetual virginity would explain why a scribe would have changed wife to betrothed.

---

[10] *Was Christ Born in Bethlehem?* (New York: Putnam, 1898).

[11] Cf. Ramsay, *ibid.,* p. 107.

Luke, as well as the other Gospel writers, affirms that Mary was the mother of several children, of whom Jesus was the *first-born* or eldest (cf. Luke 8:20). No real case can be made against the clear sense of the text in these passages. Had Luke wished to say that Jesus was an only child, he would have used the appropriate word *monogenēs*.

The humble circumstances of the birth of Jesus are depicted in the story. The word translated *inn* properly means room. An influx of guests had preempted all the places in the room in which travelers slept. The parents of Jesus were required to seek lodging in the stable or perhaps even in an open pen. The first cradle to receive their son was a *manger*, a feeding trough. Thus did this "Man for others" begin his life. And appropriately so, for there are no barriers in a stable. Superficial categories of race and class, as well as fussy notions about germs and dirt are unimportant there. All the poor, insignificant, forgotten people of the world can gather around the manger and dare to believe that the Babe who lies there really belongs to them.

b. Announced to Shepherds (2:8–14)

8 And in that region there were shepherds out in the field, keeping watch over their flock by night. 9 And an angel of the Lord appeared to them, and the glory of the Lord shone around them, and they were filled with fear. 10 And the angel said to them, "Be not afraid; for behold, I bring you good news of a great joy which will come to all the people; 11 for to you is born this day in the city of David a Savior, who is Christ the Lord. 12 And this will be a sign for you: you will find a babe wrapped in swaddling cloths and lying in a manger." 13 And suddenly there was with the angel a multitude of the heavenly host praising God and saying,

14 "Glory to God in the highest,
and on earth peace among men with whom
he is pleased!"

The truth that the gospel was meant for the socially despised and economically depressed is carried through by the story of the *shepherds*. The simple pastors of sheep belonged to the "people of the land," that multitude of common men who were considered to be outside the pale of religious respectability. Their occupation and manner of life made it impossible for them to meet the requirements of religious ritual for ceremonial purity. Since the shepherds were tending *their flock by night,* the scene could not have been possible in the middle of winter. The tradition which places the birth of Jesus on December 25 is relatively late, attested from the fourth century, and is unreliable.[12] Shepherds were *in the field* from March until November.

Only in the first chapter of the Gospel does Luke name the heavenly messengers who appear in his narrative. Elsewhere he follows the earlier Jewish practice of designating each one as *an angel of the Lord.* The reaction to the *glory of the Lord* or the radiance of God's presence, perhaps to be understood as a luminous cloud, was great *fear.*

The heavenly visitor's first words bring reassurance; he is a herald of *good news. Joy,* a recurring Lukan motif, is the proper response to God's saving deed. The *people (laos)* are God's people. At Jesus' birth this was Israel, which later became the church according to Luke's view of redemptive history.

The good news is the birth of a *Savior,* an unusual title for Jesus in the Gospels. In the ancient world a savior was primarily a deliverer from disease, from danger, or from the human predicament in the world. Rulers, both Greek and Roman, were called saviors. The title was often given to the Greek gods, especially to the divinities of the mystery religions. In the LXX God is called Saviour (e.g., Psalm 24:5; thus also in Luke 1:47). To proclaim Jesus as Saviour in the Hellenistic environment of the Gentile mission was to affirm that he was the universal Deliverer for whom people longed, who could do for them what neither their rulers nor their gods could accomplish. Only he could truly release men from their bondage to evil, fate, death, and corruption.

Christ the Lord is the translation of a dif-

12 See Oscar Cullmann's essay, "The Origin of Christmas," in *The Early Church,* ed. A. J. B. Higgins (abridged ed.; London: SCM, 1966), pp. **21 ff.,** for a discussion of the Christian tradition.

ficult phrase which consists of the juxtaposition of two nouns in the nominative case without the intervening article, literally "Christ Lord." Many conjectures about the meaning of this phrase have been offered. Some believe that the first word should be taken as an adjective and translated "anointed Lord." Others would render it "Christ and Lord," taking it to mean that Messiah is Yahweh. The most probable explanation is that there has been a corruption of an Aramaic original which should be translated "the Lord's Christ," as in Luke 2:26. *Lord* represents the Septuagintal translation of the divine name Yahweh and should be so understood here, although in the New Testament the title is often given to Jesus. The Saviour who has been born, therefore, is the Messiah that God had promised to Israel. When the shepherds find in David's city the newborn babe *lying in a manger,* they will know that they have discovered the child of whom the angel speaks.

The heavenly chorus is composed of the celestial servants of God described in Daniel 7:10. Their hymn opens with an ascription of praise to the transcendent God who has brought this wonderful event to pass. The second part describes the result of God's redeeming act as *peace on earth.* The alternate RSV marginal reading to v. 14, "peace, good will among men," does not have adequate support. The peace that the newborn Messiah is to bring belongs to "men of God's good pleasure," meaning those whom God has been pleased to choose for his own (cf. Luke 3:22). The peace that Jesus brought was reconciliation between God and man and the corollary reconciliation between man and his fellows. This peace is possible for individuals "of God's good pleasure" even in the midst of the chaos, tensions, and hatreds of human society. It does not depend on outward circumstances but upon a personal response to the initiative of divine grace.

c. The Shepherds' Visit (2:15–20)

15 When the angels went away from them into heaven, the shepherds said to one another,

"Let us go over to Bethlehem and see this thing that has happened, which the Lord has made known to us." 16 And they went with haste, and found Mary and Joseph, and the babe lying in a manger. 17 And when they saw it they made known the saying which had been told them concerning this child; 18 and all who heard it wondered at what the shepherds told them. 19 But Mary kept all these things, pondering them in her heart. 20 And the shepherds returned, glorifying and praising God for all they had heard and seen, as it had been told them.

Following the instructions given them, the shepherds discover the babe whom the angels had described. Thereupon they divulge to the parents all that the angel had told them about the child. According to v. 18, others were present and heard the shepherds' recital of their unusual experience.

The description of Mary's response to the shepherds' revelation implies that Luke thought of her as the original source of the information on which his account was based (cf. also 2:51). At the moment Mary can only *ponder . . . in her heart,* that is, meditate on the possible significance of the unusual signs surrounding the birth of her son. She and others only came to understand the mystery of Jesus' role in God's redemptive purpose in the light of subsequent developments, especially his death and resurrection.

2. The Early Childhood of Jesus (2:21–52)

(1) Circumcision and Presentation (2:21–40)

a. The Naming of Jesus (2:21)

21 And at the end of eight days, when he was circumcised, he was called Jesus, the name given by the angel before he was conceived in the womb.

As in the case of John, Jesus was circumcised and named on the same day (see 1:59). The notice about the circumcision shows that Jesus was a genuine child of the covenant community. But the giving of the divinely chosen name is the central event here. The circumstances attending the naming of Jesus bear witness that the child has a divinely preordained destiny.

b. Simeon's Witness About Jesus (2:22–32)

22 And when the time came for their purification according to the law of Moses, they brought him up to Jerusalem to present him to the Lord 23 (as it is written in the law of the Lord, "Every male that opens the womb shall be called holy to the Lord") 24 and to offer a sacrifice according to what is said in the law of the Lord, "a pair of turtledoves, or two young pigeons." 25 Now there was a man in Jerusalem, whose name was Simeon, and this man was righteous and devout, looking for the consolation of Israel, and the Holy Spirit was upon him. 26 And it had been revealed to him by the Holy Spirit that he should not see death before he had seen the Lord's Christ. 27 And inspired by the Spirit he came into the temple; and when the parents brought in the child Jesus, to do for him according to the custom of the law, 28 he took him up in his arms and blessed God and said,

29 "Lord, now lettest thou thy servant depart in peace,
      according to thy word;
30   for mine eyes have seen thy salvation
31   which thou hast prepared in the presence of all peoples,
32   a light for revelation to the Gentiles, and for glory to thy people Israel."

According to Leviticus 12, the rite of *purification* took place 33 days after the child's circumcision and involved the sacrifice of a year-old lamb as a burnt offering and either a pigeon or a turtledove as a sin offering. The poor who could not afford a lamb were permitted to substitute another pigeon or turtledove as a burnt offering. In this case the sacrifice of *a pair of turtledoves, or two young pigeons* places the family of Jesus among the poor.

The reference to *their purification* is puzzling since according to law the mother alone was considered to be unclean. There is slight manuscript evidence for the reading "her purification," which would be a correct understanding of the rite. The reading of the majority of manuscripts underlying the text of the RSV may indicate a reluctance which developed quite early to regard Mary as a sinner in need of purification.

For the requirement concerning the redemption of the firstborn see Exodus 13:2,12–16. According to Numbers 18:16 the price for the redemption of the male offspring was five shekels. The fulfillment

of the requirement was to take place when the child was a month old. On this occasion Jesus' parents *brought him up to Jerusalem* to the Temple, which was not necessary but appropriate. The account apparently fuses the rites of purification and of the redemption of the firstborn.

Simeon, like Zechariah and Elizabeth, inculcated the highest attributes of Jewish morality and faith. His devotion was expressed in the care with which he fulfilled the prescribed religious duties. Furthermore, he was one of a group of earnest people (cf. v. 38) who were expecting the *consolation of Israel.* This phrase was used by the rabbis for the fulfillment of the messianic hope (cf. Isa. 40:1). Since *the Holy Spirit was upon him,* Simeon possessed the prophetic energy essential for discerning the unfolding purposes of God. The fulfillment of the promise made to him took place in the *temple* which he entered "in the Spirit" (see marg. for v. 27), which means that he was in a state of prophetic ecstasy.

Simeon's brief song is called the *Nunc Dimittis,* the first two words of the Latin translation. The speaker declares that he is ready now to die, since God's promise to him has been fulfilled. He can depart *in peace,* without regret or a sense of frustration. He is one of those fortunate persons who has come to the end of the way with the conviction that life could have been no more rewarding and meaningful. Simeon calls himself God's *servant,* literally slave. He seems to represent in Luke the ideal for Israel, the servant people. In his faithfulness to the teachings of Judaism and in his recognition that Jesus is the fulfillment of the prophetic hope, Simeon takes the attitude becoming to Israel at this crucial juncture in salvation-history. Indeed, in his commitment to the best in the past and in his openness to the surprises of God's future, he could well serve as a model for God's servant in any generation.

In Jesus, Simeon sees the fruition of the prophetic utterance of Isaiah 52:10. Here the universal motif emerges distinctly in a passage woven from Isaianic texts. Parallels in Isaiah (cf. 42:6; 49:6) show how important to Luke's understanding of Jesus is the Suffering Servant concept found there.

All peoples may be used to refer only to Israel, but in this case it embraces all humanity. God's salvation is defined as *light* for Gentiles and *glory* for Jews. It is the light which will dispel the darkness in which Gentiles have dwelled. It is Israel's glory in that it is the culmination of God's redemptive work through his servant nation. Two prominent Lukan themes are set forth in v. 32: (1) the universal reach of God's salvation and (2) the fulfillment of Israel's religion in Jesus.

c. Simeon's Prediction to Mary (2:33-35)

33 And his father and his mother marveled at what was said about him; 34 and Simeon blessed them and said to Mary his mother,
"Behold, this child is set for the fall and rising of many in Israel,
and for a sign that is spoken against
35 (and a sword will pierce through your own soul also),
that thoughts out of many hearts may be revealed."

In spite of the inclusion of the story about the supernatural conception of Jesus, Luke speaks very naturally of Joseph as Jesus' *father* (see also 2:41,48). The surprise of the parents is caused by Simeon's description of the significance of the child. Here, as in 2:18-19 and 2:50-51, the point is made that Mary and Joseph do not really grasp the full meaning of all that was happening.

Noting the surprise of the parents, Simeon addresses himself to the mother for the first time. The coming of Jesus has introduced a crisis that will divide the nation. His presence constitutes a demand for decision on the part of his people. Those who reject him will fall, whereas those who accept him will be lifted up. This is in keeping with the theme of the abasement of the proud and the exaltation of the humble which is prominent in Luke. Some interpreters find in Isaiah's "stone of stumbling" (8:14, KJV) and "precious corner stone" (28:16) the key to the figure used here. (See Caird, p. 64, for another plausible explanation.)

In his own person Jesus constitutes God's *sign* to the nation, the unmistakable and irrefutable evidence of the breaking in of God's rule. This sign, however, is not molded to fit men's demands and, consequently, is unacceptable to many.

The mother will share to some extent in the suffering of the Son, for the cruelty meted out to him will be like a *sword* thrust through her *soul*. The reaction toward Jesus will be a disclosure of what man is on the inside: "the secret thoughts of many will be laid bare" (NEB). Already in this section, therefore, attention is focused on the personal nature of the crisis that Jesus will provoke. It is not the superficial distinctions of race or class that will make the difference but the quality of the individual's response to God's call in Jesus for personal decision.

d. Anna's Witness About Jesus (2:36-38)

36 And there was a prophetess, Anna, the daughter of Phanuel, of the tribe of Asher; she was of a great age, having lived with her husband seven years from her virginity, 37 and as a widow till she was eighty-four. She did not depart from the temple, worshiping with fasting and prayer night and day. 38 And coming up at that very hour she gave thanks to God, and spoke of him to all who were looking for the redemption of Jerusalem.

Luke's literary style is influenced greatly by his fondness for pairs, shown here in the way that he balances the episode about Simeon the prophet with one about *Anna* the prophetess. The description about the aged *widow* is marked by an unusual number of precise details. The passage does not speak of her endowment with the Spirit, but it does call her a *prophetess*, which is the same.

The primary concern seems to be to stress Anna's extraordinary religious devotion since her widowhood. In her attendance upon the *temple,* in *fasting,* and in *prayer* she went far beyond even the more devout of her contemporaries. She added her testimony to Simeon's by telling those *who were looking for the redemption of Jerusalem* that Jesus was the fulfillment of their hope. *Redemption of Jerusalem* is synonymous with the *consolation of Israel* (see 2:25). Involved in the messianic hope was the belief that the Jewish capital would be liberated from her captors (e.g., Isa. 52:1 ff.).

e. The Return to Nazareth (2:39–40)

39 And when they had performed everything according to the law of the Lord, they returned into Galilee, to their own city, Nazareth. 40 And the child grew and became strong, filled with wisdom; and the favor of God was upon him.

Since the trip from Jerusalem is described as a return to Galilee, we understand that Nazareth was the family residence during this period. But from Matthew's account the reader would assume that Mary and Joseph resided in Bethlehem until the flight to Egypt. After the return from Egypt, they went to Nazareth rather than to Judea because of their fear of Archelaus (Matt. 2:22 f.). It is fairly clear that both Matthew and Luke wrote independently and that their accounts of Jesus' infancy came from different sources. The materials are too limited to permit a definitive explanation of the relationship between the two accounts.

When persons possessed unusual ability, met with success and good fortune, escaped from danger, etc., they were said to be objects of *the favor of God.* In this passage the phrase affirms that even in this early period of development the young child showed that he was endowed with unusual gifts.

(2) The Boy Jesus in the Temple (2:41–52)

41 Now his parents went to Jerusalem every year at the feast of the Passover. 42 And when he was twelve years old, they went up according to custom; 43 and when the feast was ended, as they were returning, the boy Jesus stayed behind in Jerusalem. His parents did not know it, 44 but supposing him to be in the company they went a day's journey, and they sought him among their kinsfolk and acquaintances; 45 and when they did not find him, they returned to Jerusalem, seeking him. 46 After three days they found him in the temple, sitting among the teachers, listening to them and asking them questions; 47 and all who heard him were amazed at his understanding and his answers. 48 And when they saw him they were astonished; and his mother said to him, "Son, why have you treated us so? Behold, your father and I have been looking for you anxiously." 49 And he said to them, "How is it that you sought me? Did you not know that I must be in my Father's house?" 50 And they did not understand the saying which he spoke to them. 51 And he went down with them and came to Nazareth, and was obedient to them; and his mother kept all these things in her heart. 52 And Jesus increased in wisdom and in stature, and in favor with God and man.

The Law enjoined every male to go to Jerusalem to participate in the feasts of Passover, Pentecost, and Tabernacles (cf. Ex. 23:14–17; 34:23; Deut. 16:16). For the many Jews who lived after the exile in regions distant from Jerusalem, the fulfillment of this requirement became impossible. Residents of Palestine made an effort to be in Jerusalem for at least one of the feasts each year. Joseph was following current practice, i.e., acting *according to custom* as well as the Law (v. 42), in his yearly visit to Jerusalem for the Passover. Although women did not come under the requirement of the Law, many of them, like Mary, accompanied the male members of their families on these pilgrimages.

At puberty the Jewish boy became a son of the Law, a responsible member of the covenant community, obligated to fulfill the Law's requirements. Consequently, at the age of twelve Jesus joined his elders on their annual pilgrimage.

According to the Law, the Feast of Unleavened Bread, which followed immediately on the Passover celebration, was to be observed for seven days (Ex. 23:15). Nevertheless, many pilgrims departed Jerusalem after the two days required for their participation in the ritual of the Passover. In a caravan composed of *kinsfolk* and *acquaintances* from the same town or region, it was very easy for the absence of a twelve-year-old boy to pass unnoticed until time for the first night's camp.

Later legendary accounts tend to turn the young Jesus into a ·wonder boy. Thus, in the Gospel of Thomas he silences the teachers and becomes their instructor. This is not the case with the Lukan account in which Jesus is pictured as a learner, *listening to the teachers, asking them questions,* and in turn—almost certainly—answering questions directed at him. His unusual interest in religious matters and his keen insight are portrayed in the story.

Any parent who has experienced the anguish of searching for a missing child can appreciate the plaintive reproach addressed by Mary to her son. She naturally felt that she had been treated rather shabbily.

On the other hand, Jesus' reply shows his complete surprise that Mary and Joseph should not have known his whereabouts. "Only now," writes Leaney, "does it become apparent to him that they are unaware of his personal and private intuitions, which he had hitherto unconsciously assumed they shared" (p. 103).

The phrase translated *in my Father's house* can also be translated "engaged in my Father's business" (see, e.g., the KJV). The rendering of the RSV is most likely correct. The sense of Jesus' statement is that Mary and Joseph should have known that he would be found in the Temple and, therefore, they did not need to search for him.

Jesus' description of the Temple as the house of his Father affirms his relationship to the God of Israel, as over against the Gnostic teaching that denied the identification of Jesus' God with the Old Testament Yahweh (see, fn. 5).

Verse 49 also raises the enigmatic question about Jesus' consciousness of his own identity and mission, since it implies an awareness of a unique bond between him and God, his Father. Any understanding of Jesus which takes the incarnation seriously has to start with the recognition that he, like any other human being, had to learn to walk, talk, feed himself, etc. The question arises: At what stage in his life did Jesus

begin to come to the conviction about his decisive role in salvation-history, and how did this conviction develop? No dogmatic answer can be given to these questions. Nevertheless, the story about Jesus in the Temple indicates that at this early age Jesus was already moving toward an awareness of the singular character of his relationship to God.

The reader is given to understand that for the moment the experience in the Temple did not alter the status of Jesus in the home. Upon the return to Nazareth he continued to lead the normal and expected life of a child, being *obedient* to Joseph and Mary. This is the last reference to Joseph, giving rise to the conjecture that he died prior to the beginning of Jesus' public ministry.

The episodes from Jesus' childhood reported in Luke all affirm the Jewishness of his early environment and training. Five times we find the statement that an act is performed "according to the law" (e.g., 2:22,39). The setting for most of the material is the Temple in Jerusalem. On the other hand, the early years in Nazareth are covered by editorial summaries (vv. 40,52) which do not contain any specific episodes.

Verse 52 is an echo of 1 Samuel 2:26. It emphasizes the development of Jesus, alike in physical growth, moral insights, and character traits. *Favor* translates *charis,* grace. Grace can describe those qualities which make one attractive. It can also describe that attitude of approval, respect, or good will directed by others toward a gracious person.

II. Introduction to Jesus' Ministry (3:1—4:13)

1. The Ministry of John (3:1-20)

(1) John's Call (3:1-6)

[1] In the fifteenth year of the reign of Tiberius Caesar, Pontius Pilate being governor of Judea, and Herod being tetrarch of Galilee, and his brother Philip tetrarch of the region of Ituraea and Trachonitis, and Lysanias tetrarch of Abilene, [2] in the high-priesthood of Annas and Caiaphas, the word of God came to John the son of Zechariah in the wilderness; [3] and

he went into all the region about the Jordan, preaching a baptism of repentance for the forgiveness of sins. ⁴ As it is written in the book of the words of Isaiah the prophet,
"The voice of one crying in the wilderness:
Prepare the way of the Lord,
   make his paths straight.
⁵ Every valley shall be filled,
   and every mountain and hill shall be brought
      low,
   and the crooked shall be made straight,
   and the rough ways shall be made smooth;
⁶ and all flesh shall see the salvation of God."

When Augustus Caesar died in A.D. 14, *Tiberius* succeeded him as ruler of the Roman Empire. Consequently an event dated *in the fifteenth year* of his reign could occur in A.D. 28 or 29. After the death of Herod the Great, Palestine was divided among three of his sons. *Philip* (4 B.C.—A.D. 34) received Batanea, *Trachonitus, Ituraea,* and some adjacent territories. *Herod* Antipas (4 B.C.—A.D. 39) was made *tetrarch of Galilee* and Perea. Archelaus (4 B.C.—A.D. 6), the chief beneficiary of Herod's will, was named ethnarch and given Judea and Idumea. When he proved incapable of administering his region, Archelaus was deposed. Judea became an imperial province ruled over by a *governor.* Only later was this kind of official called a procurator, so that the application of the title to Pilate by Tacitus is probably an anachronism. *Pontius Pilate* (A.D. 26–36), the fifth of these governors, held office during Jesus' ministry. There are no clear data outside the New Testament about the *Lysanius* mentioned here.

Having placed the beginning of John's ministry in the political context, Luke relates it to the religious situation. Technically *Annas* was not high priest, having been deposed in A.D. 15. High priests were supposed to hold office for life, but under both Syrians and Romans they had an uncertain and often brief tenure (cf. Josephus, *Antiq.,* 20,10). *Caiaphas,* son-in-law to Annas, occupied the position during Jesus' public life. It can be assumed that Annas exerted influence and power that accrued to him from having been high priest.

The similarity between Luke 3:1 f. and the description by Thucydides of the beginning of the Peloponnesian War (II. 2) has been noted often. But parallels from the Old Testament, especially the account of Jeremiah's call (1:1–3), offer a more relevant association. The elaborate historical setting coupled with the solemn refrain *the word of God came to John* identifies John with the great prophets of the past. Luke serves notice that the silence of the centuries has been broken. Once again there is a prophet in Israel who challenges the people with God's message.

The *wilderness* is not identified, but its exact location is irrelevant. What is important are the religious ideas and historical associations evoked by the mention of the wilderness. There God had manifested himself as the savior of his people; and in the wilderness, so believed many, the final and decisive drama of redemption would begin. Thus, the wilderness was an appropriate setting for John's call. The description of John's dress and fare is omitted (cf. Matt. 3:4; Mark 1:6). Is this due to a reluctance to identify him with Elijah (Conzelmann, pp. 22 ff.)?

John is pictured as a peripatetic preacher who toured *the region about the Jordan.* There is no conclusive answer to the question about the origin of John's baptism. His practice may be linked to the baptism of proselytes (converts) to Judaism, with the significant difference that he summoned *Jews* to submit to his baptism. Because of the impossibility of establishing definitely such an early date for proselyte baptism, one cannot be dogmatic about this position. Attempts have also been made to identify John's rite with the Mandaean sacramental ritual, but the arguments rest on extremely precarious historical grounds. The efforts to relate it with the baptism required for entrance into the Qumran community are based on more plausible but far from conclusive evidence.¹³

That John's baptism was new and differ-

---

¹³ Scobie, *op. cit.,* pp. 102 ff.

ent is established by the fact that he was known as "the baptizer" (Mark 1:4). Such an appellation would not have attached to him if his practice had coincided with others widely known and used. His baptism was probably an act of prophetic symbolism, through which he brought together a community, a remnant out of Israel, in this way making "ready for the Lord a people prepared" (1:17; cf. Barrett, pp. 32 f.). It looks toward the baptism "with the Holy Spirit and with fire" to be administered by the Coming One (v. 16 below). It may have been thought of as a fulfillment of passages like Isaiah 1:16 and Jeremiah 4:14.

The Greek word *baptisma*, occurring here, is distinctive in that it is used only of the baptism practiced by John and early Christians. This sets their practice off from the baptismal rites of other groups. There is little argument against the view that this baptism was an unrepeatable experience which involved the total immersion of the body.

Repentance qualifies *baptism*, distinguishing it from ceremonies of ritual ablution. John's was a "repentance-kind" of baptism, i.e., one based on, or characterized by, or expressing an attitude of repentance. The Greek word means literally "a change of mind," but the underlying Hebrew word is *shubh*, meaning to turn or to return. Repentance is both a turning from sin and a turning to God, a fundamental and decisive change of direction in life.

For the forgiveness of sins does not mean that forgiveness is determined by a human attitude or act. Neither repentance nor baptism robs God of his sovereign freedom to act as he will. The preposition *for* (*eis*) has a forward-looking significance; it describes motion toward. In the eschatological context of John's preaching, the phrase introduced by "for" sets forth the hope of the baptized, repentant person. He looks forward to receiving forgiveness instead of condemnation at the time of judgment.

The passage from Isaiah 40:3–5 (vv. 4–6) originally was a prophecy of the re-

turn of the exiles from Babylon to Palestine. The *wilderness* was the wasteland separating the captives from their homeland—a symbol of the hopelessness of their situation. But God was to lead them, as a mighty King, over a highway prepared for him through the difficult terrain. In the Masoretic Text the phrase *in the wilderness* modifies *prepare*, as can be seen in the RSV translation of Isaiah 40:3. The LXX, the version followed by Luke, makes it modify *the voice of one crying*. Thus, it is appropriately applied to John, the prophetic *voice* proclaiming in the wilderness that the time had arrived for the mighty visitation so long awaited. Luke extends the quotation beyond Mark to include Isaiah 40:4–5 because of the universal motif. The *salvation* to be revealed is not limited to Israel but is destined for the whole human race. Also he omits the citation from Malachi 3:1 found at Mark 1:2. This probably is because Luke knows that it does not come from Isaiah.

(2) John's Preaching (3:7–14)

7 He said therefore to the multitudes that came out to be baptized by him, "You brood of vipers! Who warned you to flee from the wrath to come? 8 Bear fruits that befit repentance, and do not begin to say to yourselves, 'We have Abraham as our father'; for I tell you, God is able from these stones to raise up children to Abraham. 9 Even now the axe is laid to the root of the trees; every tree therefore that does not bear good fruit is cut down and thrown into the fire."

10 And the multitudes asked him, "What then shall we do?" 11 And he answered them, "He who has two coats, let him share with him who has none; and he who has food, let him do likewise." 12 Tax collectors also came to be baptized, and said to him, "Teacher, what shall we do?" 13 And he said to them, "Collect no more than is appointed you." 14 Soldiers also asked him, "And we, what shall we do?" And he said to them, "Rob no one by violence or by false accusation, and be content with your wages."

John's denunciation brings out the necessity of genuine repentance prior to baptism. In Luke his preaching is directed toward the *multitudes* rather than the "Pharisees and Sadducees," as in Matthew

3:7. *Vipers* signifies poisonous snakes. The issue is the evil of the people, unrecognized and unrenounced by them as yet. Their insincerity and religious superficiality are apparent. They are simply trying to save themselves from the impending holocaust. It is apparent that John did not ascribe magical powers to baptism. The rite does not have any value apart from a sincere individual response to God. John requires his hearers to prove themselves by a new quality of life expressed in appropriate acts that can be described as *fruits that befit repentance.*

The special pride of the Jews was their descent from *Abraham;* in this also was based their hope for the future. Moses had pleaded with God to stay the destruction of the people out of regard for Abraham, Isaac, and Israel (Ex. 32:13). Such a plea will not suffice in the crisis proclaimed by John. Race will not be a factor in God's judgment. The Jewish hearers are not to suppose that they are essential to God's purposes, because he can make sons out of stones. This may be a play on words, since the two nouns are also very similar in Hebrew.

John conceives of himself as a prophet of the end-time. The final crisis is impending. The coming of Yahweh signifies both salvation and judgment in the Old Testament. So also for John, but he was dominated by the idea of judgment. Perhaps this was because of his sensitivity to the sins of his people. He understood that his ministry was a prelude to judgment—the last moment of opportunity for repentance. The remaining period of history is so brief that it can be compared to the moment of time required for the woodsman to raise his *ax* to deliver the first blow at the trunk of the tree. In John's message the *trees* represent individuals, which means that judgment is to be on a personal basis. Unrepentant, fruitless individuals face the consuming *fire* of the wrath of God.

When the people ask for guidance, John replies with a description of righteousness in terms of concrete social relationships.

This is in keeping with the best insights of the prophets. Amos characterized the unrighteous as those "who trample upon the needy, and bring the poor of the land to an end" (8:4). From the same perspective Isaiah said that the righteous man shares his bread, brings the homeless into his house, and covers the naked (58:7).

Coats were the inner garment or tunic, not the essential outer garment or cloak (cf. Luke 6:29). Travelers often wore two tunics but did not actually need more than one. Rather than keep more than the essential for oneself, the fortunate person should *share* with another human being in need.

According to this account John attracted the same kinds of people that gravitated to Jesus. *Tax collectors* mentioned in the New Testament were for the most part minor revenue agents. The payment of imposts, always disagreeable, was rendered even more repugnant by the exploitation commonly practiced by tax officials. A man to whom a region had been farmed out on the basis of competitive bids could enrich himself by demanding far more in taxes than he in turn had to hand over to his superiors. Among Jews tax collectors were regarded as a particularly odious lot because, as tools of a hated foreign power, they enriched themselves by bleeding their own countrymen.

The proper amount of revenue to be collected was determined by law or custom. Tax collectors were instructed by John not to charge more. There is an implicit sanction of the payment of taxes. Apparently John repudiated the firebrand revolutionaries of his day.

The context gives the impression that the *soldiers* are Jews, for John addresses only his countrymen. Plummer's suggestion (p. 92) that they were Jews recruited to assist local tax collectors is plausible. The emphatic use of the personal pronoun is well translated in the text: *And we, what shall we do?* It implies that the soldiers are identified with the tax collectors. They are told also not to use the power of their position to increase their income. This whole section separates the origins of Christianity from the revolutionary currents that finally erupted in rebellion against Rome in the war of A.D. 66–70. At the same time, it is certainly not warranted to think of the functions of a pagan state as determining the Christian attitude toward questions of government, war and peace, etc. The situation of Christians in pagan, totalitarian Rome meant that their possibilities were much more limited and their responsibilities for the state much less than those of Christians in a western democratic society.

(3) John and the Coming One (3:15–17)

15 As the people were in expectation, and all men questioned in their hearts concerning John, whether perhaps he were the Christ, 16 John answered them all, "I baptize you with water; but he who is mightier than I is coming, the thong of whose sandals I am not worthy to untie; he will baptize you with the Holy Spirit and with fire. 17 His winnowing fork is in his hand, to clear his threshing floor, and to gather the wheat into his granary, but the chaff he will burn with unquenchable fire."

The preaching of the wilderness prophet ignited a fervor of messianic expectation and provoked speculation about John's role in the approaching crisis. The text conveys well the attitude of uncertainty denoted by the optative mood of the verb: *whether perhaps he were the Christ.* John did not demonstrate the expected characteristics of the Messiah. He was not a descendant of David; neither did he perform the mighty deeds expected of the Messiah. There are evidences of a belief that the Messiah was present among the people incognito, unrevealed because of their sins. Perhaps some people thought that John was this hidden Messiah.

John's reply to the speculation of the people is a forthright rejection of the idea. Instead he points them to one who *is coming.* The "coming one," a participial form of the verb used in his reply, appears to have been a messianic title.[14] The crowds ac-

[14] See Scobie, *ibid.,* pp. 63 ff. for a discussion of this idea. Cf. article by Johannes Schneider in Kittel's *Theological Dictionary of the New Testament,* II, 670.

claimed Jesus as Messiah and referred to him as the Coming One upon his approach to Jerusalem (Luke 19:38). John's question to Jesus through his intermediaries was: "Are you the coming one?" (Luke 7:19).

John's denial of messiahship is phrased in a most emphatic way. So far is he from being the Messiah that he is *not worthy to untie the thong* of his sandals. According to the Talmud, one of a slave's duties was to take off his master's shoes (cf. Strack-Billerbeck, II, 1). In effect, John avows that he is not even worthy to be Messiah's slave.

John's baptism is *with water.* This is, his ministry was one of preparation, of calling people to repentance so that they would be ready for the onset of the new age. By contrast the Coming One would baptize with the *Holy Spirit and with fire.* The puzzling nature of this phrase is indicated by the variety of interpretations suggested for it. First of all, the text of a few manuscripts and Fathers does not have "Holy." It has been suggested that *Holy Spirit* is an early Christian gloss that does not represent John's teaching. Nevertheless, there is no reason why John could not have predicted the outpouring of the Spirit as the sign and blessing of the messianic age, an idea which was already in existence (Ezek. 36:27; Isa. 44:3; Joel 2:28). Too, the overwhelming weight of the textual evidence is for the retention of the phrase.

If the interpreter allowed the grammatical structure of the sentence to be decisive, he would be forced to conclude that baptism by the *Spirit* and by *fire* are aspects of the same experience. Both words seem to refer to the same group of people. In this case, fire would be understood as the purifying, refining process to be accomplished by the Spirit. Nevertheless, fire is always connected with judgment in John's preaching and should probably be understood as the coming fire of God's wrath to be poured out by the Messiah. Thus, John points beyond himself to another, a coming one, who will be the bearer both of God's redemption and his wrath.

In primitive threshing procedures, grain

is separated from chaff by tossing it into the air. The heavier grain falls to the floor, while the wind carries away the lighter chaff. John declares that God's judgment will be like this threshing process in that it will separate the genuine Israelites from those who are false and useless. After the time of threshing, farmers disposed of the chaff by destroying it with fire. By contrast the fire of God's judgment will be *unquenchable.* That is, it is inescapable, and once it begins, nothing can stay its course.

(4) John's Imprisonment (3:18–20)

[18] So, with many other exhortations, he preached good news to the people. [19] But Herod the tetrarch, who had been reproved by him for Herodias, his brother's wife, and for all the evil things that Herod had done, [20] added this to them all, that he shut up John in prison.

Luke recognizes that his report of the Baptist's teaching is condensed; John also uttered *many other exhortations.* Since his preoccupation was with the coming judgment and the terrible fate of those unprepared for it, his preaching was hardly *good news* to those against whom it was directed. But the good news of God's redemption also brings men under the judgment of God and makes them responsible for their decisions.

The notice about his imprisonment concludes the account of John's ministry. For reasons of his own Luke evidently desired to finish his sketch of John insofar as possible prior to beginning his presentation of Jesus' ministry (cf. Conzelmann, p. 21).

In his denunciation of *Herod* Antipas' immorality John shows that he is deserving to be ranked with his great predecessors like Elijah and Nathan. They, too, did not fear to expose evil in high places. Luke does not name *Herodias'* first husband, who was half brother to Antipas. Josephus called him Herod. Mark refers to him as Philip, but he is not the tetrarch of Ituraea (Mark 6:17).

In order to marry Herodias, Herod Antipas had divorced the daughter of Aretas, the neighboring Nabataean monarch, precipitating a crisis of international proportions. When John reproved the tetrarch for his actions, he was imprisoned. The New Testament interprets this as a guilt reaction on the part of Antipas; but it may also have been politically motivated, as Josephus suggests (*Antiq.*, 18,5,2). The pointed reprimands of the popular prophet could have aggravated an already sensitive political situation. Antipas was not acting out of character in his abuse of John, for this was just another in a succession of *evil things* done by him. Herod's subsequent defeat by the aggrieved Aretas was popularly interpreted as God's judgment on him for the execution of John the Baptist.

2. The Preparation of Jesus (3:21—4:13)

(1) The Baptism (3:21–22)

[21] Now when all the people were baptized, and when Jesus also had been baptized and was praying, the heaven was opened, [22] and the Holy Spirit descended upon him in bodily form, as a dove, and a voice came from heaven, "Thou art my beloved Son; with thee I am well pleased."

Certain problems were produced in the early Christian community by the baptism of Jesus. The fact that he had been baptized by John was used by some of John's followers as evidence of the superiority of the Baptist. Also Jesus accepted a "repentance-kind" of baptism to which sinners were summoned. But "in his own teaching there is no suggestion that he ever experienced the alienation from God which is the most baleful consequence of sin" (Caird, p. 76).

The Gospel accounts come to grips with these difficulties in various ways. Matthew shows that John was a reluctant baptizer of Jesus, who yielded only to the insistence of the candidate (3:14–15). John does not mention Jesus' baptism at all. Luke describes the event with a passive participle, which removes the necessity of mentioning John's name in connection with it. Jesus' baptism is also isolated from that of the people. The extreme grammatical awkwardness of vv. 21–22 is concealed by the translators' more grammatical English construction. The passage seems to say: (1) The baptism of Jesus followed the baptism of *all the people,* that is, the multitude with whom John had been conducting a dialogue. (2) The descent of the Spirit followed the baptism of Jesus. (3) This experience occurred while Jesus was praying.

In all the Gospels the coming of the Spirit on Jesus is compared to the descent of a dove. This identification of the Spirit of God with a dove is unusual. The closest parallel seems to be the one found in the Targum on the Song of Solomon 2:12, which says that the "voice of the turtledove" is the "voice of the Holy Spirit of . Redemption." Barrett has a good discussion of the symbolism of the dove (ff. p. 35). Luke removes the possibility of a metaphorical interpretation of his description by the phrase *in bodily form.* He affirms that the Spirit's descent was subject to visual verification.

There is a serious textual question related to v. 22. The weight of the manuscript evidence is on the side of the text adopted by the translators of the RSV. Nevertheless, in some very important witnesses, the heavenly message is a quotation of Psalm 2:7 (marg.). Some scholars believe that this was the original reading and that it was rejected by later scribes because it implies an adoptionist Christology.[15] This judgment is difficult to sustain. The author of Hebrews applies the same text to the preexistent Christ (1:5), showing that he saw no incongruity in such an application. Early Fathers like Justin, Clement of Alexandria, and Augustine did not sense a theological problem in the use of the text. It is probable, therefore, that the best attested reading (that of the text) is correct and that the variant represents a later assimilation to the Old Testament text.

Beloved may be a messianic title (cf. Eph. 1:6). The pronouncement would then read: "Thou art my Son, the Messiah." The message of the heavenly voice is very similar to the version of Isaiah 42:1 in Matthew

---

15 The idea that Jesus became the Son of God by adoption at his baptism, which, of course, involves a denial of his preexistence.

12:18. This seems to identify Jesus as the Isaianic Suffering Servant. The baptism of Jesus and the associated experience of the Spirit's descent constitutes his ordination for a ministry as Suffering Servant-Messiah. On his part, the baptism is his public commitment to God's will for his life. As such, it involved in anticipation the suffering and sacrifices which would ensue, specifically his death.

Just when and how Jesus arrived at the conviction that he was to play such a singular role in salvation-history must remain a mystery. His baptism was probably the climax of a long period of reflection, inner struggle, and deepening insight. At any rate, the baptism is considered to be the event with which Jesus' public ministry is initiated.

(2) The Genealogy (3:23–38)

23 Jesus, when he began his ministry, was about thirty years of age, being the son (as was supposed) of Joseph, the son of Heli, 24 the son of Matthat, the son of Levi, the son of Melchi, the son of Jannai, the son of Joseph, 25 the son of Mattathias, the son of Amos, the son of Nahum, the son of Esli, the son of Naggai, 26 the son of Maath, the son of Mattathias, the son of Semein, the son of Josech, the son of Joda, 27 the son of Joanan, the son of Rhesa, the son of Zerubbabel, the son of Shealtiel, the son of Neri, 28 the son of Melchi, the son of Addi, the son of Cosam, the son of Elmadam, the son of Er, 29 the son of Joshua, the son of Eliezer, the son of Jorim, the son of Matthat, the son of Levi, 30 the son of Simeon, the son of Judah, the son of Joseph, the son of Jonam, the son of Eliakim, 31 the son of Melea, the son of Menna, the son of Mattatha, the son of Nathan, the son of David, 32 the son of Jesse, the son of Obed, the son of Boaz, the son of Sala, the son of Nahshon, 33 the son of Amminadab, the son of Admin, the son of Arni, the son of Hezron, the son of Perez, the son of Judah, 34 the son of Jacob, the son of Isaac, the son of Abraham, the son of Terah, the son of Nahor, 35 the son of Serug, the son of Reu, the son of Peleg, the son of Eber, the son of Shelah, 36 the son of Cainan, the son of Arphaxad, the son of Shem, the son of Noah, the son of Lamech, 37 the son of Methuselah, the son of Enoch, the son of Jared, the son of Mahalaleel, the son of Cainan, 38 the son of Enos, the son of Seth, the son of Adam, the son of God.

Since he was born prior to the death of Herod the Great (4 B.C.) and entered his ministry in the fifteenth year of Tiberias' reign (A.D. 28–29), Jesus must have been at least 32 and possibly 36 years of age at his baptism. Luke says that Jesus was *about thirty,* which leaves room for adjustments required by the data.

The description of Jesus' anointing as Messiah is accompanied by conventional proof that he fulfilled requirements for the office by being David's Son. This may be why the genealogy is placed here rather than with the birth narratives where it would seem to fit more logically. The arrangement may also be influenced by the fact that the birth narratives and the genealogy came from different sources.

There are a number of variations between the lists of Jesus' ancestry offered by Matthew and Luke. Only Luke deals with the period from Adam to Abraham. From Abraham to David there is general agreement between Matthew and Luke. The problem of sources did not arise because the Old Testament tables were authoritative (1 Chron. 1—2). Luke traces the descent from *David* through *Nathan,* whereas Matthew's line goes through Solomon. *Zerubbabel* and *Shealtiel* are the only two names of David's descendants found in both lists.

Attempts have been made to reconcile the two tables by suggesting that Luke traces Jesus' genealogy through Mary, in contrast to Matthew who traces it through Joseph. In this case, the whole phrase *as was supposed of Joseph* is considered parenthetical. Verse 23 is then interpreted as saying that Jesus was really *the son* [grandson] *of Heli,* Mary's father, although it was supposed that he was the son of Joseph. Aside from the implausibility of this exegesis, it assumes a practice contrary to the normal. Ancestry was commonly traced through the father. Furthermore, Luke's acceptance of the supernatural conception of Jesus would not rule out his tracing Jesus' ancestry through Joseph as a valid way of establishing a claim to Davidic descent.

The significant feature of Luke's genealogy is the extension of it back to *Adam.* This establishes Jesus' connection to the whole of humanity. No one group can claim him for its own; he belongs to all. By the same token, his mission was not narrow and provincial. It was universal in its sympathy and reach. Furthermore, anyone who identifies himself with this son of Adam, in so doing, transcends his own exclusive racial or social circle. He takes his stand in the much wider context of the "new race" of God's people, gathered from all lands and tribes.

(3) The Temptation (4:1–13)

[1] And Jesus, full of the Holy Spirit, returned from the Jordan, and was led by the Spirit [2] for forty days in the wilderness, tempted by the devil. And he ate nothing in those days; and when they were ended, he was hungry. [3] The devil said to him, "If you are the Son of God, command this stone to become bread." [4] And Jesus answered him, "It is written, 'Man shall not live by bread alone.' " [5] And the devil took him up, and showed him all the kingdoms of the world in a moment of time, [6] and said to him, "To you I will give all this authority and their glory; for it has been delivered to me, and I give it to whom I will. [7] If you, then, will worship me, it shall all be yours." [8] And Jesus answered him, "It is written,
'You shall worship the Lord your God,
   and him only shall you serve.' "
[9] And he took him to Jerusalem, and set him on the pinnacle of the temple, and said to him, "If you are the Son of God, throw yourself down from here; [10] for it is written,
'He will give his angels charge of you, to
   guard you,'
[11] and
'On their hands they will bear you up,
   lest you strike your foot against a stone.' "
[12] And Jesus answered him, "It is said, 'You shall not tempt the Lord your God.' " [13] And when the devil had ended every temptation, he departed from him until an opportune time.

The public commitment to the divine purpose for his life, i.e., to be God's Messiah, is followed by a period of solitude and reflection in which Jesus struggles with the meaning of his experience and the direction that his life should take. There is an existential validity to the juxtaposition of the two narratives of the baptism and the temptation. In a fleeting moment Jesus had seen what others could not see, had heard what they could not hear. Now the question arises: Will the recent experience stand the test of reflection and criticism? What at one moment seems so real, so right, so authentic can begin in retrospect to appear dim, unreal, foolish, visionary.

The temptations marked the beginning of Jesus' ministry, but they also reveal the tension in which it proceeded. There was a basic clash between his commitment and the ideas of his contemporaries. The strong pressures of his environment attempted to force him into the messianic mold fashioned by popular ideas and ambitions. He struggled against these forces from the wilderness experience through the agony of Gethsemane.

The key to the interpretation of the temptations is given by the author of Hebrews, who affirmed that Jesus was "tempted as we are" (4:15). The temptations are genuine; the struggles described, real. Thus, the account has meaning for human beings who find themselves overwhelmed in the pressures of life. The dramatic form in which the narrative is cast should not be allowed so to influence the interpreter that he understands the temptations in mythical terms, totally unrelated to the real life situation.

Luke tells us that Jesus *returned from the Jordan.* But to what place? The description of his movements is hardly clear. In the parallels (Mark 1:12; Matt. 4:1) Jesus goes directly from the Jordan to the wilderness. *Full of the Holy Spirit* is a Lukan note. Peter, Stephen, Barnabas, and Paul are also so described. They are distinguished from others whose possession by the Spirit is less marked, more sporadic. Jesus was led *in* rather than *by* the Spirit: the Greek preposition *en* should be given its locative force. His days in the desert were spent in the environment of the Spirit. The variation from Mark 1:12 may reflect an effort to avoid the suggestion that Jesus was subordinate to the Spirit. The

wilderness is not named but that is not important. It is the place of testing. In the Old Testament *forty days* is the usual period for this kind of experience. Moses (Deut. 9:9) and Elijah (1 Kings 19:8) both fasted forty days.

The *devil* (Satan in the Markan parallels) is God's adversary, seeking to alienate men from their Creator. He tempts them with a view to bringing about their downfall and destruction (cf. Stagg, pp. 21 ff.). The clash between Jesus and Satan is a power struggle between two kingdoms, the kingdom of God and the kingdom of evil.

The hunger from which Jesus suffers is the occasion for the first temptation. The voice at the baptism had declared that he was God's Son. But, is not his experience of hunger and deprivation in God's world a mocking contradiction of this relationship? He needs bread, but all around there are only stones. Would not a genuine proof of his identity be an exhibition of control over creation by turning a *stone* into lifesaving bread? Such is the struggle that followers of Jesus also experience. If we are God's children, why should we suffer while others enjoy health? Why should we be poor while others prosper?

But faith in God should not depend on the amount of bread that one has. This had been Israel's sin (Ex. 16:2 f.) when confronted by a situation similar to the one in which Jesus finds himself. To turn stones into bread will not prove his sonship. In fact, it will demonstrate the very opposite. Sonship is not expressed in the exercise of some kind of magical power, but by a calm, confident faith in God in the midst of life's most difficult circumstances. Neither is God's love proved by how much bread one has (nor by the number of cars in the garage, for that matter). Jesus refuses to commit Israel's ancient sin. He will not cease to depend on God's loving care to supply what he needs (cf. 12:22–31). Nor will he subordinate the primary concern with God's rule to the secondary physical needs of life. He rejects the temptation with a reference to the lesson which God taught Israel in the wilderness (Deut. 8:3). Man is more than a stomach to be filled, a body to be clothed. He is God's child who must depend always on his creative and sustaining word for the deepest needs of his existence, with the assurance that all other things will be provided as well (Matt. 6:33).

The second temptation illustrates a major tension of Jesus' life. Many people expected the Messiah to be a world ruler who would "restore the kingdom to Israel," a task which many believed would involve military conflict. Although one cannot actually see *all the kingdoms of the world* simultaneously, it is not impossible for a man to visualize himself as the ruler of the world and make this his ambition. This is the prize that Satan dangles before Jesus.

The biblical faith rests upon the conviction that *authority* over the world belongs ultimately to God. God may grant authority to another power or permit him to exercise it. Thus, in the New Testament Satan is called "the ruler of this world" (John 12: 31) or, even more vividly, "the god of this world" (2 Cor. 4:4). But this is only to be taken in a limited sense. He is the ruler of an age that is passing away. The sovereignty of God ultimately will be established over all the recalcitrant elements of the universe.

Here Satan claims to be able to transfer the domain under his sovereignty at will. To Jesus he offers world rule, demanding as his price that Jesus *worship* him. To worship the devil is to adopt satanic methods, to choose the weapons of power, violence, and destruction to attain one's ends. Perhaps this narrative should be understood as a commentary on the nationalistic ambitions that surged so strongly in some Jewish breasts. They would be categorized as satanic. Once again Jesus replies with a scriptural quotation (Deut. 6:13). He will serve only God, which means, translated into a life style, that he will walk the road of redemptive suffering and reject the way that seems to offer popular acceptance— success in the conventional sense—and

temporal power.

The scene of the third temptation is the *temple* in *Jerusalem*. The identification of the *pinnacle* is uncertain. It was probably the summit of a wall or battlement where the distance to the ground was great, such as the Royal Cloister on the south side overlooking a ravine (Josephus, *Antiq.,* 15,11,5).

The Temple, the center of Jewish religious life in which throngs of volatile, fervent, patriotic worshipers crowded on feast days, was the place for a dramatic, sensational demonstration of messianic power (cf. John 7:2 ff.). Such a maneuver would serve to rally the people and initiate the liberation of Jerusalem and the reestablishment of the Davidic dynasty.

The challenge is based on the hypothesis as the first temptation: *If you are the Son of God.* It is even justified by a proof text from Psalm 91:11–12—a good illustration of the weakness of this approach to understanding the Bible. Jesus rejects the suggestion that he should *tempt* God, that is, put him to such a test. To yield to this kind of temptation, no matter how pious the rationalization, results in an effort to force God's hand by putting him into a corner and making him act on other than his own terms. This was the kind of sin that the children of Israel were guilty of (Ex. 17:2) and which Moses warned them not to repeat (Deut. 6:16). These words of warning constitute Jesus' reply to the temptation. He will not repeat Israel's sin. God must be allowed to act in his own way and in his own time. The only attitude appropriate to a child of God is one of confident faith and patient waiting on him.

The temptations of Jesus stand in close relationship with the testing of Israel in the wilderness. The symbolism of the 40 days, the character of the temptations and especially the replies of Jesus, all taken from Deuteronomy, point to the earlier trials of Israel. There is one great difference. Whereas the children of God had succumbed to the trials in the wilderness, this strong Son of God emerges victorious over every temptation.

After exhausting the possibilities of the moment, the devil departs until an *opportune time*. This looks ahead to the notice in Luke 22:2 about the renewed attacks mounted against Jesus by the devil. Between these two notices the ministry of Jesus will run its appointed course.

III. The Ministry in Galilee (4:14—9:50)

1. Teaching in the Synagogues (4:14–30)

(1) Acceptance in Galilee (4:14–15)

[14] And Jesus returned in the power of the Spirit into Galilee, and a report concerning him went out through all the surrounding country. [15] And he taught in their synagogues, being glorified by all.

This editorial comment provides a transition between the baptism and temptation and the subsequent ministry in Galilee. Matthew (4:12) and Mark (1:14) connect Jesus' return to Galilee and the beginning of his public ministry with the arrest of John the Baptist. But Luke has already described John's arrest. The reference to the *Spirit* establishes a close relationship between the preceding accounts of the baptism and temptation and the following report of the Galilean ministry. *The power of the Spirit* which descended on Jesus at his baptism, enabling him to win the victory in his struggle with Satan, will be demonstrated in the public ministry which now begins. It is especially his power to cast out demons and to heal. Of the Evangelists only Luke thus associates the power of God with the Spirit (1:35; cf. Acts 1:8).

Jesus soon became the center of much public attention, as the *report concerning him* spread. Luke, with the other Evangelists, mentions the synagogue as the center of Jesus' teaching in the early stages of his ministry. Increasing hostility to him by religious leaders apparently forced him out of the synagogues or caused him to decide on pursuing his teaching and other activities in the open. The popular reaction to him was positive as described in the comment *being glorified by all*. To glorify in this sense means to praise. But this is not the real glory of Jesus. He will dedicate himself to the path that leads to the glory of God, which involves taking a course that will cause people to misunderstand him. His ministry begins with his being glorified by men and ends with his being glorified by God.

(2) Rejection in Nazareth (4:16–30)

[16] And he came to Nazareth, where he had been brought up; and he went to the synagogue, as his custom was, on the sabbath day. And he stood up to read; [17] and there was given to him the book of the prophet Isaiah. He opened the book and found the place where it was written,

[18] "The Spirit of the Lord is upon me,
   because he has anointed me to preach good
      news to the poor.
He has sent me to proclaim release to the
   captives
and recovering of sight to the blind,
   to set at liberty those who are oppressed,
[19] to proclaim the acceptable year of the
   Lord."

[20] And he closed the book, and gave it back to the attendant, and sat down; and the eyes of all in the synagogue were fixed on him. [21] And he began to say to them, "Today this scripture has been fulfilled in your hearing." [22] And all spoke well of him, and wondered at the gracious words which proceeded out of his mouth; and they said, "Is not this Joseph's son?" [23] And he said to them, "Doubtless you will quote to me this proverb, 'Physician, heal yourself; what we have heard you did at Capernaum, do here also in your own country.'" [24] And he said, "Truly, I say to you, no prophet is acceptable in his own country. [25] But in truth, I tell you, there were many widows in Israel in the days of Elijah, when the heaven was shut up three years and six months, when there came a great famine over all the land; [26] and Elijah was sent to none of them but only to Zarephath, in the land of Sidon, to a woman who was a widow. [27] And there were many lepers in Israel in the time of the prophet Elisha; and none of them was cleansed, but only Naaman the Syrian." [28] When they heard this, all in the synagogue were filled with wrath. [29] And they rose up and put him out of the city, and led him to the brow of the hill on which their city was built, that they might throw him down headlong. [30] But passing through the midst of them he went away.

The report about Jesus' rejection in Nazareth is transposed—according to most interpreters—from its Markan context (Mark

6:1–6) to this place. Several considerations support this conclusion: (1) It fits much better in the Markan context, which allows time for the development of Jesus' ministry and sets the stage for the kind of reaction to him described therein. (2) Although he follows Mark closely in his presentation of the Galilean ministry, Luke omits the Markan account of the Nazareth experience when he comes to it. He shows thereby that he has already used this material. (3) The mention of mighty deeds in Capernaum (4:23) would follow more naturally on the description of Jesus' activities in that city (4:31 ff.).

That the transposition was deliberate is hardly debatable. The reason for the freedom with which Luke handles the material is likewise clear. In this way Luke secures an episode appropriate to his purpose with which to introduce Jesus' public ministry. As it is presented in Luke, the Nazareth episode is highly representative of the picture the author is seeking to portray in his total work. In fact, it is a microcosm of the whole—Luke-Acts in miniature, one might say. In outline it corresponds closely to the Markan account, but the variations and elaborations give the distinctive Lukan emphases. Especially does the Jewish-Gentile dialectic as seen from Luke's perspective unfold in the story.

Nazareth, Jesus' home town, is the first stop on the Galilean preaching itinerary as outlined in the third Gospel. Jesus first offers the good news to his own people and forces upon them the necessity of making a decision about him. The pluperfect *had been brought up* infers that Jesus had been absent from Nazareth for some time prior to this visit. Luke stresses that his visit to the *synagogue . . . on the sabbath* was consonant with his *custom.* This serves to link Jesus with pious Jewish practice, one of the motifs that we saw in the birth and childhood stories.

In synagogue services the first Scripture reading was from the Torah and followed a schedule of 155 defined lessons designed to complete the entire Pentateuch in three-year cycles. In Palestine and Babylon the reading of each verse of the Hebrew text was followed by a translation into Aramaic, the lingua franca of the Middle East. The reading from the prophets followed the lection from the Torah. It is not clear if the selection of this passage was made by the head of the synagogue. Perhaps the choice was left to the reader's discretion. Any person could be invited to read the Scripture lesson, which was followed by a sermon when a competent teacher was present. Commonly, Scripture was read while standing, but the sermon was delivered while seated (see vv. 16,20).

The quotation from Isaiah is a rather free rendering from the Septuagint of portions of Isaiah 61:1–2 and 58:6. The reference to the Spirit harks back to the baptismal experience, when Jesus was anointed for his messianic mission. The nature of Jesus' ministry is delineated in terms of the prophetic word. There is a significant difference between Mark and Luke at this point. Mark says that Jesus proclaimed the nearness of the kingdom and urged repentance and faith as the acceptable responses (Mark 1:14–15). Luke generally avoids the theme of the imminence of the kingdom, emphasizing instead that Jesus' teaching and preaching were concerned with its nature (cf. 4:43; 16:16). Jesus is the bearer of the *good news* intended for the dispossessed, the afflicted, and the oppressed. The *poor,* the *captives,* the *blind,* etc., describe the spiritual bankruptcy and distress to which the good news brought by Jesus answers. The gospel is directed toward those whose only hope is that God will act on their behalf to accomplish liberation and healing. The good news is the disclosure that this is in fact what God is doing. The words that describe the people for whom the gospel is intended must not be given an exclusively symbolic meaning, however, because Luke shows that Jesus did indeed identify primarily with the socially, religiously, and economically excluded people of his day. The *acceptable year of the Lord* is the messianic age which has now begun in the person and work of Jesus.

The *attendant* who received the Isaiah scroll in order to return it to the chest was the chazan. He seems to have functioned as an assistant to the head of the synagogue in a role similar to that of deacon in the early church.

The story now takes on a highly dramatic note. Jesus *sat down* in a hushed atmosphere in which *the eyes of all . . . were fixed on him.* The stillness is broken by the solemn cadence of a sensational disclosure: *Today this scripture has been fulfilled in your hearing.* He, the one whom the Spirit had anointed to be the Isaianic Servant of Yahweh, had read the passage that set forth his program to the congregation. They had been ushered into the messianic age, since they were in the presence of God's Messiah. The time of waiting was over; the time of decision had arrived. Their confrontation with Jesus was the crucial moment when God spoke the decisive "now" of prophetic fulfillment.

The initial response was favorable. The congregation found his words *gracious,* that is, winsome and attractive. But they do not really understand who Jesus is. To them he is *Joseph's son,* a conclusion that stands at an infinite distance from the genuine understanding that he is God's Son, as portrayed in Luke.

Will quote (v. 23) is taken by some interpreters to be a prophetic future, describing the reaction that Jesus' reported deeds in Capernaum will produce in his own town (cf. Conzelmann, p. 34). The proverb that follows was current in the ancient world. It does not apply to the situation neatly, since Jesus is required to perform mighty deeds before his compatriots by healing others rather than himself. Nevertheless, the general sense is clear. Just as a physician is challenged to prove his capacity by exercising his healing arts on his own infirmities, Jesus is challenged to do for his own people what he has done in a neighboring town. His claims will have to be backed up with signs. The uncompromising nature of the attitude is emphasized by *doubtless* which is a strong affirmative. It is the story of the temptations illustrated by the events of Jesus' ministry: "If you claim to be the Messiah, you must do the deeds expected of the Messiah here before us."

The attitude of the congregation is an illustration of the axiom that *no prophet is acceptable in his own country.* In Luke the rejection of Jesus is part and parcel of the consistent rejection of the prophets by their own people (Acts 7:52). Jesus uses two Old Testament illustrations to justify his refusal to accede to the demands of his people for a sign. *Elijah* and *Elisha* both performed mighty works for outsiders which they did not do for their own people. Several points emerge which are important in the development of Luke-Acts: the hostility to the message of the Old Testament by the very people who claim it as their own; the reference to Gentiles which lays the groundwork for the spread of the gospel beyond the Jewish race; the murderous rage of the assembly at the implication that despised Gentiles receive benefits denied to them.

The *brow of the hill* has been variously identified. The traditional site is a precipice 80 to 300 feet in height to the southeast of Nazareth, which itself is built on the slope of a hill. It is certain that the reader is to understand that Jesus' escape from the attempt to murder him was accomplished by supernatural powers. There is a relation between this incident and the third temptation. The reader perceives that Jesus actually possessed the powers that he refused to use under the wrong kind of pressure. Another connection may be in the author's mind as he looks forward to the story to be related in the book of Acts. There he will tell how the gospel triumphantly survived similar acts of hostility and rejection on the part of Jews.

2. The Mighty Works of Jesus (4:31—5:16)

(1) The Demon-Possessed Man (4:31–37)

³¹ And he went down to Capernaum, a city of Galilee. And he was teaching them on the

sabbath; [32] and they were astonished at his teaching, for his word was with authority. [33] And in the synagogue there was a man who had the spirit of an unclean demon; and he cried out with a loud voice, [34] "Ah! What have you to do with us, Jesus of Nazareth? Have you come to destroy us? I know who you are, the Holy One of God." [35] But Jesus rebuked him, saying, "Be silent, and come out of him!" And when the demon had thrown him down in the midst, he came out of him, having done him no harm. [36] And they were all amazed and said to one another, "What is this word? For with authority and power he commands the unclean spirits, and they come out." [37] And reports of him went out into every place in the surrounding region.

Luke now begins to follow Mark and does so through 6:19, except for the interruption occasioned by the insertion of 5:1–11. *Capernaum,* an important town on the northwest shore of the Sea of Galilee, was the center of Jesus' Galilean ministry. His deeds and the reception accorded to him there contrast markedly with the experience in Nazareth. The visitor to Tell Hûm, site of the ancient city of Capernaum, will find the excavated ruins of a synagogue dating from the third century. It may be located on the site of the synagogue in which Jesus taught.

The most significant aspect of his work was the *authority* of his word. Ultimate authority belongs to God. It is the unlimited and incontestable right and power to act which belongs to him as the Creator and Ruler of the universe. It is exercised uniquely by Jesus because of his relation to God as Son. It is, therefore, his freedom and capacity to act as God's Son. The instrument of his authority is his word, which is the creative and life-giving word of God. Mark, in the parallel passage, notes by way of commentary that Jesus did not teach as the scribes (1:22). In other words, he did not document his teaching with opinions from the Jewish sages. This comment is omitted by Luke for whom the authority of Jesus' word is demonstrated first of all by his power over demons and disease (v. 36). The acts of exorcism and healing performed by Jesus are direct and unmediated, accomplished solely by the power of his word. Word and deed, therefore, are

practically synonymous; Jesus' word is his deed.

The man who is the beneficiary of the first demonstration (in Luke) of Jesus' power is said to have the *spirit of an unclean demon.* The phrase is unusual. Elsewhere in the New Testament we find "spirit," "unclean spirit," "evil spirit," or "demon," and a few such expressions as "dumb spirit." Demons in Jewish and Christian thought are evil or unclean by definition, and the use of such descriptive adjectives is, therefore, redundant. Perhaps Luke's phrase is an accommodation to the Hellenistic thought-world of his audience in which demons could be good or evil.

Ancients explained erratic, aberrational behavior caused by emotional disturbances in terms of demon possession. Demon-possessed persons were thought by the Jews to be inhabited by a power alien to them and hostile to God. Demons were in the service of the "prince of this age." Thus, the utterances of the man are not considered to be his own but to proceed from the power that has taken control of his personality. The demon possesses supernatural powers which enable him to know who Jesus is. The designation *Jesus of Nazareth* is set over against *the Holy One of God.* The former is what men thought him to be, while the latter describes his true status. *Holy One* means basically one who is consecrated to God. The demon recognizes that Jesus and demons have nothing in common; they represent two antithetical, opposing forces. The only fate that the demon can anticipate in such a situation is that he will be expelled from his chosen abode and dispatched to the nether world where he belongs (see 8:31).

Jesus rebuked the demon, commanding silence; he would not accept the testimony that comes from such sources. At Jesus' command the demon departed from the man, the moment of his departure being marked by a severe convulsion. The amazement of the onlookers stemmed from the authority by which Jesus exorcised the demon rather than from the fact of the exorcism itself. Exorcism, after all, was common in the ancient world. The demon was exorcised by a single word of command, a memorable demonstration of the authority of Jesus' word.

The miracle as it stands in the synoptic material is a witness to the fact that in Jesus the kingdom of God was breaking in upon man. The rule of Satan was challenged in such a way as to show clearly its limits and to prophesy its eventual destruction. The modern reader can hardly appreciate the tremendous message contained in stories like this for the people who first heard the gospel. To them the very air was peopled by evil spirits which were the source of all kinds of afflictions. The Christian message invited men to trust in God whose sovereignty extended over all the powers of evil in the universe and who, therefore, could guarantee their freedom and their future (cf. Rom. 8:38–39). The earnest of the gospel's promise was provided by the deeds of Jesus who liberated unfortunate creatures from the demonic forces that enslaved them.

(2) Healings Outside the Synagogue (4: 38–41)

38 And he arose and left the synagogue, and entered Simon's house. Now Simon's mother-in-law was ill with a high fever, and they besought him for her. 39 And he stood over her and rebuked the fever, and it left her; and immediately she rose and served them.
40 Now when the sun was setting, all those who had any that were sick with various diseases brought them to him; and he laid his hands on every one of them and healed them. 41 And demons also came out of many, crying, "You are the Son of God!" But he rebuked them, and would not allow them to speak, because they knew that he was the Christ.

In this passage Luke mentions Simon for the first time, but he omits the names of the accompanying disciples given in Mark 1:29. Mark tells of the call of the disciples prior to his account of the Capernaum ministry (1:16–17). Since Luke did not use that material in deference to the narrative presented at 5:1–11, he refrains from mentioning the disciples at this juncture.

We learn now that Capernaum is the home town of Simon Peter. The healing of his mother-in-law is the second specific illustration of the authority of Jesus' word. In neither case does Jesus actually seek out opportunities to display his power, but he acts in response to challenges that are presented to him. In other words, he is no wandering miracle worker or sensation monger. In this instance persons plead with Jesus to intervene on behalf of the sick person. Although the woman's illness is not equated with demon possession, it is an example of the helplessness of human beings who are victimized by the powers of this "present, evil age" (see Stagg, pp. 22–23). Consequently, Jesus' approach is the same as in the preceding case of demon possession: he rebuked the fever (cf. 4:35). The validity and completeness of the cure is proven in that the woman is able to fulfill her household duties.

It is not correct to understand the miracle as a wonder story, proof within itself of Jesus' divinity (Richardson, pp. 20 ff.). People believed in the possibility of miraculous cures, so the ability of Jesus to cure did not by itself set him apart from others of his day. This incident should be understood as a sign. What was new and different was the authority with which Jesus confronted the disease, i.e., the immediate power of his word. He showed himself thereby to be God's Messiah, bearer of the good news of the kingdom to the distressed, liberating them from the forces that oppress them. Jesus represented the challenge of the new age to the old age of darkness, sin, and disease. Once again, in the cure of Simon's mother-in-law, he demonstrated decisively that the age of salvation had dawned.

Since the Jewish day was from sunset to sunset, the setting of the sun marked the end of the sabbath (v. 31). Released from the prohibitions against work, the inhabitants of the city could bring their sick to Jesus. The power of Jesus over both demon possession and disease was now demonstrated on a much larger scale.

The laying on of hands may be related to

the descent of the Spirit, or it may signify that power to heal flowed from Jesus to the sick person. It has already been shown, however, that Jesus can heal by his word alone. The demons recognize him whose power is superior to theirs, but they are prevented from revealing that he is the *Christ*. Is this because he does not want the testimony that comes from such a source? Or, is it because he is reluctant to accept the title of Christ (Messiah) due to its nationalistic connotations?

(3) The Departure from Capernaum (4: 42–44)

⁴² And when it was day he departed and went into a lonely place. And the people sought him and came to him, and would have kept him from leaving them; ⁴³ but he said to them, "I must preach the good news of the kingdom of God to the other cities also; for I was sent for this purpose." ⁴⁴ And he was preaching in the synagogues of Judea.

Jesus is not to be possessed by any one group; nor can the gospel be fenced in by human desires and plans. His life is under the imperative of the divine will, which stands against the human will expressed by the residents of Capernaum. This sense of divine imperative is expressed first by the verb *must* and second by the verb *was sent*. These verbs express the idea that Jesus is under an obligation to fulfill a mission on which God has sent him. For the first time Luke refers to the *kingdom of God*, the central theme of Jesus' ministry (see on 4:18–19). The divine imperative under which Jesus lives involves the preaching of the good news in all Jewish territory. Subsequently the church will be placed under the same obligation to go beyond this "to the end of the earth" (Acts 1:8). At least this is the understanding of salvation-history that Luke conveys. Some manuscripts have Galilee instead of *Judea* (see marg.). But Judea is preferable both on the basis of manuscript evidence and on intrinsic grounds. It is the more difficult and, therefore, the preferred reading. Luke means to say that Jesus' ministry covered all Jewish territory, which included

Judea as well as Galilee (Conzelmann, pp. 40 f.).

(4) The First Disciples (5:1–11)

¹ While the people pressed upon him to hear the word of God, he was standing by the lake of Gennesaret. ² And he saw two boats by the lake; but the fishermen had gone out of them and were washing their nets. ³ Getting into one of the boats, which was Simon's, he asked him to put out a little from the land. And he sat down and taught the people from the boat. ⁴ And when he had ceased speaking, he said to Simon, "Put out into the deep and let down your nets for a catch." ⁵ And Simon answered, "Master, we toiled all night and took nothing! But at your word I will let down the nets." ⁶ And when they had done this, they enclosed a great shoal of fish; and as their nets were breaking, ⁷ they beckoned to their partners in the other boat to come and help them. And they came and filled both the boats, so that they began to sink. ⁸ But when Simon Peter saw it, he fell down at Jesus' knees, saying, "Depart from me, for I am a sinful man, O Lord." ⁹ For he was astonished, and all that were with him, at the catch of fish which they had taken; ¹⁰ and so also were James and John, sons of Zebedee, who were partners with Simon. And Jesus said to Simon, "Do not be afraid; henceforth you will be catching men." ¹¹ And when they had brought their boats to land, they left everything and followed him.

We may assume an acquaintance between Jesus and the disciples that antedates the call to discipleship. But the isolated pericopes about Jesus' initial contacts with the disciples do not furnish enough information out of which to reconstruct their prior relationship. Luke passed over the Markan story of the call of the first disciples (Mark 1:16–20) in favor of the narrative placed here. The especially significant role played by Peter in Luke-Acts is foreshadowed by his prominence in this account in which other disciples are mentioned only incidentally. The call of Peter is attached to a miracle, which should be understood as a sign. The call of Jesus is the demand of the kingdom of God whose power has been demonstrated in the preceding miracle.

The scene is set at the *Lake of Gennesaret*, a designation sometimes used in this period instead of the more frequently encountered Sea of Galilee. Verses 1–3 show how Jesus and Simon happen to be in the boat together and, in this manner, set the stage for the main point of the narrative. Again the authority and power of the word of Jesus are underlined. The response required of a disciple to this authority is unconditional obedience. Thus, at the *word* spoken by Jesus, Simon lets down the nets, in spite of the apparent futility of attempting to catch fish after a long night of fruitless endeavor. The power of Jesus' word is illustrated by the immediate and overwhelming success of the fisherman's venture.

The supernatural demonstration of Jesus' wonder-working power produced in Simon Peter a sense of fear and of unworthiness. Peter's later failure at the crucial moment of Jesus' arrest and crucifixion became fixed indelibly in the memory of the community of early believers. Here his personal confession of sin is recorded for all to see that from the very beginning of his association with Jesus Peter recognized himself to be a *sinful man.*

Simon's position in the apostolic community is shown to rest not on his personal qualifications, but on the authority of Jesus' summons to discipleship. The word of Jesus to him is both assurance and call. The disciple, aware of his weakness, requires the word of assurance before he can receive the call. He is not capable of discharging the responsibility of *catching men,* any more than he had been capable of catching fish the previous night. But the work of God's kingdom does not depend on the capabilities of those called to be the instruments of its power. Their effectiveness is guaranteed by the sovereign power of the one who calls them into his service. When they act in response to the word of Jesus, they meet with success, even when efforts seem futile.

The earliest disciples were fishermen, but this does not mean that they were improvident. They were businessmen with a considerable investment in ships, equipment, and fishing rights. We are told that *they left everything* to follow Jesus. He who is called must be willing to deny the demands of his old involvements in order to live under the ultimate demand of his new commitment to Jesus.

(5) The Cure of a Leper (5:12–16)

12 While he was in one of the cities, there came a man full of leprosy; and when he saw Jesus, he fell on his face and besought him, "Lord, if you will, you can make me clean." 13 And he stretched out his hand, and touched him, saying, "I will; be clean." And immediately the leprosy left him. 14 And he charged him to tell no one; but "go and show yourself to the priest, and make an offering for your cleansing, as Moses commanded, for a proof to the people." 15 But so much the more the report went abroad concerning him; and great multitudes gathered to hear and to be healed of their infirmities. 16 But he withdrew to the wilderness and prayed.

Luke now returns to his Markan source, which he follows through 6:19. The healing of lepers had special messianic significance (cf. Matt. 11:5; Luke 7:22), for the Jews expected the extirpation of this disease would be one blessing of the messianic age (Strack-Billerbeck, I, 593 ff.).

As a social outcast, the leper was cut off from association with all but wretches in the same miserable condition (Lev. 13:45–46). But Jesus dared to touch even the leper! He would lead no sanitary, safe existence behind walls that keep human disease, filth, and misery at a comfortable and safe distance.

Rather than make public proclamation of his healing, the man is to follow the Mosaic requirements pertaining to persons cured of leprosy (Lev. 13–14). Jesus says that this is to serve as a *proof to the people.* The best supported text reads, literally, "as a witness to them." The following alternatives are possible interpretations of the difficult phrase: (1) Jesus was interested in the man's complete rehabilitation, which involved reintegration into society. This was possible only if he fulfilled the legal requirements and was pronounced well by the proper authorities. (2) Jesus wished to show that he was no iconoclast, bent on the destruction of the Law. His instructions are a proof of his respect for it. (3) The RSV translation implies that the man's cure was to be a proof to the people of Jesus' messianic power. The verdict of the priest would prove that the cure was complete and valid. The last suggestion is probably best.

The incident, noised abroad in spite of Jesus' admonition, added to his considerable popularity. So besieged was he that he found it necessary to withdraw to some secluded area where he wished to meditate. We find here one of the seven Lukan references to the prayers of Jesus without parallels in the other Gospels.

3. Conflicts with Religious Leaders (5:17 —6:11)

(1) The Healing of a Paralytic (5:17–26)

17 On one of those days, as he was teaching, there were Pharisees and teachers of the law sitting by, who had come from every village of Galilee and Judea and from Jerusalem; and the power of the Lord was with him to heal. 18 And behold, men were bringing on a bed a man who was paralyzed, and they sought to bring him in and lay him before Jesus; 19 but finding no way to bring him in, because of the crowd, they went up on the roof and let him down with his bed through the tiles into the midst before Jesus. 20 And when he saw their faith he said, "Man, your sins are forgiven you." 21 And the scribes and the Pharisees began to question, saying, "Who is this that speaks blasphemies? Who can forgive sins but God only?" 22 When Jesus perceived their questionings, he answered them, "Why do you question in your hearts? 23 Which is easier, to say, 'Your sins are forgiven you,' or to say, 'Rise and walk'? 24 But that you may know that the Son of man has authority on earth to forgive sins"—he said to the man who was paralyzed—"I say to you, rise, take up your bed and go home." 25 And immediately he rose before them, and took up that on which he lay, and went home, glorifying God. 26 And amazement seized them all, and they glorified God and were filled with awe, saying, "We have seen strange things today."

The unusual introduction to this story prepares us to anticipate that it will be different from the previous accounts of Jesus' mighty acts. An august body of religious leaders from every village of Galilee and Judea and from Jerusalem had assembled (cf. Mark 2:2). The Pharisees, or "separatists," constituted one of the most influential Jewish parties in New Testament times. Although the derivation and meaning of the name are not clear, it probably described the members of the sect in terms of their efforts to avoid contamination by unclean things and persons. In addition to the Hebrew Scriptures, consisting of the Torah, the Prophets, and the Writings, the Pharisees also accepted the oral tradition, the interpretative and legal comments on Scripture, as authoritative. Teachers of the law is a characteristic Lukan term for the scribes. They were the experts in the Law who were dedicated to its interpretation and application.

The power of the Lord is a Lukan touch. The Lord (kurios) is used often in Luke's writings to refer to Jesus. Here one would assume that it is equivalent to the Septuagintal translation of Yahweh. Leaney remarks that the ambiguity may be deliberate (p. 124).

The cures performed by Jesus are initiated in various ways. Here Jesus acts in response to the faith of the men who had gone to such great lengths to place the paralytic before him. Thus, we are shown that the faith of the believing community also has an important role to play in bringing wholeness to the afflicted. Through the tiles indicates that Luke's mental picture is a Roman house with a tiled roof rather than the sod roof common in Palestine presupposed in Mark 2:4.

Until this point Jesus' cures had been directed toward the physical malady. The powers of evil, expressed in demon possession, leprosy, and other afflictions which held men in their grip, had been challenged and defeated. But there is a deeper illness, whose symptoms are not always so apparent, for which a cure is also needed. No man is whole so long as he is a prey to guilt with its train of fears, anxiety, and emotional disturbances.

The rabbis also taught the fundamental need of forgiveness in complete healing. Consequently, it was not the fact that Jesus dealt with the need of forgiveness that caused the problem. It was his approach— the direct and confident manner with which he also assumed authority over sins. In rabbinic theology man could be an instrument of healing, but only God could forgive sins. Nor is there any basis in Jewish writings for the idea that the Messiah would grant the forgiveness of sin in his own right (Strack-Billerbeck, I, 495). In the eyes of the religious leaders Jesus overstepped the boundaries between humanity and deity; and, for the first time in Luke, they begin to express hostility toward him.

Blasphemies—the emotion-laden word with a capacity to raise hostility to the point of murderous fury—is uttered. The religious leaders understood Jesus all too well. He proposed to act in his own name, so much so that the word spoken by him was the direct, unmediated word of God.

Jesus points out the logical inconsistency in his critics' attitude. After all, he had been performing the other acts of healing in the same authoritative way. They themselves believed that divine healing was preceded by forgiveness. Therefore, to speak the word of forgiveness is essentially no more than to speak the word of healing. They are simply two sides of the same coin (v. 23).

But that you may know is not an accommodation to the critics' blindness. Rather, Jesus meets their challenge forthrightly. The word of healing is spoken in such a way as to illustrate the authority which Jesus expressed in forgiving the man's sins. *I say to you* emphasizes his authority clearly and unequivocally. There is no calling on another power, no invocation of the name of deity, no magical words or motions. It is true that Jesus had been performing his other acts of healing in the same authoritative manner, but only now does the meaning become really clear. In effect, Jesus throws down the gauntlet to his enemies. One who can command a paralytic to walk in such fashion can also forgive sins. The evidence is there for them to see that *the Son of man has authority on earth to*

forgive sins. They are clearly confronted by the enigma: Whence came such authority?

Son of man can simply mean man. This is the connotation in Ezekiel where the term is employed in God's communications to the prophet. It can also refer to the glorious apocalyptic figure of the end-time, who was expected to come in power to deliver the righteous and judge the wicked. This connotation goes back to Daniel 7:13 which says, "with the clouds of heaven there came one like a son of man." The concept of a glorious, apocalyptic figure associated with the end of the age is elaborated in the Book of Enoch.

Sometimes "Son of man" is used in contexts where it seems to mean simply "I." Most of the time it has affinities with the messianic figure of Daniel and Enoch. Nevertheless, there are significant modifications, which were produced by blending the Son of man concept with the Suffering Servant figure of Isaiah. Thus, we find the paradox of a Son of man who is rejected and suffers. But he is also the resurrected and exalted One whose church confidently expects his coming in power and glory. As it is used in Daniel, the term seems to be a corporate one, representing the "saints of the Most High." This corporate idea is also important to an understanding of the New Testament usage. At times the Son of man is reduced to one, i.e., Jesus; at other times it includes the people of God and bears similarities to the Pauline concept of the body of Christ (see on 6:22). Stagg (pp. 58 ff.) gives a fuller discussion of the title. In Acts 9:4 Paul, the persecutor of the saints, is accused of persecuting Jesus, an illustration of the importance of the corporate idea in Lukan thought.

The term is used outside the Gospels only in Acts 7:56 and Revelation 1:13; 14:14. It is Jesus' preferred self-designation and may have been selected to avoid the title of Messiah because of the undesirable connotations attached to this term and because of the paradoxical possibilities mentioned above.

The cure of the paralytic produces

amazement and awe. There is a general recognition that the power of God has been seen at work. *All* probably should not be thought to include the critics, because their hostility continues to be expressed in the succeeding episodes.

(2) Association with Outcasts (5:27–32)

27 After this he went out, and saw a tax collector, named Levi, sitting at the tax office; and he said to him, "Follow me." 28 And he left everything, and rose and followed him.

29 And Levi made him a great feast in his house; and there was a large company of tax collectors and others sitting at table with them. 30 And the Pharisees and their scribes murmured against his disciples, saying, "Why do you eat and drink with tax collectors and sinners?" 31 And Jesus answered them, "Those who are well have no need of a physician, but those who are sick; 32 I have not come to call the righteous, but sinners to repentance."

Where Luke has only *Levi*, Mark identifies him as the son of Alphaeus (2:14). The Matthean parallel (9:9) has Matthew instead of Levi. The various relevant references are puzzling. Neither Luke nor Mark uses this name in the lists of the apostles, but they do include the name Matthew (Luke 6:15; Acts 1:13; Mark 3:18). These lists mention James the son of Alphaeus, which is also an alternate reading in a few manuscripts to Mark 2:14. Traditionally, Matthew has been identified with Levi, but the evidence outlined above is hardly conclusive.

Levi was probably engaged in collecting customs levied on commerce flowing along the Damascus-Acre highway. The remarkable aspect of the story is that Jesus not only associated with people like Levi but included them in his most intimate group of followers.

The command is brief and simple: *Follow me.* But it implies a great deal. To be a follower of Jesus meant that one had to be prepared to take the risks that he took. It also meant that there could be no competing loyalties. So we are told that Levi *left everything* and "began to follow" (imperfect tense) him. This involved giving up a lucrative position and embarking on a new

and dangerous venture for which there were no guarantees.

All the Gospels tell of Jesus' relationship to tax collectors and sinners, but Luke gives special prominence to it. The fact that Jesus ate with them constituted a threat to the accepted social conventions. To have business dealings with them was one thing, but to eat with them in their homes or to invite them to your home was quite another. "Decent people" simply did not socialize with such men.

The *sinners* were the "people of the land" (*'am-ha-aretz*), that multitude of common folk who either did not have the zeal or lacked the opportunity for observing the mass of religious traditions that were considered essential in dealing with ritual defilement.

The criticism against Jesus in Mark (2:16) is broadened to include the *disciples* in Luke 5:30. In this way the incident is made contemporaneous with the later time. The followers of Jesus in their disregard of accepted norms and social barriers considered that they were but following the example of their Lord. And indeed they were! The remarkable phenomenon is that many professing followers of Jesus now shut the doors of their homes, clubs, and even churches to others because of considerations of race and class.

The reply of Jesus to the criticism is couched in irony. The *righteous* are those who think themselves righteous. They measure themselves by the failure of others to live by their accepted norm. In this way, the righteous exploit the sinners. They are really glad that there are sinners, for otherwise they could not claim to be righteous. Their situation will remain unchanged until they recognize their own spiritual bankruptcy. Then they will see that before God all such categories as Pharisee, tax collector, and sinner become irrelevant. *To call* means also to invite, as, e.g., to the meal in which Jesus participated. The ambiguity has more point in the Markan context where Jesus seems to be the host and where, also, we do not find the phrase *to repentance.* Only *sinners,* that is, those who know themselves to be sinners, are called, because they are the only ones who will respond.

(3) The Question of Fasting (5:33–39)

33 And they said to him, "The disciples of John fast often and offer prayers, and so do the disciples of the Pharisees, but yours eat and drink." 34 And Jesus said to them, "Can you make wedding guests fast while the bridegroom is with them? 35 The days will come, when the bridegroom is taken away from them, and then they will fast in those days." 36 He told them a parable also: "No one tears a piece from a new garment and puts it upon an old garment; if he does, he will tear the new, and the piece from the new will not match the old. 37 And no one puts new wine into old wineskins; if he does, the new wine will burst the skins and it will be spilled, and the skins will be destroyed. 38 But new wine must be put into fresh wineskins. 39 And no one after drinking old wine desires new; for he says, 'The old is good.' "

Various examples of fasting are found in the Old Testament, especially in times of sorrow, repentance, national emergency, etc. But only the fast on the Day of Atonement was prescribed by law. After the destruction of Jerusalem, four days of fasting were established to commemorate this catastrophe (Zech. 7:3,5; 8:19). In Judaism, fasting came to be considered an especially meritorious practice, a signal mark of religious piety.

We are told about only one experience of fasting in the ministry of Jesus (Luke 4:2). Unlike similar experiences in the Old Testament (e.g., Moses in Ex. 34:28), this fast did not precede but followed the reception of a divine revelation. Fasting apparently was not a practice with Jesus and his followers, except on the Day of Atonement and possibly on the four days mentioned above. The rejection of this practice accords with Jesus' disregard for other traditional religious practices. His attitude also identifies him with the prophets who recognized the danger of such superficial interpretations of piety (e.g., Isa. 58:1 ff.).

In keeping with the tradition that Moses went up on Mount Sinai on Monday and returned on Thursday, pious Pharisees fasted twice each week (Luke 18:12), as evidently did followers of John the Baptist. Jesus' disregard of this practice of fasting furnished his critics with another vantage point from which to attack him.

In his reply Jesus removes fasting from the category of a pious act and interprets it in the Old Testament sense as an appropriate response to sorrow or crisis. The wedding banquet furnished a good analogy, because it was a festive and gay occasion for the groom and his party. The guests were relieved from the obligation to fast so that the merriment would not be marred. The point is that the disciples were not living in times of sorrow but in times of joyous fellowship with Jesus. Jesus invited men to a feast not a fast. Moments of crisis and sorrow would follow when fasting would be more suitable.

Two commonplace but pointed figures illustrate the folly of trying to press the new force which Jesus had set in motion into the old forms of Judaism. *No one* does with garments or wine what the critics want to do with Jesus and his gospel. The point of the analogy is that this involves forcing a harmony which does not exist, i.e., *the new will not match the old* (but see Mark 2:21). Judaism cannot be patched with elements from the Christian gospel. The *new wine* which it constitutes will destroy the old wineskins, which represent Judaism. In this way the basic irreconcilability between the teaching of Jesus and contemporary Judaism is stressed. According to the Lukan thesis, this irreconcilability existed because of the failure of the Jewish leaders to see that the Christian movement represented the ongoing stream of genuine Judaism.

No matter what its merits, any new thing will be rejected by some people who prefer the comfortable forms of the old. Verse 39 probably expresses a common Jewish attitude encountered by early Christians. Claims for the superiority of Judaism over Christianity were based on its more ancient vintage.

(4) Disregard for Sabbath Traditions (6:1–5)

¹ On a sabbath, while he was going through the grainfields, his disciples plucked and ate some ears of grain, rubbing them in their hands. ² But some of the Pharisees said, "Why are you doing what is not lawful to do on the sabbath?" ³ And Jesus answered, "Have you not read what David did when he was hungry, he and those who were with him: ⁴ how he entered the house of God, and took and ate the bread of the Presence, which it is not lawful for any but the priests to eat, and also gave it to those with him?" ⁵ And he said to them, "The Son of man is lord of the sabbath."

In some manuscripts *sabbath* is modified with a peculiar word, which may be translated literally as "second first" (see marg.). This is most probably a gloss. If not, we can only conjecture as to its meaning. It may distinguish this as the "second sabbath after the first" one mentioned in Luke's Markan source (4:31 f.; see Plummer, pp. 165 f.).

Disregard for the sacred traditions of the sabbath struck a blow at the nerve center of Judaism. Sabbath observance and circumcision were the two most vital expressions of the covenant relation between Israel and Yahweh. The penalty for failure to observe the sabbath was exclusion from the community (Ex. 31:14), or even death (Num. 15:32–36); but there is no evidence that violators *were* punished so severely in Judaism.

The Decalogue contains a general proscription of work on the sabbath (Ex. 20:8 and parallels). The oral tradition, the "hedge" which had been built around the Law, defined this commandment in precise and minute terms for Jews of the first century. The disciples were guilty of a multiple violation of these traditions. They broke the prohibition against reaping when they *plucked* the *grain*. By *rubbing them in their hands* they disregarded the laws against threshing and winnowing.

Jesus demonstrates the inconsistency in Jewish legalistic morality by appeal to a scriptural precedent for the disciples' action (cf. 1 Sam. 21:1–6). The *bread of the Presence* was the twelve loaves placed on a table before the Lord in the sanctuary. Each sabbath the old loaves were replaced and subsequently eaten by the priests in the sanctuary. According to tradition, David had performed the act described in 1 Samuel 21:1–6 on a sabbath. By eating the bread normally reserved for priests, David and his men subordinated religious rules to the satisfaction of physical needs, as the disciples had also done.

Luke omits the saying, "The sabbath was made for man, not man for the sabbath" (Mark 2:27). There is a similar rabbinical teaching, "The sabbath was committed to you, not you to the sabbath" (Mekilta on Ex. 31:13). But in the interpretation and application of this principle Jesus differed drastically from the rabbis. This is borne out by the affirmation: *The Son of man is lord of the sabbath.* If we read man for "Son of man," Mark 2:28 is a logical and significant development on 2:27. The Markan context, therefore, almost requires us to give "Son of man" the meaning of man (see on Luke 5:24). The rabbis would never have gone so far as to say that man is lord over the sabbath.

Thus the story illustrates the basic conflict between two diametrically opposed approaches to religion. In one, religious rules and ritual requirements are made the center. Man is dehumanized and depersonalized because he is subordinated to the rules. In Jesus' approach man is put at the center. Human welfare and need take precedence over any rule or ceremony. To say that man is lord of the sabbath, one of the two most important Jewish religious institutions, is to subordinate all others to him. The story shows that Jesus was not against the sabbath as such. He was simply opposed to an interpretation of it that disregarded the primary worth of human beings.

(5) The Man with the Withered Hand (6:6–11)

⁶ On another sabbath, when he entered the synagogue and taught, a man was there whose right hand was withered. ⁷ And the scribes and

the Pharisees watched him, to see whether he would heal on the sabbath, so that they might find an accusation against him. [8] But he knew their thoughts, and he said to the man who had the withered hand, "Come and stand here." And he rose and stood there. [9] And Jesus said to them, "I ask you, is it lawful on the sabbath to do good or to do harm, to save life or to destroy it?" [10] And he looked around on them all, and said to him, "Stretch out your hand." And he did so, and his hand was restored. [11] But they were filled with fury and discussed with one another what they might do to Jesus.

This narrative contains a number of characteristic Lukan touches (cf. Mark 3:1–6). Luke specifically states that it was the *right hand* that was affected. He also refers to the presence of hostile *scribes* and *Pharisees* at the beginning rather than at the end of the story. He omits the reference to Herodians, perhaps in keeping with his political apologetic.

The rabbis taught that the sabbath prohibitions could be disregarded in order to save a life. For example, a child trapped in a locked room could be released on the sabbath even if the door had to be broken down (*Tos. Shabbat* 15:11 f.). The healing of this crippled man, however, could not take precedence over the law of the sabbath because his life was not in danger. Presumably he would suffer little more to wait until sundown, at which time the healing could be accomplished legitimately.

Again there is a collision of two divergent approaches to religion. The sabbath was interpreted largely in negative terms in Judaism. True, there was the positive side, for it was also a day of joyous worship. Man's relation to God was stressed, but not the corollary responsibility to fellow human beings. Jesus interpreted the sabbath positively. The primary question is not the negative one: What shall I refrain from doing? Rather, it is: What good can I do on the sabbath?

The answer to the question is apparent. There is a man who needs healing. By doing this good act on the sabbath one also serves God.

Luke omits the reference to Jesus' anger toward his critics (Mark 3:5), caused by their callous disregard for the welfare of a fellow human being. He does describe the *fury* incited by Jesus' act. To the religious leaders this seems to be an impertinent and arbitrary affront to one of their most sacred institutions. They now comprehend that Jesus represents a serious threat with which they must cope.

4. The Choice and Instruction of the Twelve (6:12–49)

Luke uses two episodes from Mark to set the stage for Jesus' great sermon. The sequence in which he gives them represents a transposition of the Markan order. The choice of the twelve (cf. Mark 3:13–19) is placed before the notice about mighty works performed among a multitude (cf. Mark 3:7–12).

The sermon is presented as the culmination of a connected series of events. Jesus spends the night *in prayer* (6:12). At dawn he assembles his *disciples* and selects the *twelve* from them (6:13). He then descends from the hill top with the twelve and the other disciples to a *level place* where there is a waiting multitude (6:17). After healing the sick and demon-possessed among the multitude (6:18–19), Jesus delivers the sermon, which he addresses specifically to the *disciples* (6:20).

At 6:20 Luke begins to use sources other than Mark and continues to do so through 8:3. This block of material is often referred to as the "small interpolation."

It is generally agreed that Q is the source of both the "Sermon on the Level Place" in Luke 6:20–49 and the Sermon on the Mount in Matthew 5:1—7:27. There are many similarities between the two sermons. Both begin with a series of beatitudes, and both end with the parable about the two builders. There is no parallel in Matthew to the series of woes found in Luke 6:24–26. In addition, parallels to Luke 6:39–45 are found elsewhere in Matthew but not in the sermon. Otherwise, the content of the Lukan sermon is represented in the Sermon on the Mount. The sermon in Matthew, however, is much longer than the one in Luke. At least to some extent, this is due to Matthew's propensity to group related materials in the same section. Much of the Sermon on the Mount appears in other contexts in Luke. A notable exception is the almost complete absence of the kind of material found in Matthew 5:17 ff. and 6:1 ff.

(1) The Naming of the Twelve (6:12–16)

12 In these days he went out into the hills to pray; and all night he continued in prayer to God. 13 And when it was day, he called his disciples, and chose from them twelve, whom he named apostles; 14 Simon, whom he named Peter, and Andrew his brother, and James and John, and Philip, and Bartholomew, 15 and Matthew, and Thomas, and James the son of Alphaeus, and Simon who was called the Zealot, 16 and Judas the son of James, and Judas Iscariot, who became a traitor.

Only Luke tells us that Jesus prayed *all night* before selecting the twelve. This gives a note of great solemnity to the crucial event. The *twelve* are selected from the larger group of *disciples*. The number, which corresponds to the number of Israel's tribes, is doubtless significant. The symbolism indicates that the community created by Jesus is none other than Israel reconstituted and that he is its King-Messiah.

Outside of Luke *apostles* usually has the general sense of missionaries. It is used frequently by Luke as a designation of the inner circle of Jesus' associates. Matthew and Mark have only one such usage (Matt. 10:2; Mark 6:30). Mark says that the purpose of selecting the twelve was that they might "be with him" and "be sent out to preach." In other words, they were Jesus' chosen delegates, to be sent out bearing the authority of his appointment as heralds of his message. In order for them to fulfill this role, it was necessary for them to spend some time with Jesus. In Luke's writing the apostles are primarily witnesses who guarantee the historical authenticity of the church's message.

Most of the twelve are no more than names to us. *Simon* is mentioned first as befits his position as the leader and spokesman of the group. The epithet given to Simon by Jesus is translated *Peter*. It would be preferable to translate it into the English equivalent "rock." The hopes entertained for Simon by Jesus and the possibilities for greatness which Jesus saw in this yet unstable man are seen in the name. Jesus saw in a person not only what he was at the moment but also what he could become, and he willed this for his life.

Last place is given to *Judas*, who is remembered primarily for his treachery. The meaning of *Iscariot* is obscure. Some have understood it to describe Judas as the "man from Kerioth." Oscar Cullman [16] believes that the meaning is "zealot."

Luke's list of the twelve differs from Mark's in that he identifies *Andrew* as Simon's brother, omits the description of *James* and *John*, translates the transliterated "Cananaean" correctly as *Zealot*, and has *Judas the son of James* instead of Thaddeus.

(2) The Setting of the Sermon (6:17–19)

17 And he came down with them and stood on a level place, with a great crowd of his disciples and a great multitude of people from all Judea and Jerusalem and the seacoast of Tyre and Sidon, who came to hear him and to be healed of their diseases; 18 and those who were troubled with unclean spirits were cured. 19 And all the crowd sought to touch him, for power came forth from him and healed them all.

The selection of the twelve marks a new stage in the ministry of Jesus. From this time on he is accompanied in his travels by this specially chosen group. The encounter with the *multitude* occurs on a *level place*, not a plain but a place still in the mountains suitable for the gathering of such a crowd. The notice in 7:1 indicates that this series of events is located in the vicinity of Capernaum. Three groups of people are now present: the twelve, *a great crowd of his disciples* and the *multitude of people*. The size of the crowd is stressed, as is also its representative nature. *All Judea* proba-

16 *The State in the New Testament* (New York: Scribner's, 1956), p. 15.

bly means the Jewish homeland, including Galilee and Perea. Luke characteristically mentions *Jerusalem* separately from other Jewish territory (cf. 5:17; Acts 1:8). The people have been drawn to Jesus for two reasons: they desire *to hear him* and *to be healed.* Sometimes the power of Jesus to heal is described almost as if it were "a physical fluid transferable to others by touch" as in this passage where Luke writes that *power came forth from him* (Barrett, p. 75).

(3) The Beatitudes (6:20–23)

20 And he lifted up his eyes on his disciples, and said:
"Blessed are you poor, for yours is the kingdom of God.
21 "Blessed are you that hunger now, for you shall be satisfied.
"Blessed are you that weep now, for you shall laugh.
22 "Blessed are you when men hate you, and when they exclude you and revile you, and cast out your name as evil, on account of the Son of man! 23 Rejoice in that day, and leap for joy, for behold, your reward is great in heaven; for so their fathers did to the prophets.

Beatitudes are common in ancient literature among both Hebrews and Greeks. The beatitudes of Jesus, however, are characterized by unusual originality and force. In this sermon they are all stated in the form of paradox. The blessed are the poor, the hungry, the sad, the persecuted. The beatitudes emphasize the nonmaterialistic, eschatological grounds for blessedness. Blessedness is not due to long life, health, wealth, and kindred benefits, but to the possession of the kingdom of God. The first beatitude states this, and the last three simply interpret what it means to possess the kingdom of God.

The passive construction of the final clause, which gives the reason for blessedness, is circumlocution to avoid mentioning the divine name. It is God who gives the kingdom, satisfies hunger, causes laughter, and rewards the persecuted. The beatitudes are predicated on the sovereignty of God. This accounts for the conviction that the ultimate nature of things will constitute

a reversal of the human scene with all its inequities and injustice. They are also based on Jesus' conviction that in his word God's judgment and grace become immediate and decisive for those who hear. The beatitudes and the woes that follow (vv. 24–26) constitute God's saving word in the first instance and his call to repentance in the second (Walter Grundmann, p. 141). Jesus confronts men with the reality of God's future in which is implicit the demand for them to make the necessary adjustments with reference to the present. His utterance of the beatitudes is the fulfillment of the prophetic word in Isaiah 61:1. Thus, they are far more than wisdom sayings, teachings, or moral principles. They are the breaking in of the kingdom of God, the challenge of the old aeon by the decisive word of God.

Blessed denotes the happiness or good fortune of those who receive God's salvation. In the beatitudes Jesus defines what happiness is. But he does so in a way that completely contradicts the ideas and values of a materialistic, sensual society which equates happiness with house, car, or bank account.

In keeping with his messianic program Jesus first proclaims "good news to the poor" (cf. 4:18). Surprisingly, Jesus says that the happy, fortunate, or blessed are the *poor.* Poverty is basically a social and economic category. Teachings about the poor figure prominently in the Old Testament. They must be provided for (Lev. 19:10); God heeds their cry (Psalm 34:6); the wealthy are condemned for their exploitation of the poor (Amos 5:11). The demand for social and economic justice is written large in the Law and the Prophets. Poor also came to have a religious connotation. The "pious poor" were those who placed their faith in God alone rather than in the security offered by worldly possessions.

In v. 20 *you poor* is descriptive of the disciples. Matthew qualifies poor with the phrase "in spirit." This is an illuminating interpretation. Poverty in itself is not a source of happiness. To the contrary, it can be debilitating, degrading, and enslaving. But a change of values from a lower to a higher level is liberating and ennobling. Some disciples had recognized the depth of their poverty (even in the midst of material sufficiency) and had come to depend on God alone. They had exchanged a false security for a genuine security, since their future now belongs to God.

Jesus declares that these people who depend completely on God possess his *kingdom.* Kingdom means primarily the rule of God. It cannot be equated with territory, race, or culture, since God is in fact the ruler of the whole universe. The rule of God, therefore, cannot be promoted by man. It can only be acknowledged, affirmed, and proclaimed. The man who possesses the kingdom of God has come under the sovereign rule of God with all that this means for the present and the future. Implicit in this confidence in the sovereignty of God is the conviction that God's rule will be established completely. This involves the elimination of all evil.

The word *hungry,* similar to the word *poor,* has a double connotation. Hunger itself can be a terrible, tragic experience. As these lines are written, sensitive consciences everywhere are deeply troubled by terrible pictures of little bloated children dying of starvation in a besieged region of Africa. There is nothing blessed or Christian about that. The emphasis in the beatitude is on the present tense. The blessed are those who *hunger now.* That is, they do not find their satisfaction from the sources offered by the world. Perhaps they also hunger physically. Many early Christians suffered economic deprivation because of the estrangement between them and their world caused by their commitment to a pilgrimage whose goals lie beyond the petty and superficial satisfactions of the present. Their hunger is the only kind that will certainly be satisfied since God alone can satisfy the deepest longings and needs of mankind.

Paradoxically, men who have turned to God and who confidently face the future which he provides *weep now.* They weep because of their sins and their sorrows. They weep also because they are sensitive to the injustices and wrongs which they see in their world. They weep because of racism, the exploitation of the poor, the tragic slavery of people bound by drugs and alcohol, and the heartache and suffering of men. They will *laugh* because God's right will prevail. Love, forgiveness, reconciliation, and healing are the forces that will determine the ultimate shape of things. God has so willed, and it must come to pass. This is the kind of conviction which underlies the beatitudes and makes possible the prophetic assurances with which they are spoken.

The kind of persecution described in v. 22 is exclusion from the Jewish religious community, the synagogue. Those who are persecuted because of the *Son of man* are also pronounced blessed. The Son of man can have the sense of a corporate personality. This idea is present in Daniel where the Son of man seems to represent the "saints of the Most High" (cf. Dan. 7:14 and 18). Thus, Son of man can refer to a person, i.e., Jesus, or it can also include the community which is constituted by him. To suffer *on account of the Son of man* in this instance means to suffer as a disciple, as one who is identified with Jesus as a member of the new Israel, the church. Rather than producing consternation and perplexity, persecution should be an occasion for jubilation. *Leap for joy* translates the same word that occurs in 1:44. In the midst of suffering, the disciples can experience the joyous anticipation of a great *reward.* Reward should not be taken in a crass, materialistic sense (see on 6:35). Whatever men receive from God comes from his grace. It is not, therefore, a question of balancing books, that is, of paying man something which he has earned. Furthermore, an interpretation of reward must be consonant with the character of God and with the character of the disciple as disciple. The commitment to discipleship is made on the basis of self-giving and self-forgetfulness, which rules out a scheming, calculating approach to the service of God. The second cause for joy in persecution is that the disciple thus becomes a part of a great company of heroic men, the *prophets*, who experienced the same kind of treatment. But early Christians preferred to identify themselves with Jesus himself in their suffering (cf. Phil 3:10).

(4) The Woes (6:24-26)

24 "But woe to you that are rich, for you have received your consolation.
25 "Woe to you that are full now, for you shall hunger.
"Woe to you that laugh now, for you shall mourn and weep.
26 "Woe to you, when all men speak well of you, for so their fathers did to the false prophets.

This series of woes, found only in Luke, is a prophetic condemnation of the limited perspective of people who are controlled by purely secular values. Jesus declares that the miserable, unfortunate people are those who are *rich*, who are *full now*, and who *laugh now*.

The key to the meaning of the woes is the stress on the present tense. The rich are not condemned because they possess wealth—an awesome responsibility but in itself no sin. It is their attitude toward wealth that is at issue. They think they are rich, i.e., do not recognize their real poverty and deep need. Those who are full now are the people who get their satisfaction out of the present and the temporal. They do not hunger for that which God provides. Those who laugh now are the people who get their enjoyment out of the near, the tangible, the ephemeral. They are unconcerned and untouched by the hurt and misery of fellow human beings.

The persons about whom *all men speak well* are classed with the *false prophets*. They are the priests of the status quo who do not challenge the injustices and wrongs of society in the name of the God of justice and mercy.

(5) Love for Enemies (6:27-31)

27 "But I say to you that hear, Love your enemies, do good to those who hate you, 28 bless those who curse you, pray for those who abuse you. 29 To him who strikes you on the cheek, offer the other also; and from him who takes away your cloak do not withhold your coat as well. 30 Give to every one who begs from you; and of him who takes away your goods do not ask them again. 31 And as you wish that men would do to you, do so to them.

How are the needy and persecuted (vv. 20-23) to respond to those who exploit and oppress them? Jesus' answer is *love your enemies*. The command is absolute, without any loopholes or support for evasive rationalizations. But how can love be commanded? Of course, it cannot if we interpret love as only a sentiment or an emotion. We are attracted to and repelled by people for reasons that we only dimly perceive at best. But love is much more than a sentiment. It is a way of living with and relating to other human beings. We can act in creative, helpful, and redemptive ways toward people for whom we do not feel attracted—even toward those who are hostile and vindictive. This way of acting is subject to the control of mature people who have been liberated by the gospel; and, therefore, it can be commanded.

The succeeding phrases interpret what Jesus meant by his command. It is illuminating that the stress is primarily put on action—*do good, bless, pray for*. The action prescribed for the disciple is the opposite of the hostile action directed against him. Jesus' disciple does not have the right to reply in kind to injury. His weapons are not the harsh word, the club, nor the gun. He is armed only with active love, goodwill, kindness, and forgiveness. Jesus gives some concrete illustrations of what he means. There is no insult any more direct or provocative than being struck on the *cheek*. What is the disciple to do in such a case? Is he just to stand there and submit to the indignity? No! He is to seize the initiative in a wholly unexpected and incredible manner. He must *offer the other also.* If a man is robbed of his *cloak* (the outer garment), he must be willing to let the criminal have his *coat* (the inner garment). The principle is laid down that hostility and violence are to be met with active goodwill expressed in deeds that are in exact contrast to what might be anticipated.

Love requires us to be generous and openhanded. This is emphasized by the startling illustrations given in v. 30. The question might well be raised as to whether love does not at times require the refusal of requests in the interest of the other person's welfare. But that is not at issue here where Jesus is describing the limitless, unqualified generosity that should characterize his followers.

In one form or another the Golden Rule (v. 31) is found in the heritage of various cultures. It was also not lacking in Judaism, as, e.g., in Tobit 4:15: "And what you hate, do not do to anyone." Jesus puts it in the positive form, which is more in keeping with the foregoing teachings. His disciples are not only to refrain from doing harm to others. They must also give to men the understanding and help which all people desperately need from their fellows.

(6) The Nature of Genuine Love (6:32–36)

32 "If you love those who love you, what credit is that to you? For even sinners love those who love them. 33 And if you do good to those who do good to you, what credit is that to you? For even sinners do the same. 34 And if you lend to those from whom you hope to receive, what credit is that to you? Even sinners lend to sinners, to receive as much again. 35 But love your enemies, and do good, and lend, expecting nothing in return; and your reward will be great, and you will be sons of the Most High; for he is kind to the ungrateful and the selfish. 36 Be merciful, even as your Father is merciful.

Credit translates the Greek word for grace, which is used in the New Testament with subtle distinctions difficult to express in English translations. Grace is God's overflowing goodness poured out on undeserv-

ing people. But the grace of God also elicits grace in the individual, so that he who is its recipient becomes the instrument for the expression of the same compassion toward others. Jesus affirms that we do not need to possess any special grace or generosity of spirit to be able to respond to people who are loving and good to us. Nor does it require a spirit of sacrifice or liberality to invest in people when we have the assurance of receiving at least as much in return. *Even sinners,* i.e., anybody, can trade favor for favor.

But to love hostile, critical people and to love them much more than they deserve to be loved—this is grace. To invest one's life and substance in people who either cannot or will not reciprocate—this is also grace. It is the concrete expression in human relations of the presence and activity of God in his people. This kind of "love is not motivated by the goodness or beauty of the other. It seeks to bring about goodness and beauty in others." [17]

People who act in this way are assured that their *reward will be great* (cf. v. 23 above). What kind of reward does a man want who loves people who are difficult to love and who invests in them without hope of return? His reward is essentially his relationship with God and man. He is one of the *sons of the Most High.* A true son bears the character and inculcates the spirit of his father. So it is with genuine sons of God. What makes them different is that the spontaneous, undeserved, transforming love of God flows through them to others. This kind of relationship with God in self-giving to others is the highest of all rewards, since it is the genuine expression of life's real purpose.

In Matthew's parallel to v. 36 the word is "perfect" rather than *merciful.* But both have substantially the same meaning in this context. The tension under which the disciple lives is the character of God. The character of God is described as merciful,

17 Stagg, Frank, *Studies in Luke's Gospel* (Nashville: Convention, 1967), p. 58.

which means that he is constantly performing his mercies, i.e., concrete acts of love, toward people who do not deserve them. The disciple is to perform the same kinds of acts that God performs to the same kind of people. The imperative of the gospel demands that we become by living in this way what God in grace has already made us, that is, *sons.*

(7) A Warning Against Judging (6:37–38)

37 "Judge not, and you will not be judged; condemn not, and you will not be condemned; forgive, and you will be forgiven; 38 give, and it will be given to you; good measure, pressed down, shaken together, running over, will be put into your lap. For the measure you give will be the measure you get back."

To *judge* means basically to exercise discrimination, but here it is based on the assumption that one has the capacity to separate good people from bad. To *condemn* carries the idea a step further, for it means to judge the other person to be guilty. The desire of censorious, critical people is to establish not innocence but guilt. They want to discover the worst in people. This self-righteous, judgmental attitude is the very opposite of the generous spirit which Jesus demands. The fact is that our impressions about others are necessarily limited and superficial, distorted by our own prejudices and passions. Judgment cannot be just unless it takes all the facts into consideration. Since God alone is in possession of the whole truth about any of us, he is the only one capable of being judge. The person who judges usurps the place that belongs only to God. He is guilty of the worst kind of idolatry because he denies his own limitations as creature in his attempt to play God.

When men sit in judgment on their fellows, they in effect remove themselves from the category of sinners and thereby cut themselves off from mercy. When they *forgive,* they open their lives to grace. The only way that a person can be open to God's grace is for him to recognize that he himself is also a sinner. The inescapable corollary of this kind of self-knowledge is

the recognition that in his sin and need he stands on the same level as his brother. He and his brother are equally in need of forgiveness. We see then that it is impossible to be open to God and closed at the same time to our brother. Jesus does not teach that God's forgiveness is a mechanical reaction, subsequent to and dependent on the human act of forgiveness. To the contrary, the capacity to receive forgiveness and the ability to forgive are two sides of the same coin. Both of these are grounded in the fact that God's grace reaches out to us and to our brother at the same time.

Jesus assures us that we do not need to be afraid to *give* love and understanding. If we launch out on the kind of adventure to which he calls, we shall find that the resources which take the place of what we give away are never exhausted. We shall always receive an overflowing *measure* of God's love and goodness which more than replenishes our supply. *Lap* refers to the fold of the garment which fell down over the girdle and served as a pocket.

For the measure you give is not a threat. Nor does it transform God into a kind of celestial bookkeeper. It is a simple statement of the way things are.

(8) The Log and the Speck (6:39–42)

39 He also told them a parable: "Can a blind man lead a blind man? Will they not both fall into a pit? 40 A disciple is not above his teacher, but every one when he is fully taught will be like his teacher. 41 Why do you see the speck that is in your brother's eye, but do not notice the log that is in your own eye? 42 Or how can you say to your brother, 'Brother, let me take out the speck that is in your eye,' when you yourself do not see the log that is in your own eye? You hypocrite, first take the log out of your own eye, and then you will see clearly to take out the speck that is in your brother's eye.

The sayings in this series do not have an obvious relationship to one another. The first two appear in Matthew in other contexts and probably were inserted by Luke into the sermon. In Matthew the "blind guides" are the Pharisees (15:14). In the first Gospel the saying found in v. 40*a* is used to warn the disciples that they can expect no better treatment than their Master received (Matt. 10:24*a*).

Perhaps in the Lukan context the sayings are related to the general subject of judging, introduced in the preceding passage. They may be thought of as directed toward the twelve who have a special responsibility as leaders and teachers in the early community (Grundmann, p. 152). The *teacher* is not a judge of others. Yet, he functions as something of a critic by the very nature of the case. People who come under his influence will determine their course of action by his orientation. If the teacher is to be helpful to others, he must keep his own life under constant and rigorous self-examination. The teacher who is *blind* to his own faults can hardly help others to see theirs. Indeed the *disciple* cannot be expected to rise above the level of his teacher. On the contrary, the disciple *fully taught*, i.e., on whom the teacher has exerted a maximum influence, *will be like his teacher*. Blind teachers will produce blind disciples.

The disciples are not to judge, but they must not be indifferent to the moral needs of their brothers. This is just as bad in its way as judging them. Jesus teaches that we are responsible for the moral and spiritual welfare of others (cf. Gal. 6:1 ff.). The brother always has a *speck* in his eye, and he needs help in order to get it out. Anyone who has ever had to call on someone to help him get a small, foreign particle out of his eye can appreciate the appropriateness of the figure. But we cannot assist others with their problems if we assume a position of moral superiority. The sin of our brother in comparison to our own must always be seen in the ratio of a *speck*, a tiny splinter, to a *log*, the main supporting beam of the house. People generally turn the equation around so that the sin of the brother becomes the log, whereas their own is the speck. This lays one open to the charge of being a *hypocrite*. The Greek word for actor was hypocrite, and from this comes

the meaning of one who pretends to be something he is not. The self-righteous person is a hypocrite because he is unaware of his need for grace. So long as he is so insensitive to his own need, he cannot be helpful to others with their moral burdens.

(9) *The Springs of Character* (6:43–45)

43 "For no good tree bears bad fruit, nor again does a bad tree bear good fruit; 44 for each tree is known by its own fruit. For figs are not gathered from thorns, nor are grapes picked from a bramble bush. 45 The good man out of the good treasure of his heart produces good, and the evil man out of his evil treasure produces evil; for out of the abundance of the heart his mouth speaks.

The quality of a man's outward acts is determined by his inner nature. This is illustrated by the analogy of the two kinds of trees. *Bad* can mean either rotten or useless, but the latter is indicated here. *Figs* and *grapes* are examples of good fruit. *Thorns* and *bramble* bushes are types of useless plants. The tree is commonly judged by its product; but, on the other hand, the quality of the tree determines the kind of product. There is this kind of basic relationship between a man's character and his deeds.

Deeds that are good and loving proceed from a generous, compassionate *heart.* The heart is the center of man as an intelligent, volitional, emotional being. If a man is not right at the center of his being, his deeds are contaminated from the source. Even so-called good acts can be evil if performed for the wrong motive. The proverbial hypocrite is the very religious man who prays long and gives to worthy causes, but all for the wrong reasons.

Of course, goodness or evil can be only relative evaluations when applied to human beings. Good and evil are mixed in the same individual. Nevertheless, genuinely good acts and words proceed from a genuine inner goodness.

(10) *Profession and Deeds* (6:46–49)

46 "Why do you call me 'Lord, Lord,' and not do what I tell you? 47 Every one who

comes to me and hears my words and does them, I will show you what he is like: [48] he is like a man building a house, who dug deep, and laid the foundation upon rock; and when a flood arose, the stream broke against that house, and could not shake it, because it had been well built. [49] But he who hears and does not do them is like a man who built a house on the ground without a foundation; against which the stream broke, and immediately it fell, and the ruin of that house was great."

Two different building processes underlie the parallel passages in Matthew and Luke (cf. Matt. 7:24–27). In Matthew the two men indicate their wisdom or lack of it by their selection of the kind of ground on which to build their houses. In Luke the wise builder goes to the trouble of digging down to the rock in order to find a secure *foundation* for his house, whereas the other fails to take this precaution. In Matthew the houses are buffeted by the forces of a storm, i.e., by wind, rain, and flood. The man who loses his house made the mistake of building in a dry wadi which in a winter storm becomes a raging torrent. In Luke both houses are battered by the flash flood of a rising river. This is not an uncommon occurrence in arid countries where rain can suddenly fill the beds of rivers that have long been dry, such as is the case with the Palestinian wadis.

The problem with which the parable deals is perennial, namely, the discrepancy between profession and practice on the part of members of the Christian community. Jesus teaches that verbal protestations of allegiance are not a secure foundation on which to face the flood of God's impending judgment.

Lord had a variety of meanings in New Testament times. They range from a title of respect equivalent to "sir" to the translation in the LXX of Yahweh, the sacred name for God. Rulers were called lords, as were also deities of the eastern world. In the East the deified ruler was given the title of lord in its religious sense. This produced grave problems for early Christians to whom there could be only one "Lord, Jesus Christ" (1 Cor. 8:6). The title took

on various shades of meaning in the development and expression of the Christian community's Christology vis-à-vis the Hellenistic world. An underlying and unifying concept in all its usages is the emphasis on authority, which is primary in this passage.

What does it mean to accept the authority of Jesus? It means much more than just using words, no matter how sacred they may be. The contours of one's life are to be determined by his demands. A person witnesses the lordship of Jesus in his life by both hearing and doing his words, some of the most difficult of which are contained in the sermon which ends with this warning.

5. The Nature of Jesus' Mission (7:1–50)

(1) Messiah's Mighty Acts (7:1–17)

a. The Centurion's Slave (7:1–10)

[1] After he had ended all his sayings in the hearing of the people he entered Capernaum. [2] Now a centurion had a slave who was dear to him, who was sick and at the point of death. [3] When he heard of Jesus, he sent to him elders of the Jews, asking him to come and heal his slave. [4] And when they came to Jesus, they besought him earnestly, saying, "He is worthy to have you do this for him, [5] for he loves our nation, and he built us our synagogue." [6] And Jesus went with them. When he was not far from the house, the centurion sent friends to him, saying to him, "Lord, do not trouble yourself, for I am not worthy to have you come under my roof; [7] therefore I did not presume to come to you. But say the word, and let my servant be healed. [8] For I am a man set under authority, with soldiers under me: and I say to one, 'Go,' and he goes; and to another, 'Come,' and he comes; and to my slave, 'Do this,' and he does it." [9] When Jesus heard this he marveled at him, and turned and said to the multitude that followed him, "I tell you, not even in Israel have I found such faith." [10] And when those who had been sent returned to the house, they found the slave well.

Matthew also has the story of the healing of the centurion's slave after the Sermon on the Mount (8:5 ff.) but separated from it by the healing of a leper. In Luke the centurion enters into contact with Jesus only through intermediaries, whereas in Matthew the contact between the two is direct.

The healing of the centurion's slave had great significance as a justification for the wider mission to the Gentiles which developed soon after the close of Jesus' ministry. The oft-mentioned symbolism of the narrative is apparent. Jesus heals at a distance with a word, as he also heals another Gentile, the Syrophoenician woman's daughter (Mark 7:24 ff.). This depicts the situation of Gentiles in the later Christian mission who had contact with Jesus through his word of power but not through his physical presence.

A *centurion* was technically the commander of a "century," a hundred infantrymen, of a Roman legion. The size of his command, however, varied with the size of the legion. Since Galilee was not under the direct rule of Rome, the centurion was an officer in the service of Herod Antipas. One of the chief functions of troops stationed in Capernaum, a border town, was to provide armed support for the tax collectors who levied customs on goods entering the region (see on 3:12–14). Although it is not stated that the centurion was a Gentile, it is implied at various points in the story.

Characteristically, the gravity of the illness is brought out, as is the worth of the sick person. *Dear* could refer to the economic value of the slave, but here it undoubtedly describes the great affection and esteem felt for him by his owner. Not presuming to approach Jesus personally, the Gentile army officer sends a delegation of Jewish *elders.* The title probably means only that they were important citizens. There is noteworthy similarity between this centurion and the officer in Acts 10. The centurion of Capernaum probably should also be described as a "God-fearer," one of a large number of Gentiles attracted to Judaism by its monotheism and high ethical standards who had not yet taken the steps to become proselytes. His appreciation of Judaism had been expressed by the generous gesture of bearing the cost of constructing the local *synagogue.*

The centurion's hesitation to enter into direct contact with Jesus stemmed from the fact that he was a Gentile. But there is no hesitation at all on Jesus' part in going to him (cf. on Matt. 8:7). The trip is interrupted by the second delegation, composed of *friends.* It is apparent that the centurion possesses two great characteristics, humility and faith. Although the Jewish delegation has described him as *worthy,* he himself protests that he is *not worthy* either to talk to Jesus or to receive him in his house. He is convinced that this is not necessary anyway. Jesus does not have to be present; he can heal with his *word.* Such is the confidence that he has in Jesus' *authority* over the powers that affect men. And he knows what authority is from two perspectives. His superiors have only to speak and he executes their orders. On the other hand, his word is sufficient to secure the obedience of those under his command. In like manner, Jesus' simple word of command will be sufficient to obtain the obedience of powers subject to him.

The story is the vehicle to carry the saying of Jesus (v. 9), which is its climactic and most significant element. A Gentile can have *faith*—not only so, he can have faith superior *even* to that which Jesus has found among the Jews. Only this man has perceived the real nature of the authority of Jesus. Luke ends the story with the characteristic note about the effectiveness of the miracle. Upon their return the messengers find the slave *well,* a word which means that he is in good health.

b. The Widow's Son (7:11–17)

[11] Soon afterward he went to a city called Nain, and his disciples and a great crowd went with him. [12] As he drew near to the gate of the city, behold, a man who had died was being carried out, the only son of his mother, and she was a widow; and a large crowd from the city was with her. [13] And when the Lord saw her, he had compassion on her and said to her, "Do not weep." [14] And he came and touched the bier, and the bearers stood still. And he said, "Young man, I say to you, arise." [15] And the dead man sat up, and began to speak. And he gave him to his mother. [16] Fear seized them all; and they glorified God, saying, "A great

prophet has arisen among us!" and "God has visited his people!" [17] And this report concerning him spread through the whole of Judea and all the surrounding country.

Nain, the modern village of Nein, was near Shunem where Elisha had raised a boy from the dead (2 Kings 4:21–37). It could be reached by traveling southwest from Capernaum some nine hours on foot. Only in this story, which belongs to Luke's special material, is Nain mentioned in the Synoptic Gospels.

The people accompanying Jesus are divided into two groups, the *disciples* and the *crowd,* a characteristic distinction after the events of 6:12–19. Prior to reaching the city gates of Nain they encounter a funeral procession on its way to the burial grounds outside the city. To accompany a corpse to burial was considered a meritorious work among the Jews. The tragic plight of the grieving mother is clear to all who are acquainted with ancient society. She is a *widow* who has now lost her *only son.* Since Jesus addresses the son as *young man* (v. 14), we may assume that the woman has been left alone at a relatively young age. She lived in a man's world in which a woman had no legal rights. The testimony of women and slaves was unacceptable in judicial proceedings (Sifre Deut. on 19:17). Thus a woman without a man to represent her was particularly helpless and defenseless. The Gospels testify that Jesus had *compassion* on people like this.

Jesus is called *Lord,* a particularly significant title for the exalted Christ in the Gentile Christian community. The earliest Christian confession of faith was "Jesus is Lord." The title is especially meaningful in a narrative which describes the power of the Lord of life over death, the ultimate enemy.

He *touched the bier,* in spite of the fact that contact with the dead was avoided because it rendered one unclean (Num. 19:11). At this signal the pallbearers stop, and Jesus commands the young man to come back to life. In the context *arise* means to arise or wake up from the dead. The command is prefaced by the direct, authoritative *I say to you* (cf. on 5:24). Through Jesus' word alone the young man is brought back to life. The completeness of the mighty act is shown by the fact that the young man *began to speak. And he gave him to his mother* is identical with the Septuagintal phrase in 1 Kings 17:23, evidence of the close relationship with the similar miracle performed by Elijah.

The deed of Jesus reminds the onlookers of the mighty acts performed by the great prophets Elijah and Elisha (1 Kings 17:17–24; 2 Kings 4:21–37). *Has arisen* is the same verb Jesus used in v. 14 and possibly has the same meaning (cf. 9:19). Perhaps they think that God has raised Elijah or Elisha from the dead. The belief that a *great prophet* has appeared indicates a conviction that the messianic age is at hand. The verb "to visit" is used to speak of God's intervention in the history of his people in acts of judgment and salvation. Here it is used, as also in the Greek text of 1:68, 78, with reference to the inauguration of the messianic age. The account concludes with a remark about the widespread dissemination of the report about Jesus' mighty act, setting the stage for the following episode.

(2) John's Question (7:18–23)

[18] The disciples of John told him of all these things. [19] And John, calling to him two of his disciples, sent them to the Lord, saying, "Are you he who is to come, or shall we look for another?" [20] And when the men had come to him, they said, "John the Baptist has sent us to you, saying, 'Are you he who is to come, or shall we look for another?' " [21] In that hour he cured many of diseases and plagues and evil spirits, and on many that were blind he bestowed sight. [22] And he answered them, "Go and tell John what you have seen and heard: the blind receive their sight, the lame walk, lepers are cleansed, and the deaf hear, the dead are raised up, the poor have good news preached to them. [23] And blessed is he who takes no offense at me."

All these things are the reports that were circulating about Jesus' mighty deeds, including the healing of the centurion's slave and the raising of the widow's son. Having already mentioned that John was in prison, Luke does not repeat that detail here (cf. Matt. 11:2). From Josephus we learn that he had been incarcerated by Herod in Machaerus, a fortress east of the Dead Sea.

John sends *two disciples* to transmit his question to Jesus, the minimum number of eyewitnesses necessary to establish a fact in judicial proceedings. They are to bring back eyewitness accounts as opposed to the secondhand reports John had received.

Luke does not necessarily imply that John's question was prompted by lack of faith. Nevertheless, the whole episode brings into focus the tension between what John had expected and the actual course of Jesus' ministry. John had proclaimed that the Messiah would initiate the eschatological judgment. He would hew down the fruitless trees (3:9) and destroy the useless chaff (3:17), but neither has taken place. Herod is still in power, while the prophet is in his prison.

He who is to come translates a participle, "the coming one." This was probably a messianic title (see on 3:16). It may have affinities with the concept of a glorious Son of man who was to come on the clouds (Dan. 7:13).

Jesus' answer to the query is given in the form of deeds which represent the fulfillment of his messianic program. He asks the two men simply to report what they *have seen*, from which John can draw his own conclusions. The list of deeds outlined by Jesus begins with the giving of *sight* to the *blind* and ends with the preaching of the *good news* to the *poor*. Both of these were mentioned in the program outlined in 4:18–19. The others are not mentioned there, but all testify to the breaking in of the sovereignty of God.

To take *offense* means to trip or to fall over something. From this comes the usage often found in the New Testament of being tripped up morally or caused to fall into sin. Men who were dominated by preconceived notions of what the Messiah was supposed to do would find Jesus' words and deeds offensive. Jesus was rejected to a great extent because he was a surprise. He did not fit the mold that men had prepared for him, one that was shaped largely by their own desires for revenge and glory. They wanted a Messiah who would destroy their enemies and end their national humiliation. They supported their expectations with Scripture. But even with Scripture men cannot predict God, otherwise man with Scripture would become God. This is a perennial idolatry that continues to reappear in pious circles. The *blessed* person is he who is sensitive to what God is doing and is able to respond without the handicap of preconceived notions. Moffatt translates the phrase: "And blessed is he who is repelled by nothing in me" (v. 23).

(3) Jesus' Evaluation of John (7:24–30)

24 When the messengers of John had gone, he began to speak to the crowds concerning John: "What did you go out into the wilderness to behold? A reed shaken by the wind? 25 What then did you go out to see? A man clothed in soft raiment? Behold, those who are gorgeously appareled and live in luxury are in kings' courts. 26 What then did you go out to see? A prophet? Yes, I tell you, and more than a prophet.
27 This is he of whom it is written,
'Behold, I send my messenger before thy face,
who shall prepare thy way before thee.'
28 I tell you, among those born of women none is greater than John; yet he who is least in the kingdom of God is greater than he." 29 (When they heard this all the people and the tax collectors justified God, having been baptized with the baptism of John; 30 but the Pharisees and the lawyers rejected the purpose of God for themselves, not having been baptized by him.)

What was Jesus' evaluation of John? That question is answered now. Recent events may have affected the popular attitude toward John. Crowds are notoriously fickle. Possibly the people had begun to dismiss the man helplessly penned up in Herod's fortress prison. After all, the fate which he had met seemed to contradict the message that he had preached.

Neither *reeds* nor men clothed in *soft raiment* would be found in semiarid regions of the *wilderness*. Reeds were aquatic plants which served as a symbol of weakness (1 Kings 14:15; Ezek. 29:6), as brought out by the phrase *shaken by the wind*. The pampered sons of affluence are to be found at the centers of power, wealth, and gaiety, which in earlier times were the *kings' courts*. By contrast, the wilderness is the environment par excellence of the prophet who eschews the debilitating, enervating influence of society's gay circles and who is not interested in sumptuous meals or gorgeous clothes. To have gone into the desert expecting to find a weak, vacillating, soft man would have been as foolish as going there to look for reeds or sycophants of the court. The people had gone to a prophet's environment looking for a man suited to it. And that is the kind of man that they had found.

But Jesus goes further: John was *more than a prophet*. He was the herald of the Messiah, the fulfillment of Malachi 3:1. John stands at the boundary of two periods and, therefore, plays a unique role in salvation-history. Jesus affirms that no greater human being than John ever lived. And yet, paradoxically, the *least in the kingdom is greater than he*. The question is clearly not one of inherent personal worth. Jesus has already settled that. It is rather that of the relative importance of the two aeons. John belonged to the time of the prophets, an essential but preparatory phase of redemption. But it is not to be equated with the time of salvation inaugurated by Jesus in which the least of the disciples shares.

Verses 29–30 are put in parentheses to indicate that they represent editorial comment rather than the words of Jesus. Plummer (pp. 205 f.) takes the opposite point of view that they are part of the comments of Jesus.

In John's message Israel had been confronted by God's demand for repentance to which there had been two contrasting responses. By their submission to baptism, the sign of repentance, the *people* (cf. 3:21) and the *tax collectors* (cf. 3:12) had *justified God*. They had acknowledged that

God was just in his judgment on their sins and in his claims on their lives. The religious leaders, *Pharisees* and *lawyers* had refused to repent. In their stubborn insistence on their own righteousness they refused to recognize the just claims of God. The acknowledgement of sin is a confession of the righteousness of God. On the other hand, blindness to one's sin is a rejection of God's righteousness.

Thus we are confronted by the paradoxical situation that the experts in religion were the very ones who came under God's judgment. *Lawyers* (*nomikoi*) is a word used often in Luke but seldom elsewhere. It is a synonym for scribes, the teachers of Jewish law.

(4) The Children at Play (7:31–35)

³¹ "To what then shall I compare the men of this generation, and what are they like? ³² They are like children sitting in the market place and calling to one another,

'We piped to you, and you did not dance;
    we wailed, and you did not weep.'
³³ For John the Baptist has come eating no bread and drinking no wine; and you say, 'He has a demon.' ³⁴ The Son of man has come eating and drinking; and you say, 'Behold, a glutton and a drunkard, a friend of tax collectors and sinners!' ³⁵ Yet wisdom is justified by all her children."

The *men of this generation* are specifically those who had rejected John and Jesus. They are compared to peevish, capricious children who always want to determine the kind of game that is played and who are extremely unhappy if their playmates do not fall in line with their suggestion. *Piped* refers to playing a kind of clarinet at weddings, banquets, and funerals. Since dancing is called for, the game must be "wedding." When the game is changed to "funeral," the response is the same. The playmates will not take their cue from the funeral dirge and play the part of the mourners.

People acted in the same arbitrary and peremptory fashion toward John and Jesus. John was an ascetic, a strange man who did not eat what others ate. He isolated himself from the centers of society and sustained himself with desert fare. There was no gaiety or lightness about this prophet of judgment. The people wanted John to be sociable and gay, i.e., to play at "wedding," but he would have no part of their game. *He has a demon* is idiomatic for "he is crazy," an age-old way of disposing of someone who does not fit the common mold.

Jesus, on the other hand, spent much of his time in the towns in contact with people. He was a guest at weddings, banquets, and other social affairs. The passage implies that he had a zest for life and enjoyed being with people. Now the ones who were dissatisfied with John want to change the game to "funeral" and are unhappy because Jesus will not cooperate. They hurl exaggerated criticisms at him, *glutton and drunkard,* and they sneer about his associates who are nothing but a crowd of *tax collectors and sinners.*

The meaning of v. 35 is problematical. Matthew (11:19) has "deeds" instead of *children. Wisdom* is the wisdom of God and is a periphrasis for God's name. Both John and Jesus had been sent by God. Does "children" refer to them or to the people who have responded favorably to their ministry? Perhaps the latter. Only people who were receptive to God's revelatory and redemptive activity could appreciate the appropriateness of both John and Jesus to his purposes. Their acceptance of God's message from both men was a vindication of his course of action.

(5) *The Penitent Woman (7:36–50)*

36 One of the Pharisees asked him to eat with him, and he went into the Pharisee's house, and sat at table. 37 And behold, a woman of the city, who was a sinner, when she learned that he was sitting at table in the Pharisee's house, brought an alabaster flask of ointment, 38 and standing behind him at his feet, weeping, she began to wet his feet with her tears, and wiped them with the hair of her head, and kissed his feet, and anointed them with the ointment. 39 Now when the Pharisee who had invited him saw it, he said to himself, "If this man were a prophet, he would have known who and what sort of woman this is who is touching him, for she is a sinner." 40 And Jesus answering said to him, "Simon, I have something to say to you." And he answered, "What is it, Teacher?" 41 "A certain creditor had two debtors; one owed five hundred denarii, and the other fifty. 42 When they could not pay, he forgave them both. Now which of them will love him more?" 43 Simon answered, "The one, I suppose, to whom he forgave more." And he said to him, "You have judged rightly." 44 Then turning toward the woman he said to Simon, "Do you see this woman? I entered your house, you gave me no water for my feet, but she has wet my feet with her tears and wiped them with her hair. 45 You gave me no kiss, but from the time I came in she has not ceased to kiss my feet. 46 You did not anoint my head with oil, but she has anointed my feet with ointment. 47 Therefore I tell you, her sins, which are many, are forgiven, for she loved much; but he who is forgiven little, loves little." 48 And he said to her, "Your sins are forgiven." 49 Then those who were at table with him began to say among themselves, "Who is this, who even forgives sins?" 50 And he said to the woman, "Your faith has saved you; go in peace."

Jesus is shown in the kind of situation that served as the basis for the distorted criticisms mentioned in the preceding episode (v. 34). The gospel accounts leave the impression that he was a sought-after and welcome guest at festive occasions. He was also not excluded from the homes of *Pharisees,* which indicates that for at least a part of his ministry the Pharisaic hostility against him was not total. For this glimpse of Jesus' relation to some of the Pharisees we are indebted to Luke, who tells of two other occasions when Jesus ate with them (11:37; 14:1). Although he identified primarily with people in the lower levels of society, no person or home was off limits to him. Strictly speaking, *sat at table* is not correct. People reclined on couches around the table when they ate.

On such occasions middle eastern hospitality required that the door be barred to no one. It was common for people to come in from the streets and stand around observing the festivities. The woman who enters is called a *sinner,* which carries the general connotation of ritual impurity (see on 5:30). Nevertheless, this woman of many sins (v. 47) is probably a prostitute.

(Am haAretz)

The absolute use of sinful woman occurs in this sense in rabbinic literature (Strack-Billerbeck, II, 162).

The scene that ensues is one of the most poignant and beautiful in the New Testament. The woman's every gesture indicates great humility and sense of unworthiness in the presence of a Person who is genuinely good. And yet we also perceive that she is confident that this good person does not have the attitude that the Pharisee has. Because his feet extend behind him as he reclines at the table, the woman can approach Jesus unobtrusively to anoint his feet with the ointment that she brought for this purpose. Before she can carry out her mission, however, she is so overcome with emotion that she weeps over his feet and, having no other recourse, dries them with her hair.[18] To kiss a person's feet was a sign of deep respect.

The Pharisee jumps to certain conclusions which betray his own presuppositions. Since a good man like Jesus surely would not allow this kind of woman to touch him, he must not know what sort of creature she is. Consequently he is not a *prophet*, for a man with a prophet's gifts would discern her character.

Jesus shows that he possesses prophetic gifts by discerning the Pharisee's own unworthy thoughts. We now learn that the host's name is *Simon* (cf. Mark 14:3). The parable of the two debtors serves to illustrate simultaneously man's relationship to God and to other men (cf. Matt. 18:23 ff.). Before God he is a hopeless debtor. What difference does it make whether the debt is *five hundred denarii* or *fifty* if one cannot pay? With relationship to others, man is a fellow-debtor whose pretensions of moral and religious superiority are completely irrelevant. Five hundred denarii represents

---

[18] The story has affinities with two others in the gospels (Mark 14:3 ff.; John 12:1 ff.) Luke's omission of Mark's story in his passion narrative may be due to its similarity to the one given here. Creed believes that the striking parallel between John 12:3 and Luke 7:38 is explained by John's dependence upon Luke (p. 110). However, the whole question of the literary relationship between John and Luke is an enigmatic one to which no satisfactory solution has been given.

---

the sins of the woman; fifty, the sins of Simon. But this is the picture from man's side and not from God's. All are hopelessly in debt, but some delude themselves into believing that theirs is not so great by comparison with others. The parable also teaches that God is not like men, harshly demanding his pound of flesh. He freely forgives men their debts.

The parable is the basis for a humiliating comparison between the righteous man and the prostitute. In Luke people who pride themselves on their piety and who have no sense of personal need are set alongside the persons who are objects of their contempt in order to dramatize the danger of moral pride (cf. 18:10 ff.; 21:1 ff.). Simon's attitude toward Jesus is seen in his failure to offer the accepted social amenities: no water to wash the dust from his feet, no kiss of greeting, no oil for the head as a gesture of honor.

Jesus turns to the woman, bringing her by this gesture into the circle. *Do you see this woman?* No! Simon had not seen her. He had classified her and dismissed her as one beneath his notice. He had depersonalized her by thinking of her as being just like all others of her ilk. But on every count the woman is shown to be Simon's superior. She has a much greater capacity for love and gratitude, based, as Jesus teaches, on her capacity to receive.

From the time I came in implies that the woman had followed Jesus into the house. In the light of the succeeding dialogue it is probable that her experience of being forgiven by Jesus preceded the scene described here. Her act was an expression of gratitude for the acceptance and love that she had already encountered.

Verses 47–48 seem to be at odds with the parable of vv. 41–42. In the parable love is the response to forgiveness, whereas the natural interpretation of vv. 47–48 is that forgiveness is a response to love. The difficulty is removed if we translate: "The great love she has shown proves that her many sins have been forgiven" (v. 47a TEV). This brings the first part of the verse into harmony with 47b (omitted by D) and the preceding narrative. Jesus' public declaration that the woman's *sins are forgiven* provokes a hostile reaction (see on 5:20 ff.).

The woman's *faith is her belief that Jesus' word of forgiveness was no less than God's.* Faith does not actually save a person, for man is saved only by the grace of God. But faith is the essential receptivity to God's redeeming activity. She is declared to be a possessor of the messianic *peace,* a word that is practically equivalent to salvation. There is now no tension between the sinner and God. Because she knows herself to be accepted and forgiven by God, she can forgive herself and hold her head up before other people. The miracle of Jesus' acceptance is clearly seen. Under its influence prostitutes discover their own personal worth as daughters of the living God.

6. An Itinerant Mission (8:1–56)

(1) Jesus' Companions (8:1–3)

¹ Soon afterward he went on through cities and villages, preaching and bringing the good news of the kingdom of God. And the twelve were with him, ² and also some women who had been healed of evil spirits and infirmities: Mary, called Magdalene, from whom seven demons had gone out, ³ and Joanna, the wife of Chuza, Herod's steward, and Susanna, and many others, who provided for them out of their means.

Soon afterward marks the transition to another phase of Jesus' activities for which the Evangelist now provides an introduction. Jesus is now on the move, dedicating himself to an itinerant preaching ministry which calls for rapid visits to a number of *cities* and *villages.* He goes through these centers of population, pausing only long enough to proclaim his message. The content of the *preaching* is the *good news of the kingdom of God* (see on 4:43).

Luke stresses the meaning of kingdom as good news for the people who are living between the time of Jesus and the Parousia, still subject to the hostile pressures of the powers of this age.

Jesus is accompanied by two groups of witnesses, the *twelve* and *some women.* Three of the women's names are given. In Mark we also find the names of three women who accompanied Jesus, including Mary Magdalene. The same women, two of whom are mentioned in the Lukan parallel (24:10), are witnesses to the resurrection (Mark 16:1). The notice in Luke 8:2 establishes the fact that the women who were the first witnesses to the resurrection had also been with Jesus during his Galilean ministry. This may be of value in an anti-Gnostic polemic, since the witnesses are able to identify the crucified and risen one as Jesus of Nazareth (see below on 23:49,55; 24:10).

In the lives of the three women the good news of the kingdom had become a reality. The power of God's reign operating through Jesus had liberated them from their bondage to *evil spirits* and *infirmities.* *Mary Magdalene* is identified by tradition with the sinner in the house of Simon (Luke 7:36 ff.). Such a conjecture is mere guess, lacking support in the text. *Seven demons* does not refer to gross immorality, i.e., prostitution, but to the disintegrated mental and emotional state from which Jesus had freed Mary. *Chuza* as *Herod's steward* occupied a place of confidence and responsibility in the administration of Herod Antipas.

Mark says that the women "ministered" to Jesus (15:41). Luke adds *out of their means.* They cared for the modest financial needs of Jesus during his itinerant ministry.

After this introduction Luke returns to the Markan source for the material found in 8:4—9:50. Some passages from the source are omitted, most notably the so-called "great omission" (Mark 6:45—8:26) after 9:17 (on which see Introduction).

(2) The Parable of the Soils (8:4–8)

⁴ And when a great crowd came together and people from town after town came to him, he said in a parable: ⁵ "A sower went out to sow his seed; and as he sowed, some fell along the path, and was trodden under foot, and the birds of the air devoured it. ⁶ And some fell on the rock; and as it grew up, it withered away,

because it had no moisture. 7 And some fell among thorns; and the thorns grew with it and choked it. 8 And some fell into good soil and grew, and yielded a hundredfold." As he said this, he called out, "He who has ears to hear, let him hear."

Mark puts this parable in a teaching session conducted by the lake (4:1). Having already given a similar setting to the teaching activity which preceded Jesus' call of Simon Peter (5:1-3), Luke does not use it here. Rather he connects the parable to the itinerant preaching mission conducted by Jesus in cities and villages (vv. 1-3 above). Now people from those places gather to him in an unspecified locality. Jesus speaks to the assembled crowd *in a parable* ("parables" in Mark 4:2; Matt. 13:3). He addresses himself to the problem raised by the varied reactions of the people to his proclamation of the good news of the kingdom.

There have been four kinds of response which correspond to the types of soil with which the Palestinian farmer had to contend in his struggle to raise a crop. Thus the name "parable of the sower" is not so appropriate as is "parable of the soils."

The sower's experience was a commonplace of everyday life in Palestine. At the time for planting the farmer scattered the seed broadcast in his field and subsequently turned them under with his primitive plow. Consequently the seed fell indiscriminately on good and bad soil.

The *path* is the hardened, bare trail hammered out by the feet of people who have been passing through the farmer's field since the last harvest. Seed falling on it are particularly vulnerable to the rapacious *birds*, who are the farmer's special enemy at the time of sowing.

Mark's "rocky ground" (4:5) is preferable to *rock*. In places the thin soil covers an underlying layer of sandstone, which now and again comes to the surface. Lacking depth for the development of adequate root systems, the young plants are defenseless against the scorching sun.

The Palestinian farmer had to contend with a variety of weeds, some of which

bore nettles or thorns. The *thorns* growing more rapidly than the young plants rob them of the space and nutrient necessary to their growth.

Some of the seed falls on *good soil*. This is where the farmer's efforts meet with success. As he sows, he knows that some of his seed will be lost to birds and that some of it will never come to fruition owing to the nature of the soil or the growth of pernicious plants. But he sows in the confidence that the good soil will reward his efforts.

So it is with the proclamation of the kingdom of God. There is good soil; the seed sown in it will come to fruition, producing a *hundredfold*. Luke does not reproduce Mark's "thirtyfold" and "sixtyfold," perhaps, as Leaney (p. 151) suggests, to avoid the Gnostic teaching that there were gradations of knowledge to be attained by initiates after baptism. The parable expresses the confidence of Jesus in the kingdom of God. He is sure "that God has made a beginning, bringing with it a harvest of reward beyond all asking or conceiving" (Jeremias, p. 92).

This faith in God's sovereign power is the basis for the joy of Jesus in the midst of the frustrations of his ministry. The incredible blindness of the people, including the dullness of his disciples, is not the factor that determines the future. In spite of unpromising beginnings, God guarantees that the harvest will exceed all human expectations.

For Jesus the harvest is the joyous celebration of the ingathering of the fruits produced by his sowing. The element of judgment is not lacking, however, for he concludes with a solemn call to repentance. Those who have *ears to hear*, that is, who possess the capacity to perceive that Jesus' preaching has confronted them with demands of a sovereign God on their lives, must respond without delay.

(3) Explanation of the Parable (8:9-15)

9 And when his disciples asked him what this parable meant, 10 he said, "To you it has been given to know the secrets of the kingdom of

God; but for others they are in parables, so that seeing they may not see, and hearing they may not understand. 11 Now the parable is this: The seed is the word of God. 12 The ones along the path are those who have heard; then the devil comes and takes away the word from their hearts, that they may not believe and be saved. 13 And the ones on the rock are those who, when they hear the word, receive it with joy; but these have no root, they believe for a while and in time of temptation fall away. 14 And as for what fell among the thorns, they are those who hear, but as they go on their way they are choked by the cares and riches and pleasures of life, and their fruit does not mature. 15 And as for that in the good soil, they are those who, hearing the word, hold it fast in an honest and good heart, and bring forth fruit with patience.

The interpreter of the parables of Jesus is confronted by two basic questions. First, what did they mean in the context of Jesus' life and teaching? Second, what did they mean in the life and witness of the early church which used and preserved them? To this second question the interpretation of the parable of the soils is addressed.

Why did people not understand and respond to the teachings of Jesus contained in his parables? The answer is that they are vehicles of revelation to those who are perceptive, the disciples, but their truth is hidden from the others. Is their lack of understanding due to the fact that the truth is deliberately made inaccessible to the hearers? Or, is it not rather that the spiritual blindness of those who reject the message of Jesus prevents them from seeing that which is right before their eyes? Admittedly God could have chosen to reveal himself in ways more acceptable to the prejudice and arrogance of human beings.

But he chose rather to give a veiled revelation of his majesty and power in the person of a Galilean whose life and works were an offense to the proud and self-righteous (cf. 1 Cor. 1:18–25).

Mark calls that which is veiled the "secret of the kingdom of God" (4:11). The secret is the breaking in upon men of the kingdom of God in the person of Jesus (Bornkamm, TDNT, IV, 817 ff.). This is what people could not grasp. The plural

secrets corresponds to Luke's emphasis on the nature of the kingdom. These secrets include the relation of Jesus to the kingdom, the nature of his program, the demands which the kingdom lays upon men, its relation to the present moment, and the manner of its coming.

The *word of God* is the effective, creative power of God which can take root in the life of the receptive person and produce the fruits of the kingdom. The first group of people are those who reject the word outright. Followers of Jesus must not because of this become disillusioned, for it does not mean that the *word* is ineffective. Rather the *devil*, God's adversary, has taken *away the word from their hearts* so that it cannot do its effective work.

A second group of people who create problems in the Christian community are those who joyously start out along the way and then *in time of temptation fall away.* Temptation has the meaning here of testing and trial, chief of which was the suffering of persecution. The cause of failure is described as superficiality of commitment, a characteristic which is often unrevealed until the time of testing brings it to the surface.

A third group are those who become involved in the world and its attractions, who do not leave all to follow Jesus. Luke has the unusual verb *does not mature* instead of Mark's "proves unfruitful" (4:19). The fruit appears but is not carried through to maturity.

The last group is composed of those who manifest a lifelong commitment to the gospel. They both hear and hold fast. Consequently, in their lives the word is able to come to fruition. *Patience,* a typical Pauline word, is the quality of steadfastness and loyalty in the times of crisis, especially in persecution.

(4) A Secret to Be Made Known (8: 16–18)

16 "No one after lighting a lamp covers it with a vessel, or puts it under a bed, but puts it on a stand, that those who enter may see the light. 17 For nothing is hid that shall not be

made manifest, nor anything secret that shall not be known and come to light. [18] Take heed then how you hear; for to him who has will more be given, and from him who has not, even what he thinks that he has will be taken away."

The meaning of these three sayings is obscure. We can only guess as to the sense in which Jesus uttered them (see Jeremias, pp. 96 f., fn. 34). Each one has a doublet in another context in Luke as well as parallels in the other Synoptic Gospels (8:16—11:33; 8:17—12:2; 8:18—19:26). Here they must be understood in connection with the parable of the soils. Having received the revelation of the mysteries of the kingdom of God, the disciples must face up to their responsibility. The simile of the *lamp* teaches that they have a mission to perform. Revelation is often spoken of in terms of illumination. For the disciples to hide the light of the gospel which they have received is unthinkable. They are to allow the light to shine forth so that others (Gentiles?) may see to enter the kingdom. Luke has in mind a house after the Roman style in which the lamp is placed in the vestibule to furnish light for those *who enter*. The picture in Matthew 5:15 is a one-room, Palestinian house which is illuminated by the lamp.

God has not destined that the kingdom of God shall be the private possession of an esoteric group (v. 17). The *secret* of the kingdom of God is intended for anyone who will receive it. It shall be made public in the widest possible manner.

The third and concluding saying gives a further warning about the responsibility of hearing. Those who respond to the proclamation of the good news will have continuing and greater opportunities. On the other hand, those who reject it will find their original opportunities withdrawn from them, as illustrated in vv. 19–21 (see below).

(5) Jesus' True Family (8:19–21)

[19] Then his mother and his brothers came to him, but they could not reach him for the crowd. [20] And he was told, "Your mother and your brothers are standing outside, desiring to see you." [21] But he said to them, "My mother and my brothers are those who hear the word of God and do it."

The episode has been moved from its Markan context (3:31–35) and inserted by Luke at this point. Why was this done? Conzelmann (pp. 48 f.; see also pp. 34 f.) suggests that it is placed here as an illustration of v. 18. Jesus had made his appearance in Nazareth and had been rejected by his own people. As a result, Capernaum had become the center of his activities. Now, according to Conzelmann, Jesus' relatives have come to take him back to Nazareth. *To see you* is interpreted to mean that they want to see him perform miracles there (see on 23:8). But the result of their rejection is that Jesus' relatives and townsmen have lost the opportunity which they had. On the other hand, those who have responded to Jesus have the additional opportunities that his continuing presence affords.

The situation of the *mother* and *brothers* is set forth graphically. The *crowd* stands between them and Jesus. They have to remain *outside,* since they are not a part of the intimate, inner circle. Jesus affirms that a claim made on him based on family relationship is not valid. He has become the center of a new community of people who stand together under the sovereignty of God in a new relationship that transcends all human categories. His true relatives are those who are committed with him to the fulfillment of the purposes of God their King. They not only *hear* but also *do* God's will (as in 6:47).

(6) The Stilling of the Storm (8:22–25)

[22] One day he got into a boat with his disciples, and he said to them, "Let us go across to the other side of the lake." So they set out, [23] and as they sailed he fell asleep. And a storm of wind came down on the lake, and they were filling with water, and were in danger. [24] And they went and woke him, saying, "Master; Master, we are perishing!" And he awoke and rebuked the wind and the raging waves; and they ceased, and there was a calm. [25] He said to them, "Where is your faith?" And

they were afraid, and they marveled, saying to one another, "Who then is this, that he commands even wind and water, and they obey him?"

With only a brief and quite general introductory phrase and no transition from the preceding section, Luke gives us the first of a series of three mighty works performed by Jesus. These are drawn from Mark where the transition is clear. Jesus had spent the day teaching by the Sea of Galilee, after which he decided to cross over to the other side (Mark 4:1,35). Luke consistently and correctly calls the Sea of Galilee a *lake,* an enclosed body of water. In Mark we are told that the crossing took place at evening (4:35), which explains why Jesus fell asleep.

The crossing of the lake is marred by the sudden descent of a dangerous squall of the type that could occur so quickly on Galilee. The implied rebuke of Jesus by his disciples is missing in Luke (cf. Mark 4:38), who consistently omits this kind of material. In like manner the harshness of Jesus' question to the disciples is softened in v. 25 (see Mark 4:40). Luke will not imply that the disciples have no faith, only that they are not calling on it in the moment of crisis.

Jesus *rebuked the wind,* as he had already rebuked demons and disease (see 4:35,39). In the realm of natural phenomena storms are equivalent to demon possession and disease in human beings. They are evidence that the original harmony of nature has been disrupted, signs of recalcitrance and rebellion against God's order in the universe (Psalms 65:7; 46:3; 89:9-10).

It was part of the hope of the Jewish people that the disunity of the universe would be overcome by the sovereign power of God so that the end would be equivalent to the beginning (Isa. 11:6-9). In the manifestation of Jesus' lordship over the rebellious forces of nature we find one more sign of the breaking in of the kingdom of God. He is the one who stills "the roaring of the seas, the roaring of their

waves, the tumult of the peoples" (Psalm 65:7). His act serves as a basis for the assurance that the rule of God will extend over all the universe and bring all into a final and lasting harmony (cf. Rom. 8:19-23).

Who then is this? The disciples are still asking the question. In their lives there is yet tension between belief and unbelief. The question points toward the moment when Jesus himself will ask them this same question (9:18 ff.).

(7) The Gerasene Demoniac (8:26-39)

26 Then they arrived at the country of the Gerasenes, which is opposite Galilee. 27 And as he stepped out on land, there met him a man from the city who had demons; for a long time he had worn no clothes, and he lived not in a house but among the tombs. 28 When he saw Jesus, he cried out and fell down before him, and said with a loud voice, "What have you to do with me, Jesus, Son of the Most High God? I beseech you, do not torment me." 29 For he had commanded the unclean spirit to come out of the man. (For many a time it had seized him; he was kept under guard, and bound with chains and fetters, but he broke the bonds and was driven by the demon into the desert.) 30 Jesus then asked him, "What is your name?" And he said, "Legion"; for many demons had entered him. 31 And they begged him not to command them to depart into the abyss. 32 Now a large herd of swine was feeding there on the hillside; and they begged him to let them enter these. So he gave them leave. 33 Then the demons came out of the man and entered the swine, and the herd rushed down the steep bank into the lake and were drowned.

34 When the herdsmen saw what had happened, they fled, and told it in the city and in the country. 35 Then people went out to see what had happened, and they came to Jesus, and found the man from whom the demons had gone, sitting at the feet of Jesus, clothed and in his right mind; and they were afraid. 36 And those who had seen it told them how he who had been possessed with demons was healed. 37 Then all the people of the surrounding country of the Gerasenes asked him to depart from them; for they were seized with great fear; so he got into the boat and returned. 38 The man from whom the demons had gone begged that he might be with him; but he sent him away, saying, 39 "Return to your home, and declare how much God has

done for you." And he went away, proclaiming throughout the whole city how much Jesus had done for him.

For the first and only time in Luke, Jesus journeys beyond the boundaries of Jewish territory and sets foot on pagan soil. The alternate readings given by the RSV reflect the early confusion about the identification of the place where Jesus landed. *Gerasenes* is the best attested reading for Luke and Mark (5:1); Gadarenes, for Matthew (8:28). Conjectures about the location of the region revolve around three cities: Khersa on the east shore of Galilee, Gadara eight miles south of the lake, and Gerasa about 40 miles away. The place where Jesus landed is called the *country* (district) *of the Gerasenes*. A district could extend for some distance from the town from which it took its name. Of the places mentioned above, Khersa best fits the requirements of the Synoptic narrative.

Luke underlines the exceptional nature of Jesus' excursion with the phrase *which is opposite Galilee* (cf. Mark 5:1). He clearly defines it as being outside the normal sphere of Jesus' activities. Upon stepping out of the boat, Jesus is met immediately by a demon-possessed man. The plural *demons* (cf. Mark 5:2) indicates that his condition is very serious. Jesus must have landed close to the town's burial place, because the naked man took shelter in the *tombs.* Burial usually took place in natural caves or in those dug in the side of a hill. In these the madman could find protection from the elements. His isolation from society is explained in v. 29*b*. So violent were the seizures from which he suffered that he could not be restrained even when bound heavily with *chains* and guarded. One of the varied connotations of the *desert* was its association with demons (cf. Matt. 12:43).

Although men do not recognize Jesus, the evil powers know him. He is the *Son of the Most High God,* that One who rules in unequalled sovereignty over all powers of the universe, both human and suprahuman. The demons see in Jesus a power hostile to

them which is also superior to them. *Do not torment* is a plea to be allowed to remain in the man in whom they have established their abode. This aspect of the story teaches that evil "cannot exist by itself, but only in so far as it can gain a foothold in the good" (Richardson, p. 73).

Legion means that the man was inhabited by a host of demons. The armies of evil powers as well as the hosts of God could be called legions (cf. Matt. 26:53). Here in Gentile territory, therefore, Jesus meets the greatest challenge to his authority over demons. But the combined strength of the evil spirits in the man is no match for the power of Jesus.

The demons plead not to be sent into the *abyss,* the nether world which is the prison for Satan and demons (cf. Rev. 9:1,2; 17:8; 20:1,3). The reference to the *herd of swine* tells us that this is Gentile land. The destruction of the swine has caused many people to decide that this narrative is inappropriate to the Gospel account. It does not fit into their concept of the character of Jesus. We must remember, however, that swine were considered unclean by the Jews, a much more appropriate house for evil spirits than for a human being (Richardson, p. 73). Also the story ends with a somewhat ironic twist. The demons, who begged not to be returned to the abyss, but to be allowed to enter the swine, do not escape their destiny. They are carried into the depths by the swine who plunge into the lake. The sea was associated with the abyss in ancient thought.

Since the tale of the frightened swineherds draws a crowd from the city and countryside to the scene, the *city* was not far away. The inhabitants find that their erstwhile notorious madman, whom they could subdue neither by physical force nor chains, is now quite capable of integration into society. He is seated tranquilly *at the feet of Jesus,* i.e., as a disciple and as one who recognizes his lordship. An involuntary slavery to demons has been replaced by a glad and free submission to Jesus.

The rejection of Jesus by the pagans is

due to their superstitious fear of his strange power. Because of their concept of gods who act quite arbitrarily and often vengefully, they are afraid of further demonstrations of his divine power. They will feel much safer with Jesus beyond their shores.

The new Gentile disciple wishes to return with Jesus to Jewish territory, but his place is in the region where he has lived his life. It is here that he can be most effective. Is he a model for the later Gentile mission of the church? He is to be a witness to what *God has done*. When Jesus acts, it is equivalent to God's own act. This is the ultimate meaning of the incarnation. In the person of Jesus, God acted to liberate, heal, forgive, and reclaim men. The evidence that Jesus' power was greater than the combined power of demons whose name was "Legion" is simply a manifestation of the kingdom of God on a grander scale. In keeping with his tendency to eliminate strictly Gentile territory from his account of Jesus' ministry, Luke never mentions Decapolis, the primarily trans-Jordanian federation of Greek cities (cf. Mark 5:20).

(8) A Double Miracle (8:40–56)

40 Now when Jesus returned, the crowd welcomed him, for they were all waiting for him. 41 And there came a man named Jairus, who was a ruler of the synagogue; and falling at Jesus' feet he besought him to come to his house, 42 for he had an only daughter, about twelve years of age, and she was dying.

As he went, the people pressed round him. 43 And a woman who had had a flow of blood for twelve years and could not be healed by any one 44 came up behind him, and touched the fringe of his garment; and immediately her flow of blood ceased. 45 And Jesus said, "Who was it that touched me?" When all denied it, Peter said, "Master, the multitudes surround you and press upon you!" 46 But Jesus said, "Some one touched me; for I perceive that power has gone forth from me." 47 And when the woman saw that she was not hidden, she came trembling, and falling down before him declared in the presence of all the people why she had touched him, and how she had been immediately healed. 48 And he said to her, "Daughter, your faith has made you well; go in peace."

49 While he was still speaking, a man from the ruler's house came and said, "Your daughter is dead; do not trouble the Teacher any more." 50 But Jesus on hearing this answered him, "Do not fear; only believe, and she shall be well." 51 And when he came to the house, he permitted no one to enter with him, except Peter and John and James, and the father and mother of the child. 52 And all were weeping and bewailing her; but he said, "Do not weep; for she is not dead but sleeping." 53 And they laughed at him, knowing that she was dead. 54 But taking her by the hand he called, saying, "Child, arise." 55 And her spirit returned, and she got up at once; and he directed that something should be given her to eat. 56 And her parents were amazed; but he charged them to tell no one what had happened.

In contrast to the rejection by Gentiles on the other side of the lake, Jesus is *welcomed* by the waiting *crowd* when he returns. The reference is presumably to the same crowd that had gathered to hear him prior to his departure (8:4). Both Luke and Matthew greatly condense the succeeding Markan narrative, losing thereby some of its dramatic quality as well as its clarity.

The *ruler of the synagogue* was its president, whose primary responsibility was to care for the physical arrangements for the worship services. Besides *Jairus* two others are mentioned by name in the New Testament (Acts 18:8,17), both also in Lukan writings. Jairus' direct address in Mark 5:23 is turned into indirect speech by Luke (v. 42), who also adds that the child was an *only* daughter (cf. 7:12; 9:38).

Before Jesus reaches the home of Jairus another miracle is performed. This is the only narrative in the Gospels in which the account of one miracle is set in the context of another. In the huge throng that surrounded Jesus, there was a woman who suffered from a constant discharge of blood. Here we note the famous omission of Mark's apparently derogatory statement about the treatment she had received from physicians (cf. Mark 5:26). In all fairness it should be said that the remark was not intended to reflect unfavorably on the medical profession but rather to emphasize the gravity of the woman's condition and her hopelessness. Luke also stresses that she *could not be healed by any one.* The case was one, therefore, for which there was no human remedy.

Seeking to be as unobtrusive as possible, the woman approaches Jesus from behind and only touches the fringe of his garment. *Fringe* can be the hem of the cloak or the tassels sewn on at the four corners as specified in the Law (Deut. 22:12). The outer robe was made in the form of a square and doubled at night as a blanket.

The reasons for the woman's furtive movements are quite understandable. Aside from the fact that she is a woman, the discharge from which she suffers makes her unclean (Lev. 15:25 ff.). Three types of uncleanness were serious enough to call for exclusion from society: leprosy, a bodily discharge, and contact with the dead. The woman had no right to be where she was nor to do what she did. The Gospels relate that on various occasions Jesus disregarded the demands of ceremonial purity (e.g., 5:13; 7:14). Jesus' contact with unclean persons did not defile him; it cleansed them.

Terrified by what she had done, the poor woman seeks to hide in the crowd. But she is forced to come forward to give a public testimony to the miracle that had taken place. Because of the nature of the disease, only she could verify the fact of the miracle. Others could only know of it through her witness. Why was the woman required to tell her story when so often in the Gospels Jesus demanded secrecy? Perhaps it was because the woman could not receive the complete liberation which Jesus wanted to give her until she heard his assuring word (v. 48). The story may have been used in the early church to encourage the timid and fearful to give their witness publicly.

Alan Richardson (p. 63) cautions us against confusing these miracles with socalled faith-healing. He rightly says that faith is used here in the sense of a "saving, personal, believing relationship with Christ." Furthermore, there is no suggestion in the Gospels "that Jesus could not have worked a miracle if the belief that a cure would be effected had been lacking." Faith illuminates the meaning of the miracles rather than being their effective cause.

Jesus' words to the woman are identical in the Greek text to those spoken in 7:50. The different English translations are due to the context. But the validity of the different renderings is questionable. Ostracized by the rules of her religion from society, this woman also considered a sinner had a deep sense of guilt which marred her relationship with God. But Jesus has now spoken to her the word of salvation and peace.

Jesus' remarks to the woman are interrupted by the arrival of a messenger from the house of Jairus with word that the *Teacher* would not be needed because the child had died. It was believed that the power to heal was a divine authentication of a rabbi's ministry (cf. John 3:2). Jairus' request need have been based on nothing more than the belief that Jesus was a great teacher with healing power. But the raising of the dead was quite another matter. Their circumscribed understanding of who Jesus really was is shown by the fact that they were convinced that he could not cope with death. Only Israel's greatest prophets had possessed this power.

In the crisis Jesus' response is one of assurance. The ultimate enemy death is not exempt from God's rule which he represents. Faith, therefore, is the key to confronting even such a crisis as this. To *believe* signifies once again a personal trust in Jesus which involves the confidence that he will gain the victory over death.

The scene of mourning is typical. Against it are set the words of Jesus. Death need not cause such consternation; whatever power it has is only temporary. *She is sleeping* presents the Christian view of death because it betokens the confidence of an awakening. This point of view meets with ridicule: *they laughed at him.*

The Markan narrative is clearer at this

point. There we are told that Jesus put all others out and entered the room accompanied only by the mother and father (Mark 5:40). Luke also characteristically omits the phrase in Aramaic (Mark 5:41). The command is to *arise*, i.e., from the dead. Luke's explanation of the phenomenon is that *her spirit returned*. The fact of the resurrection is to be verified by giving the girl something to eat (cf. 24:41–43).

7. Revelations to the Twelve (9:1–50)

(1) The Mission of the Twelve (9:1–6)

[1]And he called the twelve together and gave them power and authority over all demons and to cure diseases, [2] and he sent them out to preach the kingdom of God and to heal. [3] And he said to them, "Take nothing for your journey, no staff, nor bag, nor bread, nor money; and do not have two tunics. [4] And whatever house you enter, stay there, and from there depart. [5] And wherever they do not receive you, when you leave that town shake off the dust from your feet as a testimony against them." [6] And they departed and went through the villages, preaching the gospel and healing everywhere.

The *twelve* now undertake a mission which is an extension of Jesus' own work. As we have seen in the story of the draught of fishes (5:1–11), they possess no inherent power for such an enterprise. Consequently Jesus gives them *power* for healing and *authority* over unclean spirits.

Thus armed, the disciples are *sent out*. They are apostles or "sent ones" whose function corresponds to the role of the Hebrew *shalicha*. The latter, a legal term, designates a person delegated for a specific task who exercised the authority of the sender in the discharge of his responsibility. A rabbinical source says: "The one sent by a man is as the man himself" (*Ber.* 5,5). The twelve are to confront people with the proclamation of the *kingdom of God*, validated by a demonstration of its contemporary, effective power in miracles of healing and exorcism.

The tenor of the narrative indicates that this is an urgent mission to be accomplished with all possible haste. No preparations at all are to be made for the journey.

Jesus instructs his apostles to *take nothing*, not even the essentials for existence (see Mark 6:8 where a staff is permitted). A *staff, bag, bread* and *money* would be the basic equipment that a traveler would normally carry on such a trip (see on 3:11 for *two tunics*).

For lodging the disciples are to depend on the hospitality of people who receive their proclamation. This is the pattern of the early Christian mission in which itinerant missionaries and teachers depended on local hospitality for their subsistence. The brevity of time to be spent in each town and the urgency of their mission there make it necessary for the disciples to remain in the *house* that receives them.

Moreover, no time is to be wasted on people who reject them and their message. Their proclamation of the kingdom in word and deed calls for decision. The hoped-for decision is repentance (Acts 2:37–38), but rejection is decision nonetheless. Having given a rebellious town its opportunity, the disciples are to move on, shaking the *dust* of the place from their *feet*. It was customary for Jews sensitive to such matters to shake the contaminating dust of pagan lands from their feet upon entering Palestine. A similar gesture by the disciples was tantamount to classifying a Jewish community as heathen territory.

(2) The Perplexity of Herod (9:7–9)

[7] Now Herod the tetrarch heard of all that was done, and he was perplexed, because it was said by some that John had been raised from the dead, [8] by some that Elijah had appeared, and by others that one of the old prophets had risen. [9] Herod said, "John I beheaded; but who is this about whom I hear such things?" And he sought to see him.

The comment on the reaction of Herod Antipas to the reports circulating about Jesus constitutes an interlude between the departure of the twelve and their return. Luke's account is an adaptation of the much longer Markan passage (Mark 6:14–29). The list of differing opinions which gave rise to Herod's perplexity sets the stage for the confession scene (see on

vv. 18–22 below). In general these opinions seem to connect Jesus with the messianic age, but only as its herald or the sign of its beginning rather than as its central figure, the Messiah. The reader's first intimation of John's untoward fate comes when he learns of the popular conjecture *that John had been raised from the dead*. The tetrarch dismisses the speculations about John (but see Mark 6:16). John I beheaded is a summary of and substitute for Mark's more detailed narrative of John's execution.

Who is this? Here is the central question with which the Gospels come to grips. It is a unifying motif in this part of the third Gospel. Luke is telling his readers who Jesus is, aware of the fact that the conviction of his own faith is but one of the alternatives among which men can choose. Herod's problem is the problem of the whole Jewish nation, confronted as it was by the disturbing enigma of Jesus' person. How is one to interpret these reports of mighty deeds? But Herod is not content with *hearing;* he wishes to *see* Jesus, that is, to see him perform the kinds of miracles that people are talking about. Eventually Herod and Jesus come face to face, but the desire of the ruler is not satisfied (cf. 23:8). The truth of the matter is that even those who have seen Jesus perform miracles have not really seen him in the sense of perceiving who he really is. This is apparent from the opinions that they hold of Jesus, all of which miss the mark.

(3) The Feeding of Five Thousand (9: 10–17)

[10] On their return the apostles told him what they had done. And he took them and withdrew apart to a city called Bethsaida. [11] When the crowds learned it, they followed him; and he welcomed them and spoke to them of the kingdom of God, and cured those who had need of healing. [12] Now the day began to wear away; and the twelve came and said to him, "Send the crowd away, to go into the villages and country round about, to lodge and get provisions; for we are here in a lonely place." [13] But he said to them, "You give them something to eat." They said, "We have no more than five loaves and two fish—unless we are to go and buy food for all these people." [14] For there were about five thousand men. And he said to his disciples, "Make them sit down in companies, about fifty each." [15] And they did so, and made them all sit down. [16] And taking the five loaves and the two fish he looked up to heaven, and blessed and broke them, and gave them to the disciples to set before the crowd. [17] And all ate and were satisfied. And they took up what was left over, twelve baskets of broken pieces.

From Matthew's account we would conclude that the withdrawal of Jesus and the disciples from Galilee was due to the hostility of Herod Antipas (14:13). Luke implies what Mark states expressly (6:31), that Jesus wished to escape the pressures of the crowd for a while. In Luke the withdrawal is to *Bethsaida*, whereas Jesus departs for Bethsaida after feeding the multitude in Mark 6:45. Geographical references often reveal more about Luke's theological perspective than they do about locations of events. Conzelmann has a thoroughgoing theological interpretation of Lukan geographical references. His helpful suggestions sometimes go beyond the limits warranted by the data (pp. 18 ff.). The organization of the Gospels is determined by factors other than the chronological and geographical reconstruction of the course of Jesus' ministry. A specifically Lukan characteristic is the tendency seen here to place events in or near cities.

Although Jesus' desire to be alone with the disciples is frustrated by the arrival of the *crowds*, Luke affirms that he *welcomed* them. The activities of Jesus during the day are described in the usual Lukan manner. He taught them about the kingdom of God and healed the sick. The remarks of the *twelve* at the conclusion of the day tell us that they are not in the city but in a *lonely place*. In Luke the need to *lodge* as well as get food is recognized by the disciples (cf. Mark 6:36).

The feeding of the five thousand is the one miracle found in all four Gospels (Matt. 14:13–21; Mark 6:32–44; John 6:1–14), which indicates its importance in the life of the early church. *Loaves* and *fish* are symbols of the Eucharist found on the walls of Christian catacombs in Rome. The use of these symbols shows that early Christians interpreted this miracle as a prototype of the Lord's Supper. The similarity between Jesus' actions prior to the distribution of the bread to the multitude and those during the Last Supper (Mark 14:22; Matt. 26:26) also bears out the close identification between the two.

In Luke the miracle seems to provide a special link between Herod's question and the disciples' confession. Through the distribution of the bread Jesus reveals who he is, in keeping with the motif that he makes himself known to disciples "in the breaking of bread" (24:35). By feeding the people in the desert, Jesus shows that he is the new Moses, the Prophet that God has promised to raise up among the people (Deut. 18:15). The abundance of the messianic age, anticipated in popular expectation, has become a reality. All the people ate until they were *satisfied,* and yet there was more. *Twelve baskets,* one for each apostle, were filled at the conclusion of the meal. Even though they shared with the multitude, the *twelve* still have far more than the five loaves and two fish with which they had begun. Moreover, the miracle has an eschatological significance in that it points toward the heavenly messianic banquet that Jesus will share with his followers.

It is noteworthy that we do not find the typical conclusion to this narrative. There is no reference to awe and praise as responses to almighty work. Nor is there any indication that anyone but the twelve was aware of what had really taken place. The wonder of Jesus' act is subordinated to its significance as a vehicle for revealing who Jesus was.

(4) The Great Confession (9:18–22)

[18] Now it happened that as he was praying alone the disciples were with him; and he asked them, "Who do the people say that I am?" [19] And they answered, "John the Baptist;

but others say, Elijah; and others, that one of the old prophets has risen." [20] And he said to them, "But who do you say that I am?" And Peter answered, "The Christ of God." [21] But he charged and commanded them to tell this to no one, [22] saying, "The Son of man must suffer many things, and be rejected by the elders and chief priests and scribes, and be killed, and on the third day be raised."

The omission of the long section from Mark (6:45—8:26) has the consequence of bringing the confession of the disciples into a close relationship with the notices about Herod and the feeding miracle. Whether fortuitously or by design, the question about the identity of Jesus becomes the dominant theme of a large part of Luke which reaches its climax in the disciples' confession.

Luke omits the reference to Caesarea Philippi (Mark 8:27), possibly because the city lay in Philip's domain outside of what might be properly considered Jewish territory. He alone introduces the scene with the information that Jesus *was praying*. In addition to stressing the importance of the subsequent episode, this lets us know that Jesus and the disciples are no longer with the multitude.

The confession is the watershed of Mark's Gospel, the distinct dividing line between two phases of Jesus' ministry. After the confession the Markan narrative proceeds rapidly and directly to the passion. The difference in Luke is due largely to the insertion of a great body of distinctive material (Luke 9:51—18:14) into the Markan framework.

Jesus first questions the disciples about the opinions of the *people*. This is not simply an introductory, incidental question. Faith is not lived out in a vacuum but in the world where men hold opposing and conflicting views. Consequently, a sheltered faith can never be a mature faith. The conviction held by believers is only one of the options open to men, and they must always understand this. The response of the disciples corresponds to the speculations reported to Herod Antipas (see v. 9).

The time comes, however, when one

must quit talking about the opinions of others and assume the responsibility of personal decision. The disciples have gone beyond the people in their perception of Jesus' identity. They recognize in him the central figure of the messianic age. As spokesman for the twelve, Peter's confession expresses the conviction of the group that Jesus is Yahweh's Messiah, or the Christ of God (see on 2:11,26). This is the first time since the opening chapters of the third Gospel that anyone other than demons has recognized—at least declared—who Jesus is.

The confession is followed by a command to secrecy. In the context of the third Gospel there are at least two ways to understand this. First, Jesus has consistently refused to make any direct assertions of his messiahship. His deeds and words contain the clue to his identity. It is the responsibility of the people who witness them to respond on the basis of what they see and hear (cf. 7:22–23).

Second, although Jesus apparently accepts the ascription of the title Messiah, he is aware that it carries certain unacceptable connotations. He is the Messiah, but not the kind that people expect—not even the kind that the disciples have in mind. Consequently, the disciples' confession is followed by Jesus' interpretation of his own destiny. Instead of Messiah, he uses his favorite self-designation Son of man (see on 5:24), which also carries connotations of power and glory but with apocalyptic rather than nationalistic associations. The power and glory which belong to the Son of man are not to be achieved through self-assertion. Indeed, quite the opposite is true; it is through subjection to humiliation and suffering that glory is to be reached.

This is said by Jesus to be necessary. The impersonal verb dei (must) signifies the necessity of divine purpose and control. The path of suffering is not an optional one. It has been marked out by God. Any other way, e.g., the way of a nationalistic messianic movement, would be satanic (see on 4:5–8). The cross opposes and judges the power philosophy of the world. The rebuke by Peter, which illustrates the incapacity of the disciples to accept the idea of a suffering Messiah, and Jesus' harsh reply are omitted (cf. Mark 8:32–33).

(5) The Cost of Discipleship (9:23–27)

23 And he said to all, "If any man would come after me, let him deny himself and take up his cross daily and follow me. 24 For whoever would save his life will lose it; and whoever loses his life for my sake, he will save it. 25 For what does it profit a man if he gains the whole world and loses or forfeits himself? 26 For whoever is ashamed of me and of my words, of him will the Son of man be ashamed when he comes in his glory and the glory of the Father and of the holy angels. 27 But I tell you truly, there are some standing here who will not taste death before they see the kingdom of God."

A disciple is a person who follows Jesus. The word mathētēs (disciple) signifies apprentice or learner, an adequate definition for the disciple of a rabbi or a peripatetic Greek philosopher. But it falls woefully short of describing a disciple of Jesus Christ. Since Jesus is destined to experience rejection and death, the person who actually follows him will inevitably share that experience. The followers of Jesus were finally to be faced with a simple, stark test: Will you die with Jesus? They were called on to stake their lives on the faith that the last word was not spoken by the Sanhedrin, by Pontius Pilate, nor by the soldiers who casually drove spikes into another condemned man's hands. They were called on to believe, as Jesus did, that beyond the hard, cruel realities of this age there stood the greater, ultimate reality of the kingdom of God. The New Testament tells us that they failed that first test; but they passed subsequent ones.

To affirm allegiance to Christ requires a person to deny himself. The disciple is to give up all claims on his own existence, surrendering his personal ambitions for prominence and power. Rather than attempting to contrive his own future, the disciple is called to follow Jesus in utter abandonment, believing that God guarantees his future.

To *take up* one's *cross* was the ultimate humiliation, the ignominy forced on condemned criminals who were required to carry the instrument of their own execution. But for the Christian it is a joyous and willing choice. To the phrase *take up his cross*, Luke adds *daily* (cf. Mark 8:34). This takes the cross out of the past and makes it part of contemporary existence. It is not only the instrument on which Christ died but also a way of life—the daily offering up of one's self to the will of God.

Paradoxically the man who equivocates and recoils in the time of testing in order to *save his life* actually loses it. Jesus taught that man is more than a body to be clothed and a stomach to be filled. He is confronted by the possibilities of a future that transcends life and death. The self-seeking man who follows the principles of looking out for himself so successfully that he *gains the whole world* has made a bad bargain in the long run. He may gain the world, that is, reach the absolute ultimate in materialistic success by possessing all wealth and power. But he cannot finally save himself for the final destiny of a human being is determined by God alone.

To be *ashamed* of Jesus means to be unwilling to acknowledge him under social, economic, or political pressures, when perhaps even life is at stake. The disciple is required to affirm his allegiance in the most trying circumstances. For him, therefore, the future contains both threat and promise. The *glory* of which Jesus speaks is the complete revelation of God's sovereign power in the Parousia of the *Son of man.* The *angels* are the heavenly hosts who serve God and do his bidding.

In v. 27 Luke omits "come with power" with which Mark concludes the prophetic word of Jesus (Mark 9:1). The statement is clearly removed from any association with the end of the age. To *see the kingdom* "means that although the kingdom cannot actually be seen, it can be perceived" (Conzelmann, p. 105). This is true because "the life of Jesus [is] a clear mani-

festation of salvation in the course of redemptive history" (*ibid.*).

(6) The Transfiguration (9:28–36)

28 Now about eight days after these sayings he took with him Peter and John and James, and went up on the mountain to pray. 29 And as he was praying, the appearance of his countenance was altered, and his raiment became dazzling white. 30 And behold, two men talked with him, Moses and Elijah, 31 who appeared in glory and spoke of his departure, which he was to accomplish at Jerusalem. 32 Now Peter and those who were with him were heavy with sleep but kept awake, and they saw his glory and the two men who stood with him. 33 And as the men were parting from him, Peter said to Jesus, "Master, it is well that we are here; let us make three booths, one for you and one for Moses and one for Elijah"—not knowing what he said. 34 As he said this, a cloud came and overshadowed them; and they were afraid as they entered the cloud. 35 And a voice came out of the cloud, saying, "This is my Son, my Chosen; listen to him!" 36 And when the voice had spoken, Jesus was found alone. And they kept silence and told no one in those days anything of what they had seen.

According to Mark the transfiguration took place six days after the confession (9:2). Luke gives an approximate estimate of the time lapse, *about eight days after.* In both instances a week is meant. The time reference is given to bind the passion saying and the transfiguration closely together. Jesus' ultimate destiny is exaltation, but glory is impossible apart from suffering and death.

Several distinctive features mark the narrative in the third Gospel, i.e., the prayer vigil of Jesus, the sleepiness of the disciples, the subject of conversation between Jesus and the heavenly visitors, and the omission of the dialogue about John the Baptist (cf. Mark 9:2–13; Matt. 17:1–13).

The three chosen to ascend the mountain with Jesus, *Peter, John,* and *James,* are the disciples also associated with him in the agony of Gethsemane (Mark 14:33—omitted by Luke). Apparently they constituted a sort of inner circle within the twelve who continued to exert leadership in the early church (cf. Gal. 2:9). Although some have guessed that the transfiguration took place on Mount Hermon, the *mountain* does not necessarily mean a specific mountain. It is the place of prayer and revelation. As was true at the descent of the Spirit after his baptism, Jesus is also in prayer when the transfiguration occurs.

The appearance of his countenance was altered is a circumlocution for Mark's one word "he was transfigured (*metemorphōthē*)." The Hellenist Luke must have been sensitive to the pagan associations of a word used to describe the capacity of the gods to assume different forms at will. To this point Jesus' true identity has been veiled by a Galilean face and common Galilean clothing. "The rulers of this age" were convinced that they had crucified a Galilean peasant and did not know that they had really killed the "Lord of glory" (1 Cor. 2:8).

For the moment, however, both face and clothing take on a heavenly appearance. The countenance was *altered*. His clothing became dazzling bright like lightning. The language is eschatological. Similar terminology is used to describe God (Dan. 7:9), the exalted Son of man (Rev. 1:13 ff.), martyred saints (Rev. 6:11; 7:14), heavenly visitors (Luke 24:4), etc. The real identity of Jesus is projected visibly. For a moment the disciples catch a glimpse of the exalted Lord as he will be after the struggle which looms immediately ahead.

Moses and *Elijah* appear *in glory*. This simply means that they do not revert to human appearance but are seen as heavenly beings with shining countenance and white clothing. Since they have already passed through the struggles and suffering of a life of service into the presence of God, they are now in glory. Both Moses and Elijah, the two great figures of the age of the Law and the Prophets were associated with messianic expectations. Both also had unusual departures from this life. The subject of their conversation is the *departure* or death of Jesus, literally his "exodus." This means that they talked about the death of Jesus, the fulfillment of the "law of Moses and the prophets," as

the necessary gateway to glory (cf. Luke 24:44–46). The word exodus may also associate the death of Jesus with the liberation of Israel from Egypt under the leadership of Moses. It is the new Exodus through which the new Israel is liberated and brought into being.

The three disciples were *heavy with sleep*, which brings out the detail that the experience occurred at night. For the disciples the transfiguration is both assurance and call. The assurance is that the way Jesus has taken leads to glory. The call is for them to follow him. So a fleeting glimpse of glory, a fragile vision in the night is the only proof given that following Jesus, that is, self-renunciation and death, leads to participation in glory. This is what the disciples had to balance against the "solid facts" of the "real world." And so it has always been. On the one side is the allure of what men can count, feel, possess now—a bank account, a luxurious home, social acceptability. On the other side, there is the vision in the night, the gleam of a reality seen briefly and dimly (through sleepy eyes) that summons men to renounce all in dedicating their lives to the service of God and man.

Peter's suggestion about building the *three booths* is a rejection of Jesus' teaching about the necessity of his suffering. He wants to seize the moment of glory and extend it, thereby eliminating all the struggles and doubts inherent in the future to which Jesus has called him.

The overshadowing cloud is an expression of the presence of God (cf. Ex. 13:20 f.; 19:16 ff.; 33:9 ff.). It is this association that brings fear to the disciples (cf. esp. Ex. 19:21 ff.). Although the syntax is not clear, we would assume that the cloud *overshadowed* the three glorified figures and that *they*, not the disciples, *entered the cloud.*

The affirmation of sonship uttered at the beginning of Jesus' ministry is restated here where it has become clear that Jesus has faced and accepted rejection by his people. He is rejected by men but not by

God. Jesus is called his **Chosen.** The variant "Beloved" (marg.) is an assimilation to the baptismal statement (3:22). The title "Chosen" (Elect) affirms once again that Jesus is God's Messiah. His suffering is not evidence of rejection by God but is instead proof of his obedience to God. *Listen to him* points to the prophet like Moses about whom it was said, "Him you shall heed" (Deut. 18:15). The words of Jesus are to take precedence over all others, including those of Moses and Elijah. Furthermore, the teachings of Jesus about the nature of his messiahship are to be accepted instead of those held by the disciples and their contemporaries. Luke says that the disciples told no one (cf. Mark 9:9). They cannot talk of his glory because they do not understand its relationship to his suffering. This will come later (cf. Acts 2:33).

(7) The Healing of an Epileptic (9:37–43a)

37 On the next day, when they had come down from the mountain, a great crowd met him. 38 And behold, a man from the crowd cried, "Teacher, I beg you to look upon my son, for he is my only child; 39 and behold, a spirit seizes him, and he suddenly cries out; it convulses him till he foams, and shatters him, and will hardly leave him. 40 And I begged your disciples to cast it out, but they could not." 41 Jesus answered, "O faithless and perverse generation, how long am I to be with you and bear with you? Bring your son here." 42 While he was coming, the demon tore him and convulsed him. But Jesus rebuked the unclean spirit, and healed the boy, and gave him back to his father. 43 And all were astonished at the majesty of God.

The *crowd* waits at the foot of the mountain for Jesus' return. As Moses descended from Sinai to encounter a faithless people (Ex. 32:15 ff.), so does Jesus upon his descent find his disciples discredited and humiliated. This is not brought out so clearly here as it is in Mark 9:14 ff. Finding Jesus gone, an anxious father had turned to his disciples. Because their attempts to exorcise the demon failed, the man now begs Jesus to *look upon* his son. The verb means to take an interest in with a view to help-

ing. Luke says that the boy was an *only child*. The description of the boy's malady indicates that he was subject to epileptic seizures.

The disciples' failure is seen as an example of the faithless and rebellious spirit of a whole *generation* that fails to appropriate the opportunities afforded by the presence of Jesus. The condemnation is phrased in language similar to Deuteronomy 32:5. It emphasizes the fact that the opportunity afforded by his presence among men is limited in time.

The boy is healed and given *back to his father* (cf. 7:15). The story is condensed by the omission of the dialogue between Jesus and the father, in which the man's unusual faith is apparent (Mark 9:23–24), and the conversation between Jesus and his disciples (Mark 9:28–29). The power of Jesus over demons is an evidence of God's *majesty,* a word found nowhere else in the Gospels.

(8) The Second Passion Saying (9:43b–45)

But while they were all marveling at everything he did, he said to his disciples, 44 "Let these words sink into your ears; for the Son of man is to be delivered into the hands of men." 45 But they did not understand this saying, and it was concealed from them, that they should not perceive it; and they were afraid to ask him about this saying.

Since Luke did not indicate that Jesus departed from Galilee (see Mark's itinerary: 7:24,31; 8:10,22,27), he omits the notice about his return (Mark 9:30). The second passion saying is set alongside the preceding miracle in which Jesus once again manifested his power as God's Messiah. This dialectic between strength and weakness is integral to the Gospel portrait of Jesus. He is the strong Son of God; at the same time, he is the "helpless one" who is the victim of evil's power, i.e., *delivered into the hands of sinners.* The phrase means that men had no power over him but that which God permitted them to exercise.

Let these words sink into your ears is a solemn appeal for the disciples to comprehend the paradox of the suffering *Son of man.* Luke's explanation of the disciples' dullness is that the mystery *was concealed from them,* an intimation that this concealment was a part of the divine purpose. The conjunction *that* may express result as well as purpose. Their blindness was not the fulfillment of God's purpose but was rather the *result* of the fact that God had chosen to act in what was to them incomprehensible ways.

Aware that they are confronted with a mystery, they are *afraid* to press the matter further. Does Luke mean that the demeanor of Jesus was so solemn as he spoke about the future that they were intimidated? At any rate, the statement answers a question which must have been raised in later years: Why did the disciples not pursue the questions raised by Jesus' revelations until they came to understand what he was trying to tell them?

We need not be surprised at their blindness to the real meaning of Jesus' life and teachings. Contemporary disciples are still unwilling apparently to accept the significance for them of Jesus' suffering. By keeping the cross safely locked up in the remote past as doctrine we show that we do not understand what it means to follow him. thus we can be religious and still live in splendid isolation from the world's hurts and needs.

(9) Concerning Greatness (9:46-48)

⁴⁶ And an argument arose among them as to which of them was the greatest. ⁴⁷ But when Jesus perceived the thought of their hearts, he took a child and put him by his side, ⁴⁸ and said to them, "Whoever receives this child in my name receives me, and whoever receives me receives him who sent me; for he who is least among you all is the one who is great."

Since Luke does not follow Mark in setting this incident in Capernaum (Mark 9:33), the resultant effect is to relate it closely to the preceding passion saying. In this way the disciples' obtuseness is illustrated by the report of the power struggle in which they engage so soon after Jesus talked to them about dying. The basis of their rivalry is their already demonstrated misconception about the messianic kingdom (cf. Matt. 18:1). Because they still believe that they are following a leader who will win victory over Israel's enemies and establish a glorious kingdom, they covet leading roles in the reestablished Davidic dynasty.

Had they understood Jesus' statements about his destiny, they would have perceived that he conceived of himself as servant rather than as a national messianic hero. From this perspective he interprets for them the requirements of discipleship. Jesus uses an act of prophetic symbolism to present the lesson. By a minor variation from Mark, Luke makes the act even more meaningful. Mark says that Jesus placed the child "in the midst of them" (9:36); but in Luke we find that Jesus *put him by his side.*

Now the question is: How is the disciple to serve Jesus? The answer is: By ministering to the child by his side. The child is the symbol of the unprotected and weak person in the human family. Not that we should equate the underprivileged and defenseless people with God. But commitment to God in following Jesus is expressed primarily in acts of mercy and love. In the Bible God is closely identified with victims of injustice and prejudice. Jesus also identified with them—so closely indeed that he can say that to receive them, i.e., to give them protection and help, is to receive him and is to receive God.

The "religious" way to avoid the impact of Jesus' demands is by establishing a "Jesus cult." We can meet in buildings, sing songs about Jesus, wax sentimental about him, weep over him, and then emerge to walk with unseeing, dry eyes through a world of misery and need without reaching out to the kinds of people that he served. When we do this, religion becomes evil, providing an escape sanctified by the name of Jesus from the severity of his demands on our lives (cf. Matt. 25:31 ff.).

In the second place, the child represents

the *least* in the group. Conditioned as he
was by the authoritative environment in
which he lived, the child had no misunderstanding about his place. It would have
been inconceivable for him to argue with
the disciples about a position of prominence. The child was greater than the disciples exactly because he was devoid of
pretensions. Consequently, the disciple
who wants to be *great* paradoxically must
give up all ambitions to be great.

(10) Concerning Outsiders (9:49–50)

⁴⁹ John answered, "Master, we saw a man
casting out demons in your name, and we
forbade him, because he does not follow with
us." ⁵⁰ But Jesus said to him, "Do not forbid
him; for he that is not against you is for you."

Luke makes a slight but significant
change in the Markan narrative which
makes the point of contention vivid. The
disciples claim that the unnamed exorcist
was not following *with* them (cf. Mark
9:38). That is to say, he was following
Jesus but not as a part of their group. By
casting out demons in the *name* of Jesus,
he was exercising the prerogatives of discipleship without having what they considered to be valid credentials.

The question of the validity of forms and
functions has exercised the Christian community since its earliest days. Is membership in a certain group the test of authenticity? Is a theory of apostolic succession or
some variation of it adequate grounds for
determining the validity of the disciple's
ministry?

Jesus teaches that the test of validity is
not a fulfillment of formal requirements
laid down by the group. The reality of a
person's relationship to Jesus is expressed
in the quality of his life and acts, especially
the fulfillment of the servant role. The man
whom the disciples had rebuked was ministering to broken lives in the name of Jesus.
In a verse omitted by Luke, Mark underlines Jesus' emphasis on the servant role as
the determining characteristic of the disciple (Mark 9:41).

Jesus' principle is contained in the words

he that is not against you is for you (cf.
Phil. 1:15–18). Through the centuries
some Christian groups have turned this
around to say: "He who is not following
with us is against us."

IV. From Galilee to Jerusalem: Part One (9:51—13:30)

The large central section (9:51—19:27)
which gives to Luke's Gospel so much of its
distinctive character begins now. The Markan source is put aside and will not be used
again until the latter part of the section
(18:15 ff.).

The central section seems to represent in
part Luke's solution to the problem of what
to do with a large amount of the material
that he had collected concerning the life of
Jesus. He was able to put much of it into
the "slot" provided by Mark's account of
Jesus' final journey to Jerusalem (cf. Mark
10:1,17,32). The various references to a
journey give a kind of literary unity to this
part of Luke (9:51,57; 10:38; 13:22,33;
17:11; 18:31; 19:1,11,28). Nevertheless,
the contents consist of more or less heterogeneous passages which do not shed light
on the actual chronological or geographical
sequence of Jesus' ministry. In other words,
they cannot be fitted into an actual journey
to Jerusalem.

Primarily the journey to Jerusalem provides the theological motif for the central
section. It puts all that occurs after 9:51
under the influence of the cross. The end is
now known. We are not allowed to forget
that Jesus' destiny is Jerusalem. We know
that Jesus will confront Israel in the capital
city with his "veiled" messianic claims. We
also know that he will be rejected and
executed. Although the journey does not
help us to draw up Jesus' itinerary to Jerusalem, it does set forth the destiny of his
life. No matter where he is at any given
moment, no matter what may have been
the original setting of the isolated pericope
that forms a part of the section, everything
leads to a climax in Jerusalem.

Various attempts have been made to discover an underlying, unifying plan in the

central section. One of the most noteworthy is C. F. Evans' suggestion that it was designed as a Christian "Deuteronomy." [19] We are probably not justified by the evidence, however, in going beyond W. G. Kuemmel's summary statement: "In 9:51—19:27 the Lord, who goes to suffer according to God's will, equips his disciples for the mission of preaching after his death." [20]

1. The Beginning of the Journey (9:51–62)

(1) Rejected by Samaritans (9:51–56)

51 When the days drew near for him to be received up, he set his face to go to Jerusalem. 52 And he sent messengers ahead of him, who went and entered a village of the Samaritans, to make ready for him; 53 but the people would not receive him, because his face was set toward Jerusalem. 54 And when his disciples James and John saw it, they said, "Lord, do you want us to bid fire come down from heaven and consume them?" 55 But he turned and rebuked them. 56 And they went on to another village.

Verse 51 makes a decisive turning point in Luke's presentation of Jesus' ministry. It introduces a new section that ends with his approach to Jerusalem. The passage contains an unusual number of Semitisms (cf. Plummer, pp. 262 f.), which are obscured in the English translation. "When the days were fulfilled" brings out better than does the phrase *drew near* the conviction that all which transpires is under divine control. *To be received up* translates a noun in the Greek text which can be rendered "assumption." Assumption may mean death, but Luke uses it to comprehend the whole complex of death, resurrection, and ascension. It is entirely possible that Luke is evoking associations with the apocryphal story of the assumption of Moses and with the Old Testament account of the translation of Elijah.[21]

Jesus voluntarily accepts the divine im-

perative under which his life has been placed as he sets *his face to go to Jerusalem.* The paradox of divine election and human responsibility is seen nowhere more clearly than in the teaching about the death of Jesus. The New Testament writers were anxious to show that the death of Jesus did not mean a defeat for God. Man had not taken over—not even for a moment. God had been in charge all the way. Furthermore, early Christians were convinced that Jesus was not a helpless, unwitting victim of circumstances. He chose to walk the road that he took, fully aware of his bitter destiny but also convinced that in losing his life he would gain it. Nevertheless, this does not absolve the men who murdered Jesus from their guilt at all. God "delivered [him] up" (Acts 2:23); Jesus willingly accepted death; but men (not God) killed him in an act of lawlessness (Acts 2:23; cf. Stagg, pp. 128–135).

Messengers are sent on ahead, apparently to seek lodging for the night. The hostility between Jews and Samaritans was deep and of long standing. Samaritans took special pains to manifest ill will toward pilgrims who took the direct route through their territory to join in the Passover celebration in Jerusalem (Josephus, *Antiq.,* 20,6,1). Because Jesus is on his way to Jerusalem, the people will not receive him.

James and John were called "sons of thunder" (Mark 3:17—omitted by Luke). They now justify their nickname by their bloodthirsty attitude toward the Samaritans. The RSV marginal reading "as Elijah did" is probably an interpolation, but the suggestion made by the disciples is reminiscent of 2 Kings 1:10. It is only in an incident involving foreigners that the disciples want to take such drastic measures. They also take it for granted that God shares their contempt for Samaritans and will rain destructive fire on them. They have not learned that their mission is not to destroy but to transform and heal. Their evil attitude is *rebuked* by Jesus.

This story was useful in the later mission to Gentiles which proceeded against the

---

[19] See "The Central Section of St Luke's Gospel" in *Studies in the Gospels,* ed. D. E. Nineham (Oxford: Basil Blackwell, 1955), pp. 37–53.

[20] *Introduction to the New Testament,* Paul Feine and Johannes Behm; reedited by Werner George Kuemmel, tr. A. J. Mattill, Jr. (New York: Abingdon Press, 1966), p. 99.

[21] Evans, *op cit.,* pp. 50 ff.

hostility of a wing of the Jewish Christian community. It shows that Jesus was against this age-old spirit of enmity between the two racial groups. Although the longer text of vv. 54–56 (see marg.) must be judged an interpolation, it is an excellent interpretation of Jesus' attitude.

(2) Jesus' Severe Demands (9:57–62)

57 As they were going along the road, a man said to him, "I will follow you wherever you go." 58 And Jesus said to him, "Foxes have holes, and birds of the air have nests; but the Son of man has nowhere to lay his head." 59 To another he said, "Follow me." But he said, "Lord, let me first go and bury my father." 60 But he said to him, "Leave the dead to bury their own dead; but as for you, go and proclaim the kingdom of God." 61 Another said, "I will follow you, Lord; but let me first say farewell to those at my home." 62 Jesus said to him, "No one who puts his hand to the plow and looks back is fit for the kingdom of God."

The call to discipleship is a call to share Jesus' commitment and the suffering inherent in it. The lot of the disciple can be no different from the lot of the one whom he follows. Now we learn from three concrete examples what Jesus demands of those who want to follow him. The first two have parallels in Matthew 8:19–22; the third is found only in Luke.

The first prospective disciple is a volunteer, but he is not aware of the implications of his decision. Perhaps he thought that the *road* along which Jesus traveled led to success and power. But we know differently. It led to Gethsemane and Golgotha. Jesus would have no superficial commitment. He was an evangelist of the kingdom of God; but, unlike so many who have claimed to represent him, he indulged in no cheap evangelistic methods. Jesus' words to the man follow immediately on the experience in which Jesus was denied lodging. But they look ahead to a much more tragic moment when he will be rejected and killed (cf. John 1:10–11). To follow Jesus means to share his homelessness in the world, and ultimately, his rejection and death.

The second man is willing to follow Jesus

but only after he has discharged a most sacred obligation. The highest duty of a son was to care for his father in his old age and finally to give him an honorable burial. Because it is such a shocking contradiction of Jewish piety, the reply of Jesus throws into bold relief the all-consuming claims of the kingdom of God. There are people who are *dead*, i.e., dead spiritually in that they have not responded to the claims of God, to take care even of such important responsibilities as burying the man's father. The urgency of the hour and the task demands that those few who have submitted to the rule of God give themselves to the proclamation of the *kingdom*. This can take second place to no other loyalty or responsibility.

The third man finds it difficult to cut the ties that bind him to his past and his culture. He lacks the decisiveness and commitment with which one must face the future to which God has called him. In order to plow a straight furrow the farmer must choose a point of orientation and move toward it. He must keep his eye fixed on the goal. In the same manner the kingdom of God is all-absorbing, all-demanding, requiring that those who give themselves to it do so without qualifications, reservations, or regrets.

2. The Mission of the Seventy (10:1–24)

(1) Instructions to the Seventy (10:1–12)

1 After this the Lord appointed seventy others, and sent them on ahead of him, two by two, into every town and place where he himself was about to come. 2 And he said to them, "The harvest is plentiful, but the laborers are few; pray therefore the Lord of the harvest to send out laborers into his harvest. 3 Go your way; behold, I send you out as lambs in the midst of wolves. 4 Carry no purse, no bag, no sandals; and salute no one on the road. 5 Whatever house you enter, first say, 'Peace be to this house!' 6 And if a son of peace is there, your peace shall rest upon him; but if not, it shall return to you. 7 And remain in the same house, eating and drinking what they provide, for the laborer deserves his wages; do not go from house to house. 8 Whenever you enter a town and they receive you, eat what is set before you; 9 heal the sick in it and say to

them, 'The kingdom of God has come near to you.' [10] But whenever you enter a town and they do not receive you, go into its streets and say, [11] 'Even the dust of your town that clings to our feet, we wipe off against you; nevertheless know this, that the kingdom of God has come near.' [12] I tell you, it shall be more tolerable on that day for Sodom than for that town.

The recurring Lukan title *Lord* underlines the authoritative role of Jesus in relation to the disciples whom he sends forth. *Appointed* is often used in the sense of appointment to public office. It comes over into Luke "from the political sphere and the institution of the seventy has the character of a public and official action" (Heinrich Schlier, TDNT, II, 30). The number 70 (72?) likely has symbolic significance. A possible Old Testament association is with the number of elders (70) appointed by Moses to aid him in administration (Num. 11:16,24). The spirit descended on two others, Eldad and Medad, bringing the total to 72 (Num. 11:26). More likely, however, the number is a symbol for the Gentile nations of Genesis 10. In the Masoretic Text the number is 70, whereas in the LXX the number is 72. This explains the vacillation of the authorities between 70 and 72 in the text of Luke 10:1 (see marg.). In the thinking of Luke and his readers, the mission of the *seventy* probably represented the Christian mission to the Gentiles.

The verb *sent* indicates that these are Jesus' authoritative representatives or *shaliahs* (cf. 9:1). As witnesses to the kingdom of God, they are sent out *two by two* after the pattern of Deuteronomy 19:15. The testimony of two men is reliable and worthy of trust. Their task is described as one of preparation for a subsequent mission to be undertaken by Jesus himself.

In Matthew the comment on the *harvest* and *laborers* is related to Jesus' own itinerant ministry (9:37–38). The harvest is a figure for the coming kingdom of God in both its aspects, that of saving and that of judging (3:17). The fact and extent of the harvest is never in doubt because it is determined by the sovereignty of God and is not conditioned by factors extraneous to that sovereignty. This does not, however, obviate the need for *laborers.* They are the heralds of the kingdom, the men who announce it and call others to decision. But even they are furnished by the *Lord of the harvest.* In no sense, therefore, is the harvest dependent on purely human efforts and plans. People who are concerned about the critical nature of the times have one recourse: they can beseech God for additional heralds.

The messengers are sent out as *lambs in the midst of wolves.* As Jesus was in the world, so are his disciples to be in the world—unarmed and exposed to its rejection and violence.

The seventy will travel completely divested of provisions. They are not to take *purse* (money bag), a *bag* for provisions, possibly of the kind used by beggars, or even *sandals* for their feet. They will not have the security of possessing enough even for one future meal. The urgency of their mission is brought out by the command: *salute no one on the road.* Oriental greetings were so ceremonious and time-consuming that the messengers could not indulge in the required delay.

The greeting to be used by the disciples was the ancient Semitic *shalom* or *peace,* which was basically a wish for the other's well-being. But the greeting takes on new meaning. It stands for the peace of the messianic age which can be possessed now by persons who wish to share in it. In contrast to rabbinic usage, it is an individual and personal matter based on one's relationship to God. It is, therefore, synonymous with salvation (cf. 7:50).

A *son of peace* is a person awaiting the "consolation of Israel" (2:25), who can be expected to welcome the heralds of the kingdom. Presumably a person's hostility toward the preachers will be evidence that he is not a son of peace. In such a case, their peace will return. As the pronouncement of the messianic salvation, peace is viewed as something more or less objective. The messianic salvation can be repulsed, in which case the gift of God is thought of as returning to those from whom it went out.

The seventy are not to be concerned about the quality of their hospitality. Their preoccupation is to be with their mission. Nor are they to have a sense of guilt about subsisting on the generosity of others. Those who bear the message of the kingdom of God are worthy of being supported by its recipients (cf. 1 Cor. 9:4 ff.). Furthermore, they are relieved of the burdens and restrictions imposed by the Jewish food laws. They must eat what is set before them. One of the major problems faced by Jewish evangelists in the Gentile mission had to do with table fellowship. Paul apparently solved it in the way indicated by the text (1 Cor. 10:27), but others found it difficult to eat Gentile food with Gentiles (cf. Gal. 2:11 ff.).

In vv. 9 and 11 we find the statement, unusual in Luke: *The kingdom of God has come near you.* This does not mean that the final day of salvation and judgment is at hand. For Luke the kingdom of God was present in the world in the person of Jesus. Since the seventy are his authorized representatives, their healing of the sick and proclamation of the kingdom bring it near to the inhabitants of the towns whom they visit. People can appropriate its benefits and join those who look forward confidently to the final manifestation of the kingdom.

The missionaries go out with the word of salvation, but the result of their mission may be judgment. They are to *wipe off* the dust of a hostile town *against* its rebellious inhabitants, a dramatization of the fact that it is under God's judgment (see on 9:5).

That day (v. 12) is the day of judgment. *Sodom* was the epitome of wickedness in the Old Testament. But the most wicked city of antiquity will fare better in the judgment than the town which rejects Jesus' envoys.

(2) Consequences of Rejection (10:13–16)

13 "Woe to you, Chorazin! woe to you, Bethsaida! for if the mighty works done in you had been done in Tyre and Sidon, they would have repented long ago, sitting in sackcloth and ashes. 14 But it shall be more tolerable in the judgment for Tyre and Sidon than for you. 15 And you, Capernaum, will you be exalted to heaven? You shall be brought down to Hades.
16 "He who hears you hears me, and he who rejects you rejects me, and he who rejects me rejects him who sent me."

Chorazin, mentioned in the New Testament elsewhere only in the Matthean parallel (11:21), was approximately two miles north of *Capernaum. Bethsaida,* a short distance to the east, was located on the north shore of Galilee on the other side of the Jordan. The *mighty works* included the healing of the sick, cleansing of lepers, exorcism of demons, and raising of the dead mentioned in the account of the Galilean ministry. These mighty acts had not caused the people to renounce their rebelliousness and submit to the rule of God.

Tyre and *Sidon* were Gentile cities, Phoenician ports, looked upon as centers of idolatry and evil. Jezebel, daughter of the king of the Sidonians, was a Phoenician who was responsible for much of the idolatry of the Northern Kingdom during the ministry of Elijah. But these idolatrous cities would have been more responsive to Jesus' presence than were the Galilean centers of his work. *Sackcloth,* coarse material made of goat's or camel's hair, was worn as a symbol of great mourning over sins. To sit in *ashes* carried the same meaning.

Capernaum had been the headquarters of Jesus' Galilean ministry. But the arrogant city had self-righteously rejected Jesus' message and had refused to humble herself in repentance. The words with which Jesus prophesies the downfall of the city are taken from Isaiah 14:13,15, where they predict the eventual humiliation of the proud king of Babylon. *Hades* is the realm of the dead or death itself and is always so used in the New Testament with one exception (Luke 16:23). Instead of life Capernaum has chosen the way of death.

Verse 16 follows v. 12 more logically than v. 15 since it continues the thought of vv. 10–12 where the theme is the rejection of the disciples' ministry. As Jesus' personal delegates the seventy represent the sender in person, word, and deed. To *hear* them is to hear Jesus. The person who hears the word of God in this sense appropriates it. Often in Scripture, hearing is practically synonymous with faith (Gerhard Kittel, TDNT, I, 216 ff.).

The rejection of the missionaries is tantamount to the rejection of Jesus who *sent* them. It is also a rejection of God, because God sent Jesus as his *Shaliah* to speak and act for him.

(3) The Return of the Seventy (10:17-20)

¹⁷ The seventy returned with joy, saying, "Lord, even the demons are subject to us in your name!" ¹⁸ And he said to them, "I saw Satan fall like lightning from heaven. ¹⁹ Behold, I have given you authority to tread upon serpents and scorpions, and over all the power of the enemy; and nothing shall hurt you. ²⁰ Nevertheless do not rejoice in this, that the spirits are subject to you; but rejoice that your names are written in heaven."

When the seventy return, they are filled with the *joy* of liberated men. No longer need they live in constant fear of the demon's evil power. The demons are *subject* to them, the representatives of the messianic Deliverer. The victories of the disciples, however, were not contrived, personal triumphs for which they could take credit, for they were accomplished in the *name* of Jesus. Since the name stands for the person, the demons had yielded to the authority of Jesus. Consequently, disciples are not independent of their *Lord,* as the use of the title implies.

In Job, *Satan* is pictured as being in heaven as man's accuser (1:6; 2:1). In Revelation, he is the evil spiritual power who challenges the authority of God in heaven, the very seat of that authority (12:7 ff.). The inevitable failure of Satan's challenge is prefigured in victory of the delegates sent out by Jesus over the demons which represent Satan's power in the world. His *fall* will be like *lightning,* which is to say, his defeat will be sudden and completely decisive.

Serpents and *scorpions* stand for sinister and evil forces. Here they are symbols of the enmity and deadly power of Satan. Jesus declares that the disciples are safe from the harm which Satan would do them (based on Psalm 91:13). In their exorcism of demons they had been treading on serpents and scorpions by means of the *authority* which Jesus had given to them. Does this mean that the time of Jesus' ministry, the time of salvation, is a period when the disciples are safe from Satan's onslaughts (Conzelmann, pp. 28, 80 ff., etc.)? If so, the time of Jesus is like the new age which will be ushered in by the Parousia (cf. Rev. 21:3-4). The time when Jesus was on earth becomes the basis of the confidence and hope of the beleaguered and persecuted church as it looks forward to the consummation of history. Ultimately *nothing* can *hurt* the followers of Jesus.

Jesus cautions the seventy not to exaggerate the importance of the deeds that they have accomplished. The exorcisms are "a sign of the approaching salvation, but they are necessarily of less import than the fact that the disciples are elect participants in the salvation itself" (Barrett, p. 64). The symbol of a heavenly book is common in the literature of Judaism and appears also in the New Testament (Phil. 4:3; Heb. 12:23; Rev. 3:5). To have one's name *written in heaven* is to be assured of eternal life in the presence of God. It is not the disciples' victories but God's ultimate sovereignty over evil which is the ground of their hope and the basis of their rejoicing.

(4) The Rejoicing of Jesus (10:21-24)

²¹ In that same hour he rejoiced in the Holy Spirit and said, "I thank thee, Father, Lord of heaven and earth, that thou hast hidden these things from the wise and understanding and revealed them to babes; yea, Father, for such was thy gracious will. ²² All things have been delivered to me by my Father; and no one knows who the Son is except the Father, or who the Father is except the Son and any one to whom the Son chooses to reveal him."
²³ Then turning to the disciples he said privately, "Blessed are the eyes which see what you see! ²⁴ For I tell you that many prophets and kings desired to see what you see, and did not see it, and to hear what you hear, and did not hear it."

Rejoiced in the Holy Spirit is a characteristic Lukan phrase (cf. 2:27) which would normally indicate that a person is in a state of prophetic ecstasy. In the pattern of acceptance and rejection with which his work has been greeted, Jesus sees evidence of the working out of the purposes of God. He expresses gratitude to God because his work of redemption proceeds along such paradoxical lines. *Father* is Jesus' affirmation of his consciousness that as Son he sustains a unique relationship to God. But the one who is Father is also Creator and King, the *Lord of heaven and earth.*

The *wise and understanding* are the scribes, the men who are learned in the traditions of their religion. The *babes* are the simple people, the folk without arrogance and pretensions. The people who are seeking to become masters of the knowledge of God are blind to what God is doing among them. On the other hand, the people who are religiously illiterate are receptive to God's work. As a person God makes himself known through revelation. He can only reveal himself to those who, humbly aware of their need, turn to him in openness to his judgment and grace. To all others he remains unknown.

Gracious will translates the same word found in a different case at 2:14, where it is rendered "with whom he is pleased." It means God's good pleasure and refers specifically to the will of God seen in the choice of those whom he has called to himself. It was his good pleasure to choose the unsophisticated rather than the *wise,* i.e., those who consider themselves wise.

All things is indefinite as is *these things.* It includes all that God has given the Son in the realms of both wisdom and power. Knowledge means primarily the understanding that arises out of personal relationship rather than the mastery of theological dogmas or words about the attributes of God. Only one person stands in the kind of relationship to God that affords the possibility of knowing him, and that one is the Son. Likewise, only the Father really

knows who the Son is. Jesus' consciousness of his identity as Son and Suffering Servant-Messiah arose out of God's revelation to him and was independent of popular opinions about him.

The special function of the Son is to be the revealer of the Father (John 14:9). Jesus is in the world as a human being, accepting the consequences which include a lack of understanding and awareness of who he is, in order that he may reveal the Father to men of God's good pleasure.

The *prophets* and *kings* of Israel belonged to the time of preparation. Prophets had lit the lamp of messianic hope. Kings had looked forward to the coming of the Messiah, the descendant of the great king David. The disciples have the privilege of seeing in Jesus the fulfillment of those longings and that faith.

3. Teachings About Relationships (10:25–42)

(1) The Lawyer's Question (10:25–28)

25 And behold, a lawyer stood up to put him to the test, saying, "Teacher, what shall I do to inherit eternal life?" 26 He said to him, "What is written in the law? How do you read?" 27 And he answered, "You shall love the Lord your God with all your heart, and with all your soul, and with all your strength, and with all your mind; and your neighbor as yourself." 28 And he said to him, "You have answered right; do this, and you will live."

The *lawyer,* a Lukan synonym for scribe, assumes the role of the learner and puts Jesus in the role of the rabbi by calling him *teacher.* We are made aware that he has an ulterior motive. He wants to put Jesus *to the test* and show him up as inept and unsophisticated in theological discussion.

In Mark 12:29–31 it is Jesus who combines the demand for love of God (Deut. 6:4–5) with the demand for love of neighbor (Lev. 19:18). Here he responds to the lawyer's question with a question, a common rabbinic teaching method. No version of Deuteronomy 6:5 gives the fourfold predicate found in v. 27a. In Hebrew thought *heart* and *mind* are synonymous. The two Greek phrases probably represent independent translations of the Hebrew word for heart which were then conflated to form the text which lies behind the New Testament citations (Leaney, p. 182). The meaning is that man is to love God with the totality of his being.

Love for the neighbor is made dependent on one's attitude toward one's self. Without a proper concept of one's own value as a human being, it is impossible to have the right attitude toward a fellow man. Arrogance, contempt for others, and prejudice are basically an expression of low self-esteem and inner insecurity.

Do this, Jesus demanded. So the ability to give the right answer to theological questions does not guarantee that one *will live.* One weakness of orthodoxy, whether Jewish or Christian, is the mistaken belief that one can satisfy God by giving the accepted answers to questions which are framed by the expert himself. The decisive test is whether our lives are governed by love for God and for our fellow man.

(2) The Good Samaritan (10:29–37)

²⁹ But he, desiring to justify himself, said to Jesus, "And who is my neighbor?" ³⁰ Jesus replied, "A man was going down from Jerusalem to Jericho, and he fell among robbers, who stripped him and beat him, and departed, leaving him half dead. ³¹ Now by chance a priest was going down that road; and when he saw him he passed by on the other side. ³² So likewise a Levite, when he came to the place and saw him, passed by on the other side. ³³ But a Samaritan, as he journeyed, came to where he was; and when he saw him, he had compassion, ³⁴ and went to him and bound up his wounds, pouring on oil and wine; then he set him on his own beast and brought him to an inn, and took care of him. ³⁵ And the next day he took out two denarii and gave them to the innkeeper, saying, 'Take care of him; and whatever more you spend, I will repay you when I come back.' ³⁶ Which of these three, do you think, proved neighbor to the man who fell among the robbers?" ³⁷ He said, "The one who showed mercy on him." And Jesus said to him, "Go and do likewise."

The lawyer finds himself in a somewhat embarrassing situation. Why did he ask a question to which he knew the answer? He finds it necessary to *justify himself* by

pursuing the matter a step further. The love for God is clearly without limits, but love for one's neighbor can be limited by the definition of neighbor. *Who is my neighbor* was a legitimate question in contemporary theological discussions.

The definition of neighbor often depends on who is doing the defining. Your neighbor may be another person's enemy. For a Jew a neighbor was a fellow Jew or a full proselyte. Pharisees would limit it even more to exclude people like tax collectors and sinners. Jesus answered the question with a parable that made havoc of these accepted modes of thought.

The first character in the drama is a *man.* We do not know whether he was white or black, Jew or Gentile, religious or nonreligious. He is a human being who like so many other human beings becomes the helpless victim of evil.

The first man to come down the road after the tragedy occurred is a *priest.* Because priests passed this way each week after their service in the Temple (see on 1:23), this was not unusual. After serving God for a week, he is confronted with an opportunity to serve man. But the situation is complicated for him because he is a religious man. For all he knows, the unconscious man may be dead. If he touches the body to determine if he is alive, he can become defiled (Lev. 21:1). Also, there is no way of determining who the man is. A naked, beaten man has no badges of social position or religious affiliation. He can be a tax collector—or even a Samaritan! In this case he is not a neighbor whom the priest is required by his interpretation of the Law to help. The best thing to do in this doubtful situation, therefore, is to pass by as far from him as possible. A *Levite,* one of the helpers in the Temple, follows the priest's example, no doubt for the same reasons.

What Jesus has done is to present a concrete situation in which people act out their understanding of the two commandments recited by the lawyer. Conflicts between their religious rules and whatever humanitarian instincts they had are resolved in favor of the former. The two people act as the lawyer himself probably would have acted.

The third man to come along is a *Samaritan.* What shock and anger Jesus' example must have produced among his hearers! We can understand how they felt only if we have the same kind of prejudice toward people of another race that Jews and Samaritans had for one another.

The Samaritan "loved" the helpless victim. From the story we see that love is not a weak sentiment. We also learn how you "do" love (see v. 28). The Samaritan did the practical, common sense things required by the man's condition. He poured mixed *oil* and *wine,* a common remedy of ancient times, in the man's wounds, *bound* them up, put the unconscious man on his own animal, and took him to an *inn.* There he made all the arrangements necessary to care for his immediate and future needs.

In order to love his *neighbor,* a man has to be a neighbor, sensitive to the responsibility placed on him by the need of any other human being. Who was the neighbor? The lawyer is forced to answer the question. He cannot bring himself to say the hated word Samaritan, so he uses a circumlocution. But he cannot evade the point of the story. There can be no conflict between love for God and love for another human being. Then Jesus adds the crowning rebuke. The example for this arrogant scholar is not the pious and orthodox priest or Levite but the hated Samaritan. The English text does not have the emphatic personal pronoun of the Greek: *You* do likewise.

(3) *Mary and Martha* (10:38–42)

38 Now as they went on their way, he entered a village; and a woman named Martha received him into her house. 39 And she had a sister called Mary, who sat at the Lord's feet and listened to his teaching. 40 But Martha was distracted with much serving; and she went to him and said, "Lord, do you not care that my sister has left me to serve alone? Tell her then to help me." 41 But the Lord answered her, "Martha, Martha, you are anxious and troubled about many things; 42 one thing is needful.

Mary has chosen the good portion, which shall not be taken away from her."

Only in this story is there a reference to Martha and Mary in the Synoptic Gospels. The fourth Gospel gives a prominent role to Mary, Martha, and their brother Lazarus (11:1 ff.; 12:1 ff.). Luke says that Martha had a house in a *village.* John identifies the place where they lived as Bethany, a small village about one and a half miles east of Jerusalem. For Jesus to be in Bethany at this juncture, however, does not fit into the pattern required by a journey to Jerusalem, for Jesus does not even enter Judea until 18:35 ff. (See comment on Luke 9:51 ff.)

The scene is easily visualized. Jesus is the rabbi surrounded by his disciples. Mary was also there sitting at the *Lord's feet.* To sit at a person's feet was the idiom equivalent to our expression "to study under someone" (cf. Acts 22:3). So Mary is pictured as a student, in itself a revolutionary innovation, for rabbis did not teach women.

Martha's sense of responsibility as a hostess will not allow her to follow Mary's example. Moreover, she becomes incensed because she feels that her sister is taking advantage of her. Her appeal is to Jesus, the guest whose needs must be met and whose word will be recognized as authoritative by her sister.

The interpretation of Jesus' answer to Martha's complaint is complicated by a very difficult textual problem. There are five variations each of which has strong support in the authorities: (1) *one thing is needful* (RSV); (2) few things are needful; (3) few things are needful, or only one; (4) D omits 42a; (5) other Western witnesses omit everything between "Martha, Martha" and "Mary" (41b and 42a). From the point of view of textual evidence more weight would generally be given to (3) because it has the support of the great forth-century Uncials א and B. If it is original, the reply of Jesus would be understood thus: "few things are necessary— really only one." That is to say, basically only the spiritual part chosen by Mary is essential. If the reading is (2), we would understand the remark to refer to dishes. Martha need not have occupied herself with the preparation of so many dishes. If (1) is original, which seems likely, the *one thing* would refer to the choice made by Mary. The incident then would be an illustration of the principle: "Man does not live by bread alone, but by everything that proceeds out of the mouth of the Lord" (Deut. 8:3; cf. Luke 4:4). Martha was concerned about bread for the stomach; Mary was more interested in hearing the word of God. Since Mary has made the right choice, she will not be deprived of it.

4. Teachings on Prayer (11:1–13)

(1) The Lord's Prayer (11:1–4)

¹ He was praying in a certain place, and when he ceased, one of his disciples said to him, "Lord, teach us to pray, as John taught his disciples." ² And he said to them, "When you pray, say:
"Father, hallowed be thy name. Thy kingdom come. ³ Give us each day our daily bread; ⁴ and forgive us our sins, for we ourselves forgive every one who is indebted to us; and lead us not into temptation."

Two of Matthew's seven petitions, the third and the last, are missing in Luke's version of the model prayer (cf. Matt. 6: 9–13). Also, those contained in Luke show a few slight variations from the Matthean parallels.

There are many variants in the authorities from the generally adopted Lukan text of the prayer, but most were produced by the tendency to assimilate it to Matthew's longer version. An interesting and important variant is found in a few authorities which substitute "Let thy Holy Spirit come upon us and cleanse us" for the second petition. On intrinsic grounds, i.e., Luke's interest in the Holy Spirit, a good case can be made for the originality of the reading. Nevertheless, the text of the prayer underlying the RSV has the support of the best manuscripts and is accepted by most scholars as the original.

The practice of private prayer by Jesus furnishes the occasion for the disciple's petition. The request is explained by the phrase *as John taught his disciples*. It was not unusual for a disciple to request instruction in prayer from his rabbi. The unnamed disciple would know the public prayers which he and his fellow worshipers recited as a part of the synagogue service. But such prayers were not adequate for the new life into which Jesus had led his disciples.

Jesus taught his followers to address God as *Father*. This, at least in part, is the revelation that Jesus the Son of God gives of God. He knows him as Father and leads others into a filial relationship with him. The idea of the fatherhood of God is also found in the Old Testament (e.g., Deut. 32:6; Psalm 89:25 ff.; Isa. 1:2; 63:16; Mal. 3:17). But it was a minor aspect of Jewish teaching about God. Nor was God spoken of as Father in the personal, intimate way that Jesus used. A Jew might use the liturgical term *Abbi* ("my Father") or he might set it in parallel to a title such as King, as in the sixth of the "eighteen benedictions." Or he might address God as "Father in heaven," using a qualifying phrase to emphasize the distance between man and God. (The phrase in Matt. 6:8 is a liturgical expansion equivalent to Jewish usage.)

Jesus' use of *Abba* (Father) must have seemed shockingly intimate to his contemporaries, because it was the word that little children used in addressing their fathers. The nearest equivalent is the English term "daddy" used in some regions. All the dependence, confidence, and love that a little child feels for his father is expressed in the term. And it also expresses all the tenderness, love, and care with which God relates to his children. Jesus revealed that God was not first of all a majestic Creator or august Sovereign and that he was not at all a vindictive tyrant before whom his children have to tremble in fear. Above all, he is Father.

The first two petitions are parallel and look toward the end of the age which will bring the final resolution of the problems of sin and rebellion. They are both phrased in the passive, a grammatical device to avoid the use of the divine name. In each case, however, it is God who is to be the subject of the action. He will sanctify his name; he will cause his kingdom to come.

Name stands for the person, in this case the person of God. God is already holy and cannot be made any more so. Nevertheless, men do not reverence and worship him as they should. They sin against him and in so doing profane his name. The petition then calls on God to bring about the day when he will be everywhere recognized as holy. God is already King, but he is not everywhere recognized as sovereign Lord. The prayer for his *kingdom* to come is a prayer for the beginning of the future age when there will no longer be incoherence and rebellion in the universe.

The two petitions are eschatological pleas for the consummation of history. But they are also intensely personal and contemporary. The fragmented nature of the universe is but a picture of the fragmented state of our own inner lives in which there is much which is not under the rule of God. No one can pray earnestly for God to be everywhere recognized as holy Sovereign unless he longs for God to rule completely over his own life.

Included in the prayer is a request for life's physical necessities. The word translated *daily* is one of the most enigmatic words in the New Testament. It is found in only one papyrus fragment outside the comments by Christian writers on this text. "For tomorrow" is one likely meaning, but some interpreters reject it because they feel that Jesus' teaching rules out anxiety about bread for tomorrow, i.e., the needs of the future. Another possibility is "necessary" (Werner Foerster, TDNT, II, 590 ff.). In this case, the disciple is taught to depend on God as did Israel in the wilderness for the sustenance essential for each day. Luke has the imperative *give* in the present tense and the phrase *each day*. Matthew puts "give" in the aorist tense and has "this day" (6:11). We may interpret Luke's request as follows: "Give us day by day the bread which is necessary for that day." By contrast, most of us want bread laid up for the next ten or twenty years.

Although the wording is slightly different, both Luke and Matthew show that God's forgiveness of us is inseparably related to our forgiveness of our fellow man. Jesus never allows us to escape from our fellow man into communion with God. Rather, he teaches that those who go to God are at the same time confronted with their brothers. Jesus challenges us to base our claim to God's forgiveness on our willingness to forgive others, a challenge that few of us would be willing to accept.

Temptation is testing which could cause a person to fall into sin. The petition is not an oblique indictment of God, for he does not will that man should sin. On the contrary, it is intended as a pattern for the humble prayer of a disciple who recognizes his own weakness. The person who prays: "Lead me not into temptation" is really saying: "I am weak, and there are many situations with which I cannot cope." The meaning of the prayer is illustrated in the Gethsemane experience. Jesus urged his uncomprehending, unprepared disciples to pray that they not be thrust into a situation of testing for which they were unprepared (Mark 14:38). Had they heeded his counsel, their actions in the succeeding hours might have been much nobler and more courageous.

(2) The Insistent Friend (11:5–13)

5 And he said to them, "Which of you who has a friend will go to him at midnight and say to him, 'Friend, lend me three loaves; 6 for a friend of mine has arrived on a journey, and I have nothing to set before him'; 7 and he will answer from within, 'Do not bother me; the door is now shut, and my children are with me in bed; I cannot get up and give you anything'? 8 I tell you, though he will not get up and give him anything because he is his friend, yet because of his importunity he will rise and give him whatever he needs. 9 And I tell you, Ask, and it will be given you; seek, and you will find; knock, and it will be opened to you. 10 For every one who asks receives, and he who seeks finds, and to him who knocks it will be opened. 11 What father among you, if his son asks for a fish, will instead of a fish give him a

serpent; [12] or if he asks for an egg, will give him a scorpion? [13] If you then, who are evil, know how to give good gifts to your children, how much more will the heavenly Father give the Holy Spirit to those who ask him!"

The parable of the insistent friend teaches the need for persistence in prayer. Its structure indicates that this application is probably secondary (cf. Jeremias, p. 118). The problem is not that man has to overcome the reluctance of God to hear and answer his prayers. To the contrary, the problem is located in the one who prays. If God does not respond immediately and on his terms, then the individual is apt to lose faith, either in God's existence or in his character as a loving Father. Persistence in prayer is an act of faith, a testimony to our belief in a loving, personal God.

During certain times of the year, the intense heat in the Middle East will cause a person to travel either early or late. It was not uncommon for a person traveling on foot to reach his destination late at night. Since bread was baked daily in accordance with the anticipated need for the day, households often had no bread left after the last meal. But it was considered a disgrace not to welcome a weary and hungry traveler with food. For this reason the man who receives an unexpected guest at midnight goes to such lengths to secure bread for him.

The humor of the scene is inescapable. All the children have at last gone to sleep. The door has been bolted for the night and the weary man himself has finally lain down, when a knock is heard on the door. *My children are with me in bed* does not mean that they are all sleeping in the same bed. The sense is "my children, as well as I, are in bed." All are sleeping in the single room of a poor man's hut.

The crisis provoked by his guest's unexpected arrival is so great, however, that the neighbor will not accept refusal. *Because of his importunity* is translated by Leaney picturesquely "for his unblushing persistence" (p. 187).

Finally, of course, the poor man has to arise, unbolt the door, awakening all the children in the process, and give his friend *whatever he needs,* not necessarily just what he has requested.

The three imperatives *ask, seek, knock* are in the present tense which brings out the need for persistence—keep on asking, keep on seeking, keep on knocking. The believer must never falter in his assurance that God will respond to the seeking of his children.

This does not mean at all that prayer is an exercise in magic by which we control God. All subsequent requests are governed by the first petitions of the model prayer. On our side we seek God and those gracious gifts which will help us to be better children. On his part, the response of God to our prayers must be consonant with his fatherly wisdom and love.

The section on prayer is concluded by an argument that moves from the lesser to the greater, from the human to the divine Father. If a *son* asks for that which is wholesome and nourishing, a *fish* or an *egg,* a human *father* will not give him that which is poisonous and dangerous, a *serpent* or a *scorpion* (cf. Matt. 7:9–10).

If men, therefore, with all their *evil* normally seek the best for their *children,* how much more will God, who alone can be called good (18:19), give what is necessary for his children. Matthew has "good gifts" (7:11) where Luke has *Holy Spirit.* Of all the good gifts that God can give his children, the Holy Spirit is considered in Luke to be the greatest of all. Through the Spirit man is able to live in fellowship with God and joyously anticipate the full consummation of his salvation (cf. Eph. 1:13–14).

5. Unfavorable Responses to Jesus (11:14–54)

(1) The Beelzebul Controversy (11:14–23)

[14] Now he was casting out a demon that was dumb; when the demon had gone out, the dumb man spoke, and the people marveled. [15] But some of them said, "He casts out demons

by Beelzebul, the prince of demons"; [16] while others, to test him, sought from him a sign from heaven. [17] But he, knowing their thoughts, said to them, "Every kingdom divided against itself is laid waste, and house falls upon house. [18] And if Satan also is divided against himself, how will his kingdom stand? For you say that I cast out demons by Beelzebul. [19] And if I cast out demons by Beelzebul, by whom do your sons cast them out? Therefore they shall be your judges. [20] But if it is by the finger of God that I cast out demons, then the kingdom of God has come upon you. [21] When a strong man, fully armed, guards his own palace, his goods are in peace; [22] but when one stronger than he assails him and overcomes him, he takes away his armor in which he trusted, and divides his spoil. [23] He who is not with me is against me, and he who does not gather with me scatters.

The healing of the *dumb man* is a proclamation of the presence and demand of the kingdom of God. The presentation of the claims of God to rule over his universe always forces upon those to whom they are presented the necessity for making some kind of decision. There can be no neutrality. When the dumb man speaks, incontrovertible evidence that he has been freed from his malady, the witnesses immediately divide into three groups. The *people* (crowds) *marveled*, an indication that they recognized that God had performed a mighty deed before them. This response, however, is still this side of that which is adequate, which is submission to God's rule so mightily demonstrated.

Unable to deny that a supernatural display of power had taken place, some accused Jesus of being in league with *Beelzebul, the prince of demons*. According to them he exercised some kind of black magic. If hostile, evil men cannot deny a good man's deeds, they can destroy his influence by attributing it to sinister motives.

Still others do not find the sign of Jesus' mastery over demons convincing enough. Before they will believe that he is Messiah, he must perform a sign to fit their own specifications. *A sign from heaven* indicates that they desired some astral phenomenon (Strack-Billerbeck, I, 727 ff.).

Jesus discerns the thoughts of his critics, i.e., the second group, and demonstrates the weakness of their accusation. First, he points out that it is illogical. If from Beelzebul he received the power to cast out another evil spirit, this would mean that Satan's forces were embroiled in a self-destructive civil war. *House falls upon house* depicts the destruction in a city torn apart by civil conflict. This kind of reasoning is absurd on the face of it.

Second, Jesus shows that their judgment is arbitrary. Only on the basis of prejudice can they judge Jesus' acts to be demonic while at the same time attributing to the power of God similar acts performed by people of their own group. *Your sons* are members of the rabbinic circles. *They shall be your judges* means that their deeds will furnish evidence to prove how inconsistent and dishonest Jesus' enemies were.

The third hypothesis suggested by Jesus is the correct one. The expression *the finger of God* refers to a direct, unmediated act of God (Ex. 8:19;31:18; Deut. 9:10; Psalm 8:3). The closest Old Testament parallel to its usage here is Exodus 8:19, where the acts of God are shown to be beyond the power of the Egyptian magicians to duplicate. Here also Satan's servants, the demons, had been vanquished by a superior power, that is, the power of God. The authority of God exerted over demons showed that his *kingdom* (rule) had come upon those who witnessed what Jesus had done. Instead of owning God as king, they were rejecting the signs of his rule.

The *strong man* is Satan. But *one stronger than he*, that is, Jesus, has attacked him and gained a victory before their eyes. Possession of the defeated foe's armor was evidence of the victor's triumph. By custom the goods of the vanquished were confiscated by the victor, who divided part of them with his own troops. Jesus, the conqueror of Satan, divides among believers the fruits of his victory— liberation from Satan's power and freedom from fear.

Finally Jesus affirms that there can be no middle ground (v. 23). Neutrality is as much an expression of unbelief as is open hostility.

(2) The Unclean Spirit (11:24–26)

24 "When the unclean spirit has gone out of a man, he passes through waterless places seeking rest; and finding none he says, 'I will return to my house from which I came.' 25 And when he comes he finds it swept and put in order. 26 Then he goes and brings seven other spirits more evil than himself, and they enter and dwell there; and the last state of that man becomes worse than the first."

Although exorcism is one of the most important signs of the messianic triumph over the powers of evil, Jesus teaches that the mere expulsion of demons is not enough. After departing from his victim, the *unclean spirit* or demon goes *through waterless* places, another example of the association of evil spirits with the desert (see 8:29). He is not satisfied, however, without a victim. He needs a body through which to express his demonic nature (see on 8:32). His *house* is the body of the man formerly possessed, which is now clean but has not been filled. Perhaps the reason for bringing *seven spirits* is in order to take complete control of the man (cf. 8:2), whose *last state* is much *worse than the first.*

In the exorcism of demons the possessed individual was a passive recipient of the benefits of God's rule. But it was also necessary for him as well as those who witnessed the mighty deed of God to respond positively to the proclamation of the kingdom. By faith they could be filled with the power of God that would arm them against any future assaults by demons.

(3) Reply to a Woman's Praise (11:27–28)

27 As he said this, a woman in the crowd raised her voice and said to him, "Blessed is the womb that bore you, and the breasts that you sucked!" 28 But he said, "Blessed rather are those who hear the word of God and keep it!"

Jesus is interrupted by a woman who pronounces a blessing on his mother. Although Mary figures more prominently in Luke than in any other Gospel, an effort is also made to prevent the distortion of her place in salvation-history. In the ancient world a woman's chief purpose was to bear children, especially sons. Since the fulfillment of her life was in her children, the mother of a famous son was considered especially blessed.

Perhaps the connection with the preceding passages is to be found in the fact that Mary, like the man liberated from the demon, had been an instrument for the revelation of God's power in the world. But it is not enough to be a recipient of God's mercies. One must also act in response to the revelation of his presence. The essential nature of man's response is to *hear the word of God and keep it,* which parallels the demand expressed in 8:19–21.

At this time Mary does not fall in the category of those who were ordering their lives in keeping with the word of God. For this reason it is inappropriate to call her *blessed.* Jesus reserved that term for those who had come under the rule of God (6:20 ff.). Luke himself shows that Mary did become a part of the believing company, after which she is mentioned no more (Acts 1:14).

(4) The Sign of the Son of Man (11: 29–32)

29 When the crowds were increasing, he began to say, "This generation is an evil generation; it seeks a sign, but no sign shall be given to it except the sign of Jonah. 30 For as Jonah became a sign to the men of Nineveh, so will the Son of man be to this generation. 31 The queen of the South will arise at the judgment with the men of this generation and condemn them; for she came from the ends of the earth to hear the wisdom of Solomon, and behold, something greater than Solomon is here. 32 The men of Nineveh will arise at the judgment with this generation and condemn it; for they repented at the preaching of Jonah, and behold, something greater than Jonah is here.

The theme for this passage is provided by the request for a *sign from heaven* made by some of the people who witnessed the cure of the dumb man (v. 16 above). The demand for a sign is consistently refused by Jesus. Such a request is characterized as *evil*, an expression of the perversity and rebellion of the people. It is a rejection of what God has already done among them, as well as an attempt to make God prove himself on their terms.

In Matthew the *sign of Jonah* is the parallel between Jonah's experience in the belly of the fish and Jesus' death (12:40). In Luke the sign is Jonah's call to repentance, unsupported by wonders, to which the people of Nineveh responded. Jesus is to his generation what Jonah was to the Ninevites. In his person he is the sign God has given to them. In his deeds and words the call to repentance has been presented.

The idea that Gentiles would witness against Israelites in the judgment entered into violent shock with contemporary ideas. Jews looked forward to the judgment as the time of vindication for righteous men, among whom the religious leaders classified themselves. They also believed that the judgment would bring about the destruction of the wicked, which included most Gentiles.

The *queen of the South* is the queen of Sheba of 1 Kings 10:1–10. Josephus identifies her as the queen of Egypt and Ethiopia (*Antiq.*, 2,10,2; 8,6,5–6). According to a national tradition, the royal line of Abysinnia is descended from the union of Solomon and the Queen of Sheba. These traditions lack adequate historical foundations. More likely she was from a tribe of northwestern Arabia.

The *ends of the earth* denotes the limits of the known world. By going to such lengths to verify personally the rumors that she had heard about the grandeur of Solomon, the queen had shown that she was honest. By contrast Jesus' contemporaries betray their inherent dishonesty in being unwilling to act on the evidence which they have. Their guilt is all the greater because *something greater than Solomon* is in their midst. It is difficult to say what the neuter *something greater* includes. Perhaps it is a reference to the total event of Jesus' presence in the world. They are blind to a

glory and grandeur which far exceed the wonders of Solomon's reign.

Likewise the *men of Nineveh* will serve as witnesses in the *judgment* to prove the blindness of the people who reject Jesus. The Assyrians, whose capital was Nineveh, were among the most ruthless and barbaric people of antiquity. The very fact that they responded to the preaching of Jonah confirms the guilt of those who reject Jesus. On the one hand, there is the contrast between Jonah as God's preacher to the Ninevites and the much more decisive, demanding call to repentance presented by Jesus—*something greater than Jonah*. If wicked Ninevites repented at the preaching of Jonah, there is no hope for Israelites who reject the claims of God represented by Jesus.

(5) Receptivity to Light (11:33–36)

33 "No one after lighting a lamp puts it in a cellar or under a bushel, but on a stand, that those who enter may see the light. 34 Your eye is the lamp of your body; when your eye is sound, your whole body is full of light; but when it is not sound, your body is full of darkness. 35 Therefore be careful lest the light in you be darkness. 36 If then your whole body is full of light, having no part dark, it will be wholly bright, as when a lamp with its rays gives you light."

Three disparate and apparently originally unconnected sayings are linked together by the catchword *lamp*. The result is a passage which presents great difficulties for the interpreter. The first saying (v. 33) has already been used by Luke in another connection (8:16; cf. Mark 4:21). It is also used by Matthew in a different context (5:15).

Here the lamp is God's call to repentance, i.e., the ministry of Jesus. Luke has continually mentioned the crowds, who have been present to see and hear Jesus' deeds and words. His activity has not been private or esoteric. He has not gone off in the desert with a select few and isolated himself from the people. Just as a person who lights a lamp intends for it to be seen, so also does God intend for people to receive the revelation given in Jesus.

In the second saying the lamp is the *eye,* the member through which light enters to illuminate the *body.* Of course, the body depends upon a *sound eye* to receive light. A diseased or blind eye shuts out the light. (See on Matt. 6:22 f. for a different use of the idiom *sound* [single] *eye.*) The analogy in this case is to the faculty of spiritual perception. The problem with Jesus' contemporaries is that they are spiritually blind and, therefore, incapable of receiving the light.

The light in you is probably best understood as the organ of spiritual perception, the heart (Creed, p. 164). Responsibility for sensitivity to the light is placed on the individual, who is urged to *be careful* to keep his lamp in good order.

As it stands, v. 36 is confusing and impossible to interpret, due perhaps to a "very early corruption" (Creed). C. C. Torrey [22] suggests that the original Aramaic saying of Jesus should have been translated: "If however your whole body is lighted up, with no dark part, then all about you will be light, just as the lamp lights you with its brightness." This means that the Christian, illuminated by Christ, is to be a light shining in a dark world.

(6) Controversy over Washing (11:37–41)

37 While he was speaking, a Pharisee asked him to dine with him; so he went in and sat at table. 38 The Pharisee was astonished to see that he did not first wash before dinner. 39 And the Lord said to him, "Now you Pharisees cleanse the outside of the cup and of the dish, but inside you are full of extortion and wickedness. 40 You fools! Did not he who made the outside make the inside also? 41 But give for alms those things which are within; and behold, everything is clean for you.

A dinner scene, for which Luke has a predilection, provides the setting for Jesus' denunciation of Jewish religious leaders. The *Pharisee's* surprise arises from the presupposition that Jesus will perform the traditional ablutions prior to eating. The pur-

[22] *The Four Gospels: A New Translation* (London: Hodder and Stoughton, 1933), pp. 309 f.

pose of washing the hands was to remove any defilement that the person might have incurred by coming into contact with something or somebody who was unclean. By his unvoiced disapproval of Jesus' ceremonial negligence the Pharisee places himself in the category of those to whom religion is legalistic, outward conformity to certain traditional requirements. Over against this is set the position represented by Jesus that genuine religion is inward and spiritual, having to do primarily with the kind of human being a man is and how he relates to God and persons in the world.

The same criticisms of Jewish religionists appear also in Matthew 23. Additional material is found in the longer Matthean passage, which is also arranged quite differently from this one. The target of Jesus' denunciations in Matthew, the scribes and Pharisees, are grouped together. Luke divides his six woes into two groups of three, the first directed toward the *Pharisees* and the second group addressed to *lawyers.*

The *Pharisees* are characterized as men who are concerned about exterior righteousness but neglect to come to grips with their inner depravity. Such a superficial concept of righteousness is based on a superficial concept of sin. When sin is seen as something "out there," exterior to the person, the problem becomes how to avoid contamination. This is achieved by omitting certain practices, by isolation from certain kinds of people, and by careful observance of prescribed religious duties. But Jesus taught that sin has its roots in the inner nature of every man and demanded that each one face up to the fact that he is himself a sinner. The self-righteous person is a self-deceived person. His religion is a means of escaping from his real self.

The meaning of v. 40 is not clear. *He* may refer to God who created the total man, both the *inside* and the *outside.* Consequently, he cannot be satisfied with a religion that is concerned with the *outside of the cup,* disregarding the much more important inner nature. Verse 41 is very difficult. Taken as it stands, it may be understood as an injunction to offer up as a gift to God one's very self, that which he is on the inside.[23] This contrasts with the legalistic piety of the Pharisees of which almsgiving was an important part. Wellhausen conjectured that an original Aramaic *dakki* (cleanse) was misunderstood as *zakki* (give alms). A "brilliant conjecture," according to Matthew Black.[24] This suggestion is strengthened by the fact that it brings the injunction into line with its parallel (Matt. 23:26). We would then understand the statement in this way: if the inside is cleansed, there is no need to be concerned about the outside.

(7) Woes on the Pharisees (11:42–44)

42 "But woe to you Pharisees! for you tithe mint and rue and every herb, and neglect justice and the love of God; these you ought to have done, without neglecting the others. 43 Woe to you Pharisees! for you love the best seat in the synagogues and salutations in the market places. 44 Woe to you! for you are like graves which are not seen, and men walk over them without knowing it."

The Pharisees were extremely scrupulous in observing the requirements of the law relating to secondary matters. They tithed even the herbs used for seasoning. One text (P[45]) has "dill" instead of *rue*, as does also Matthew 23:23. Dill is doubtless original, because rue was not subject to the tithe. But Jesus accuses the Pharisees of being deficient in what are called "the weightier matters of the law" in the Matthean parallel (cf. Micah 6:8). *Justice* means primarily a concern for the plight and right of the oppressed. To some people justice denotes almost exclusively the apprehension and punishment of criminal elements. But there is no just society which does not place foremost the protection and vindication of its weaker elements, such as racial minorities, the culturally and physically handicapped, and little children. *Love*

23 Karl Heinrich Rengstorf, *Das Evangelium nach Lukas* in *Das Neue Testament Deutsch*, ed. Gerhard Friedrich (Goettingen: Vandenhoeck and Ruprecht, 1967), p. 154.
24 *An Aramaic Approach to the Gospels and Acts* (Oxford: Clarendon, 1954), p. 2.

of God is love *for* God, but we have already seen that this cannot be isolated from love for man.

Instead of loving God, the Pharisees are accused of loving honor and recognition. A basic evil of legalistic religion is that it contributes to human pride. Righteousness is interpreted in such a way that it is made attainable by human efforts. Those who make the effort are apt to do so because it is one way of achieving social prominence and respect. *The best seats in the synagogue* were the ones reserved for the most important persons in the assembly. Another sign of prestige were the *salutations in the market places*, the greetings from an awed public whose religious and social standards were imposed on them by the persons who profited most from them.

Since touching the dead was especially defiling, care was also used to avoid contact with *graves*. A person could be rendered unclean by contact with an unmarked grave and have no knowledge of his defilement. The Pharisees' attention to outward ritual masked their inward corruption. They were sources of defilement who contaminated an unsuspecting public. In this vivid way Jesus set forth the failure of the religious leaders to achieve their major goal, that is, religious purity.

(8) Woes on the Lawyers (11:45–54)

45 One of the lawyers answered him, "Teacher, in saying this you reproach us also." 46 And he said, "Woe to you lawyers also! for you load men with burdens hard to bear, and you yourselves do not touch the burdens with one of your fingers. 47 Woe to you! for you build the tombs of the prophets whom your fathers killed. 48 So you are witnesses and consent to the deeds of your fathers; for they killed them, and you build their tombs. 49 Therefore also the Wisdom of God said, 'I will send them prophets and apostles, some of whom they will kill and persecute,' 50 that the blood of all the prophets, shed from the foundation of the world, may be required of this generation, 51 from the blood of Abel to the blood of Zechariah, who perished between the altar and the sanctuary. Yes, I tell you, it shall be required of this generation. 52 Woe to you lawyers! for you have taken away **the key of**

knowledge; you did not enter yourselves, and you hindered those who were entering."
⁵³ As he went away from there, the scribes and the Pharisees began to press him hard, and to provoke him to speak of many things, ⁵⁴ lying in wait for him, to catch at something he might say.

Lawyers is Luke's synonym for scribes, the experts in the interpretation of the Torah. They are generally grouped with the Pharisees as "scribes and Pharisees" or "scribes of the Pharisees." By the nature of the case, the scribes were associated with and supported by the party of the Pharisees to which the majority of them apparently belonged. These "doctors of the law" developed the traditions by which the Pharisees undertook to live.

The burdens laid upon the people were the casuistic interpretations which defined what was lawful and unlawful and so complicated the daily lives of the people who sought to live by them. Moreover, Jesus accused the "scholars" of not making the slightest effort—i.e., not touching with *one of your fingers*—to aid the people in bearing their burden of constantly multiplying legal observances. But they were very adept at devising loopholes through which they themselves could escape the requirements of their traditions when self-interest so demanded.

The second woe pronounced on the lawyers is unclear. How does building the *tombs of the prophets* involve them in the guilt of their fathers? In the Matthean parallel (23:29 ff.) it is said that they witness against themselves by acknowledging their relationship to the murderers of the prophets. Perhaps the meaning of the whole is that they honor dead prophets but react as their fathers did to living ones. Dead prophets are not disturbing and threatening; living ones are. Just so do we praise Jesus and the apostles while disavowing the messengers who come in his name to challenge us to a new commitment to justice and openness to all humanity.

The *Wisdom of God said* corresponds to rabbinic phrases like "the Holy Spirit says" and "the divine righteousness says"

(Strack-Billerbeck, II, p. 189). It is equivalent to "God says." *Prophets* and *apostles* probably also includes persecuted witnesses of the early church, e.g., Stephen, whose speech declared that the murder of Jesus was in keeping with the treatment afforded prophets by earlier generations (Acts 7:52). *Zechariah* is the son of Jehoida the high priest whose murder is recounted in 2 Chronicles 24:17–22 (but see on Matt. 23:35). Since Chronicles is the last book of Hebrew Scripture in the Masoretic Text, all the martyrs of the Old Testament are included in the span from *Abel* to *Zechariah.* The perversity and rebellion seen in Jewish history is thought of as reaching its climax in the treatment of Jesus and the first Christian witnesses. Early Christians understood this to be the reason for the devastating defeat of the Jews and the destruction of Jerusalem in the Jewish-Roman War of A.D. 66–70.

Just as the "clean" Pharisees are denounced for their uncleanliness, so are the "wise" scholars denounced for their ignorance. The Scriptures are the *key of knowledge* (objective genitive) when rightly interpreted (cf. 24:45 ff.). That is, they point to what God is doing in Jesus. But instead of understanding the Scriptures, the teachers have distorted them. By their wrong interpretations they have shut both themselves and the people that they influence out of the kingdom of God (cf. Matt. 23:13).

In the concluding statement Luke substitutes the synonym *scribes* for lawyers. As a result of Jesus' denunciation of them, the hostility of the *scribes* and *Pharisees* toward Jesus becomes more intense. They now begin to put pressure on him in order to provoke him into making some kind of compromising statement which can be used to destroy his influence.

6. Admonitions for Persecution (12:1–12)

(1) A Warning Against Hypocrisy (12:1–3)

¹ In the meantime, when so many thousands of the multitude had gathered together that they trod upon one another, he began to say to

his disciples first, "Beware of the leaven of the Pharisees, which is hypocrisy. 2 Nothing is covered up that will not be revealed, or hidden that will not be known. 3 Whatever you have said in the dark shall be heard in the light, and what you have whispered in private rooms shall be proclaimed upon the housetops.

A series of rather loosely connected teachings to the disciples and to the crowd begins with 12:1 and goes through 13:9. Luke brings us back from the plots of the Pharisees to the activities of Jesus with the phrase *in the meantime.* The setting of the teaching of Jesus is characteristic, as is also the distinction between the *multitude* and the *disciples.* Although it is possible to take *first* as the opening word of Jesus' address to his disciples, it more likely belongs to the introductory phrase. Jesus first teaches the disciples, and then he addresses the multitude (beginning at v. 54).

Because of the way that it permeates a batch of dough, *leaven* was generally a symbol of the corrupting influence of evil. It is identified here as the *hyprocrisy* of the *Pharisees* (but see on Matt. 16:6; Mark 8:15). Their corrupt inner condition is masked by their exterior religiosity. Perhaps Jesus is warning the disciples against being deluded by the Pharisees' outward show of righteousness. More likely, he is cautioning them against falling into the kind of legalism represented by the Jewish religious leaders. There is to be coherence between the disciples' inner being and outward acts. The warning of Jesus is particularly pertinent now due to the fact that the institutions formed by people who claim to follow him tend to take on the nature of the ones that he challenged. The "good" Christian is then defined, like the Pharisee, as the man who is faithful in his performance of religious acts, such as going to church, giving it financial support, and refraining from a cluster of contaminating acts.

Jesus assures his disciples that the mask will be stripped off and that people and things will be revealed as they really are. God does not judge man by his exterior show but by what he really is. Just as the inner reality of the Pharisees will come to light, so also will the disciples' message become the subject of the widest proclamation. In Matthew (10:27) it is the word spoken by Jesus to his disciples that will be proclaimed publicly. The variation here (v. 3) is a characteristic transition from the time of Jesus to the next generation.

The faith of the disciples in their small, limited, apparently insignificant groups will be the subject of missionary proclamation. The same sovereign power which guarantees that hidden wickedness will be brought to light also guarantees that the truth of the gospel will be proclaimed in spite of the odds against it. By the time Luke is written, the gospel has been preached in the marketplaces of the great cities and is known from Jerusalem to Rome.

(2) God's Care in Danger (12:4-7)

4 "I tell you, my friends, do not fear those who kill the body, and after that have no more that they can do. 5 But I will warn you whom to fear: fear him who, after he has killed, has power to cast into hell; yes, I tell you, fear him! 6 Are not five sparrows sold for two pennies? And not one of them is forgotten before God. 7 Why, even the hairs of your head are all numbered. Fear not; you are of more value than many sparrows.

For their part in the publication of the gospel, Christian witnesses will provoke the hostility of governing authorities which have the power to execute them. But Jesus points them to One whose jurisdiction transcends the geographic and temporal limits of the world's courts.

This is the only time in the Synoptic record that Jesus calls the disciples *friends* (cf. John 15:14). It is their relationship to Jesus that places them in a precarious position in the world. But it is also the ground of their security for the future.

Jesus explains that the most the disciples have to fear from other men is the loss of life. But God has authority that extends beyond death. His judgment, therefore, can be much more serious, for he has the *power to cast into hell.* Gehenna (hell) appears first in Jewish apocalyptic literature of the second century B.C. as the place of punishment for apostate Jews. By the time of Jesus it is generally a place of punishment for the godless. The name comes from the Valley of Hinnom. In this valley, located southwest of Jerusalem, the city garbage was burned, for it had been polluted by fireworship and human sacrifice during the reign of Ahaz (2 Kings 16:3).

If one is to be awed by power, clearly God must take precedence over human judges. The disciples, however, are not to be driven to be faithful by quaking fear of God. The power of God is rather the ground of confidence because it is used on their behalf. The central teaching of Jesus is that the great sovereign God is a loving Father who cares for his children. *Sparrows* are so cheap that men consider them practically worthless. Yet God is concerned for them. The disciples can be assured that a God who is interested in the least of his creatures will not forget those who are his children. God will see to it that not a *hair* of their heads is lost. This is another way of saying that they are perfectly secure in God's care (cf. Rom. 8:38).

(3) Confessing Christ Before Men (12:8–12)

8 "And I tell you, every one who acknowledges me before men, the Son of man also will acknowledge before the angels of God; 9 but he who denies me before men will be denied before the angels of God. 10 And every one who speaks a word against the Son of man will be forgiven; but he who blasphemes against the Holy Spirit will not be forgiven. 11 And when they bring you before the synagogues and the rulers and the authorities, do not be anxious how or what you are to answer or what you are to say; 12 for the Holy Spirit will teach you in that very hour what you ought to say."

The pressures of persecution will subject followers of Jesus to the most difficult kind of test. The disciples are to be aware of the consequences of affirming and denying their relationship to him. If in an hour of crisis they affirm their allegiance to him, they can be assured that he will be their advocate in the time of eschatological crisis

that lies beyond this age. Luke is thinking here of judgment, the great and final assize before the assembled hosts of heaven. While it is true that the language does not require the identification of Jesus with the *Son of man,* this was no doubt the identification made by early Christians and by Luke. (Matt. 10:32 has "I," which, as Creed says [pp. 171 f.], may be original.)

Those who yield to the pressures and deny Jesus cannot expect to have an advocate at the judgment. In his teaching, Jesus constantly drives home the severity of the gospel's demands. By his actions, however, he shows that the love of God is not withdrawn from the weak and cowardly. The early church remembered well that the persons who denied Jesus in the hour of crisis were forgiven and restored to places of trust.

The gospel is always both grace and demand. Without demand grace becomes cheap; without grace demand leads to despair. So those of us who have denied him because of social and business pressures or for other reasons must hear the word of grace, which brings us once more under the demand to be true whatever the cost.

The teaching about blasphemy against the Holy Spirit is somewhat easier to understand in the Matthean context (see on Matt. 12:31–32). *A word against the Son of man,* is a word against Jesus, present in the world as a man rather than the apocalyptic figure of the end-time. Hostility to him does not cut a person off from the possibility of forgiveness. Indeed, some of those who at the moment reject him, including his own family, will become a part of the community of believers. Even after they condemned him unjustly and crucified him, the Jewish nation will be given another opportunity in the Christian mission. After the earthly ministry of Jesus, however, those who reject the work of the Holy Spirit as evil will have no other avenue to God (Grundmann, p. 255).

The disciples are not to be concerned about how they will answer charges which may be brought against them. *Synagogues*

. . . rulers . . . authorities presupposes hearings before both Jewish and pagan courts and judges. Followers of Jesus can face the threats of the future because they will have the ministry of the *Holy Spirit* in the hour of need. He will *teach* them how they must answer when confronted by the world's hostility and power.

7. Teachings About Wealth (12:13–34)

(1) The Rich Farmer (12:13–21)

13 One of the multitude said to him, "Teacher, bid my brother divide the inheritance with me." 14 But he said to him, "Man, who made me a judge or divider over you?" 15 And he said to them, "Take heed, and beware of all covetousness; for a man's life does not consist in the abundance of his possessions." 16 And he told them a parable, saying, "The land of a rich man brought forth plentifully; 17 and he thought to himself, 'What shall I do, for I have nowhere to store my crops?' 18 And he said, 'I will do this: I will pull down my barns, and build larger ones; and there I will store all my grain and my goods. 19 And I will say to my soul, Soul, you have ample goods laid up for many years; take your ease, eat, drink, be merry.' 20 But God said to him, 'Fool! This night your soul is required of you; and the things you have prepared, whose will they be?' 21 So is he who lays up treasure for himself, and is not rich toward God."

The request of a man from the multitude provides the occasion for Jesus' teachings about the proper attitude toward material possessions. The older *brother* presumably assumed proprietorship of all his father's goods at death and had not given the younger the share allotted to him by the Law. A *teacher* or rabbi could be expected to interpret how the provisions of the Law would apply in this specific case (cf. Num. 27:8 ff.; Deut. 21:17). The distinctions between religious and civil matters did not exist in Israel, for all of life was under the hegemony of the law of God. As a Jew, the older brother might be expected to follow the ruling of a person whose authority as a teacher he recognized. Jesus, however, rejects the office that the man seeks to thrust on him.

Jesus cannot be a party to the amassing of wealth since he considers the pursuit of it to be a prostitution of man's energies and talents. *Covetousness* would probably best be rendered greed. The story illustrates how man can give too much value to material possessions, not the sin of desiring what belongs to another. The maxim of Jesus is the antithesis of secularism. *Possessions* do not equal *life*. We say that we know this, but we betray our secular values by such expressions as: that man is worth a million dollars.

The story is called a *parable.* It is really an illustrative story comprehended in the very general category of the Hebrew *mashal,* usually translated parable. Basically *mashal* denotes a comparison. In popular usage it came to designate a wide variety of literary forms, such as a riddle, a proverb, an oracle, an allegory, a taunt song, etc. This general application of the Hebrew synonym influenced the use of the Greek word for parable in the New Testament.

The main character in the story is already *rich.* Consequently the abundant harvest simply increased his wealth and confronted him with a dilemma. But he consults neither God nor man. The solution is sought in a conversation with himself, which sets forth his grand isolation from the world and its need.

What shall I do? This is the question that each human being has to face when he possesses more than he needs to sustain his own life. Conceivably there were many things that the rich man could have done with his surplus. But his is the solution of the callous egoist. He will fill new *barns* rather than hungry stomachs.

He has spoken of *my crops . . . my barns . . . my grain . . . my goods.* But now he goes a step further when he says *my soul.* Soul is not embodied spirit. It means life and describes man as an animate being. On biblical grounds it is God's creation and gift (Gen. 2:7). Life belongs to God and is under his dispensation. Man is on earth as a steward, responsible to God for the life he has given.

The man has reached the place where

he is satisfied that his possessions will be sufficient for the years ahead. He has reached the goal toward which he has been working. So he decides to retire one day— and is dead the next. The *many years* were exactly what he could not provide. *Ample goods* do not guarantee *many* years; just as less goods would not have meant fewer years.

His neighbors no doubt called him intelligent; God called him a *fool.* A fool is a man whose decisions about the present do not take into consideration the possibilities of the future. What a poor, futile little life he had lived! He had spent all his years amassing goods; now another, perhaps just as foolish, will fall heir to them. He had the temporary responsibility for houses and lands and had failed to face up to it as a human being. The foolish rich man belongs to a large tribe. They walk the face of the earth talking arrogantly about "my house, my land." In just a few years somebody else will also be saying, "my house, my land." The irony is that they will be talking about the same property.

The application (v. 21) is not in D and some allied manuscripts. It may be a later addition to Luke. *Rich toward God* is the antithesis to laying up treasures for one's self. How does one become rich toward God? By taking a direction opposite to that of the rich man—by being sensitive to humanity's needs and hurts and ministering to them in the name of God.

(2) The Sin of Anxiety (12:22–31)

22 And he said to his disciples, "Therefore I tell you, do not be anxious about your life, what you shall eat, nor about your body, what you shall put on. 23 For life is more than food, and the body more than clothing. 24 Consider the ravens: they neither sow nor reap, they have neither storehouse nor barn, and yet God feeds them. Of how much more value are you than the birds! 25 And which of you by being anxious can add a cubit to his span of life? 26 If then you are not able to do as small a thing as that, why are you anxious about the rest? 27 Consider the lilies, how they grow; they neither toil nor spin; yet I tell you, even Solomon in all his glory was not arrayed like

one of these. 28 But if God so clothes the grass which is alive in the field today and tomorrow is thrown into the oven, how much more will he clothe you, O men of little faith! 29 And do not seek what you are to eat and what you are to drink, nor be of anxious mind. 30 For all the nations of the world seek these things; and your Father knows that you need them. 31 Instead, seek his kingdom, and these things shall be yours as well.

The parable of the rich farmer from Luke's special source is followed by related teachings taken from Q, paralleled in Matthew 6:25–33 as a part of the Sermon on the Mount. The introductory phrase affirms that these are instructions intended for disciples.

Jesus continues to teach that life is far too precious for a man to exhaust his energies by fruitless anxiety over mere physical needs. Anxiety is the corrosive, futile, self-defeating worry as to whether or not we shall have physical necessities and luxuries in a future that we are helpless to guarantee. This does not mean that one is not to be a responsible human being, using his energies in wise and planned ways to provide for the physical necessities of those who depend on him. Constructive effort to provide for the necessities of life for today is legitimate (see 11:3); worry about what we are to eat and wear next year is not.

Such anxiety implies a low view of life rather than a high one. When a person understands who he is, he is not going to dedicate his best thought and talent to the purely physical aspects of life. The basis of Jesus' teaching is his concept of the nature of man as (1) created in the image of God and (2) having a future which extends beyond the narrow and provincial concerns of physical existence. *Life* (literally, soul) and *body* will exist in a resurrected state beyond death. Since this fact is more important than the narrow existence between birth and death, man should direct his thoughts toward his higher needs and responsibilities.

God cares for the physical needs of his creatures. An example is the *ravens* (Psalm 147:9), for whom God has made provision.

Their physical existence depends on God's daily provision, because they do not have man's facilities in which to store food for future consumption. Since people are worth more than birds, they too can have confidence in God's day-by-day care for them.

The futility of anxiety is seen in that it makes no contribution at all to that which is the source of its concern, i.e., the preservation and extension of life. A *cubit* is the distance from the tip of the middle finger to the elbow, about 18 inches. The word translated correctly *span of life* can also be translated "stature" (as in the KJV). But it would be no *small thing* (v. 26) to add 18 inches to one's height. Anxiety cannot extend life one moment. To the contrary, and ironically, it shortens the lives of those who indulge in it. People who are most worried about whether they will have enough to eat and wear ten years hence are really those least likely to need such commodities.

The *lilies* furnish another example of God's care for those things subject to his will. With all his wealth, Solomon could not buy a wardrobe to compete with the glory of God's flowers. Once again the argument is from the lesser to the greater. Men, who rank much higher than lilies in God's creation, should be able to trust him who has so lavished his care on flowers that have no future beyond this moment.

Moreover, anxiety is pagan. The *nations of the world* are the non-Jewish or heathen nations. In Christian thought the phrase describes the people who do not know God as Jesus revealed him. It was not that pagans were atheists. They believed in divine powers. But their gods acted arbitrarily and were self-centered, not motivated by love. The God whom Jesus revealed to his disciples was their *Father.* Insecurity on the part of the disciples was in fact a repudiation of belief in a loving Father who was personally concerned about each of his children.

When one does believe, not just with the top of the head but deep within his being,

in this kind of God he is freed from anxiety about the future. His future is secure in the best possible hands. He is liberated to direct his energies toward goals worthy of men rather than those of a mere animal level. That goal is described by Jesus as the *kingdom.* The concern of the man who genuinely believes in God should be to bring his life under God's rule. Once he has properly related himself to God, all other things also have their proper relationship to his life. Here we see the real problem in our world. People are starving to death, although the technical knowledge and resources are available to solve these problems of human physical need. But man's greed and selfishness, which express rebellion against God's rule, are the elements which thwart his will for his world.

(3) Heavenly Treasure (12:32–34)

32 "Fear not, little flock, for it is your Father's good pleasure to give you the kingdom. 33 Sell your possessions, and give alms; provide yourselves with purses that do not grow old, with a treasure in the heavens that does not fail, where no thief approaches and no moth destroys. 34 For where your treasure is, there will your heart be also.

Those people who seek the kingdom rather than things are assured that they need not fear disappointment. Jesus is the shepherd who guides his *little flock* in the right direction. His followers can have confidence in what he tells them about their *Father.* Furthermore, it is God's *good pleasure* to give them the *kingdom.* They are the ones whom God in his gracious will has chosen for his own (see on 2:14 and 10:21). The possibility of their choosing God as their king is based on the fact that he has chosen them for his subjects. They can confidently expect to receive the blessings of God's rule, especially the joys which will come at the future consummation.

The disciples can dispense with earthly riches, which are both unnecessary and dangerous, because they possess heavenly riches. Even the purses in which men put their money deteriorate. But the disciples can acquire *purses that do not grow old.*

This expression emphasizes the security of the heavenly investment which a person makes when he lives his life for God. Earthly *treasure* is transitory, subject to the ravages of time, the elements, and human greed (cf. Matt. 6:19–20). Life which is eternal should be invested in the kinds of values which are also eternal.

In biblical thought *heart* denotes primarily the mind, purpose, will. Jesus is talking about what we call the "bent" of one's life. The direction of a person's life, his purposes, ideals, and dedication, will be determined by his standard of values. Life can be lived either toward God and that which is permanent or toward things, which have a limited and dubious value.

8. Proper Attitudes Toward the Future (12:35—13:9)

(1) The Unexpected Return (12:35–40)

35 "Let your loins be girded and your lamps burning, 36 and be like men who are waiting for their master to come home from the marriage feast, so that they may open to him at once when he comes and knocks. 37 Blessed are those servants whom the master finds awake when he comes; truly, I say to you, he will gird himself and have them sit at table, and he will come and serve them. 38 If he comes in the second watch, or in the third, and finds them so, blessed are those servants! 39 But know this, that if the householder had known at what hour the thief was coming, he would have been awake and would not have left his house to be broken into. 40 You also must be ready; for the Son of man is coming at an hour you do not expect."

What is to be the attitude of men whose hearts are fixed on the kingdom in the period prior to the time when it is ushered in in its fullness? These passages about the future answer some of the questions and problems that arise in this interim. The disciples are not to become indifferent or lazy, nor are they to be lulled into sleep by the delay in the coming of their Lord. They are to be prepared at all times for his arrival. The *loins* must *be girded,* which means that the long oriental robe, which could impede swift movement, is to be caught up and tied around the waist. The

lamps are to be kept *burning* continually so as to furnish light for the master's entrance. Thus when he *knocks,* the servants will be prepared to open *at once.* They do not set the time of the master's return. This is his prerogative. This means that each moment is pregnant with the possibility of his return. The servants, therefore, must be equally alert at every moment.

The master leaves a *marriage feast,* a picture of the joyous heavenly fellowship. On his arrival there will be a feast, a picture of the renewed fellowship between Jesus and his disciples. Surprisingly, Jesus says that the Lord will serve the servants. As he was in his earthly ministry so will he be when he returns. He is the Lord whose greatness is demonstrated by his servant qualities. Thus in the kingdom of the future the same values will still hold true. The greatest will be the servant of all (Matt. 23:11). This overturns all purely materialistic and selfish expectations for the future and runs contrary to the crude, popular concepts of heavenly reward. A temporary hut here in exchange for an eternal mansion is a pretty good bargain in any language. But why are we to think that a person who receives joy from serving now will be deprived of that joy in the future?

The Jews divided the night into three watches. The servants who are ready for their Lord's arrival, even though he does not come before the night is almost over, are called *blessed.* Delay in his return is not to serve as an excuse for sleeping or giving up hope.

The second parable illustrates the same warning. The Son of man is to come like a "thief in the night" (1 Thess. 5:2; 2 Peter 3:10; Rev. 3:3). The *thief* does not forewarn the *householder* about the hour when he will dig through the thick walls of sundried brick or mud. Only by remaining awake through the night can the householder be sure of not being caught off guard. Followers of Jesus are to remain alert through the night of his absence, awaiting his return. Otherwise, they will be unprepared when he comes.

Jesus teaches that the future belongs to
God. It is this faith that determines the
believer's attitude toward the present. The
end may come at any moment, brought
about by death or the end of the age. Each
moment is the last moment, as it were.
From this point of view the present moment must be taken seriously and lived
responsibly before God from whom it
comes as a gift.

(2) The Unfaithful Servant (12:41-48)

⁴¹ Peter said, "Lord, are you telling this parable for us or for all?" ⁴² And the Lord said,
"Who then is the faithful and wise steward,
whom his master will set over his household, to
give them their portion of food at the proper
time? ⁴³ Blessed is that servant whom his master when he comes will find so doing. ⁴⁴ Truly I
tell you, he will set him over all his possessions. ⁴⁵ But if that servant says to himself, 'My
master is delayed in coming,' and begins to
beat the menservants and the maidservants,
and to eat and drink and get drunk, ⁴⁶ the
master of that servant will come on a day when
he does not expect him and at an hour he does
not know, and will punish him, and put him
with the unfaithful. ⁴⁷ And that servant who
knew his master's will, but did not make ready
or act according to his will, shall receive a
severe beating. ⁴⁸ But he who did not know,
and did what deserved a beating, shall receive
a light beating. Every one to whom much is
given, of him will much be required; and of
him to whom men commit much they will
demand the more.

Verses 42-46 are paralleled in Matthew
24:45-51. Peter's question (v. 41), as well
as the application of the parable (vv.
47-48), is found only in Luke and determines the characteristic Lukan coloring of
the passage.

Peter speaks for the twelve. He asks
whether the preceding teachings, containing promises of blessings as well as warnings against laxity, apply only to the twelve
or to other followers as well. In this question and in the teachings which answer it,
we can discern Luke's preoccupation with
a perennial problem of the Christian movement. Power does tend to corrupt, and
especially so in religious circles where its
use can be sanctified in the name of God.
The problem of the misuse of leadership

must have arisen early in the Christian
community. Peter's question provides the
opportunity for warnings directed against
the abuse of leadership. On the first plane
it is addressed to the twelve, but beyond
that to others who will have responsible
places. According to Jeremias (p. 124)
the words of Jesus were originally addressed to the Jewish leaders, especially
scribes.

What the Lord expects of his *steward* is
described in two words: *faithful* and *wise*.
The fool is the man who acts as though he
is not a steward (12:20). He uses his master's belongings as though they were his
own. The faithful and wise steward uses
the goods entrusted to him according to his
master's wishes, that is, to care for and
sustain those for whom he is responsible.
And what will be his reward? More responsibility!

The steward can take another approach.
Lulled into false security by the delay in
his master's return, he can abuse his position. This is done by mistreating those who
have been delivered to his care and appropriating his lord's goods for his own selfish
ends. In those times a servant could expect
the harshest kind of punishment for his evil
deeds. *Will punish him* is literally "will cut
him in two," a grisly ancient form of execution (see marg.). *Unfaithful* is in contrast
with *faithful* of v. 42. The servant who
exploits his position shares neither the
character nor the destiny of the responsible
steward. *With the unfaithful* is "with the
hypocrites" in Matthew 24:51, which is
probably original. It makes the parable pe-
culiarly applicable to Jewish leaders who
have abused their responsibility.

The thought is carried a step further to
point up how serious it is to be a religious
leader. Greater knowledge implies greater
responsibility. The person who knows but
does not do his *master's will* is more guilty
than the person whose errors arise out of
ignorance. In other words, the Christian
leader who guides people in the wrong
direction is guilty of an evil much more
serious than that of the deceived people

who follow. To be a steward over God's household is not an honor to be sought but an awesome responsibility to be discharged "in fear and trembling." *Much* has been given to the leaders; much will be required in return.

(3) The Crisis Provoked by Jesus (12: 49–53)

49 "I came to cast fire upon the earth; and would that it were already kindled! 50 I have a baptism to be baptized with; and how I am constrained until it is accomplished! 51 Do you think that I have come to give peace on earth? No, I tell you, but rather division; 52 for henceforth in one house there will be five divided, three against two and two against three; 53 they will be divided, father against son and son against father, mother against daughter and daughter against her mother, mother-in-law against her daughter-in-law and daughter-in-law against her mother-in-law."

Scholarly opinions are divided about the symbolic meaning of *fire*. In the teaching of John the Baptist it represents judgment, but this probably is not the meaning here. It could refer to the purifying, refining process through which his followers are to pass. Or, it might refer to the divisions which are precipitated by the work of Jesus. In the context of Luke-Acts another possibility is the sending of the Holy Spirit to the disciples on the day of Pentecost (Grundmann, p. 270). This last seems to be indicated by v. 50. The fire cannot be cast upon the earth at the moment. Jesus is prevented from doing this until after his *baptism,* which is his death (Mark 10:38). After his death will come the *fire.*

Jesus did not come to institute the state of *peace* which men expected in connection with the messianic kingdom (cf. Isa. 11:6–9; Micah 4:3–4). He came to call men to decision. Inherent in such a mission is the possibility of divisions and antagonisms. The sword of Jesus' proclamation (cf. Matt. 10:34) cuts across the closest human relations. This picture of the consequences of his mission is set forth in terms found in Micah 7:6, which describes the apocalyptic anguish which precedes the end. In Micah (also in Matt. 10:35) the young couple rebel against their parents. In Luke the antagonism cuts both ways.

(4) The Blindness to the Times (12:54 –56)

54 He also said to the multitudes, "When you see a cloud rising in the west, you say at once, 'A shower is coming'; and so it happens. 55 And when you see the south wind blowing, you say, 'There will be scorching heat'; and it happens. 56 You hypocrites! You know how to interpret the appearance of earth and sky; but why do you not know how to interpret the present time?

Jesus' presence is the sign of the time, God's urgent summons to decision. Some few have responded, but most people are still unaware of the significance of his presence among them.

A *cloud rising in the west,* from the direction of the Mediterranean Sea, is laden with moisture and brings rain. A *south wind* from off the parched Negev Desert brings scorching heat. (See also on Matt. 16:2–3 where the idea is the same but the content and context are different.) Jesus upbraids the multitudes because they are sensitive to the signs which denote changes in the weather but are impervious to those which speak to them of the changes God has brought about in the times. A new epoch of salvation-history has begun, and they are not even aware of it. The *present time* is a decisive new period in God's dealing with man. *Time* (*kairos*) is a word with important religious connotations. It means basically the decisive moment as determined by God. It is an auspicious moment of opportunity because God calls the people to repent. But it is also a moment freighted with the possibility of danger and tragedy. The *kairos* is also a fleeting moment. Today God addresses them in the person of Jesus; tomorrow he will be gone, and the *kairos* will have passed.

(5) Preparation for Judgment (12:57–59)

57 "And why do you not judge for yourselves what is right? 58 As you go with your accuser before the magistrate, make an effort to settle with him on the way, lest he drag you to the

judge, and the judge hand you over to the officer, and the officer put you in prison. [59] I tell you, you will never get out till you have paid the very last copper."

The meaning of Jesus' illustration is clearer here than it is in the Matthean context (6:25–26). It is an injunction for men to get right with God while there is still time. *What is right* will be explained in 13:5. The only way that men can settle with God is through repentance.

In former times indebtedness was considered a felony and was punished by the severest sort of penalties. An intelligent debtor would make every effort to resolve his problem with the man to whom he was indebted before the case was brought to court. Presumably he would settle by coming to some agreement about the method of payment. Once hailed before the *judge* it could be too late to take such measures. If the judge found him guilty of indebtedness, he would be delivered to the *officer* who was responsible for collecting the debt. The debtor was commonly placed in *prison* until his family could make arrangements to pay what he owed. In such a situation he would not be liberated until every cent was paid.

Men who are on their way to face God's judgment would be well-advised to do the sensible thing by settling the debt that they owe to him. Among the Jews, sin was often spoken of as a debt (as in Matt. 6:12).

(6) The Necessity of Repentance (13:1–5)

[1] There were some present at that very time who told him of the Galileans whose blood Pilate had mingled with their sacrifices. [2] And he answered them, "Do you think that these Galileans were worse sinners than all the other Galileans, because they suffered thus? [3] I tell you, No; but unless you repent you will all likewise perish. [4] Or those eighteen upon whom the tower in Siloam fell and killed them, do you think that they were worse offenders than all the others who dwelt in Jerusalem? [5] I tell you, No; but unless you repent you will all likewise perish."

Now Luke turns to his special source from which vv. 1–17 are taken. But the urgent need for repentance, the theme already introduced in 12:54–59, continues to be stressed through v. 9.

Some present is perhaps better translated "some arrived." They came up *at that very time*, that is, as Jesus was exhorting the people to get right with God while they had the opportunity. The tragic story told by them provides the occasion for Jesus to correct popular misconceptions about the relation of suffering to sin and to reiterate his urgent plea for Israel to repent.

Josephus, who gives detailed accounts of Pilate's relation with the Jews, does not tell about the slaughter of the Galileans. Nevertheless, the incident is entirely coherent with the character of Pilate. He was finally removed from office for the attack in A.D. 35 on some misguided Samaritan worshipers on Mount Gerizim and the subsequent execution of Samaritan leaders. The Galileans were probably slain in the Temple as they were killing the animals which they intended for sacrifices (Strack-Billerbeck, II, 192 f.). Since Galilee was a breeding ground for Jewish revolutionaries, it is natural to suppose that the unfortunate men belonged to some kind of rebel band.

Jesus' question (v. 2) implies that the a priori theological assumptions of his hearers caused them to jump to the conclusion that the fate of the Galileans was the result of their unusual sins. But Jesus asserts that all Israelites are equally sinners; all stand on the same level before God. Israel as a nation must *repent* or *perish*. If the people continue in the same course, a disaster similar to that of the Galileans will be the fate of the whole nation. If the Galileans were revolutionaries, this may be a warning against the increasingly militant, revolutionary attitude toward the Romans, which is in essence a rejection of Jesus' call for Israel to identify with him as the Suffering Servant.

Jesus himself cites another, perhaps recent tragedy in which some men lost their lives accidentally. The *eighteen* were probably construction workers engaged in building the *tower of Siloam,* which may have been a defense post intended to guard the water supply of Jerusalem in the event of siege. From Josephus we learn how Pilate's plans to use Temple monies to construct an aqueduct in Jerusalem sparked a popular protest. It was quelled by troops who used clubs on the hostile crowd with whom they had mingled, dressed in civilian clothes (*Antiq.,* 18,3,2; *Wars,* 2,9,4). If the men were employed on this project, their death was probably considered by other Jews to be an act of divine retribution for their irreverence.

But Jesus repudiates the inference that the eighteen were worse sinners than the other inhabitants of Jerusalem. Just as the tower had fallen on those men, so would the rubble of a destroyed city fall on the heads of its inhabitants if they persisted in their rebellion against God. Jesus teaches that the tragedies of life should not be used to feed the self-righteousness of those who escape them. They should instead speak to all of us about our frailty as human beings. They tell us that we are creatures, not gods, and that we need to turn to the God who calls to us even in tragedy.

(7) The Peril of Fruitlessness (13:6–9)

6 And he told this parable: "A man had a fig tree planted in his vineyard; and he came seeking fruit on it and found none. 7 And he said to the vinedresser, 'Lo, these three years I have come seeking fruit on this fig tree, and I find none. Cut it down; why should it use up the ground?' 8 And he answered him, 'Let it alone, sir, this year also, till I dig about it and put on manure. 9 And if it bears fruit next year, well and good; but if not, you can cut it down.' "

The *vineyard* is an Old Testament figure for Israel (Isa. 5:1–7). The symbolism of the fig tree is uncertain; but it also probably represents Israel, as it does in Mark 11:12 ff. It was customary for Palestinians to plant fruit trees in their vineyards.

The *parable* invites allegorical interpretation. The owner of the vineyard is Israel's God. For *three years,* an indefinite but limited period of time, he has been patient with the tree that has not borne the expected fruit. The *vinedresser* who secures more time for the tree can be thought to represent Jesus, whose intercession has gained another opportunity for Israel. By digging around the tree to cut away the grass and weeds and by fertilizing it, every reason for fruitlessness extraneous to the tree itself is removed.

Nevertheless, the story is a parable and not an allegory. As a parable it has one major point. Israel is being given one last opportunity. If she does not bear fruit, she will be cut down. The *fruit* which God expects are the deeds which express genuine response to his call to repentance (3:8).

9. The Cure of a Crippled Woman (13: 10–17)

10 Now he was teaching in one of the synagogues on the sabbath. 11 And there was a woman who had had a spirit of infirmity for eighteen years; she was bent over and could not fully straighten herself. 12 And when Jesus saw her, he called her and said to her, "Woman, you are freed from your infirmity." 13 And he laid his hands upon her, and immediately she was made straight, and she praised God. 14 But the ruler of the synagogue, indignant because Jesus had healed on the sabbath, said to the people, "There are six days on which work ought to be done; come on those days and be healed, and not on the sabbath day." 15 Then the Lord answered him, "You hypocrites! Does not each of you on the sabbath untie his ox or his ass from the manger, and lead it away to water it? 16 And ought not this woman, a daughter of Abraham whom Satan bound for eighteen years, be loosed from this bond on the sabbath day?" 17 As he said this, all his adversaries were put to shame; and all the people rejoiced at all the glorious things that were done by him.

The notice that Jesus is teaching in *one of the synagogues* signals a change in the direction of the narrative. Only here do we find him in a synagogue during the latter part of his ministry. The phrase *on the sabbath* prepares us for the conflict scene which follows.

Spirit of infirmity intimates that illness is related to the power of demons. Jesus takes the initiative in healing the woman who had been badly crippled for *eighteen years*. After proclaiming her liberation (in keeping with 4:18), Jesus lays his hands upon her, whereupon she is *made straight*.

The anger of the *ruler of the synagogue* (see on 8:41) is caused by Jesus' violation of the sabbath traditions. Such an action threatens the stability of the religious establishment of which he is a part. The ruler assumes the role of a teacher of the Law. His interpretation is an example of the misuse of religious leadership that Jesus has already condemned (11:42 ff.).

Jesus addresses the ruler but includes also those who accept his interpretation. *Hypocrites* describes people who give attention to the observance of religious rules but who are not committed to "justice and the love of God" (11:42). They loose animals on the sabbath out of concern for their physical welfare; Jesus has just *loosed* a woman. An interpretation of religion which makes animals more important than people is simply wrong from Jesus' point of view.

Satan had bound the woman; God had liberated her. Infirmities are not, therefore, the will of God. Rather, the woman's crippled condition was a frustration of God's purposes in creation. Jesus accepted the fact that suffering was a necessary ingredient in his own commitment to the will of God. But it was suffering that resulted from a course freely chosen, which is vastly different from the suffering of helpless victims of pain and disease.

In the editorial comment the assembly is characteristically divided into *adversaries* and the *people*. The logic of Jesus' argument overwhelms his critics. The *glorious things* which cause the people to rejoice include mighty deed and marvelous word.

10. The Nature of the Kingdom (13:18–30)

(1) The Mustard Seed and the Leaven (13:18–21)

18 He said therefore, "What is the kingdom of God like? And to what shall I compare it? 19 It is like a grain of mustard seed which a man took and sowed in his garden; and it grew and became a tree, and the birds of the air made nests in its branches."
20 And again he said, "To what shall I compare the kingdom of God? 21 It is like leaven which a woman took and hid in three measures of meal, till it was all leavened."

Under cultivation the *mustard* plant, a wild annual, grew to a height of eight to ten feet. The difference between the smallness of the seed and the eventual size of the plant it produced was proverbial. If pressed literally, the details of the parable do not conform to exact scientific data. The *mustard seed* denoted by the Greek word was not "the smallest of all seeds" (Matt. 13:32; Mark 4:31). This detail is omitted by Luke, for whom the size of the plant rather than the smallness of the seed is the principal point. Furthermore, it seems doubtful that birds could have made their *nests in its branches,* since the plant did not reach maturity until long after the nesting season had passed. Some interpreters would remove this difficulty by understanding *made nests* as "settle or roosted upon."

It is unnecessary to be overly concerned about the detailed scientific accuracy of an illustration. Moreover, the reference to the *birds* is probably a reminiscence of Daniel 4:20–21. There the kingdom of Nebuchadnezzar is compared to a giant tree "in whose branches the birds of the air dwelt." There is both similarity and contrast, for the *kingdom of God* has a greatness and permanency which did not belong to the Babylonian's rule.

The parable expresses Jesus' confidence in the triumph of the rule of God. This confidence was not based on numerical statistics. Those who had made a genuine response to his preaching were few in number; his opponents were numerous and powerful. But Jesus believed that God was King and that his sovereignty was not threatened by the combined hostility of the evil forces in the universe.

Leaven was a piece of fermented dough saved from a previous mixture. *Three measures of meal* was an extraordinarily large amount, "a bushel of flour" (TEV). When baked, this would produce bread for 162 persons (Jeremias, p. 90, fn. 4). Leaven elsewhere is often a symbol of evil. But because a small bit of it irresistibly permeates such a large quantity of dough, it also is a good figure of the kingdom of God.

Leaven does its work silently, mysteriously. This may be seen as an apt illustration of the way God's rule works in human society. Early Christians, including Luke, would also see in the parable a promise fulfilled in the miraculous growth of the church in the world. To Jesus, however, the main point was probably the irresistibility and ultimate victory of God's rule which no force could stay.

(2) Surprises of the Kingdom (13:22–30)

[22] He went on his way through towns and villages, teaching, and journeying toward Jerusalem. [23] And some one said to him, "Lord, will those who are saved be few?" And he said to them, [24] "Strive to enter by the narrow door; for many, I tell you, will seek to enter and will not be able. [25] When once the householder has risen up and shut the door, you will begin to stand outside and to knock at the door, saying, 'Lord, open to us.' He will answer you, 'I do not know where you come from.' [26] Then you will begin to say, 'We ate and drank in your presence, and you taught in our streets.' [27] But he will say, 'I tell you, I do not know where you come from; depart from me, all you workers of iniquity!' [28] There you will weep and gnash your teeth, when you see Abraham and Isaac and Jacob and all the prophets in the kingdom of God and you yourselves thrust out. [29] And men will come from east and west, and from north and south, and sit at table in the kingdom of God. [30] And behold, some are last who will be first, and some are first who will be last."

We are reminded in an editorial note that Jesus is *journeying toward Jerusalem.* Perhaps the question raised by *some one* is prompted by the anticipation that the messianic kingdom will be inaugurated upon Jesus' arrival in Jerusalem. The number to be included in the kingdom was a live subject for debate in Jewish religious circles. Would all Jews or only a *few,* as claimed by certain sects, be *saved* when the crisis came? This exercise in futility is still practiced by certain people who are anxious to

establish the exact boundaries which exclude the lost from the select group of the righteous. Of course, persons who engage in this futile debate are always smugly sure that *they* belong to the insiders. The answer of Jesus brings the listener up short and destroys all his false security. He is told to classify himself with those on the outside who should be concerned about entering the kingdom.

God opens the *door* between the two aeons. By his grace it is possible to pass from one to the other. But the door is *narrow,* not easily or frivolously entered. The salvation to which it beckons is costly. No one will enter who makes only a half-hearted gesture in the direction of the kingdom. *Strive* is a Pauline word (e.g., *agonizō,* 1 Cor. 9:25; Col. 1:29) which describes the strenuous effort demanded of the athlete in a contest. It is a present imperative—"keep on striving." The door is narrow in the sense that it is entered at the exclusion of all other interests. It is the door of repentance which calls upon man to renounce his arrogance and self-will.

Those who do not strain every nerve now to enter the narrow door *will seek to enter* it, that is, after the time of opportunity has passed (Plummer, p. 346). Difficult to enter when it is open, entrance is impossible once it is closed. The man who has let opportunity pass him by *will not be able* to force the closed door open.

The one who opens the door will also *shut* it. Then those who spurned it will begin to *knock* at it. Although they had once sneered at Jesus as the son of a local carpenter, they will then call him *Lord.* Where once they had despised him, they will be seeking to claim a relationship with him. They had known him and had heard his teaching. But their superficial claims will be of no avail. Mere exposure to the teachings of Jesus is not enough. Now those who had rejected him because his credentials were not adequate find the situation reversed. Since they have spurned the offer of God through Jesus to make them sons, their past does not fit them for the glories of God's future. The irony is that people who spent so much time tracing their ancestry, which they felt made them members of the chosen race, will not have the correct lineage. Those who failed to be doers of the word that Jesus had taught in their streets will be called *workers of iniquity.*

The people who pride themselves so much on being descendants of *Abraham* will be cut off from their fathers, because God's people are not selected on the basis of race. The *prophets,* whom their fathers had persecuted and whose teachings they reject in rejecting Jesus, will be there. But the crowning blow is that the body of Israel will be fleshed out or composed by Gentiles from despised and lowly nations. Weeping and gnashing of teeth will express the despair and regret of those on the outside looking in. Their frustration will be compounded by the fact that they, like the unknown interrogator of v. 23, were so sure that they were among the elect.

Jesus emphasizes repeatedly that in the coming age God will overturn the values and categories of this age. The righteous are the sinners; the sinners are the righteous. The excluded are the included; the included are the excluded. It is always true that "tax collectors and harlots go into the kingdom" before "religious" people (Matt. 21:31), not because of their sin but because they recognize that they are sinners. In the gospel of Jesus the sinner is addressed by the word of grace; the self-righteous, by the word of judgment.

V. *From Galilee to Jerusalem: Part Two* (13:31—19:27)

1. *Jesus' Destiny and Jerusalem (13:31–35)*

31 At that very hour some Pharisees came, and said to him, "Get away from here, for Herod wants to kill you." 32 And he said to them, "Go and tell that fox, 'Behold, I cast out demons and perform cures today and tomorrow, and the third day I finish my course. 33 Nevertheless I must go on my way today and tomorrow and the day following; for it cannot be that a prophet should perish away from Jerusalem.' 34 O Jerusalem, Jerusalem, killing the prophets and stoning those who are sent to you! How often would I have gathered your children together as a hen gathers her brood under her wings, and you would not! 35 Behold, your house is forsaken. And I tell you, you will not see me until you say, 'Blessed is he who comes in the name of the Lord!' "

At that very hour ties this to the preceding passage. We do not know what the relationship between the *Pharisees* and *Herod* was. Whether they were friendly to Jesus or willing tools of a crafty ruler cannot be surmised. Evidently Herod's stratagem was to try to get Jesus out of his realm without arousing the people's wrath. Some of the same reasons which caused him to eliminate John might also have caused him to fear Jesus, who had also become a popular figure.

Jesus refuses to be swayed by the threat. *Fox* may symbolize craftiness. Most likely, in accord with its most frequently attested use, it describes Herod as an insignificant, inferior person (Strack-Billerbeck, II, 200 ff.). Although the exact meaning of Jesus' reply is far from clear, the principal idea is that his future is charted and that Herod is impotent to stay the God-ordained course of his ministry. He will complete what he has come to do. First, there is the time of proclamation characterized by the mighty acts of messianic sovereignty. Then there comes the consummation when Jesus will *finish* his *course.* This refers to the climactic events to take place in Jerusalem. One way of resolving the lack of clarity in the text is to understand *today and tomorrow* as day-by-day and *the third day* as a subsequent day beyond this period. Black translates verse 32: "Behold I cast out demons, and I do cures day by day, but one day soon I shall be perfected." [25]

Jesus' decision to go to Jerusalem is, therefore, not due to the pressure exerted by Antipas but to his commitment to his own destiny. Death in some obscure village of Galilee or Perea would be relatively meaningless. The death of a prophet in

25 *Ibid.,* p. 152.

Jerusalem is a judgment on the whole nation. There is the center of its worship, the Temple. There sits its most august and authoritative council, the Sanhedrin.

The lament over Jerusalem should probably be understood as the word of God uttered after the manner of the prophets (as in Hos. 11:1 ff., for example). God has attempted to bring Jerusalem under his sovereign and loving care through the word of *prophets*. If the apostrophe is taken as Jesus' own lament over Jerusalem, various problems in interpretation arise. *How often* (v. 34) presupposes activities in Jerusalem for which Luke gives no background. The final quotation also would present difficulties, since it can only refer to a coming in judgment rather than the entry into Jerusalem (19:38).

Instead of receiving the prophets, Jerusalem had *killed* and *stoned* them. The consequences of this pattern of rejection which will reach its climax in the rejection of Jesus is the withdrawal of God from among the people. The *house* is the Temple, symbol of the presence of God. But it will be *forsaken*. Redemptive activity will cease and judgment will come. *He who comes* is probably a title for Messiah (see on 3:16). But his coming to Jerusalem does not mean its liberation but its destruction.

2. Teachings at a Meal (14:1–24)

(1) The Man with Dropsy (14:1–6)

¹ One sabbath when he went to dine at the house of a ruler who belonged to the Pharisees, they were watching him. ² And behold, there was a man before him who had dropsy. ³ And Jesus spoke to the lawyers and Pharisees, saying, "Is it lawful to heal on the sabbath, or not?" ⁴ But they were silent. Then he took him and healed him, and let him go. ⁵ And he said to them, "Which of you, having an ass or an ox that has fallen into a well, will not immediately pull him out on a sabbath day?" ⁶ And they could not reply to this.

In Judaism the observance of the *sabbath* was colored negatively by abstention from activities classified as work by the oral tradition. But positively it was a day of celebration. Feasting was a particularly appropriate way for Israelites to express their joy over being special objects of God's grace in that they were included in the covenant community (*Jubilees* 2:31; 50:9 f.). The sabbath meal, prepared on Friday, was often shared by invited guests. Contemporary customs, therefore, furnish the background for the meal in the Pharisee's house, which probably followed attendance on the service in the synagogue.

The host was a *ruler*, an influential man, who belonged to the sect of the *Pharisees*. Perhaps his guests were fellow members of a particular society of Pharisees. The meal determines the outline of the succeeding developments. Before it begins, a man is healed. As the guests recline at the table, or shortly thereafter, Jesus addresses rebukes to the guests and host in turn. Participation in the meal itself furnishes the atmosphere for the concluding parable.

The sick man is not one of the invited guests. He probably was one of the curious persons who had wandered in off the street to observe the festivities. On these occasions a man's door was open to the public. *Dropsy* designates a physical condition characterized by an excess of fluids in the body. It could be caused by kidney or heart disorders or some other organic malfunction. On the basis of a "cause and effect" theology, it was attributed by some to sexual immorality (Strack-Billerbeck, II, 203).

The guests *were watching* to see if Jesus would disregard their traditions by healing the man on the sabbath. To the question about the legality of healing on the sabbath there was silence. From their point of view the Pharisees could give no unequivocal answer. Sometimes it was lawful to heal; but the life of the person healed had to be in jeopardy. Generally it was not considered legal to perform such an act. On this issue Jesus differed with his contemporaries. The law of love was the weightiest commandment and took precedence over all others. To do good to another human being was always right. In keeping with this principle he healed the unnamed man, who left the house. This is one of five acts of this kind performed on the sabbath as related by Luke.

The healing is greeted with silent condemnation. To this Jesus speaks further. The law allowed an animal to be rescued from a *well* on the sabbath (an application of Deut. 22:4). The text of v. 5 presents critical problems. The variant "son" for *ass* is well-attested and, on the basis of good critical principles, is probably the prior one. Matthew Black [26] believes that the generic Aramaic word for beast of burden was mistaken in translation as the similar word for son. Whatever the explanation for the Greek text, Jesus with Deuteronomy 22:4 in mind must have referred to animals. The whole challenge to the contemporary system is based on the implied greater duty to a man who finds himself in untoward circumstances.

Not being able to refute his argument, the guests greet it with silence. At no time is there praise of God. At no time is there joy over a life reclaimed. The religious leaders are interested in maintaining the status quo. Jesus is interested in people. The two approaches invariably clash, for the status quo is always relatively unjust and uncharitable.

(2) Instructions to Guests (14:7–11)

7 Now he told a parable to those who were invited, when he marked how they chose the places of honor, saying to them, 8 "When you are invited by any one to a marriage feast, do not sit down in a place of honor, lest a more eminent man than you be invited by him; 9 and he who invited you both will come and say to you, 'Give place to this man,' and then you will begin with shame to take the lowest place. 10 But when you are invited, go and sit in the lowest place, so that when your host comes he may say to you, 'Friend, go up higher'; then you will be honored in the presence of all who sit at table with you. 11 For every one who exalts himself will be humbled, and he who humbles himself will be exalted."

At first glance the instructions given by Jesus are no more than rules of etiquette and have been so interpreted. But as Luke says, Jesus' words are a *parable*. This puts us on the alert to the fact that the scene moves on two different levels. A meal is

also a figure for the eschatological feast in the messianic kingdom (cf. Isa. 25:6).

Jesus notes that among these religious people there is a scramble for the *place of honor*, those nearest the host. This is an example of how their religion breaks down in the area of human relations, exactly where it should be most effective.

In a *marriage feast*, the example chosen by Jesus, social protocol required that guests be seated according to order of their importance (Plummer, p. 357). The kind of jockeying for position that Jesus had observed could lead to public embarrassment on such a formal occasion. But what Jesus is really talking about is God's order of things. Egotism and disregard for others disqualify a man for a position of honor in the heavenly banquet. This is simply another way of saying that God's judgments are a blow to man's arrogance.

Conversely, the attitude of humility is a mark of greatness. The man who does not seek to be preferred over others is the one whom God honors. He will be placed near the head of the table in the messianic banquet.

This does not mean that humility is a weak, self-deprecating attitude. The humble man knows that he is a child of God, whose worth is established in terms of this relationship. Because he is secure, he is freed from the need to engage in the mad scramble for the little badges of recognition afforded by human society. Nor can he engage in activity to exalt himself at the expense of his brother.

The application is given in v. 11. The passive voice avoids the use of the divine name. God humbles and exalts; but he humbles the proud and exalts the humble. How we relate to our fellow man is decisive in determining our position before God.

(3) Instructions to the Host (14:12–14)

12 He said also to the man who had invited him, "When you give a dinner or a banquet, do not invite your friends or your brothers or your kinsmen or rich neighbors, lest they also invite you in return, and you be repaid. 13 But when

26 *Ibid.*, p. 126.

you give a feast, invite the poor, the maimed, the lame, the blind, [14] and you will be blessed, because they cannot repay you. You will be repaid at the resurrection of the just."

The host is just as self-centered as his guests. His social relationships are based on the principle of reciprocity. A glance around the table sufficed to show that he had made up his guest list with an eye to future personal benefits. Jesus criticizes the egocentric structure of society of which the closed circle around the table was a microcosm.

The man is urged to break out of his social circle to invite guests from whom he can expect to receive no benefit (cf. 6:32–36). The words of Jesus were far more of a shock to social sensibilities than we probably imagine. Physical defects had religious implications. The *maimed*, the *lame*, and the *blind* were excluded from full participation in the religious community. Classed among sinners, they were unfit for intimate association with the righteous who enjoyed privileged position in the community. Jesus urges his host to invite to his most intimate social functions the very people whom his group would rule out completely.

If Jesus were speaking to us, he would use other categories. But we may be sure that he would urge us likewise to open our homes and social functions to the very people against whom we have the deepest prejudice and would most likely exclude.

The people who act in the way that Jesus counsels can expect to be *repaid*, for God will compensate them. At first glance this seems to threaten the purity of Christian ethic. But their payment is that they will be recipients of the love of God, which also goes out to people who cannot possibly reciprocate his favors. They will not be excluded from God's feast.

In some Jewish theological circles there was a belief that the resurrection would be limited to the *just*. It would be a mistake, however, to attribute such a belief to Jesus, Luke, or the contemporary Christian communities on the basis of this one phrase

(see, e.g., Acts 24:15). Jesus affirms that unselfish love and goodwill transcend death and have eternal significance.

(4) The Great Banquet (14:15–24)

[15] When one of those who sat at table with him heard this, he said to him, "Blessed is he who shall eat bread in the kingdom of God!" [16] But he said to him, "A man once gave a great banquet, and invited many; [17] and at the time for the banquet he sent his servant to say to those who had been invited, 'Come; for all is now ready.' [18] But they all alike began to make excuses. The first said to him, 'I have bought a field, and I must go out and see it; I pray you, have me excused.' [19] And another said, 'I have bought five yoke of oxen, and I go to examine them; I pray you, have me excused.' [20] And another said, 'I have married a wife, and therefore I cannot come.' [21] So the servant came and reported this to his master. Then the householder in anger said to his servant, 'Go out quickly to the streets and lanes of the city, and bring in the poor and maimed and blind and lame.' [22] And the servant said, 'Sir, what you commanded has been done, and still there is room.' [23] And the master said to the servant, 'Go out to the highways and hedges, and compel people to come in, that my house may be filled. [24] For I tell you, none of those men who were invited shall taste my banquet.' "

To *eat bread in the kingdom of God* means to be among those who participate in the joys of the messianic kingdom. The pious platitude is uttered by a man who is smugly sure that he is among the righteous who will be included. His unwarranted self-assurance is challenged by the parable with which Jesus responds. For a similar story see Matthew 22:1–10. The differences are so great, however, that this parable must have come from Luke's special source.

Social customs are mirrored in the story. First, guests were invited to a banquet. Subsequently, those who accepted the invitation were advised when the banquet was ready. The parable follows the outline of salvation-history presented in Luke-Acts. The *many* in Israel had received an invitation to the messianic banquet through God's messengers, the prophets. But when the announcement is made that the time for the feast has arrived, those who were invited act in an extremely insulting manner. They *all* alike begin to make excuses. Three representative examples of the excuses are given. Involvement with land, animals, and family take priority over their host's invitation. Thus it is that involvement in the affairs of this age cause men to make the wrong decision when God's invitation is sent out.

It now becomes clear that those who receive the first invitations are the religious leaders, specifically the Pharisees, who prided themselves in occupying the first rung of Judaism's ladder of religious categories. The story implies that very few of the religious elite became followers of Jesus. The invitation now goes out to the people who are on the social and religious fringes of Israel (see above on v. 13). Those who cannot participate fully in Israel's worship are the ones who will sit at the table in place of those who arrogantly reject God's invitation.

All of the places are not taken by those who respond to the invitation. There is *still room.* With this "postscript" the story moves beyond Israel as it places the mission to the Gentiles in God's divine purpose. The meaning is similar to the idea elaborated by Paul in Romans (11:11 ff.). Israel's rejection means salvation for the Gentiles. The *highways* and the *hedges* are the roads leading from the city where travelers of varied background will be found. But no lines are drawn. From this variegated collection will come guests to fill the empty places.

The verb *compel* does not justify any attempt to coerce people either by political force or by psychological tricks into the kingdom of God. The invitation finally goes out to people to whom it is a surprising and unexpected occurrence. The servant must take the steps necessary to assure the people that they have really been invited, overcoming a natural reluctance to respond to such an unexpected development.

I in v. 24 is Jesus. He speaks directly to the guests around the table. To receive an invitation does not guarantee participation in his banquet. This was the unwarranted assumption of the man who had uttered his pious platitude (v. 15). The proper response must be made at the decisive moment. Jesus lays claim to the messianic banquet when he calls it *my banquet.* Those Israelites who fail to respond to the invitation which he issues will not be included.

3. The Terms of Discipleship (14:25-35)

25 Now great multitudes accompanied him; and he turned and said to them, 26 "If any one comes to me and does not hate his own father and mother and wife and children and brothers and sisters, yes, and even his own life, he cannot be my disciple. 27 Whoever does not bear his own cross and come after me, cannot be my disciple. 28 For which of you, desiring to build a tower, does not first sit down and count the cost, whether he has enough to complete it? 29 Otherwise, when he has laid a foundation, and is not able to finish, all who see it begin to mock him, 30 saying, 'This man began to build, and was not able to finish.' 31 Or what king, going to encounter another king in war, will not sit down first and take counsel whether he is able with ten thousand to meet him who comes against him with twenty thousand? 32 And if not, while the other is yet a great way off, he sends an embassy and asks terms of peace. 33 So therefore, whoever of you does not renounce all that he has cannot be my disciple. 34 "Salt is good; but if salt has lost its taste, how shall its saltness be restored? 35 It is fit neither for the land nor for the dunghill; men throw it away. He who has ears to hear, let him hear."

Attention now shifts from the Pharisees, the religious elite who will not attend God's summons, to the *multitudes.* The people who accompany him have a decidedly erroneous idea about his destiny. They do not have the slightest suspicion that anything so grim and terrifying as a cross stands at the end of the road down which Jesus journeys. So the terms of his invitation must be made clear. Those who accept must be willing to offer up all other relationships, interests, and ambitions on the altar of their commitment.

In Matthew the demand of Jesus is phrased in somewhat milder terms. There we find the phrase "loves more" instead of Luke's *does not hate* and also "is not worthy of me" for Luke's harsher *cannot be my disciple* (cf. Matt. 10:37–38). Family relations can compete with the claims of the kingdom in various ways. The closest members of the family may be hostile to one's commitment to discipleship. Or the family may make demands that conflict with responsibilities to the kingdom. In any case of competing loyalties, the issue can only be resolved in one way. The disciple is also called on to hate *even his own life*. He must be willing to affirm the interests of the kingdom rather than his own ambitions to the point of being ready to die if circumstances so demand.

Under Roman rule Jews had learned what it meant to *bear* a *cross* and to die on one, so the figure used by Jesus was not foreign to his hearers. The cross to be borne by the Christian, however, can only be understood with relation to the experience of Jesus. To follow him requires unswerving commitment to the will of God for one's life in the face of the greatest threats and dangers. To bear a cross is to accept fully the consequences of discipleship—the shame, the loneliness, the hostility that men direct toward a life that is the channel of God's truth, justice, and love. Therefore, a *disciple* is not a person who memorizes vast amounts of religious tradition so that he can give the orthodox answers to theological questions. He is a person who follows after Jesus, gladly sharing in his redemptive suffering.

Not wanting to make disciples on the wrong basis, Jesus stressed the possibilities inherent in the decision to follow him. Admittedly there is no guarantee that the person who faces up realistically to the cost of discipleship will persevere to the end. Nevertheless, he will be prepared for crises and will be more likely to weather them. Decisions prompted only by emotions have a way of evaporating when subjected to the stern tests of day-by-day reality.

People do not—or at least, should not—attempt costly ventures without a realistic estimate of what will be demanded of them to carry the project through to completion. Jesus illustrates this principle with two examples. The first is about a man who plans to construct a *tower*, perhaps of the kind people built in their vineyards. He first *sits down*, however, to *count the cost*. He takes time to think about what is involved. If he does not, he may not get any further than the *foundation*.

The *king* who faces the prospect of *war* measures his forces against the challenge that they must face. The point at issue is the common sense approach with which the king evaluates his resources. If in the face of overwhelming odds he concludes that his troops are no match for the enemy, he *asks terms of peace* or "submits" (Creed, p. 195). Naturally the figure must not be pressed because Jesus does not counsel his followers to surrender. But he does warn people against following him without an awareness of the consequences and a willingness to accept them.

What is the cost of discipleship? Nothing less than the renunciation of everything. Luke gives special emphasis to the "costly grace" of Jesus, perhaps as a reflection of a time when some Christians were growing fainthearted and others were cowardly, bringing discredit to Jesus and the church.

When, for whatever reason, the disciple fails to manifest the characteristics of true discipleship, he becomes worthless—like *salt* that *has lost its taste*. Of course, pure salt can never lose its taste; sodium chloride is always sodium chloride. But the salt taken from the Dead Sea was adulterated, mixed with gypsum and other substances. This impure salt was subject to losing its salty taste. So long as it was salty, it was *good* for the purposes for which people used it, as a condiment and preservative. But once it had lost its characteristic qualities as salt, it was good for nothing, not even for fertilizer. It could neither be applied directly to the land nor deposited temporarily on the manure heap (see also on Matt. 5:13; Mark 9:50). The only thing to do with worthless salt is to *throw it away.*

4. God's Joy over the Recovery of the Lost (15:1–32)

(1) The Attitude of the Leaders (15:1–2)

¹ Now the tax collectors and sinners were all drawing near to hear him. ² And the Pharisees and the scribes murmured, saying, "This man receives sinners and eats with them."

The inclusion of Israel's rejected people in the kingdom of God is made concretely visible when Jesus receives them in table fellowship. His acceptance of these people is no less than the extension to them of God's forgiving grace. Their eating together with him is the new fellowship established among them under the rule of God. In his association with the people beyond the boundaries of respectability Jesus was flying in the face of all the conventions. He threatened pious people so much because he who was clearly not a sinner and who ought to have associated with "good" people simply ignored boundaries established by religious and social conventions.

The joyous fellowship between Jesus and the *tax collectors* and *sinners* aroused the displeasure and indignation of the *Pharisees* and *scribes.* Their justification for this attitude was that Jesus was contaminating himself by association with transgressors of the Law.

The three parables which follow speak to the attitude expressed by the religious leaders. Verses 1–2 should be considered as the introduction to each parable, especially to the last one in which the two sons represent the two groups, the righteous and the sinners.

The parable of the lost coin and the lost son are found only in Luke. Matthew has the parable of the lost sheep (Matt. 18:12–14). There, however, it is directed toward the disciples and teaches a different lesson—their responsibility toward "little ones," i.e., the weaker and humbler members of the community. Luke's parable comes from his special material, probably forming a pair with the parable of the lost coin prior to Luke's use of it.

(2) The Lost Sheep (15:3–7)

³ So he told them this parable: ⁴ "What man of you, having a hundred sheep, if he has lost one of them, does not leave the ninety-nine in the wilderness, and go after the one which is lost, until he finds it? ⁵ And when he has found it, he lays it on his shoulders, rejoicing. ⁶ And when he comes home, he calls together his friends and his neighbors, saying to them, 'Rejoice with me, for I have found my sheep which was lost.' ⁷ Just so, I tell you, there will be more joy in heaven over one sinner who repents than over ninety-nine righteous persons who need no repentance.

Any person who has lost something which is precious to him makes an effort to recover it. The knowledge that he still has *ninety-nine* sheep does not compensate for the owner's sense of loss and concern when he discovers that one is missing. To what limits will he go to recover the lost sheep? Jesus says that he does not stop searching *until he finds it.* All can appreciate the sudden relief and the joy that replace concern when at last he has found the sheep. He throws it over his shoulders in order to hasten back home with it. Once there he calls in his acquaintances to share his joy.

The presupposition of these parables is that the acceptance of Jesus' fellowship by the sinner is repentance and that the acceptance of the sinner by Jesus is forgiveness. The life of Jesus is God's quest for his lost sheep. When one is recovered, there is rejoicing *in heaven,* which is a circumlocution for the name of God.

Jesus' antagonists would rejoice over the recovery of their lost animals, but they are filled with dismay when men are reclaimed. They are dour and resentful about that which makes God glad! Jesus deals their pride a severe blow. They are convinced that they are more important in God's sight than these despised tax collectors and sinners. But Jesus declares that the recovery of one of these lost persons brings more joy to God than *ninety-nine* people like them. Is *righteous persons* a bit of irony, actually meaning self-righteous? It is more apt to designate people who lived by the standards of orthodox Jewish piety than to designate those who are right before God. Jesus had no criticism for the high standards which governed the Pharisees' personal morality. Neither did he shut his eyes to the bad in others. He had no "predilection for immorality." [27]

The Pharisees' problem was not their immorality but their attitude toward their fellow man. Like so many good, religious people, they were hard, judgmental, unforgiving. Their contempt of persons who did not meet the standards was an important facet of their lack of humility before God. They failed to recognize their need of grace. And, not having been the recipients of grace, they had none to give.

It is not, therefore, the sinner's sin which causes rejoicing but his *repentance*. It is not the Pharisee's righteousness that excludes him from the glad fellowship of the kingdom but his attitude toward other men.

(3) The Lost Coin (15:8–10)

[8] "Or what woman, having ten silver coins, if she loses one coin, does not light a lamp and sweep the house and seek diligently until she finds it? [9] And when she has found it, she calls together her friends and neighbors, saying, 'Rejoice with me, for I have found the coin which I had lost.' [10] Just so, I tell you, there is joy before the angels of God over one sinner who repents."

One *silver coin,* a drachma, was worth only about twenty-five cents. Some persons would hardly miss a quarter and would spend little time to look for one if they lost it. But two things must be understood in order to appreciate the woman's anguish. *Ten silver coins* was all that she had, her total wealth. Furthermore, although one was not worth much by modern standards, a drachma was the wage of a laborer for a whole day of hard work.

The persistence of the woman is stressed. Since her little hut is poorly lighted even in the daytime, it is necessary

[27] Cf. Guenther Bornkamm, *Jesus of Nazareth,* trans. Irene and Fraser McLuskey and James M. Robinson (New York: Harper, 1960), p. 79.

to *light a lamp* in order to see the coin. By sweeping the hard clay floor, she will eventually bring it into the light. Others are called in to share her joy. They know what it is to be poor—how much it hurts to lose one precious drachma—and what a relief and joyous feeling one has when it is found.

The one who rejoices before the heavenly hosts is God himself. If the recovery of *one sinner* produces joy, how great must be God's exultation over the large group who have entered the fellowship of which Jesus is the center! The parable is really an invitation—an invitation for the critical religious leaders to join in a joyous, heavenly celebration. In other words, it is an invitation for them to repent also.

(4) The Lost Son (15:11–32)

a. The Prodigal's Father (15:11–24)

[11] And he said, "There was a man who had two sons; [12] and the younger of them said to his father, 'Father, give me the share of property that falls to me.' And he divided his living between them. [13] Not many days later, the younger son gathered all he had and took his journey into a far country, and there he squandered his property in loose living. [14] And when he had spent everything, a great famine arose in that country, and he began to be in want. [15] So he went and joined himself to one of the citizens of that country, who sent him into his fields to feed swine. [16] And he would gladly have fed on the pods that the swine ate; and no one gave him anything. [17] But when he came to himself he said, 'How many of my father's hired servants have bread enough and to spare, but I perish here with hunger! [18] I will arise and go to my father, and I will say to him, "Father, I have sinned against heaven and before you; [19] I am no longer worthy to be called your son; treat me as one of your hired servants." ' [20] And he arose and came to his father. But while he was yet at a distance, his father saw him and had compassion, and ran and embraced him and kissed him. [21] And the son said to him, 'Father, I have sinned against heaven and before you; I am no longer worthy to be called your son.' [22] But the father said to his servants, 'Bring quickly the best robe, and put it on him; and put a ring on his hand, and shoes on his feet; [23] and bring the fatted calf and kill it, and let us eat and make merry; [24] for this my son was dead, and is alive again;

he was lost, and is found.' And they began to make merry.

The third parable of the series represents even more vividly than the previous two the dynamics of the situation to which all three speak. The whole problem is one of relationships—the relationship of a father to two sons, of the sons to the father, and of the sons to each other. The two sons represent "the sinner and the Pharisee," neither of whom is denied by a God whose father-love is broad enough to include both and is expressed by an unceasing, questing concern for both. The story shows that man's love is narrow, shortsighted, contingent, selfish. On the other hand, God's love is boundless, profound, reconciling, unreserved. Each, the Pharisee and the sinner, in his own way had sinned against that love.

The two sons are decidedly different; but they have one thing in common that should transcend all divisive tendencies. They have the same father. One son, the younger, is typical of the rebellious adolescent, driven by the desire to escape the family situation in order to be "his own man." We must recognize that the story flows on two levels. Although a young man needs to establish his own identity and independence as a mature, responsible adult, no person ever becomes so mature that he can declare his independence of God.

The usual custom was for property to be divided among the sons after the death of the father and in accordance with his last will. Property could be settled on children as a gift, however, during the life of the parent. They then had no further claim on the family possessions. Usually the profits from property so acquired would begin to go to the beneficiary only after the death of the father. In this case, however, the son acquires the right to exchange his property immediately for negotiable wealth.

The command to honor parents was understood concretely as the responsibility to care for them in old age. But the young man severed relations with his father and journeyed to a *far country*, i.e., outside Palestine to a Gentile land. The sin of the son was not that he requested his share of the property. It was rather that he cut himself off from his father's love and care and denied his just claims. In so doing he also denied his own status as son. This was the condition of the sinners whom Jesus had called to repentance. They had forgotten who they were. It is a condition which all men share who in their passion for the exotic pleasures of some far country or in their stubborn self-will take the control of their lives into their own hands.

Since he no longer has access to the wealth of his father, the young man is limited to what he actually possesses. This is rapidly squandered. Alienated from his father and visited by the consequences of his own choices, the younger son discovers that he is the victim of his own self-will and self-deceit. He left home thinking that he would discover life's meaning and fullness in the exhilarating company of new friends. Instead, he finds himself destitute and forsaken. He had left back home the only person who really loved him.

The prodigal's personal financial problems are complicated by the economic conditions of the region, gripped by famine just when he had spent all he had. His fortunes reach such a low ebb that he, a Jew, is forced to take the most repugnant kind of employment. The Jew's attitude toward swine was governed by the law which says: "Of their flesh you shall not eat, and their carcasses you shall not touch; they are unclean to you" (Lev. 11:8). His hunger is so great that he is ready to eat the pods of the carob trees, eaten only by the very poor or used as feed for domestic animals.

There now arises a decisive distinction between this and the former two parables, which told about the loss and recovery of things and animals. No longer is the focus only on the questing concern of the person who has lost something. Since that which is lost is a person, he cannot be found until he himself desires to be found. It was necessary for him to *come to himself*—to emerge from the dream world of unreality and illusion into which he had fled in order to see himself and his situation in a true light. Now he understands what he had given up when he had in effect renounced his sonship. Even the people who work for wages in his father's house have more than enough to eat. He also sees how wicked was the pride and how selfish the motivations that led him to turn his back on his father.

So the decision is made to return. He still uses the title *father,* although he realizes that he has lost all right to be considered a *son.* He will return and confess his sin. *Against heaven* means against God. A sin against the father was also a sin against God, for one of the weightiest commandments enjoined honor for parents. Having forfeited all rights, he will return to his father simply as a hungry man asking for a job. He prefers to live in his father's house as a hired hand to living elsewhere on his own resources. So he arises and begins the difficult trek back to his home. Repentance is just such a turning. It is a turning from self-will and self-indulgence; it is a turning toward God and a glad submission to his rule of love.

The kind of homecoming a prodigal son can expect always depends on the kind of father he has to go back home to. The father in the story is simply waiting for the son to come back. He waits in that peculiar agony known only to fathers who love their prodigal sons. It is an agony compounded of hope and fear. Each day brings fresh hope for the son's return; each moment is pregnant with the terrible dread that the son may destroy himself in the far country. The boy does not even have to get all the way home. From a distance the *father saw him.* Neighbors would have seen the rags, the dirt, the bare feet. They would have classified him—just another alcoholic, or bum, or hippie, or whatever the current categories might be. A common human tendency is this failure to see people as persons. But the father saw *him!*

The father does not give the son a reluctant, grudging, reserved reception. Just the opposite! The father *ran* to embrace and kiss his son. The son begins his little memorized speech, but the father cuts him short. He is not interested in speeches. Neither wounded pride nor resentful recriminations play a part in the story. Here we get a glimpse of what it means for God to forgive a person. God asks only for an opportunity to lavish his love on his wandering children. All they have to do is to start back to the Father to receive his immeasurable and unreserved forgiveness. The rags are to be stripped off. A clean, fresh robe—the *best* —is to be put on the son. He is received as the father would receive an honored guest who arrives weary and dusty after a long trip. A *ring,* the symbol of sonship, is to be placed on his finger. He arrives barefoot like a slave, but that must be changed. *Shoes* are required for his feet. The *calf* that is being fattened against an occasion that calls for feasting must now be killed. A joyous celebration is to end this memorable day. From all this we see that sonship is not based on the worth of the prodigal but on the love of the father. Those who resented Jesus' reception of tax collectors and sinners knew a great deal about human depravity, but they knew nothing at all about divine love.

Dead is parallel to *lost; alive again,* to *is found.* Someone greatly loved has been raised from the dead. Something infinitely precious has been found. It is a day for celebration and not for long faces.

b. The Elder Brother (15:25–32)

25 "Now his elder son was in the field; and as he came and drew near to the house, he heard music and dancing. 26 And he called one of the servants and asked what this meant. 27 And he said to him, 'Your brother has come, and your father has killed the fatted calf, because he has received him safe and sound.' 28 But he was angry and refused to go in. His father came out and entreated him, 29 but he answered his father, 'Lo, these many years I have served you, and I never disobeyed your command; yet you never gave me a kid, that I might make merry with my friends. 30 But when this son of

yours came, who has devoured your living with harlots, you killed for him the fatted calf!' 31 And he said to him, 'Son, you are always with me, and all that is mine is yours. 32 It was fitting to make merry and be glad, for this your brother was dead, and is alive; he was lost, and is found.' "

What has the elder brother been doing during the prodigal's absence? As it turns out, he has been living by the rules—dutifully, conscientiously, joylessly. Typically he is *in the field* when his brother returns. Upon discovering the motive for the merrymaking, he refuses to enter.

The father who had run to meet his younger son now seeks out the elder to reason with him. But his jealousy makes the older brother unyielding. *I have served you* is literally "I have slaved for you." Also he has not been a transgressor of his father's wishes, *never* having *disobeyed* his orders. This presents a typical picture of legalistic piety.

It appears to him that his brother's wantonness has been rewarded, while his own faithfulness is unappreciated. A *kid* is much less valuable than a calf, but the father has not even given him one of these lesser animals for a feast. *This son of yours* has a resentful, contemptuous ring. By implication the elder brother blames the father for having such a son and at the same time disavows his own relationship to his brother.

The father points out that the very faithfulness of the older son had ruled out such a celebration. Never having been lost, the father could not rejoice over his having been found. Further, the relationship between the father and the son had not been changed at all by the arrival of the younger brother. He was still to receive everything that was coming to him as the elder son and heir. Just as the father exults over finding a lost son, so should the elder son rejoice over finding a lost *brother*. The father will not allow him to disavow his relationship. No one can really say "Father" who is not ready to say "brother."

The story ends on the invitation to join in the merriment of the feast. We are not told that the older brother accepted. Perhaps he continued to stand outside the house, glowering and resentful because of the happiness within. God does not reject either of his two sons—neither the sinner because of his waywardness nor the Pharisee because of his self-righteousness. There is a place at his banquet table for both—if there is repentance.

The parable is an invitation to the critical, self-righteous churchmen to shed their resentment and join in a happy feast with Jesus and the prodigals who had returned to the Father. Their isolation from the group and their resentment of Jesus' relationships with such people have implications that go far beyond the moment. In excluding themselves from their prodigal brothers they are also disavowing their relationship to their Father—who is God.

5. More Teachings About Wealth (16:1–31)

(1) The Shrewd Steward (16:1–9)

1 He also said to the disciples, "There was a rich man who had a steward, and charges were brought to him that this man was wasting his goods. 2 And he called him and said to him, 'What is this that I hear about you? Turn in the account of your stewardship, for you can no longer be steward.' 3 And the steward said to himself, 'What shall I do, since my master is taking the stewardship away from me? I am not strong enough to dig, and I am ashamed to beg. 4 I have decided what to do, so that people may receive me into their houses when I am put out of the stewardship.' 5 So, summoning his master's debtors one by one, he said to the first, 'How much do you owe my master?' 6 He said, 'A hundred measures of oil.' And he said to him, 'Take your bill, and sit down quickly and write fifty.' 7 Then he said to another, 'And how much do you owe?' He said, 'A hundred measures of wheat.' He said to him, 'Take your bill, and write eighty.' 8 The master commended the dishonest steward for his prudence; for the sons of this world are wiser in their own generation than the sons of light. 9 And I tell you, make friends for yourselves by means of unrighteous mammon, so that when it fails they may receive you into the eternal habitations.

Jesus now turns *to the disciples*, but the Pharisees toward whom the parables of chapter 15 were directed are still in the picture, serving as foils for some of the teachings in chapter 16. The unifying theme of this chapter is the right attitude toward and the right use of wealth.

The main figure in the parable of the shrewd steward is an unsavory character, completely devoid of moral scruples and wholly devoted to his own welfare. Consequently, we are not to think that Jesus is holding him up as a person to be admired and imitated, as is the case in an example story like the parable of the good Samaritan. Rather this is a parable in the strictest sense. There is a lesson that can be learned even from a rascal like this. Our task then is to discover the specific point which Jesus wished the unusual story to convey. Jeremias (p. 127) surmises that the story was not a product of Jesus' creative imagination but an actual occurrence familiar to the people to whom he was talking. If this be the case, Jesus simply picked up a current subject of conversation and used it to press home a relevant lesson.

A *steward* or administrator of a household was often a capable and trusted slave. In this instance the steward or "business manager" is a free man. He had exceptionally large responsibilities, extending to the management of his employer's business affairs. In that he was in charge of property that did not belong to him, the steward's situation is parallel to that of every person who has material possessions. Whatever we own has been entrusted to us by the God who created it and to whom we are responsible for its use.

Since there was no such thing as a yearly audit of books in those days, knowledge of mismanagement often came to the owner in the form of *charges* of wrongdoing pressed by a third party. There seems to be no question about the man's guilt. The owner takes it as proven, and the steward's subsequent actions are those of a man without a defense against the accusations. *Turn in the account* is probably an order for him to turn in the records of business transactions as a prelude to the termination of his employment.

Faced with the bleak prospects of unemployment, the incompetent administrator foresees a real crisis in the immediate future. He is not able to work; he is *ashamed to beg.* If he cannot make some arrangements which promise a measure of financial security, he will starve. With time about to run out for him, he decides to take advantage of the powers that he still exercises to perform a deed that will place his master's creditors under obligation to him. In his hour of need he then will be able to turn to them. The *debtors* may have been tenants whose debt was the share of the produce that they owed to the owner. More likely they were merchants who had received merchandise from him for which they had not as yet settled their accounts.

The debts are quite substantial. A *measure* of oil was between eight and nine gallons. The first man's debt was reduced, therefore, by approximately 438 gallons. A *measure* of wheat was 10–12 bushels, which means that the second man's debt was reduced by approximately 220 bushels.

As it stands, v. 8 is awkward. The remark that the *master* praised the steward seems strange to say the least in view of the fact that he had just been bilked out of a sizable sum by the rascal. The second part (8b) must be understood as Jesus' comment on the fellow's one outstanding characteristic. This conclusion is based, however, on the sense rather than the construction of the sentence. To the contrary, the conjunction *for* prepares us for learning the reason for the astonishing commendation of the dishonest steward by his erstwhile employer.

Because of these difficulties some interpreters take *master* (lord) as a reference to Jesus. But the sudden change to the first person in v. 9 argues against this. It has been conjectured that v. 9 is an interpolation, which would solve the problem. Nevertheless, it seems best to take the story as it stands in spite of the difficulties. The owner might be the kind of shrewd fellow who would appreciate just such a neat trick as that pulled off by his steward, even at his own expense.

By the use of the adjective *dishonest* Jesus indicates his general disapproval of the low standards by which the man acted. The comment in *8b* contains the lesson of the parable, the one thing that can be learned from an otherwise reprehensible person. In the light of his values, needs, and possibilities, he had acted "wisely." The wise man is one whose actions in the present moment are based on the possibilities of the future. Naturally the man's concept of the future was very limited. He was a *son of this world,* who acted by the distorted and superficial concepts of this age. But he did look ahead, taking the measure available to him to prepare for the inevitable crisis that lay in the future.

The sons of light belong to the new age of God's redemption and rule. In their future there is a time of crisis when as stewards they will be required to give an account of their stewardship. Jesus calls on them to act as prudently in the light of this knowledge as did the dishonest steward within his limited understanding of the future.

Unrighteous mammon is material possessions. In itself wealth is amoral, capable of being used for great good or great evil. Because of a desire for greater profit, a landlord can force a tenant to rear his children in a slum environment that will scar them for life. Another man can invest his money in schools that help to liberate the same children from ignorance. Money, however, is most often used selfishly, which is why it bears such a stigma.

In keeping with his commitment to follow Jesus, the disciple should use money to help the kinds of people that his Lord came to liberate. Our use of money is to be conditioned by the fact that we know that it is limited and temporary in its usefulness. The example of the rich farmer (12:16 ff.) shows exactly *when it fails*—when a man dies. By using it to *make friends* money is given a lasting significance as it is invested in relationships which transcend death. We see, therefore, that "money can serve to unite people, although normally it divides them." [28] *They* is probably a circumlocution for the name of God (Strack-Billerbeck, II, 221). God, who has a special concern for the poor, receives his faithful steward who has been a channel of the divine love to the poor into *eternal habitations.*

(2) The Right Use of Wealth (16:10-13)

10 "He who is faithful in a very little is faithful also in much; and he who is dishonest in a very little is dishonest also in much. 11 If then you have not been faithful in the unrighteous mammon, who will entrust to you the true riches? 12 And if you have not been faithful in that which is another's, who will give you that which is your own? 13 No servant can serve two masters; for either he will hate the one and love the other, or he will be devoted to the one and despise the other. You cannot serve God and mammon."

Between the two parables with which chapter 16 begins and ends is a collection of sayings of Jesus brought together under the theme of the use of wealth (vv. 10–18). Because they circulated originally in isolated form, the connection between the sayings is difficult to perceive. Especially is this true with vv. 16–18, where one cannot be sure at all as to the exact meaning of the verses in the Lukan context.

First of all, the character of God's steward is sharply distinguished from that of the man in the preceding parable. He must be *faithful* in using the goods entrusted to him according to the will of God, who is their owner.

In vv. 10–13 there is a play on the contrast between worldly wealth and heavenly treasure. The *little* consists of the material goods for which a person is responsible in the use of which he must prove that he can be trusted with *much,* i.e., the eternal riches that God will give to him. *Unrighteous mammon* is the false, illusory wealth of the world in contrast to the *true riches* that God bestows on faithful stewards beyond this life. An individual's earthly existence is thought of as the testing ground in

28 Stagg, *Studies in Luke's Gospel,* p. 105.

which his character is revealed. A basic test is his attitude toward material possessions.

Moreover, the things of the world are said to be *another's*. A man may have a temporary, transient responsibility for a more or less small fraction of God's world. But God has not given the world to man as his private possession. He retains ownership of it. That which God will give to men beyond death, however, really belongs to them, since there will be no temporal limitations on their use.

A person's concept of the values of life is determined by the *master* which he serves. The verb translated *serve* (v. 13) is literally "be a slave to." The principle is that no man can be enslaved to two masters simultaneously, that is, he cannot give his ultimate allegiance to two persons at the same time. Man does not have the privilege of deciding whether he will be a servant (Luke's word; cf. Matt. 6:24). Inherent in his creaturehood is the fact that he is not complete master of his life. He is only free to decide which master will receive his allegiance.

Life can go in one of two directions, but it cannot go in both. We can find our values and goals within the narrow limits of birth and death and in the things which are susceptible to vision, taste, and touch. On the other hand, we can give ourselves to goals that transcend the demands of body and ego. If we make things our gods, we shall spend life and energy acquiring, guarding, and selfishly using them. But if we make the Creator of all things our God, we shall be liberated to devote ourselves to higher and more meaningful values.

(3) Comments to Some Pharisees (16:14–18)

14 The Pharisees, who were lovers of money, heard all this, and they scoffed at him. 15 But he said to them, "You are those who justify yourselves before men, but God knows your hearts; for what is exalted among men is an abomination in the sight of God.
16 "The law and the prophets were until John; since then the good news of the kingdom of God is preached, and every one enters it violently. 17 But it is easier for heaven and earth to pass away, than for one dot of the law to become void.
18 "Every one who divorces his wife and marries another commits adultery, and he who marries a woman divorced from her husband commits adultery.

Exit disciples; enter *Pharisees.* Throughout this section the Pharisees and disciples are both present. In 17:1 the teaching of Jesus will once again be addressed to disciples.

Although the service of God and love for money are mutually exclusive, this is not necessarily true of religion and love for money. Those who interpret religion in a legalistic and individualistic way often do not see any contradiction between it and the amassing of wealth. Many churchmen, like the Pharisees, attribute their success to their righteous character which has caused God to favor them in a special way. They often resent the poor, convinced that underprivileged people would have no problems if they were only virtuous and hardworking. The Pharisees *scoffed* at the connection that Jesus had made between the use of wealth and the service of God.

One way that the rich can show themselves to be pious, i.e., *justify themselves before men,* is through the performance of prescribed religious acts. In Matthew 6:1 ff. Jesus attacks this ostentatious practice of righteousness expressed in pious acts, such as almsgiving, prayer, and fasting. But *God knows your hearts,* or the motive, for what people do. Pious acts are robbed of their significance by the wrong motive. When one acts in a religious way, like going to church or giving money, to prove to men that he is righteous, he has chosen a course which leads to ultimate self-defeat. Men may exalt him, but by the same token he goes down in God's scale of values.

Keeping the Law was the ultimate goal of pharisaism. But this is no longer a valid goal. The Law and the Prophets constituted a phase of redemptive history that ended with John, the last prophet of that era.[29]

Now, however, another period has begun—the time of fulfillment to which the Law and the Prophets pointed. Now the *good news . . . is preached;* the door of the kingdom is open; decision is called for.

Everyone enters it violently is one of the most difficult phrases in the New Testament. The verb translated *enters violently* in the middle voice usually means "to force, oppress, constrain." In the passive sense it is "to be forced, etc." Black[30] believes that the original Aramaic saying of Jesus was "Everyone oppresses it," i.e., the kingdom.

It probably retains a sense similar to this in Matthew 5:18, but the structure of the phrase and its context are different in Luke. Here it should probably be given the sense, "Everyone is eagerly pressing into it." *Every one* is taken as hyperbole, referring to the people who are responding to the proclamation of the gospel. This interpretation would fit well into Luke's missionary and universalistic emphasis (Gottlob Schrenk, TDNT, I, 609 ff.)

The statement in v. 17 accords with Jewish dogma that the Torah is eternal. But the passage shows that the purpose of the Law is interpreted in a completely different sense. The Law is not considered the final, ultimate revelation of God. It is not a question of the Law becoming void but of the fulfillment of its purpose. The Law's function is to lead up to and point toward the preaching of the gospel. A *dot* is an ornamental flourish added to one letter (Strack-Billerbeck, I, 249).

One instance is cited which shows how the time of the preaching of the gospel advances beyond the time of the Law. According to the Law a man could divorce his wife—"for any cause" in the opinion of

some rabbis (Deut. 24:1–4). But the time of the kingdom is to be as the time of the beginning. And in the beginning God had created man and woman and established a unity between them to be broken only by death (cf. Mark 10:2–12; also Matt. 5:31–32; 19:7–10). Jesus insists that the radical demands of the kingdom of God go beyond those of the Law. But we misuse his teaching on the ideal for marriage if it becomes the point of departure for establishing a new legalistic casuistry to be used as the basis for distinguishing between "good" people and "bad." This subtle snare of legalism, which makes Christianity the very kind of institution that Jesus attacked, must be avoided.

In its Lukan context the passage must mean that Jesus' teachings supersede the Pharisaic ideas about righteousness and wealth based on their interpretation of the Law. The present moment is under the aegis of the kingdom of God. Heavenly treasures must be the goal of life.

(4) The Rich Man and Lazarus (16:19–31)

[19] "There was a rich man, who was clothed in purple and fine linen and who feasted sumptuously every day. [20] And at his gate lay a poor man named Lazarus, full of sores, [21] who desired to be fed with what fell from the rich man's table; moreover the dogs came and licked his sores. [22] The poor man died and was carried by the angels to Abraham's bosom. The rich man also died and was buried; [23] and in Hades, being in torment, he lifted up his eyes, and saw Abraham far off and Lazarus in his bosom. [24] And he called out, 'Father Abraham, have mercy upon me, and send Lazarus to dip the end of his finger in water and cool my tongue; for I am in anguish in this flame.' [25] But Abraham said, 'Son, remember that you in your lifetime received your good things, and Lazarus in like manner evil things; but now he is comforted here, and you are in anguish. [26] And besides all this, between us and you a great chasm has been fixed, in order that those who would pass from here to you may not be able, and none may cross from there to us.' [27] And he said, 'Then I beg you, father, to send him to my father's house, [28] for I have five brothers, so that he may warn them, lest they

---

[29] Luke 16:16 is one of the key verses on which Conzelmann (pp. 16 f.; cf. pp. 20 ff.) bases the understanding of Luke's view of redemptive history outlined in his book.

[30] *Op. cit.,* p. 84.

also come into this place of torment.' 29 But Abraham said, 'They have Moses and the prophets; let them hear them.' 30 And he said, 'No, father Abraham; but if some one goes to them from the dead, they will repent.' 31 He said to him, 'If they do not hear Moses and the prophets, neither will they be convinced if some one should rise from the dead.' "

The parable is coherent with and illustrates themes already presented in Luke. Especially do we call to mind the blessings on the poor and woes on the rich in the great sermon (6:20 ff.). Stories on a similar theme, the fate of the poor just man and the unjust rich man, were current in both Egypt and Palestine. One of these must have furnished the outline for Jesus' parable. The story is double-edged. Not only does it point out how God reverses the categories and values of human society; it also teaches that a sign, even one so sensational as a resurrection, will not serve to convince the incredulous.

With great economy of words Jesus paints a vivid picture of two men who represent the extremes of human society. One man is *rich*. He dresses exceptionally well; his meals are daily banquets. *Purple* was the expensive outer garment worn by royalty. The word originally designated the expensive dye which was used in the manufacture of the cloth. The rich man's inner garment was made of costly *linen*, the production of which had become a fine art in Egypt.

The rich man is anonymous, along with all the other characters in Jesus' other parables. The only exception to the rule is this poor beggar. In our time we would, of course, know the name of the wealthy person, for the poor are the anonymous members of human society. The name *Lazarus* means God helps, which is probably significant. Lazarus is one of those people who in their extremity turn to God in whom they rest all their hope as they uncomplainingly accept life's inequities. Since he *lay at the gate*, we gather that he was crippled or made helpless by his illness. One symptom of his illness was a body covered with *sores*, a condition not unusual in people

who subsist on an extremely deficient diet and live in unsanitary conditions.

Bread served as napkins in those days. After it was used, it was thrown under the table. Lazarus had established himself at the entrance to the rich man's palatial home in order to get some of that bread. Since the language does not imply that he was refused, we would suppose that he kept himself alive by eating discarded bread. So helpless and weak was he that the poor beggar could not fend off the *dogs* that roamed the streets of the city and aggravated his sores by licking them.

The poor man died—to no one's surprise. Indeed the wonder was that he had lived so long. A prevalent idea among the Jews was that *angels* carried the dead to their eternal destination. *Abraham* is the first participant at the messianic feast mentioned in 13:28. The phrase *in his bosom* means that the beggar's place was right next to the father of all Israel, in his bosom, at the place of honor.

But the rich man had not followed the principle laid down by Jesus (12:33). Now we begin to see the consequences. *The rich man also died.* There is the shock. It does not seem right to us that the rich and powerful should succumb to the same diseases that strike down the poor. But death is the great mocker of our pretensions and arrogance, of our petty social divisions based on race and wealth. In the end we see that all alike are made of the same frail substance. The rich man had a decent and honorable burial, the fitting touch at the end for a man so singularly "blessed." From birth to death, the story is the same. No expression of God's judgment in earthly misfortune or failure is mentioned in the story.

Hades is used here only in the New Testament as a synonym for Gehenna (cf. 12:5). It is usually the equivalent of the Hebrew *Sheol*, the place of the departed dead. Now the situation is reversed. Lazarus had been on the outside looking in piteously while the rich had banqueted. It is the rich man's turn to be on the outside looking in.

The rich man is also a descendant of Abraham, a relationship which is claimed by the man and acknowledged by Abraham. But race is not decisive in determining a man's relationship to God. Now we come to the real reason for the surprising reversal of the situations of the two men in eternity. The rich man received in life his *good things.* He had no basis for complaint. Having made good clothes and good food his goal, he had enjoyed them both in abundant measure. His life had been a closed circle in which there was money, food, clothes, good times, etc. But he had left God out. Not that he was necessarily irreligious. He had simply appropriated what belonged to God for himself and had allowed one of God's creatures to die in misery at his gate. All his prayers, fasting, almsgiving, and sacrificing in the Temple could not change the fact that he was a practical atheist. On the other hand, Lazarus had looked to God for help and also was successful in that he received what he wanted most.

A great chasm makes it impossible for Lazarus to go to the rich man. We ask: Who dug the chasm? The answer is clear —the rich man. It is the chasm that had separated him in his abundance from Lazarus in his misery. The only thing that he had not bargained for was that God was on the same side of the chasm as Lazarus. In shutting out Lazarus, the rich man had shut out God.

Now he thinks of his brothers. If Lazarus cannot traverse the chasm between them, perhaps he can reappear in life to *warn* his brothers who have the same set of values that he had lived by. Abraham replies that *Moses and the prophets* will speak to the brothers if they will but listen. *Moses* was a contemporary synonym for the Pentateuch or Torah. The rich man also had these Scriptures, but he complains that they are insufficient. The only thing that will deter the brothers from their doom is a great, supernatural spectacular—a resurrection from the dead. But Abraham affirms that

people who are deaf to Moses and the prophets will hardly be convinced even by a resurrection. The problem is not that they lack evidence; they simply ignore the evidence that they have. Perhaps this is an explanation of why the risen Lord appears only to believers. It is only to them that his resurrection has meaning, for genuine conversion is not a product of sensationalism.

6. The Character of the Disciple (17:1–10)

(1) Responsibility for Others (17:1–4)

¹ And he said to his disciples, "Temptations to sin are sure to come; but woe to him by whom they come! ² It would be better for him if a millstone were hung round his neck and he were cast into the sea, than that he should cause one of these little ones to sin. ³ Take heed to yourselves; if your brother sins, rebuke him, and if he repents, forgive him; ⁴ and if he sins against you seven times in the day, and turns to you seven times, and says, 'I repent,' you must forgive him."

We are put on notice by the introductory comment that the teachings which follow it were intended for *disciples.* In this paragraph Jesus speaks to the problem of relationships within the community constituted by his followers.

Temptations to sin translates a Greek word *skandala,* which originally designated the bait stick of a trap. In the New Testament its prevailing meaning is the lure which causes a person to fall into sin. The harsh word, the thoughtless deed, the frivolous remark—these injurious facets of human relations are inevitable. But that does not lessen the seriousness of the deed nor the responsibility of the offender.

The person who is guilty of actions which harm another were better off had he died first. The *millstone* is the kind whose motor power was furnished by a mule or an ass. A person about whose neck such a stone was attached would plummet rapidly to the bottom of the sea. *Little ones* probably does not refer specifically to children, although they would be included. The *little ones* are less important members of the community, who would be more vulnerable to the actions of the leaders. In the Greek text *one* is put in an emphatic position. It is a terribly serious matter to offend even one of the persons who might be considered insignificant by common social standards. The verse division is not good; v. 3a is the conclusion of the warning in vv. 1–2.

The disciple is responsible for fellowship under any and all conditions—responsible to see that his actions do not affect it and responsible when another threatens it by offending him. We are not allowed to retreat behind walls to nurse wounds inflicted by others. The teaching of Jesus does not permit us to say, "He is the guilty party; therefore, he must come to me." Jesus says that we are to *rebuke* our offending brothers. This does not mean that we are to attack him with arrogant accusations and demands for apology. Rather, we are to seek the brother out, expose the problem in its seriousness to him, and express the desire for fellowship. If his attitude is right, he will adopt the proper attitude without coercion. This teaching presupposes a desire for fellowship on his part also.

How often is one to forgive? *Seven times in the day,* which means that there is no limit to forgiveness (cf. Matt. 18:21–22). There never comes the time when the follower of Jesus can say, "I shall go no further. I will not forgive again." The attitude toward the brother is always to be one of forgiveness which seeks only an opportunity to express itself. Furthermore, forgiveness is not judgmental. It causes one to accept a fellow human being at face value without reading into his actions hypocrisy or a lack of seriousness. Forgiveness must be granted as often as it is requested.

(2) The Need for Faith (17:5–6)

⁵ The apostles said to the Lord, "Increase our faith!" ⁶ And the Lord said, "If you had faith as a grain of mustard seed, you could say to this sycamine tree, 'Be rooted up, and be planted in the sea,' and it would obey you.

The disciples ask either for *faith,* i.e., "Give to us faith," or for a greater faith, as

in the text. The underlying Greek allows either translation. Perhaps the plea expressed by the *apostles* is to be understood as a reaction to the extremely demanding teachings that they have just heard. To relate to others on the terms laid down by Jesus is beyond human capacity. A mere man needs faith to rise above the usual patterns of human relations.

Jesus' reply shows that it is not a question of little faith or great faith. The problem is whether a person has any faith at all. The *mustard seed* is proverbially small. Consequently, the smallest amount of faith is enough to enable the person who has it to accomplish astounding deeds. Matthew has a similar saying in two different contexts (17:20; 21:21; cf. also Mark 11:23). In the first Gospel the figure is the moving of a mountain rather than the uprooting of a tree. But the difference in figures is hardly important, since either is completely incredible.

Note that faith is demonstrated by the power of the believing word. The man who has faith speaks, and the power of God is demonstrated. This accords with the Synoptic emphasis on the power of Jesus' word and is further illustrated by statements made by Paul (Rom. 15:18–19; 1 Cor. 2:4, 4:20). The statement is not to be watered down by spiritualizing it. It simply means that the person who has the smallest possible amount of real faith becomes the instrument of God's unlimited power. On the other hand, we must recognize that faith is not a magic by which we control God. Nor is it synonymous with presumption. We cannot use it to back God into a corner and force him to produce a sensational show which will enable us to make the headlines.

(3) Unconditional Service (17:7–10)

⁷ "Will any one of you, who has a servant plowing or keeping sheep, say to him when he has come in from the field, 'Come at once and sit down at table'? ⁸ Will he not rather say to him, 'Prepare supper for me, and gird yourself and serve me, till I eat and drink; and afterward you shall eat and drink'? ⁹ Does he

thank the servant because he did what was commanded? [10] So you also, when you have done all that is commanded you, say, 'We are unworthy servants; we have only done what was our duty.'"

Since the ownership of slaves was common in ancient times, this is another of those illustrations which draws upon the common fund of human experience. The story cannot be used to justify slavery any more than the story of the dishonest steward can be used to justify trickery. There is no indication that any of the disciples was either a land-holder or a slave-owner. Jesus, therefore, was simply saying: "Given these circumstances, this is the way people normally act." Obviously no man can make traffic with other human beings who takes seriously the command to love one's neighbor as oneself.

The person envisioned in the example has only one slave, the correct translation of the Greek *doulos* (*servant*). Because of this the poor fellow must do double duty, as a farm hand and domestic servant. Only a person who has had the experience of plowing all day can imagine how tired the slave must be when the day finally ends. But his duties as a slave are not ended. He must yet prepare the evening meal and serve his master at the table before he can eat and rest. Even after such long hours of arduous work, he can still expect no gratitude. Why? Because he has only done what he as a slave is expected to do. The master commands, the slave obeys. That is the way things are.

The application of the story is found in v. 10. When God commands, man as servant should obey. If he does everything that he is commanded to do, he should not expect this to bring him any special distinction. *Unworthy servants* does not imply a deprecation either of self or of the worth of the work done. The phrase only means that God's faithful servant must not boast of his accomplishments but should remind himself that he does no more than his *duty*.

We must remember that Jesus thought of himself as servant. As servant he lived

and died, asking no more than to do the will of God. Paul also referred to himself as God's slave (e.g., Rom. 1:1, marg.). What is at issue here is not God's attitude toward us and our work nor our attitude toward others and their work. It is our attitude toward what we ourselves do in the service of God.

On the one hand, the gospel refers to the goodness and love of God poured out on his children. On the other hand, it includes our response of loving obedience as servants of God. But care must be taken to stress the fact that God's goodness is always to be received as grace (unmerited favor) rather than as payment for services rendered. God is never in debt to man. Neither can any man on the basis of statistics about hours worked or services rendered expect to be treated as God's favorite child.

7. The Healing of Ten Lepers (17:11–19)

[11] On the way to Jerusalem he was passing along between Samaria and Galilee. [12] And as he entered a village, he was met by ten lepers, who stood at a distance [13] and lifted up their voices and said, "Jesus, Master, have mercy on us." [14] When he saw them he said to them, "Go and show yourselves to the priests." And as they went they were cleansed. [15] Then one of them, when he saw that he was healed, turned back, praising God with a loud voice; [16] and he fell on his face at Jesus' feet, giving him thanks. Now he was a Samaritan. [17] Then said Jesus, "Were not ten cleansed? Where are the nine? [18] Was no one found to return and give praise to God except this foreigner?" [19] And he said to him, "Rise and go your way; your faith has made you well."

In Plummer's outline (p. 402) of Luke, the third and last part of the "journey" section begins here. *Between Samaria and Galilee*, i.e., on the frontier between the two regions, is probably the correct interpretation of the prepositional phrase. It is possible to render the phrase "through the middle of Samaria and Galilee." Nevertheless, there is no way to make the notice fit into a scheme of orderly progress from Galilee to Jerusalem, beginning with 9:51 and ending with 19:40. After Jesus was rejected by a Samaritan village (9:52 f.), we would assume that he then took the circuitous route through Perea. In Luke he is in fact said to enter Judea from this direction through the border town of Jericho. But even as the journey narrative draws to a close, Jesus is placed here once again on the border between Galilee and Samaria.

Conzelmann (p. 68 ff.) cites this as evidence of Luke's erroneous notion of Palestinian geography. But there are places in Luke and Acts, especially the latter, where a genuine familiarity with the geography of the region can be detected. Perhaps the incongruities of v. 11 are best explained by the fact that other considerations overruled strictly geographical ones. First, the readers are reminded once again that Jesus is on the way to Jerusalem, which is primarily a theological motif in Luke (see on 9:51). Second, the narrative inserted here demands a congruous setting. In the border region one might expect to encounter a mixed group of Jewish and Samaritan lepers, whose racial differences were transcended by the bonds of common misery.

According to Leviticus 13:46, the leper was to be isolated from social intercourse with all but his kind. Since this band of *ten lepers* maintain some distance from Jesus and his party, they have to raise their voices in order to make their plea heard. *Master* translates a Lukan word found elsewhere only on the lips of disciples. It along with teacher served as synonym for the Semitic "Rabbi."

Jesus answers the piteous plea of the ostracized, diseased men with a command rather than an act of healing: *Go and show yourselves to the priests.* After he was cured, the leper was required by the Law to submit to an examination by a priest, who would determine officially if the man were ready to be reintegrated into society (see Lev. 13—14). Jesus' command, therefore, is a demand for faith. The diseased men are to go to their priests in the confidence that prior to their arrival they will be healed. All alike obey the command of Jesus, and all alike are healed.

In those days of limited medical resources and knowledge, a leper could hope only for a miracle from God. His healing was considered a signal act of God's mercy. Upon discovering that he is healed, one of the ten starts back to Jesus, *praising God with a loud voice.* Not only does he praise God, but he falls at the feet of Jesus in homage to the one who had been the instrument of his cure. Only now do we learn the man's racial identity. The personal pronoun *he* is emphatic (v. 16b), which underlines the fact that of the ten only the one who returned was a non-Jew, a *Samaritan.* The questions Jesus asks (vv. 17–18) are rhetorical, raised to contrast the action of the grateful Samaritan with that of the Jews who accepted the cure as their due. He is described as a *foreigner,* a representative in this Gospel of all non-Jewish people. Samaritans figure more prominently in Luke than in any other Gospel because they prefigure for him the mission to Gentiles. This incident is a sign of the rejection of the gospel by Jews and its enthusiastic reception by aliens, developments which had become established facts by A.D. 85.

All the lepers believed in God, that is, in the possibility of miraculous healing, or they would not have heeded Jesus' instructions. How then can the Samaritan alone be addressed by the word: *your faith has made you well?* Faith must involve something more than belief in the miracle-working power of God. It also involves the recognition that his mercies are undeserved, which means that gratitude is an essential concomitant of faith. Nine of the men had been healed in vain in that their selfish spirits had not been changed. Only one had responded spontaneously to God's goodness and had recognized the relationship between Jesus and God's mighty acts. Therefore, only one really had faith.

8. The Kingdom of God and the Son of Man (17:20—18:14)

(1) The Kingdom in the Midst (17:20-21)

20 Being asked by the Pharisees when the kingdom of God was coming, he answered them, "The kingdom of God is not coming with signs to be observed; 21 nor will they say, 'Lo,

here it is!' or 'There!' for behold, the kingdom of God is in the midst of you."

Whereas we find apocalyptic material in Matthew and Mark concentrated in one chapter (Matt. 24; Mark 13), Luke has two such passages, the first of which begins here. This is the first of four passages in which the question of the time of the Parousia is dealt with specifically in Luke-Acts (also 19:11; 21:7; Acts 1:6).

The exchange between Jesus and the Pharisees is found only in Luke. Discussions about signs that could be identified as pointing to the dawning messianic kingdom evidently agitated Pharisaic circles considerably.[31] The question posed by the Pharisees was for them, therefore, an important one. There is no hint that it is asked with other than a serious intent in the hope that Jesus as a teacher might be able to throw some light on the discussion. But he simply denies the validity of the question because the answer is not accessible to human beings. Jesus taught that the future belongs to God and that he must be trusted with it. *With signs to be observed* translates a prepositional phrase found only here. There is no possibility of being dogmatic about its meaning in Greek, nor about any underlying Aramaic phrase. Nevertheless, the general sense is clear. There is no basis on which men can predict the date for the beginning of the future consummation. Jesus' teachings about the future call men from foolish speculations about times and seasons to an awareness of the seriousness of the present moment. Each moment is charged with as much potential as any other moment. No moment of the future can be any more critical than this one that we are living in, for anything that can happen in the future can happen *right now.*

31 Strack-Billerbeck, IV, *Zweiter Teil*, pp. 977 ff. A long excursus on "Preliminary signs and calculations of the days of the Messiah" gives examples from the Talmud. Although these are later than the ministry of Jesus, we can conclude that similar calculations designed to determine the beginning of the kingdom were also made in Pharisaic circles contemporary to Jesus. G. R. Beasley-Murray in *Jesus and the Future* (pp. 173 ff.) points out that by way of contrast there is "no trace of mathematical calculations" in Mark 13. The same can also be said of the other similar passages in the Gospels.

All questions about the time of the revelation of the kingdom of God are futile; likewise also are the speculations about place. People were asking how they could recognize the coming kingdom when really they were blind to the presence of the kingdom in their midst. Jesus calls his questioners back from fruitless speculations about the future to a confrontation with the kingdom in the present.

The meaning of the Greek preposition *entos* (*in the midst of*) is still much debated. The two possibilities are "within" or "among." We can dismiss the idea that Jesus thinks of the kingdom as an immanent, spiritual reality with unlimited evolutionary possibilities. This idea is in direct opposition to its primary meaning in Jewish thought and the New Testament. The kingdom is the transcendent rule of God that guarantees the establishment of a new order in the universe, which spells doom to the present age of darkness and rebellion. In Luke the kingdom of God is present in the life and teaching of Jesus whose words and acts become the basis for faith in it and an understanding of its nature. But even so we can still speak of the kingdom as being both "within" man and "among" men. In Jesus the kingdom of God lays its claim upon the heart, i.e., upon man's will and loyalties, and demands a decision. It is not, therefore, a question of what is "out there" either in time or space, but what is "in there" in terms of their inward response to the demands of the kingdom here and now.

At the same time, the Son of man is "among" the Jewish people at the time when they look for him "out there." He is the decisive reality with which they have to do. Instead of useless speculations about the time and place of the future kingdom, they need to respond to this manifestation of God's rule by repenting, i.e., by turning to God and making him their king.

(2) The Days of the Son of Man (17:22–37)

22 And he said to the disciples, "The days are coming when you will desire to see one of the days of the Son of man, and you will not see it.

23 And they will say to you, 'Lo, there!' or 'Lo, here!' Do not go, do not follow them. 24 For as the lightning flashes and lights up the sky from one side to the other, so will the Son of man be in his day. 25 But first he must suffer many things and be rejected by this generation. 26 As it was in the days of Noah, so will it be in the days of the Son of man. 27 They ate, they drank, they married, they were given in marriage, until the day when Noah entered the ark, and the flood came and destroyed them all. 28 Likewise as it was in the days of Lot— they ate, they drank, they bought, they sold, they planted, they built, 29 but on the day when Lot went out from Sodom fire and brimstone rained from heaven and destroyed them all—30 so will it be on the day when the Son of man is revealed. 31 On that day, let him who is on the housetop, with his goods in the house, not come down to take them away; and likewise let him who is in the field not turn back. 32 Remember Lot's wife. 33 Whoever seeks to gain his life will lose it, but whoever loses his life will preserve it. 34 I tell you, in that night there will be two men in one bed; one will be taken and the other left. 35 There will be two women grinding together; one will be taken and the other left." 37 And they said to him, "Where, Lord?" He said to them, "Where the body is, there the eagles will be gathered together."

The problem of the interim, the period between the ministry of Jesus and the Parousia, had become especially acute for the Christian community by the time Luke wrote his Gospel. Two dangers in particular had to be confronted. The first was the possibility of despair and loss of faith. The other was the deceptive appeal of apocalyptic sensationalism. These are the kinds of considerations that determined Luke's selection and use of sayings of Jesus here and elsewhere in the Gospel. The teachings and warnings are addressed to the *disciples*, i.e., to the church.

The intense desire of a pilgrim, martyr church will be to reach the destination toward which it moves. Like the Pharisees, the disciples will also be concerned about the end of the age. *The days of the Son of man* is taken by Leaney (p. 68 ff.) to refer to the manifestations beginning with the transfiguration in which the disciples beheld the glory of Jesus as the Son of man. Such an experience would bring inspiration and renewed hope to help them face the

problems of life in this age. This interpretation is possible but hardly likely here. The whole passage is dealing rather with the problems of a Parousia that does not occur when expected and longed for. *Days of the Son of man* is synonymous with "days of the Messiah," a rabbinic expression for the messianic age (Strack-Billerbeck, II, 237). According to Conzelmann, "the plural indicates that the Eschaton is no longer imagined as one complete event, but as a succession of events distinct from one another" (p. 124). What they long to see is the dawn of the new age. But the longing will be in vain; "not because it will never come; but because it will not come in those days of longing" (Plummer, p. 407).

In this situation followers of Jesus will be especially susceptible to the authoritative pronouncements of the apocalyptists. But any effort to identify the place and time of the Parousia is to be rejected. Such claims are incongruous with what Jesus teaches about the end of the age. Early in the history of the church problems were created by people who taught that the Parousia had already occurred (cf. 2 Thess. 2:2). It is this kind of claim that Jesus' warning nullifies.

Signs will be totally unnecessary because who the Son of man is and what he is will be unmistakably clear to all. He will be as bright as a flash of *lightning* that illuminates the whole sky (as he was at the transfiguration—9:29). Note the slight but significant difference from the parallel in Matthew 24:27. There it is the Parousia which will be like a flash of lightning; here it is the Son of man himself.

But before the Parousia of the Son of man can take place, he must *first* suffer. Perhaps this also hints that the way of suffering is also essential for the church before it can experience the glory of the new age.

The experience of *Noah's* generation is used as an illustration of the unpredictability of the end-time. There were no signs. Life was going on in the daily routine, when the *flood* suddenly began without warning and *destroyed them all*. Fanciful preaching to the contrary, the Old Testament account does not say anything about a warning even from Noah. The same situation prevailed at the destruction of *Sodom.* Life in the wicked city was proceeding as usual until *the day when Lot went out.* The only days that were different were the days of catastrophe.

By the same token, life in this age will go on until the day of the Parousia. The basic view from which this is said is apocalyptic, but it is apocalypticism divested of its sensational aspects. It is apocalyptic in that it expresses the pessimistic view that the present world order is essentially and hopelessly corrupt. It is also based on the conviction that the kingdom of God is a transcendent reality that will interrupt the corrupt processes of this age. The messianic age is not thought of as a utopia that is the final stage of an inevitable evolution toward good.

The warnings in v. 31 fit better in their context in Matthew 24:17–18 and Mark 13:15–16, where they refer to the destruction of Jerusalem. Here they stress the need to be prepared and ready when the *Son of man is revealed.* The commitment to God must be so complete that it rules out any desire to hold on to the things of this age. In this connection the reference to Lot's wife is relevant (v. 32). Instead of resolutely facing the future she looked back with longing to the past, something which the disciples must not do at the last moment. This attempt to save one's life (with existence interpreted in terms of possessions and status in this age) will cause one to lose it, i.e., the future that God has prepared for the people who are ready for that kind of life.

When the end comes, it will cut across the closest relationships of this world order. The coming is pictured as taking place toward the end of the last watch (cf. 12:38), that is, when the fainthearted have given up hope. The men are still in bed,[32]

---

[32] "Men" is not required by the Greek text; the masculine "two" could also stand for a man and his wife. Also v. 36 does not appear in the RSV text since it is omitted from the best manuscripts.

but the women are already in the initial stages of the arduous task of preparing bread for the day. *Will be taken* means to be taken into salvation by God, probably by his angels.

The disciples are still asking *where.* The reply is another one of those difficult sayings to which no dogmatic interpretation can be given. Leaney (p. 232), along with others, identifies *eagles* as Roman standards, whose emblem was the eagle. It is taken as a reference to the conquest of Jerusalem by the Roman army. But it seems better to relate the passage to the Parousia. The *eagles* (perhaps vultures) are symbols of judgment. There is no answer to the questions of time and place. Jesus simply affirms that judgment is inevitable and that it will take place when in God's purposes the time has come.

(3) The Importunate Widow (18:1–8)

[1] And he told them a parable, to the effect that they ought always to pray and not lose heart. [2] He said, "In a certain city there was a judge who neither feared God nor regarded man; [3] and there was a widow in that city who kept coming to him and saying, 'Vindicate me against my adversary.' [4] For a while he refused; but afterward he said to himself, 'Though I neither fear God nor regard man, [5] yet because this widow bothers me, I will vindicate her, or she will wear me out by her continual coming.' " [6] And the Lord said, "Hear what the unrighteous judge says. [7] And will not God vindicate his elect, who cry to him day and night? Will he delay long over them? [8] I tell you, he will vindicate them speedily. Nevertheless, when the Son of man comes, will he find faith on earth?"

A parable from Luke's special source concludes the foregoing teachings about the future. Addressed to the disciples, it is concerned specifically with the problem of the interim. When the longings and expectations of the followers of Jesus, living in a hostile, alien age, are not fulfilled by the coming of the kingdom, there is always the danger of despair. They must be careful, therefore, not to *lose heart.*

Set over against this spirit of despair is a life of continual prayer, which is a constant testimony to the believer's faith. The presupposed central petition is the plea of the early community: *maranatha* ("Our Lord, come!" 1 Cor. 16:22). Jesus' parable establishes the basis of this life of prayer. Believers *ought always to pray* because there is one who hears their petitions and who will surely respond.

The effective use of contrast is characteristic of a number of the parables of Jesus. Here once again the leading figure is a man of totally reprehensible character, the exact reverse of what a judge should be. In the Old Testament the basis for the conscientious discharge of judicial responsibilities was the fear of God, i.e., the recognition that there was a higher Judge to whom all human judges had to answer (e.g., Ex. 23:6–7). But this judge did not fear God. Neither did he have respect for other human beings and so could not be moved by consideration for them. Since he acted only from self-interest, his judgments were always determined by the size of the bribe which the plaintiffs offered to him.

This then is the type of judge before whom the case of a poor widow was pending. A single judge could decide this kind of case involving financial disputes (Strack-Billerbeck, I, 289). Someone owed the widow money or in some way was attempting to defraud her. A widow is used in the parable because she is the epitome of helplessness and defenselessness (see on 7:12). She had neither the money to bribe nor the power to influence a selfish and greedy judge. Her only recourse was to keep bothering him, hoping eventually to be granted relief from her adversary, the opposing party in the suit. Finally the self-centered judge acted in character. He decided to render a verdict in her favor, i.e., *vindicate her*, simply to free himself from her ceaseless pleading.

The argument is from the lesser to the greater. If a corrupt judge will attend the pleas of a poor widow for whom he has no concern, how much more will God be moved by the cries of *his elect*. As Caird remarks, if "election means favoritism, it is because God has a bias in favour of the innocent victims of persecution" (p. 201).

The vindication for which they look will take place in the judgment, at the end of this age. The oppressed, helpless victims of hostility and injustice who rest their case with God will find their faith justified.

Verse 7b is difficult. It can hardly carry the meaning given in the RSV text, which sets it at odds with the context of the parable and, indeed, of the entire Gospel. In Luke the teaching is that the time of the end is unknown; hence, the period prior to the Parousia may be longer than expected. But it is sure to take place. We can give the Greek phrase its usual translation and put it in the form of an affirmation: "and he is patient with them" (Jeremias, p. 116). Unlike the unrighteous judge, God listens patiently to the petitions of his children. *Speedily* in v. 8 probably should be "unexpectedly."

God will be faithful, but can the same be said about man? By the time of the Parousia, *when the Son of man comes,* will all men have despaired so that no one still believes in the eventual triumph of the sovereign rule of a just God?

(4) The Pharisee and the Tax Collector (18:9–14)

⁹ He also told this parable to some who trusted in themselves that they were righteous and despised others: ¹⁰ "Two men went up into the temple to pray, one a Pharisee and the other a tax collector. ¹¹ The Pharisee stood and prayed thus with himself, 'God, I thank thee that I am not like other men, extortioners, unjust, adulterers, or even like this tax collector. ¹² I fast twice a week, I give tithes of all that I get.' ¹³ But the tax collector, standing far off, would not even lift up his eyes to heaven, but beat his breast, saying, 'God, be merciful to me a sinner!' ¹⁴ I tell you, this man went down to his house justified rather than the other; for every one who exalts himself will be humbled, but he who humbles himself will be exalted."

To the parable of the importunate widow is added another, connected to it by the theme of prayer. In the former a woman figures prominently; in the latter, a man—a good example of Luke's fondness for pairs. A change in audience as well as theme is indicated by the introductory statement. The parable is the first in a series of episodes in which the requirements for entrance into the kingdom of God are delineated.

Since the *temple* is the setting, the incident takes place in Jerusalem. Two men who stand religiously and socially at the opposing poles of Judaism go to *the temple to pray*, at the time either of morning prayer, around 9:00 A.M., or of afternoon prayer, around 3:00 P.M. We are prone to have a distorted view of the Pharisee, who personifies self-righteousness, hypocrisy, and other evils. But if this kind of person were unique in the history of religion, he would hardly serve any purpose as illustration. The fact of the matter is that the sins and weaknesses as well as the virtues of the Pharisees were those which religious people are apt to possess. Consequently they illustrate the perennial danger of institutionalizing piety, of making religion a set of rules, and of failing to grasp the centrality of relationships with God and man.

Prayer was generally offered from a standing position. Either the *Pharisee stood . . . with himself,* away from the common crowd, or he *prayed* with himself. The latter indicates that his prayer was a monologue rather than a dialogue with God. The first word uttered is God's name. But because a person uses God's name and other pious phrases does not mean necessarily that he is talking to God. Rather than being a prayer, the Pharisee's monologue was an exercise in self-congratulation. Morality conceived in negative terms is of central importance in the legalistic concept of righteousness. The righteous man is one who does not transgress the law. He does not commit the kinds of acts of which people like the tax collectors are guilty.

After claiming to be no transgressor of the Law, the Pharisee mentions two significant areas in which he has expressed his righteousness by going beyond the Law's demands. By law Jews were required to fast on the Day of Atonement only (cf. on 5:33 ff.). But the more pious of them had adopted the practice of fasting *twice a week* considering it an act of special religious merit. As stated in Deuteronomy 14:22 ff., the Law required a tithe of certain agricultural products, specifically of grain, wine, oil, and the firstlings of herds and flocks. But the Pharisee claims to go beyond this. He tithes *all* that he gets.

This phrase is susceptible to three meanings (Strack-Billerbeck, II, 244 ff.). (1) The Pharisees had extended the tithe to cover all agricultural products, including the herbs of their gardens (see 11:42). (2) The more pious Jews also made it a practice to tithe all the agricultural products that they bought for fear that they might be using untithed goods. (3) The phrase *all that I get* could refer to the man's total acquisitions whether from farming or business, whereas the law of the tithe included only agricultural products.

The problem with legalism is that it defines righteousness in such a way that it is attainable by men. Having attained the standards by which they judge such matters, men are prone to fall into the sin of moral pride. There are two sides to this coin. On the one is erroneous judgment of the self; on the other is a contempt for those who do not meet the standards.

In contrast to the arrogance and self-assurance of the Pharisee, we see the humility and despair of the *tax collector. Standing far off* cannot mean that he was in some other area of the Temple, e.g., the Court of the Gentiles, because the Pharisee sees him. But he does not feel worthy to approach the sanctuary, the symbol of God's presence, which stood before the Court of Israel (see on 1:9–10). Nor will he look toward *heaven,* i.e., toward God, with sinful eyes. He *beat his breast,* a poignant expression of the agony of his guilt. He is oblivious to the presence of the Pharisee, for he can see no other's sins but his own. Having absolutely no basis for self-justification, he possesses only one ground of hope —that God is indeed *merciful.* It goes without saying that if the Pharisee was really talking to God, then the tax collector was doomed. From the God of the Pharisee a person like him could expect only contempt, rejection, and punishment. On the other hand, if God actually responds to the heartbroken cry of the tax collector, the Pharisee's religious ideas are untenable.

Note the direct, authoritative *I tell you* (v. 14). Jesus assumes the prerogative to speak for God. In him the eschatological judgment becomes actual, contemporary. The passive voice avoids the mention of God's name. God justifies the tax collector. This statement takes us back to v. 9. Self-righteousness rules out the possibility of receiving God's righteousness. To say that the tax collector was *justified* is to say that he was forgiven and that a new relationship between him and God had been established.

Jesus does not implicitly or otherwise condemn the good in the Pharisee nor condone the evil in the tax collector. The Pharisee is not condemned because of his virtues but because of his sins. They are different from those of the tax collector but none the less real. We can assume that the tax collector had abused men financially by extorting from them more in customs duty than they owed. By his prejudice and pride the Pharisee abused people in ways that could be even more damaging. Like many a good churchman among us, he would not think of taking illicit profits from others but did not hesitate to treat them with contempt if he judged their racial or religious background to be inferior.

The recurring principle of the reversal of human values by the judgment of God is stated again in 14*b*. All men are sinners; all need forgiveness. Consequently, all stand on the same level before God. The good news proclaimed by Jesus is that God is not like the God of the Pharisee; he is like the father of the prodigal son.

9. Entrance into the Kingdom (18:15–30)

(1) Jesus and the Children (18:15–17)

¹⁵ Now they were bringing even infants to him that he might touch them; and when the disciples saw it, they rebuked them. ¹⁶ But Jesus called them to him, saying, "Let the children come to me, and do not hinder them; for to such belongs the kingdom of God. ¹⁷ Truly, I say to you, whoever does not receive the kingdom of God like a child shall not enter it."

Luke now returns to his Markan source which furnishes the material for the rest of the chapter (Mark 10:13 ff.). He describes the children who are brought to Jesus as *infants,* a minor variation from Mark's "children" (10:13). *They,* presumably the parents who wanted Jesus to bless the children, find their way blocked by the *disciples.* This is a serious misinterpretation by the disciples of their role. They view themselves as guardians of Jesus' dignity and time. The teacher is not to be bothered by unimportant, little people. Jesus has taught that he is especially accessible to such people and that the disciples should be especially careful not to offend them. Evidently they have not yet learned this lesson.

Jesus overrules the disciples and receives the children, using them as a vehicle for stressing a major theme of his teaching. The *kingdom of heaven* belongs to "children." That is, it is composed of people who know themselves to be God's children, who call him Father, and who accept their state of dependence.

The kingdom of God is not a prize to be won, a premium for faithfulness to an intensive moral and religious program. It is a gift to be received, a relationship into which one enters. In the preceding parable the Pharisee was outside the kingdom because he clung to an illusion of self-sufficiency and autonomy. Since God is the Father, we do not have to earn his love. All we have to do is to enter into the relationship that his love makes possible, aware of the fact that we are little children and that we need him as Father.

(2) The Rich Ruler (18:18–30)

¹⁸ And a ruler asked him, "Good Teacher, what shall I do to inherit eternal life?" ¹⁹ And Jesus said to him, "Why do you call me good? No one is good but God alone. ²⁰ You know the commandments: 'Do not commit adultery, Do

not kill, Do not steal, Do not bear false witness, Honor your father and mother.' " [21] And he said, "All these I have observed from my youth." [22] And when Jesus heard it, he said to him, "One thing you still lack. Sell all that you have and distribute to the poor, and you will have treasure in heaven; and come, follow me." [23] But when he heard this he became sad, for he was very rich. [24] Jesus looking at him said, "How hard it is for those who have riches to enter the kingdom of God! [25] For it is easier for a camel to go through the eye of a needle than for a rich man to enter the kingdom of God." [26] Those who heard it said, "Then who can be saved?" [27] But he said, "What is impossible with men is possible with God." [28] And Peter said, "Lo, we have left our homes and followed you." [29] And he said to them, "Truly, I say to you, there is no man who has left house or wife or brothers or parents or children, for the sake of the kingdom of God, [30] who will not receive manifold more in this time, and in the age to come eternal life."

Luke describes the seeker as a *ruler;* Mark does not identify him (10:17). This is the second man in Luke who asks what he must *do* in order *to inherit* eternal life (see on 10:25). For the other man the question was a subterfuge, but for this one it is of crucial personal importance. *To inherit eternal life* is synonymous with "to enter the kingdom." Jesus has just answered the question: "You must receive it as a little child." But what does this mean specifically in the life and experience of this particular man?

We note a fundamental problem at the very beginning. Jesus had used the verb receive, whereas the man uses *do.* He is under the wrong impression that he can wrest eternal life from God by the dint of personal effort.

Jesus challenges and rejects the use of the adjective *good.* (Note the variation in Matt. 19:16–17. Because early Christians thought of Jesus as wholly good, they had difficulty in accepting his rejection of the adjective.) Pharisaic Judaism had clearly defined who a good man was: he kept the Law in the manner prescribed in the traditions. Of primary importance, therefore, was what he did *not* do (cf. 18:11). It is dangerous to use the word *good.* The man

so described may take it seriously and become convinced that he is good because he lives by accepted standards. Or the man who uses it may be trapped into thinking that he can be good if he rises to the prescribed standard of moral and religious conduct. *God alone* is good. This means that there is no place for religious pride. No matter how much he tries, man can never be good—in an absolute sense. So he never reaches a point that he does not need grace; nor does he ever reach a level from which he can look down with contempt on people who are not good.

Characteristically, Jesus points the ruler to the *commandments.* The answer to the question about eternal life is found in the Scriptures which the ruler accepts and ostensibly is following (cf. 10:26; 16:29,31). We note that Jesus does not mention those commandments in the Decalogue which have to do with man's relation to God. Rather he begins with the seventh command, reciting a list (all the last five) that the ruler also knows by heart. Jesus is aware that he can respond as he in fact does: *All these I have observed from my youth,* i.e., ever since becoming a son of the Torah at about 12 years of age (cf. Phil. 3:6).

Luke does not have the question that we find in Matthew 19:20: "What do I still lack?" But this only makes explicit what is implied here. The natural assumption is that Jesus will continue in the same vein and mention the first commandments, to which the ruler would have also replied in the same way. Instead Jesus demonstrates where he has missed the real meaning of those commandments. He does this by presenting him with an unmistakably clear but immensely difficult choice. He is required to do only one thing, that is, sell all his possessions, *distribute* the proceeds to the *poor,* and *follow* Jesus.

Instead of receiving joyfully the answer to the burning religious question which had so preoccupied him, the ruler becomes *sad.* To be required to give a tenth or even half would be acceptable, but to give all of a huge fortune away and become a penniless pauper with no financial security is more than he can bring himself to do.

Jesus has put his finger on the problem. The man who had boasted about keeping the commandments is really a transgressor of the Law. He is an idolator! He is attempting to worship God and mammon at the same time. But when the test is put to him, it is obvious that his property is his real god. Jesus asks him to divest himself of his property and trust God alone for the needs of the future. He must cease his efforts to lay up treasures on earth and begin to lay up heavenly treasures. For one man wealth is an idol; for another it may be social acceptance, political power, or any one of a host of things. In every case loyalty to God demands the putting away of such gods, no matter how painful the process may be.

Now we see what it means to receive the kingdom as a little child. The child's destiny is in the hands of his father. Whether he starves or is well-nourished depends on how his father provides for him, since he normally has no other resources. Just so a person must trust God for everything, depending completely on his care and love.

The tendency to trust mammon is overriding. No attempt should be made to mitigate the analogy in v. 25. It is *easier* for a *camel* to pass through the *eye* of a sewing *needle* than for the *rich* to enter the *kingdom*—in other words, a clear impossibility.

Then who can be saved? is a logical question if the entrance into the kingdom is so small. Can anyone at all make it through the "needle's eye?" But the outlook is not so bleak as the disciples suppose. It is *impossible* for man to negotiate the entrance to the kingdom by his own efforts. But what is beyond man's capacity to achieve is in God's power to give. In any case salvation is a miracle brought about by the grace of God rather than the power of man.

Peter speaks for the disciples when he affirms that they have fulfilled the requirements laid down by Jesus for the ruler.

Luke has *our homes* where Mark has "everything" (10:28). Jesus' reply is a renewed assurance that no man chooses in vain the kingdom of God in preference to competing loyalties. There are slight differences in Luke's list of such loyalties and the one found in Mark 10:29. He has *wife,* combines "brothers" and "sisters" into *brothers* and "mother" and "father" into *parents,* and omits "fields."

The rewards of single-minded loyalty are immeasurable both in the present age and in the age to come. The problem is that most people prefer the more tangible, material emoluments that come from the treasures and relationships of this age. They deprecate the values that stem from service to God and the new relationships of the kingdom (see the part of Mark 10:30 which Luke omits).

10. The Approach to Jerusalem (18:31 —19:27)

(1) The Third Passion Saying (18:31–34)

31 And taking the twelve, he said to them, "Behold, we are going up to Jerusalem, and everything that is written of the Son of man by the prophets will be accomplished. 32 For he will be delivered to the Gentiles, and will be mocked and shamefully treated and spit upon; 33 they will scourge him and kill him, and on the third day he will rise." 34 But they understood none of these things; this saying was hid from them, and they did not grasp what was said.

Now the fateful events which are to take place in the Jewish capital draw near. Once again the disciples are reminded of their destination and are confronted with an explanation of what it means. They have the idea that the glorious triumph of the Messiah will occur in Jerusalem. Although they find his words inadmissible and, therefore, incomprehensible, Jesus iterates in this third passion saying that Jerusalem is the place of rejection and death.

The disciples share with others a basic misunderstanding of the Scriptures. The prophets have written that suffering is an essential prelude to glory, and what they have written *will be accomplished,* or better, "will be fulfilled." There is no detailed account in the prophets of a death like the one described in vv. 32–33, nor is there a prediction that there will be a resurrection like the one described in v. 33. How can the experience of Jesus, therefore, be interpreted as a fulfillment of the things *written . . . by the prophets?* The answer is that the prophets speak of two figures who will play a part in the drama of redemption. One is the Suffering Servant of Isaiah; the second is the Son of man of Daniel, along with the King-Messiah of the Psalms and elsewhere. In the experience of Jesus these two figures merge and become one Person. God's Servant is to suffer; this is equated with the cross. He is to rule in glory; this is equated with the resurrection, ascension, and Parousia. This is the way that Jesus fulfills what the prophets declared about the suffering and glory of God's Servant, the Son of man.

Jesus' countrymen will play a decisive role in this drama when they hand him over to the Gentile representatives of Rome, specifically Pilate and the soldiers who crucify him. The Jews conspire to bring about his death; Gentiles accomplish it. But God, not man, has the last word: the Son of man *will rise.* The disciples do not understand the relation between suffering and glory. This they will comprehend only in the light of the events which are immediately ahead. Then they will see that they must walk the same road. Suffering for them is also a necessary prelude to glory (as in the experience of Stephen, Acts 7:54—8:1a).

(2) The Healing of a Blind Man (18:35–43)

35 As he drew near to Jericho, a blind man was sitting by the roadside begging; 36 and hearing a multitude going by, he inquired what this meant. 37 They told him, "Jesus of Nazareth is passing by." 38 And he cried, "Jesus, Son of David, have mercy on me!" 39 And those who were in front rebuked him, telling him to be silent; but he cried out all the more, "Son of David, have mercy on me!" 40 And Jesus stopped, and commanded him to be brought to him; and when he came near, he asked him,

41 "What do you want me to do for you?" He said, "Lord, let me receive my sight." 42 And Jesus said to him, "Receive your sight; your faith has made you well." 43 And immediately he received his sight and followed him, glorifying God; and all the people, when they saw it, gave praise to God.

In Mark the blind man is healed when Jesus and his company are leaving Jericho (10:46 ff.), whereas in Luke the healing takes place as they enter the city. Mark identifies him as Bartimaeus the son of Timaeus, a tautology which is omitted by Luke. The entrance to a city was a favorable spot for a blind beggar to make his appeal to the travelers who came and went. The sound of an unusually large group of people passing along the highway arouses the blind man's curiosity. Since Jesus (Joshua) was a common name among the Jews, it is necessary to identify him with reference to his home town *Nazareth.*

Apparently the fame of Jesus is such that the blind man knows immediately who he is and recognizes his particular moment of opportunity. *Son of David* is a messianic title the use of which probably has a special significance at this time. The blind man recognizes Jesus as the descendant of David whom the Jews expect to bring an end to their national humiliation by freeing Jerusalem and assuming the scepter of their greatest ruler. The blind man's acknowledgement that Jesus is the anticipated Messiah comes just prior to his entrance into Jerusalem. There Jesus will present himself as Messiah but in terms which are not congenial to the nationalistic aspirations of many of his contemporaries.

Like the tax collector in the Temple, the poor blind man can only cry for *mercy.* He presents no claim on God based on his own achievements. Is the rebuke of the blind man an expression of the same attitude shown toward the children by the disciples (18:15)? He is also one of the world's little people, too insignificant to merit attention during these crucial hours preceding the fateful entrance into Jerusalem. On the other hand, the command to silence may indicate that the title *Son of David* has dangerous revolutionary and political overtones. It could be misinterpreted easily in these tense days of inflamed passions.

Whatever the case, Jesus attends the poor man's cry, just as he consistently gave attention to little people. The beggar is required to define precisely his desires. In his reply we note once again the use of *Lord*, the prominent post-resurrection title of Jesus so often found in Luke. The man's request is based on an implicit faith in Jesus' mastery over the forces that have made him blind—a confidence that is justified in the cure that follows. *Faith*, a grain of which can uproot trees (17:6), has made him *well*. The verb "to make well," ambiguous in Greek, can refer to physical healing as well as salvation. Faith is not the power that heals, but it is the receptivity that has caused the power of God to be brought to bear on his problems. This reference to the blind man's faith as well as his subsequent act of discipleship (he *followed* Jesus) indicates that he was *made . . . well* of both physical and spiritual blindness. Both the healed man and the people recognize the cure as an act of *God*, the correct interpretation of such events.

This is the last of the miracles of healing performed by Jesus and understood as messianic signs in the Synoptic material. In the light of the messianic program embraced by Jesus at the beginning of his ministry, it is an especially appropriate sign to come toward its end (cf. 4:18–19).

(3) The Conversion of Zacchaeus (19:1–10)

¹ He entered Jericho and was passing through. ² And there was a man named Zacchaeus; he was a chief tax collector, and rich. ³ And he sought to see who Jesus was, but could not, on account of the crowd, because he was small of stature. ⁴ So he ran on ahead and climbed up into a sycamore tree to see him, for he was to pass that way. ⁵ And when Jesus came to the place, he looked up and said to him, "Zacchaeus, make haste and come down; for I must stay at your house today." ⁶ So he made haste and came down, and received him joyfully. ⁷ And when they saw it they all mur-

mured, "He has gone in to be the guest of a man who is a sinner." ⁸ And Zacchaeus stood and said to the Lord, "Behold, Lord, the half of my goods I give to the poor; and if I have defrauded any one of anything, I restore it fourfold." ⁹ And Jesus said to him, "Today salvation has come to this house, since he also is a son of Abraham. ¹⁰ For the Son of man came to seek and to save the lost."

References to the entourage accompanying Jesus in the preceding episode (18:35–43) set the stage for the narrative of Jesus' encounter with *Zacchaeus*, found only in Luke. *Jericho* was an important city on the border of Judea some 15 miles northeast of Jerusalem. Not only did the commerce from the east pass through this city, but it was also the center of a fertile agricultural region, noted especially for its palm and balsam groves. Because of its warmer climate the Herods used Jericho as their winter capital. Their numerous construction projects in the city during this period were patterned after Roman architecture.

Zacchaeus, therefore, had an important post which must have paid handsomely. *Chief tax collector* is a position about which nothing is known, but we may surmise that he was the head of a district with a number of subordinate collectors responsible to him. Personal and property taxes were collected directly by the Roman government; but customs on goods were farmed out, a system which gave rise to unlimited opportunities of exploitation. In spite of the fact that his name means pure or righteous one, Zacchaeus probably was guilty of the evils common to his profession.

The circumstances leading up to the remarkable meeting with Jesus are described. The *crowd* is huge, no doubt getting larger all the time as other pilgrims on their way to celebrate the Passover in Jerusalem are attracted to it. Zacchaeus is too short to see over the crowd, which is so tightly pressed around Jesus that he cannot penetrate it. No one would be likely to make way for a hated tax collector. In order to be able to see Jesus, the little man runs along the main route through the city until he gets ahead of the crowd. He climbs up into a *sycamore tree* so as to secure a guaranteed vantage point, for had he remained on the ground he might have been shoved out of the way by the pressure of the throng. The sycamore, a tree which produced a type of fig used as food by the poor, was easy to climb because of its large, low-hanging branches.

In the circumstances Jesus' acceptance of and identification with the despised Zacchaeus constitute a bold, public act. No other story gives more vivid evidence of the remarkable liberty exercised by Jesus in his association with people. Where the welfare of a man was at stake, he ignored all the taboos and social protocol. Not only does he recognize and speak to Zacchaeus but he chooses to make the house of an unclean man his rest stop, thereby shocking all the religious people in the crowd.

Zacchaeus' eager and joyful response to the totally unexpected turn of events is understandable. No self-respecting Jew would have anything to do with him. None would greet him or extend the basic courtesies, much less offer warmth and friendship. Then along comes this man who speaks to him without censure, declaring in front of all the people that he is going to the tax collector's house.

Acceptance of the "outsider" involves identification with him to the extent that one becomes the target of the hostility and abuse heaped on him: *they all murmured.* Jesus' acceptance of Zacchaeus was unconditional. He did not say: "If you will give up your job and stop doing the things that make it costly for me to associate with you, I will go to your house."

Under the impact of unconditional acceptance by Jesus, a transformation is worked in the life of Zacchaeus. The sign of that transformation is a radical change in his attitude toward wealth. It is no longer his god. *Half* of his property will be given to the *poor* (cf. 12:33). The rest will be used to right the wrongs that he has committed. *If I have defrauded* does not imply the possible innocence of Zacchaeus of

such wrongs. The meaning is: "In those cases in which I have defrauded." When a person who unjustly acquired the property of another took the initiative in recognizing and confessing his wrong, he was required to return the property plus one-fifth of its value as compensation (Lev. 6:5; Num. 5:7). But Zacchaeus goes far beyond this in a voluntary decision to give the compensation imposed for stealing a sheep, *fourfold* restitution (Ex. 22:1; 2 Sam. 12:6).

The reply of Jesus is more appropriately addressed to the attitude of the critics than to the declaration of Zacchaeus. The meaning of Jesus' entrance into his house is given in the words *salvation has come to this house.* Just as the mighty acts of Jesus were concrete demonstrations of God's power, so also were his acts of acceptance and grace concrete expressions of God's salvation. The clause *since he also is a son of Abraham* does not make race the basis of Zacchaeus' salvation. The explanation of the remark is v. 10. Although the tax collector is a son of Abraham, he is a despised outsider among his people, the kind of person that Jesus came seeking. The *lost* are the tax-gatherers and prostitutes. They are also the multitudes of people who did not live up to the religious demands of the traditions. They were excluded from the inner circle of the religious community, objects of scorn and deprecation. As the shepherd goes after the lost sheep, so does Jesus also seek out these lost, neglected sons of Abraham. It is with just such people that he lays the foundation of the new Israel.

(4) The Ten Pounds (19:11–27)

11 As they heard these things, he proceeded to tell a parable, because he was near to Jerusalem, and because they supposed that the kingdom of God was to appear immediately. 12 He said therefore, "A nobleman went into a far country to receive kingly power and then return. 13 Calling ten of his servants, he gave them ten pounds, and said to them, 'Trade with these till I come.' 14 But his citizens hated him and sent an embassy after him, saying, 'We do not want this man to reign over us.' 15 When he returned, having received the

kingly power, he commanded these servants, to whom he had given the money, to be called to him, that he might know what they had gained by trading. [16] The first came before him, saying, 'Lord, your pound has made ten pounds more.' [17] And he said to him, 'Well done, good servant! Because you have been faithful in a very little, you shall have authority over ten cities.' [18] And the second came, saying, 'Lord, your pound has made five pounds.' [19] And he said to him, 'And you are to be over five cities.' [20] Then another came, saying, 'Lord, here is your pound, which I kept laid away in a napkin; [21] for I was afraid of you, because you are a severe man; you take up what you did not lay down, and reap what you did not sow.' [22] He said to him, 'I will condemn you out of your own mouth, you wicked servant! You knew that I was a severe man, taking up what I did not lay down and reaping what I did not sow? [23] Why then did you not put my money into the bank, and at my coming I should have collected it with interest?' [24] And he said to those who stood by, 'Take the pound from him, and give it to him who has the ten pounds.' [25] (And they said to him, 'Lord, he has ten pounds!') [26] 'I tell you, that to every one who has will more be given; but from him who has not, even what he has will be taken away. [27] But as for these enemies of mine, who did not want me to reign over them, bring them here and slay them before me.' "

As they draw near Jerusalem, the disciples' expectation that the kingdom will be ushered in after they arrive continues to gain in intensity. They anticipate the Parousia rather than the crucifixion, indicating that they have not yet perceived the true course of redemptive history. Theirs is a "wrong conception of both Christology and eschatology" (Conzelmann, p. 74). The request of the sons of Zebedee, omitted by Luke, is further evidence that the disciples associated their arrival in Jerusalem with the coming of the kingdom (Mark 10:35–45). In Luke's Gospel the fact and purpose of the interim between Jesus' ministry and the Parousia are stressed as a corrective to the expectations of an immediate Parousia held by contemporary Christians. In the story three points about this subject are made: (1) There will be an interim; (2) the interim is a time of testing for the disciples; (3) there will be a time of reckoning, i.e., a Parousia.

Luke's parable is similar to the parable of the talents contained in Matthew, which also is given an eschatological application (Matt. 25:14–30). There are, however, many differences. The Lukan parable is more complex and cumbersome, largely because it brings together two motifs: the responsibility of the disciples in the period prior to the Parousia and the fearful consequences attendant on the Jewish rejection of Jesus. Scholars have long suggested that to a parable about the responsibility of servants to an absent lord has been fused an allegory about a king who was rejected by his subjects.

This conjecture is not required, because the two themes of the story are closely related. Jerusalem is not the city where the kingdom will be inaugurated but the place where it is to be rejected. As a result of this rejection the doom of Jerusalem is sealed. It will be destroyed. But this destruction, which is a consequence of the city's failure to accept her king, is not to be associated with the events of the end. This is a significant chain of thought in the third Gospel.

The parable of the pounds probably incorporates historical reminiscences from the experiences of Archelaus. Although named in Herod's will to the most important part of his kingdom and to the title of king, Archelaus was opposed by a Jewish embassy in Rome. The emperor confirmed Herod's will but named him tetrarch. Archelaus returned to take over a rebellious territory which he was able to rule for only ten years.

It may well be, therefore, that the pattern for the *nobleman* is Archelaus and the *far country* is Rome. Before his departure the nobleman gives one *pound*, approximately 20 to 25 dollars, to each of *ten . . . servants*. They are to prove their devotion and ability by the use of this small sum (see 16:10) in the master's absence. Because he travels to a far country, a long and indefinite period will elapse prior to his return.

The second group of people now come

into the picture. They are the *citizens* who reject the rule of the nobleman. In them we have a picture of the Jewish people who reject Jesus their King.

Upon his return the nobleman first has a reckoning with his *servants*. We are told of only three, who are representatives of the whole group. The first one has been very successful, but in his modest reply he does not boast of his own industry or ingenuity. It is his master's *pound* that has earned *ten* more. Nevertheless, the nobleman's praise of his servant is effusive. Because he has proved himself *in a very little*, he will now be able to bear a large responsibility in the nobleman's rule. Perhaps the second possesses less talent or is less industrious, but he also has been successful. He is able to present *five* additional pounds to his lord. He also is given a proportionate share in the responsibilities of the kingdom.

In contrast to the previous servants, the third has to make quite a speech to justify his failure to match the achievements of the others. He can claim only the accomplishment of having faithfully and carefully guarded what his master gave to him. He is similar to the legalists, the teachers who have built a fence around the Law, carefully guarding it against encroachment. But they have also decisively prevented God's gifts from bearing their intended fruit in the world. The man's problem is his concept of his master, whom he pictures as a hard, unjust man. If the servant of God has a similar concept of his Lord, he too will be so overly fearful of violating the "don'ts" that he will not have the liberty to engage in a life of joyous, creative service.

The ruler points out the lack of logic in his servant's defense. If his concept of his master was what he had described, intelligence should have dictated another course of action. The money would have been just as safe with bankers as it was in his *napkin*. In addition it would have collected *interest*, i.e., harvested what the owner had not sown.

Because of his failure the servant is deprived of the little that had been entrusted

to him. Verse 25 may be intended as an exclamation from those who listen to Jesus' story, and who protest involuntarily the ruler's severe decision. Or it may be a part of the story, an exclamation from members of the court. There is also the possibility that this verse is an interpolation into the text, because it is omitted by important textual witnesses. The master's decision is in accord with a basic principle which presupposes each person's responsibility for the capacities and opportunities which are given to him. Their faithful use will open up greater possibilities of service and trust. But people who do not put their gifts to the proper use will lose them.

Now the parable shifts to the nobleman's decision about his rebellious subjects. Their punishment is similar to the terrible fate meted out to rebels by offended Oriental monarchs. This is an allegorical reference to the destruction of Jerusalem, which is seen as the fearful consequence resulting from Israel's rejection of her King. A terrible slaughter of its inhabitants followed the fall of the capital to the merciless legions commanded by Titus.

VI. The Ministry in Jerusalem (19:28— 23:56)

1. Jesus' Presentation of His Messianic Claims (19:28–48)

(1) The Approach to Jerusalem (19:28– 40)

28 And when he had said this, he went on ahead, going up to Jerusalem. 29 When he drew near to Bethphage and Bethany, at the mount that is called Olivet, he sent two of the disciples, 30 saying, "Go into the village opposite, where on entering you will find a colt tied, on which no one has ever yet sat; untie it and bring it here. 31 If any one asks you, 'Why are you untying it?' you shall say this, 'The Lord has need of it.'" 32 So those who were sent went away and found it as he had told them. 33 And as they were untying the colt, its owners said to them, "Why are you untying the colt?" 34 And they said, "The Lord has need of it." 35 And they brought it to Jesus, and throwing their garments on the colt they set Jesus upon it. 36 And as he rode along, they spread their garments on the road. 37 As he was now draw-

ing near, at the descent of the Mount of Olives, the whole multitude of the disciples began to rejoice and praise God with a loud voice for all the mighty works that they had seen, [38] saying, "Blessed is the King who comes in the name of the Lord! Peace in heaven and glory in the highest!" [39] And some of the Pharisees in the multitude said to him, "Teacher, rebuke your disciples." [40] He answered, "I tell you, if these were silent, the very stones would cry out."

We are now carried into a new phase of Jesus' experiences, the last days prior to his crucifixion. For his account of the events which occurred in these last days Luke is primarily dependent on Mark.

After coming to grips with the false hopes raised by the pilgrimage to Jerusalem, Jesus takes up his journey again, leading the large crowd of followers toward the city. No matter what the direction from which he approached it, the traveler was always thought of as *going up to Jerusalem.* Away from Jerusalem was always down. *Bethphage,* whose exact location is unknown, was probably east of *Bethany,* a village about one and a half miles east of Jerusalem. According to John, Bethany was the home of Lazarus and his sisters, Martha and Mary (John 11:1). In the vicinity of these two villages Jesus pauses until the disciples can procure the *colt* on which he will complete his journey to Jerusalem.

The *village* where the *colt* is to be found is unnamed. Only an animal that had never been used as a beast of burden was considered suitable for sacred purposes (Num. 19:2; 1 Sam. 6:7). A *colt* ridden by no other person must be used for the climactic entrance of Israel's King into the capital city. Prior arrangements for the animal may have been made by Jesus. But the passage also may imply supernatural knowledge, as indeed is indicated in v. 32. The experience of the disciples who procure the animal corresponds exactly to what they expected as a result of the instructions of Jesus. Their simple reply to the owner's question seems to satisfy him. Only in Mark 11:3, the parallel to v. 31, do we find the same use of the title *Lord* encountered so often in Luke.

As David's ministers placed Solomon on his father's mule for his royal procession (1 Kings 1:33), so now do the disciples place another and greater Son of David on a colt for his royal entry into Jerusalem. As on another occasion Israelites paved the path of the newly anointed Jehu with their own garments and hailed him as king (2 Kings 9:13), so also do these Israelites pave the path of their King whom they now acclaim. Luke omits the reference to spreading branches along the road (Mark 11:8; Matt. 21:8).

Both he and Mark omit the citation from Zechariah 9:9 (cf. Matt. 21:5): "Lo, your king comes to you; triumphant and victorious is he, humble and riding on an ass, on a colt the foal of an ass." Nevertheless, both understood that Jesus entered Jerusalem in a manner that fulfilled this prophecy. By so doing Jesus presents his claim to Israel: he is Israel's King-Messiah. But he does so in a way that repudiates the militaristic, nationalistic ambitions which were projected on the Messiah. Both his humility and his mission of peace are symbolized by the animal on which he, God's Anointed, rides. Luke's description of Jesus' approach to Jerusalem differs from that of the parallels because he sets the stage for the lament over Jerusalem, which is found only in the third Gospel. The party is described as coming to the top of the *Mount of Olives,* from where they catch their first glimpse of the city of Jerusalem. Here the crowd begins to burst out in praises to God. *All the mighty works* were those powerful acts of Jesus that disclosed to perceptive people that in him the power of the kingdom was at work in the world.

The shout of the multitude contains a part of Psalm 118:26, a psalm that was sung as pilgrims entered the Temple during the feast of the Tabernacles. It is now used in the coronation procession of the messianic *King,* "the coming one" (see on 3:16). By using *The King, who comes in the name of the Lord* instead of "the kingdom of our father David that is coming" (Mark 11:10), Luke softens the possible revolutionary implications of the crowd's acclamation. The conclusion is similar to the song of the angelic choir which announced Jesus' birth (2:14). *Peace in heaven* is the guarantee of the triumph of peace in the universe. In Jesus' obedient submission to God's redemptive purposes is the seed of the triumph of God over the forces of evil and disintegration in the world. For "hosanna" (Mark 11:10) Luke has *glory* (*doxa*), a word of praise which is more understandable to Gentile readers. There is no doubt but that the company with which Jesus enters Jerusalem understood at least in part the meaning of his entrance and thought of him as Messiah.

In Luke alone do we find the objection voiced by the *Pharisees*. The people hail Jesus as *King*. The Pharisees persist in calling him *teacher*. An exaggerated and politically volatile enthusiasm such as that generated in the people surrounding Jesus is from their point of view both wrong and dangerous. They consider it to be his responsibility to stop it. But Jesus instead rebukes the Pharisees. So appropriate is the acclamation by his followers that the *stones* would raise the same chorus were there no human voices to do it. He implies that God would use stones before he would turn to the Pharisees (cf. 3:8)!

(2) The Lament over Jerusalem (19:41–44)

⁴¹ And when he drew near and saw the city he wept over it, ⁴² saying, "Would that even today you knew the things that make for peace! But now they are hid from your eyes. ⁴³ For the days shall come upon you, when your enemies will cast up a bank about you and surround you, and hem you in on every side, ⁴⁴ and dash you to the ground, you and your children within you, and they will not leave one stone upon another in you; because you did not know the time of your visitation."

As the singing crowd comes to the top of the mountain, they catch their first glimpse of the *city*. The sight of Jerusalem brings home to Jesus with sudden force the tragedy which hangs over it. *Wept* is a strong verb which is used to describe the heart-broken sobbing of people at a funeral (e.g., 7:13,32; 8:52). The attitude of Jesus toward the rebellious city is vastly different from that of the cruel despot toward his subjects as depicted in the parable in v. 27.

Jerusalem, which means "mount of peace," is pursuing a course that leads to inevitable confrontation with the power of Rome. Instead of embracing Jesus and his interpretation of the kingdom of God, the Jews will attempt to make their desires for a kingdom become a reality through the force of arms. The door of opportunity opens, but it also closes with grim finality. The unseeing eyes of the people fail to perceive that for a little while they have had in their midst the only one who can bring *peace*.

A prediction of the siege and destruction of Jerusalem is given in vv. 43–44. Many scholars assume that it was influenced by the actual events, which had already taken place before Luke was written. There is nothing in the prediction, however, that makes this conclusion necessary. It is no more specific than similar predictions by the prophets that the Babylonians would destroy Jerusalem. It is a rather general statement based on a knowledge of current military tactics on the one hand, and an awareness of the overwhelming power of Rome on the other. The rejection of Jesus was due in part to a blind dedication to the kind of messianic nationalism that was leading to eventual clash with Rome which would inevitably issue in the total destruction of Jerusalem.

The only way that a fanatically defended Jerusalem could be taken was by a long siege. Cut off from supplies and surrounded by a superior force that could wait patiently for the inevitable, sooner or later the city would be overwhelmed. *Dash you to the ground* can also mean "lay you level with the ground," i.e., destroy you. The inhabitants of Jerusalem are called her *children* (cf. 23:28). Jerusalem's fate is attributed to her failure to see that in Jesus, God had visited his people and offered them salvation. Their *time* (*kairos*) of visitation came and went without their being aware of it.

(3) The Cleansing of the Temple (19:45–48)

⁴⁵ And he entered the temple and began to drive out those who sold, ⁴⁶ saying to them, "It is written, 'My house shall be a house of prayer'; but you have made it a den of robbers."
⁴⁷ And he was teaching daily in the temple. The chief priests and the scribes and the principal men of the people sought to destroy him; ⁴⁸ but they did not find anything they could do, for all the people hung upon his words.

Several differences between Mark and Luke appear at this point (cf. Mark 11:11–25). In Luke the cleansing of the Temple follows immediately on the account of the triumphal entry. There is no mention of the lodging in Bethany, of the fruitless fig tree, nor of the associated teachings. Also the cleansing of the Temple, told by Luke in only 25 words, greatly abbreviates Mark's account of 60 words.

Luke does not say that Jesus entered the city at this time (cf. Mark 11:11,15; Matt. 21:10). Reference is made only to his activities at the Temple. A profitable commercial enterprise had developed there to supply what the worshipers required to fulfill their religious obligations. Animals and fowls that met the ritual requirements were sold in the Court of the Gentiles for use in the sacrifices. Travelers who came from other countries could exchange their foreign money for the half-shekel needed by male Jews to pay the Temple tax (Mark 11:15b—omitted by Luke). Since there was a heavy demand for these goods and services, especially during feasts, the Temple authorities were operating what must have been a very profitable concession. Luke omits the rather violent scene which Mark describes. But the traders were not intimidated by the physical force of a lone man. It was rather the power of his righteous anger and the impact of his lordship over men coupled with a sense of their own guilt that brought at least a temporary halt in their traffic. The words of Jesus are

based on a combination of Isaiah 56:7 and Jeremiah 7:11. The Temple is no longer the *house* of God; it is now a *den of thieves,* where people use religion for commercial exploitation. The whole episode is probably to be taken as a fulfillment of Malachi 3:1: "And the Lord whom you seek will suddenly come to his temple."

After cleansing the Temple, Jesus uses it for his last days of teaching (cf. Conzelmann, pp. 75–78). But this occupation is only a temporary interlude which does not alter the fact that it, along with the city, is destined for destruction. *Teaching daily* implies a longer ministry in Jerusalem than the time assigned to it in the traditional Passion Week. This is also implied in Luke's source, where Jesus says: "Day after day I was with you in the temple teaching" (Mark 14:49).

Jesus' drastic action in the Temple was a direct affront to the high priestly family and to the Sadducees whose power base was the Temple and the Sanhedrin. *Chief priests, scribes,* and *principal men* are the various groups from which the Sanhedrin's seventy members were drawn. The high priest was the presiding officer of this the highest Jewish court and governing body. Now the power structure is united in the determination to destroy Jesus. The leaders are convinced that they must pick up the gauntlet which Jesus has thrown down. There is, however, one major obstacle to their design. Jesus is extremely popular with the *people.* They are no longer susceptible to the counsel of their leaders because of their attraction to Jesus. This cleavage between the Jewish leadership and the people is a characteristic aspect of Luke's Gospel.

2. Controversies in the Temple (20:1—21:4)

(1) The Question of Authority (20:1–8)

¹ One day, as he was teaching the people in the temple and preaching the gospel, the chief priests and the scribes with the elders came up ² and said to him, "Tell us by what authority you do these things, or who it is that gave you

this authority." ³ He answered them, "I also will ask you a question; now tell me, ⁴ Was the baptism of John from heaven or from men?" ⁵ And they discussed it with one another, saying, "If we say, 'From heaven,' he will say, 'Why did you not believe him?' ⁶ But if we say, 'From men,' all the people will stone us; for they are convinced that John was a prophet." ⁷ So they answered that they did not know whence it was. ⁸ And Jesus said to them, "Neither will I tell you by what authority I do these things."

In Mark the question about Jesus' authority is related closely to the measures which he took to halt commercial activities in the Temple area (Mark 11:27–33). By the interposition of the editorial comment in v. 1, Luke implies that the question was provoked by Jesus' teaching and preaching activities in the Temple, i.e., by the way he had taken charge of it and was conducting himself as one who had official sanction for his activities. These are described as *teaching* and *preaching the gospel*. The latter translates a verb which means to proclaim good news. In this phase of his ministry Jesus performs no more mighty works. He chooses to present himself to Jerusalem's inhabitants in ways that speak of the fulfillment of Israel's messianic expectations. As Messiah he approached the city. As Messiah he cleansed and took charge of the Temple. Now as Messiah he teaches the *people* the true meaning of the Law and the prophets and proclaims to them the good news of the coming kingdom.

Jesus is challenged by those who represent Israel's highest official authority, the members of the Sanhedrin, composed of *chief priests, scribes,* and *elders.* After the deposition of Archelaus (A.D. 6), Judea was made part of an imperial province ruled over by a governor. The governor, Pontius Pilate at this time, was responsible primarily for maintaining order and collecting taxes. Internal affairs were largely left to the jurisdiction of the Sanhedrin, composed of 71 (70?) members, including the high priest, the presiding officer. Some of these were religious leaders, i.e., priests and scribes; others were leading Jewish citizens or *elders.*

In his teaching ministry in the Temple Jesus assumed the place of the ordained rabbis without the consent of Temple authorities or the Sanhedrin. He was able to do this temporarily because the people, impervious to constituted authority, were supporting him. Thus the authority and role of the Sanhedrin in Jewish life was brought under specific challenge. The leaders could not afford to let this challenge go unheeded and so rose to the attack.

Two questions are asked, meaning: (1) "What is the nature of your authority?" and (2) "Who is its source?" Clearly the source was not an official one.

In good rabbinic method a question is often answered with a question. Jesus will not answer their question in a vacuum. His work and teaching must be placed in the context of recent redemptive history. Any discussion about his authority must proceed from a consideration of the authority of *John.* His ministry is related to John's, since he had accepted John's baptism and had been the beneficiary of John's witness. Both had proclaimed the kingdom of God. The identity of their message is clearer in Mark and Matthew than in Luke where more of a distinction between John and Jesus is made (cf. Mark 1:14; Matt. 3:1; 4:17). An adequate appraisal of John's ministry involves a recognition of the continuity between him and Jesus.

John had appeared, calling Jews to repentance and baptizing them in preparation for the coming crisis. The question is: What authority did he have to do such a thing? *From heaven* means from God. Consequently, the Jewish leaders are called on to make a public judgment. Did John, who also acted in no official capacity and without official sanction, have a higher authority, that is, God's? Or did he act on an independent, and therefore unacceptable, human decision?

Now the situation is suddenly reversed; the religious leaders, who are expected to give authoritative answers to such queries, are put in an untenable situation. They huddle to discuss the three possible alternatives. They can acknowledge that John's authority was divine, the authority of the prophet rather than the official sanction of the religious institution. But they had refused to heed his message and accept his baptism. So one question will only lead to another embarrassing one: *Why did you not believe him?* Another option is to deny John's divine authority, which in effect they had done by refusing to heed his call to repentance. But this will get them, instead of Jesus, into trouble with the people. Luke explicitly states that they were afraid of being stoned (cf. Mark 11:32). In public opinion John was a *prophet*, which involved the belief that he was "sent from God" (John 1:6). The leaders choose the third option. Being unwilling to face up to the question, they confess ignorance. By so doing, they make further discussion of the question which they had raised impossible.

(2) The Rebellious Tenants (20:9–18)

9 And he began to tell the people this parable: "A man planted a vineyard, and let it out to tenants, and went into another country for a long while. 10 When the time came, he sent a servant to the tenants, that they should give him some of the fruit of the vineyard; but the tenants beat him, and sent him away empty-handed. 11 And he sent another servant; him also they beat and treated shamefully, and sent him away empty-handed. 12 And he sent yet a third; this one they wounded and cast out. 13 Then the owner of the vineyard said, 'What shall I do? I will send my beloved son; it may be they will respect him.' 14 But when the tenants saw him, they said to themselves, 'This is the heir; let us kill him, that the inheritance may be ours.' 15 And they cast him out of the vineyard and killed him. What then will the owner of the vineyard do to them? 16 He will come and destroy those tenants, and give the vineyard to others." When they heard this, they said, "God forbid!" 17 But he looked at them and said, "What then is this that is written:
'The very stone which the builders rejected
    has become the head of the corner?'
18 Every one who falls on that stone will be broken to pieces; but when it falls on any one it will crush him."

Luke follows Mark's order in placing the parable of the rebellious tenants after the discussion about Jesus' authority (Mark 12: 1–12). There is a relationship between the parable and the song of the vineyard of Isaiah 5:1–7. From the time of Isaiah the *vineyard* was a symbol for Israel. Luke omits the Markan details which describe the extent of the owner's initial investment in time and effort (cf. Mark 12:1). It appears that he handed over the vineyard to *tenants* as an act of trust, because he then began a journey which took him away, as Luke adds, *for a long while.* When the *time came*—i.e., after the *fruit of the vineyard,* the wine, had been prepared—he sent servants to collect his share of the product of his vineyard.

The parable is more of an allegory than the others which we have considered. Mistreated prophets are represented by the mistreated servants. Luke mentions only three where Mark (12:5) speaks of "many others." In Mark the third servant in addition to others is killed. In Luke only the son is slain. Thus the parable in Luke builds to a climax. Each servant is treated more shamefully than the first, leading up to the fourth and climactic deed, the murder of the son. By the use of a literary method reminiscent of the repetition in Amos of the phrase: "For three transgressions . . . and for four" (Amos 1:3, etc.), the stage is set for the declaration that the time of judgment has arrived.

Contrary to the expectations of the owner, the tenants do not *respect* his son. *Beloved son* may intentionally call to mind the words at the baptism of Jesus (3:22). The detail which places the son's death outside the vineyard makes Luke's story correspond more closely to the actual experience of Jesus than does the Markan parallel. Israel's sin in rejecting Jesus is depicted as the renunciation of God's sovereignty over Israel. The religious leaders to whom God had entrusted his people have betrayed their stewardship and attempted to shut God out of his own vineyard.

The owner of the vineyard destroys the usurping tenants and gives their place to others. The point is not lost on the hearers who exclaim *God forbid,* literally, "may it not happen." This protest, missing from Mark, provides a transition from the story to the scriptural quotation (Psalm 118:22). This psalm was probably a frequently used messianic proof text in the early church. Instead of continuing the quotation with the addition of Psalm 118:23, which Mark gives, Luke has a statement reminiscent of Daniel 2:34,44, and Isaiah 8:14. The figure is now changed, and God's people are thought of as a temple rather than a vineyard. The stone that is rejected is Jesus, who becomes the *head of the corner* of a new edifice. But the stone is also a stone of judgment. It is not susceptible to destruction by its enemies. All efforts against the stone shatter to *pieces.* Furthermore, it falls in judgment on those who reject it. The verb rendered *crush* means primarily to winnow, but early versions support the RSV translation.

(3) *The Question of Tribute (20:19–26)*

¹⁹ The scribes and the chief priests tried to lay hands on him at that very hour, but they feared the people; for they perceived that he had told this parable against them. ²⁰ So they watched him, and sent spies, who pretended to be sincere, that they might take hold of what he said, so as to deliver him up to the authority and jurisdiction of the governor. ²¹ They asked him, "Teacher, we know that you speak and teach rightly, and show no partiality, but truly teach the way of God. ²² Is it lawful for us to give tribute to Caesar, or not?" ²³ But he perceived their craftiness, and said to them, ²⁴ "Show me a coin. Whose likeness and inscription has it?" They said, "Caesar's." ²⁵ He said to them, "Then render to Caesar the things that are Caesar's, and to God the things that are God's." ²⁶ And they were not able in the presence of the people to catch him by what he said; but marveling at his answer they were silent.

So infuriated are the official representatives of Judaism by the implications of the preceding parable that they are kept from seizing Jesus on the spot only by fear of the *people.* The picture of these last days as presented in Luke is a very dramatic one. On the one side is Jesus, a lone man who has assumed control of Israel's central religious institution. On the other side are the members of the Sanhedrin, infuriated but wary. In between are the people—volatile, unpredictable, but for the moment throwing the weight of their protection around Jesus.

In this situation his enemies determine on a course that they hope will cause Jesus to give some grounds for a charge of treason against Roman rule. Rather than openly attacking him, they send agents who plant themselves in his audience in order to raise provocative questions under the guise of a sincere desire for guidance and a respect for his teaching. The editorial introduction to this episode (v. 20) lays the foundation for the subsequent trial of Jesus where he is in fact accused of hostility to the emperor, a charge which Luke proves by this narrative to be false (cf. on 23:2). It should be noted that Luke does not here or elsewhere mention the Herodians (cf. Mark 12:13).

The flattery of the *spies* has the purpose of influencing Jesus to make bold statements against the government. *Show no partiality* means that he does not allow power or position to influence him. *The way of God* is the way that a person should live as delineated by the will of God. They hope that his loyalty to God will cause him to take a position which may be interpreted as disloyalty to the emperor.

Tribute is the personal, direct tax required by the Roman government of the citizens of Palestine. It was a constant, inflammatory reminder to them of their subjugation by a foreign power. In A.D. 6 when a census was ordered for the purpose of composing the tax rolls, it provoked an abortive revolt led by Judas of Galilee. The question of tribute was, therefore, a burning issue among the people.

Characteristically, Luke's story in comparison to Mark's is somewhat abbreviated, which makes it less dramatic. In response to Jesus' demand, one of his audience produces a silver denarius, the coin with which the tax was paid. The point is that they themselves were carrying coins that bore Caesar's image. To this extent, therefore, they were submitting to Caesar's rule (Tiberius) and accepting its benefits. The prerogative of the ruler of a region was the minting and distribution of coins, which were considered by ancient practice to belong to him. Consequently, the Jewish people are using coins that really belong to the emperor. If he asks for one of them, he is only requesting what rightfully belongs to him. The principle is clear: *render,* or better, give back, *to Caesar* what belongs to him.

But he does not stop there. The use of coins or of anything else inscribed with images was shunned by Jews as a violation of the Second Commandment. Emperor worship was already widely practiced in the East. For this reason the image of Caesar on his coins had a religious connotation. To some it was the image of a god (cf. Leaney, pp. 252 ff.). Therefore, Jesus warns against giving to Caesar the worship and service that belong only to God.

Because Jesus had so little to say directly about the state, this one affirmation has been made to bear an enormous weight of ideas and interpretations. He certainly never intended that life should be divided into two spheres, the secular and the spiritual. Jesus' teachings emphasize that God is King over all. There are no autonomous areas where men can escape his ethical and moral demands. Caesar is to receive a coin, a mere pittance. But man must give his total life to God. God's will must be determinative in every decision in politics, economics, or personal morality.

Patently the spies fail in their efforts to trap Jesus. He has answered their question without identifying his mission with that of the radical nationalists. At the same time he has held up before all of them the basic truth of his message: God alone is really King.

(4) The Question of the Resurrection (20:27-40)

[27] There came to him some Sadducees, those who say that there is no resurrection, [28] and they asked him a question, saying, "Teacher, Moses wrote for us that if a man's brother dies, having a wife but no children, the man must take the wife and raise up children for his brother. [29] Now there were seven brothers; the first took a wife, and died without children; [30] and the second [31] and the third took her, and likewise all seven left no children and died. [32] Afterward the woman also died. [33] In the resurrection, therefore, whose wife will the woman be? For the seven had her as wife."

[34] And Jesus said to them, "The sons of this age marry and are given in marriage; [35] but those who are accounted worthy to attain to that age and to the resurrection from the dead neither marry nor are given in marriage, [36] for they cannot die any more, because they are equal to angels and are sons of God, being sons of the resurrection. [37] But that the dead are raised, even Moses showed, in the passage about the bush, where he calls the Lord the God of Abraham and the God of Isaac and the God of Jacob. [38] Now he is not God of the dead, but of the living; for all live to him." [39] And some of the scribes answered, "Teacher, you have spoken well." [40] For they no longer dared to ask him any question.

On the opposite end of the spectrum from the radical nationalists stood the Sadducees. Organized around the high priesthood, their base of power was the Temple and the Sanhedrin. In the absence of national independence the high priest, as presiding officer of the Sanhedrin, was the highest ranking Jewish political figure in the imperial province. To the Sanhedrin, as we have seen, Rome gave much of the responsibility for administering internal affairs of the province. Because they benefited from the status quo, the Sadducees were basically opposed to political change. They were also conservative religiously. They disagreed with many Pharisaic ideas on the grounds that they were innovations. Rejecting in toto the oral traditions, they accepted as their religious authority only the Pentateuch, in which they claimed to find no basis for belief in a resurrection.

The hypothetical situation which the Sadducees put to Jesus in an attempt to embarrass him must have been a commonly used ploy in their arguments with persons of the Pharisaic persuasion. The example, which is purposely carried to the point of absurdity, is based on the prescription for levirate marriage in Deuteronomy 25:5–10. The word is derived from *levir,* meaning brother. According to the Deuteronomic passage, the obligation applies to two brothers who live together. If one dies, the other is to cohabit with his widow. The first son of such a union bears the name of the deceased.

There is one significant difference between Luke and the Markan parallel (Mark 12:18–27). The third Gospel speaks of *those who are accounted worthy to attain . . . to the resurrection from the dead* (v. 35). In Mark's parallel we find "when they rise from the dead" (12:25). This difference is often interpreted as evidence that Luke's theology anticipates a resurrection of the just only. But dogmatic conclusions cannot be based on such meager hints (see on 14:14).

Jesus answers the Sadducees' riddle with a simple affirmation. Their question does not take into consideration the basic distinction between the two ages. Involved in the concept of the resurrection is also the belief that the resurrected person is transformed. Because of this, relationships in this age are not decisive in determining those of the coming age. After death the resurrected ones become a part of the heavenly host, equivalent to *angels.* Many see in this a reference to Enoch 15:6, in the passage which tells of the fallen angels. As participants in the coming age, these transformed persons are no longer mortal. Consequently, provisions, like levirate marriage, which arise to meet the circumstances brought on by mortality, do not apply to a situation that will not be affected by death. Since the population of heaven will not be decimated by death, marriage will not be a pertinent institution.

The categories of family and race are abolished in an existence in which all God's children are related to each other in the same way. The only family in the coming age is the family of God. There is only one Father, who is *God;* all others are *sons* or children. *Sons of the resurrection* is a Semi-

tism which means resurrected ones.

After answering their question, Jesus challenges the rejection of the resurrection by the Sadducees. He does it not by questioning their concept of authority but by questioning their interpretation of the Pentateuch, which they do accept as authoritative. In Exodus 3:6 the **Lord** (Yahweh) identifies himself as the **God of Abraham . . . Isaac and . . . Jacob.** This proves that these men, though they had died, were still alive at that time as resurrected servants of God. Otherwise the title Moses gave to God was a complete contradiction. To speak of a God of dead people is an absurdity.

Momentarily *some of the scribes* forget their hostility to Jesus in their glee over this discomfiture of their theological opponents. They compliment Jesus for an adroit defense of the resurrection in which he has turned the weapons of the Sadducees against them.

With this encounter Luke brings to a close the series of attempts on the part of Jesus' enemies to discredit him. In so doing he omits the question about the greatest commandment (Mark 12:28–34). But the introduction to the parable of the good Samaritan (10:27) bears strong similarities to the Markan passage. This may have induced the omission at this place.

(5) *The Question About the Messiah (20:41–44)*

41 But he said to them, "How can they say that the Christ is David's son? 42 For David himself says in the Book of Psalms,
'The Lord said to my Lord,
Sit at my right hand,
43 till I make thy enemies a stool for thy feet.'
44 David thus calls him Lord; so how is he his son?"

With his enemies put to rout by the sagacity of his replies to their loaded questions, Jesus now becomes the interrogator. He challenges the nationalistic messianic concept embodied in the popular understanding of the title *David's son.* The problem was not that people thought of the coming Messiah as David's son. **Christ,** "anointed one," is a transliteration of the Greek word which translates the Hebrew word Messiah. The early church, including Luke, also understood Jesus to be the son of David. But Jesus rejected the idea that the Messiah's role was to reestablish the Davidic dynasty in Jerusalem and vindicate the humiliated Jewish people by raising them to a position of supremacy over Gentile nations.

The point in the quotation from Psalm 110:1 is that the Messiah must be more than David's son, the heir to his throne. The statement the Lord (Yahweh) said to my Lord (the Christ) is used to prove that David thought of the Messiah as something more than a son. A man would hardly call his son my Lord. So not only is the Messiah David's son; he is also David's Lord.

(6) The Condemnation of the Scribes (20:45-47)

[45] And in the hearing of all the people he said to his disciples, [46] "Beware of the scribes, who like to go about in long robes, and love salutations in the market places and the best seats in the synagogues and the places of honor at feasts, [47] who devour widows' houses and for a pretense make long prayers. They will receive the greater condemnation."

Luke has already given another and longer criticism of the religious leaders derived from his Q material (11:37 ff.; cf. Matt. 23:13 ff.). This shorter passage is based on Mark 12:38-40. The introduction to the story, however, is Lukan. It tells that Jesus' warning against the scribes is directed to both the people and the disciples.

Desire for public recognition and unscrupulous greed are the sins with which Jesus charges the scribes. The prophetic note so prominent in the teaching of Jesus again surfaces here. A person's lack of concern for helpless, defenseless people is unmistakable proof that his religion is hollow mockery. No amount of religious activity can make this palatable to God.

The scribes are accused of devouring widow's houses. We are not told just how they did this. Perhaps they took advantage

of the widows' unquestioning faith in their religious leaders. Plummer suggests that they accepted "hospitality and rich presents from pious and weak women" (p. 474). This is a very common way of using religion to exploit others. On the other hand, the houses may have been security for loans and debts (Leaney, p. 256).

As is so often the case, chapter 21 makes an unfortunate division in material which belongs together. The condemnation of the scribes is intended to be seen in contrast to the following commendation of the widow, a representative of their helpless victims.

(7) The Commendation of the Widow (21:1-4)

[1] He looked up and saw the rich putting their gifts into the treasury; [2] and he saw a poor widow put in two copper coins. [3] And he said, "Truly I tell you, this poor widow has put in more than all of them; [4] for they all contributed out of their abundance, but she out of her poverty put in all the living that she had."

The criticism of the scribes is followed by the commendation of a widow. Jesus looked up because he was in the sitting position of a teacher. The treasury was a row of chests with trumpetlike openings into which the offerings were put. Among the rich who approached the treasury to cast in their handsome gifts was a poor widow, who must have seemed out of place in such company. She made a very insignificant offering of two copper coins, worth less than a penny.

Surprisingly, Jesus declares that her offering was of more value than the total contributions of all the others. They had contributed out of their abundance and were no worse off after they had contributed than before. By contrast, the coins given by the widow represented her total wealth. Her gift was a genuine expression of her faith that God in his providence would supply her future needs.

The rich had shown no such faith. They had not forfeited any of their financial security. At the same time, they believed that they had earned God's favor with an offering of money.

3. Teachings About the Events of the End (21:5–38)

(1) The Danger of Being Led Astray (21:5–9)

5 And as some spoke of the temple, how it was adorned with noble stones and offerings, he said, 6 "As for these things which you see, the days will come when there shall not be left here one stone upon another that will not be thrown down." 7 And they asked him, "Teacher, when will this be, and what will be the sign when this is about to take place?" 8 And he said, "Take heed that you are not led astray; for many will come in my name, saying, 'I am he!' and, 'The time is at hand!' Do not go after them. 9 And when you hear of wars and tumults, do not be terrified; for this must first take place, but the end will not be at once."

Mark attributes a direct statement about the Temple to one of the disciples, commenting that it was made as Jesus led the disciples from the edifice (13:1). In Luke *some* of the people in Jesus' audience call attention to the massiveness and beauty of the *temple*. The *offerings* were the "votive gifts" (Moffat) that various people, including King Herod and Caesar Augustus himself, had contributed to the Temple.

Herod the Great began what amounted to a reconstruction of the second Temple in 19 B.C. This third Temple, a complex of buildings covering some 13 acres on Mount Moriah, may not have been completely finished at the outbreak of the first Jewish-Roman War. Josephus informs us that the Temple was constructed of massive blocks of white marble, which from a distance looked like a gleaming, snowcapped mountain peak. It was ornamented with gold, precious stones, and costly tapestries.

Jesus replies to the admiring comments about this Temple with a prediction that the imposing edifice which possessed such an air of permanency would one day be reduced to rubble. In A.D. 70 the Romans put the Temple to the torch and subsequently under Caesar's orders leveled its walls in their systematic demolition of the city. When they had finished, the place where Israel's proud capital once stood was

an uninhabited wasteland (Josephus, *Wars* 7, 1, 1–3). Just as Jeremiah had foreseen the destruction of the first Temple as the result of Judah's disastrous foreign policy (26:6), so did Jesus anticipate that Herod's Temple would suffer the same fate.

Mark tells us that Peter, James, John, and Andrew questioned Jesus about his prediction "as he sat on the Mount of Olives opposite the temple" where the impressive structure was in full view (13:3). The Temple, however, is the Lukan setting for all of Jesus' teaching activities during these last days. There unidentified persons ask him when the predicted destruction will take place and how they will be able to anticipate it. They presuppose that a *sign* will be given that will put those who recognize it on the alert for the impending occurrence. Evidently the destruction of the Temple is presumed to be an eschatological event closely associated with the end-time.

From Jesus comes first of all a word of warning. His hearers are not to be susceptible victims of false expectations. As he does also in Mark, Jesus here issues a caution against messianic pretenders.[33] The most famous Jewish claimant to the title in subsequent history was Bar Cochba who, acclaimed as messiah by no less a person than Rabbi Akiba, led the Jews in their last abortive rebellion against Rome (A.D. 132–135). Luke also contains Jesus' warning against attempts to fix a specific time for the end, which is not found in Mark. The unexpected, sudden nature of the Parousia is a consistent eschatological motif in the third Gospel.

Wars and *tumults* are not to be interpreted as signs of an imminent *end* of the age. *Tumults* denotes civil disturbances of the type that afflicted the Roman Empire

---

[33] Manson (p. 231) argues that "persons who come in Jesus' name must be Christians claiming his authority." He removes the difficulty in the way of this interpretation with the suggestion that "I am he" means "the Messiah has come." The warning in this case would be against a premature proclamation of the Parousia. This interpretation has much merit.

from the death of Nero until the accession of Vespasius (A.D. 68). This word is found in Luke instead of Mark's "rumors of wars" (13:7). By the introduction of the modifiers *first* and *at once* into the Markan text, Luke makes it clear that chaotic, frightening historical disturbances are separate from the events of suprahistorical character with which this age will be brought to an end. In the concept of eschatology found in Luke certain historical developments must take place before the end, but not any of them is a sign itself of an imminent Parousia.

(2) Disturbances and Persecutions (21: 10–19)

¹⁰ Then he said to them, "Nation will rise against nation, and kingdom against kingdom; ¹¹ there will be great earthquakes, and in various places famines and pestilences; and there will be terrors and great signs from heaven. ¹² But before all this they will lay their hands on you and persecute you, delivering you up to the synagogues and prisons, and you will be brought before kings and governors for my name's sake. ¹³ This will be a time for you to bear testimony. ¹⁴ Settle it therefore in your minds, not to meditate beforehand how to answer; ¹⁵ for I will give you a mouth and wisdom, which none of your adversaries will be able to withstand or contradict. ¹⁶ You will be delivered up even by parents and brothers and kinsmen and friends, and some of you they will put to death; ¹⁷ you will be hated by all for my name's sake. ¹⁸ But not a hair of your head will perish. ¹⁹ By your endurance you will gain your lives.

International conflict, earthquakes, famines, plagues, and unusual astral phenomena have all been associated at various times with divine displeasure, impending catastrophe, and judgment. In Christian circles they have often been thought to indicate the imminent return of the Lord and God's final judgment. This kind of Christian apocalyptic thought has its roots in Jewish apocalypse. The plagues inflicted on Egypt preceding the release of Israel from captivity are a symbol of the wonders that will presage Israel's eschatological redemption. But as this writer views the subject, in this Lukan passage these phenomena are not associated with the impending end of the age. The omission of the phrase, "this is but the beginning of the sufferings" (Mark 13:8b), is decisive in this regard.

Of more immediate concern for the followers of Jesus, however, is the persecution that they must endure. In times of intense suffering, believers are susceptible victims of false hopes. Apocalyptic literature is a product of periods of crisis and distress, when people despair of any relief except through the direct intervention of God. It expresses the hope that God will act to overthrow the evil powers that oppress them. Two types of persecution are anticipated in our text. Christians will be hailed before Jewish synagogue courts. They will also be brought to trial before Gentile *kings* and *governors* for his *name's sake*, i.e., because they publicly acknowledge their allegiance to Jesus. Paul was a victim of both kinds of persecution (2 Cor. 11:23 ff.).

Instead of associating persecution with an imminent Parousia, followers of Jesus are to understand that it is the time for witnessing and spreading the gospel. Persecution will give them an opportunity to give their *testimony* to their faith. Acts contains a number of illustrations of the way Christian leaders used public judicial hearings as opportunities to proclaim the gospel.

The verb *to meditate* (v. 14) means to prepare a speech. In experiences of persecution disciples will not be shut up to their own resources. Jesus promises to give them a *mouth*, i.e., words, and *wisdom*, i.e., God's wisdom. Mark says that the Holy Spirit will speak for believers (13:11b). There is no essential difference in the meaning of the Lukan statement. This is seen, for example, in Acts 4:8 where Peter is "filled with the Holy Spirit" prior to beginning his defense.

Followers of Jesus must be prepared to pay a heavy price for their loyalty. They will be betrayed by the people who are closest to them, *parents, brothers,* etc.

Some will suffer martyrdom. By the end of the seventh decade the ranks of the Christian movement had already been hard hit by the loss of leaders like Stephen, James, Peter, and Paul. *Hated by all* describes general hostility to be directed toward Christians by society. Because they were already viewed with deep suspicion and dislike, Christians were logical scapegoats on which Nero could unload the blame for causing the great fire in Rome. Extensive efforts were made later to eliminate Christianity completely from the Empire.

The context shows that the statement *not a hair of your head will perish* does not mean that disciples are to escape all physical harm (see on 12:4). It is an assurance that they can trust in God, who cares for them so much that even "the hairs of their heads are numbered" (12:7). Although men can take their lives, they cannot rob believers of their ultimate security. They will *gain their lives*—not their physical existence but life in the age to come. Christians can confront the perils of a precarious existence in this age because they know that *endurance,* which is steadfastness in times of persecution, has its reward. This emphasis on endurance underlines the fact that Jesus' followers cannot expect their suffering to be cut short by the Parousia.

(3) The Destruction of Jerusalem (21:20– 24)

20 "But when you see Jerusalem surrounded by armies, then know that its desolation has come near. 21 Then let those who are in Judea flee to the mountains, and let those who are inside the city depart, and let not those who are out in the country enter it; 22 for these are days of vengeance, to fulfil all that is written. 23 Alas for those who are with child and for those who give suck in those days! For great distress shall be upon the earth and wrath upon this people; 24 they will fall by the edge of the sword, and be led captive among all nations; and Jerusalem will be trodden down by the Gentiles, until the times of the Gentiles are fulfilled.

Now an answer to the question raised in v. 7 is given. When the Roman armies close in on Jerusalem, this is the sign that its capture and destruction are imminent. *Jerusalem surrounded by armies* replaces the Markan phrase "the desolating sacrilege set up where it ought not to be" (cf. Dan 9:27; 11:31; 12:11). Perhaps this is due to the apocalyptic connotations of the latter. The destruction of Jerusalem is presented in such a way as to show that it is not associated with the Parousia.

Furthermore, Christianity is dissociated from those nationalistic aspirations of the Jewish people that will lead to so terrible a fate. Before Jerusalem is completely sealed off by the besieging army, Christians are to flee the city. The fourth-century historian Eusebius tells that Christians were warned by a prophet to flee Jerusalem prior to its fall. Whatever may be the historical merit of that notice, we know that Jewish Christians did retreat to the city of Pella in Perea in time to avoid the fate of their fellow citizens who remained in the city. This failure to support their nation in its resistance against Rome made definitive the already wide gulf between Christianity and Judaism.

Days of vengeance defines the fate of Jerusalem as the judgment of God. Perhaps it is thought of as the fulfillment of Ezekiel 9:1: "Draw near, you executioners of the city, each with his destroying weapon in his hand" (cf. Jer. 5:29; Hos. 9:7). The destruction of Jerusalem is the fate of a nation that, obstinately clinging to its rebellious nationalism, rejected God's Messiah because he did not fit into their own ideas of the kingdom of God.

Pregnant women or those with nursing babies will be in special danger because they will not be able to travel swiftly enough to escape. Luke has *distress* instead of Mark's "tribulation" with its more apocalyptic connotation. *Earth* is better translated land, i.e., of Palestine. *Wrath upon this people* is parallel to *distress . . . upon the earth,* repeating the interpretation of the destruction of Jerusalem as an act of divine judgment. Josephus relates that 1,100,000 Jews were slain in the siege of Jerusalem and in addition 97,000 were taken as prisoners. Although these figures must be exaggerated, the toll of the rebellion was terribly costly indeed.

It is so often the case that wars of national liberation and expansion bring results which are the very opposite of those hoped for by their promoters. Instead of becoming the seat of a proud, independent Jewish nation, Jerusalem became the site of a Gentile settlement. *The times of the Gentiles* embraces a concept similar to that expressed by Paul in Romans (see especially Rom. 11:25). The Jewish rejection of God's will and the consequent catastrophe initiated a period of missionary expansion among the Gentiles. Luke himself was living in the *times of the Gentiles.* This phrase will hardly bear the weight of elaborate apocalyptic schemes that interpret the return of Jews to Jerusalem as the fulfillment of prophecy and the beginning of the end. Especially is this true since the teaching in Luke expressly divorces all historical developments from the end itself, ruling out just this kind of prediction. The phrase expresses the conviction that the mission to the Gentiles is a part of God's redemptive movement which will run its full course before the end comes.

(4) The Coming of the Son of Man (21:25-28)

25 "And there will be signs in sun and moon and stars, and upon the earth distress of nations in perplexity at the roaring of the sea and the waves, 26 men fainting with fear and with foreboding of what is coming on the world; for the powers of the heavens will be shaken. 27 And then they will see the Son of man coming in a cloud with power and great glory. 28 Now when these things begin to take place, look up and raise your heads, because your redemption is drawing near."

To this point, the direction of this apocalyptic passage has been rather clearly indicated. The part which begins here (vv. 25–31) is much more difficult. It is usually interpreted in association with the return of the Lord and the end of the age. This is the interpretation indicated by the reference to the *world,* a word which means the whole inhabited earth (v. 26), to the *coming* of the *Son of man* (v. 27), and to the nearness of the *kingdom* (v. 31), in addition to the usual associations of the apocalyptic language which appears here. Leaney takes another position and attributes the language to "the desire to invest the fall of Jerusalem . . . with catastrophic solemnity" (p. 262). That such language could be applied to an act of God in the history and experience of the earliest community is seen in Acts 2:16 ff. There the wonders of Pentecost are declared to be a fulfillment of an apocalyptic passage from Joel 2:28–32.

Also Luke must assume that the words of Jesus are addressed to his immediate hearers and are, therefore, relevant to them. The simplest interpretation of v. 32 (see below) is to take it in connection with the first generation of Christians. Furthermore, the giving of *signs* (v. 25) that indicate the drawing near of the Parousia seems to contradict the consistent teaching in Luke that the return of the Lord will be a surprise for the world and that it will catch Christians off guard unless they are always alert. We have the option, therefore, of interpreting the passage in relation to events which fall within the lifetime of the earliest Christian generation.

After the signs depicted in vv. 25–26 the *Son of man* will come in a cloud, not "in clouds" as in Mark 13:26. Leaney (pp. 71–72) interprets this as a manifestation of the Son of man similar to that at the transfiguration (9:28 ff.) and the resurrection-ascension (Acts 1:9), both of which also mention a cloud. He further understands *redemption* (v. 28) as a reference to an "event wrought by God in history" (p. 262). It is entirely possible that the salvation of Christians in the impending disaster is conceived as another revelation of the *power* and *glory* of the *Son of man.*

(5) The Sign of the Fig Tree (21:29-33)

29 And he told them a parable: "Look at the fig tree, and all the trees; 30 as soon as they come out in leaf, you see for yourselves and

know that the summer is already near. ³¹ So also, when you see these things taking place, you know that the kingdom of God is near. ³² Truly, I say to you, this generation will not pass away till all has taken place. ³³ Heaven and earth will pass away, but my words will not pass away.

The sprouting of the *fig tree* and *all the trees* (a Lukan addition to Mark 13:28a) is a sure sign that summer is on the way. In like manner the tribulations of which Jesus has been speaking are a certain indication that *the kingdom of God is near.* The question is whether this refers to the last crisis of the world which immediately precedes the consummation of the kingdom. In the only other use in Luke of the phrase *the kingdom of God is near,* it did not have this connotation (10:11). The manifestation of the power of God to preserve his people and ensure the progress of his redemptive work may also indicate the nearness of his kingdom.

Generation can be "humanity in general" (Conzelmann, p. 131). Ellis (p. 247) says that it is "the generation of the end of time" to which Jesus spoke and which extends from the preresurrection mission to the Parousia. But it is more likely to refer to those who were contemporaries of Jesus, some of whom were still alive at the time of the conflict with Rome. Verse 33 is a solemn assurance that nothing will stay the fulfillment of what Jesus has spoken. This statement invests Jesus' words with the finality and authority of Torah (cf. 16:17).

Luke omits Mark 13:32, perhaps because he shuns a statement that affirms the Son's ignorance about the time of the Parousia. He also does not use Mark 13:33–37, which is similar to material already incorporated in his narrative (12:35–40). Some manuscripts have the pericope of the adulterous woman after v. 38 (see John 7:53—8:11 marg.).

(6) The Need to Be Alert (21:34–36)

³⁴ "But take heed to yourselves lest your hearts be weighed down with dissipation and drunkenness and cares of this life, and that day come upon you suddenly like a snare; ³⁵ for it will come upon all who dwell upon the face of the whole earth. ³⁶ But watch at all times, praying that you may have strength to escape all these things that will take place, and to stand before the Son of man."

These words stand at the end of the apocalyptic passage in Luke, whereas Mark 13 is brought to a close with a parable. Although different in content the two endings are similar in theme. There are also pronounced Pauline characteristics in the passage (cf. 1 Thess. 5:1–10), which contains a large number of characteristic Lukan words and expressions.

An ever-present danger for Christian disciples is that they who are "sons of the resurrection" will become too involved with life in this age. Debauchery and drunkenness will deaden the senses; concentration on the *cares of this life,* i.e., food, clothing, financial security, etc., will take the mind (*hearts*) off the concerns of the kingdom. For those who become so immersed in affairs of this age, *that day,* the day of the Lord, will come *suddenly like a snare.* It will not be greeted joyously but will be an unexpected, unpleasant event.

As compared to the limited judgment on the land of Palestine and Jerusalem, the Parousia will be a time of judgment for *all* upon the *whole earth.* There will be no escape from this final, universal crisis. Disciples are to remain alert for the Parousia, praying in the meantime for strength to emerge victorious from the trials and distress about which Jesus has spoken. If they exercise such prayerful vigilance, they will be able to *stand,* vindicated and unashamed, *before the Son of man.* The faithful followers of Jesus have nothing to fear in the final crisis that ushers in the new age.

(7) The Temple Ministry (21:37–38)

³⁷ And every day he was teaching in the temple, but at night he went out and lodged on the mount called Olivet. ³⁸ And early in the morning all the people came to him in the temple to hear him.

With this editorial note Luke brings his presentation of the public ministry of Jesus to a close. The newly cleansed *temple* was the scene of his teaching. Each evening he left the Temple and spent the night on the *mount called Olivet.* According to Mark, Jesus spent the first night after the triumphal entry in Bethany, which was just beyond the Mount of Olives (11:11). He is also placed at Bethany in Mark 14:3. Luke omits this story of the anointing in Bethany, which is very similar to the episode already recounted at 7:36 ff. Mark 11:19 tells us that Jesus at evening "went out of the city," probably also to Bethany since he and the disciples pass the withered fig tree on their return (see Mark 11:12–14).

Each morning the *people* thronged into the Temple to hear him. Once again we note Luke's fondness for the word *all.* Their attitude is contrasted throughout Luke with that of their leaders, who do not attend Jesus' new exposition of the Scripture.

4. Preparation for the Passion (22:1–53)

(1) The Plot to Kill Jesus (22:1–6)

¹ Now the feast of Unleavened Bread drew near, which is called the Passover. ² And the chief priests and the scribes were seeking how to put him to death; for they feared the people. ³ Then Satan entered into Judas called Iscariot, who was of the number of the twelve; ⁴ he went away and conferred with the chief priests and captains how he might betray him to them. ⁵ And they were glad, and engaged to give him money. ⁶ So he agreed, and sought an opportunity to betray him to them in the absence of the multitude.

Instead of Mark's specific notice of time (14:1), "two days before the Passover," we find here a more indefinite one. This adds to the general impression of a rather prolonged ministry in Jerusalem. Technically the *feast of Unleavened Bread* and the *Passover* were different. The Passover designated the ritual slaying of the paschal lamb on the 14th of Nisan, which was followed by the domestic meal that evening, the beginning of Nisan 15 (cf. Ex. 12:3 ff.). The seven-day feast of Unleavened Bread was observed from 15 to 21 of Nisan. But already in popular usage Passover and Unleavened Bread were used indifferently of

the two festivals because of their close relation in time. Josephus (*Antiq.,* 14, 2, 1) writes about the "feast of Unleavened Bread which we call the Pascha," although elsewhere he also distinguishes the two.

The *chief priests* and the *scribes,* members of the Sanhedrin, had determined that Jesus was to be eliminated. Their only problem was *how* to do it, for they felt obliged to find a method that would not stir up popular wrath. According to Mark 14:2, they first decided against consummating their plans "during the feast, lest there be a tumult of the people." Because the Passover was a popular pilgrim festival, there may have been 100,000 pilgrims or more in Jerusalem at this season of the year. With this number of Jews in the city, many of them ardent nationalists, the possibilities of a popular explosion with the inevitable savage repression and reprisals by the Romans were great.

Apparently the dilemma of the hostile leaders was solved with the help of a member of Jesus' inner circle. For the first time since the temptation narrative, Jesus' adversary *Satan* is mentioned. This serves notice that the ministry of Jesus has now run its course (cf. 13:32). Satan had attempted to destroy Jesus at the beginning by perverting his program. Having failed that, he returns to the attack in order to encompass his death with the aid of *Judas.* Luke mentions that Judas *was of the number of the twelve,* preparing the way for the story of the filling of his place (Acts 1:15 ff.). That place becomes vacant now, not later when Judas commits suicide.

There are two important questions raised by Judas' treachery. The first is, Why did he do it? To say that *Satan entered him* hardly answers the question specifically. It simply means that Judas is now identified with the hostile powers (the kingdom) opposed to the rule of God. There have been many guesses. Perhaps the best is that Judas was a disillusioned man. He had followed Jesus in the high hopes that he would share in Messiah's glorious rule. But now he sees that Jesus has no intention of taking the steps that promise to fulfill his ambitions.

Another view is that Judas betrayed Jesus in order to force him to exercise the miraculous powers which he as Messiah possessed. In this way, the act of betrayal would be regarded as a sort of perverted act of loyalty on the part of one who wished to precipitate the onset of the messianic kingdom. Perhaps the least satisfactory conjecture is that Judas performed the deed only for the thirty pieces of silver.

The second question is, What did Judas do? Apparently he was able to give Jesus' enemies the information and help that they needed in order to accomplish their purpose. Guided by Judas they took Jesus into custody at a time and place when he was isolated from the crowds.[34] So he met with the *chief priests* and *captains,* who were happy to get this assistance from a totally unexpected quarter. The *captains* commanded the Temple guards in the service of the Sanhedrin. They would be used to apprehend Jesus. In conference they agreed on a plan and Judas' role in it; in return the priests promised him *money,* "thirty pieces of silver" according to Matthew 26:15.

(2) The Last Supper (22:7–38)

a. The Place of the Supper (22:7–13)

7 Then came the day of Unleavened Bread, on which the passover lamb had to be sacrificed. 8 So Jesus sent Peter and John, saying, "Go and prepare the passover for us, that we may eat it." 9 They said to him, "Where will you have us prepare it?" 10 He said to them, "Behold, when you have entered the city, a man carrying a jar of water will meet you; follow him into the house which he enters, 11 and tell the householder, 'The Teacher says to you, Where is the guest room, where I am to eat the passover with my disciples?' 12 And he will show you a large upper room furnished; there make ready." 13 And they went, and

found it as he had told them; and they prepared the passover.

Five New Testament passages relate events which occurred on the night of Jesus' betrayal (1 Cor. 11:23 ff.; Mark 14:17 ff.; Matt. 26:20 ff.; Luke 22:14 ff.; John 13:1 ff.). They all agree that Jesus partook of a meal with his disciples on that night. Critical problems, however, are raised by a comparison of the various accounts, especially of the Synoptic and Johannine versions. The Synoptic narratives identify the meal as a Passover celebration, while certain passages in John indicate that it was not. John introduces the narrative with the phrase: "Now before the feast of Passover" (13:1). In 18:28 we read that Jews "did not enter the praetorium, so that they might not be defiled, but might eat the Passover" (cf. also 19:31). The Johannine narrative seems to place the death of Jesus at about the time that the paschal lamb was slain. [35] It has also been suggested that Paul's statement: "For Christ, our paschal lamb, has been sacrificed," is also based on this coincidence (1 Cor. 5:7). We must add to this the fact that Paul does not identify the Last Supper with the Passover (1 Cor. 11:23).

Joachim Jeremias [36] has made a very convincing case for the position that Jesus' last meal with his disciples prior to his crucifixion was indeed a Passover meal. It is just possible that Jesus and the disciples celebrated this Passover prior to the day called for by the Jewish calendar. Such an act would not be without precedent (Ellis, pp. 249–250). In this case both John and the Synoptics would reflect what actually took place. This is but one possible explanation for a very complex problem to which no wholly satisfactory answer can be given on the basis of the extant data.

---

34 According to Albert Schweitzer, (*The Quest of the Historical Jesus.* Tr. W. Montgomery [New York: Macmillan, 1950] p. 396.) Judas betrayed the "messianic secret," thus giving Jesus' enemies a basis for charging him with sedition, for which until this occurred they did not feel that they had sufficient evidence.

35 Consult the exegesis of the pertinent passages in the Commentary on John in this volume. Also see Frank Stagg, *New Testament Theology,* pp. 240–242, for a suggestion that harmonizes John with the Synoptic Gospels. In pp. 235–249 of the same work is found a more complete discussion of the Supper than can be given in this work.

36 *The Eucharistic Words of Jesus,* trans. Arnold Ehrhardt (Oxford: Basil Blackwell, 1955).

The two disciples chosen by Jesus to make arrangements for the Passover, unnamed in Mark 14:13, are identified as *Peter* and *John* by Luke. This responsibility was usually discharged by the leader of a group of pilgrims, in this case Jesus; but the passage implies that the opposition to him made open movement in the city dangerous. Preparation for the Passover meal included the purchase, sacrifice, and cooking of a lamb, and the provision of unleavened bread, bitter herbs, and wine.

Under the crowded conditions which existed during this season, rooms available to pilgrims for the celebration of Passover must have been limited. Evidently Jesus had already made arrangements for a room. According to prevailing custom, residents of the city ceded the use of rooms upon request to pilgrims during the Passover. In return they received the skins of the sacrificial sheep. The two disciples were to be led to the house by *a man carrying a jar of water*, likely a prearranged signal. Since this was considered a woman's task, the man would be easily identified. The story may imply, but not necessarily so, that Jesus' instructions were based on prescient knowledge. Probably the *householder* was a resident of Jerusalem who had become a disciple and to whom Jesus would also be the *teacher* or rabbi.

Preparations had already been made by the householder to the extent that he had *furnished* the room for the meal, i.e., provided it with cushions or couches and perhaps a low table. Our popular conception of Jesus and his disciples sitting around a table comes from religious art, especially da Vinci's *Last Supper*. But this picture is foreign to the customs in Palestine, where guests reclined to eat the Passover.

b. The Cup and the Bread (22:14-23)

14 And when the hour came, he sat at table, and the apostles with him. 15 And he said to them, "I have earnestly desired to eat this passover with you before I suffer; 16 for I tell you I shall not eat it until it is fulfilled in the kingdom of God." 17 And he took a cup, and when he had given thanks he said, "Take this, and divide it among yourselves; 18 for I tell you that from now on I shall not drink of the fruit of the vine until the kingdom of God comes." 19 And he took bread, and when he had given thanks he broke it and gave it to them, saying, "This is my body. 21 But behold the hand of him who betrays me is with me on the table. 22 For the Son of man goes as it has been determined; but woe to that man by whom he is betrayed!" 23 And they began to question one another, which of them it was that would do this.

Luke's narrative of the Supper is longer than that found in the other Synoptic gospels. Characteristically the meal is used by Jesus as an occasion for instructing those present. Some of the sayings are found in other contexts in Matthew and Mark, and some occur only in Luke. The extent and nature of the differences between the third Gospel and Mark indicate that Luke was using an independent source in addition to his primary one. The most noticeable variation is the reversal of the order of the elements, which, of course, changes not at all the meaning of the Supper. Undoubtedly the liturgical practices of various Christian communities are reflected to some degree in the narratives of the Supper left to us by the three Evangelists and Paul.

Sat at table would be more accurately translated "reclined at the table." The twelve (Mark 14:17) are called *apostles* by Luke.

I have earnestly desired could imply that Jesus did not himself partake of the meal.[37] The same Greek verb is used in 15:16 and 17:22 with the sense of "unfulfilled desire." This position is supported to some degree by the affirmation in v. 16, which does not contain the word "again" according to the best evidence (note the marg.). Nevertheless, the interpretation is rather doubtful. It can hardly be doubted that Jesus did share in a meal with his disciples on the night of his betrayal.

Jesus' introductory statement serves two

---

37 Jeremias, *ibid.*, p. 165.

purposes: (1) It indicates that this meal alone stands between him and his suffering. (2) It identifies the Last Supper with the messianic banquet which Jesus will share with his disciples in the coming kingdom. This eschatological note is seen also in the other narratives (Mark 14:25; Matt. 26:29; 1 Cor. 11:26). But here it is given a more prominent emphasis and is in keeping with the characteristic Lukan association of a meal with fellowship in the kingdom. The meal is an act of prophetic symbolism which will be *fulfilled in the kingdom of God.*

Although the loaf precedes the cup in Paul's outline of the order followed in the Supper (1 Cor. 11:23–26), in 1 Corinthians 10:16 the cup is mentioned before the loaf. This may indicate that the order was not universally fixed in the practice of the churches. In common practice each person had his own cup in the celebration of the Passover. But here all the disciples drink from Jesus' cup. Not only does this point up the unity of their fellowship with one another in him, but it also reminds disciples that they are called on to drink the same cup of which he drank, that is, to share in his sufferings (cf. Mark 10:39 in a passage omitted by Luke). In a parallel this time to the other Synoptic accounts, another reference is made to the messianic banquet at which Jesus will drink again with his disciples when *the kingdom of God comes.*

The giving of the cup is followed by the giving of the bread accompanied by the words: *This is my body.* There has been long and heated controversy over the meaning of the verb *is,* which ironically enough would not be present in the underlying Aramaic statement. "This means my body" is just as appropriate a translation. But this does not solve the basic question about how the bread represents the body of Christ. In Pauline thought the body of Christ is not the bread but the people who partake of the bread (1 Cor. 11:27–29). The bread does not stand for the "broken" body of Christ (John 19:36). This word is not in the best text of 1 Corinthians 11:24

and is, in fact, out of harmony with Paul's teaching there.[38] The important aspect of the experience is that they all partake of the one loaf, an expression of the oneness of the new community created by the redemptive self-giving of the Son of man.

At this point there is a serious textual problem. The RSV follows the Western text in omitting vv. 19b–20 (see the KJV). The longer text, however, is supported by many of the best authorities. The decisive argument against the inclusion of 19b–20 is its similarity to 1 Corinthians 11:24–25. It is difficult to avoid the conclusion that it is an interpolation from that source. If it is not original, Luke has no parallel to the reference in the other Synoptics to "my blood of the covenant" (Matt. 26:28; Mark 14:24). This phrase ties the death of Jesus more closely to the Passover experience and the escape from Egypt. A new liberation from bondage has taken place, a new exodus has occurred, a new Israel has come into being, and a new covenant has been instituted. So for the Christian community the Supper took the place of the Jewish Passover.

Mark's narrative begins with the prediction of betrayal, which is placed here by Luke (Mark 14:17). The enormity of the treachery is compounded by the fact that it was committed by one who shared table fellowship with Jesus, i.e., whose hand was with him on the table (v. 21). In Semitic social circles only a blackguard would so betray his host. *As it has been determined* replaces Mark's "as it is written of him" (14:21), a characteristic Lukan change to strengthen the teaching that Jesus' death was a divine necessity.

Although Jesus dies because of his obedience to the will of God, this does not lessen the guilt and responsibility of the betrayer. He must bear the consequences of his deed. Judas is not pictured as a helpless pawn who was necessary to God's purposes. He did not serve the purposes of God but those of God's enemy. God did not

---

38 See Stagg, *New Testament Theology,* pp. 236 ff.

kill Jesus; evil men accomplished the deed because they could not tolerate living in the same world with him. The dialogue in Mark 14:19 is replaced by Luke's indirect statement in v. 23.

c. The Dispute over Greatness (22:24–27)

24 A dispute also arose among them, which of them was to be regarded as the greatest. 25 And he said to them, "The kings of the Gentiles exercise lordship over them; and those in authority over them are called benefactors. 26 But not so with you; rather let the greatest among you become as the youngest, and the leader as one who serves. 27 For which is the greater, one who sits at table, or one who serves? Is it not the one who sits at table? But I am among you as one who serves.

This is a passage which only Luke places here, but it is related in content to Mark 10:42–45 (cf. Matt. 20:25–28). It also reminds us of Jesus' teachings in John's account of the Last Supper (13:3–16).

In their *dispute* the disciples are following the patterns of the pagan world. In the structures of Gentile society, the great, noble, and honored people are those who possess and exercise power over others. *Benefactor* was a rather common title bestowed on Gentile rulers.

But the normal patterns of society are to be completely reversed in the fellowship of believers. The *greatest* is to *become as the youngest*. Age was an extremely important factor in ancient society, especially in family relationships. The *youngest* was the least important member of the family, the one who had to do the most menial tasks and could expect the smallest reward. The *leader as one who serves* is parallel to the preceding statement. From this point of view the greatest persons in the Christian fellowship are those who in humility and love give themselves in service to others. Instead of vying to get ahead of others, we who follow Christ are to vie in serving others. Much denominational and church politics comes under the judgment of Jesus' teaching. Many a person who has reached the top of the ladder in his denomination after years of seeking public recognition can consider that he holds a receipt from

God marked "paid in full" (cf. Matt. 6:2,5,16).

In the normal organization of human society the man who *sits at* table is considered superior to the person who *serves him* his food. But the life of Jesus has instituted a new set of values, a completely revolutionary approach to human relations, for his followers. For he has been among men as a servant (as in John 13:3 ff.). And he came to be followed in his service. No one can truly call himself a follower of Jesus who is not ready to adopt this new set of values.

Note that Luke does not have anything that corresponds to Mark's "and to give his life a ransom for many" (10:45). Luke emphasizes the divine necessity rather than the redemptive significance of Jesus' death.

d. The Promise of the Kingdom (22:28–30)

28 "You are those who have continued with me in my trials; 29 as my Father appointed a kingdom for me, so do I appoint for you 30 that you may eat and drink at my table in my kingdom, and sit on thrones judging the twelve tribes of Israel.

Because Jesus has chosen to be in the world *as one who serves,* he must accept the consequence of his choice, i.e., his *trials.* The same word is translated temptation in 4:13. It may refer to the continuing pressures exerted on him to assume the messianic role shaped by popular desire, such as the demand for a sign. More probably his trials are the hostility and threats which now beset him. We think at once of the desertion of Jesus even by the twelve at the moment of crisis just a few hours in the future. But the text looks beyond this failure to the subsequent loyalty of these same men whose sacrifices wipe out the fact of their tragic lapse.

Satan had offered a kingdom to Jesus, a kingdom of this world (4:5–7). At that time Jesus repudiated present, tangible, worldly goals and affirmed his loyalty to God. Now he faces the consequences of that choice. But in the moment of helplessness before the onrushing tides of human evil and passion, he affirms his conviction that God is the King of the universe. So he who will soon hang on a cross as the victim of the hate and injustice of the world's rulers confidently talks about a *kingdom* which his *Father* has already *appointed* for him. It should be noted that even when he is called on to suffer he still calls God *Father*. In so doing he leaves an example for all of us weaker ones who sometimes turn on God when life becomes difficult. Sharing in Christ's victory is related intimately with sharing his trials (cf. Phil. 3:10–11).

The kingdom that God appoints for Jesus, that is, his position of authority and glory, is the basis for the hope of his disciples. Our confidence for the future is thus ultimately bound up with our confidence that Jesus is in fact the Son of God whose resurrection represents victory over the inequities and injustices of life. Belief in his future was for the disciples belief also in their future. It was in the moment when they lost this faith in his future that they became afraid and despaired of their own.

Jesus makes a twofold promise to the twelve. They will share in the fellowship of his kingdom, i.e., *drink* at his *table* in the messianic banquet. They will share in the authority of his rule as judges of the *twelve tribes of Israel*. There probably is an analogy between the relation of the patriarchs to Israel of the past and that of the disciples to the new Israel. The twelve represent the beginning of the new community, the people of the new covenant.

e. The Prediction of Peter's Denial (22:31–34)

31 "Simon, Simon, behold, Satan demanded to have you, that he might sift you like wheat, 32 but I have prayed for you that your faith may not fail; and when you have turned again, strengthen your brethren." 33 And he said to him, "Lord, I am ready to go with you to prison and to death." 34 He said, "I tell you, Peter, the cock will not crow this day, until you three times deny that you know me."

Mark places the prediction of Peter's denial after the supper en route to the Mount of Olives (14:26–31). The repetition *Simon, Simon* gives solemnity to the subsequent words and expresses deep concern. *Satan* is pictured in Job (1:6–12; 2:1–6) as the accuser of men before God and also as the one who attempts to destroy their faith in God by the use of those means allowed to him. *Satan demanded*, i.e., of God, which underlines the teaching that evil is not ultimate in the universe. The power of Satan is limited both as to time and scope. *Sifting* describes the process of testing by which the genuine is separated from the false, the good from the bad. *You* (v. 31) is plural, referring to all the disciples, for the loyalty of all will be put to the test by the events of the night.

Over against the demands of Satan are placed the prayers of Jesus for his own. Jesus is their advocate when Satan is their accuser (cf. 1 John 2:1). From this we should not get a distorted idea of a neutral or distant God, influenced on the one hand by the demands of Satan and on the other hand by the prayers of Jesus. The Christian view of God is that he was "in Christ, reconciling the world to himself" (2 Cor. 5:19). To say that Christ is for men who are weak and sinful is to say that God does not abandon them in their hour of need.

Jesus had prayed for Simon (singular *you* in v. 32) who will be the instrument used to strengthen the other disciples. *Faith* is the kind of commitment to Christ that makes one acknowledge him publicly when it is costly to do so. Simon's denial will be only a temporary episode. He will turn again, i.e., renew his commitment to follow Jesus. He will be the first of the twelve to be confronted by the risen Lord and to grasp the fact of the resurrection (cf. 24:34). Then he will be able to help those who labor under the doubt caused by the crucifixion. The role of Simon as the leader of the early Christian community is attested by this text. But the other disciples are called *brethren*. The relation is not hierarchical but familial. All of the artificial distinctions between clergy and laity are a distortion of our relationship to one another. All of us are children of God; all of us are brothers to one another.

The intimation that Peter will fail the immediate test spurs him to protest. He is willing to go to *prison* or to *death*. Prison is mentioned only in Luke (cf. Mark 14:31). Acts tells how boldly Peter reacted to imprisonments and threats after the resurrection (cf. e.g., 4:19 f.). But this was later, after he had understood the nature of the kingdom better. Now he still is dominated by ideas of earthly power and greatness. In order to help Jesus gain his messianic kingdom he was ready to die. And he was telling the truth. History is filled with the names of men who have died reaching for power. But those who have been willing to die a redemptive kind of death are few in number.

Jesus predicts that Peter will deny him before dawn. The cock crow is the third watch of the night according to Roman time. The hour intended is around 3:00 A.M., the end of the third Roman watch (see also Mark 13:35). *This day* is found instead of "this very night" (Mark 14:30). The Jewish day began at evening.

f. Instructions to the Disciples (22:35–38)

35 And he said to them, "When I sent you out with no purse or bag or sandals, did you lack anything?" They said, "Nothing." 36 He said to them, "But now, let him who has a purse take it, and likewise a bag. And let him who has no sword sell his mantle and buy one. 37 For I tell you that this scripture must be fulfilled in me, 'And he was reckoned with transgressors'; for what is written about me has its fulfilment." 38 And they said, "Look, Lord, here are two swords." And he said to them, "It is enough."

This difficult passage is found only in Luke. *Purse* and *sandals* are not mentioned in the charge of the twelve (cf. 9:3) but in that delivered to the seventy (cf. 10:4). Perhaps the lack of coincidence is due to an oversight in editing, when the materials from the various sources were put in their final form. The basic meaning of the text is not affected. Jesus is contrasting the earlier mission with the moment of danger and conflict into which they now enter. Previously the disciples had not needed supplies for their journey; homes were open, and people were hospitable.

Now the situation has changed, denoted by the references to Satan's renewed activity (22:3,31). The disciples must be prepared to face hostility. They will find that the hand of their fellowman is against them. Their attitude and actions must now be determined by the new atmosphere. Jesus cautions them to carry provisions and to provide themselves with a sword, even if they have to sell their *mantle* to buy one. The mantle was the indispensable outer garment that served as both coat and bed.

We are confronted by an obvious problem. How can Jesus, who consistently rejected the use of force, now counsel his disciples to procure a sword? Almost certainly, the answer is that his statements are to be understood metaphorically. What he means is that the disciples are in grave danger and they need to be realistically aware of it.

Their danger arises from their association with him. He will be put to death as a lawless person, i.e., *reckoned with transgressors*. Even though Jesus' self-understanding as well as the Gospel portrait of him are greatly influenced by Isaiah 53, this quotation is the only one that comes directly from it. The normal sequel to the execution of a rebel leader is for his followers to be hunted down and exterminated. This is the danger that became so real to Simon Peter just a few hours later. We can only guess what might have happened had Peter acknowledged then his relationship to Jesus.

The disciples misunderstood Jesus, hardly realizing that *two* (or eleven) *swords* would not provide protection. That Jesus did not intend for violent weapons to be used is shown clearly enough in vv. 49–51 below. *It is enough* makes little sense if we interpret the phrase to mean that two swords are sufficient. After all, Jesus has just counselled each one to obtain a sword. Probably we should understand the reply to mean: "That is enough talk about swords." Jesus abruptly terminates a discussion whose real meaning his followers had failed to grasp.

(3) On the Mount of Olives (22:39–46)

39 And he came out, and went, as was his custom, to the Mount of Olives; and the disci-

ples followed him. ⁴⁰ And when he came to the place he said to them, "Pray that you may not enter into temptation." ⁴¹ And he withdrew from them about a stone's throw, and knelt down and prayed, ⁴² "Father, if thou art willing, remove this cup from me; nevertheless not my will, but thine, be done." ⁴³ And there appeared to him an angel from heaven, strengthening him. ⁴⁴ And being in an agony he prayed more earnestly; and his sweat became like great drops of blood falling down upon the ground. ⁴⁵ And when he rose from prayer, he came to the disciples and found them sleeping for sorrow, ⁴⁶ and he said to them, "Why do you sleep? Rise and pray that you may not enter into temptation."

Leaving the upper room, Jesus went *as was his custom to the Mount of Olives.* The phrase indicates that his movements are not furtive or secretive (Grundmann, p. 411). He is now following his normal course of activity (as in 21:37–38). Luke omits Gethsemane (Mark 14:32), probably in keeping with his practice of omitting Semitic names, and has only *the place.* He also does not tell that Peter, James, and John accompanied Jesus beyond the spot where the other disciples stopped (Mark 14:33). Instead of three separate periods of prayer followed in each case by a return to the three disciples, Luke condenses the episode into one prayer vigil and one return. The condensation of Markan narratives is characteristic of both Luke and Matthew.

Now that the evil powers have arrayed themselves against the kingdom of God, the disciples are called on to *pray* that they *may not enter into temptation.* Temptation here refers to the hostility, anguish, and pressures to which the disciples will soon be subjected. In Mark, Jesus explains the basis for his injunction: "The spirit indeed is willing, but the flesh is weak" (14:38). In other words, the disciples are simply not ready for the crisis which is about to erupt. In their present condition their only recourse is to pray that they not get involved in a situation which will cause them to sin.

Jesus then removes himself from them *about a stone's throw,* that is, close enough so that the disciples could witness his strug-

gle. We note that Jesus still addresses God as *Father.* Even now when he is forced to walk a lonely, terrifying road he affirms the basic relation between him and God. *This cup* signifies his suffering and death. Clearly, Jesus was no masochist who sought death. He pleads with God to spare him the terrible ordeal that lies immediately ahead. While no one can fathom his dread crucible, Jesus' agony in Gethsemane may be explained in part by the fact that he faced rejection by his own people, those to whom he had given himself and to whom he had opened the door of the kingdom. Furthermore, he is burdened by the terrible consequences of that rejection, which he has portrayed so vividly. In this hour of trial, however, Jesus once again wins the victory. He will not be deterred from his commitment. Nor will he shrink before its ultimate consequences.

All Jesus needed to do in order to escape death was to leave Gethsemane for some safe retreat—to refuse to confront his people with the necessity of making their ultimate, fateful choice. But had he left Gethsemane, there would have been no gospel, no New Testament, no Christian hymns, no churches. Gethsemane is the place where the drive to save one's self comes into direct conflict with God's summons to redemptive self-giving. In such situations we generally choose to save ourselves. But he chose to lose himself to save us. His prayer ends, therefore, as should every prayer offered by one who is committed to God: *not my will, but thine, be done.*

Verses 43–44 are omitted from some manuscripts, including B (Vaticanus), one of the leading textual authorities. A majority of the manuscripts, including some of the best, have these verses. They are also well-attested in the Fathers. Nevertheless, some scholars have suggested that they are an anti-Gnostic interpolation. Most probably, however, their omission in some manuscripts is due to the tendency to play down Jesus' struggle. They tell us that Jesus was not abandoned in this crisis but that he received heavenly strength. They also describe the depth of his *agony.* Agony means anxiety, inner tension. We are not to think of it as "fear of death, but concern for victory in face of the approaching decisive battle on which the fate of the world depends" (E. Stauffer, TDNT, I, 140).

In this crucial hour the disciples are not praying; they are asleep! And only a stone's throw from the arena where Jesus had been engaged in a titanic struggle! Luke, who tends to defend the disciples, adds the phrase *for sorrow* as an extenuating explanation. He also omits Mark 14:41–42, perhaps because of its lack of clarity, and closes the episode with a repetition of the injunction of v. 40.

(4) The Arrest of Jesus (22:47–53)

⁴⁷ While he was still speaking, there came a crowd, and the man called Judas, one of the twelve, was leading them. He drew near to Jesus to kiss him; ⁴⁸ but Jesus said to him, "Judas, would you betray the Son of man with a kiss?" ⁴⁹ And when those who were about him saw what would follow, they said, "Lord, shall we strike with the sword?" ⁵⁰ And one of them struck the slave of the high priest and cut off his right ear. ⁵¹ But Jesus said, "No more of this!" And he touched his ear and healed him. ⁵² Then Jesus said to the chief priests and captains of the temple and elders, who had come out against him, "Have you come out as against a robber, with swords and clubs? ⁵³ When I was with you day after day in the temple, you did not lay hands on me. But this is your hour, and the power of darkness."

The arriving crowd interrupts the injunctions of Jesus to his disciples. It is led by *Judas*, who in this way fulfills his compact with the enemies of Jesus. Again we are reminded that he was one of the *twelve*. He alone knew exactly where Jesus would be. Even in the darkness, illuminated poorly at best by the flickering light of torches, he could easily identify Jesus because of his intimate relation with him. The situation demanded that the arrest be consummated with dispatch in order to provoke as little trouble as possible. Mark tells us that the kiss was the prearranged signal of identification (14:44). Luke does not have this, giving instead the remark addressed to Judas by Jesus. *With a kiss* comes first in the Greek text—the emphatic

position. The act of betrayal is consummated with an ostensible gesture of love.

Only Luke has the question from the companions of Jesus: *shall we strike with the sword?* Without waiting for an answer the deed is done. Luke with John (18:10) tells us that the *right ear* of the high priest's *slave* was cut off. Only Luke tells us that Jesus repaired the damage. *No more of this* is an enigmatic phrase susceptible of various interpretations (cf. Plummer, p. 512). Literally it is "allow it up to this." With Creed we may interpret: "Let events take their course—even to my arrest" (p. 274). It is a repudiation by Jesus of the act of violence. Whatever is meant by the statement in v. 36, this passage shows that the actual use of a sword is not envisaged.

Luke differs from the parallels by including elements of the Sanhedrin, *chief priests* and *elders,* in the contingent that has come to arrest Jesus. The leaders are a constant factor in the action from the apprehension of Jesus through his crucifixion. The Temple guards come armed to arrest Jesus, as though he were a *robber.* This word is used of members of the quasi-revolutionary, armed bands who were a continuous problem to the Roman government, especially in Galilee. Jesus' enemies had come prepared as though to deal with an insurgent who might be defended by his followers— a perverse interpretation in the light of Jesus' teaching and public conduct. He is no rebel who has been hiding from the authorities.

The lack of real moral conviction on the part of the Jewish leaders has been demonstrated by their failure to apprehend Jesus as he appeared daily in the Temple. Only under the cover of darkness do they dare bring their purposes to fruition. *This is your hour* indicates that the forces of evil appear to have the upper hand for the moment. Demonic forces are loose in the world whose authority (*power*) comes from the *darkness.* The enemies of Jesus are tools of this dark power. But every event and deed is evaluated in the light of the eternal, ultimate sovereignty of God.

The *power* (authority) *of darkness* is, therefore, limited and temporary; it is for an *hour* only.

Luke does not tell of the flight of the disciples (Mark 14:50) nor of the strange episode of the young man's escape (Mark 14:51–52).

VII. The Passion of Jesus (22:54—23:56a)

1. The Trial of Jesus (22:54—23:25)

(1) The Denial by Peter (22:54–62)

⁵⁴ Then they seized him and led him away, bringing him into the high priest's house. Peter followed at a distance; ⁵⁵ and when they had kindled a fire in the middle of the courtyard and sat down together, Peter sat among them. ⁵⁶ Then a maid, seeing him as he sat in the light and gazing at him, said, "This man also was with him." ⁵⁷ But he denied it, saying, "Woman, I do not know him." ⁵⁸ And a little later some one else saw him and said, "You also are one of them." But Peter said, "Man, I am not." ⁵⁹ And after an interval of about an hour still another insisted, saying, "Certainly this man also was with him; for he is a Galilean." ⁶⁰ But Peter said, "Man, I do not know what you are saying." And immediately, while he was still speaking, the cock crowed. ⁶¹ And the Lord turned and looked at Peter. And Peter remembered the word of the Lord, how he had said to him, "Before the cock crows today, you will deny me three times." ⁶² And he went out and wept bitterly.

The large number of distinctive aspects in the Lukan passion narrative constitutes one of the arguments used by advocates of a Proto-Luke (see Introduction). According to this theory, Markan elements were interpolated into a primary narrative of the passion already composed by Luke. Luke does in fact make extensive use of other materials in this section, but the basic framework is still Markan.

Luke does not identify the **high priest** (cf. 3:2). John says that Jesus was first led to Annas (18:13). Possibly Annas and his son-in-law, Caiaphas, the high priest at this time, lived in the same house. According to Mark, there was a hearing in the night, involving "the chief priests and the whole council" (14:55). There is no evidence in rabbinic literature that an official meeting, which would be highly irregular if held at night, was ever conducted at the **high priest's house.** Perhaps Mark refers to an informal interrogation. Luke tells of only one meeting of the council, which he places after daybreak. It is often his practice to telescope the material of his source in this manner.

Peter's denial follows immediately on the notice of Jesus' arrest and detention in the house of the high priest. Whatever our judgment of Peter, we must remember that he at least had the temerity to follow Jesus, although furtively, *at a distance.* The Passover occurred in March-April at which time the nights were still cold on occasions. Because of this, *they kindled a fire.* We are not told how the *maid* identified Peter as one of Jesus' companions. Caught in the glare of the spotlight that her accusation throws on him, Peter's courage drains away. He denies any acquaintance with Jesus. Plummer remarks: "It was not Pilate, nor any of the Sanhedrin, nor a mob of soldiers, but a single waiting-maid, who frightened the self-confident Apostle into denying his Master" (p. 516). This is really unfair. Probably his weakness can better be explained as that of a disillusioned man whose dreams lie in ruins about him. Rather than being led by Jesus to conquest, it appears more likely that he will be the victim of fast-moving events that have turned hope into despair. To die when there is hope for victory is one thing; to die for a lost cause, quite another.

All the Gospels record a threefold accusation and a threefold denial. There are some variations in details, particularly in the identity of Peter's accusers. *Some one else* (v. 58) is the same maid in Mark 14:69. *Still another* (v. 59) replaces "the bystanders" in Mark 14:70. Peter's regional dialect could have betrayed the fact that he was a *Galilean.* It was only natural to infer that a Galilean was a follower of Jesus. In keeping with his tendency, Luke spares the apostle by not telling that "he began to invoke a curse on himself and to swear" (Mark 14:71).

Only the third Gospel records the poignant scene which occurs as the cock crows: *And the Lord turned and looked at Peter.* From where? Perhaps through a window or door overlooking the courtyard. The crowing of the cock and the look of the Lord bring home to Peter the enormity of his deed. He does not excuse himself, as he might well have done. After all, he hardly has acted more poorly than the others who had deserted the Lord. *He went out and wept.* This is the moment when grace can begin its work—when a man is stripped of his arrogance and stands before God naked in his need. Verse 62, an exact parallel to Matthew 26:75b, is omitted from the text by old Latin manuscripts. It may well be an interpolation.

(2) The Mocking of Jesus (22:63–65)

63 Now the men who were holding Jesus mocked him and beat him; 64 they also blindfolded him and asked him, "Prophesy! Who is it that struck you?" 65 And they spoke many other words against him, reviling him.

Jesus is mocked by the Roman soldiers after his trial before Pilate, according to Mark 15:16–20. Luke does follow Mark at that point. He tells that Jesus was mocked and beaten by his captors—perhaps Temple guards. It was evidently a kind of cruel pastime to while away the hours until daybreak. The game that they played with Jesus as victim shows that he had gained a widespread reputation as a prophet. A prophet has deep insight into the purposes and activity of God. Indeed he sees what others cannot see and hears what they cannot hear. But this is totally different from clairvoyance or magic. The tormentors shared the popular misunderstanding of the prophet's real function. The main point is the depth of Jesus' humiliation and shame. He held out to men the hand of love; they replied with the clenched fists of hate and mockery.

(3) Jesus Before the Council (22:66–71)

66 When day came, the assembly of the elders of the people gathered together, both chief priests and scribes; and they led him away to their council, and they said, 67 "If you are the Christ, tell us." But he said to them, "If I tell you, you will not believe; 68 and if I ask you, you will not answer. 69 But from now on the Son of man shall be seated at the right hand of the power of God." 70 And they all said, "Are you the Son of God, then?" And he said to them, "You say that I am." 71 And they said, "What further testimony do we need? We have heard it ourselves from his own lips."

After daybreak the Sanhedrin convenes in official session. As we have noted, Luke telescopes Mark's narrative of two hearings before the Sanhedrin into one. Also it is possible that he is following another source which has only one hearing. The question asked in Mark 14:61 is here divided into two. First, members of the *council* ask Jesus if he is the *Christ* (Messiah). Second, they ask if he is the *Son of God.*

From all the evidence, we conclude that Jesus did not publicly claim for himself the title of Messiah during his ministry. He lived and acted according to the program depicted in Isaiah 61:1–2 and impelled people to make their own decision. Lacking the kind of direct evidence that they need, the interrogators want Jesus to admit publicly that he is the Messiah. They can then interpret this in political terms, accusing Jesus of being a revolutionary. In the hearing at night in Mark, Jesus answers affirmatively (14:62). Here he refuses to answer on the basis that it is useless for him to try to defend himself. No matter what he claims, they will not believe and they will not respond if he in his own defense questions them. It was accepted judicial procedure for the defendant to be allowed to raise questions. Western textual authorities add "or release me" to v. 68, which may represent the original reading. The meaning of Jesus' reply is that the case against him has been so prejudged that no honest decision can be reached.

Characteristically Luke does not mention the coming of the Son of man "with the clouds of heaven" (Mark 14:62). The enemies of Jesus can work their will, but after his death he will be seated at the *right hand* of God. To Mark's "Power" (14:62) Luke has added the explanatory phrase *of*

God for Gentile readers. Since God was the source of all power, the word could be used in an absolute sense as a name for God. To be seated at God's *right* hand is to occupy the place of highest honor in heaven.

Son of God became the supreme title for Jesus in the church. But the church's conception of Jesus as God's Son has its foundation in his own consciousness of a unique relationship with God expressed, for example, in the way that he spoke of God as his Father. For him this was no abstract, metaphysical dogma of the Trinity. It was an existential conviction that his life belonged uniquely to God. For us also the theological dogmas which attempt to delineate the undefinable are often without real meaning. The conviction that Jesus is the Son of God may mean much that we cannot grasp. But at least it means that there is not nor can there be any other revelation of God in history so clear and so profound as this. Jesus is the key to our understanding of God and the world, of ourselves and our fellow men, of history and the future.

You say that I am is difficult. Apparently it means: "You are the ones who use the phrase, not I." But it also must surely imply assent, because the judges now claim that Jesus has incriminated himself. In the case of confession by the accused, witnesses were unnecessary. The sin of which Jesus is guilty in the eyes of the court is blasphemy. This is a crime from the perspective of Jewish law, but such an accusation will not stand up in a Roman court.

(4) Jesus Before Pilate (23:1–5)

¹ Then the whole company of them arose, and brought him before Pilate. ² And they began to accuse him, saying, "We found this man perverting our nation, and forbidding us to give tribute to Caesar, and saying that he himself is Christ a king." ³ And Pilate asked him, "Are you the King of the Jews?" And he answered him, "You have said so." ⁴ And Pilate said to the chief priests and the multitudes, "I find no crime in this man." ⁵ But they were urgent, saying, "He stirs up the people, teaching throughout all Judea, from Galilee even to this place."

As Mark phrases it, "the whole council held a consultation," after which Jesus was delivered to Pilate (15:1). Since the Sanhedrin evidently did not have authority to execute a capital sentence, the appearance of Jesus before it must have had the character of an informal hearing. Instead of being Jesus' judge, the council played the role of prosecutor before Pilate. Because their purpose was to secure the execution of Jesus, the Jewish leaders had to make a case against him that would achieve the desired end. Therefore, *the whole company*, i.e., the entire council, accuses him of the crime of treason.

Although the difference is primarily a matter of emphasis, Luke stresses the guilt of the Jewish leaders in the death of Jesus more than any other Evangelist. Mark says they accused him of many things (15:3). In Luke three specific, related charges are preferred against Jesus by the council. *Perverting our nation* means that he was undermining its loyalty to Rome. The payment of *tribute* was an acknowledgment of sovereignty. An attempt to induce citizens not to pay it was also a treasonable act. *Christ* (Messiah) is interpreted in a political sense. He was seeking to become the *king* of the Jews. All three of these charges are patently false in the light of Luke's presentation of the teaching and acts of Jesus. He has repudiated extreme nationalism, has in effect acknowledged Caesar's right to collect tribute, and has interpreted his mission in nonpolitical terms.

The accused is questioned by Pilate with regard to his political ambitions. When he asks Jesus if he is king of the Jews, he really means: "Are you a revolutionary seeking to establish an independent Jewish state?" *You have said so.* That is, "You are using the terminology with its political implications, not I."

The reply must have been taken by Pilate as a denial of the charge, for he now declares his conviction that Jesus is innocent. This is the first of three such clear declarations by Pilate, a distinctive Lukan feature of the passion narrative. All the Evangelists portray Pilate as an unwilling tool of Jesus' Jewish enemies, but none other makes it quite so clear.

His verdict is not acceptable to the people who have determined that Jesus must die. They insist that he is an agitator who threatens the peace of Rome's Jewish subjects. *Judea* is the equivalent of Palestine. According to the charge Jesus is not just an insignificant person who can be dismissed lightly. His influence has been exerted from *Galilee* to *Jerusalem,* i.e., from the outer limits to the center of Palestine.

(5) Jesus Before Herod (23:6–12)

⁶ When Pilate heard this, he asked whether the man was a Galilean. ⁷ And when he learned that he belonged to Herod's jurisdiction, he sent him over to Herod, who was himself in Jerusalem at that time. ⁸ When Herod saw Jesus, he was very glad, for he had long desired to see him, because he had heard about him, and he was hoping to see some sign done by him. ⁹ So he questioned him at some length; but he made no answer. ¹⁰ The chief priests and the scribes stood by, vehemently accusing him. ¹¹ And Herod with his soldiers treated him with contempt and mocked him; then, arraying him in gorgeous apparel, he sent him back to Pilate. ¹² And Herod and Pilate became friends with each other that very day, for before this they had been at enmity with each other.

Only Luke gives the episode of Jesus' appearance before Herod Antipas (cf. 3:1). The statement about Jesus' activities in Galilee causes Pilate to raise the question of jurisdiction. If he were a Galilean whose activities constituted a menace to the political peace in that region, his case should be decided by Herod. Presumably the Galilean tetrarch is in Jerusalem for the celebration of the Passover. The Herods were Jews, although as descendants of an Idumean whose people had been forced to become proselytes by John Hyrcanus, their ancestry was not the best. They were more Hellenistic than Jewish in their personal lives and attitudes, but it would not be unusual for them to appear in Jerusalem to participate in a high holy feast.

This is the second reference to Herod's desire to see Jesus (cf. 9:7–9). It is now explained that Herod wished to see a miracle performed by Jesus. The Hellenistic Antipas probably entertained the idea that Jesus might be a divine being of some kind who could prove his divinity by a magical display of power. But miracles are not performed on request (cf. 4:16–30). Furthermore, Jesus will not take this route to save himself. His power is used to help and redeem others, not in his own behalf. Herod's questions are greeted with silence. The silence of Jesus before his accusers is mentioned by the other Synoptics, although in a different connection (cf. Mark 15:5; Matt. 27:14). No doubt this illustrates the reference to the silence of Suffering Servant in Isaiah 53:7.

Over against the uncomplaining silence of Jesus are set the vehement accusations of *chief priests* and *scribes,* members of the Sanhedrin. They are also a part of this new scene where they presumably press the same charges.

Herod's contempt for Jesus and the little credence given to the charges against him are shown in the treatment accorded the prisoner. Since he concludes that Jesus is no god, Herod treats him as a powerless and inconsequential human being. Herod's *soldiers* (cf. 3:14) make of Jesus a pitiful plaything for the amusement of their master. Jesus is arrayed in *gorgeous apparel,* the white robe of royalty, to mock his messianic pretensions. After having his sport with Jesus, Herod sends him back to Pilate. He has concluded that Jesus is no threat to his rule. The contact that Herod and Pilate have as a result of their involvement in the proceedings against Jesus serves to break down the hostility between them so that they become *friends.* There is no other evidence which throws light on this relationship between Herod and Pilate.

(6) The Condemnation of Jesus (23:13–25)

¹³ Pilate then called together the chief priests and the rulers and the people, ¹⁴ and said to them, "You brought me this man as one who was perverting the people; and after examining him before you, behold, I did not find this man

guilty of any of your charges against him; 15 neither did Herod, for he sent him back to us. Behold, nothing deserving death has been done by him; 16 I will therefore chastise him and release him."

18 But they all cried out together, "Away with this man, and release to us Barabbas"— 19 a man who had been thrown into prison for an insurrection started in the city, and for murder. 20 Pilate addressed them once more, desiring to release Jesus; 21 but they shouted out, "Crucify, crucify him!" 22 A third time he said to them, "Why, what evil has he done? I have found in him no crime deserving death; I will therefore chastise him and release him." 23 But they were urgent, demanding with loud cries that he should be crucified. And their voices prevailed. 24 So Pilate gave sentence that their demand should be granted. 25 He released the man who had been thrown into prison for insurrection and murder, whom they asked for; but Jesus he delivered up to their will.

Pilate calls the accusers together for his second declaration of Jesus' innocence. The *priests,* the *rulers,* and the *people,* representing the nation of Israel, hear the pronouncement. In a strange development, the judge, the Roman governor, becomes the attorney for the defense. We really do not have enough evidence to be able to understand completely the dynamics of the situation. What impact did Jesus have on Pilate? How much was Pilate motivated by a sense of judicial responsibility? With all of the inequities and cruelty in the Roman Empire, the government maintained great pressures on its representatives to uphold justice in their decisions. How much did Pilate's antipathy against the Jews influence his actions? He is certainly not exonerated by the Evangelists, but he is placed in the best possible light in view of the circumstances. Of course, the Evangelists were not interested in rehabilitating Pilate. They were motivated by a desire to show that Jesus was not guilty of the crime for which he was executed. He was God's Messiah and mankind's Saviour, not a disappointed, defeated revolutionary.

Luke shows that the two men who represent Rome as rulers of the major regions of Palestine concluded that Jesus was innocent. According to Jewish law the corroborating witness of two men is decisive. Pilate understands that Herod would not have sent Jesus back to him had he concluded that the prisoner was a Galilean agitator (v. 15).

The milder·*chastise* instead of "scourge" is another indication of the Lukan tendency to soften the part that Pilate played in the suffering of Jesus. The fact that Jesus is scourged at the orders of Pilate (Mark 15:15), a common treatment of prisoners scheduled for execution, is omitted in Luke. Chastise can involve corporal punishment but not necessarily so. It can mean simply to warn.

Pilate's third attempt to release Jesus brings into the picture a criminal by the name of *Barabbas.* Many important manuscripts omit v. 17 altogether (see marg.). A few Western witnesses place it after v. 19. It is an interpolation inserted to explain why the people demanded the release of Barabbas. Once again Pilate's defense of Jesus meets with determined opposition.

According to Mark 15:7, Barabbas was one of a group of rebels who had been thrown into prison. In other words, Barabbas was guilty of the very crime of which Jesus had been falsely accused. He had been involved, perhaps as a messianic pretender, in an insurrection. According to Luke, this took place in Jerusalem itself.

Their choice of Barabbas clearly defines the stance of the Jewish leaders. They who accuse Jesus of hostility to Rome are Caesar's real enemies, for their sympathies are with a man who is guilty of a violent revolt. The story shows that the trial of Jesus was the grossest miscarriage of justice. In the final analysis Pilate allowed the enemy of his ruler to go free and allowed a man to be executed who had no ambitions to rule an earthly kingdom.

Jesus' enemies really pronounce sentence on him. In opposition to the attempts by Pilate to release him, they cry for him to be crucified. For the third time Pilate declares Jesus to be innocent. In response to the clamor for his crucifixion, the governor avers that he has committed no capital crime. Again he renders his own sentence. He will *chastise* and *release* Jesus. But the will of the Jewish leaders is stronger than the will of Pilate. The governor passes a sentence that represents the *demand* of Jesus' enemies rather than his own conviction. The Roman official was not true to the principles of justice that his government required him to follow. Furthermore, he freed the insurrectionist whose release the Jewish leaders desired. Jesus' death is carefully shown to be a rejection by his own people and not the will of Rome's administrators. They and not Pilate must bear the major burden of guilt. At the same time, Pilate is definitely portrayed as a poor administrator of Roman justice.

The contemporary meaning of the cross is a judgment on the evil of all humanity. For centuries men have deftly avoided the implications of the cross by a very simple maneuver; they have placed the blame for the murder of Jesus on Jews. The idea has been shamefully cultivated that the Jews who conspired in the death of Jesus were a special breed of people, extraordinarily evil and perverse. But the truth is that they were people *just like all people*, the present generation included—with the same ambitions, the same weaknesses, the same problems. Racial prejudice, institutionalized religion, social injustice—these were the evils that Jesus challenged. Who among us dares to deny that the same evils are present in our society?

Jesus' own people reacted to his challenge by trying to shove God out of his world. Instead of coming to terms with the word of God, they decided to silence the disturbing voice which proclaimed it. We also try to push God out of his world, take it over for ourselves, use it for our own ambitions. This is the ultimate idolatry. In this sense the crucifixion is not only something that happened a long time ago; it takes place every day in our own world.

2. The Crucifixion (23:26–56a)

(1) The Weeping Women (23:26–31)

26 And as they led him away, they seized one Simon of Cyrene, who was coming in from the country, and laid on him the cross, to carry it behind Jesus. 27 And there followed him a great multitude of the people, and of women who bewailed and lamented him. 28 But Jesus turning to them said, "Daughters of Jerusalem, do not weep for me, but weep for yourselves and for your children. 29 For behold, the days are coming when they will say, 'Blessed are the barren, and the wombs that never bore, and the breasts that never gave suck!' 30 Then they will begin to say to the mountains, 'Fall on us'; and to the hills, 'Cover us.' 31 For if they do this when the wood is green, what will happen when it is dry?"

Except for v. 26 this description of Jesus' journey to the cross is found only here in the Gospels. It brings out the relationship between Jerusalem's rejection of Jesus and the city's ultimate destruction, an important Lukan motif.

Simon is identified as a native of *Cyrene*. This city, capital of the North African district of Cyrenaica, had a sizable Jewish population. Either Simon was in Palestine for the celebration of the Passover, or he had emigrated to the land of his fathers. Mark 15:21 identifies him as the father of Alexander and Rufus, who must have been well-known members of the early Christian community. The conjecture that Simon subsequently became a Christian is, therefore, a logical one. The *cross* is the beam to which the executed person's arms were affixed. Condemned criminals were forced to carry it as a part of the public spectacle made of their execution, a warning to other possible violators. Why did Jesus not carry his own cross beam? Perhaps the scourging to which he had been subjected (Mark 15:15) had been so severe that he was physically unable to do so. Simon seems to represent for Luke the ideal of the disciple who follows behind Jesus, carrying his cross. No disciple was there to do what a stranger was compelled to do.

There is a funeral procession for Jesus prior to his death. Women played an important part in the ritual of the Jewish funeral. They were the ones who sang the funeral dirges.[39] Women in the multitude

[39] See articles by Gustav Stählin in TDNT, III, 148–155 and 830–860, for a discussion of the Greek words translated "bewailed" and "lamented."

bewailed and *lamented* Jesus. This means they beat their breasts, uttered the customary lamentations, and wept (according to v. 28). This amounts to a public acclamation of Jesus, which went against all customary treatment of a condemned man.

If they really understood the meaning of the event which evokes their lamentations, the women would be crying out to God for mercy for themselves and their children. Jesus rejects their mourning for him, issuing a call for tears to be shed over a doomed city. This is in effect a prophetic summons to repentance. They are to recognize their own guilt, their solidarity with the city's rejection of Jesus, and the inevitability of judgment.

Jerusalem faces days of terrible suffering and tragedy. In those days sterility will be considered a blessing and motherhood a curse, the very opposite of the normal attitude. Childless women will be glad that they did not bear and nurture children to experience the tortures which will attend the death of the city. The inhabitants will seek in vain for a place to hide from their fate, in their desperation calling for the protection of *mountains* and *hills* (cf. Hos. 10:8).

They (v. 31) must refer to the Roman masters of Jerusalem. If these Gentiles crucify a person like Jesus in the spring, *when the wood is green*, what will happen in the fall, *when it is dry?* Spring is the time of sowing; fall, the time of reaping. Jerusalem is sowing seeds now that will bear a harvest of bitter fruits. Only three crosses pierced the landscape on that fateful day. But we are informed that the Roman conquerors crucified an untold number of Jews after the fall of Jerusalem.

(2) The Execution of Jesus (23:32–38)

32 Two others also, who were criminals, were led away to be put to death with him. 33 And when they came to the place which is called The Skull, there they crucified him, and the criminals, one on the right and one on the left. 34 And Jesus said, "Father, forgive them; for they know not what they do." And they cast lots to divide his garments. 35 And the people stood by, watching; but the rulers scoffed at him, saying, "He saved others; let him save himself, if he is the Christ of God, his Chosen One!" 36 The soldiers also mocked him, coming up and offering him vinegar, 37 and saying, "If you are the King of the Jews, save yourself!" 38 There was also an inscription over him, "This is the King of the Jews."

Jesus is accompanied to the place of execution by two evildoers, destined for the same fate. They are called robbers by Mark (15:27). The place of crucifixion is unknown, but it was outside the city (Heb. 13:12 f.) along a main traffic artery. Luke omits the Semitic name Golgotha and gives only the translation, *The Skull*. Perhaps the hill bore configurations that gave the impression of a skull.

Crucifixion had been borrowed by the Romans from the Phoenicians and Persians. This unusually barbaric form of execution was generally reserved for non-Romans. The victim's hands and feet were either nailed or lashed to the cross. His body was supported by a peg affixed to the main member of the cross, which he straddled. Often he hung alive on the cross for several days, subject to the torture of elements, insects, the jeers of passersby, and physical pain and exhaustion. Death was caused by hunger, thirst, shock, and fatigue. Very little if any blood was actually shed. To say that Jesus "shed his blood" means that he gave his life. The criminals were crucified on either side of Jesus.

Jesus' prayer for his enemies (v. 34) is absent from a number of excellent authorities and is judged by some scholars to be an insertion into the original text. Grundmann (pp. 432 ff.), however, argues persuasively on the basis of intrinsic evidence for its genuineness. There is, for example, a close relationship between the prayers of Jesus and of Stephen (Acts 7:60). Apostolic preaching also declares that the Jewish people have another opportunity to repent because the crucifixion was contrived in ignorance (Acts 3:17). Moreover, the prayer is in keeping with the character and teaching of Jesus (cf. Luke 6:28) as portrayed in the Gospels. While Jesus prays, the hardened soldiers determine by casting *lots* which of them will get his clothing.

The people watch; the rulers scoff—the distinction is a characteristic Lukan touch. A redemptive life is not sufficient proof to the leaders that Jesus is the Messiah. If he is the Christ, he must prove it by using his power on his own behalf. They cannot conceive of power or position not being used for self. Nor do they understand that saving one's self is incompatible with saving others. Neither can they believe that God would allow his **Chosen One** to be so humiliated. Their God is a projection of their own self-interests and ideas. So they assume that he would act in the same way that they would in such circumstances.

The *soldiers* who carried out the crucifixion also join in the jeering. *Vinegar* is the cheap sour wine drunk by the common people. It is offered here in mockery to Jesus, accompanied by a jeering challenge. Roman soldiers would understand *King of the Jews* in a political sense. They think of Jesus as a frustrated and defeated pretender to Jewish rule. This is some King who cannot save himself!

It was customary to write the accusation against the executed person on a placard and affix this to the cross or hang it around his neck. According to the charge, Jesus was executed as a rebel against Rome.

(3) The Penitent Thief (23:39–43)

³⁹ One of the criminals who were hanged railed at him, saying, "Are you not the Christ? Save yourself and us!" ⁴⁰ But the other rebuked him, saying, "Do you not fear God, since you are under the same sentence of condemnation? ⁴¹ And we indeed justly; for we are receiving the due reward of our deeds; but this man has done nothing wrong." ⁴² And he said, "Jesus, remember me when you come in your kingly power." ⁴³ And he said to him, "Truly, I say to you, today you will be with me in Paradise."

This is another episode told only by Luke. Mark states: "Those who were crucified with him also reviled him" (15:32b). Luke tells us that one of these men perceived who Jesus was. He rebukes his fellow criminal on the basis that the hour of death is hardly the appropriate moment for an evildoer to revile an innocent man. Having been sentenced by the Roman court, they are soon to be ushered through death before the judgment of God.

Then the penitent robber turns to Jesus with a plea to be remembered when he comes in his *kingly power*. Some good manuscripts have "when you come into your kingdom." The text followed by the RSV is supported by excellent authorities and fits the context better. The dying man asks to be remembered at the Parousia, an expression of faith in Jesus as Messiah.

In his reply Jesus assures the man that he will not have to wait until a future date in order to be remembered. It is possible to place the comma after *today*, but the punctuation in the text is more appropriate. Anyone, therefore, who turns to Jesus even in the last moment is granted fellowship with him. Death is presented in a new light, since it is necessary to the fulfillment of Jesus' word to the dying man. Both Jesus and the man must die for them to be in *Paradise*, a word of Persian origin meaning heaven. So death is not a defeat. It is rather a necessary experience if one is to enter into glory. Death is interpreted as entrance into God's presence, both for Jesus and for those who believe in him.

(4) The Death of Jesus (23:44–49)

⁴⁴ It was now about the sixth hour, and there was darkness over the whole land until the ninth hour, ⁴⁵ while the sun's light failed; and the curtain of the temple was torn in two. ⁴⁶ Then Jesus, crying with a loud voice, said, "Father, into thy hands I commit my spirit!" And having said this he breathed his last. ⁴⁷ Now when the centurion saw what had taken place, he praised God, and said, "Certainly this man was innocent!" ⁴⁸ And all the multitudes who assembled to see the sight, when they saw what had taken place, returned home beating their breasts. ⁴⁹ And all his acquaintances and the women who had followed him from Galilee stood at a distance and saw these things.

Mark tells us that Jesus was crucified at "the third hour," i.e., 9:00 A.M. According to Luke, two significant signs occurred while Jesus was on the cross. *The sun's light failed,* from noon until 3:00 P.M. (the *ninth hour*), which emphasizes the cosmic significance of the death of Jesus. This is the fleeting moment when the "power of darkness" (22:53) seems to be victorious. *The curtain of the temple* separated the Holy of Holies from the rest of the sanctuary. The high priest went behind it once each year to make atonement for the sins of the people. The parting of the curtain means that through Christ direct access to God has been opened, making the sacerdotal institution unnecessary. Also, it may be taken as an omen of the judgment of God on a doomed Temple.

The death of Jesus was unusually rapid. Perhaps this was due to the effect of scourging by Roman soldiers. Men often died under the lash. Luke omits the cry of dereliction taken from Psalm 22:1 (cf. Mark 15:34). The last saying of Jesus in the third Gospel is a quotation from Psalm 31:5. Even in this final hour Jesus does not falter in his confidence that God is his *Father.* Beyond the pain and despair, beyond the loneliness and the hate, God stands waiting to receive his Son.

The centurion was the officer who had supervised the execution of Jesus. He adds his verdict to that of Pilate and Herod: *This man was innocent* (cf. Mark 15:39). Thus all the official representatives of Rome's presence in Palestine mentioned in the narrative agree that an innocent man was executed. The *multitudes* left the scene *beating their breasts,* an expression of remorse. Jesus' Galilean followers stand *at a distance* and witness the crucifixion and death of Jesus. The qualifications of these witnesses to the risen One are carefully pointed out by Luke. They see him die; they see him buried; and they discover the empty tomb. The *women* mentioned here are those referred to in 8:2 and again in 23:55 and 24:10 (see comment on 8:2). An anti-Gnostic motif is likely here, for Luke takes great care to establish solidly the identity of the One who died, was buried, and arose.

(5) *The Burial of Jesus* (23:50–56a)

⁵⁰ Now there was a man named Joseph from the Jewish town of Arimathea. He was a member of the council, a good and righteous man, ⁵¹ who had not consented to their purpose and deed, and he was looking for the kingdom of God. ⁵² This man went to Pilate and asked for the body of Jesus. ⁵³ Then he took it down and wrapped it in a linen shroud, and laid him in a rock-hewn tomb, where no one had ever yet been laid. ⁵⁴ It was the day of Preparation, and the sabbath was beginning. ⁵⁵ The women who had come with him from Galilee followed, and saw the tomb, and how his body was laid; ⁵⁶ then they returned, and prepared spices and ointments.

Care for Jesus' body comes from a surprising source—from a member of the very *council* that had contrived the crucifixion. Usually *Arimathea* is located in the Judean hill country northwest of Jerusalem, but its exact site is unknown. Joseph's is no one-sided or superficial piety. He is *good* toward his fellowman and *righteous* toward God, in a class with Zechariah (1:6) and Simeon (2:25). Luke explains that Joseph had not agreed with fellow members of the council in the conception and execution of their plan to get rid of Jesus. Furthermore, like Simeon (2:25) he was expectantly awaiting the fulfillment of the prophetic word about the *kingdom of God*. This may explain his interest in Jesus who had proclaimed the nearness of the kingdom.

As a *righteous* man, Joseph may also have been motivated by the commandment against leaving the body of an executed man hanging on a tree overnight (Deut. 21–23). He requested and received from Pilate permission to bury Jesus. The naked body was wrapped in *linen shroud,* a sheet wound around the body of the dead. Matthew tells us that Joseph was rich (27:57), which is supported by the fact that he possessed a *rock-hewn tomb*. Luke makes the additional comment: *where no one had ever yet been laid*. Since it is new, it is appropriate for such sacred use.

Preparation is the Jewish word for Friday. At this time of the year the sabbath would begin at approximately 6:00 P.M. All the Gospels agree that Jesus was crucified on Friday and that the tomb was discovered to be empty on the first day of the week. The *women* verify that Jesus is buried (see v. 49 above). *Spices* and *ointments,* aromatic substances used to anoint the bodies of the dead, are made ready against the next opportunity for a visit to the tomb.

VIII. The Resurrection of Jesus (23:56b— 24:53)

Luke's resurrection narrative is divided into three episodes which are put together in such a way as to form a connected, excellently constructed literary unity. Only in the first episode does one find parallels with the other Gospels, but even this unit is distinctive. At two significant places we find variations from Mark's story of the empty tomb: (1) In Mark the angel tells the women to convey to the disciples the message that Jesus will meet them in Galilee (Mark 16:7; cf. Luke 24:6–7). (2) According to Mark 16:8, the women "said nothing to anyone, for they were afraid" (cf. Luke 24:9). But the Markan account naturally presupposes that the women eventually told their story, or it could not have found its way into the Gospel.

The remaining stories are found only in Luke. They are set in Jerusalem or its immediate environs. The manner of presentation is determined to a great extent by certain Lukan motifs and concepts. In Luke the action in the life of Jesus moves from Galilee to Jerusalem. The Jewish capital then becomes the center from which the witness of the early church begins. The flow of action is from Jerusalem to Rome in the book of Acts. Consequently Luke does not relate any Galilean appearances. If we had this Gospel only, we would be forced to conclude that Luke conceived of all the experiences he records as taking place on resurrection Sunday, climaxed by the as-

cension. But in Acts he tells of appearances over a 40-day period prior to the ascension.

1. The Women at the Tomb (23:56b— 24:11)

On the sabbath they rested according to the commandment.

¹ But on the first day of the week, at early dawn, they went to the tomb, taking the spices which they had prepared. ² And they found the stone rolled away from the tomb, ³ but when they went in they did not find the body. ⁴ While they were perplexed about this, behold, two men stood by them in dazzling apparel; ⁵ and as they were frightened and bowed their faces to the ground, the men said to them, "Why do you seek the living among the dead? ⁶ Remember how he told you, while he was still in Galilee, ⁷ that the Son of man must be delivered into the hands of sinful men, and be crucified, and on the third day rise." ⁸ And they remembered his words, ⁹ and returning from the tomb they told all this to the eleven and to all the rest. ¹⁰ Now it was Mary Magdalene and Joanna and Mary the mother of James and the other women with them who told this to the apostles; ¹¹ but these words seemed to them an idle tale, and they did not believe them.

It is explained that adherence to the Jewish law of the sabbath kept the women from going to the tomb, perhaps because it lay at a distance exceeding a sabbath day's journey from the place where they were lodged.

According to Luke and Mark, the purpose for which the women went to the tomb was to embalm the body with spices. Mark says that they "bought spices when the sabbath was past" (16:1). They went at *early dawn,* as soon as there was a bit of light that enabled them to see. The first day of the week had begun at 6:00 P.M., some 12 hours previously.

The heavy stone placed at the entrance of the tomb to protect the body from animals was rolled away when they arrived. Within there was no *body.* Many authorities follow body with the phrase "of the Lord Jesus," a title not found elsewhere in the Gospels. This is the first of a number of readings in this chapter omitted by Western textual sources, most of which are judged generally to be interpolations.

The failure to find the body produces

perplexity and not faith. The resurrection narrative in Luke emphasizes that the empty tomb of itself is no proof of a resurrection. Belief in the resurrection is based on the appearance of the risen Lord. But it was also important for the church to show that it was the actual body of Jesus of Nazareth that was raised in order to counter Gnostic speculations.

Two men arrayed as heavenly messengers explain the meaning of the empty tomb. Mark 16:5 says "a young man." Luke is fond of pairs, consonant with the witness motif so prominent in his writing. At the ascension "two men . . . in white robes" again appear (Acts 1:10) to define the proper attitude of the church toward the departure and return of her Lord. Leaney (pp. 291 f.) holds that the two men serve to link the resurrection with the transfiguration. He identifies them as Moses and Elijah.

The messengers tell the women that they have come to the wrong place to look for Jesus. Since he is alive, he is not to be found in a tomb. Some authorities insert: "He is not here, but is risen," an apparent interpolation from Mark 16:6.

In Mark the women receive instructions to tell "his disciples and Peter" that Jesus will meet them in Galilee (16:7). Luke, however, restricts his account of the resurrection to Jerusalem. The women are reminded that Jesus predicted the resurrection during the Galilean ministry (Luke 18:32–33). *They remembered his words,* i.e., they now interpret the empty tomb in the light of Jesus' prophecy. The women understand that the body has not been removed, but that Jesus has risen. From the narrative we presume that the disciples have been staying together during this period. Returning to them, *the eleven* and *all the rest,* they divulge what they have experienced. But their recital is dismissed as fantasy. We may have here a reflection of the polemic of the early church. Enemies of Christianity possibly characterized the report of the resurrection as simply an emotional tale of excited, deluded women.

The narrative discloses that this was exactly the reaction of the earliest disciples. They did not believe the women until they had become convinced of the resurrection by their own personal experience.

Three of the women are named, two of whom were mentioned at 8:3. Mark names Mary Magdalene, Mary the mother of James the younger and Joses, and Salome as witnesses to the crucifixion (15:40). Only Luke mentions *Joanna,* while he does not refer to Salome. These are the Galilean witnesses who follow him to Jerusalem, watch him die, see him buried, and discover the empty tomb. Verse 12, omitted from Western authorities, is probably an interpolation based on John 20:4–6.

2. The Appearance to Two Disciples (24:13–35)

(1) Conversation on the Way to Emmaus (24:13–27)

13 That very day two of them were going to a village named Emmaus, about seven miles from Jerusalem, 14 and talking with each other about all these things that had happened. 15 While they were talking and discussing together, Jesus himself drew near and went with them. 16 But their eyes were kept from recognizing him. 17 And he said to them, "What is this conversation which you are holding with each other as you walk?" And they stood still, looking sad. 18 Then one of them, named Cleopas, answered him, "Are you the only visitor to Jerusalem who does not know the things that have happened there in these days?" 19 And he said to them, "What things?" And they said to him, "Concerning Jesus of Nazareth, who was a prophet mighty in deed and word before God and all the people, 20 and how our chief priests and rulers delivered him up to be condemned to death, and crucified him. 21 But we had hoped that he was the one to redeem Israel. Yes, and besides all this, it is now the third day since this happened. 22 Moreover, some women of our company amazed us. They were at the tomb early in the morning 23 and did not find his body; and they came back saying that they had even seen a vision of angels, who said that he was alive. 24 Some of those who were with us went to the tomb, and found it just as the women had said; but him they did not see." 25 And he said to them, "O foolish men, and slow of heart to believe all that the prophets have spoken! 26 Was it not necessary that the

Christ should suffer these things and enter into his glory?" 27 And beginning with Moses and all the prophets, he interpreted to them in all the scriptures the things concerning himself.

The rest of the Lukan resurrection narrative is peculiar to Luke. *Two of them* are from the group of disciples who had heard the women's story, but they are not of the eleven (v. 33 below). *That very day* is the day when the tomb had been discovered empty. The location of *Emmaus* is uncertain, but it may be the modern village of Kolonieh.

When Jesus joins the disciples on the way to Emmaus, they do not recognize him. Luke's resurrection account stresses the continuity between the crucified and the risen Jesus, but it also indicates that there was a difference. Here the interpretation is that *their eyes were kept from recognizing him,* that is, it was part of the divine plan. Their ignorance of their companion's identity provides an occasion for him to expound the meaning of the experiences about which they had been talking.

The two are amazed that the stranger has to ask about the subject of their discussion. *Are you the only visitor* can also be translated "are you the only one who is such a stranger in Jerusalem, etc." His apparent ignorance causes them to conclude that he has arrived since the events which disturbed the city took place.

Their response to the request for information presents their understanding of the crucifixion as the frustration of the high hopes that had been inspired by Jesus. He was a *prophet;* his death has not changed this conviction. He had shown himself to be a prophet in both *deed* and *word. Before God and all the people* means in God's sight or estimation as well as in popular opinion. God's evident power expressed in the life of Jesus was a sign of divine approval on his ministry. The responsibility for the death of this prophet is laid once again on the shoulders of the Jewish leaders.

The disciples had hoped that he was the Messiah. But they conceived the mission of the Messiah to be the redemption of Israel from its subjection to Rome. To them, therefore, his death signified that he was not Israel's redeemer.

There is one other element in the story. Their slain leader's *body* was missing from the *tomb.* The women had discovered it empty and had reported an encounter with *angels* who affirmed that Jesus was alive. *Some of the disciples* had verified that at least a part of the women's story was true. The tomb was indeed empty. But an empty tomb was not taken as proof that Jesus was raised from the dead.

Jesus accuses the two disciples of failure to *believe all that the prophets have spoken.* For this reason they had a distorted concept of Messiah's life and mission. Two things were essential: (1) *that the Christ should suffer* and (2) *enter into his glory.* Jesus now teaches what the Scriptures say, i.e., expounds the necessity of suffering as a prelude to glory. *Moses* was a contemporary designation of the Torah. The *prophets* was the second of three major sections of Hebrew Scriptures accepted as authoritative by the Pharisees and the majority of Jewish people. In every section of Scripture there are *things concerning* Jesus in the light of which the disciples can interpret recent events.

(2) Recognition in Emmaus (24:28–35)

28 So they drew near to the village to which they were going. He appeared to be going further, 29 but they constrained him, saying, "Stay with us, for it is toward evening and the day is now far spent." So he went in to stay with them. 30 When he was at table with them, he took the bread and blessed, and broke it, and gave it to them. 31 And their eyes were opened and they recognized him; and he vanished out of their sight. 32 They said to each other, "Did not our hearts burn within us while he talked to us on the road, while he opened to us the scriptures?" 33 And they rose that same hour and returned to Jerusalem; and they found the eleven gathered together and those who were with them, 34 who said, "The Lord has risen indeed, and has appeared to Simon!" 35 Then they told what had happened on the road, and how he was known to them in the breaking of the bread.

The "unknown expositor" of Scripture is *constrained* to remain with the disciples in Emmaus, for the day is almost over. It is only when he is *at the table with them* and the old fellowship is restored that the two men finally recognize Jesus. When he fed the multitude, he revealed who he was to the disciples in the blessing and breaking of bread (9:16). This is the way that he is known in the community of the resurrection. When believers gather around the table they know him as the center of their fellowship and the essence of their being. When his body was brought forth from the grave, his body, the church, was also given life. The witness of its joyous communion with him and with one another is to this day the greatest "proof" of the resurrection. After the blessing and breaking of bread, Jesus disappears. As a result of his death and resurrection, the Christian community no longer depends on his actual physical presence (Leaney, p. 293).

In the light of this new revelation, the two disciples remember unusual aspects of their experience with Jesus on the Emmaus road: their hearts had *burned* within them as he had interpreted to them the *scriptures*. Immediately they return to Jerusalem to share with the other disciples the joyous news that Jesus is alive. They find, however, that the others also now believe that Jesus has risen because of Peter's witness to them (cf. 22:32). In Paul's list of the appearances of the risen Christ to disciples, he mentions first the appearance to Cephas (1 Cor. 15:5). Following that are listed the appearances to the twelve, to "more than five hundred brethren," to James, to "all the apostles," and then to Paul himself.

3. The Appearance in Jerusalem (24:36–53)

(1) Proof of the Resurrection (24:36–43)

³⁶ As they were saying this, Jesus himself stood among them. ³⁷ But they were startled and frightened, and supposed that they saw a spirit. ³⁸ And he said to them, "Why are you troubled, and why do questionings rise in your hearts? ³⁹ See my hands and my feet, that it is I myself; handle me, and see; for a spirit has not flesh and bones as you see that I have." ⁴¹ And while they still disbelieved for joy, and wondered, he said to them, "Have you anything here to eat?" ⁴² They gave him a piece of broiled fish, ⁴³ and he took it and ate before them.

As they were saying this places the appearance of Jesus to the assembled disciples on the evening of the first Easter. It is *Jesus* who stands among them. The major purpose of this passage is to stress the corporeality of the resurrected body and the identity between the risen One and Jesus of Nazareth. According to some manuscripts, Jesus greeted the disciples with the salutation: "Peace to you." Most likely this is an interpolation from John 20:19*b*.

The disciples first think that a *spirit* has appeared to them. This idea is identical with Gnostic dogma which denied any relationship between the Christ, who is pure spirit, and the flesh, which is essentially evil. But this is plainly presented as an error. The verb *supposed* stresses that this initial idea was contrary to fact. This episode shares motifs with the Johannine literature, which also repudiated the Gnostic error. The disciples are invited to see and feel in order to verify that this is really a body of *flesh and bones* and no *spirit* (cf. 1 John 1:1). Verse 40 is rejected on the basis of its absence from Western witnesses as an interpolation from John 20:20.

But the invitation to *see* and *handle* does not quite convince the disciples that their initial supposition was in error. *They still disbelieved for joy* is characteristic of the Gospel which shows the apostles in the best possible light. They have difficulty in accepting the incredible, wonderful fact of the resurrection. Their doubts are dispelled only when Jesus eats a *piece of broiled fish . . . before them.*

(2) Interpretation of Scripture (24:44–49)

⁴⁴ Then he said to them, "These are my words which I spoke to you, while I was still with you, that everything written about me in the law of Moses and the prophets and the psalms must be fulfilled." ⁴⁵ Then he opened their minds to understand the scriptures, ⁴⁶ and

said to them, "Thus it is written, that the Christ should suffer and on the third day rise from the dead, [47] and that repentance and forgiveness of sins should be preached in his name to all nations, beginning from Jerusalem. [48] You are witnesses of these things. [49] And behold, I send the promise of my Father upon you; but stay in the city, until you are clothed with power from on high."

In his last association with the disciples recorded in the third Gospel, Jesus gives them the proper perspective for the understanding of Scripture. Here only in the New Testament are the *psalms* mentioned with the *law* and the *prophets*. They constituted one of the major sources of messianic texts for the early church. Naturally not all of Hebrew Scripture can be related to the suffering and resurrection of Jesus. What Jesus helps the disciples to understand is *everything written about* him.

But now the motif of prophecy and fulfillment is taken a step further. What had been written about Jesus had been fulfilled. There yet remains, however, a prophetic expectation that is unfulfilled. The gospel must now be preached *to all nations*. The time of the church is also foreseen in Scripture (cf. Luke 2:32; 3:6; Acts 13:47, etc.). Luke does not understand salvation-history in terms of three periods (Conzelmann, p. 16), but in terms of two. The first is the time of prophecy. The second is the time of fulfillment, which takes place in two stages. First, there is the fulfillment of Scripture in the life of Jesus. Subsequently, there is the fulfillment in the life of the church. Clearly this has the effect of separating the life of Jesus from the Parousia.

It is noteworthy that in this whole postresurrection section in Luke there is no word at all about the coming of the Lord. The emphasis is on his entrance into glory and not on his expected return. In the unfolding of the divine plan the church must patiently play her part and leave the end of history in the hands of God (Acts 1:7–8).

The gospel is to be preached to the Gentiles *in his name*. As apostles to the nations, believers are representatives of their Lord. Their mission proceeds under his authority. They do not need to appeal to any higher authority as a justification for calling men to repentance (Acts 2:38). In the preaching of the gospel they are acting according to his will. *Jerusalem* is to be the starting point for the mission that will embrace the nations of the world.

They who accompanied Jesus from Galilee, who watched him die, and to whom he had appeared have a special function in God's redemptive work. They are the *witnesses of these things*, the foundation for the historical trustworthiness of the gospel. That a man like Jesus lived, that he died, and that he rose from the dead is vouchsafed by their testimony. Luke claims that the foundation of his Gospel is the message of these "eyewitnesses and ministers of the word" (1:1–4).

The Lord from glory will *send the promise of* the *Father*. As interpreted in Acts, this promise is the message of Joel invoked by Peter on the day of Pentecost (Acts 2:16 ff.). The church's Lord is in glory, but the church is not left without direction. The vacuum that is left by the removal of the physical presence of Jesus will be filled by the Spirit. The disciples are instructed not to leave Jerusalem until they are *clothed with power from on high*. Jerusalem, the city from which the church must begin her mission, is also the place where she will be equipped for it. After the experience of Pentecost believers will possess resources of strength and leadership for their task.

(3) The Final Parting (24:50–53)

[50] Then he led them out as far as Bethany, and lifting up his hands he blessed them. [51] While he blessed them, he parted from them. [52] And they returned to Jerusalem with great joy, [53] and were continually in the temple blessing God.

The resurrection narrative is telescoped in the Gospel into what appears to be the compass of one day, the first Easter. After blessing the disciples, Jesus *parted from them.* Some manuscripts add "and was carried into heaven." This interpolation probably correctly interprets v. 51 as a description of the ascension of Jesus, although we cannot draw a dogmatic conclusion. In his recapitulation of Jesus' ministry to the disciples after the resurrection, Luke says that his appearances to them took place over a period of 40 days (Acts 1:3). In the resurrection narrative in the Gospel, the author is not governed by the desire to give a chronological sequence of the post-resurrection experiences of the disciples in the manner of a modern news report. He is dominated principally by the need to conclude the story about Jesus in an appropriate manner by bringing into focus certain indispensable motifs.

Jerusalem and the Temple are still centers of the believers' life and worship. The Christian community is still Jewish. The central institution of Judaism is still of great importance in its life and worship. Also the first task of the community will be to confront Jerusalem with the message of the gospel and give the city that crucified Jesus yet another opportunity to repent and claim the promise of God, becoming part of the New Israel (Acts 2:38–39).

Hopelessness and frustration have been transformed into *joy* by the disciples' resurrection faith. They now understand how much better and higher was God's will and purpose than their own earlier limited and distorted understanding of it. Theirs is the sacrifice of unbroken praise to God who has shown them how suffering and glory are indissolubly linked. Their Lord has been exalted to God's right hand. From there he beckons to them as they also walk through suffering to glory in obedience to the purpose that he has set before them (cf. Rom. 8:17). The story of that triumphant pilgrimage remains to be told in the book of Acts.

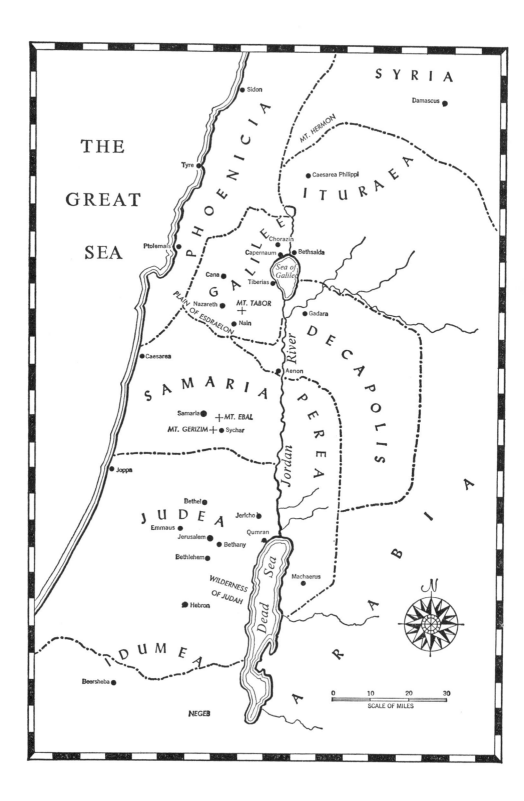

SYRIA

Sidon

Damascus

THE

GREAT

SEA

PHOENICIA

MT. HERMON

ITURAEA

Tyre

Caesarea Philippi

Ptolemais

GALILEE

Chorazin

Capernaum ● Bethsaida

Cana

Sea of
Galilee

Tiberias

Nazareth ✝ MT. TABOR

PLAIN OF ESDRAELON

Nain

Gadara

DECAPOLIS

Caesarea

Aenon

SAMARIA

PEREA

River Jordan

Samaria ● ✝ MT. EBAL

MT. GERIZIM ✝ ● Sychar

Joppa

Bethel ●

JUDEA

Jericho ●

Emmaus ●

Jerusalem ● ● Bethany

Qumran

Bethlehem ●

WILDERNESS
OF JUDAH

Dead Sea

Machaerus ●

A R A B I A

Hebron ●

IDUMEA

N

Beersheba ●

0   10   20   30
SCALE OF MILES

NEGEB

John

WILLIAM E. HULL

Introduction

The Gospel of John is at once the easiest and the hardest book in the Bible to understand. Here simplicity and sublimity are inseparably united. Theology has been put into monosyllables, yet they express one of the most breathtaking visions of ultimate reality to be found in Scripture.

The supreme challenge of any Gospel is to clarify the meaning of Jesus Christ for the life of mankind. The central problem is that of the relation between faith and history. In Johannine categories, what does it mean for the "Word" to become "flesh" (1:14); i.e., for the self-disclosure of the eternal God to become limited by time and space? That issue has two aspects: To what extent does the Gospel of John purport to offer a reliable witness to the earthly life of Jesus? Conversely, to what extent is the Gospel trying to convey those eternal realities which are beyond temporal and spatial categories?

Efforts to solve the Johannine problem may best be approached from three perspectives. First, in no other book is an awareness of the historical setting more important. The dialogue of the fourth Gospel with its milieu largely determined both the material to be included and the meaning which it conveyed. Further, in a literary sense no other book has been more carefully constructed. An adequate assessment of its content is impossible apart from an appreciation of its form. Finally, no book is more self-consciously theological in its attempt to root the Christian faith in the historical life of Jesus. The purposes occasioning this effort and the methods used to carry it out must be discerned if the bold contribution for which John is justly famous be given its due.

I. The Setting of the Fourth Gospel

The Gospel of John was consciously involved on three fronts in a balanced attempt to preserve its Jewish heritage from the past, to clarify its Christian faith in the present, and to prepare for its missionary responsibilities to the Gentiles in the future. This explains why reflections of all three worlds are found on its pages.

1. The Christian Setting

The Synoptic Gospels. Since all four Gospels are concerned with the historical ministry of Jesus, it is only natural to suppose that there was some original connection between them. The most common position in modern study has been that John, as the latest Gospel, made use of one or more of the Synoptics, especially Mark and Luke, a view still defended with vigor by C. K. Barrett in his major commentary of 1955. However, since the pioneering work of Percy Gardner-Smith, *Saint John and the Synoptic Gospels* (Cambridge: University Press, 1938), scholars have come increasingly to see that the differences are too great to allow for a direct dependence of John on any Synoptic source. The conclusion that the fourth Gospel was independent of the other three has now been

189

given strong support by C. H. Dodd in his massive study of *Historical Tradition in the Fourth Gospel* (Cambridge: University Press, 1963).

There is not space here to exhibit the complex evidence bearing on this issue, but some of the more prominent features may be summarized. First, material central to the Synoptics is missing in John: the birth narratives, the baptism and temptations of Jesus, the public preaching of the kingdom of God, the demon exorcisms, the teachings in parables, the Lord's Prayer, the association with publicans and sinners, the ministry centered in Galilee around Capernaum, the confession at Caesarea-Philippi and the transfiguration, the one climactic visit to Jerusalem, the eschatological discourse on the Mount of Olives, the institution of the Lord's Supper, and the agony in Gethsemane. Conversely, the most distinctive material in John has no place in the Synoptic accounts: the changing of water to wine, the visit of Nicodemus, the early Judean ministry before the arrest of John, the Samaritan woman, the healing at Bethezda, the ministry centered in Jerusalem, the "I am" (*egō eimi*) claims, the healing of a man born blind, the raising of Lazarus as the turning point precipitating Jesus' death, the washing of the disciples' feet, the farewell discourses and prayer of consecration, and the role of the beloved disciple.

To be sure, there is some material common to John and the Synoptics, but even it is presented in strikingly different ways. For example, both include the cleansing of the Temple, but John puts it at the outset of the ministry, whereas the Synoptics place it at the end. Both describe the calling of disciples, but John records their confessions of faith in Jesus as Messiah from the beginning, whereas the Synoptics reserve this commitment until much later. Both know that Jesus died on Friday, but John dates this on the eve of the Passover (Nisan 14), whereas the Synoptics date it on the first day of the Passover (Nisan 15). Beyond these and other major differences

are a host of minor divergencies which strongly suggest that the fourth Evangelist did not write with any Synoptic source before him.[1]

Those who assume that John was aware of the Synoptics usually infer thereby that a major purpose for writing the fourth Gospel was either to supplement, correct, or replace the other three. It is very doubtful, however, if any of these intentions were in the mind of the Evangelist. A much more plausible case can be made for the view that John was concerned to clarify the faith for those within his own Christian community rather than to improve on Gospels issued by other Christian groups.

The Johannine Literature. Traditionally, the fourth Gospel, the three Johannine epistles, and the Apocalypse have been associated together on the assumption of a common authorship by John the son of Zebedee. In actuality, only in the Apocalypse does the author claim to be a man named John (Rev. 1:1,4,9; 22:8); in the second and third epistles he refers to himself as "the elder" (2 John 1; 3 John 1), while in the first epistle and the Gospel he is identified only by the pronouns "I" and "we" (1 John 1:1 ff; 2:1,7,12 ff; John 21:24–25). Comparisons of content make it virtually certain only that 2 John and 3 John are by the same person. In other cases, there are strange mixtures of similarities and dissimilarities which have often been explained either by a theory of multiple authorship or by the contention that one man wrote all five books over a long period of time under widely varying circumstances.

The view taken here is that a number of individuals contributed to the composition of the five Johannine writings over a period of perhaps one or two decades, thus accounting for specific divergencies of

---

[1] A possible exception may have been some contact between John and the special material in Luke (designated as L). See J. A. Bailey, *The Traditions Common to the Gospels of Luke and John* ("Supplements to *Novum Testamentum*," VII [Leiden: E. J. Brill, 1963]); Pierson Parker, "Luke and the Fourth Evangelist," *New Testament Studies*, 9 (1963), pp. 317–336.

thought, but that these individuals contributed their literary efforts to the same Christian "school" or community, thus accounting for broad convergencies of thought.[2]

On this view, the other Johannine writings do not help us to understand the author of the fourth Gospel as much as they supply valuable perspectives on the life setting in which the Gospel took shape and to which it was addressed. For example, from the Johannine corpus we see a Christianity in Asia Minor near the end of the first century in which relations with the Jewish synagogue had become intolerably strained (Rev. 2:9; 3:9), in which schism threatened the unity of the church (1 John 2:19), in which ministerial authority was hotly debated (3 John 9–10), in which an incipient Gnosticism advocated a docetic Christology (1 John 4:2–3), in which Roman persecution sought to coerce absolute submission to Caesar as king (Rev. 13:1–2). So directly did the fourth Gospel speak to these and related concerns that it was very likely a part of the world from which they came.

Other Early Christian Literature. The originality of the Gospel of John limits the possibility of comparison with writings of the New Testament other than the Synoptics and the Johannine corpus. A possible exception is Paul. In addition to the basic convictions which they share with the rest of the New Testament, both develop a Christ-mysticism which is strikingly similar in thought if not in terminology. The greatest areas of agreement are not between John and the earlier Pauline epistles, for the Gospel does not show the central concern of these letters with the great debate over justification by faith versus works of the law and circumcision. Rather, John is much closer to Colossians, where the Wisdom-Christology of 1:15–20 anticipates the Logos-Christology of the Prologue, and to Ephesians, where the theme of the unity of the church parallels John 10 and 17.

2 See H. E. Dana, *The Ephesian Tradition* (Kansas City: Kansas City Seminary Press, 1940).

Since Ephesians may have been the final Pauline writing (apart from the question of the Pastorals) and since it likely circulated in Asia Minor around Ephesus (although "at Ephesus" is to be omitted in Eph. 1:1), this writing may provide the closest link between Paul and the Gospel of John. It is striking to observe the way in which both utilize cosmic categories (world above/world below) to describe the Christological drama. In the crucial area of eschatology and its effect on ecclesiology it may be contended that John has modified the Synoptic thrust in somewhat the same way that Ephesians had modified the earlier letters of Paul. No direct connection need be established between the Ephesian epistle and the Ephesian (?) Gospel. It is sufficient to see in this form of maturing Paulinism one factor affecting the larger context in which John was set.

2. The Jewish Setting

The Old Testament. John makes quantitatively less use of the Old Testament than the other Gospels, referring directly to scriptural texts in only 14 passages (1:23; 2:17; 6:31; 6:45; 7:38; 7:42; 10:34; 12:13–15; 12:38–40; 13:18; 15:25; 19:24; 19:28; 19:36–37).[3]

However, these quotations and allusions are strategically placed at pivotal points in the narrative: e.g., the preaching of John the Baptist, the cleansing of the Temple, the feeding of the five thousand, the triumphal entry, the rejection of Israel, the betrayal by Judas, and particularly the crucifixion. Moreover, Old Testament themes are woven deeply into the texture of the Gospel: e.g., the great pilgrim feasts, the new exodus motif, the "I am" claims, the messianic titles, and the basic images for Israel. Clearly the fourth Gospel understood both Jesus and his church fundamentally in biblical categories.

This deliberate employment of a scrip-

3 For a detailed study of each passage see E. D. Freed, *Old Testament Quotations in the Gospel of John* ("Supplements to *Novum Testamentum*," XI [Leiden: E. J. Brill, 1965]).

tural setting for the fourth Gospel reflects two convictions by the author. First, it represented his unalterable commitment to the Israel of God as the soil from which the faith had sprung. No matter how partisan the Evangelist became in the fierce conflict that raged between Christians and Jews, he could not repudiate his kinship with true Israel for to do so would result in a kind of spiritual amnesia, a forgetfulness of the family of faith from whence he had come. At the same time, to embrace the Old Testament did not leave him uncritical of all Jews who shared his sonship with Abraham, for on its pages he found prophetic denunciations directed not to the heathen but to unrepentant Israel. Thus both his affirmations and his condemnations of Judaism sprang from a common source. For all his severity, John was never harder on the Jews than Isaiah had been on their predecessors (cf. comment on 12:36b–43).

Rabbinic Judaism. In the time of Jesus the Pharisaic movement nourished the scribal study of the Old Testament and the oral traditions surrounding it. With the fall of Jerusalem and collapse of the Temple in A.D. 70, the rabbis became the undisputed religious leaders of normative Judaism and the synagogue its dominant institution. The fourth Gospel, in chapters 1—12, shows more explicit interest in these developments than does any other writing in the New Testament. Clearly the "book of signs" (John 2—12) was deeply involved with the identity crisis through which Jewish officialdom passed in the second half of the first century.

Illustrations abound on every page. Jesus devoted virtually his entire public ministry to Jerusalem where the religious establishment was concentrated (see comment on 2:1—12:50). Most of his debates were with those such as Nicodemus, who represented the Sanhedrin or who supported its efforts to maintain the status quo (e.g., 3:1; 7:45–52; 9:28–29; 11:45–53). Often these controversies turned upon rabbinic arguments and exegesis (e.g., 5:10–18, 37–47; 7:15–24; 8:13–19; 10:31–38). Elsewhere, disputes with the Jews were related to the synagogue (6:59; 9:18–23) and reflected homiletical materials in the rabbinic Haggadah (see comment on 6:1–71). In particular, the Christology of John reflects rabbinic concerns with its interest in the origin and nature of the Messiah (e.g., 7:25–31,40–44; 12:34), with the claim of Jesus to be the "I am" (*egō eimi*) or "name" of God (see comment on 5:1—10:42), and with the presentation of Jesus as Logos (see comment on 1:1–18).

Apocalyptic Judaism. At first glance, the Gospel of John shows little or no reflection of Jewish apocalyptic; indeed, this is often pointed to as one of its most striking contrasts with the Synoptics. On closer inspection, however, behind an apparent indifference lurks a clear awareness of such thought and a deliberate strategy for dealing with it. The probable connections between the Gospel and the Apocalypse of John (see above) make it likely that the Evangelist was familiar with this mode of expression. That presumption is confirmed by the Gospel's use of typically apocalyptic concepts; e.g., Son of man (e.g., 1:51; 3:13–14), kingdom (3:3,5; 18:36), judgment (5:27–29), tribulation (16:33), and resurrection (11:23–26). More generally, John shares with apocalyptic thought a concern to unveil the world beyond and see God himself in his heavenly splendor (cf. Rev. 4:1; John 1:51).

At the same time, John has subtly transmuted the apocalyptic idiom in applying it to the historical Jesus. Now that the Revealer has already come in the past, temporal futurity no longer has the same meaning for his followers as it did for the Jewish apocalyptist. Spectacular symbolism (dragons, thrones, fire) is not needed to depict a future age because the realities of the eternal realm have already been disclosed through the historical imagery (water, bread, light) used by Jesus. In place of visions, dreams, and raptures, one now "sees" God by looking at the earthly Jesus (cf. 1:18; 3:32; 5:19; 6:40; 14:7–9). To be sure, the future is still crucial for the Christian as the time both of the clarifying work of the Holy Spirit (14:25–26; 16:4*b*–15) and of the climactic triumph of Christ (5:25–29; 6:38–40,54; 17:24–26), but the future is no longer a mystery needing to be solved by esoteric instruction.

Just as it would be an oversimplification to assume that John ignored apocalyptic, so it would equally oversimplify to conclude that the Gospel rejected it. Probably John wrote shortly after the fall of Jerusalem when apocalyptic hopes as popularly interpreted by the Jews lay in shambles. His strategy was to conserve the enduring convictions which apocalyptic mediated from its Old Testament heritage but to restate the issues with which apocalyptic had grappled in a form less suspect to those in the Hellenistic world.

Sectarian Judaism. Post–World War II discoveries at Qumran near the Dead Sea have greatly enlarged our awareness of sectarian groups within first century Judaism. In the surviving literature of this somewhat monastic Essene community we find closer contacts with certain aspects of Johannine thought and terminology than anywhere else. This does not necessarily imply a relationship of direct dependence between the two groups that produced John and the Scrolls, but it does suggest the likelihood that these respective communities were open to several common influences because they both coexisted together in the same general Judean region for almost a half-century.

Numerous similarities substantiate this hypothesis. Both John and Qumran reflect a modified (i.e., monotheistic rather than metaphysical) dualism which is described, for example, as an eschatological and ethical struggle between light and darkness. Both groups stressed the communal solidarity of the sons of light and the brotherly love that should bind them together over against the sons of darkness in the world. Each shared a dissatisfaction with the Jerusalem Temple and a conviction that true worship was being spiritualized within its midst. On the other hand, Johannine Christianity did not embrace many of the ceremonial, legalistic, and sacerdotal emphases

at Qumran, nor did the sectarians know the sense of fulfillment that had already come to Christians in the person of Jesus Christ.

Schismatic Judaism. One of the emphases which the fourth Gospel (4:1–42; 8:48) shares in common with the special material in Luke (9:52; 10:30–37; 17:11–19) is an interest in the Samaritans (mentioned nowhere in the other Gospels except for the negative reference in Matt. 10:5). Living in the central highlands of Palestine between Judea and Galilee, this group had long been ostracized by orthodox Judaism for its interracial marriages, its syncretistic theology, and its competing temple center. Like the Essene sectaries, the Samaritans claimed to perpetuate an even purer form of Israel's faith than did other groups within Judaism; e.g. they venerated their edition of the Torah (Pentateuch) as the one true form of the Scriptures. Unlike the Qumran community, however, they were not accepted within the broadest definition of the Jews as legitimate members of the household of Israel; e.g., Josephus seriously considered becoming an Essene (*Life*, 10–12) but he would never have thought of becoming a Samaritan. As the early Christians began to separate from Judaism they found themselves in a parallel position to the Samaritans at the point of being considered neither fully Jewish nor fully pagan.

It is noteworthy that a primary interest of John in the Samaritans concerns the transformation of Temple worship (4:16–26), which is also a point of contact with Qumran. Scholars are just beginning to piece together bits of available evidence which may establish historical links between the Samaritans, the Hellenists of Stephen, the nonconformist Judaism seen at Qumran, and the Johannine group responsible for chapter 4, particularly at the point of a common attitude toward the Temple.[4]

Hellenistic Judaism. When the church began to move out into the Graeco-Roman

---

[4] Oscar Cullmann, "A New Approach to the Interpretation of the Fourth Gospel," *The Expository Times*, 71 (1959), pp. 8–12, 39–43.

world, its first missionaries confronted the same challenge that had long faced Diaspora Judaism, that of commending to non-Jews a religion rooted in the Hebraic faith of the Old Testament, while at the same time attempting to win Hellenistic Jews as well. There are many indications that the fourth Gospel, more than any other, adapted some of the methods which had been developed by Hellenistic Judaism in response to its pagan environment. This may be seen best by comparing John with the Wisdom of Solomon (in the Old Testament Apocrypha) and the writings of Philo, both products of Alexandrian Judaism just before and during the first Christian century. For example, the Logos doctrine in the Prologue shares with these writings the realization that to speak of divine attributes and activities in personified fashion would help build a bridge to the world of pagan thought (see comment on 1:1–18).

3. The Graeco-Roman Setting

John understood that to translate a message for a new matrix requires a creative adaptation of the conceptual materials available in that setting. We turn now to an assessment of the way in which the fourth Gospel interacted with certain features of pagan thought in order to penetrate its inner life with the claims of Christ.

Greek Philosophy. By the first century, the classical philosophy of Plato had become a quasi-religious outlook which increasingly supplanted traditional polytheistic mythologies. Although this popular monism was disseminated by itinerant interpreters, it did not assume the form of an institutional religion but of a pervasive mood which exercised a strong appeal to thoughtful citizens of cosmopolitan centers in the Hellenistic world.

There are several indications that the Gospel of John was sensitive to this situation. Speaking to the Platonic notion of an invisible world of eternal reality in contrast to the visible world which is its imperfect, transient copy, Jesus is pictured in 8:23 as

"from above" (*ek tōn anō*), his opponents as "from below" (*ek tōn katō*). Similar ideas are expressed in 3:31 and in 18:36. The frequently used adjective "true" (*alēthinos*) may have carried the connotation of "real" or "archetypal" when used with light (1:9), bread (6:32), and vine (15:1). At the same time, the philosophical meaning was not primary, for the central concern was to link "true" light, bread, and vine not with the ideal world above but with the historical person of Jesus Christ.

This caution suggests that the Gospel of John was not interested in borrowing as much as in meeting. The inquiring skeptic would realize that its author was aware of and interested in his problems but equally aware that he was giving them a decisively new answer. Yet this independence of conviction never became an indifference to other efforts to solve the great issues of human existence. In popular Platonism the Evangelist found elements that enhanced his presentation of Christ to the Greeks without compromising the integrity of his message.

Stoicism.[5] True to the eclectic temper of the New Testament era, a kind of "Platonizing Stoicism" became widely disseminated by popular missionary preachers of morality who reacted against the degeneracy of their times. In the face of skepticism and even fatalism it affirmed that a unity of purpose (*logos*) ran through all the universe. The "wise man" who perceived this providential ordering of things should cultivate a lofty inner detachment (*apatheia*, lit., apathy) from the apparent evil and suffering in the world coupled with a strong sense of brotherhood and philanthropy toward others.

The fourth Evangelist appears to have highlighted those characteristics of Christ which confirmed the best insights in Stoicism. In this Gospel Jesus is presented primarily not as a man of sorrows acquainted with grief (the term "compassion" never

---

[5] On Stoicism and the Gospel of John see R. H. Strachan, *The Fourth Gospel* (3rd. ed.; London: SCM Press, 1941), pp. 52–70.

occurs in John) but as a divinely self-sufficient Son (10:17–18) who was in complete control of every human claim upon him (2:4; 6:15; 7:3–9; 11:3–7), who moved through his passion with the poise of a king (e.g., no Gethsemane; see comment on 18:1—19:42), who conferred "peace" upon his disciples in the midst of tribulation (14:27; 16:33), and who devoted himself completely to his brethren (13:1,34) and to good works for others (5:17).

None of this means, of course, that John embraced the beliefs of Stoicism. The God of this Gospel is intensely personal, not pantheistic. Although immanent in the world in a revelatory sense (1:3–4,9), he was primarily incarnate in the world in a redemptive sense that experienced the full reality of pain and anguish (11:33,35,38; 12:27; 13:21). The ministry of Jesus was guided by the will of God (4:34) rather than by some natural determinism. The Evangelist willingly made contact with Stoicism both to identify its valid contributions and to invite a consideration of fundamental changes in its outlook.

Gnosticism. By far the most difficult, most controversial, and possibly most important question of backgrounds concerns the relationship of the Gospel of John to Gnosticism. Some scholars insist that Gnosticism provides the key to an understanding of our Gospel, while others emphasize with equal vigor that there was no connection between them and, indeed, that Gnosticism as such did not even exist as early as the time of the Gospel. Because of the great complexity of the matter there is space here only to summarize one possible approach.

During the Hellenistic Age (ca. 300 B.C.—A.D. 300), conquests by Alexander and the later consolidation by Rome accelerated a process of religious assimilation in which diverse elements from East and West coalesced to create a new mood of alienation aptly described by Gilbert Murray as "the failure of nerve." Wearied by almost unbelievable cruelty, languishing under totalitarian power structures, men began to feel estranged from any sense of the divine presence in the world below. A specific impetus to this growing sense of futility was the collapse of Jewish apocalyptic hopes in the national crisis of A.D. 66–73.[6]

In this climate of ferment and frustration, Gnosticism began to emerge, not at first as an institutional religion but as a pervasive world-view which emphasized the radical dualism that separated God from man and thus viewed the world as a cosmic tyranny imprisoning men in time and space. The only hope of redemption lay in discovering by means of *gnosis* (knowledge) the divine spark within the individual that needed liberation in order to ascend to the realm of light from whence it had fallen. Gnosticism was an attitude of thoroughgoing introspection or passionate subjectivity (akin to certain types of modern existentialism) that sought salvation in self-understanding because of its fatalistic view of life.[7]

The fourth Gospel seems to have been concerned to interact with certain tendencies that may fairly be called incipient or nascent Gnosticism, and that in two ways. First, the Gospel occasionally utilizes the thought forms employed by Gnosticism in picturing the world as the realm of darkness (8:12; 12:35,46), where men are divided into two groups: those who are saved because they "know" the truth (8:32; 17:3) and those who are condemned to bondage in sin because they have rejected the word of truth (8:33–34). Into this world Jesus is "sent" from the realm above as the bearer of light (8:12) and truth (18:37) to reveal his glory to men of faith. Secondly, the Gospel is at the same time concerned to correct the Gnostic emphasis on otherworldliness

6 The thesis that Gnosticism arose out of the debris of shattered apocalypticism has been argued by Robert M. Grant, *Gnosticism and Early Christianity* (rev. ed.; New York: Columbia University Press, 1966).

7 Generally on the ethos of Gnosticism see Hans Jonas, *The Gnostic Religion* (rev. ed.; Boston: Beacon Press, 1963).

by asserting both the role of the Logos in creation (1:3) and the full incarnation of the Logos in the historical life of Jesus (1:14). Knowledge of the truth about Jesus does not lead to escape from the world but a life of service to the world in the spirit of love (13:1–20).

Hermetism. The Corpus Hermeticum is a collection of writings from the second and third Christian centuries attributed to Hermes Trismegistus, supposedly a sage of ancient Egypt. Although later than the fourth Gospel, the Hermetic literature contains many striking parallels because it, too, has assimilated elements from Platonism, Stoicism, Gnosticism, and the Mysteries.[8] For example, in the tractate "Poimandres" there are references to the need for rebirth, the importance of knowledge, the role of the Logos, the dualism of light and darkness, the descending and ascending heavenly man, and the importance of spirituality in the life of the believer.

The Corpus Hermeticum provides a basis of comparison for discerning the impact which the Christ-event had on the religious notions of that day because it is in so many respects like the Gospel of John except for this decisive factor. When the two are set side-by-side it becomes clear that although John took seriously the points of contact offered by his environment, he took even more seriously the responsibility of confronting that environment with the cruciality of Christ.

II. The Shaping of the Fourth Gospel

From a confessional perspective, the dominant impulse to create the Gospel of John was provided by divine inspiration given in the life of Jesus and mediated through his Spirit. From a historical perspective, this inspiration is seen to have permeated a complex process of literary composition stretching over several decades. If the book had been produced at only one place in a brief period of time, it

[8] See C. H. Dodd, *The Interpretation of the Fourth Gospel* (Cambridge: University Press, 1953), pp. 10–53.

would hardly have been as sensitive to the many environmental factors identified above. In what follows, the formation of the Gospel will be traced from the time of the events which it records to its present place in the Christian Scriptures.

1. The Origin of the Fourth Gospel

We begin by asking when and where, by whom and for whom, the book appeared. With these fixed points established we can then trace what went before and after.

Authorship. From a study of the English Bible it is quite easy and natural to assume that the author of a book is indicated by the title given to it, in this case "The Gospel According to John" (RSV). Such a title was not an original part of the Gospel, however, having been added in the second century after the four Gospels had been completed, circulated, and collected into a literary unit. The proper way to approach the question of authorship is through a balanced assessment of external and internal evidence.

External evidence is drawn from the earliest and most reliable references to authorship outside the Gospel itself. Since there is no direct mention of the fourth Gospel in any contemporary sources, including the New Testament, we are here dependent entirely on later second-century sources which yield a somewhat confusing picture. On the one hand, Irenaeus affirmed (ca. A.D. 180–200) that the Gospel was published by "John the disciple of the Lord, who also had leaned upon his breast" (*Against Heresies*, III, 1:1; cf. I, 8:5; II, 22:5; III, 3:4; note Eusebius, *Ecclesiastical History*, III, 23:1–4; IV, 14:3–6), although this tradition cannot be traced back with consistency through Irenaeus' sources. On the other hand, the slowness of the Gospel to be received in the church (see below), including outright opposition from some quarters, "makes it impossible to believe that it had been published with the full authority of apostolic authorship" (Barrett, p. 97).

Turning to internal evidence within the book itself further complicates the picture. Properly speaking, the Gospel is anonymous, although very significant but indirect statements are made about authorship, especially in 21:24–25. There, we see clearly that the process of composition was not limited to any single author but involved at least three distinct stages:

(1) The underlying foundation of the Gospel is claimed to rest on the testimony of an eyewitness ("he") who beheld the crucified (19:35) and risen (21:24) Christ. The context in both passages indicates almost certainly that this witness was the beloved disciple.

(2) John 21:24 then refers to a community ("we") which accepted the testimony of the beloved disciple; use of the first person plural implies that this group was also bearing its witness through the publication of the Gospel (cf. 1:14; 1 John 1:1–4). This cannot be the editorial "we" of the beloved disciple since he is referred to separately in the same verse (21:24— "*we* know . . . *his* testimony").

(3) A community, however, cannot write a book except through some representative, and this individual is identified in 21:25 ("I"). Again, coming in the same context, this person cannot, logically, be identified with the beloved disciple.

To summarize: the pronominal progression "him—we—I" in 21:24–25 points to a threefold process of composition. Trustworthy testimony regarding Jesus Christ was declared by a uniquely qualified participant in his ministry whose spiritual sensitivity won for him a special place in the affection of the Master. Some Christian congregation embraced this witness and joined in proclaiming its validity (20:31) through various oral and literary materials which one of their number edited in final form. This is all that the fourth Gospel itself asserts regarding authorship. (For another reflection of the long and complicated process in which the "author" of a Gospel participated, see Luke 1:1–4).

We are now in a position to ask whether that beloved disciple who functioned as the primary witness contributing to this Gospel may be identified with "John the disciple of the Lord," as was done in ecclesiastical tradition a century later. Despite numerous efforts to justify this connection, the cumulative force of the evidence is to the contrary.[9] Consider, for example, the following:

✓ (1) John was a Galilean. There he was called and there he worked with Jesus. Yet the fourth Gospel shows little interest in Galilee, its geographical knowledge being limited almost entirely to the south.

(2) John was a fisherman, yet, in contrast to the Synoptics, the fourth Gospel displays little interest in fishing or activities around the sea except in the supplementary chapter 21.

(3) John had a brother, James, and the two of them, along with Simon Peter, formed an inner circle in the disciple band. There is no hint of this triumvirate in the fourth Gospel, and James is never mentioned (but cf. 21:2).

(4) John was called a "son of thunder" by Jesus (Mark 3:17), apparently describing a wrathful man. The beloved disciple was obviously noted for his loving disposition, a characteristic never attributed to John in the Synoptics.

(5) John once expressed a vengeful attitude towards the Samaritans (Luke 9:54), whereas the fourth Gospel manifests an unusually positive attitude toward the Samaritans.

(6) John was interested in demon exorcisms. Presumably he was present for all such healings recorded in the Synoptics; he was commissioned to cast out demons (Mark 3:15); and he showed concern when an unauthorized exorcist was found doing so (Mark 9:38). Yet this subject is never mentioned in the fourth Gospel.

9 The classic defense of the son of Zebedee as author of the fourth Gospel is by B. F. Westcott, *The Gospel According to St. John* (London: James Clarke & Co., 1958), pp. v–xxxii. On the arguments against this identification see Pierson Parker, "John the Son of Zebedee and the Fourth Gospel," *Journal of Biblical Literature,* 81 (1962), 35–43.

(7) As a member of the inner circle, John in particular was permitted to witness the transfiguration following the Caesarea Philippi confession, to hear the great eschatological discourse on the Mount of Olives, to prepare for and participate in the institution of the Lord's Supper, and to share in the agony of Gethsemane. Yet these are precisely the climactic episodes omitted from the fourth Gospel.

As indicated by 21:24–25, the beloved disciple was not the final editor of the fourth Gospel but only its eyewitness source. Thus we might allow for a number of secondary characteristics to develop unrelated to the son of Zebedee. However, the internal evidence suggests that John did not contribute even the basic approach found here (see above on the relation of the fourth Gospel to the Synoptics). It is not an exaggeration to conclude that nothing which we know about the son of Zebedee from the Synoptics fits what we know about the beloved disciple from the fourth Gospel.

If this be so, then at least two questions regarding authorship need to be raised. First, who was the beloved disciple? The most intriguing suggestions among many identify this shadowy figure either with Lazarus [10] or with John Mark.[11] It is true that Lazarus is explicitly described as the disciple whom Jesus loved (see comment on 11:3,5) and that he does occupy a climactic place in the witness of the Gospel. Also, it is striking to discover that extant information about John Mark fits remarkably with our inferences regarding the author of the fourth Gospel—including the convenient fact that he was named John! At best, however, these and similar hypotheses must remain conjectural for lack of decisive evidence. At the same time, they do serve to keep the question open

and to illustrate the difficulty of devising a solution that fits all pieces of the puzzle together. It may even be that the final editor intended for the identity of the beloved disciple to remain obscure so that attention would focus not on who he was but on the One to whom he bore witness.

The second remaining question springs naturally from the state of the evidence as we have surveyed it thus far: how, then, was the name "John" eventually connected with the fourth Gospel? The second-century situation is most confusing but two likely possibilities present themselves. One is that John the son of Zebedee may have migrated to Asia Minor and, venerated as the only original apostle to live out his days in that vicinity, gave his name to the Gospel produced there. Admittedly the evidence that John ever lived at Ephesus is slight, but it is not implausible (no NT evidence; cf. Justin, *Dialogue with Trypho,* LXXXI, 4, with Eusebius, *Ecclesiastical History,* IV, 18:6–9; the tradition that John suffered an early martyrdom is weak). The other possibility is that the attribution of the Gospel to John may have arisen because of its relation, not to the son of Zebedee, but to the "elder" mentioned in 2 and 3 John. Papias, in a very disputed passage quoted by Eusebius (*Ecclesiastical History,* III, 39:1–8), identified a "presbyter John" as one source of living words of truth from the Lord and seems to imply that he, too, was from Ephesus. Although the "elder" could hardly have been the beloved disciple, many scholars suppose that he was the final editor of the fourth Gospel, whatever the role of the son of Zebedee may have been, and thus may have given to the book his name (see the full discussion in Bernard, I, xxxiv–lxxi).

Date of Writing. Several considerations suggest that the book in final form is to be dated nearer the end of the first century than its midpoint. Quite obviously, relations with Judaism had deteriorated past the breaking point (9:22; 12:42; 16:2). A distinctively Christian theology which built on the Old Testament but went well be-

---

[10] See Floyd V. Filson, "Who Was the Beloved Disciple?" *Journal of Biblical Literature,* 63 (1949), pp. 83–88; J. N. Sanders, "Who Was the Disciple Whom Jesus Loved?" *Studies in the Fourth Gospel,* ed., F. L. Cross (London: A. R. Mowbray, 1957), pp. 72–82.

[11] See Pierson Parker, "John and John Mark," *Journal of Biblical Literature,* 79 (1960), 97–110.

yond it had now been elaborated (e.g., in the Prologue and in the doctrine of the Paraclete). Chapter 21 makes the most direct contribution to dating by implying that the apostolic generation had died out, including both Peter (21:18–19) and the beloved disciple (21:22–23), before the arrival of the Parousia. These factors, plus the general situation depicted in the other Johannine literature, point to a period no earlier than the last decade of the first century.

At the same time, other factors suggest that the latest date could hardly go beyond the first decade of the second century. Already by A.D. 125–135 copies of the Gospel were circulating in Egypt as established by a fragmentary papyrus find containing John 18:31–33, 37–38, which is to be dated ca. A.D. 135–150 (P⁵², Rylands Papyrus 457). Some knowledge of John seems to be assumed in both Ignatius (ca. A.D. 110) and Justin (ca. A.D. 150). Use of the fourth Gospel on equal footing with the Synoptics in the Papyrus Egerton 2 (ca. A.D. 150) and in Tatian's *Diatessaron* (ca. A.D. 175) suggests that it had gained widespread acceptance by virtue of having been in circulation for a similar period of time. Thus we are left with a plausible date of ca. A.D. 100 with a leeway of some ten years on either side.

Place of Writing. External evidence cited above in the discussion of authorship clearly favors the province of Asia in general and the city of Ephesus in particular as the locale of the fourth Gospel. This identification tends to be confirmed by internal evidence which, while silent on the subject of place, does depict a life situation remarkably similar to that in the Johannine epistles and the Apocalypse, writings which almost certainly originated in this region (see above on the Johannine writings). Other suggestions include Alexandria because of close connections with Philonic and Wisdom literature, as well as Antioch because of possible ties with Ignatius, but there is little direct evidence to support either claim.

2. The Composition of the Fourth Gospel

Assuming that the fourth Gospel originated from Ephesus in final form ca. A.D. 100, we must now attempt to trace the stages of its composition beginning with those events in Palestine ca. A.D. 30 on which all of the Gospels ultimately rest. Since this long process was nowhere described in early Christian literature, we must reconstruct its major phases entirely by inference from the nature of the Gospel itself.

Sources. As the great stream of Christian testimony to Jesus was gradually reduced to writing, several major sources eventually utilized in the composition of the fourth Gospel began to appear. Probably the chief period for the production of these materials was ca. A.D. 50–80 as Christianity began for the first time to withdraw from Judaism, to penetrate new cultures, to defend itself against persecution, and to attack various threats to internal unity. So different are some of these sources in content and emphasis that they may be clearly distinguished within the Gospel. Three of these are sufficiently important to deserve special mention here (for details see the introductions to each of these sections in the commentary).

First, the "backbone" of the Gospel was contributed by the "book of signs" now comprising chapters 2—12. This material was probably consolidated on Palestinian soil shortly after A.D. 70 to meet the problem of the collapse of Temple worship with the fall of Jerusalem.

Second, this highly Jewish source in chapters 2—12 was balanced for Hellenistic readers with a very original "upper room" source now comprising chapters 13—17 which shows almost no interest in the Jews. The emphasis shifts from the institutional to the personal, and a mystical idiom is employed which is particularly suited to the private worship of small bands of Greek converts.

Third, the passion narrative now in John 18—20 was probably one of the earliest sources to be formulated, since the story of the death and resurrection of Jesus was from the outset at the very center of Christian preaching. All of the Gospels have this kind of source, the one in John seeming to be earlier than A.D. 50 because of its contacts with the special (Judean?) passion source in Luke. However, when it became attached to chapters 13—17 to form the "book of the passion" in the second half of the Gospel, several features designed to appeal to Greek readers were included.

Probably these three sources were joined to make an early draft of the Gospel which the final editor refers to as those things "written" by the beloved disciple (21:24). If so, then the editor himself was responsible for adding three minor sources: a hymnic Prologue to serve as a liturgical introduction (1:1–18); a cycle of material on John the Baptist (1:19 ff), fragments from which may be scattered in such passages as 3:22–36; 5:33–35; 10:40–42; and a supplementary epilogue (21:1–23) designed to meet questions which had been raised about the first draft of the Gospel.

Unity. The very fact that the Gospel utilized several sources has led many scholars to question whether they were edited correctly. Many theories have been devised to challenge the literary integrity of the work in its present form.

Theories of displacement are the most common and in some ways the most plausible because they seek to correct the obvious geographical and chronological discontinuities in the narrative. To explain these phenomena it is sometimes conjectured that individual papyrus sheets were accidentally dislocated in the final stages of publication. The most glaring instances of seams or breaks in the text will be noted in the commentary and the position taken that the present order was intended primarily for theological or dramatic reasons (cf. comment on 5:1–47; 13:1—17:26).

Theories of redaction assume an early dislocation of the text which may be repaired by a careful discrimination of the basic sources. Such reconstructions are of ambiguous value because they yield nei-

ther the original sequence of the authoritative words of Jesus nor the intended sequence of the canonical Gospel but only the possible sequence of some now unrecoverable document lying at an intermediate stage between the two.

Literary Method. Preoccupation with problems of disunity has the disadvantage of drawing attention away from the skill of the Evangelist in the utilization of his sources. Several characteristic techniques heighten the dramatic power of his presentation: Frequent use is made of words with double meanings (e.g., *anōthen* = anew/from above; *pneuma* = wind/Spirit; *hupsōthēnai* = lifted up on cross/lifted up in exaltation). At times, whole sentences may have a second meaning which is the opposite of that intended by the speaker (e.g., 11:50–52; 12:19; 19:5,19). At other times, a key concept will be introduced and then held in reserve to be illustrated later (e.g., "light" in 8:12 is illustrated in 9:1–41; "casting out" and "finding" in 9:34–35 is illustrated in 10:1–30; "laying down one's life for the sheep" in 10:11 is illustrated in 11:1–54). Elaborate discourses draw out first one aspect of a theme and then another (e.g., "bread" in 6:1–71; "abiding" in 15:1–17). Attention will be drawn in introductory sections of the commentary on the text to the care with which the writer organizes symmetrical cycles of material (e.g., 2:1—4:54), effects careful transitions between apparently unrelated sections (e.g., 2:23–25), and carries the reader forward by a climactic arrangement of Christological titles (e.g., 4:1–42; 9:1–41).

Structure. The supreme example of Johannine literary skill is the way in which originally diverse sources have been fused so as to give the entire Gospel a unified structure organized around the motif of the "descending" and "ascending" of Jesus as Son of man. The detailed outline printed below is designed to show how the Gospel framework resembles a "parabola of redemption" which traces the humiliation and exaltation of Jesus in the same way anticipated by the stately Prologue (see introduction to 1:1–18). This chiastic principle of organization supplies an added theological dimension to the Gospel narrative. The reader is never allowed to forget that the Jesus who appeared on earth both came from God and returned to God. The temporal was thereby set in the context of the eternal, the historical and the ontological became inseparable.

3. The Transmission of the Fourth Gospel

Having traced the composition of the fourth Gospel up to the time of its completion ca. A.D. 100, we now comment briefly on its fortunes since that time.

Reception. Surprisingly for a book which has become one of the most beloved in the Bible, the Gospel of John was not at first warmly welcomed by the church. Despite the fact that it grappled profoundly with many of the most urgent problems facing Christianity in the first half of the second century, it was not utilized directly even by writers of this period who seem to be aware of its contents (e.g., Ignatius, Polycarp, Justin). Only about A.D. 180, almost a century after its initial appearance, did the fourth Gospel come into its own as of equal standing with the Synoptics (e.g., Irenaeus, Tatian, Melito). Even at this late date, however, it was still necessary for the work to be defended by its advocates (e.g., Irenaeus, the Muratorian Canon, Hippolytus).

The reasons for this initial resistance are not difficult to discern. Even in that precritical period it was widely recognized that John was strikingly different from the other three Gospels (see Clement in Eusebius, *Ecclesiastical History,* VI, 14:5–7). Moreover, the attractiveness of the book to the Hellenistic world led it to be adopted quite early by the Gnostics. In fact, the earliest known commentary was by Heracleon, an "esteemed representative of the School of Valentinus" (Clement, *Stromateis* 4:9). Further, the teachings of the Gospel on the Holy Spirit caused it to be unpopular among those opposing Montanism; Irenaeus seems to have known those who rejected the book for this reason (*Against Heresies,* III, 11:9).

Canonization. With the arrival of the third century and the increasing stabilization of the early church, initial questioning of the fourth Gospel gave way to its traditional acceptance along with the other three. By the time that official canonical lists began to be promulgated in the fourth century, the Gospel of John was invariably included (e.g., Festal Letter of Athanasius in A.D. 367; Council of Rome in A.D. 382; Council of Carthage in A.D. 397). Since that time, it has been universally accepted within both Western and Eastern Christendom (cf. BBC, Vol. 8, pp. 18–21).

Text. As is true with all books of the Bible, no original text of John has survived. We are dependent entirely on editions produced more than a century after the Gospel was written. During the hundreds of years in which manuscripts of the fourth Gospel were laboriously copied by hand, numerous divergencies arose by a process of accidental error in transcription and deliberate editorial revision which must now be evaluated by the science of textual criticism (see BBC, Vol. 8, pp. 15–18).

In comparison with the rest of the Bible, and particularly with other ancient documents, the surviving manuscripts of John are superior in both quantity and quality. Our Gospel is to be found in virtually all of the major uncial and minuscle manuscripts of the New Testament, and in more known papyrus copies (17) than of any other New Testament book, including the recently published Bodmer papyri dating ca. A.D. 200.

III. The Significance of the Fourth Gospel

In the light of the historical setting and the literary shaping of the Johannine material, we are now in a position to assess its theological significance.

1. Theological Purposes

The striking originality of the Gospel of John is itself ample proof that the intention of the book was not to pass on some unchanging body of doctrine but to relate certain Christian convictions to the challenges facing the community in which it arose. Any writing which is more than a half-century in the making will naturally reflect several diverse concerns. We select for treatment here four interests which seem to have influenced the content of the book at various stages in its composition.

Evangelistic Interests. The stated purpose of the Gospel in 20:31 is well known: "These are written that you may believe . . ."[12] The key verb "believe" is central not only to the immediate context (3 times in 20:24–29) but to the entire book as well (98 times in John, only 34 times in all of the Synoptics together). Such believing is further said to lead to (eternal) "life," another prominent emphasis in this Gospel (36 times in John, only 16 in all of the Synoptics together). Clearly the dominant aim of the book is to facilitate a personal relationship with Jesus which will transform the very character of one's existence.

The scope of this endeavor is suggested by the two phrases which qualify the meaning of believing "in his name." First, pride of place is given to the predicate "Christ," elsewhere explained to mean the Hebrew "Messiah" or "Anointed One" (1:41; 4:25). Since this term was largely unintelligible to the Greeks, its use here points directly to the evangelization of the Jews. We know from Acts (17:3; 18:5) that early Christian missionaries sought to prove in the synagogues of the Diaspora that the crucified Jesus of history was indeed the promised Messiah of Judaism. This debate was now carried forward on the pages of the Gospel, particularly through the evidence of the signs which authenticated his ministry as the fulfillment of Scripture.

At the same time, the Evangelist is concerned to establish also belief in Jesus as the "Son of God," a concept which was as meaningless or offensive to the Jews as the

title "Christ" was to the Greeks. Despite the Jewish aversion to this unique identification of a man with God (5:18 ff.; 8:34 ff.), the concept of "Son" is central to Johannine Christology, suggesting a desire to present Jesus in meaningful categories to Greek readers. The most distinctive feature of John's evangelistic intention, therefore, is to offer the gospel of Jesus "to the Jew first and also to the Greek" (Rom. 1:16). This explains why the book is so concerned both with Judaism (ch. 2—12) and with the wider world beyond Judaism (ch. 13—20).

Ecclesiastical Interests. In urging an outreach which would gather all of the scattered children of God (cf. 11:52; 17:20–21), the fourth Evangelist was not unmindful of the internal needs of the church. The very tensions involved in uniting Jewish and Greek converts—symbolized by the union of "Christ" with "Son of God" in 20:31—were part of a larger upheaval which deeply troubled the church during the age of transition in which the Gospel was completed. Not only was Christianity spreading into new cultures. The passage of time had brought the death of the apostolic generation without the arrival of the Parousia (see comment on 21: 18–23). The very need to have a written Gospel—without which the church had gotten along for a half-century—was intensified by new pressures: subtle forms of heresy, increasingly bitter harassment from enemies, and internal disunity prompted in part by a crisis in ministerial leadership.

In response to these complex problems the Evangelist made one basic decision: the greatest single need of the church was to discover the proper connection between its contemporary life and the historical ministry of Jesus. To this end the writer insisted that Jesus continues to be known by his followers through the ministry of the Spirit and the Word (6:63; 14:26; 16:12–15). Since Jesus now abides with his own, one's hopes need not be fixed only on his future return; in an experiential though not cosmic sense, eschatology has been "realized" (13:31—14:31). In the

12 On the significance of 20:31 for an understanding of John's intention see W. C. van Unnik, "The Purpose of St. John's Gospel," *The Gospels Reconsidered* (Oxford: Basil Blackwell, 1960), pp. 167–196.

power of his presence one may face even persecution (16:1–33). His ministry furnishes the model and criterion for all true shepherds of the flock (10:1–18). His bread and water and blood give substance to the religious symbols used by the church in baptism and the Lord's Supper (e.g., 6:52–58; 13:1–17; 19:34–35). In writing a Gospel about Jesus rather than a philosophical treatise, a scriptural commentary, or an ethical code, the Evangelist was expressing his central conviction that the full meaning of Christianity lay latent in the incarnate life of Jesus rather than in some concept, book, or rule.

Apologetical Interests. In seeking to commend Jesus to the Jews, the Gospel faced a double challenge. Since Christianity had originated within Judaism, it was hardly sufficient to explain why the Jews should now enter the church as if they were outsiders. Some reason also had to be given why the earliest Christians had left the Temple and synagogue. This issue was greatly exacerbated by the revolt of A.D. 66–73, when Jewish Christians, forced to choose between their nation and their faith, opted for the latter. In the aftermath of that conflict, with Jerusalem in shambles, Judaism began to reorganize its religious life at Jamnia by excluding those Jewish Christians who had formerly been tolerated within its midst (cf. comment on 9:22; 12:42; 16:2). One has only to reflect on Jewish-Christian relations for the past two thousand years to realize the fatefulness of this rupture.

The Gospel of John seems to show a special interest in the relation of the old Israel to the new, particularly in chapters 2—12. As the commentary will show, the framework of this section was determined by the great Temple festivals in Jerusalem. The thrust of the theological argument, which often reads like a synagogue debate, is that of the superiority of Christianity not as the replacement of Judaism but as its true embodiment. Rather than renouncing the Temple in the hour of its mortal peril, the church had itself *been* the true temple as the body of Him in whom the glory of

God tabernacled upon earth (cf. 1:14; 2:19–21). To a people bereft of their ancient feasts, an apology was developed for Christ as the true Passover, Tabernacles, and Dedication. What the church had rejected was only the racial and political dimensions of Israel, not its true spiritual substance. Hence the Jews were invited to accept Christ in order to fulfill rather than to repudiate their scriptural calling.[13]

Polemical Interests. One subsidiary but significant theological purpose of the fourth Gospel was to correct misunderstandings of the proper relationship between Jesus and John the Baptist. This was accomplished by emphasizing John's denials that he was worthy to be compared with the Christ and by specifying the ways in which Jesus was his superior (cf. 1:8,15,19–34; 3:22–36; 5:33–36; 10:42). It is interesting to note that most of the passages on the Baptist do not fit well into their present contexts, suggesting the possibility that they were taken from an independent source written to meet this special problem. Apparently there were those in the movement launched by John who had not transferred their loyalties to Jesus (see comment on 3:22–28). Acts 19:1–7 refers to such a group at Ephesus, the possible home of the fourth Gospel. Further evidence of a Baptist sect is suggested in the Pseudo-Clementine literature (*Recognitions*, I, 54, 60), where the disciples of John are viewed as one of four Jewish sects opposed to the church.

Although this polemic had the negative purpose of restricting inflated claims made for John, it was equally concerned with the positive task of giving John his rightful place in Christian theology. Nowhere is the Baptist treated as an opponent as are "the Jews"; his followers do not come under attack as, for example, the Pharisees do. Rather, John is portrayed as the ideal witness (1:7) and friend (3:29) of Jesus who, in utter self-denial, fulfilled the greatest

---

[13] For details on this section see T. C. Smith, *Jesus in the Gospel of John* (Nashville: Broadman Press, 1959), especially pp. 22–56.

task of all, that of proclaiming Christ to the world.[14]

2. Theological Sources and Methods

The Fourth Gospel identifies not only the needs it sought to meet but also the basic sources of its faith. Three factors interacted to produce the theological outlook of this Gospel.

The Remembered Jesus. The primary source of religious truth for the fourth Gospel was the actual words of the incarnate Jesus (6:63,68). The first disciples were instructed from the beginning to remember his teachings (15:20; 16:4). Later converts were aided in this task by eyewitnesses who reported what they had seen and heard (19:35; 21:24; cf. 1 John 1:1–4). This remembrance was not merely a factual recall but the reflective pondering of a unique past through the help of the Holy Spirit (14:26) in the light of subsequent events (2:22). The bedrock on which the Evangelist rested all of his theology was the self-disclosure of the historical Jesus, not some revelation that had come to him through personal experience.

The Relevant Scriptures. The words of Jesus could not be understood in isolation, however, but needed to be set in the context of the inspired Scriptures. Jesus had taught his disciples that the most crucial events in his ministry should be understood as the fulfillment of Scripture (cf. 5:39,46–47; 6:31–33,44–45; 13:18; 17:12). However, the contribution of the Old Testament to a clarification of Jesus' life was not always readily apparent (20:9). After their Master's departure, therefore, the disciples embarked upon a further search for insight from its pages, a quest which did not go unrewarded (2:17,22; 12:16). When the Gospel was written, the evangelist helped the reader to grasp the richer significance of some apparently minor incidents, for example in the crucifixion of Jesus, by rooting them in the experience of Israel (19:24,28,

36,37). Without Jesus as the clue, Bible study could prove futile (5:38–40) because it was to Jesus that patriarch and prophet alike bore witness (5:46; 8:56; 12:41).

The Risen Lord. The Evangelist looked not only backward to history and outward to written record but also inward to the abiding presence of the Spirit as a source of theological insight. After Jesus was risen, the disciples were not cut off from further growth by his physical absence but were just entering their period of most fruitful discovery (2:22; 12:16; 16:23–25). Heretofore they had been able to "bear" only a small part of the "many things" that Jesus wished to say to them, but now the Spirit would guide them into "all the truth" (16:12–13). Just as Jesus was the clue to Scripture, so he was the criterion by which to "test the spirits," for the Paraclete would not speak on his own authority but would reveal only a fuller understanding of God in the life of Jesus (16:14–15).

The method of the Evangelist in combining these three sources was clearly intended to strike a dynamic theological balance. To emphasize Jesus apart from Scripture would be like cutting a flower away from its roots. Or, to champion Scripture apart from the fresh guidance of the Spirit would have limited the possibility of progress in the face of rapid change. Again, to isolate the Spirit as the one key to truth would have left no safeguards against unbridled enthusiasm. But to unify all three channels of revelation around the reality of Christ and to insist that he is known in the events of history, in the pages of a book, and in the presence of the Spirit achieved one of the most productive theological methods to be found in the New Testament.

3. Theological Emphases

In choosing to write a historical narrative, the Evangelist decided thereby not to set forth certain doctrines in systematic fashion. To tear his distinctive truths away from the tissue of the text in which they are interwoven and reduce them to topical

---

14 See Walter Wink, *John the Baptist in the Gospel Tradition* ("Society for New Testament Studies Monograph Series," 7 [Cambridge: University Press, 1968]), pp. 98–106.

summaries is to risk the danger of distortion. Here, therefore, we will only mention some of the leading religious ideas in John and use Scripture references to indicate the contexts in which they may best be studied.

Revelation. Of all the books of the Bible, John is preeminently concerned with the divine disclosure (1:51). This is seen immediately in the Prologue, where the concept of Logos as the self-expression of God is developed (1:1–18). By identifying Jesus with the eternal Word, an initial foundation is laid for the presentation of his ministry as a means of "knowing" God (10:38; 14:7,20; 17:3,7–8,25) and therefore of discovering "the truth" (1:14,17; 4:24; 8:32,40,45–6; 14:6; 17:17–19; 18:37). The miracles, for example, were not so much acts of power as they were "signs" pointing to ultimate reality (2:11; 4:54; 11:47; 20:30) which manifested the "glory" of Jesus (2:11; 11:40; 17:4–5). The great frequency of terms both for "hearing" and for "seeing" in a spiritual sense (see comment on 1:14) underscores the conviction of the Gospel that the revelation of God has been given and may be received.

God. As a Christian whose Bible was the Old Testament, the Evangelist could assume a clear conception of the God of Israel as the foundation of his theology. However, he did enrich this inherited understanding in the light of its supreme clarification by Jesus. For example, God is referred to as "Father" 119 times, despite the fact that this was not a dominant designation for the Divine among the Jews (see 5:17–18). Again, the eternal love of God for all men is strongly asserted (3:16; 17:23–26). Finally, because of the unique relationship both to the Father and to the Holy Spirit claimed by Jesus, the fourth Gospel begins to develop a trinitarianism which affirms both the solidarity and the individuality of the divine family (1:1,18; 5:19–23; 10:30; 14:18–26; 16:12–16; 17:5,22,24; 20:28).

Christology. Just as John affirmed the God of the Old Testament, so he accepted the messianic hope which it bequeathed to the church. Virtually all of the traditional titles used to describe the expected deliverer were attributed to Jesus: e.g., Christ, Son of man, Prophet, King (see comment on 1:19–51). However, parallel to the singular concentration on God as Father is a corresponding emphasis on Jesus as "the Son" (e.g., 1:14,18; 3:16–18,35–36; 5:19–23; 6:40; 8:35–36; 14:13; 17:1). This absolute or unqualified usage was particularly suited to convey both the subordination of Jesus to God and his filial intimacy with the Father. In this family analogy lies one of the deepest clues to the Christology of the fourth Gospel. Its supreme expression, however, is reflected in the use of "I am" (*egō eimi*) to identify Jesus as an historical theophany of the eternal being of God and thus to assert his full deity (see comment on 5:1–10:42).

Salvation. As the tabernacling glory of God (1:14), the coming of Jesus was like the shining of light in darkness (1:4–5,9; 3:19–21; 8:12; 9:5; 12:35–36,46). Inevitably, therefore, a process of judgment was set in motion which sifted men according to their response to Jesus (5:22–24,27,30; 8:16; 9:39; 12:31). In this dialectical situation, God determined the necessity, the alternatives, and the consequences offered to human choice, but man determined whether his response would be made in the freedom of faith or in submission to the tyranny of evil (see comment on 3:16–21; 6:66–71; 8:12–59; 9:39–41; 12:36b–50). Although in a historical sense salvation was "from the Jews" (4:22), Jesus—a Jew who came to his own (1:11)—was "the Savior of the world" (4:42) and not of one particular group. In union with him (see comment on 15:1–17) through faith (see on 2:1–4:53), the believer is given "eternal life," an existence qualitatively like that of the life which belongs to God himself (3:15–16,36; 4:14,36; 5:21–24; 6:33,35, 40,47,63; 10:10,28; 11:25; 14:6; 17:2–3; 20:31). That such life may be a present as well as a future possession shows that eschatology has already begun to be realized in Christ.

The Church. Any book dealing with the earthly life of Jesus could speak of the community which his ministry called into being only to a very limited extent. Nevertheless, more direct attention is given to the church here than in any other Gospel. Side by side with an intensely personal individualism stands a conception of the church as that collective organism which draws its life exclusively from Christ (15:1—16:33). Particular concern is expressed for the unity of this fellowship (see comment on 10:1–30; 17:11–26; 21:11), especially as it is fostered by a faithful ministry modeled after the pattern of Jesus himself (10:1–18). The mission of this body was to gather unto itself all the scattered people of God wherever they might be (cf. on 7:35; 11:51–52; 12:32; 17:20; 21:11). To that end they were authorized by Jesus to preach the gospel of forgiveness and judgment in the power of the Holy Spirit (20:19–23). So completely was the church to be an extension of Jesus' own ministry (17:18; 20:21) that its celebration of baptism and the Lord's Supper would re-present Jesus who alone is the true Water and Bread of life (see comment on 6:52–59; 13:1–11; 19:34).

Outline of the Gospel
Introduction (1:1–51)

I. The Word of God: Prologue (1:1–18)
  1. The Word and the universe (1:1–5)
  2. The Word and John (1:6–8)
  3. The Word and the world (1:9–13)
  4. The Word and the church (1:14–18)
II. The witness of men (1:19–51)
  1. Witness of John the Baptist (1:19–34)
    (1) The negative witness to himself (1:19–28)
    (2) The positive witness to Jesus (1:29–34)
  2. Witness of the first disciples (1:35–51)
    (1) Andrew and another disciple (1:35–42)
    (2) Philip and Nathanael (1:43–51)

Part One: The Book of Signs (2:1—12:50)

I. The reception of the Revealer (2:1—4:54)
  1. The new joy (2:1–12)
    (1) The first sign: water to wine (2:1–11)
    (2) The visit in Capernaum (2:12)

  2. The new worship (2:13–25)
    (1) Cleansing of the Temple (2:13–22)
    (2) Reaction to the cleansing (2:23–25)
  3. The new birth (3:1–21)
    (1) The dialogue with Nicodemus (3:1–15)
    (2) The monologue of the Evangelist (3:16–21)
  4. The New Master (3:22–36)
    (1) John the Baptist and Jesus (3:22–24)
    (2) The subordination of John (3:25–30)
    (3) The superiority of Jesus (3:31–36)
  5. The new fellowship (4:1–42)
    (1) Introduction and setting (4:1–6)
    (2) The offer of living water (4:7–15)
    (3) The offer of spiritual worship (4:16–26)
    (4) The witness of the woman (4:27–30)
    (5) The challenge to the disciples (4:31–38)
    (6) The Response of the Samaritans (4:39–42)
  6. The new life (4:43–54)
    (1) The return to Galilee (4:43–45)
    (2) The healing of an official's son (4:46–54)
II. The resistance to the Revealer (5:1—10:42)
  1. The authority of life (5:1–47)
    (1) The cure of a lame man (5:1–9a)
    (2) Criticism of the Jews (5:9b–18)
    (3) The claims of Jesus (5:19–29)
    (4) The evidence for the claims (5:30–47)
  2. The Bread of life (6:1–71)
    (1) The feeding of five thousand (6:1–15)
    (2) The crossing of the Sea (6:16–24)
    (3) The source of the Bread of life (6:25–34)
    (4) The nature of the Bread of life (6:35–51)
    (5) The reception of the Bread of life (6:52–65)
    (6) The testing of the twelve (6:66–71)
  3. The Water of life (7:1–52)
    (1) The coming of Jesus to Jerusalem (7:1–13)
    (2) Conflict over the authority of Jesus (7:14–24)
    (3) Conflict over the origin of Jesus (7:25–31)

(4) The appearance before Pilate (18:33–38a)
(5) The offer of Barabbas (18:38b–40)
(6) The effort to release Jesus (19:1–11)
(7) The condemnation of Jesus (19:12–16)
3. Jesus fulfills his passion (19:17–42)
  (1) The crucifixion and inscription (19:17–22)
  (2) The distribution of Jesus' clothing (19:23–24)
  (3) The mother of Jesus and the beloved disciple (19:25–27)
  (4) The death of Jesus (19:28–30)
  (5) The witness of blood and water (19:31–37)
  (6) The burial of Jesus (19:38–42)
III. Jesus lives for his disciples (20:1–31)
1. The appearance to Mary Magdalene (20:1–18)
  (1) The discovery of the empty tomb (20:1–10)
  (2) The discovery of the risen Lord (20:11–18)
2. The appearances to the disciples (20:19–31)
  (1) The appearance to the group (20:19–23)
  (2) The appearance to Thomas (20:24–29)
  (3) The significance of the signs (20:30–31)

Conclusion (21:1–25)

I. The revelation of Jesus in Galilee (21:1–23)
1. An Appearance by the Sea of Tiberias (21:1–14)
2. The responsibility of Simon Peter (21:15–19)
3. The death of the beloved disciple (21:20–23)
II. The conclusion to the Gospel (21:24–25)
1. The authenticity of the Gospel (21:24)
2. The selectivity of the Gospel (21:25)

Selected Bibliography

Most of the relevant contemporary literature has been collected and classified by Edward Malatesta, *St. John's Gospel: 1920–1965. A Cumulative and Classified Bibliography of Books and Periodical Literature on the Fourth Gospel.* ("Analecta Biblica," 32.) Rome: Pontifical Biblical Institute, 1967. Many of the significant findings in the 3,120 studies listed by Malatesta are reflected in the following:

BARRETT, C. K. *The Gospel According to St. John.* London: S.P.C.K., 1955.

BERNARD, J. H. *A Critical and Exegetical Commentary on the Gospel According to St. John.* Ed. A. H. MCNEILE. ("The International Critical Commentary.") Edinburgh: T. & T. Clark, 1928.

BROWN, RAYMOND E. *The Gospel According to John.* ("The Anchor Bible.") Garden City: Doubleday & Company, 1966. Vol. I, introduction and commentary on chapters 1–12; remainder in preparation.

BULTMANN, RUDOLF. *Das Evangelium des Johannes.* ("Kritisch-exegetischer Kommentar über das Neue Testament.") 17th ed. Göttingen: Vandenhoeck & Ruprecht, 1962. Translation supervised by G. R. Beasley-Murray, in preparation.

———. *Theology of the New Testament,* Vol. II. New York: Charles Scribner's Sons, 1955.

DODD, C. H. *Historical Tradition in the Fourth Gospel.* Cambridge: University Press, 1963.

———. *The Interpretation of the Fourth Gospel.* Cambridge: University Press, 1953.

HOSKYNS, E. C. *The Fourth Gospel.* ed. F. N. DAVEY (2d. ed.). London: Faber and Faber, 1947.

HOWARD, W. F. *The Fourth Gospel in Recent Criticism and Interpretation.* Fourth edition revised by C. K. Barrett. London: Epworth Press, 1955.

HUNTER, A. M. *According to John. A New Look at the Fourth Gospel.* Philadelphia: Westminster Press, 1968.

LIGHTFOOT, R. H. *St. John's Gospel.* Ed. C. F. EVANS. Oxford: Clarendon Press, 1956.

MACGREGOR, G. H. C. *The Gospel of John.* ("The Moffatt New Testament Commentary.") New York: Harper and Brothers, 1928.

SANDERS, J. N. *The Gospel According to St. John.* Edited and completed by B. A. MASTIN. ("Harper's New Testament Commentaries.") New York: Harper and Row, 1968.

SCHNACKENBURG, RUDOLF. *The Gospel According to St. John.* Trans. KEVIN SMYTH. ("Herder's Theological Commentary on the New Testament.") New York: Herder and Herder, 1968. Vol. I, introduction and commentary on chapters 1–4; remainder in preparation.

SMITH, T. C. *Jesus in the Gospel of John.* Nashville: Broadman Press, 1959.

STRACHAN, R. H. *The Fourth Gospel: Its Significance and Environment* (3d. ed.). London: S.C.M. Press, 1941.

TEMPLE, WILLIAM. *Readings in St. John's Gospel.* London: Macmillan and Co., 1940.

WESTCOTT, B. F. *The Gospel According to St. John.* London: James Clarke and Co., 1958 (reprint of 1880 edition).

Commentary on the Text

Introduction 1:1–51

Each of the four Gospels opens with a carefully wrought introduction designed to clarify the theological context in which the historical ministry of Jesus may be understood. This development began with Mark 1:1–13, was elaborated in Matthew 1:1—2:23 as well as in Luke 1:1—2:52, and reached its climax in John 1:1–51. Here, the testimony of John the Baptist is given more fully than elsewhere (1:19–36), to which is appended the corroborating witness of four other followers (1:37–49) and of Jesus himself (1:50–51). The foundations of the public ministry are traced back beyond John, Abraham, and even Adam to eternity itself (1:1). This means that the words with which Jesus claimed to reveal God (1:51) were not simply an extension of John's message (1:15), nor only the fulfillment of the word of God in the Mosaic Law (1:17). Rather, they gave voice to that primal Word by which God forever thinks his own thoughts (1:1) and by which he expressed himself in the creation of the universe (1:3).

The introduction to the Gospel clearly divides itself into two parts: (1) a majestic Prologue in 1:1–18 which is a poetic meditation on the Word of God; (2) a historical narrative in 1:19–51 which records the manifold witness of men. There is profound theological significance to the symmetry and sequence of these sections. The Word of God is primary and prior; unless God has spoken, there is no witness which men can bear. The multiple confessions in 1:19–51 are human reactions to the divine action in 1:1–18. On the other hand, the eternal Word of God is meaningless to men without earthly testimony. Every discovery of reality awaits the willingness of a witness to share what he has seen and heard.

The unity of the two sections is provided by Jesus himself who was both the unique divine Word in 1:1–18 and the supreme human witness in 1:19–51. This dual perspective is a dominant theme throughout the fourth Gospel where Jesus is both the revelation and the revealer of truth, both the object and the subject of faith. As Son of God (1:18) and Son of man (1:51), he was the one in whom divine reality descended from heaven to earth as well as the one in whom human reality ascended from earth to heaven (1:51; cf. 3:13; 6:51,62). On the one hand, he dared to declare the life-giving word of God (cf. 3:34; 5:24; 6:63,68; 8:31,47,51; 12:48; 17:8,14) which the Father himself authenticated (cf. 5:32,37; 8:18). On the other hand, he was but a lowly witness who could do nothing on his own authority (5:30–31; 18:37). In these dual roles, Jesus both confronted men with the reality of God and, at the same time, guided them to confess their acceptance of the divine claim.

I. The Word of God: Prologue (1:1–18)

The form of this beginning to the Gospel must be understood before its content can be appreciated.[1] The style is that of Semitic poetry, frequent use being made of such rhythmic devices as climactic or "stair-step" parallelism whereby a new line carries forward a key element in the preceding line; e.g., a literal translation of v. 1:

In beginning was **the Word,**
    and **the Word** was with **God,**
        and **God** is what the Word was.

Or, again (vv. 4–5):

In him life was,
and the **life** was the **light** of men,
    and the **light** in the **darkness** shines,
        and the **darkness** cannot extinguish it.

---

[1] On the Semitic poetry and four strophes in the Prologue, see Joachim Jeremias, *The Central Message of the New Testament* (New York: Charles Scribner's Sons, 1965), pp. 71–90.

The poetic features of the Prologue suggest that this material was adapted for use as a hymn in early Christian worship. As the Psalms so clearly indicate, ancient Israel often set to song its recital of God's saving deeds (e.g., Psalm 78). Here the new Israel summarized the holy history of its Messiah in hymnic form, thereby ascribing to him a transcendent dignity like that attributed to wisdom in the exalted eulogies of Proverbs 8, Ecclesiasticus 24, and Wisdom of Solomon 7–9. This means that these verses reflect not only philosophical meditation and theological affirmation but also doxological adoration of a personal Lord whose life moved his followers to burst forth in praise.

The poetic pattern found in most of the Prologue is broken by prose references to John the Baptist, particularly in vv. 6–9,15. So matter-of-fact are these sections that they seem almost an intrusion into the lyrical rhapsody which surrounds them. And yet, both styles are an integral part of the Christian faith. Here, at the outset, we are introduced both to the poetry and to the prose of the Gospel, both to the glory of the eternal Word and to the simple witness of a mortal prophet.

Once the basically poetic style of the Prologue is recognized, it is not surprising to discover that its internal structure is arranged in four strophes or hymnic stanzas which correspond to the four paragraphs in the RSV. Here the Word is depicted successively in relation to God and his universe (vv. 1–5), to John the Baptist (vv. 6–8), to the world of men (vv. 9–13), and to the confessing church (vv. 14–18). Since the sequence of these stanzas is primarily topical rather than temporal, it is misleading to make certain verses refer exclusively to the preexistent Word and others only to the incarnate Word. Just as any person is best understood in the light of his various roles or relations (e.g., to family, work, enemies, and friends), so here the basic purpose is to clarify the person of the Word by describing his significant involvements whether they came before, during, or after the days of his flesh.

At the same time, while separate statements within the four stanzas do not form a clear chronological progression, the total hymn does tell the gospel story of Jesus in connected sequence as an historical episode between two eternities. In one respect, therefore, the Prologue resembles the Jewish hymns to wisdom with their descriptions of "timeless" attributes (e.g., Wisd. Sol. 7:24—8:1), while in another sense it is more like the Old Testament cultic hymns of confession which recite the "timely" acts of God in history (e.g., Psalm 105 or 106). Individual verses may simultaneously look backward to the past, outward to the present, and upward to eternity (e.g., v. 5), but the overall outline of vv. 1–18 guides the reader successively through the main stages in the once-for-all epoch of redemption.

This external structure of the Prologue resembles the arc of a pendulum or the curve of a parabola, which is the same form reflected in some of the other early Christian hymns.[2] Philippians 2:6–11, e.g., pictures the condescension and vindication of Christ Jesus in two movements: first, the downstroke of the pendulum in humiliation (vv. 6–8); then the upstroke of the pendulum in exaltation (vv. 9–11). This symmetrically inverted structure, called chiasmus, was a favorite literary form in the ancient world especially suited to express the paradox or "great reversal" at the heart of the gospel (cf. 2 Cor. 8:9).

An emphasis on this twofold movement of descending and ascending has determined the overall structure of the Gospel. Thus it is not surprising that an opening summary would adopt the same general pattern. So understood, the Prologue resembles a gateway to God with its pillars anchored from above in eternity rather than from below in time. The humiliation

---

[2] On the hymnic and parabolic character of the Prologue, see M. E. Boismard, *St. John's Prologue*, Carisbrooke Dominicans, trans. (London: Blackfriars Publications, 1957), pp. 73–81.

of the Son of God is sketched in vv. 1–11, followed by his exaltation in vv. 12–18. The contours of this presentation may be represented by the following diagram of verses:

```
     1–2                    17–18
      3–4                     16
       5                     15
        6–8                 14
          9–10           13
           11–12
```

In less than a dozen verses the Prologue records the swift descent of the Word from complete intimacy with God (v. 1) to complete forsakenness by men (v. 11). But in this abyss the arc begins to bend upward again. The pendulum ends (v. 18) where it began (v. 1) in the perfect fellowship of the eternal Godhead—but with what a difference! For now men could know the deepest secrets of the divine silence. Now, in Jesus, God had spoken clearly to all who would listen. Between the eternity with which the Prologue began and the eternity with which it ended stood the earthly life of Christ as a definitive commentary on the nature of God. Thus the Prologue that began by speaking of the "Word . . . with God" (v. 1) ended by speaking of the "Son . . . in the bosom of the Father" (v. 18).

We turn now to a consideration of the central category in the subject matter of the Prologue, the identification of Jesus Christ (v. 17) as the Word (vv. 1,14, *Logos*). This terminology sought to interpret the significance of Jesus by viewing his life as the language of God. Such a comparison is unusually clarifying, for speech is the essential and enduring basis on which our true humanity is constituted, our personal relations are cultivated, and our deepest insights are conveyed. As a metaphor with multiple meanings, it is not surprising that Logos was one of the richest words in the religious history which prepared for the Prologue of John. Three main tributaries converged to form the background of this concept as it is used in the fourth Gospel:

the Jewish, the Greek, and the Christian.[3]

(1) The Hebraic understanding of Logos roots in the Old Testament where "the word of the Lord" was viewed as sovereign energy that could call the created order into being (Gen. 1; Psalm 33:6,9), that could burn like fire or shatter like a hammer (Jer. 23:29), that could accomplish the divine purpose (Isa. 55:11). This dynamic element, however, did not exclude a didactic aspect. The "word of the Lord" was also a revelation of his will and thus was equivalent to instruction in the Law (Psalm 119), which, in turn, was increasingly identified with the wisdom of God (Ecclus. 24). In Jewish thought of the New Testament period this cluster of concepts (Word/Law/Wisdom) came to represent personalized aspects of the activity of God in the affairs of men.

(2) The Hellenistic world tended to understand Logos more as a philosophical principle than as a personal power and thus to use the term primarily with the meaning of thought rather than of word. Heraclitus identified the Logos as the basis of order and continuity in a world of flow and flux. The Stoics saw it as the mind of God interpenetrating the universe to give it stability and coherence. The Jewish apologist, Philo, adapted Greek categories in viewing the Logos as the projected thought of the transcendent God, the clue to meaning and purpose in life, the criterion of ultimate reality, the bond of rationality between the human and the divine.

(3) The early church viewed the preaching of its gospel as a "ministry of the word" (Acts 6:4). The content of that message was Christ himself (Luke 1:2; Acts 1:21–22), who had proclaimed the word during his earthly ministry (Mark 2:2). But Jesus was more than a teacher or rabbi. The entire event of his life was a divine declaration; thus "the name by which he is called is The Word of God" (Rev. 19:13).

---

[3] For details, see Gerhard Kittel, ed., *Theological Dictionary of the New Testament*, trans. Geoffrey W. Bromiley (Grand Rapids: Wm. B. Eerdmans Publishing Company, 1967), IV, 77–136.

In the prologue to 1 John we approach the Logos concept of the fourth Gospel: "the word of life" announced in Christian witness was both "from the beginning . . . with the Father" and was also "made manifest" to the ear, the eye, and the touch (1 John 1:1–2).

From these three perspectives, then, the Word could be viewed as a divine *power,* as a rational *principle,* or as a redemptive *proclamation.* This means that a Jew might understand the Prologue as a Christian claim that its Lord is the agent of God's creative power, the fulfillment of the Old Testament Torah, the embodiment of divine wisdom. A Greek, on the other hand, could just as easily assume that he was being asked to believe in Jesus as the manifestation of unchanging truth, the perfect pattern of ultimate reality, the pointer to the meaning of the universe. To a Christian, however, the passage would help to clarify that the essential content of the Christian message lay in the life, death, and resurrection of the incarnate Christ; not in certain doctrinal propositions, mystical experiences, or ethical admonitions.

The genius of the Gospel of John lies in its ability to mediate between three worlds at once and, at the same time, to transcend all of them. The Evangelist deliberately employed that terminology with which all of his intended readers were asking the deepest questions of life. On the one hand, he sought to conserve the heritage of the Old Testament by showing how the "word of the Lord" which came to Israel was perfectly expressed in Christ. At the same time, he was equally interested in liberating the gospel to make creative contact with nonbiblical currents of thought in the Hellenistic world. In doing both, he did not forsake but rather enriched the faith of the church by giving traditional terminology a new thrust. Readers would approach his Gospel from different perspectives depending on their inherited thought forms, philosophical presuppositions, or religious commitments; but this freedom did not endanger the essential gospel message. For the unique conviction at the core of the

Prologue is that the Word as power, principle, and proclamation was fulfilled ultimately in the Word as *person.* The life of Christ transcended every human frame of reference and could not be adequately expressed by any of them. As the Logos, he is forever the power of God, the wisdom of God, and the gospel of God (cf. 1 Cor. 1:23–24).

1. The Word and the Universe (1:1–5)

¹ In the beginning **was** the Word, and the Word was with God, and the Word was God. ² He was in the beginning with God; ³ all things were made through him, and without him was not anything made that was made. ⁴ In him was life, and the life was the light of men. ⁵ The light shines in the darkness, and the darkness has not overcome it.

The first stanza of the Prologue is set in a cosmic context which considers the involvement of the Logos with God (vv. 1–2), with the creation (vv. 3–4), and with darkness (v. 5). As such, this single paragraph grapples with three of the profoundest issues in human existence: the relation of eternity to time, of spirit to matter, and of good to evil.

These five verses are reminiscent of the opening passage in the Old Testament, Genesis 1:1–5. Not only are the initial words (*In the beginning*) identical, but the content is closely parallel. In both cases, God's Word created a world in which light and darkness were differentiated. The Gospel of John begins as a new Genesis which depicts the redemptive work of Christ in bringing the creation to its intended consummation (cf. 5:17; 9:4–5).

(1) The Logos and God (vv. 1–2)

The first verse makes three claims for the Logos which are set forth symmetrically by the thrice-repeated key word *was.* Cf. the TEV (1 ed.) paraphrase:

"From the very beginning,
when God was, the Word also was;
where God was, the Word was with him;
what God was, the Word also was."

At the outset, the Prologue asserts the eternity, the proximity, and the identity of the Logos with God. Verse 2 solemnly repeats for emphasis the central claims of v. 1 as if they were too staggering to be assimilated on the basis of a single affirmation.

Since *in the beginning* suggests not only the start of the gospel story (cf. Mark 1:1) but the creation of the world as well (cf. Gen. 1:1), the implication is that the Word already was a reality even before time began. This means that God is, by eternal nature, not mute but articulate. Unlike the dumb idols (1 Kings 18:26–29; Psalms 115:3–8; 135:15–18; Hab. 2:18–19; 1 Cor. 12:2), God has always had a word. The Almighty is not speechless; all of the meaningful sounds of life are not finally negated by an ultimate silence.

Moreover, the claim is here made that the Word was prior to creation, which is to say that thought preceded act. This is indicated not only by the first phrase in v. 1—literally, "the Logos existed before anything began"—but also by the relation of v. 1 to v. 3, the sequence suggesting that God had a word before he made a world. There is a kind of pragmatic empiricism which assumes that meaning simply emerges out of events. But John is certain that God first thought through his plans before doing anything and that this Word of truth both shaped what subsequently happened and determined its deepest significance.

One basic purpose of the Prologue is to identify the historical Jesus with the eternal Logos and thereby contend that what men heard in his brief ministry is what God has always been trying to say to the world. This emphasis on the preexistence of the Word was not speculative but practical, designed to meet two current problems:

First, the Jews tended to set the veneration of Scripture above the claims of Jesus because of its great antiquity. John replied that the revelation given in Jesus was actually much older than the Old Testament, for it already existed with God before the primeval history with which Genesis 1:1 began. Jesus may have burst upon the earthly scene as a young man (8:57); but he did so as the Word antedating and inspiring the words of Isaiah, Moses, and Abraham. In reality, they spoke of him and thus are to be understood in terms of him (5:39–47; 8:53–58; 12:37–41). As the eternal Logos, Christ is the norm by which to measure all of the biblical revelation.

Second, many of the Greeks, in contrast to the Jews, attached no absolute authority to ancient scriptures. In their popular mythologies the gods were fickle and capricious, hence their words were not trustworthy. To John, the *"was-ness"* of the Word guaranteed the dependability of the Word. The Logos is forever constant, unconditioned by historical contingency. We might paraphrase v. 1a: "When God began to express himself, the content of that disclosure was not an innovation or afterthought but was the communication of his unchanging reality."

The two final phrases of v. 1 stand in creative tension with each other, stressing as they do both the separation and the connection of the Word with God. On the one hand, the Logos was face to face *with* or "in the company of" God. While such proximity does suggest a filial intimacy (cf. "in the bosom," v. 18), the primary concern was to insist on a proper distinction between the Logos and God (cf. Prov. 8:30). On the other hand, in addition to this difference, there was an equality between the two; for, as the NEB nicely puts it, "What God was, the Word was." The Word was not just one attribute of God but was rather an expression of the very being of God.

These two phrases held here in careful balance prepare for the twin Christian claims that (a) Jesus and God were distinct in person and function (e.g., Jesus did not talk to himself when he prayed; cf. 17:4–5) and yet that (b) they were identical in nature and purpose (i.e., Jesus did not merely reveal something *about* God but rather revealed God *himself;* cf. 14:9).

(2) The Logos and Creation (vv. 3–4)

The eternal being of the Logos, stressed by the threefold *was* of v. 1, is now contrasted with the temporal becoming of *all things,* stressed by the threefold *made* (lit., "became" or "has become") of v. 3. By affirming that the entire created order came into being through the agency of the Word, the Prologue implies that matter is not eternal and self-sufficient but is limited and derivative. As v. 3*b* emphasizes, "not one thing" has its existence—much less its significance—except as a creative expression of God.

The relation of the Word to creation is not here understood, however, in terms of a cosmic dualism which would posit an absolute antagonism between spirit and matter. Rather, the complete compatability of God with his world is established by the involvement of the Logos in both spheres. The very Word that was linked to God three times in vv. 1–2 is linked to the world three times in vv. 3–4 (*through him . . . without him . . . in him*). This Logos is no inferior intermediary between a perfect God and his imperfect world, as with the Gnostics. Instead, the Logos who is to be identified with the totality of the divine order (v. 1*c*) was God's agent in calling forth the totality (*all things*) of the created order (v. 3*a*). Thus two extremes are rejected: the world is neither eternal and therefore ultimate, nor is it evil and therefore worthless.

What, then, does it mean to confess that this is a Christocentric universe (cf. 1 Cor. 8:6; Col. 1:16; Heb. 1:2)? Three truths are strongly implied:

Meaning is prior to matter, thus things derive their importance from the spiritual purposes for which they are intended. This contention opposes any materialism which views reality as ultimately tangible, the world as of intrinsic rather than of instrumental importance, and life as finally fulfilled by sensory experiences.

The creation, as a Logos-activity, is part of God's effort to communicate with man (cf. Rom. 1:20; Acts 14:17). The *significance* of the physical lies in its ability to *sign*-ify or serve as a revealing *sign* of the spiritual. If the universe was shaped by the Logos, then there can be a proper analogy between the seen and the unseen. This is why Jesus spoke of God in terms of such symbols as wine (2:1–11), water (4:7–

15), and bread (6:25–59).

Christ, as agent of creation, is entitled to claim the universe as its recreator and redeemer (cf. Col. 1:15–18). His earthly presence in the world which he had made (v. 10) was a coming unto "his own things" (v. 11*a*). The incarnate Logos was invested with a cosmic authority (3:35; 13:3; 17:2) because the entire created order was but a projection of the pattern perfectly embodied in his life. This means that no area of our existence, however mundane, is exempt from finding its coherence in submission to him.

The precise interpretation of v. 4 is extremely difficult because no exact text or punctuation is possible on the basis of available manuscripts. The RSV expresses the translation dilemma by offering an alternate (marg.) reading which includes the last phrase of v. 3 with v. 4. Because it would require a complex technical discussion to set forth all of the exegetical possibilities, we may content ourselves here to follow the general line of thought, which is not seriously affected by decisions regarding individual words and phrases.[4]

Being a personal intelligence in fellowship with God, the Logos, in functioning as the agent of creation, was primarily the contributor of life. Any creative act involves more than the manufacture of inert molecules. Matter has meaning only when it lives, and the affirmation here is that *in him was* the source of *life* by which everything was given the chance to live. In a sense, the Logos had the same purpose in creation as in redemption: "I am come that you may have life" (cf. 5:26; 5:40; 10:10; 14:6). As a divine gift, this life became the *light* by which men are pointed to God (cf. 8:12; 12:46). That is, every person (v. 9*b*) ought to see that God is the powerful and thoughtful creator of the universe in the light of the miracle of life which abounds in human experience (cf. Psalm 36:9).

(3) The Logos and Darkness (v. 5)

Why, then, do so many misunderstand and even oppose the light of life active in

4 For a detailed discussion, see Boismard, pp. 12–19.

the created order? Why is life so often cheapened by prejudice, slavery, war, and a host of other threats? Supremely, why did the world destroy with savage swiftness that one life so luminous with the light of God (cf. 1:10–11; 8:12–59; 12:35–50)? The answer here is that the light shines not in some neutral moral vacuum but in cosmic conflict with the power of darkness. We are thus abruptly introduced to the problem of evil.

Having just considered the divine work of creation (vv. 3–4), the question naturally arises whether evil also has its origin in God. Was the Logos that made *all things* also responsible for the *darkness?* No such suggestion is contained in this passage. Rather, *darkness* is simply assumed and introduced without comment as the inevitable concomitant of *light.* The situation is the same as in Genesis 1:1–5 where "in the beginning," before God spoke his creative word, "darkness was upon the face of the deep."

The primary purpose of v. 5 is neither to explain nor to curse the darkness but to affirm the overriding conviction that light finally prevails (cf. 1 John 2:8). This was true in creation when the darkness fled before the word, "Let there be light" (Gen. 1:3). It was true in Christ who, though rejected by many (1:10–11), was nevertheless the Light of the world (8:12). It is still true in the church whose witness could not be extinguished by persecution (cf. 9:22; 12:42; 16:2). To be sure, the darkness will endure as long as men are evil (cf. 3:19–21), and, because it coexists with light, a decision for one or the other is inevitable. But the outcome of the struggle is never in doubt, for it is already clear that the darkness cannot master the light.

2. The Word and John (1:6–8)

⁶ There was a man sent from God, whose name was John. ⁷ He came for testimony, to bear witness to the light, that all might believe through him. ⁸ He was not the light, but came to bear witness to the light.

This second stanza of the Prologue exhibits both a strong connection and a sharp contrast with the preceding stanza. Continuity is established as the claim regarding "the light of men" (v. 4) is fulfilled in a *man* who came to bear witness to the *light.* Moreover, in John the darkness met a courageous witness to that light which can never be snuffed out (v. 5). Most important, these two stanzas are bound together by the unity of word (vv. 1–5) and witness (vv. 6–8), a concern also of this chapter and of the entire Gospel. The divine Word was ultimate in that "all things" came to exist "through him" (v. 3a), but the human witness carried forward the redemptive purpose of creation in that *all* men were called to *believe through him.*

At the same time, discontinuity is just as evident as we move abruptly from eternity to time, from the universe to the desert, from exalted claims to an insistent disclaimer (v. 8). Notice the strikingly different fashion in which the two stanzas begin (vv. 1,6). Jesus was the Word (*logos*), while John was but *a man (anthropos).* Jesus enjoyed intimate fellowship "with" (*pros*) God, while John was sent *from (para)* his side. Jesus always "was" (*ēn*), without beginning or end; whereas John "came into being" (*egeneto*) at a point in time. (The RSV obscures this final contrast by translating the two different verbs in vv. 1,6 as *was.*) Clearly, a need was felt to subordinate John to Jesus, especially in the strong negation of v. 8a (cf. 1:15; 1:19–34; 3:22–30; 4:1; 5:33–36; 10:40–41). It seems that some followers of John had not transferred their loyalty to Jesus and needed to be reminded that their master never made ultimate claims for himself (cf. Acts 18:24–26; 19:1–7).

At the same time, the lowliness of John provided the backdrop against which to perceive his true greatness. Although a lonely herald without credentials, he dared to be a prophet of the dawn in a day when the age of prophecy had been relegated to an idealized past. His only motivation was the sense of mission by which he *came,* his only purpose was to point beyond himself in *witness,* and his only message was of the *light.* We were introduced to many immensities in the first stanza of the Prologue, but here is a wonder worthy to stand beside them: a single man in touch with transcendence, a man obsessed with light when other men were content to live in the shadows, a man willing to renounce the securities of the status quo and to depend entirely upon the future to vindicate his hope.

3. The Word and the World (1:9–13)

⁹ The true light that enlightens every man was coming into the world. ¹⁰ He was in the world, and the world was made through him, yet the world knew him not. ¹¹ He came to his own home, and his own people received him not. ¹² But to all who received him, who believed in his name, he gave power to become children of God; ¹³ who were born, not of blood nor of the will of the flesh nor of the will of man, but of God.

The strong negation with which the second stanza of the Prologue ends (v. 8) prepares for the equally strong affirmation with which the third stanza begins (v. 9). Although John himself was not the promised light of God's final revelation (cf. Isa. 9:2; 42:6; 60:1–3,19–20), the Logos who *was* the *true light* did fulfill the passionate expectation of his forerunner by entering the world of men in a decisively new way. This is indicated immediately by v. 10*a*, where the emphasis in v. 9 is repeated (*he* really was *in* the world), as well as by *he came* in v. 11 and by *who received him* in v. 12. The third stanza then summarizes the earthly career of the incarnate Logos and in so doing anticipates the broad outlines of the Gospel story soon to unfold (v. 9 = ch. 1; v. 10 = ch. 2—4; v. 11 = ch. 5—12; vv. 12—13 = ch. 13—21).

The Prologue itself makes clear just how incredible was this divine intervention into human affairs. The universal light which shines on *every man* became a particular man. The one who had always existed even before the world began now *came* at a definite time in history. The agent who had created the entire cosmos now occupied a particular spot of earthly space. Once everything that had been made lived "in

him," but now he lived *in the world*. From a human perspective, it was hard enough to believe that God would prepare for his climactic coming with only one obscure herald, John the Baptist. But it was simply unthinkable that the eschatological event itself would involve the eternal becoming temporal, the infinite becoming spatial, and the spiritual becoming material; for this is precisely the reverse of that process by which redemption is usually described as taking place.

No wonder, then, that men were so unprepared for the coming of the light. Rejection is traced in two stages. First, *the world* which was his by creation, here understood as the organized life of humanity, *knew him not* in loving recognition and response. Second, having come especially to his *own home* in Israel, even the people of God who were his by covenant were unwilling to take him to themselves. The shocking assertion is here made that neither the world living by the light of natural reason nor religion living by the light of divine revelation could see the true Light of the world when it became embodied in a human life!

What was the basic reason for this blindness? In both the Greek love of wisdom and the Jewish love of works lurked a tendency to define the goal of human existence in terms of what is achieved rather than in terms of what is received. They could not see the light standing before them as a sheer gift because they were busy trying to manufacture it in their own minds and temples. Nothing is as necessary for the discovery of light as openness. Closed eyelids can thwart all the radiance of a blazing sunrise. Thus the Prologue pinpoints the crux of a positive response in the word *received* and links this receptivity with the nature of faith by identifying *all who received him* as those *who believed in his name*. Christianity is thereby defined fundamentally in terms of grace (*he gave*) which is, after all, the only way that logos and light—whether earthly or heavenly—can ever come to men. There is a kind of creative human passivity, an alert listening and looking, which permits the divine activity of speaking and shining.

It is not surprising that the gift is first described as the right or privilege (not *power* as in RSV) to become *children of God.* This figure suggests the fellowship of the family of faith. It also conveys the notion of a new beginning. The most characteristic thing about a child is that his life is still before him; the best is yet to be. Most important in this context, the implication is that men are not naturally *children of God,* whether they belong to the world created through the Logos or whether they belong to the chosen people of the Messiah as descendants of Abraham. Rather, they *become* children of God through a new creation which transcends all national, racial, and religious distinctions (cf. 8: 39–47).

This initial becoming in v. 12 is further clarified as a divine begetting in v. 13. Three negative phrases, which are virtually identical in meaning, insist that such birth is in no sense the result of biological reproduction. The way in which Christ was born into this world provides the pattern by which any man may be reborn: not by heredity or human effort but *of God* (cf. comment on 3:1–15).

4. The Word and the Church (1:14–18)

14 And the Word became flesh and dwelt among us, full of grace and truth; we have beheld his glory, glory as of the only Son from the Father. 15 (John bore witness to him, and cried, "This was he of whom I said, 'He who comes after me ranks before me, for he was before me.'") 16 And from his fulness have we all received, grace upon grace. 17 For the law was given through Moses; grace and truth came through Jesus Christ. 18 No one has ever seen God; the only Son, who is in the bosom of the Father, he has made him known.

Reference to the new birth at the end of the third stanza leads naturally to a discussion of the Christian life in the final stanza, but with one important difference in perspective. Now, for the first time in the Prologue, the pronouns shift from the third person (they) of objective description to the first person (we) of subjective confession (cf. 21:24b; 1 John 1:1–4). At the climax of the hymn, one community of those who have become "children of God" (vv. 12–13) celebrate the incarnation of the Logos (v. 14) in the light of the resultant gifts which they have received.

Such witness is borne in sober realism, however. The paradox of the Word-become-flesh which pervades the Prologue reaches its clearest expression in v. 14 as three marks of condescension in the first part of the verse are sharply juxtaposed with three marks of exaltation in the latter part. (The RSV has altered the order of the Greek text by transposing *full of grace and truth* from the end of the verse to its center; this change of sequence disturbs the symmetry of the sentence and distorts its train of thought.)

Note first the threefold limitations attributed to the Logos in v. 14 as compared with v. 1:

(1) The *Word* that always "was" in his eternal being with God (v. 1) now became a temporal event at a point in history, limited to a moment of time as was John the Baptist in v. 6. (The Greek verb *egeneto* used in v. 6 to contrast the historical John with the eternal Logos of v. 1 is now used of the historical Logos in v. 14.) He through whom all creation became (v. 3), now himself *became* a finite creature.

(2) Furthermore, *the Word* that "was God" (v. 1c) now came into being as *flesh;* i.e., he began to exist as a human being (cf. 1 John 4:2; 2 John 7). The ultimate medium chosen to convey the divine message was not an idea, an emotion, or an organization; rather, the revelation was embodied in a person. This does not mean that the Word ceased to be Word when it *became flesh,* but that ultimate meaning and earthly existence were perfectly fused in the life of a single individual.

(3) Finally, the Word that was eternally with (*pros*) God (v. 1b) now came *from* (*para*) *the Father* and *dwelt* temporarily *among us.* The verb *dwelt* may suggest the notion of pitching a tent, reminiscent of

God's tabernacling presence with his people in the wilderness (Ex. 25:8; 40:34).

This threefold lowliness did not obscure his true greatness, however, but provided the backdrop against which eyes of faith could see it even more impressively. The ultimate significance of the Logos is now affirmed in three successive phrases.

We beheld his glory. Glory is one of the richest terms in the theological vocabulary of the Bible, referring primarily to visible manifestations of God in power. The life of Jesus was radiant with the focused presence of the divine majesty. Through his earthly ministry God made a weighty impact upon men which summoned them to a new awareness of his purpose and prestige.

The only Son from the Father. The word translated *only Son* (*monogenous*) [5] could suggest the idea of "only begotten," as in the KJV, since a *father-son* relationship is usually established by the process of birth. The primary meaning of the term, however, is "only one of its kind," and the overall emphasis of the Prologue on the eternal "*was*-ness" of the Word suggests—contrary to the KJV rendering—that this *Son* is uniquely different in being *un*-begotten. In fact, a deliberate contrast between v. 13 and v. 14 may intend the implied chiasmus: We men of earth who are born in the *flesh*/Were privileged to become *children* of God/By a *begetting* not of man but of God/Because he who needed *not to be born* of God/Since he was God's eternal and incomparable *Son*/Was willing to be born of *flesh* on our behalf.

Full of grace and truth. As a man, the unique Logos was not empty of divine reality (as Phil. 2:7 is sometimes misunderstood to imply) but was *full* of that merciful love and steadfast faithfulness which were central elements in the Old Testament understanding of God (Ex. 34:6–7; Psalms 85:9–10; 89:14; 108:4). Note the balance achieved by coupling these two terms. *Grace* is an irresistible compulsion to give men more than they deserve which

[5] Dale Moody, "God's Only Son," *Journal of Biblical Literature,* 72 (1953), pp. 213–219.

springs spontaneously from the boundless generosity of God. *Truth,* on the other hand, roots in a divine determination to be consistent, predictable, and thereby trustworthy in dealing with mankind. Grace without truth is easily seen as sentimentality while truth without grace can appear to be an inflexible rigidity. In declaring the character of God, Jesus combined an infinite tenderness toward the sinner with an unswerving fidelity to the right.

Looking now at v. 14 as a whole, the two parts provide what at first appears to be a striking inconsistency. The first half describes the divine action in history as the coming of **the Word,** whereas the second half describes the human reaction in terms of what *we have beheld.* But a word is ordinarily something which one hears, not sees; conversely, glory is usually understood as something seen without a sound. This unusual combination of audition and vision in v. 14 conveys the profound truth that in Jesus God sought access to human life through the ear-gate as well as the eye-gate (cf. 1 John 1:1). As such, he appealed both to the intellect and to the imagination, both to the reflective and to the celebrative capacities of man. Moreover, the visible Logos transcended the traditional dichotomy between word and deed. There was an absolute consistency between what men heard Jesus say and what they saw him do. In an ultimate sense, they "saw" what he "said" because he perfectly practiced what he preached.

That the divine revelation would come as a human life was far from self-evident, however, for such a shocking affirmation is without parallel in any other religion. Thus the unique **Word** of v. 14 is immediately linked to the ringing witness of John in v. 15. This connection was necessary because John had been the first crucial link between Jesus and that unbroken chain of believers included in the *we* of this stanza. The present tense of the Greek verb, obscured by the RSV *bore witness,* perhaps should be taken literally in the sense that the long-dead prophet was still bearing witness through the pages of this Gospel (e.g., in vv. 19–36). He *cried* out courageously during his brief ministry, and the echo still rang a generation later as his words were written down. John, like Abel, though dead was "still speaking" (Heb. 11:4).

The content of that testimony concerned the problem of precedence in Jewish religious practice. Since Jesus was younger than John and had first come to him for baptism, it might be assumed that he intended to be his follower, for in Judaism *he who comes after me* was normally the designation for a disciple (cf. Mark 1:17; 8:34). But John reversed the relationship by insisting that Jesus actually ranked ahead of him because he was the preexistent One (cf. v. 30).

It is important that the abrupt parenthetical intrusion in v. 15 not obscure the close connection between v. 14 and v. 16. Because faith is a matter of receiving him who was *full of grace and truth,* it naturally follows that *from his fulness have we all received.* The curious phrase *grace upon grace* literally means grace "in exchange for" or "replaced by" more grace (cf. Rom. 1:17; 2 Cor. 3:18); that is, as the TEV nicely puts it, "one blessing after another." This means that we draw from his fullness as from an inexhaustible source. Once the gift has been *received,* it does not cease to grow.

To be sure, God has always been a God of grace. In the Old Testament era *the law was given through Moses,* whereas in the Christian era his unchanging *grace and truth came through Jesus Christ.* The difference lay not in the character of God as giver but in the potentialities of the gift to make him known. A living person *full* of the divine reality is a more adequate medium of revelation than commandments written on tables of stone.

Throughout vv. 14–18 the superiority of Christ to Moses is frequently implied. In Exodus 33—34, Moses, to whom God spoke "face to face" (33:11), pleaded that the divine presence also accompany the people

on their pilgrimage to the promised land (33:14–17). When God agreed, Moses asked to see his glory (33:18) but was granted only a hidden revelation, "for man shall not see me and live" (33:20). Despite this limitation, the people were allowed to know the "name" (character) of the Lord as one who abounds in "steadfast love and faithfulness" (34:6), and this was the basis of their covenant cut on two tables of stone (34:1,10,27–28). In the Prologue, however, the Logos who was face to face with God (v. 1) *dwelt among us* as the "tent of meeting" where God's *glory* was *beheld* and where the *fulness* of his *grace and truth* was *received,* not as *law* on stone but as life in *flesh.*

This comparison reaches its climax in v. 18 where the inability of Moses to "see God" (cf. also Judg. 13:22; Isa. 6:5; John 5:37; 6:56; 1 John 4:12,20) is superseded by the work of the *only Son* who *has made him known.* The precise force of this claim is complicated by textual variants, some manuscripts reading "only Son" (*monogenēs huios*) as in the RSV text, others reading "only God" (*monogenēs theos*) as in the RSV marginal note. It is almost impossible to choose with any confidence between these two alternatives, the internal evidence of the context favoring *Son* (to go with *in the bosom of the Father*) but the external evidence of the manuscripts favoring *God* (especially in the very early papyri). In the thought of the fourth Gospel, of course, these options are not mutually exclusive, since Jesus is understood both in terms of God (e.g., 1:1; 20:28) and in terms of Son (e.g., 3:16–18; 5:19–23). Here, if the word *monogenes* itself implies *only Son,* as the RSV renders it in v. 14, then combining it with *theos* could yield the translation, "God the only Son," and the entire expression might thus be paraphrased, "the one who is the unique Son because he is to be uniquely identified with God."

Reference to *the bosom of the Father* reminds us of the phrase "with God" in v. 1. Since, between these two parallel verses, the earthly life of Jesus has been described (vv. 9–14), we may assume that v. 18 refers to the exalted Lord who has completed the parabola of redemption and is now "at the right hand" of the Father in glory (Acts 2:33–34). The ascension is not emphasized, however, because this verse turns back to anticipate the gospel story which is soon to unfold and to interpret it as a record of the way in which *the only Son . . . has made (the Father) known.* The life of Jesus was a unique disclosure of the divine hiddenness (cf. 12:45; 14:9), a visible commentary (lit., "exegesis") of the unseen God, a Word which explained the Father he had known so intimately for all eternity.

II. The Witness of Men (1:19–51)

Balancing the poetic hymn to the Word of God in 1:1–18, the introduction to the Gospel now concludes with a prose narration of the witness by men in 1:19–51. The presentation of this testimony is organized around the relation of John the Baptist to Jesus. The entire section is divided into four scenes which unfold on successive days.

On the first (vv. 19–28), John alone occupies the center stage while Jesus is the unknown one who has not yet appeared. On the next day (vv. 29–34), John sees Jesus coming and speaks directly of him, but the latter still remains offstage. On the third day (vv. 35–42), however, both men appear side by side, and the disciples of John begin to transfer their loyalty to Jesus. By the final day (vv. 43–51), John goes completely unnoticed as Jesus dominates the stage. Here, to use John's own words, are the four steps by which "he must increase and I must decrease" (3:30).[6]

Within the form of this four-day cycle, the central content of the testimony is conveyed by ten Christological confessions[7] on the lips of five witnesses: John (vv.

---

[6] T. F. Glasson, "John the Baptist in the Fourth Gospel," *The Expository Times,* 67 (1956), pp. 245–46.

[7] Rudolf Schnackenburg, *The Gospel According to St. John,* trans. Kevin Smyth (New York: Herder and Herder, 1968), I, 507–14.

19–36), Andrew (vv. 37–42), Philip (vv. 43–46), Nathanael (vv. 47–49), and Jesus himself (vv. 50–51). Already in the Prologue such terms as "Word," "God," "life," "light," and "only Son" had been used. Now Jesus is identified as:

1. The (greater) one to come after John (vv. 27,30)
2. The Lamb of God (vv. 29,36)
3. The (preexistent) one before John (v. 30)
4. The one who baptizes with the Holy Spirit (v. 33)
5. The Son (or Elect/Chosen One) of God (vv. 34,49)
6. The Rabbi/Teacher (v. 38)
7. The Messiah/Christ (v. 41)
8. The one of whom Moses and the prophets wrote (v. 45)
9. The King of Israel (v. 49)
10. The Son of man (v. 51)

Unlike some of the titles used in the Prologue, these ten are more traditional Jewish designations drawn largely from the Old Testament Scriptures and intertestamental religious literature. Taken together, they form a composite picture of the expected deliverer of God's people. It is important to realize, however, that only in Jesus were the separate images unified and attributed to one historical person. Only he met all of the needs which had given birth to these titles during different periods of Israel's history.

This means that Christology is inevitably distorted when some of these roles are emphasized to the exclusion of others. For example, Jesus is equally the Lamb who deals with the problem of sin, the Rabbi who responds to the problem of ignorance, and the Messiah who meets the problem of leadership. Too often only a few of his functions are emphasized, thereby limiting an appreciation of the wide range of human needs which he came to meet.

Not only had these titles been enriched as bearers of Israel's hopes for centuries past, but they were subsequently deepened through decades of Christian devotion. By the time that the fourth Gospel was written, each phrase had come to have vastly more meaning than it could have had to newly found disciples at the outset of Jesus' ministry. The full implications of these words may be grasped only by looking backward to their roots in the faith of Israel and by looking forward to their fruits in the faith of the early church. So understood, they offer each reader of the Gospel an opportunity to make his own mature confession of faith in Christ.

Unless it is realized that a long process of development has been telescoped in the use of these titles as a sort of theological shorthand, the reader could wrongly conclude that the first followers of Jesus were spiritually reborn fully grown, that their faith ripened in an instant, that they clearly understood the nature of Jesus' person from the outset. We have abundant evidence both from this Gospel (e.g., 16:29–31) and from the Synoptics (e.g., Mark 8:27–33) that such was not the case. The pilgrimage toward spiritual insight was torturously slow, marked by many false starts and reverses.

Why, then, is there virtually no trace of this struggle in 1:19–51? Because here faith is being depicted in the light of the end to which it leads. It is, of course, important to understand just how modestly faith may begin, but it is equally important to realize the vast potential inherent in the most humble commitment. In this section we are being asked to consider not the insignificance of the seed when it is sown but the greatness of the harvest already latent within it. This does not mean, however, that the fourth Gospel is interested only in results and not causes. In the larger context, for example, a fine balance is maintained between faith as a climactic *point* in 1:19–51 (e.g., 1:29,41,45,49) and faith as a growing *process* in 2:1—4:54 (e.g., 2:22; 4:41–42,50–53).

In literary arrangement, 1:19–51 is clearly divided into two primary parts, 1:19–34 in which John bears witness and 1:35–51 in which the disciples bear witness. By means of repetition in 1:35–36, a close link between the two parts is clearly established. Each part is subdivided into two sections, giving a total of four units in 1:19–51 which correspond to the chronological framework of four days (vv. 19,29,35,43). This very careful organization of the material suggests its possible use in some confessional setting of early Christian worship (cf. especially v. 20*a*).

1. The Witness of John the Baptist (1:19–34)

This section is set apart by a very formal introductory title, "This is the *testimony* of John," and by an equally impressive conclusion, "And I have seen and have borne *witness*." In Greek, the symmetry of the arrangement is even more obvious because the words "testimony" and "witness" come from the same root. The Synoptics present John as a forerunner of the Messiah, as a preacher of repentance, as an ethical teacher, and as the baptizer of a new remnant community (Matt. 3:1–12; Mark 1:1–8; Luke 3:1–18). Here, however, these functions are all subordinated or ignored in order to concentrate exclusively on his role as a witness to Jesus.

(1) The Negative Witness to Himself (1:19–28)

19 And this is the testimony of John, when the Jews sent priests and Levites from Jerusalem to ask him, "Who are you?" 20 He confessed, he did not deny, but confessed, "I am not the Christ." 21 And they asked him, "What then? Are you Elijah?" He said, "I am not." "Are you the prophet?" And he answered, "No." 22 They said to him then, "Who are you? Let us have an answer for those who sent us. What do you say about yourself?" 23 He said, "I am the voice of one crying in the wilderness, 'Make straight the way of the Lord,' as the prophet Isaiah said."

24 Now they had been sent from the Pharisees. 25 They asked him, "Then why are you baptizing, if you are neither the Christ, nor Elijah, nor the prophet?" 26 John answered them, "I baptize with water; but among you stands one whom you do not know, 27 even he who comes after me, the thong of whose sandal I am not worthy to untie." 28 This took place in Bethany beyond the Jordan, where John was baptizing.

An unusually solemn setting is suggested by the announcement that an official delegation of priestly authorities had been dispatched by the Jewish religious leadership in Jerusalem to a particular place near the Jordan River (v. 28) in order to determine the identity of John (v. 19). It is as if they had come to subpoena his testimony (vv. 19,22,24–25) as the first witness in that great trial of Jesus which unfolded throughout his ministry (cf. 3:1–2; 5:19–47; 7:14–52; 8:12–20; 9:13–34; 10:19–39; 11:45–53; 12:44–50) and was the basis for the formal trial which determined his crucifixion (18:19—19:16). The introduction to John's response in v. 20a is prefaced by a terse formula, *He confessed, he did not deny,* strongly reminiscent of Matthew 10:32–33. Christian missionaries laboring under opposition or even persecution could take courage from this record of an unflinching confession under pressure.

While John certainly *did not deny* the faith, as we shall see later (vv. 29–34), he did find it necessary to prepare for his positive affirmation of Christ by a threefold negation of self, which grew progressively more emphatic (lit., "I am not . . . not I . . . no!"). By denying that he was *the Christ, Elijah,* or *the prophet,* John firmly dissociated himself from any of the eschatological figures expected at the end-time. Many Jews looked eagerly not only for *the Christ* as an anointed son of David (Isa. 9:2–7; 11:1–9) but for *Elijah* (Mal. 4:5–6) and for the Mosaic *prophet* (Deut. 18:15,18) as well. Both of these Old Testament figures had left this world under unusual circumstances (2 Kings 2:9–12; Deut. 34:5–12) and were expected to return either before or during the new age (cf. Mark 8:28; 9:4).

John repudiated any connection with all three of these chief actors in the messianic drama. Insistently he drew attention away from his own person (*Who are you?*), not because such questions were unimportant but because only one person deserved the ultimate status indicated by these titles. As a witness, John's role was not to receive titles (vv. 19–28) but to give them (vv. 29–34)!

Having disclaimed the three proposals of the Jewish delegation (vv. 19–21), John now met their insistent interrogations (vv. 22,25) by placing three further strictures on the importance of his ministry. (1) Rather than being himself the "Word" of the Lord, John was merely a *voice* or mouthpiece of Scripture (Isa. 40:3) calling the people to prepare a royal road for God's arrival. (2) Moreover, he baptized only *with water,* which was obviously no more than an outward, anticipatory rite much like the lustrations which the priests and Levites used in their Temple services. (3) Finally, he was *not worthy* to do even the work of a slave in untying *the thong* of the *sandal* for the hidden Messiah when he stepped forth in glory.

(2) The Positive Witness to Jesus (1:29–34)

29 The next day he saw Jesus coming toward him, and said, "Behold, the Lamb of God, who takes away the sin of the world! 30 This is he of whom I said, 'After me comes a man who ranks before me, for he was before me.' 31 I myself did not know him; but for this I came baptizing with water, that he might be revealed to Israel." 32 And John bore witness, "I saw the Spirit descend as a dove from heaven, and it remained on him. 33 I myself did not know him; but he who sent me to baptize with water said to me, 'He on whom you see the Spirit descend and remain, this is he who baptizes with the Holy Spirit.' 34 And I have seen and have borne witness that this is the Son of God."

John was not negative about himself out of some overwhelming sense of modesty, but because he had something more important to say about Jesus. The denials of the first day in vv. 19–28 are now balanced by the affirmations of the second day in vv. 29–34. The strong sense of a dramatic new revelation is conveyed by the absence of any local place setting (contrast v. 28) and by the repeated use of terms for visible disclosure: John *saw* Jesus coming and cried, *Behold.* He baptized with water that Jesus might be *revealed* to Israel. He *saw* (lit. "beheld") the Spirit descend as God had promised. Ultimately, the basis for John's entire witness rested on his solemn insistence, *I have seen.* (v. 34).

The content of this vision was summarized in a series of positive affirmations which balanced the negative denials of 1:19–28. The first of these, *the Lamb of God, who takes away the sin of the world* (v. 29), illustrated the fusion of several Old Testament theological motifs when applied to the ministry of Jesus by early Christian reflection.

In Judaism, the lamb—or a similar animal such as the goat—was: (1) the primary cultic sacrifice in the daily burnt offering (Ex. 29:38–42) and on many special occasions (Num. 28—29; Lev. 1—7); (2) the victim that bore the sins of the people on the Day of Atonement (Num. 29:7–11; Lev. 16:20–22); (3) the meat ritually slain, roasted, and then eaten for the Passover celebration (Ex. 12:1–11); (4) the symbol of the Servant suffering in silence who bore the people's griefs and the sin of many (Isa. 53); (5) the apocalyptic ram that victoriously led the flock of God (Enoch 90:38; Testament of Joseph 19:8). The versatile image of the lamb was prominent in all three of the major traditions lying behind the ministry of John: the cultic, the prophetic, and the apocalyptic.

In all of these varied strands of Jewish usage, however, it is striking that none provides the precise antecedent of a *lamb* (*amnos*) that *takes away the sin of the world.* Jesus fulfilled many of the spiritual functions symbolized by the lamb in the Old Testament, yet he transcended them all. He was the Servant who suffered as a lamb (Acts 8:32–35), the true Passover sacrifice (1 Cor. 5:7), the unblemished offering (1 Peter 1:19), and the slain but conquering leader of the flock (Rev. 5: 6,12; 7:14,17; 17:14; 22:1,3). We cannot now determine just how many of these insights would have been clustered around the concept in the thinking of John himself. Probably the Evangelist intended the paschal allusion to be central (cf. 19:36 and

Ex. 12:46). The instructed Christian reader, however, who has pondered the Old Testament and celebrated the Lord's Supper is heir to all of the multiple meanings that belong to the history of this rich symbol.

The second confession by John (v. 30) was reminiscent of a saying already recorded in the Prologue (v. 15). Although Judaism normally assumed that any *man* who came *after* a religious leader thereby became his subordinate, John insisted that among his followers was one who actually was, and had always been, his superior, *before* him in both time and rank. Certain of his own limited role as a witness, John was equally convinced that God would send someone greater, even before he or anyone else knew who it was.

The third and climactic confession (vv. 31–33) concerned the relation of Jesus to the Spirit, for only the Spirit could reveal the hidden Messiah already in their midst. Despite his prophetic vocation, John *did not know him,* nor could his *baptizing* merely *with water* cause him to be revealed to Israel (v. 31). Any external ritual, even when divinely ordained, is of limited value without the concurrent action of the Spirit. But John cherished the promise that one day he would see flesh and spirit permanently united, and in that hope he faithfully baptized with water until the Spirit did *descend* as realistically as a *dove* in flight and *remained on* Jesus. For the Spirit to *remain* (cf. 3:34) meant that one had come who could baptize (minister) not with water but *with the Holy Spirit.* The gift of the Spirit was the distinguishing mark of the new dispensation to be inaugurated by Jesus (cf. 3:5–8; 3:34; 4:23–24; 6:63; 7:37–39).

The concluding confession that Jesus was *the Son of God* may represent not another major affirmation by John but only his witness to the heavenly voice heard at Jesus' baptism authenticating him as the "beloved Son" (cf. Matt. 3:17; Mark 1:11; Luke 3:22). An important textual variant substitutes "the Elect (or Chosen) One" for *the*

Son, perhaps as an early effort to make more explicit the Servant background of the descent of the Spirit at the baptism of Jesus (cf. Isa. 42:1).

2. The Witness of the First Disciples (1:35-51)

This section develops in three ways the central theme of testimony which runs throughout 1:19-51. First, in vv. 35-37, the witness of John already given in v. 29 is carefully repeated as the crucial transition to a new series of confessions which follow. Second, in vv. 38-49, a group of disciples move beyond the preparatory work of the Baptist by expressing their allegiance on the basis of a personal attachment to Jesus. Finally, in vv. 50-51, Jesus himself delivers the climactic witness as to what the future with him will hold for these new followers.

In form, this unit is divided into two balanced parts (vv. 35-42; 43-51) consisting of parallel cycles which describe how two pairs of named disciples, plus an unnamed individual, came to Jesus. This sequence is strikingly similar to Mark 1:16-20 where first Simon and Andrew, then James and John, were called to follow Jesus. Both presentations underscore the unchanging methods of Jesus in gaining adherents and exhibit in the simplest possible manner the basic components of a Christian commitment. It is as if the narrative were saying: in case after case, this is the way Christ mastered men.

(1) Andrew and Another Disciple (1:35-42)

35 The next day again John was standing with two of his disciples; 36 and he looked at Jesus as he walked, and said, "Behold, the Lamb of God!" 37 The two disciples heard him say this, and they followed Jesus. 38 Jesus turned, and saw them following, and said to them, "What do you seek?" And they said to him, "Rabbi" (which means Teacher), "where are you staying?" 39 He said to them, "Come and see." They came and saw where he was staying; and they stayed with him that day, for it was about the tenth hour. 40 One of the two who heard John speak, and followed him, was Andrew, Simon Peter's brother. 41 He first found his brother Simon, and said to him, "We have found the Messiah" (which means Christ). 42 He brought him to Jesus. Jesus looked at him, and said, "So you are Simon the son of John? You shall be called Cephas" (which means Peter).

Having directed a general witness to his people Israel, John now offered that same witness specifically to his disciples. It is one thing to state a sweeping conviction to the masses, quite another to deliberately give up one's own devotees; but John did not flinch from dismantling the rapidly growing movement that had brought him fame and followers (cf. 3:22-30). It was a mark of his effectiveness as a witness that although two disciples *heard* John speak, they *followed Jesus.* Soon they would be attributing to him the very titles of ultimate honor which John had renounced for himself (cf. vv. 20,41).

Notice the careful balance of divine and human initiatives in the encounter of Jesus with his first disciples. From the human side, the *two disciples* of John acted resolutely upon his witness and *followed Jesus* in an effort to discover where he, an itinerant *Teacher,* might be currently staying. At the same time, the initial impulse which they received from John (v. 37) rooted ultimately in the revelation of God to him (v. 33) and thus represented a divine summons. Moreover, Jesus answered their inquiry with an invitation, *Come and see,* which proved so captivating that they immediately accepted, even though the day was far spent, *the tenth hour* being around 4:00 P.M.

As the living chain of witnesses began to grow, the same balance between divine and human initiative was carefully maintained. The *first* thing that *Andrew* did was to share with *his brother Simon* the great "Eureka" of Christian evangelism, *We have found!* This prototypal disciple voluntarily decided to become a witness, but he did so only as a result of his meeting with Jesus. He immediately *found* his earthly brother because he had already found his spiritual leader (*Messiah* is the Hebrew word and

Christ the equivalent Greek word referring to one designated by anointing for a special mission). The key word *found* (vv. 41,43,45) implies a single experience in which all of the effort involved in human discovery is combined with a recognition of the sheer givenness of that which was put "there" by God to be discovered.

Andrew had already learned from John the Baptist (vv. 36–37) that the giving of testimony to Christ is never complete until the hearer has been led beyond the spokesman to the living reality described by his witness. Thus he not only shared his discovery with Simon but also *brought him to Jesus*. It may not have been easy for this headstrong fisherman to accept the stupendous claim that his less aggressive brother, Andrew, had actually found the supreme hope of the ages. After all, misguided messianic enthusiasms were a commonplace in Palestine.

Nevertheless, when Simon agreed to come and see for himself, Jesus did not commend him for his response but rather *looked at him* with a penetrating gaze and conferred on him a new sense of identity in the change of his name. Heretofore, he had defined himself in terms of the past as *the son of John*. Now he would understand his personhood in terms of the future: *You shall be called Cephas*. This Aramaic word, which is translated *Peter* from the Greek, was not a normal proper name but a striking nickname which promised Simon that as a disciple he would become a "rock-man" (cf. Matt. 16:18).

Here again, the reciprocity of grace and faith is clearly illustrated. Simon came to Jesus in response to the initiative of Andrew. Jesus, in turn, responded with the unexpected gift of a new character for one who would willingly seek him. This mutuality of response in the divine-human encounter is characteristic of all true evangelism.

(2) Philip and Nathanael (1:43–51)

43 The next day Jesus decided to go to Galilee. And he found Philip and said to him, "Follow me." 44 Now Philip was from Bethsaida, the city of Andrew and Peter. 45 Philip found Nathanael, and said to him, "We have found him of whom Moses in the law and also the prophets wrote, Jesus of Nazareth, the son of Joseph." 46 Nathanael said to him, "Can anything good come out of Nazareth?" Philip said to him, "Come and see." 47 Jesus saw Nathanael coming to him, and said of him, "Behold, an Israelite indeed, in whom is no guile!" 48 Nathanael said to him, "How do you know me?" Jesus answered him, "Before Philip called you, when you were under the fig tree, I saw you." 49 Nathanael answered him, "Rabbi, you are the Son of God! You are the King of Israel!" 50 Jesus answered him, "Because I said to you, I saw you under the fig tree, do you believe? You shall see greater things than these." 51 And he said to him, "Truly, truly, I say to you, you will see heaven opened, and the angels of God ascending and descending upon the Son of man."

Leaving the Judean environs where John had been baptizing (1:28), Jesus decided to travel north *to Galilee*, a largely pagan territory on the upper periphery of Jewish Palestine (the name Galilee literally means "circle of the Gentiles" or "district of foreigners"). There he found *Philip*, a Jew with a Greek name from *Bethsaida*, whose home was a strongly hellenized town on the northeast shore of the Sea of Galilee. Perhaps Jesus was guided to Bethsaida (lit., "house of the fisher") because it was also *the city of Andrew and Peter*. In any case, he would find there cosmopolitan citizens especially suited to mediate between the Jewish and Greek worlds (cf. 12:20–22).

The call of Philip as recorded here has been reduced to its most essential element: *Follow me*. This phrase also lies at the core of the call to commitment in the Synoptic Gospels (e.g., Mark 1:17; 2:14; 8:34; 10:21). It defines discipleship in relational rather than in intellectual, emotional, or actional terms. Philip was not offered an idea to ponder, a mood to experience, or a task to accomplish, but a person to obey. In place of law in the sacred Scriptures or ritual at the holy Temple, Jesus dared to identify himself as the source of guidance to God. Furthermore, his summons was future-facing. Following implies an open-ended, dynamic pilgrimage, not a closed, static position. Christianity is not a place to stand but a road to walk in choice companionship with the "leader" of life (cf. Acts 3:15; Heb. 12:2).

Attachment to Jesus, however, does not draw a person out of the world but sends him forth with the responsibility of witnessing to others. Thus *Philip* soon *found Nathanael,* a Jew from nearby Cana of Galilee (21:2) who is known to us only from the fourth Gospel, and shared with him the faith of the growing disciple band. In a sense, Philip could say *We have found him* because Jesus had first found Philip. The content of the testimony identifying Jesus as *him of whom Moses in the law and also the prophets wrote* may be a specific allusion to the Mosaic prophet described in Deuteronomy 18:15–18 (cf. Deut. 34:10), although it is general enough to depict Jesus as the fulfillment of the entire Old Testament.

The identification of the cherished biblical hope with one man *Jesus,* known only as *the son of Joseph* from the obscure village *of Nazareth,* elicited from Nathanael the incredulous retort, *Can anything good come out of Nazareth?* Since rivalry between neighboring towns is proverbially strong, Nathanael may have instinctively voiced the contempt of Cana for nearby Nazareth. More likely, however, he reacted as a serious student of the Scriptures who knew that no *son of Joseph* from *Nazareth* had ever been anticipated in the promises of Scripture (cf. 7:41,52). In any case, the response of Philip offered an effective answer, whether to provincial prejudice or to biblical literalism, *Come and see.*

The strategy of Jesus was even more striking than that of Philip. No sooner did he see *Nathanael coming to him* than he praised this one who had just belittled his origins: *Behold, an Israelite indeed, in whom is no guile.* This picture of the model pious Jew confronted Nathanael with his deepest sense of identity, with

that style of life which he sought most passionately to emulate. No wonder he exclaimed in the face of such uncanny insight into his inner commitments, *How do you know me?* (cf. 2:25).

The clue to this clairvoyance was one which Nathanael in particular would appreciate. Jesus could identify him as the true embodiment of Old Testament religion because he *saw* him *under the fig tree.* This reference, whether intended to be literal or symbolic, depicted those spiritually ideal conditions under which to study the law of God (Mic. 4:4; Zech. 3:10). Jesus attached the utmost significance to a sincere study of Scripture by those earnestly searching for the messianic reign of peace (cf. 5:39,46).

So perfectly had Jesus discerned and affirmed the deepest loyalties of Nathanael's life that doubt quickly gave way to faith in the confession, *Rabbi, you are the Son of God! You are the King of Israel!* Earthly origins were forgotten as Jesus was set in an entirely new context and seen, not as one *out of Nazareth,* but as one *of whom Moses in the law and also the prophets wrote.* He was no longer viewed as *the son of Joseph,* a possible term of derision (cf. 6:42; 8:19,41), but as *the Son of God,* a title linked in the Old Testament with *the King of Israel* (Psalm 2:7). Jesus became for Nathanael the great teacher (*Rabbi*) with whom he could study the Scriptures *under the fig tree,* as well as the kingly Messiah who would usher in the new age of paradise where such a "tree of knowledge" could flourish.

Exalted as the exclamation of Nathanael was, the climactic confession of Jesus in reply was even more astonishing. Now that the master was certain of his disciples' total commitment, he could lead them beyond the Jewish foundations on which their faith had first been based. For he had not come simply to fulfill even the finest current Jewish understandings of the Old Testament but to accomplish *greater things than these.*

Here, as at Caesarea-Philippi (Mark 8:29,31), Jesus countered a typically Jewish interpretation of his mission in terms of political messiahship by substituting the more spiritual concept of the **Son of man** developed in the latter part of the Old Testament. To this title, moreover, he linked the familiar story of Jacob's dream at Bethel with the ladder to heaven on which the *angels of God* were *ascending and descending* (Gen. 28:12). A decisive difference, however, lay in the assertion that *the Son of man* was himself the ladder. Jesus claimed that he was the personal channel of revelation between God and man.

The crux of the claim for the disciples lay in the twice repeated promise *you shall see*, which was further reinforced by the solemn introductory formula, *Truly, truly.* This was no "back to Bethel" experience in which all true Israelites such as Nathanael were invited to dream the dreams of the ancestral patriarchs. Rather, the assurance was given that in their future pilgrimage of discipleship what had been for Jacob only a dream would become for them a visible reality. Nor would they have long to wait. As the next verse indicates (2:1), only three days later they did begin to see that *heaven* had been *opened* permanently and united to earth in the person of Jesus. This view of Jesus as the open link between heaven and earth, as the one who turned ancient dreams into present realities, dominates the remainder of the Gospel, especially the "book of signs." As such, 1:51 serves effectively as a text for all that is to follow in chapters 2—12.

Part One: The Book of Signs
2:1—12:50

The Gospel of John is divided into two great sections, chapters 2—12 and chapters 13—20, with chapter 1 serving as an introduction and chapter 21 as a conclusion. This literary structure corresponds to the twofold theological movement of the Gospel which traces the "descending" and "ascending" of the incarnate Logos in a "parabola of redemption" between heaven and earth. Part One focuses on the public minis-

try of Jesus to the old Israel, while Part Two is concerned primarily with his private ministry to the new Israel (cf. the summary in 1:11–12).

John 2—12, unlike the Synoptics, centers the activity of Jesus in the south around Jerusalem rather than in the north around Capernaum. This results in striking differences between the two accounts which are best explained by supposing that John was basically developing Judean sources, whereas the Synoptics had access primarily to materials originating in Galilee. The two approaches do not consciously supplement or contradict each other but move along largely independent lines. For example, John 2—12 depicts Jesus in a more cosmopolitan urban setting dealing with the hierarchy of Jewish officialdom, while the Synoptics view him in a more provincial rural setting involved with the local leaders of popular Jewish piety.

In its literary development, John 2—12 appears to have evolved from a nucleus of miracle stories which had been collected in a "signs source." This is suggested by the emphatic enumeration of the signs in 2:11 and 4:54, as well as by the sweeping references to miracles in 1:50–51 and in 20:30–31 (cf. 12:37), particularly if these verses originally prefaced and concluded such a source. Although John 2—12 includes fewer miracle stories than do any of the Synoptic accounts, they are here presented much more elaborately with a literary skill and theological subtlety unrivaled elsewhere in the Gospels.

Many expositors suppose that the signs in chapters 2—12 have been rendered even more impressive by deliberately limiting them to seven, since this number in biblical thought often symbolized completeness. On this reckoning, the seven signs are: the changing of water to wine (2:1–11), the healing of the officer's son (4:46–54), the cure of a lame man (5:1–9), the feeding of five thousand (6:1–15), the walking on the water (6:16–21), the restoration of sight to a man born blind (9:1–7), and the raising of

Lazarus (11:1-44).

However, the word sign (sēmeion) is not mentioned in reference to two of these incidents (5:1-9; 6:16-21), while the plural signs (sēmeia) is used elsewhere of several other events (2:23; 3:2; 6:2; 6:26; 7:31; 9:16; 11:47; 12:37). Thus, it is likely either that the exact number of signs was not intended to be significant or that these seven miracles were developed beyond an earlier, simpler source which referred generally to many signs.

The content of John 2—12 traces the Jewish repudiation of the Messiah in three successive stages. First, chapters 2—4 summarize his positive reception as the bearer of the powers of the new age (2:11,23; 3:2,26; 4:1,41,45,53). Then, in chapters 5—10, the mood changes from one of enthusiastic if sometimes superficial acceptance to one of conflicting opinions and deepening hostility (5:16,18,43; 6:41,52,66; 7:1,12–13,19–20,25,30–32,43–44,48; 8:13, 37,59; 9:16,22; 10:19–21,31,39). Finally, in chapters 11—12, the tempo of controversy accelerates rapidly until an irrevocable decision is reached to destroy Jesus and the rupture between him and Israel is complete (11:8,16,50,53–54,57; 12:7,24,33,37,42,48). Nowhere in all the New Testament are the dynamics of decision and the irony of rejection more profoundly analyzed. Here, from a quite different perspective, is a grappling with the same anguished problem that concerned Paul in Romans 9—11: Why does religion itself often pose the ultimate barrier to belief in Christ?

I. The Reception of the Revealer (2:1—4:54)

Each Synoptic Gospel begins with a highly theological introduction followed by a general section on the inauguration of Jesus' public ministry in power (cf. Matt. 4:23—9:34; Mark 1:14–45; Luke 4:16–44). All agree that the beginnings in Galilee were largely successful, although not without a measure of misunderstanding. The Gospel of John has carried this pattern of presentation to a climax by following his majestic introduction (1:1–51) with a comprehensive account (2:1—4:54) of the new age ushered in by Jesus. This latter section serves as a vivid commentary on 3:17. God's initial offer to man is salvation, not condemnation. Always the first word of the gospel is grace, not judgment. The rejection of Jesus which eventually developed in chapters 5—12 was essentially the result of human resistance to the offer of a new way of life in chapters 2—4.

In form, 2:1—4:54 is one of the most carefully organized sections of the Gospel. It deliberately begins (2:1) and ends (4:54) in Galilee, which may reflect a knowledge of the Synoptic approach. The opening and closing accounts in Cana serve as clamps which bracket the entire sequence to form a literary unity. In between are four other incidents set in Jerusalem, Judea, and Samaria. The swift succession of six narratives is calculated to provide a cumulative impact which confronts the reader with a comprehensive illustration of the new age now dawning. In each case, the dramatic account of Jesus' redemptive work alternates with an interpretative word by the Evangelist, providing the reader with an opportunity to pause for reflection (cf. 2:11–12; 2:21–25; 3:16–21; 3:31–36; 4:43–45; 4:54).

The purpose of 2:1—4:54 in the framework of the Gospel may be understood from its relation to the preparatory section which precedes it (1:19–51). There, the person of Jesus was clarified by attributing to him ten titles rich in Old Testament development and in early Christian devotion. Here, the work of Jesus is summarized in six highly symbolic narratives which record how he offered to Judaism those deepest spiritual realities anticipated by its ancestral religion. A sense of fulfillment pervades the entire section.

It is very significant, however, that these signs of the consummation of Israel's hopes did not come in a catastrophic manner, as many Jews supposed they would, but disclosed themselves rather to eyes of faith. In all six parts of this section, faith is singled out as the crux of the human response to the saving activity of Jesus (cf. 1:7,12).

In Cana, the disciples did not enjoy the new supply of wine but "*believed* in him" who had made it (2:11). The cleansing of the Temple became meaningful to them only after the resurrection when "they *believed* the Scripture and the word which Jesus had spoken" (2:22). Nicodemus was challenged to *believe* "heavenly things" (3:12), i.e., to have faith in him "who descended from heaven, the Son of man" (3:13), for only one who "*believes* in him may have eternal life" (3:15; cf. vv. 16,18). John the Baptist insisted that his followers shift their loyalty to Jesus, and this plea was reinforced by the affirmation that "he who *believes* in the Son" has already escaped the wrath of God (3:36). Jesus reaped a bountiful human harvest as "many Samaritans . . . *believed* in him," whether from a woman's witness or from his own word (4:39–42). Because an official from Capernaum "*believed* the word that Jesus spoke" (4:50), the official's son was rescued from death, leading to yet greater belief (4:53).

This singular concentration on faith at the climax of each unit shows both the cruciality of belief for salvation and its essential character as obedient openness to the powers of the new age now manifest in the ministry of Jesus.

Moreover, this faith is always described in John by the verb form (*pisteuein*) rather than by the noun form (*pistis*), which is never used. This means that believing is viewed primarily as an active response rather than an unchanging attitude. Such a perspective explains why faith is frequently depicted as a growing reality in John 2—4.

Following the response of faith in Cana (2:11), the disciples came to understand the cleansing of the Temple only after a long process of reflection and scriptural study 2:17,22). Nicodemus was urged to

move from belief in earthly things to belief in heavenly things (3:12). John the Baptist sought a steady decrease of allegiance to himself and a corresponding increase of allegiance to Jesus (3:22–23,26,30; 4:1). The Samaritan woman and her countrymen moved in several stages toward a deeper faith (4:15,19,29,39–42). Finally, at least three levels of faith are identified in the story of the Capernaum official (4: 48,50,53).

This does not mean, however, that faith is forever incomplete, a tentative surmise in search of that verification which the relativities of human existence can never provide. Rather, as 1:35–51 shows so clearly, faith may arise as an absolute conviction even when it is far from mature. Just as true marriage involves the pledging of irrevocable vows by two persons whose growth to mature devotion has scarcely begun, so discipleship is based on faith understood both as total allegiance and as complete openness. This is why the emphasis on faith as a decisive beginning in John 1 must always be balanced with the emphasis on faith as unending pilgrimage in John 2—4.

1. The New Joy (2:1–12)

The reference to the "third day" (2:1) at the outset of this passage provides the transitional link with the preceding section. There, Jesus had gathered a company of followers who confessed their faith that the messianic hope of Israel would be fulfilled in him (1:36,41,45,49). Scarcely could they realize, however, that this process would begin in only "three days," a biblical phrase used to indicate a very short period of time (e.g., Hos. 6:2). Almost immediately after Jesus had solemnly assured his disciples that "they would see greater things" (1:51), this apocalypse, or vision of "heaven opened," began to be realized (cf. Mark 14:62). Here is the first instance of a creative use of the phrase "three days" to suggest the swiftness with which Jesus sought to establish the new age (cf. 2:19; Mark 8:31). This mood of imminent expectation pervaded his ministry from the outset.

(1) The First Sign: Water to Wine (2: 1-11)

¹ On the third day there was a marriage at Cana in Galilee, and the mother of Jesus was there; ² Jesus also was invited to the marriage, with his disciples. ³ When the wine failed, the mother of Jesus said to him, "They have no wine." ⁴ And Jesus said to her, "O woman, what have you to do with me? My hour has not yet come." ⁵ His mother said to the servants, "Do whatever he tells you." ⁶ Now six stone jars were standing there, for the Jewish rites of purification, each holding twenty or thirty gallons. ⁷ Jesus said to them, "Fill the jars with water." And they filled them up to the brim. ⁸ He said to them, "Now draw some out, and take it to the steward of the feast." So they took it. ⁹ When the steward of the feast tasted the water now become wine, and did not know where it came from (though the servants who had drawn the water knew), the steward of the feast called the bridegroom ¹⁰ and said to him, "Every man serves the good wine first; and when men have drunk freely, then the poor wine; but you have kept the good wine until now." ¹¹ This, the first of his signs, Jesus did at Cana in Galilee, and manifested his glory; and his disciples believed in him.

A wedding feast was one of the most important and joyous occasions in the life of a Jewish family. Since marriages were usually arranged well in advance, the tiny village of **Cana in Galilee** may have eagerly anticipated this celebration for a long while. A great host of friends and relatives had doubtless been invited, including the **mother of Jesus** from nearby Nazareth. As the festivities progressed, she became aware of a potentially acute embarrassment as the carefully selected wine reserves began to run short. Turning to her son who had **also** been **invited** and was there **with his disciples,** she indirectly sought his assistance by confiding that the refreshments were now depleted (v. 3).

There is no indication of the spirit or purpose of her implicit request. We cannot determine, for example, whether this was a tactful hint that the time had come to depart or, since this story occupies a position in John similar to that of the temptation narrative in the Synoptics, whether it may have been an eager mother's effort to encourage her son to exercise his remarkable powers. The important point is the realization by Jesus that he and his mother were thinking on completely different levels. This is indicated by all three parts of his reply.

(1) In addressing her as *woman* he was not being curt or indifferent. The term could be infinitely tender, as in 19:26. Rather, he was formally redefining their relationship, much as in that incredible Synoptic question, "Who is my mother?" (cf. Mark 3:33). The use of *woman* by a son to refer to his mother was quite unprecedented in Judaism. In one sense, she would have to lose him as son in order to find him as Saviour.

(2) The idiomatic expression, **What have you to do with me?,** was not necessarily hostile (cf. Judg. 11:12; 1 Kings 17:18; Mark 1:24; Matt. 8:29), but it did serve as a forceful declaration of independence, a sharp insistence that she could lay no claim on him. His mother must not understand what followed merely as a son's dutiful effort to fulfill her wishes.

(3) This surprising detachment was prompted by the fact that his mother was concerned about a shortage of wine, whereas Jesus was absorbed with his eventual vocational destiny, here called the **hour which has not yet come** (cf. 7:30; 8:20; 12:23,27; 17:1). What he was willing to do in Cana must be consistent with—indeed, an integral part of—that ministry yet to unfold which would climax in the cross.

In the light of this impasse between mother and son, why did Jesus immediately follow his rebuff by agreeing to deal with the wine shortage? This apparently inconsistent behavior is part of a significant pattern which recurs elsewhere in the Gospel. For example, in 7:1-10 his brothers suggested that he go to Jerusalem; Jesus rejected their proposal but then went. Again, in 11:1-7 the sisters of Lazarus sent for Jesus; at first he declined to respond but shortly thereafter insisted on making the trip.

These are not instances of vacillation on Jesus' part but are reflections of his three-fold determination: (1) not to be guided by human pressures, even when based on a genuine need, (2) but rather to relate such problems to his understanding of the will of God, and (3) therefore to deal with these issues at a far deeper level than those who were troubled could imagine. Jesus was not indifferent even to the most mundane or misguided request. Rather, he was quick to discover creative ways by which to set such concerns in a redemptive context.

In this instance, Jesus saw in the wine shortage an appropriate opportunity to teach his disciples a basic truth about his ministry. With the gracious cooperation of his mother, he first instructed *the servants* to *fill* with water *six stone jars* customarily used by the Jews for ceremonial washings to remove pagan defilement. To fill these containers *up to the brim* was probably intended to be symbolical rather than practical, for to do so was not customary since *the Jewish rites of purification* involved plunging the lower part of both arms into the water (the apparent meaning of Mark 7:3–4).

Even as the disciples puzzled over such a strange procedure, their astonishment was compounded as Jesus again bade the servants to *draw some out,* this time for *the steward of the feast.* That this water was to be drawn from the well rather than from the stone jars is likely for at least two reasons: (1) the water originally in the jars presumably would have been dirty from previous use by the wedding guests; (2) the verb "to draw out" (*antleō*) usually means "to draw from a well" and is so used in this Gospel (cf. 4:7,15).[8]

On this understanding, the symbolism in-

tended by these strange instructions was both consistent and revealing. The stone jars represented the Jewish ceremonial system; that there were six of them may have further suggested the incompleteness of the old order. Jesus, however, did not ignore this heritage but rather fulfilled it (i.e., acting on his instructions the servants *filled the jars up to the brim*). Then from the well as a seventh or complete source, he had the servants draw out his own distinctive contribution to the feast. This was not the stagnant water of the stone jars but the well water drawn from an abundant gushing supply (cf. 4:14; 7:38; Jer. 2:13). According to this interpretation, Jesus wanted to show his disciples that he was concerned for the Jewish religion, else why bother to fill the six stone jars? (Note the parallel in 6:13 of twelve filled baskets.) At the same time, he sought to suggest that he could go beyond the prevailing system which provided for purification through ritual lustrations.

The final lesson for the disciples came as they watched. *The steward of the feast tasted the water* and discovered that it had *now become wine.* Knowing nothing of Jesus' actions, he immediately *called the bridegroom* and half-chidingly congratulated him on saving the best for last. Suddenly, a sagging party took on new life as the result of the transformation wrought by Jesus.

More important than the change of spirit at the marriage feast, however, was the change of faith in the disciples. They realized that this new joy which burst forth in Cana was but a sign or pointer to the *glory* (divine significance) of Jesus himself. Thus their deeper response was not to enjoy the gift but to *believe* in the giver. For them, Jesus was vastly more than "the life of the party." In his symbolical action they saw that a decisive *first* or new beginning had been made in which the eschatological joy of the messianic age was being *manifested.*

Notice how the incident concentrates entirely on the miracle worker and not on the miracle itself. The text simply states that

---

[8] The view that the water turned to wine had been drawn from the well rather than from the jars was popularized by B. F. Westcott, *The Gospel According to St. John* (London: James Clarke & Co., 1958 reprint of 1880 ed.), pp. 37–38. It is contested by reputable scholars such as C. K. Barrett, *The Gospel According to St John* (London: S.P.C.K., 1955), p. 160.

the water became wine, but there is no hint of how this happened. Jesus neither acted nor spoke in miracle-working fashion. The master of ceremonies understood nothing of the matter, nor did the bridegroom. The miracle itself took place off the stage, out of sight. Even the *servants knew* only from whence they had *drawn the water.* Unlike most miracle stories, there was no general recognition that a mighty work had been performed. The account is not concerned with the methods used to change water to wine but only with the effect of this change on the faith of the disciples.[9]

The modesty with which the miracle is treated stands in sharp contrast to stories from the cult of Dionysos (Bacchus) where the most extravagant claims of supernatural wine production were a commonplace. In the ancient world, merely to claim that Christ had turned water into wine would hardly have been unique. The basic difference between Christianity and the mystery religions lay in Jesus himself and in the quality of faith which he awakened.

The true context in which to understand the wine-wedding symbolism of the Cana story is provided by the Old Testament and the ministry of Jesus. Three themes from these sources have coalesced in this highly theological account.

(1) Wine was closely associated with *joy*, both physical and spiritual. In creation, it was a good gift of God to gladden the heart (Gen. 27:28; Psalm 104:15; Eccl. 9:7). When the land was devastated and the vineyards destroyed, the joy that wine brings became a future hope (Hos. 14:7; Jer. 31:12; Zech. 10:6-7). In the new age, the Lord was expected to make a feast of wine on his holy mountain (Isa. 25:6). This is why Jesus likened the kingdom to a banquet or wedding feast (Matt. 8:11; 22:1-10; 25:1-13; 26:29) and his followers to the friends of the bridegroom (Mark 2:19; cf. John 3:29). To the chagrin of

every religious killjoy, he openly celebrated the joy of God's salvation with tax collectors and sinners (Matt. 11:19). He both poured new wine (Mark 2:22) and was himself its source (John 15:1). At Cana, the disciples saw that when Christ intervened, men were "surprised by joy" (C. S. Lewis).

(2) Connected with the emphasis on wine as joy was the kindred theme of *abundance.* The prophets, in particular, looked forward not only to the "sending of wine" as a divine gift (Joel 2:19) but to its presence in profusion (Joel 2:24) when the mountains themselves "shall drip sweet wine" (Joel 3:18; Amos 9:13-14). An unusual expression of this motif occurs in 2 Baruch 29:5-6 where, in the future age "when all is accomplished" and "the Messiah shall then begin to be revealed" (v. 3), "the earth also shall yield its fruit ten thousandfold and on each vine there shall be a thousand branches, and each branch shall produce a thousand clusters, and each cluster produce a thousand grapes, and each grape produce a cor of wine" (cor = 120 gallons). At Cana, the fact that the servants could return to the well yet again after it had already yielded enough water to fill six pots each holding twenty or thirty gallons (v. 6) shows that the new wine of Jesus is drawn from an inexhaustible supply.

(3) In the light of these emphases on abundant joy, it is strange to find that wine was also associated with *suffering* and death. Not only did its color suggest blood, but its production involved the crushing of grape clusters in the winepress. Drinking the bitter dregs of the wine of suffering was a form of divine punishment (Psalms 60:3; 75:8). Jeremiah combined this figure with the kindred concept of the cup (Jer. 49:12; cf. Isa. 51:17,22) to yield the striking phrase, "cup of the wine of wrath" (25:15), a vivid picture of God's vengeance closely related to the poem of the winepress in Isaiah 63:1-6.

Jesus grasped the explosive consequence

[9] C. H. Dodd, *Historical Tradition in the Fourth Gospel* (Cambridge: University Press, 1963), pp. 223-28.

of offering new wine in a religious system that was brittle like old wineskins (Mark 2:22). Just as John the Baptist had been taken from his disciples, so Jesus would suffer the same fate and the joy of his wedding guests would come to an abrupt end (Mark 2:20). At Cana, lest his mother mistakenly suppose that the new age of messianic joy could come so easily, Jesus made no wine until he first reminded her that his *hour* had *not yet come,* that hour when the cup would be his "blood . . . poured out for many" unto death (Mark 14:24). The joy that erupted at Cana was short-lived, for it was but the anticipation of that enduring joy which Jesus and his disciples would know only when they drank "new in the kingdom of God" (Mark 14:25).

(2) The Visit in Capernaum (2:12)

¹² After this he went down to Capernaum, with his mother and his brothers and his disciples; and there they stayed for a few days.

This brief historical notice stands in sharp contrast to the elaborate theological narrative which precedes it. However, such a mundane reference serves to remind the reader that the one who manifested his glory by mighty works (v. 11) was no heavenly apparition but an earthly man, with *mother, brothers, and disciples,* who lived in specific places such as *Capernaum.* At the very point where the supernatural character of Jesus seemed most evident the Evangelist was concerned to give equal attention to his historicity. Several problems were raised from the outset by this editorial transition, and various efforts to solve them are reflected in the unstable text of the most ancient available manuscripts.

First, were those referred to here as *his brothers* (*hoi adelphoi*) actually blood kin by virtue of having the same mother? (The word *his* is omitted from several manuscripts and is an uncertain reading.) Roman Catholic belief in the perpetual virginity of Mary requires the assumption that

these were sons of Joseph by a previous marriage or that they were cousins of Jesus by a brother of Joseph or a sister of Mary. Although the doctrine of Mary's perpetual virginity arose early in the history of the church, there is no evidence for such a notion in the New Testament. The uniform picture in the Gospels is that Jesus did have four blood brothers (Mark 6:3) who are regularly mentioned with their mother Mary (Mark 3:31) and are consistently represented as not believing in him during the earthly ministry (John 7:5).

Second, who *stayed* in Capernaum *for a few days?* The RSV *they* translates a reading which includes mother, brothers, and disciples with Jesus in this brief sojourn. Other texts read that only "he" remained, implying that Jesus soon left for Jerusalem (2:13) but that the whole group did not go with him. Confusion is created primarily by a comparison with the Synoptic evidence at three points: (1) Jesus made his headquarters at Capernaum for an extended Galilean ministry, (2) without his mother and brothers, (3) after John the Baptist had been arrested (Matt. 4:12–13; Mark 1:14,21,29; 2:1; Luke 4:23,31). In John, however, (1) he never made Capernaum his headquarters but visited it only briefly, (2) with his mother and brothers, (3) before John the Baptist had been arrested (cf. 3:22–24).

Two important conclusions may be drawn from the data. First, the fourth Gospel is largely independent of the Synoptics in the historical materials utilized to present the ministry of Jesus. Further, since only a small portion of the relevant material could be utilized (20:30; 21:25), the arrangement of the fourth Gospel is primarily topical and theological rather than chronological and geographical. This means that 2:12 may preserve a bit of independent historical information to the effect that Jesus' family was openly associated with his ministry before a period of disenchantment set in (cf. 7:5; Mark 3:21,31). At the same time, this verse locates the time of that

Capernaum sojourn only generally during the earlier phase of his ministry.

2. The New Worship (2:13-25)

One of the most dramatic and significant features of this section is its location in relation to the overall plan of the Gospel. In the immediate context, the coupling of the cleansing of the Temple with the changing of water to wine achieves a striking balance between the dialectical themes of joy and judgment. Here is a revealing commentary on Mark 2:22. In Cana Jesus poured the new wine of messianic joy, whereas in Jerusalem he struggled against the old wineskins of brittle traditionalism. How ironic that in tiny Cana, on the periphery of Judaism, Jesus met with obedient response even from humble servants whereas in the Holy City he got no hearing from the highest religious leadership. As a result, the gladness that flooded a simple wedding celebration could not penetrate the courts of worship. The sequence, however, is significant: joy was the first word of the gospel, giving infinite pathos rather than harsh vindictiveness to the judgment that followed.

In the larger context, the Johannine placement of the cleansing of the Temple at the outset of the public ministry, long before the triumphal entry (12:12–19), stands in conspicuous contrast to the Synoptic presentation where it comes near the close of the public ministry immediately following the triumphal entry (Matt. 21:1–13; Mark 11:1–19; Luke 19:28–46). The traditional hypothesis of two cleansings seems most unlikely for so crucial an event, in which case the simple solution of accepting both dates is ruled out. Nor must we choose between the two dates, for in arranging their materials neither John nor the Synoptics were concerned primarily with chronology.

Actually, the cleansing may have been placed at opposite ends of the gospel story in these two approaches for the same reason—to underscore its primary importance. The Synoptics put the incident last because

they decided to concentrate all of the Jerusalem ministry of Jesus into one final climactic week, and this was obviously the only context in which a Temple activity could take place. In so doing, they expressed the conviction that the entire public ministry led up to this decisive showdown which, in turn, precipitated the chain of events leading to the cross. Likewise, John located this same event at the outset because of the concern which we have already noticed to disclose the end from the beginning. In what follows, Jesus will go to Jerusalem several times—indeed, most of his ministry will take place there—and the deepest clue to all the controversy which unfolded there will already be known to the reader from this frontispiece.

Whereas the Cana story hints at the cross by means of its wine imagery and reference to the "hour not yet come," the cleansing explicitly anticipates the time when the enemies of Jesus will "consume" (v. 17) and "destroy" (v. 19) him. This tends to turn the entire Gospel account which follows into an extended passion narrative. From one perspective, Jesus appears to be constantly on trial (see comment on 1:19–28), whereas, from another perspective, it is Judaism that is actually on trial; i.e., Jesus is "cleansing" (testing or sifting) the old Israel in order that the new Israel might emerge. Mark makes somewhat the same point by beginning his Gospel with a cycle of controversies (2:1—3:6) which conclude with an explicit passion reference (3:6). What all of the Gospels are trying to clarify is the conviction that Jesus did not die by accident for no good reason but rather that his entire ministry was a life-and-death struggle in which his consistent commitment to certain ultimate issues finally sealed his fate at the hands of those who understood all too well what both he and they were doing.

(1) The Cleansing of the Temple (2:13-22)

13 The Passover of the Jews was at hand, and Jesus went up to Jerusalem. 14 In the temple he

found those who were selling oxen and sheep and pigeons, and the money-changers at their business. 15 And making a whip of cords, he drove them all, with the sheep and oxen, out of the temple; and he poured out the coins of the money-changers and overturned their tables. 16 And he told those who sold the pigeons, "Take these things away; you shall not make my Father's house a house of trade." 17 His disciples remembered that it was written, "Zeal for thy house will consume me." 18 The Jews then said to him, "What sign have you to show us for doing this?" 19 Jesus answered them, "Destroy this temple, and in three days I will raise it up." 20 The Jews then said, "It has taken forty-six years to build this temple, and will you raise it up in three days?" 21 But he spoke of the temple of his body. 22 When therefore he was raised from the dead, his disciples remembered that he had said this; and they believed the scripture and the word which Jesus had spoken.

Jesus capitalized on great historic occasions to confront Israel with its religious destiny. *The Passover* was the supreme public celebration *of the Jews,* held annually in the spring, which summoned multitudes of devout pilgrims *up to Jerusalem.* In a season when spiritual sensitivity should have been strongest, however, Jesus found *in the* outer *temple* precincts the dealers in sacrificial animals, *who were selling oxen and sheep and pigeons,* as well as *the money-changers* who, for a fee, converted the Roman coinage with its hated image of Caesar into the Tyrian coinage with which the half-shekel Temple tax could be paid. This "business-as-usual" atmosphere, with its huckstering of piety for a profit, was so incompatible with the eschatological fervor of Jesus that he made a *whip of cords* and *drove them all . . . out of the temple.*

The sight of Jesus with a scourge in his hand is one of the most provocative and disturbing pictures in the Gospels. Critics have distorted the issue by charging that Jesus lost his temper, resorted to brute force, disturbed public worship, and thereby contradicted the very principles for which he stood. To answer these unwarranted accusations we must clarify three features of the account.

First, the *whip of cords* was not a cruel leather lash such as we know today. Since worshipers were not allowed to bring any sticks or weapons into the temple precincts, the scourge must have been hastily plaited out of materials readily available in the vicinity—e.g., stalks used either in worship (somewhat like our branches on Palm Sunday) or as food or bedding for the animals.[10]

Second, the Greek text may not be represented as clearly by the RSV translation, which implies that the *all* driven out of the Temple were the vendors, as by the Moffatt translation, "he drove them all, sheep and cattle together, out of the temple." Jesus herded the beasts out with a stinging "switch," but he banished the men with an equally stinging word, *Take these things away.*

Finally, Jesus did not interrupt a service of worship but sought to make a clearing where such could take place. Since this incident occurred inside the Temple grounds, merchandizing must have been allowed in the outermost Court of the Gentiles. In this one area reserved for a response to God by other races, Jesus discovered that *my* (not our) *Father's house* had become *a house of trade* (lit., an emporium). Thus, in an act fraught with eschatological finality, he repudiated in principle an establishment where trade had usurped the place of worship and sacrifice had become a substitute for worldwide compassion.

The *disciples* were so shocked by this revolutionary onslaught against the ecclesiastical status quo that they were driven to the Scriptures for an explanation. This search enabled them to *remember* a passage in Psalm 69:9 where *it was written, Zeal for thy house will consume me.* Jesus had dared to challenge the supreme institution in Jewish life out of a burning pas-

10 The RSV translation of *phragellion ek schoiniōn* by "whip of cords" may mislead the English reader. *Phragellion* is from the Latin *flagellum,* which is used of a whip for driving cattle. *Schoinion* is the diminutive of *schoinos,* meaning "rush," and refers to any small rope or cord twisted or plaited out of rushes.

sion for the true purpose of the Temple. He had not held the whip in his hand for conquest but for cleansing. Incidentals were banished in order that worship might rediscover its true purpose, that of cultivating a consuming zeal for God himself.

The word translated *consume* referred not only to the intensity of holy zeal from within but to the hostility which such zeal could provoke from without (cf. Psalm 69), thus it may also be translated "destroy" (e.g., NEB). Jesus did not simply scourge the Temple as its master (cf. Mal. 3:1; 1 Peter 4:17). Rather, he was willing to be scourged and destroyed as the living temple in which the glory of God had tabernacled among men (cf. v. 19*a*).

Without benefit of this scriptural perspective from Psalm 69, *the Jews* were at such a loss to understand the cleansing that they demanded a *sign* which would validate so highhanded an act. In response, Jesus "turned the tables" once more by charging that they themselves would *destroy this temple* if they refused to heed his cleansing; i.e., if they continued to make the house of God a privileged sanctuary of nationalistic exclusivism instead of an open center for universal evangelism. The Jews had accused Jesus of endangering the Jerusalem Temple, whereas he insisted that they were the ones whose practices were certain to reduce it to ruin.

But their failure would not finally thwart God's purposes. In the short space of *three days,* a cryptic reference to his climactic work of death and resurrection (cf. Mark 8:31), Jesus would *raise . . . up* the very reality which the Jews were tearing down but in an entirely new form. He would himself, through *his body,* the church, become the transformed center around which the worldwide worship of God with zeal could gather. This meant that the human catastrophe which was certain to befall the earthly Temple—and which did so in A.D. 70—would not interrupt the divine continuity of God's presence among men (cf. Mark 14:58; 15:29–30).

Faced with an enigmatic answer of such obvious spiritual profundity, *the Jews* could manage no better response than a reference to their building program! Herod the Great had launched an ambitious enlargement of the national worship center in 20/19 B.C. By this time, *forty-six years* had already passed (making the date A.D. 26/27), and the total project was still incomplete—indeed, it would not be finished for almost forty years more! A comparison of this monumental effort on their part with the brief and insignificant ministry of Jesus prompted a contemptuous question which concealed one of the ultimate issues of institutional religion: could one man with nothing but *zeal* for God's house do more *in three days* to *raise up* true worship than an entire nation could do working with stones for *forty-six years?*

The answer to that question awaited the verdict of history, which the writer provided from his perspective a half-century later (vv. 21–22). *The temple* to which Jesus referred was *his body.* In the flesh, that body was destroyed by his Jewish antagonists, thereby destroying the true temple in which the glory of God had dwelt on earth (1:14). But *when he was raised from the dead,* the church became the *body* of Christ. By the *three days* of his death and resurrection, Jesus transformed a band of Jewish disciples into a universal fellowship which was itself a *temple* where all men might worship God without the limitations that thwarted the highest purposes of the Jerusalem Temple (cf. 1 Cor. 3:16–17; 6:19–20; 2 Cor. 6:16; Eph. 2:11–22; 1 Peter 2:4–10; Heb. 10:19–22). Conversely, in rejecting the cleansing zeal of Jesus, the Temple keepers chose a course that led to its utter ruin at the hands of the Romans within a generation. Stones do not a temple make, even when they have been lovingly laid for forty-six years!

The passage concludes with a clarification of the process by which the disciples came to grasp the deeper significance of this incredible event. Essentially, their faith was founded on a fusion of insights from three sources: (1) they *remembered* what Jesus *had said* in the days of his flesh; (2) they searched the Old Testament and *believed the scripture* which prepared for this transformation (e.g., Amos 5:21–25; Jer. 7:1–15; Ezek. 40–48; Isa. 2:2–4; 66: 1–4); (3) they benefitted from the interpreting Holy Spirit given *when he was raised from the dead* (cf. 14:16–17,26; 15:26; 16:13–14). In a sense, all Christian theology should be based on a balanced combination of guidance from the remembered Jesus, the relevant Scriptures, and the Spirit of the risen Lord.

(2) Reaction to the Cleansing (2:23–25)

23 Now when he was in Jerusalem at the Passover feast, many believed in his name when they saw the signs which he did; 24 but Jesus did not trust himself to them, 25 because he knew all men and needed no one to bear witness of man; for he himself knew what was in man.

This editorial summary provides an effective transition between the account of the cleansing and the story of Nicodemus which follows. In his challenge to the supreme sanctuary, Jesus had called the very heart of Judaism to radical renewal. But how could an ancient religion throw off the traditional strictures whch had accumulated during almost a thousand years of national existence? That was to be the central concern of the Jewish ruler Nicodemus when he came to Jesus as a representative of the religious establishment. The urgency of such a visit was prompted not only by Jesus' disruptive tactics in the Temple but also by the popular support which such a protest had gained for him: *Now when he was in Jerusalem at the Passover feast, many believed.*

Nicodemus, in fact, reflected this widespread public sentiment in his opening remarks. Like the *many* who *believed in his name,* he affirmed that Jesus was worthy of the impressive names "Rabbi" and "teacher come from God" (3:2). Further, just as many believed *when they saw the signs which he did,* so Nicodemus justified the names he had given Jesus by reasoning that "no one can do these signs which you do,

unless God is with him" (3:2).

But *Jesus did not trust himself* to a faith based only on signs. He knew how easy it was to be a popular hero. Others had won the adulation of the festival crowds by protesting against the aristocratic Temple hierarchy, but he was not content with such superficial faith. *Because he knew* the inner motives of *all men,* Jesus *needed no one to bear witness* to the limits of their outward enthusiasms. Thus, he was not overawed either by the impressive credentials or by the exalted confession of Nicodemus, but abruptly responded to his complimentary words with a divine imperative that spoke to his deepest need. As that encounter will illustrate, Jesus did indeed know *what was in man!*

The kind of faith with which *many believed* (v. 23) is understood to lie somewhere between the true faith exhibited by the disciples in Cana (v. 11) and the complete lack of faith encountered among the Temple authorities in Jerusalem (v. 18). This Gospel is concerned to distinguish various levels of belief and particularly to describe a rather shallow faith which was awakened by signs but which did not go beyond their outward symbolism to the inner spiritual substance and recognize in Jesus the true revelation of God (cf. 4:45,48; 6:26,36; 7:3–5).

John's discriminating concern for the quality of faith provides a needed corrective to the popular assumption that any kind of belief is inherently good and thus beyond criticism. By absolutizing the action of God but relativizing the reaction of man, this Gospel warns against a temporary discipleship based upon fickle faith (e.g., 2:24; 6:66; 7:6–8). At the same time, it encourages superficial believers to seek a more mature commitment centered in Christ himself (10:37–38; 14:10–11; 20: 29–31).

3. The New Birth (3:1–21)

This passage is divided into two parts, a historical dialogue between Jesus and Nicodemus (vv. 1–15) and a theological monologue by the Evangelist (vv. 16–21). Although it is difficult to tell precisely where the former shades into the latter, the RSV is probably correct in paragraphing the separation between vv. 15 and 16. At that point, the references to Jesus shift clearly into the past tense and the third person, with no further mention being made of Nicodemus. This twofold arrangement into narrative and commentary illustrates the essential character of the Gospel as a presentation of unique historical remembrances in the light of contemporary Christian convictions.

Because of the very nature of these two parts, they reflect a creative tension between the ambiguity and absoluteness of faith. In the concrete historical situation (vv. 1–15), Nicodemus consistently illustrated the ambiguity of the official Jewish response to the ministry of Jesus (cf. comment on 2:23–25). Although unable to deny the potency of Jesus' impact upon the people or the authenticity of his motivation as a man of God, still Nicodemus could not accept the radicality of Jesus' demands either upon the sacred institutions of Judaism or upon his own role as a leader of the Jews. Torn between his attraction to Jesus (3:2) and his responsibilities to the religious establishment (cf. 12:42), Nicodemus seemed to manifest a tentative faith that wavered between courage and fear (cf. 7:50–52; 19:38–39). Indeed, it is never made clear whether he became a Christian or not!

In the appended meditation (vv. 16–21), however, there is no room for a halfway house of faith. The choice here is absolute: either one believes and has eternal life (v. 16) or one does not believe and is already condemned (v. 18). The two paragraphs are not in contradiction but rather reflect two different perspectives. At a given historical moment, from a human perspective, faith may seem to waver as it sifts the evidence and struggles with opposing forces. But in retrospect, from the divine perspective shared by the community of faith, the decision being made is seen to have ultimate consequences. The fourth Gospel is profoundly realistic in depicting how men are often confronted with an absolute decision in what for them is a highly ambiguous situation.

(1) The Dialogue with Nicodemus (3:1–15)

[1] Now there was a man of the Pharisees, named Nicodemus, a ruler of the Jews. [2] This man came to Jesus by night and said to him, "Rabbi, we know that you are a teacher come from God; for no one can do these signs that you do, unless God is with him." [3] Jesus answered him, "Truly, truly, I say to you, unless one is born anew, he cannot see the kingdom of God." [4] Nicodemus said to him, "How can a man be born when he is old? Can he enter a second time into his mother's womb and be born?" [5] Jesus answered, "Truly, truly, I say to you, unless one is born of water and the Spirit, he cannot enter the kingdom of God. [6] That which is born of the flesh is flesh, and that which is born of the Spirit is spirit. [7] Do not marvel that I said to you, 'You must be born anew.' [8] The wind blows where it wills, and you hear the sound of it, but you do not know whence it comes or whither it goes; so it is with every one who is born of the Spirit." [9] Nicodemus said to him, "How can this be?" [10] Jesus answered him, "Are you a teacher of Israel, and yet you do not understand this? [11] Truly, truly, I say to you, we speak of what we know, and bear witness to what we have seen; but you do not receive our testimony. [12] If I have told you earthly things and you do not believe, how can you believe if I tell you heavenly things? [13] No one has ascended into heaven but he who descended from heaven, the Son of man. [14] And as Moses lifted up the serpent in the wilderness, so must the Son of man be lifted up, [15] that whoever believes in him may have eternal life."

This is the most highly developed dialogue in all of the Gospels between Jesus and a named individual. Because Nicodemus is so clearly identified, it is possible to form a reasonably clear picture of his personality and of the purpose for his visit. As *a man of the Pharisees,* he belonged to the most deeply religious brotherhood in all of Judaism. As *a ruler of the Jews,* he sat on the supreme judicial body permitted by the Romans, the Sanhedrin, entrusted with the spiritual and moral leadership of the nation. As *a teacher of Israel,* he was a

Was the 'by night' not out of 'fear of the Jews' but an attempt to hide from the married ones any hint of accidentally for ... years?

trained theologian concerned with the true understanding and teaching of the revelation given by God.

Since the account gives such prominence to the official groups in which Nicodemus held membership, the view is taken here that he came to visit Jesus not just as a private individual but as a representative of the Jewish religious establishment. It was only natural to investigate an unknown and untrained young man who had suddenly appeared as a popular public teacher who was attracting many adherents (2:23), particularly after his dramatic intervention into the affairs of the Temple (2:13–20). Judaism permitted wide latitude in individual beliefs and practices, but it clearly could not condone a mass movement which seemed to threaten the very foundations of institutional religious life (cf. an earlier investigation in 1:19,24).

This does not mean, however, that Nicodemus was necessarily hostile toward Jesus. Another view maintains that he came primarily out of personal concern, and this position is reinforced by the interest which Nicodemus showed in Jesus elsewhere (7:50–51; 19:39). The two approaches are not incompatible, since Nicodemus may have been picked for this specific assignment because he had manifested a particular sympathy for the cause espoused by Jesus. In any case, Jesus dealt with him both as a private individual and as one deeply involved in his public leadership roles.

In the light of widely differing backgrounds, it is not surprising to discover a basic clash of temperament between these two men which is reflected in two contrasting expressions that recur throughout the narrative.

On the one hand, Nicodemus seemed to be preoccupied with the art of the possible. He began by admitting that Jesus *can* do signs, to which Jesus replied that it was far more crucial to determine whether or not Nicodemus can see the kingdom of God. Taken aback, Nicodemus asked how any man *can* meet the requirement of being born again since one *can* hardly enter his mother's womb a second time. To this dilemma Jesus reiterated that no one *can* enter the kingdom apart from a divine begetting of water and the Spirit. The final query of Nicodemus characterized his attitude throughout the interview: *How can this be?* The Greek verb translated "can" (*dunamai*) occurs six times between vv. 2 and 9 as the hallmark of a practical realist who was cautious, if not skeptical, of all efforts to transform human nature in the midst of this present life.

On the other hand, Jesus spoke as one convinced of divine authority rather than concerned over human ability. In answer to the questions of Nicodemus regarding what man can do, he countered by asserting what God can do. All three replies were prefaced by the solemn formula, **Truly, truly**, the repetition in each case serving to strengthen the assertion which it introduces.

The word in the original (*amēn*)[11] is one of the most tenacious terms in the religious vocabulary of mankind, having been used in Hebrew, Greek, Latin, and many modern languages as an exclamation confirming some truth just uttered in preaching, prayer, or praise. But whereas we put the "amen" at the end of our deepest convictions when offering them to God, Jesus put the "amen" at the beginning of his most urgent pronouncements, thereby indicating that what followed was already divinely validated by his own authority as its spokesman. This distinctive use gave the formula a force equivalent to the prophetic phrase in the Old Testament, "Thus saith the Lord." No problem which Nicodemus could raise caused Jesus to compromise his utter certainty that the word of the Lord was being revealed through his demands.

This fundamental difference between the two men is further clarified by their use of the pronouns throughout the dialogue.

Jesus = sure, certain, strong. N. => fearful, uncertain, confused.

11 For details on *amēn*, cf. H. Schlier in Kittel, TDNT, I, 335–338; Joachim Jeremias, *The Prayers of Jesus*, "Studies in Biblical Theology," 2d series, 6 (London: SCM Press, Ltd., 1967), pp. 112–15.

The view suggested here is that Nicodemus spoke in the plural as a representative of the ruling groups from which he had come, "Rabbi, we know." Over against this theology of consensus by the leaders of Judaism, Jesus dared to set a sovereign singular, "Truly, truly, I say." Although Jesus directly challenged Nicodemus ("I say to you—singular) with truths which each person must appropriate for himself ("unless one is born"), he also clearly enlarged his concern to include the entire Jewish religious leadership. This is seen in the shift of his demand into the plural: "You (i.e., all of you) must be born anew," a change which is not clear in English because the second personal pronoun is identical in the singular and plural. Because he was speaking both to Nicodemus and through him to an entire religious community, Jesus eventually included the witness of his own disciples in this wider appeal, but without blurring his unique authority: "I say to you, we speak of what we know."

If this reconstruction of the historical situation be correct, the Nicodemus episode was not limited to an encounter between two individuals. Rather, it involved Jesus as the leader of a dynamic renewal movement within Judaism pleading with Nicodemus as a guardian of the religious establishment to open the life of Israel to the power of the Spirit already at work in their midst. This insistent plea not only foreshadowed the later confrontation of the church with the synagogue but also anticipated the dynamics by which the people of God are called to renewal in each successive era of their existence. To be sure, the passage is of crucial importance for the matter of individual salvation, but its application may also be directed to the transformation of the religious life of those who count themselves as leaders of the Israel of God.

As a dramatic dialogue, vv. 1–15 are carefully constructed around three exchanges, each initiated by Nicodemus and completed by Jesus, which consider in turn

(1) the divine demand; (2) the human difficulty; and (3) the way of deliverance.

a. The First Exchange (vv. 2–3)

Nicodemus.—The indication that the stage setting for this drama was *by night* suggests (1) that Nicodemus had come to talk theology with Jesus, since the evening was the time set aside for busy men to study the Law after the day's work was done; (2) that the visit of so prestigious a leader to one who had recently cleansed the Temple might best be kept confidential because of the controversy which had aroused the populace; (3) that in visiting Jesus, Nicodemus was coming out of spiritual darkness into the light (cf. 13:30).

True to his mission, the opening words of the older man were a model of diplomacy, cautious but complimentary. By conceding that Jesus was a *rabbi* or *teacher come from God*, Nicodemus implicitly suggested that they discuss the main lines of his teaching and its suitability for public consumption. Jewish officialdom could not deny that Jesus had done works of evident power, proving to the people that *God* was *with him*, but such enigmatic *signs* had not made clear to trained scholars the precise purpose of his unusual ministry (cf. Mark 11:27–28; 12:14,18,28).

Jesus.—The discontinuity between the remarks of Nicodemus and the response of Jesus is startling. The younger man completely ignored the tributes from his distinguished visitor but instead confronted him with the only condition by which he or anyone else could ever glimpse the rule of God in human affairs. It was as if Jesus boldly snatched the conversation away from Nicodemus and reestablished it on entirely new foundations. The hour was entirely too urgent to be spent passing compliments. If he and any who may have sent him wanted to know the essence of his message and the passion of his ministry, they could have it in a single conviction: *unless one is born anew, he cannot see the kingdom of God.*

In utilizing the basic analogy of birth, Jesus reminded Nicodemus of the one way in which everything that lives is renewed. Just as the human race would soon grow old and perish if babies were not born, so the religious institutions of Israel, such as the Temple, could quickly grow senile without the gift of new spiritual life from its only source, God above. This is why Jesus frequently insisted that the kingdom of God is for those who become as little children (Matt. 18:3; Mark 10:15). The most significant fact about a newly born babe is that his entire life is still before him (cf. 1:13).

In calling for a new birth, however, Jesus was striking at the spiritual security of a good Pharisee, such as Nicodemus, who found his religious confidence in the fact that he was "a Hebrew *born* of Hebrews" (Phil. 3:5). John the Baptist had already encountered the Pharisees who, in the face of imminent catastrophe, would "presume to say to [themselves], 'We have Abraham as our father'" (Matt. 3:9). But initiation by circumcision into "the commonwealth of Israel" (Eph. 2:12) was not enough (contrast 1:11 with 1:13). To a man most proud of the way he had been religiously wellborn, Jesus insisted that he must be born in another way, "not . . . of man but of God" (1:13). Without minimizing the value of a great religious heritage, he was certain that pride in one's genealogy was misplaced, that physical descent could not guarantee spiritual heredity, that even the best umbilical cord could never bind Israel to God (cf. 8:37–44).

To be sure, the Pharisees did envision that in the day of the Messiah the entire world would be renewed, and they called this transformation a "rebirth" (cf. *paliggenesia* in Matt. 19:28). But Jesus demanded that now, rather than later, in one person at a time rather than universally, this eschatological reality should be existentialized. The entire Jewish heritage of the past and the hope of the future must be personally appropriated as a new possibility in the present. The rabbis often compared the conversion of a Gentile to Judaism as a "new birth." Here Jesus challenged Nicodemus to realize that achieving membership in Israel was not enough. The decisive new beginning demanded by God was needed not only by pagan proselytes but by the most eminent religious leaders of Israel!

b. The Second Exchange (vv. 4–8)

Nicodemus.—The qualifying word *anew* (*anōthen*) used by Jesus in developing the analogy of spiritual birth could mean "again" or "from above." The former connotation seemed to confront Nicodemus with an impossibility; he was already *old* and could not reverse the life process by entering *a second time into his mother's womb.* The most inexorable fact of life to the old is that the calendar cannot be turned back however much it may be desired.

Some suppose that Nicodemus was merely stupid in misunderstanding *anew* to mean "again" rather than "from above," but this is unlikely for a trained religious leader accustomed to use symbolic language. Others assume that he was seeking to ridicule Jesus by reducing his teaching to absurdity, but this would be inconsistent with the sincerity which he manifested throughout the Gospel (cf. 7:50–51; 19:38–39). More likely the mood of Nicodemus was one of incredulity in the face of Jesus' challenge to begin life all over again. An enthusiastic stranger with only a handful of disciples might well be eager for new departures, but this was not easy when one already had commitments both to the Pharisees and to the Sanhedrin as an accredited teacher of Israel.

In this context, therefore, the question of Nicodemus probably had two applications. Personally, it was the wistful rejoinder of a man whose habits were well fixed, whose role was highly visible, and whose responsibilities were sharply defined. His problem was not a lack of interest in a new birth but a realistic awareness of the difficulties of extricating himself from years of entanglement in the status quo.

Professionally, his response sought to remind the Temple-cleanser that the religion of Israel was already *old* and heavy with the weight of tradition. Perhaps Jesus had found corruption at the sanctuary, but it had been a thousand years in the making and could not be reformed overnight. Stated theologically rather than metaphorically, Nicodemus was asking whether the eschatological order could really begin to interpenetrate the established order, as Jesus supposed, or whether the *old* age would finally have to die before the new age could take its place.

Jesus.—Because the question of Nicodemus was neither foolish nor caustic but relevant and profound, Jesus readily answered by clarifying that to be born *anew* involved being born *of water and the Spirit.* When the Pharisees had sent representatives to investigate the ministry of John (1:19,24–25), they should have learned that he was baptizing "with water" in anticipation of One who would baptize "with the Holy Spirit" (1:26,31,33; cf. Mark 1:8). Now a Pharisee was told that the one whom John promised had arrived —before his very eyes!—and thus the renewal for which John prepared by means of *water* had become a present possibility through Jesus as bearer of the *Spirit* (cf. Acts 1:5).[12]

A further clarification of Nicodemus' question was provided by the fundamental difference between the earthly realm of the *flesh* and the heavenly realm of the *spirit.* Nature begets its own kind. Any offspring *of the flesh* (i.e., of man) *is flesh,* which does indeed grow old and die. But to be *born of the Spirit* (i.e., of God) is to live as *spirit* in a sphere that transcends the temporal order. Nicodemus and his fellow Jewish leaders should *not marvel* at this thrice-

repeated imperative of birth anew by the Spirit since it was a well developed expectation in their Scriptures (e.g., Isa. 11:2; 32:15; Joel 2:28–29; Ezek. 36:25–27).

At this point, the dialogue began to move easily from the analogy of birth to the kindred analogy of breath, for the most basic evidence of life is the ability to breathe. In both Hebrew (*ruach*) and Greek (*pneuma*), the same word may mean breath, wind, and spirit, permitting a subtle play on these connotations which is not possible in English. Such is the case in Ezekiel 37:1–14, where Israel in exile (v. 11) was likened to "dry bones" (the spiritually dead) that can "live" (be renewed) when "breath" from the four "winds" blows upon them (v. 9), i.e., when God puts his "Spirit" within them (v. 14). In contending for the renewing power of the Holy Spirit, Jesus was not advancing some novel doctrine but was grappling with a problem as old as the Exile and doing so in the very way indicated by the Scriptures which Nicodemus and his associates should have known so well.

Perhaps at this juncture in the conversation a fresh breeze began to blow, furnishing the basis on which to develop further the breath/wind/spirit analogy. Nicodemus obviously did *not know* either the *whence* or the *whither* of the wind, but he was convinced of its reality because he could *hear the sound of it.* Just so, one may experience the effect of the Spirit without understanding either its origin or its destination. There is a sovereign spontaneity in the realm of the spiritual just as in the realm of the physical: *the wind blows where it will.* Only God controls that animating power by which the people of God do not grow old and "breathe their last" but "catch a second wind" and begin to live all over again.

c. The Third Exchange (vv. 9–15)

Nicodemus.—True to the cautious realism that had characterized his contribution to the dialogue from the outset, Nicodemus concluded with the stock question of the

---

[12] On the many interpretations of v. 5, see Ray Summers, "Born of Water and the Spirit," *The Teacher's Yoke: Studies in Memory of Henry Trantham,* eds. E. J. Vardaman and J. L. Garrett, Jr. (Waco: Baylor University Press, 1964), pp. 117–28.

pragmatist: *How can this be?* Presumably, his mood was not one of incredulity but of genuine concern, for Jesus did take his question seriously. Perhaps he wished a list of specific reforms at the Temple which he and his colleagues might consider undertaking. Nicodemus would hardly question the claim of Jesus that God's Spirit could effect new birth, but he was concerned about the human (Jewish) responsibility for bringing it about.

Jesus.—As a *teacher of Israel,* Nicodemus should have been able to understand that *this* kind of transformation is never something men can do but is rather something of which they may *speak* in *witness* to what God has done. By shifting to the plural pronoun *we,* Jesus involved his disciples in this testimony, thereby inviting Nicodemus and his colleagues (the *you* in v. 11 is also plural) to share their corporate life in which the powers of the new age were already operative.

But how had God renewed this remnant band of disciples? Since Judaism did *not* *receive* their *testimony* to a divine transformation, Jesus had sought through a leading representative, Nicodemus, to lead his people (references to *you* in v. 12 are plural) to *believe* by speaking of *earthly things;* i.e., by discussing such simple symbols as womb, water, and wind to illustrate the way God works. But if they would *not* even begin to *believe* on the basis of the seen, how could they grasp the reality of unseen *heavenly things?*

The only possible answer was to realize that God himself had met the problem of moving from *earthly things* to *heavenly things* by reversing the process and providing something greater than a human analogy. In an ultimate sense, *no one has* ever *ascended into heaven* (cf. 1:18); i.e., man cannot grasp divine reality directly even with the help of simple illustrations. Those who do believe through the help of earthly things know God only indirectly (analogically). But now ultimate reality has *descended from heaven* in personal form as *the Son of man* (cf. 1:51). Unlike the

wind, Jesus was more than a metaphor of what God was like. Although he descended and thereby became an earthly thing, he was the locus of the divine presence, the embodiment of heavenly things.

In other words, belief is not a matter of man somehow ascending up to heaven by his spiritual ingenuity and then descending back to earth with the faith which he discovers there. Precisely the reverse: the Son of man first descends from heaven, bringing God to man, then ascends back again, bringing man to God. Stated pictorially, the gateway to God is an arch swung downward from above, anchored in eternity, rather than swung upward from below, anchored on earth (cf. introduction to 1:1–18).

These descending and ascending strokes of the divine pendulum characterized the entire ministry of Jesus (cf. 1:51; 17:11,13), but the descent was decisively inaugurated with the incarnation and the ascent was supremely climaxed in the atonement or "lifting up" on the cross. Here the divine reversal of human effort reached its ultimate paradox. Men try to ascend by flights of mystical ecstasy or apocalyptic speculation, but the Son of man *must* ascend by being *lifted up* in brutal death which, paradoxically, is his greatest glory. Once again, an earthly thing served as a preparatory analogy, in this case *the serpent* that *Moses* had *lifted up in the wilderness* (Num. 21:9). At best, however, this was but a symbol which became reality in the death of Jesus.

The dialogue concludes with a generalizing transition that both summarizes the final point of the passage and prepares for the meditation which follows. *Whoever* would believe *heavenly things,* which is the only way that new birth can begin, must believe in the Son of man. He is the only one in whom both the earthly analogy and the heavenly reality are perfectly united. Therefore, to become his disciple here and now in a moment of history is at the same time to *have* the *eternal life* of God.

(2) The Monologue of the Evangelist (3:16–21)

16 For God so loved the world that he gave his only Son, that whoever believes in him should not perish but have eternal life. 17 For God sent the Son into the world, not to condemn the world, but that the world might be saved through him. 18 He who believes in him is not condemned; he who does not believe is condemned already, because he has not believed in the name of the only Son of God. 19 And this is the judgment, that the light has come into the world, and men loved darkness rather than light, because their deeds were evil. 20 For every one who does evil hates the light, and does not come to the light, lest his deeds should be exposed. 21 But he who does what is true comes to the light, that it may be clearly seen that his deeds have been wrought in God.

Nicodemus has now disappeared completely as the writer guides his readers to step back and ponder the implications of a faith which focuses entirely on the person of Jesus (v. 15—"believes in him"). The terminology in vv. 16–21 is distinctively Johannine, suggesting that the Evangelist has here provided his own understanding of the cruciality of Christ. The paragraph reads much like the summary of a sermon on the words of Jesus recorded in 12:44–50 (other fragments of which may be found in 3:31–36). As such, it provides a commentary not only on the Nicodemus episode but on the entire ministry of Jesus as presented in the "book of signs" (chs. 2—12).

The paragraph is divided into two carefully balanced parts. In vv. 16–18, the content is strongly Christological, **the Son** being mentioned six times (note the elaborate designation in v. 18c, **the name of the only Son of God**). Here the connection with the preceding section is established by the recurring **believes in him.** Everything hinges on faith in the one whom **God sent** to save the world. But in vv. 19–21, the Son is alluded to only in connection with **the light,** which has a strongly ethical character in contrast with **darkness/evil.** Here everything hinges on man's **deeds,** or whether he **does what is true** and so **comes to the light.** This paragraph, therefore, con-

tends for the unity of theology and morality in Christ by representing him as the key both to God's action in conversion and to man's reaction in conduct.

The divine initiative is nowhere more clearly and comprehensively interpreted than in vv. 16–18. Despite the many difficulties which the ministry of Jesus presented to Judaism (2:13—3:15), his life was an overwhelming gift by **God** of his **only Son** (cf. 1:14), an act of grace intended to awaken faith in order that even religious rulers (such as Nicodemus) **should not perish.**

For God to lavish his love on the entire **world** (kosmos), which obviously did not love him, rather than to limit it to his chosen people, meant that the everlasting mercy bestowed in Christ had now gone far beyond the boundaries of the ancient covenant with Israel. (Divine love in the OT, chesed, was primarily covenant love, not world love.) The purpose of such love was **that the world might be saved** from its own perverse love of darkness. Christ, as the incarnation of love, forgave and accepted all men who came to him in faith, thus delivering them from fear of judgment (1 John 4:17–18) and causing them to cry with Paul, "There is therefore now no condemnation" (Rom. 8:1).

If **judgment** was not the purpose of Christ's coming, it was the inevitable result. For human life is mercilessly devastated by its refusal to be loved and to love in return. Since Christ has already confronted mankind with the ultimate expression of God's love, salvation or condemnation is now determined by whether one **believes** or **does not believe.** Nicodemus had been taught the possibility of a spiritual birth long after one is physically born. Now the reader learns the obverse, the possibility of a spiritual death long before one has physically died. Judgment is not arbitrarily dispensed by God in the afterlife but is clearly determined by men in the present life on the basis of their response to the **only Son of God.**

The dynamics of this ultimate decision

are carefully traced in vv. 19–21. The issue involves not the flaunting of some legal or moral code but the love of the human heart for *darkness* once *the light has come into the world.* But rather than abandon all hope for men *because their deeds* are *evil,* an alternative option is strongly distinguished in dialectical fashion, much like descriptions of the "two ways" familiar in Judaism and elsewhere in the New Testament (e.g., Matt. 7:13–27). Rather than being captive to a fatalistic determinism, each person may choose between being (1) either one who *does evil and hates the light* or one who *does what is true;* (2) either one who *does not come to the light* or one who *comes to the light;* (3) either one whose *deeds* are not *exposed* or one whose *deeds* are *clearly seen* to *have been wrought in God.* God determines the necessity, the alternatives, and the consequences of the decision, but this only reinforces the urgency and clarity with which each man determines what his response will be.

4. The New Master (3:22–36)

Jesus, like the church after him, had to define his ministry not only in relation to official Judaism but in relation to John the Baptist as well. In the former instance, the danger was that of expecting too little, of allowing the weight of tradition to absolutize the status quo and so stifle the winds of renewal that were beginning to blow. In the latter instance, the danger was that of expecting too much, of assuming that John the Baptist was himself the agent of the new age because he had been the first to call for a radical reformation of the religious establishment. Having defined the ultimate superiority of Jesus to Pharisaic Judaism in 3:1–21, the Gospel now clarifies his preeminence over John the Baptist in 3:22–36.

As was also true in the two preceding chapters, an effective theological balance is maintained between these two parts of chapter 3. In vv. 1–21, the emphasis is on new birth, i.e., on the transformation which

is required to begin the life of discipleship and on the discontinuity of that life with the past. In vv. 22–36, however, the emphasis is on the increasing centrality of Christ to the believer, i.e., on the gradual shift of loyalties from the earthly leader with whom the pilgrimage may have begun in water to the heavenly Lord with whom it must develop in spirit (cf. 3:5). In other words, vv. 1–21 focus on the new being and vv. 22–36 on the new becoming. Each is an equally crucial component of the Christian faith, for true belief involves both a point of irrevocable commitment and a process of unending growth, both a looking back to the certainty of initial conversion and a looking forward to the fulfillment of its latent implications.

Translated into contemporary terms, the concern of vv. 22–36 to transfer loyalties from John to Jesus speaks to one of the most urgent tasks confronting the church, that of guiding immature believers away from dependence upon some forerunner whose witness resulted in faith to that One who is himself the object of every witness and the content of true faith. God uses many go-betweens, often gifted preachers who make a great impact on those whom they baptize. But the work of the baptizer is not done when he has served as the human instrument of a new birth, for he must then lead the grateful convert beyond an understandable but improper pride in his newfound spiritual hero to a singular and total attachment to Jesus. In this passage, the prophet who had more right than any to claim his own personal following made clear why any form of competition with Christ is unthinkable.

(1) John the Baptist and Jesus (3:22–24)

²² After this Jesus and his disciples went into the land of Judea; there he remained with them and baptized. ²³ John also was baptizing at Aenon near Salim, because there was much water there; and people came and were baptized. ²⁴ For John had not yet been put in prison.

This editorial summary contains three items of historical information regarding the ministry of Jesus not otherwise known from the gospel record: (1) That *Jesus and his disciples* exercised an early ministry in *the land of Judea* (i.e., in the outlying environs around Jerusalem). The Synoptics tell only of a late Judean ministry of Jesus just before his final visit to Jerusalem (Matt. 19:1; Mark 10:1; but cf. Luke 4:44; Matt. 23:37). (2) That Jesus ministered publicly before *John had been put in prison.* The Synoptics begin Jesus' ministry in Galilee "after John was arrested" (Mark 1:14). (3) That Jesus *baptized* adherents (this is clarified in 4:2 to mean that Jesus sponsored such activity by his disciples, not that he administered the rite himself). The Synoptics never mention that Jesus either baptized or authorized anyone else to do so during his public ministry.

In addition, two otherwise unknown items regarding the ministry of John the Baptist are summarized here: (1) That John, contrary to the impression created by 1:29–37, continued an independent baptismal movement even after Jesus had begun to gather disciples. This is implied both by the absence of any mention that the *people* who *came* to John for baptism were transferred to Jesus, and by the reference to John's disciples. (2) That John relocated his *baptizing at Aenon near Salim.* The precise identification of this site where *there was much water* is disputed, but it was probably in Samaria, to the north of Judea, which would mean that John preceded Jesus in ministering to that area (cf. 4:38*b*).

Two important inferences may be drawn from these remarkable data. To begin with, it is apparent that at the outset of his ministry Jesus was much more closely associated with John than the Synoptics indicate. From this description it would seem that he largely modeled his pattern of activity on that of the forerunner. Perhaps John moved from the popular Judean locale (Mark 1:5) to the much less promising Samaritan region in order to give his successor maximum opportunity to establish his own ministry.

This Gospel has recorded the overlapping of their current ministries so as to establish more securely than the Synoptics the original link which existed between them. This was needed because the movement launched by John had never been completely assimilated into the movement guided by Jesus (cf. Mark 2:18; Acts 19:1–7), resulting in a division which neither founder would have desired.

At the same time that this Gospel dares to relate just how similar John and Jesus once were, it indirectly helps us to understand just how different they eventually became. After John had been arrested, Jesus clearly abandoned the pattern of his predecessor by going to a region where John had never worked, there launching a new type of ministry in which water baptism played no part. Perhaps this deliberate change in strategy contributed to the uncertainty reflected in John's question to Jesus from prison (Matt. 11:2–6). In any case, these verses help us to realize the extent both of the continuity and of the discontinuity between Jesus and John.

(2) The Subordination of John (3:25–30)

25 Now a discussion arose between John's disciples and a Jew over purifying. 26 And they came to John, and said to him, "Rabbi, he who was with you beyond the Jordan, to whom you bore witness, here he is, baptizing, and all are going to him." 27 John answered, "No one can receive anything except what is given him from heaven. 28 You yourselves bear me witness, that I said, I am not the Christ, but I have been sent before him. 29 He who has the bride is the bridegroom; the friend of the bridegroom, who stands and hears him, rejoices greatly at the bridegroom's voice; therefore this joy of mine is now full. 30 He must increase, but I must decrease."

In the time of Jesus many sectarian groups practiced ritual lustrations in the Jordan valley, giving rise to considerable *discussion* over the relative merits of such acts in meeting the scriptural demand for *purifying.* In the context of such debate, an unidentified *Jew* may have advanced the supposition that Jesus' rite was superior to John's since *here he is, baptizing, and all are going to him.* Such reasoning was hardly acceptable to John's disciples because they remembered that their master had begun his work first, that Jesus had gone to him *beyond the Jordan* to be baptized, and that the *witness* which John *bore* to him was the basis on which Jesus had attracted his first followers (cf. 1:35–37). How easily a theological argument over religious forms can degenerate into a competitive quarrel over personalities!

The graciousness of John's spirit in dealing with the wounded pride of his devotees sprang from a clear understanding of the nature of grace. No one, whether himself or Jesus, could *receive anything* that really mattered—be it popularity, or followers, or theological approbation—*except* as it was *given* by God *from heaven.* Thus John could rejoice both that a little band had gathered about himself and that a much larger number had turned to Jesus, for every believer is a divine gift over which to celebrate rather than a human trophy over which to boast (cf. 6:37,44; 17:6). As for taking precedence over Jesus because he had preceded him in time, John simply reminded his followers that he had always said, *I am not the Christ but I have been sent before him* (cf. 1:15,20,30).

John further clarified his true role by comparing himself to *the friend of the bridegroom.* In Jewish wedding practice, this was the groomsman who brought the *bride* to the *bridegroom* and then stood guard over the nuptial chamber. Although he could hear *the bridegroom's voice* exclaiming in joy over the consummation of his union, he would not think of interfering with such intimate proceedings.[13] Indeed, ancient Near Eastern law strictly forbad giving the bride to this "best man" (cf. Judg. 14:20—15:6; 2 Cor. 11:2). Just so,

John would never consider wooing the bride, Israel, away from Jesus (cf. Isa. 54:5; 62:4–5; Jer. 2:2; 3:20; Ezek. 16:8). Rather, *this* kind of *joy* that only a matchmaker could know was *now* already *full* because of his successful work as a go-between. With this transitional task now done, Jesus *must increase* in influence while John *must decrease,* like a light that has burned brightly but then begins to wane (cf. 5:35).

(3) The Superiority of Jesus (3:31–36)

[31] He who comes from above is above all; he who is of the earth belongs to the earth, and of the earth he speaks; he who comes from heaven is above all. [32] He bears witness to what he has seen and heard, yet no one receives his testimony; [33] he who receives his testimony sets his seal to this, that God is true. [34] For he whom God has sent utters the words of God, for it is not by measure that he gives the Spirit; [35] the Father loves the Son, and has given all things into his hand. [36] He who believes in the Son has eternal life; he who does not obey the Son shall not see life, but the wrath of God rests upon him.

Just as the section on Jesus' relation to Judaism (3:1–15) was concluded with a theological meditation (3:16–21), so this section on Jesus' relation to John the Baptist (3:22–30) ends with a strikingly similar passage (3:31–36) that may have come from the same source. The transition from v. 30 to v. 31 is so smooth that the reader could suppose that John the Baptist was continuing to speak, yet the style and theology of the Evangelist are evident. It is almost as if we have here the witness which John would have wanted to bear had he been a Christian at the time when this Gospel was written. In this sense, vv. 31–36 summarize a sermon on his text in v. 30, advancing three reasons why Jesus must increase but John must decrease.

First, as the one *who comes from above* (cf. 1:51; 3:13), Jesus is *above all,* whereas John, as a man (1:6) *of the earth belongs to the earth.* Since one *bears witness* only to what he has *seen and heard,* John was limited to what God had revealed to him on *the earth,* but Jesus could testify

---

[13] For the details of the wedding practices which seem implied by v. 29, see J. Jeremias in Kittel, TDNT, IV, 1101; A. van Selms, "The Best Man and Bride—From Sumer to St. John," *Journal of Near Eastern Studies,* 9 (1950), 65–75; J. D. M. Derrett, "Water into Wine," *Biblische Zeitschrift,* Neve Folge, 7 (1963), pp. 81–83.

directly to that transcendent realm from whence he had come. *No one receives* heavenly *testimony* on the basis of earthly understanding except as he becomes convinced and certifies (*sets his seal*) that Jesus revealed what is true of God (cf. Matt. 16:17*b*).

Second, to John, as to the prophets of the Old Testament, God gave his Spirit *by measure*, i.e., at the time when they spoke under divine inspiration (Num. 11:25; 1 Sam. 10:5–11; Jer. 1:4–10). But Jesus did not utter *the words of God* only on occasion, for it was *not by measure* that God had given him the Spirit (cf. 1:31–34). In fact, so great was the love of the *Father* for *the Son* that he *has given all things into his hand* (cf. Matt. 28:18). In Jesus, the paradox of grace reached its perfect expression: by claiming nothing he was given everything.

Third, John could do nothing more than prepare for the impending judgment, but Jesus was himself the basis on which the judgment was carried out. To respond to John meant to place oneself in readiness for a new day, but to respond to Jesus meant to decide one's ultimate destiny: *he who* now *believes* already *has eternal life,* whereas he *who does not* now *obey* already experiences *the wrath of God* (cf. Rom. 1:18) abiding upon his life (cf. 3:18). The reason why eschatology is so decisively realized is that in Jesus salvation has already come. Quite clearly a final judgment lies in the future (e.g., 5:25–29), but it will not offer any opportunities or alternatives not already present in Jesus. Although the possibility of new decisions is not foreclosed, one does anticipate the eventual verdict of heaven by virtue of the response made to Christ on earth.

5. The New Fellowship (4:1–42)

The scene now shifts to Samaria, a region in the central hill country of Palestine between Judea and Galilee whose inhabitants were of particular interest to this Gospel, as to Luke-Acts. Following the conquest of the Northern Kingdom by Assyria

in 722 B.C., the extensive resettlement of both Israelites and foreigners resulted in intermarriages and the infiltration of pagan religious influences, both of which were intolerable to the Jewish religious leadership of Jerusalem (2 Kings 17). Centuries of mounting hostility reached a climax with the erection by the Samaritans on Mount Gerizim of a rival temple, which was destroyed by John Hyrcanus in 128 B.C. By the time of Jesus, Samaria had become a despised ghetto with an introverted culture, a schismatic religion, and a static theology.[14]

This means, therefore, that almost insurmountable obstacles stood in the way of any meaningful contact between the Jewish man Jesus and a Samaritan woman. Three major barriers are identified in this account:

Racial. Even Jews who showed reasonable tolerance of other races were openly contemptuous of Samaritans as half breed descendants of the former ten tribes of Israel whose racial purity had been corrupted by foreign settlers (2 Kings 17:24). Nothing would be calculated to infuriate Jews more than the way in which their most cherished patriarchs were also proudly claimed as ancestors by the Samaritans.

Sexual. The rabbis frowned on a man talking with a woman in public—even his own wife! "He who talks much with womankind brings evil upon himself and neglects the study of the Law and at the last will inherit Gehenna" (*Aboth* 1:5). To be in a strange setting, at an unusual hour, with a woman of questionable background only compounded the problem for Jesus. From her side, the woman had good cause to distrust men since so many of them had discarded her like a worn out shoe.

Religious. Because Deuteronomy 27:4 had identified Mount Ebal (beside Mount

---

14 On the Samaritans see James A. Montgomery, *The Samaritans* (New York: Ktav Publishing House, 1968 reprint of 1907 edition); John Macdonald, *The Theology of the Samaritans* (Philadelphia: Westminster Press, 1964).

Gerizim, near Shechem) as the place to build an altar, the Samaritans resented the later centralization of the sanctuary on Mount Zion in Jerusalem. On one occasion, for example, they retaliated by scattering human bones in the porticoes and throughout the Temple while the major Passover festival was in progress (Josephus, *Antiq.*, XVIII, 29–30).

How did Jesus transcend the bitter prejudices which had accumulated for centuries among both Jews and Samaritans? Five steps were involved in his evangelistic strategy:

(1) He made contact at the point of common physical need. "Give me a drink" implied that they were both thirsty. Once the woman recognized that all persons, however different, do have the same basic physical needs, she would have to reckon with the possibility that everyone also shares the same spiritual needs.

(2) He used the inability of earthly resources to meet physical needs as the basis for pointing to analogous heavenly resources that do meet spiritual needs. The woman knew that the problem of physical thirst could be met only temporarily by drawing a bucket of water from the deep well. Jesus awakened new hopes with the announcement that this limitation did not apply to the satisfying of spiritual thirst for which there was available an endless supply of living water "welling up to eternal life."

(3) He broadened the scope of her religious concerns with a reminder of her sinful relationship to others. Instead of seeking spiritual gifts only for herself, she should be prepared to share them with her closest companions.

(4) He met her need for forgiveness through worship with a dynamic understanding of God. The past had led to the localizing of cultic response in a few geographical centers, but the future would find a universal Father worshiped wherever men were open to the power of the divine Spirit.

(5) He pointed to himself as the em-

bodiment of those spiritual realities which he offered to others. This made explicit not only the nature of "living water" but its source as "the water that I shall give."

It is instructive to observe that Jesus dealt with this heterodox Samaritan woman (4:1–26) in many of the same ways as he did with the orthodox Pharisee, Nicodemus (3:1–15). In both cases he began with a basic reality by which physical life is sustained (birth/water) in order to suggest, by analogy, the need for corresponding religious realities that renew the spiritual life (birth anew/living water). In response, both persons quickly identified the difficulty of his teaching from an earthly perspective (birth when one is old?/water when the well is deep?). Not to be deterred, Jesus met the dilemma by developing his analogy in new directions (the wind blows/the water flows) and by explaining that the Spirit of God is the source of this dynamic power (3:8; 4:24). When the interlocutor questioned how the promised Spirit of the new age could function already in the present (3:9; 4:25), Jesus went beyond analogy by pointing to himself as the eschatological agent who had begun to fulfill the future here and now (3:13–15; 4:26). These striking parallels suggest that in both cases the central issue remained the same: Was the religious status quo open to renewal by the power of the Spirit operative in the ministry of Jesus?

The crucial change which Jesus sought in this particular situation is reflected in the Samaritan response which he elicited. At first, the woman viewed him only in terms of his race—as "a Jew," whereas she was soon forced to acknowledge that he was also "a prophet." Following the entire dialogue, she dared to wonder if he could possibly be "the Christ," but the Samaritan villagers who heard her witness soon went even further to confess that he was indeed "the Savior of the world."

The issue for them was not *whether* to believe but in *what* to believe. The Samaritans were a deeply religious people, fanatics in the eyes of some, but the practical effect of their piety had been to turn them inward upon themselves in spiritual isolation. By offering them a broader faith in a Father God whose worship was as universal as his Spirit, Jesus came to be seen in the light of his deepest intention as the Saviour of the *world*.

The key phrase, "Neither on this mountain nor in Jerusalem," shows again the essential link between this story and the Nicodemus account. Restricting Mount Gerizim to the Samaritans was just as bad as restricting Mount Zion to the Jews. In the new age, both of these cultic centers would have to be "cleansed" of narrow provincialisms. The Pharisees suffered from a sense of religious superiority which built barriers to keep others out. The Samaritans suffered from a sense of religious inferiority which built protective defenses to shut themselves in. But none of these manmade boundaries belonged in the new age of the Spirit. Neither Jews nor Samaritans could confine God in their religious structures any more than they could control the rushing wind that blows across the open skies or the gushing water that flows from underground springs.

(1) Introduction and Setting (4:1-6)

¹ Now when the Lord knew that the Pharisees had heard that Jesus was making and baptizing more disciples than John ² (although Jesus himself did not baptize, but only his disciples), ³ he left Judea and departed again to Galilee. ⁴ He had to pass through Samaria. ⁵ So he came to a city of Samaria, called Sychar, near the field that Jacob gave to his son Joseph. ⁶ Jacob's well was there, and so Jesus, wearied as he was with his journey, sat down beside the well. It was about the sixth hour.

The connection with the preceding section (3:22-36) is established by vv. 1-3, which indicate that Jesus *left Judea* because *the Pharisees had heard* that he was *making and baptizing more disciples than John* (cf. 3:26). Unlike the Baptist, Jesus could not counter such invidious comparisons by stressing his own subordination (cf. 3:28-30), so he chose instead to remove the appearance of competition by depart-

ing for **Galilee**. Since *his disciples* were actually the ones administering baptism to those who came to Jesus, they could have succumbed to petty jealousies—as did certain followers of John (3:25-26)—had they continued to work in an atmosphere distorted by rumor.

In leading his disciples northward, Jesus *had to pass through Samaria,* not as a geographical necessity but as a divine constraint. The typical Jewish pilgrim would have deliberately avoided this direct route by traveling through Transjordan to the east, but Jesus knew that his disciples needed to learn how to witness not only in Jerusalem (2:13—3:21) and in all Judea (3:22-36) but in *Samaria* as well (cf. Acts 1:8).

A suitable setting was provided by *a city of Samaria, called Sychar, near the field that Jacob gave to his son Joseph* (Gen. 48:22). The identification of this village is not certain today, unless Sychar (*sucher*) is a corruption of Shechem (*suchem*), but its general location is not in doubt since it was obviously close to *Jacob's well* which still survives at the foot of the twin mountains Ebal and Gerizim some forty miles north of Jerusalem.

The distance being covered by Jesus on foot explains why he was *wearied . . . with his journey* upon reaching the well in the heat of high noon. Jewish time was reckoned from sunrise to sunset, thus *about the sixth hour* would be near 12:00, a most suggestive reference for the drama about to begin (cf. the stage setting of the Nicodemus episode at night in 3:2). In the first century, as today, women were accustomed to fetch water in the cool of the early morning and evening, never at midday. Was the woman whom Jesus encountered so disreputable that she sought to avoid the crowds that gathered around the well at other hours?

(2) The Offer of Living Water (4:7-15)

⁷ There came a woman of Samaria to draw water. Jesus said to her, "Give me a drink." ⁸ For his disciples had gone away into the city

to buy food. ⁹ The Samaritan woman said to him, "How is it that you, a Jew, ask a drink of me, a woman of Samaria?" For Jews have no dealings with Samaritans. ¹⁰ Jesus answered her, "If you knew the gift of God, and who it is that is saying to you, 'Give me a drink,' you would have asked him, and he would have given you living water." ¹¹ The woman said to him, "Sir, you have nothing to draw with, and the well is deep; where do you get that living water? ¹² Are you greater than our father Jacob, who gave us the well, and drank from it himself, and his sons, and his cattle?" ¹³ Jesus said to her, "Every one who drinks of this water will thirst again, ¹⁴ but whoever drinks of the water that I shall give him will never thirst; the water that I shall give him will become in him a spring of water welling up to eternal life." ¹⁵ The woman said to him, "Sir, give me this water, that I may not thirst, nor come here to draw."

Like the conversation with Nicodemus (3:1–15), this part of the encounter is described in the form of a dialogue with three exchanges. In the former instance, Nicodemus took the initiative because he had come to raise a sensitive issue with Jesus, whereas in this case Jesus guided the discussion because he was the Jewish intruder into hostile Samaria.

a. First Exchange (vv. 7–9)

Jesus.—Combining simplicity with surprise, Jesus startled a strange woman with the request, *Give me a drink.* At first sight this appears to have been a quite natural suggestion, since he was hot, tired, and thirsty, as well as temporarily without the assistance of *his disciples,* who *had gone away into the city* nearby *to buy food.* It might seem to us that ordinary courtesy would dictate an affirmative response to this appeal for help.

The woman.—In that setting, however, it was unthinkable that *a Jew* would *ask a drink* of her, *a woman of Samaria,* because, as the Evangelist parenthetically explains, *Jews have no dealings with Samaritans.* This does not mean that the Jews never had any direct contact with the Samaritans but that they would not share the same food vessels with them for fear of ritual contamination (cf. TEV, "Jews will

not use the same dishes that Samaritans use"). The proposal of Jesus was astonishing because Jews did not drink from a cup that Samaritan lips had touched, and Jesus had no utensils of his own.[15]

b. Second Exchange (vv. 10–12)

Jesus.—Characteristically, Jesus responded to this dilemma with a divine contrast: *If you knew the gift of God* (cf. 3:16,27,35). So often, as here, it is the nature of man to withhold, but it is always the nature of God to bestow. If only the woman knew *who* Jesus was, that he was an agent of heavenly generosity and not of Jewish narrowness, she *would have asked him* instead of being asked by him, and he *would have given* to her instead of having been refused by her, and the water that he provided her would be *living* or flowing in endless supply rather than only one drink such as she could provide from the well.

The woman.—As was the case with Nicodemus, the woman at first refused to explore the spiritual implications of Jesus' symbolic language because of its difficulties at the physical or literal level. She knew that Jacob's well was fed by an underground spring (*pēgē*), which she assumed Jesus was referring to as *living water,* but this source lay at the bottom of a *well* or shaft (*phrear*) that was *deep.*[16] How could Jesus *get* to that *living water* far below since he had *nothing to draw with?* Just as Nicodemus questioned whether Jesus could provide a new birth to one who was old because of the difficulty of returning to the womb (3:4), so the woman was dubious of his ability to provide living water from the well because it was deep and he had nothing with which to draw.

Further, just as Nicodemus was skeptical of Jesus' ability to change the religious sta-

---

15 On this interpretation of v. 9 see David Daube, "Jesus and the Samaritan Woman: The Meaning of *sugchraomai,*" *Journal of Biblical Literature,* 69 (1950), pp. 137–47.

16 The well today is 75 feet deep but partially filled with debris. Thus it may have been nearly 100 feet deep in the time of Jesus. See D. C. Pellett, "Jacob's Well," IDB, II, 787; J. N. Sanders, *The Gospel According to St. John* (New York: Harper & Row Publishers, 1968) p. 140, fn. 1, and p. 142, fn. 1,

tus quo because it had existed since the days of the patriarchs, even so the woman questioned, *Are you greater than our father Jacob?* The venerable patriarch had been forced to draw water laboriously up through the long shaft and for more than a millennium this system had not changed. Jesus' talk about a gushing fountain was as dubious to a tired woman as his talk about a newborn babe had been to an old man.

c. Third Exchange (vv. 13-15)

Jesus.—There was no need to solve the limitations of the literal well since, whatever the problems of reaching its depths, the more serious inadequacy lay in the obvious fact that *everyone who drinks of this water* once it is drawn *will thirst again* (cf. 6:26-27). The only adequate answer was to discover *the water that* Jesus himself could *give,* for *whoever* drinks of it *will never thirst* (cf. 6:35)—literally, "will not ever thirst throughout the [new] age." Far from leaving a person thirsty again once it is drunk, this water is not lost but *will become in him* who receives it a permanent source of supply. The "new Jacob" did not dig his wells deep into the earth but deep into the human heart. Moreover, as the modifier "living" has already implied, this spiritual reality at the center of life does not accumulate there like still water in a cistern but leaps with power like *a spring . . . welling up to eternal life.*

The woman.—Having been led from need through curiosity to desire, the woman exclaimed in the very words with which Jesus began, *Give me this water.* How quickly the tables were turned. At the outset, the one who had descended from above spoke of earthly things in order that one who was of the earth might ascend in her aspirations and learn to ask for heavenly things (cf. 3:12-13,31). To be sure, the basis for her petition was superficial if not selfish: *that I may not thirst, nor come here to draw.* But at least she had begun to search for something better and, more important, she had learned the right person to ask (cf. v. 10).

(3) The Offer of Spiritual Worship (4:16-26)

16 Jesus said to her, "Go, call your husband, and come here." 17 The woman answered him, "I have no husband." Jesus said to her, "You are right in saying, 'I have no husband'; 18 for you have had five husbands, and he whom you now have is not your husband; this you said truly." 19 The woman said to him, "Sir, I perceive that you are a prophet. 20 Our fathers worshiped on this mountain; and you say that in Jerusalem is the place where men ought to worship." 21 Jesus said to her, "Woman, believe me, the hour is coming when neither on this mountain nor in Jerusalem will you worship the Father. 22 You worship what you do not know; we worship what we know, for salvation is from the Jews. 23 But the hour is coming, and now is, when the true worshipers will worship the Father in spirit and truth, for such the Father seeks to worship him. 24 God is spirit, and those who worship him must worship in spirit and truth." 25 The woman said to him, "I know that Messiah is coming (he who is called Christ); when he comes, he will show us all things." 26 Jesus said to her, "I who speak to you am he."

Unlike the interview with Nicodemus which was limited to a single dialogue on one subject (3:1-15), the conversation with the Samaritan woman consisted of two parts—on the subjects of water (vv. 7-15) and of worship (vv. 16-26). This latter section, which functions in the story of the Samaritan woman somewhat as did the cleansing of the Temple (2:13-22) in relation to the Nicodemus account, is also arranged in the form of a dialogue with three exchanges.

a. The First Exchange (vv. 16-17a)

Jesus.—In v. 15 the woman had voiced a legitimate request for water but had limited it to the meeting of her own thirst and the ending of that daily chore which necessitated trudging to the well at high noon. In response, Jesus abruptly instructed her, *Go, call your husband, and come here.* The motive for this request is not indicated. Some suppose that he was trying to overcome her self-centeredness by reminding her of her obligations to others. On this view, "Go call your husband" means "Don't you want your family to share in the discovery of living water?" Others, however, hold that Jesus already knew of her sexual failures and was trying to expose the problem of unresolved guilt. On this view, his instructions were designed to breach her defenses and prompt a confession of sin.

The woman.—Suddenly confronted with the claim which God's gift placed upon her life, the woman sought to sidestep the issue by an evasive reply, *I have no husband.* As we shall see, in one sense her answer was technically correct, since she had been married to many husbands, but this does not alter the likelihood that she was deliberately attempting to be deceptive. In her immature ethic, truth was determined more by accuracy of words than by integrity of motive.

b. The Second Exchange (vv. 17b–20)

Jesus.—With gentle irony, Jesus applauded her answer as *right in saying* that she had *no husband.* But, alas, this was *said truly* only because she had actually been married to *five husbands,* and the man with whom she then lived was *not* her *husband.* The woman's negative evasion had exposed the deeper truth that her domestic life was in shambles. The rabbis sanctioned a maximum of three marriages, whereas she had already failed beyond that limit. Her personal history in one sense recapitulated the national history of her country, for Samaria had "intermarried" with more than five foreign tribes, each with its own god (2 Kings 17:29–34).

The woman.—So swiftly had Jesus stripped away the mask of pretense that the woman was forced to acknowledge that he was *a prophet* with supernatural insight into her life (cf. 2:25). Now that her sin was exposed, she supposed that her immediate need was to find forgiveness in the experience of worship. Whether this response was sincere or was born of evasion, in either case her search for a suitable place of sacrifice was thwarted by the religious divisiveness that had long separated Samaritan and Jew. Her countrymen *worshiped on* Mount Gerizim nearby, even

after the temple there was destroyed by John Hyrcanus, whereas the Jews insisted that *in Jerusalem* was *the place where men ought to worship.* Unfortunately, racial hostility had infiltrated even the worship of God and resulted in segregated shrines where all were not equally welcome.

c. The Third Exchange (vv. 21–25)

Jesus.—Whereas the woman defined the problems of the present on the basis of traditional practices in the past ("Our fathers worshiped"), Jesus answered in terms of the promised potentialities of the future: *The hour is coming.* The worship of the new age would not be limited by any geographical center, whether *this mountain* or *Jerusalem,* but would be universal in scope (cf. Isa. 66:1).

This does not mean that Jesus gave sweeping endorsement to religion in general wherever it might be found. He knew that many people, including Samaritans, sought to *worship* that which they did *not* clearly *know,* whereas his own people (1:11) did *worship* on the basis of a unique revelation of God given to Israel in its long history. In that sense the parenthetical comment is added that *salvation is from the Jews,* a strong affirmation of the particularity of God in electing Israel as the agent of his redemptive purpose. Jesus had symbolized his freedom from prejudice on the Jewish side by offering to drink from a Samaritan bucket. Now the woman was invited to overcome her Samaritan prejudices by acknowledging that her salvation could come from him, a Jew.

Note the paradox created by vv. 21–22. Because God has become known *somewhere* (e.g., in Israel), he can become known *everywhere* (e.g., far beyond Israel). Now that faith is founded on a distinctive history recorded in Scripture, it need not be unified by a single sanctuary located on a mountain. This means that true worship is exclusive in origin but inclusive in outreach. One of the deepest antinomies in human thought is rooted in the tension between paticularity and universality. Here the two are brilliantly balanced by the conviction that in Jesus the historical particularity of the old Israel coincides with the eschatological universality of the new Israel.

This polarity is also seen in v. 23, where the *hour* of cultic transformation *is* both *coming* in the future (i.e., the old age with its divisiveness still exists) and *now is* in the present (i.e., the new age of oneness has already begun to arrive). Both of these apparently contradictory affirmations can be true in the sense that the decisive hour when the new day dawns *is coming* in the future for most of the world, but it already *now is* a reality for the disciples of Jesus, in whose ministry the future is proleptically present. Now that Jesus has made God known as the universal *Father* of all mankind, it is possible for anyone to be a *true worshiper*—not by virtue of *where* one worships (Gerizim or Jerusalem) but by virtue of *how* one worships (*in spirit and truth*). Notice that the qualifications for participation in the new age are not determined by race, sex, or religion, but by *God* himself who *is spirit*.

To worship *in spirit* does not mean that all holy places and material aids should be abandoned but that the creative, life-giving power of God should infuse whatever human forms are utilized by the cultus. The Samaritan woman must learn that worship is not validated by a traditional place but by a transcendent power. The addition here of *in truth* points to the claim that this divine reality was being uniquely revealed in the ministry of Jesus. A profound theological synthesis is achieved by this characteristic coupling of universal divine *spirit* with particular historical *truth* (cf. 14:17; 15:26; 16:13).

The woman.—As the implications of these ultimate assertions began to dawn, the Samaritan woman acknowledged her belief in a future *Messiah* (*Christ*) yet to come who *will show us all things* (cf. 11:24). Although this comment may have represented her one last evasion, an effort to escape the claims of Jesus by indulging

in Christological speculation, it was more likely a wistful rejoinder similar to that of Nicodemus' question (3:9); i.e., "How can all of this talk about worshiping in the power of God's Spirit come true before the great figure appears who will usher in the messianic age?"

In reply, Jesus concluded the dialogue with a climactic surprise: *I who speak to you am he.* This absolute self-assertion, by which Jesus identified himself as the mediator of eschatological reality, parallels the final answer given to Nicodemus (3:13–15). Just as one need not be bound by the heritage of the past, so one need not wait for the hopes of the future. The total sweep of God's purpose from the first patriarchs to the final Messiah was concentrated in Jesus. This is further hinted in the form of the sentence in Greek. A literal translation designed to convey the original force might read, " 'I am'—he is the one speaking to you." This use of "I am" (*egō eimi*) anticipates its explicit use later (e.g., 8:58) as a revelatory formula announcing the presence of the eternal God in the midst of history (cf. Ex. 3:14; Isa. 43:10).

(4) The Witness of the Woman (4:27–30)

27 Just then his disciples came. They marveled that he was talking with a woman, but none said, "What do you wish?" or, "Why are you talking with her?" 28 So the woman left her water jar, and went away into the city, and said to the people, 29 "Come, see a man who told me all that I ever did. Can this be the Christ?" 30 They went out of the city and were coming to him.

At this point the *disciples* of Jesus, who had gone into the nearby city to buy food (v. 8), *came* upon Jesus and the Samaritan *woman* deep in conversation. So unthinkable was this breach of religious scruple that *they marveled*, but so unpredictable was their Master that *none* dared to interrupt. Perhaps because of their sudden return—and the chagrin written on their faces—the woman departed in such haste that she *left her water jar*. But it mattered little. In the light of what Jesus had told her, she would be back soon. No need to be encumbered with a large pot as she ran to bear her witness (allusion to 2:6 ff.?) for now she was more concerned with "living water" that is carried within the heart. Perhaps Jesus could use the jar in her absence (cf. v. 11) since he was free from the prejudice which prohibited Jews from using Samaritan vessels (v. 9b).

On the basis of her brief encounter with Jesus, the woman's witness upon reaching *the city* was superficial and tentative at best. Her initial testimony was not to the person of Jesus but to his clairvoyance in discerning the secrets of her heart (cf. 2:23; 3:2). Whether he was more than *a man* she could only guess. Her question is better translated, "This one couldn't possibly be the Christ, could he?" Nevertheless, discovery mingled with doubt did prompt others to see for themselves. However defective her witness, it brought the people *out of the city* to Jesus. What a large harvest God can grow from such small seed!

(5) The Challenge to the Disciples (4:31–38)

31 Meanwhile the disciples besought him, saying, "Rabbi, eat." 32 But he said to them, "I have food to eat of which you do not know." 33 So the disciples said to one another, "Has any one brought him food?" 34 Jesus said to them, "My food is to do the will of him who sent me, and to accomplish his work. 35 Do you not say, 'There are yet four months, then comes the harvest'? I tell you, lift up your eyes, and see how the fields are already white for harvest. 36 He who reaps receives wages, and gathers fruit for eternal life, so that sower and reaper may rejoice together. 37 For here the saying holds true, 'One sows and another reaps.' 38 I sent you to reap that for which you did not labor; others have labored, and you have entered into their labor."

At the same time that the woman was sharing what she had learned at Jacob's well, *the disciples* were illustrating their need to grasp the same truths. Like the woman, they were at first preoccupied with physical sustenance: *Rabbi, eat.* In reply, Jesus illustrated that he already possessed those abiding inner resources which he had offered the woman: *I have food to eat of which you do not know.*

Misunderstanding his reference to spiritual food just as the woman had misunderstood his allusion to spiritual drink, the disciples wondered to themselves if someone (the woman?) had *brought him food.* Sensing their confusion, Jesus explained that his *food* was *to do the will* and *work* of God (contrast v. 15, where the woman wanted inner sustenance primarily for personal reasons). Because the disciples did not yet share his deep sense of being *sent* on mission (cf. 17:18; 20:21), they could not understand his utter preoccupation with the needs of people that made him oblivious to the need for food.

When talking with the Samaritan woman, Jesus had used the analogy of a flowing fountain to illustrate the endless abundance of spiritual drink. Now, he shifted the disciples' attention to the metaphor of harvest in an effort to show them that spiritual food also multiplies bountifully. Normally, it was necessary to wait for an interval of *four months* after sowing before it was time for *the harvest* to *come.* But Jesus did not see himself at an early point in the spiritual crop cycle but at its end point. Even then his disciples could *lift up* their *eyes*—toward the Samaritans coming from the city (v. 30)?—and *see how the fields* were *already white* (ripe) *for* a human *harvest* (cf. Matt 9:36–38). Just as God's water wells up with the power of an underground stream, so God's food grows up with the potency of a planted seed (cf. Mark 4:3,29,32). The one *who reaps* a harvest of this spiritual food is doubly rewarded with both *wages* and *fruit* not for a season but *for eternal life* (cf. v. 14b).

The disciples could begin to reap such a harvest without delay because of a division of labor reflected in the proverbial saying, **One sows and another reaps.** They had **not** done the **labor** of sowing. Others had preceded them, such as Jesus himself (4:7–26), possibly John the Baptist (3:23), plus a host of Old Testament prophets beginning with Moses. Now that harvest time had at last come, the disciples could enter *into* that *labor* of preparation in their new role as reapers.

This does not mean that someone else had done all of the work while they would get all of the credit. In the solidarity of the people of God, *sower and reaper . . . rejoice together* when the entire process is complete. If anything, the privilege of reaping carried with it the urgent responsibility of bringing to fruition the efforts of so many for so long. This paradox of grace and demand is implicit in Christ's commission to every disciple: *I sent you to reap that for which you did not labor.* Today, more than ever, we inherit as grace the foundational work of the centuries. How imperative, therefore, that we be good stewards of the sickle in gathering a bountiful harvest.

(6) The Response of the Samaritans (4:39–42)

³⁹ **Many Samaritans from that city believed in him because of the woman's testimony, "He told me all that I ever did." ⁴⁰ So when the Samaritans came to him, they asked him to stay with them; and he stayed there two days. ⁴¹ And many more believed because of his word. ⁴² They said to the woman, "It is no longer because of your words that we believe, for we have heard for ourselves, and we know that this is indeed the Savior of the world."**

The response of the Samaritans provided a dramatic illustration of the abundant harvest which could be reaped as a result of the preparatory work of Jesus. At first he had been one tired and thirsty man alone beside a well (vv. 6–7), but now he was accepted as the *Savior of the world.* At first he was viewed as a Jew who would have no dealings with Samaritans (v. 9), but now he was invited *to stay with them* and did so for *two days.* At first he had partially convinced only one disreputable woman (v. 29), but now *many Samaritans* from her city *believed in him.*

This summary is concerned to trace the stages by which faith arose among the Samaritans. Initially, many believed in Jesus *because of the woman's testimony,* despite the fact that it had two limitations. First, the content of her witness, **He told me all**

that I ever did (cf. vv. 16–19,29), was based more on a recognition of Jesus' power than on a deeper knowledge of his person. This confession did not really convey any of the central truths revealed in vv. 7–26. Second, her *words* mediated an indirect relationship to Jesus, whereas *his* own self-witness enabled them to hear for themselves in an unmediated direct encounter. Thus, as was true also in the case of John the Baptist (3:26), *many more believed because of his word* than because of the secondary report of the woman. This Gospel was written in the conviction that the faith which is called forth by the testimony of believers finds its ultimate expression in response to the self-witness of Jesus made personal and immediate by the ministry of the Holy Spirit (cf. 14:26; 15:26–27; 16:13–15).

6. The New Life (4:43–54)

With this passage we reach the climactic section in a cycle of six accounts which illustrate the new age inaugurated by Jesus (chs. 2—4). Having seen how Christ came to fulfill the old order by offering new joy (2:1–12), new worship (2:13–25), new birth (3:1–21), new leadership (3:22–36), and new fellowship (4:1–42), it now becomes clear that his supreme gift was new life itself. This had already been hinted in the raising up of a destroyed temple (2:19), in the possibility of being "born anew" (3:3), in the present possession of "eternal life" (3:16,36), and in the description of both living water and harvested fruit as "to/for eternal life" (4:14,36).

Now, however, these anticipations are made explicit in the threefold refrain, "Your son *lives*" (vv. 50–51,53). Since the fourth Gospel everywhere else uses both the verb to live (*zaō*) and the noun life (*zōē*) to refer to God's qualitatively different kind of existence, it is likely that this miracle of physical restoration is meant to reflect—as will the raising of Lazarus (11:25)—the power of Jesus to confer enduring spiritual life.

Both in its location and in its literary

form, this unit is designed to conclude the first major section in the "book of signs" (chs. 2—4). The mention of Galilee in general, and of Cana in particular, is deliberately reminiscent of 2:1–12, as the Evangelist was concerned to point out (4:46,54). The structure of the second Cana miracle is strikingly similar to the first. In both cases, an unexpected request was thrust before Jesus (2:3; 4:47), only to meet his initial rebuff (2:4; 4:48). The continuing concern of the petitioner (2:5; 4:49), however, did prompt an immediate intervention by Jesus in which his surprising instructions were submissively obeyed (2:6–8; 4:50). This led, in turn, to the discovery that a dramatic change had taken place (2:9–10; 4:51–53a), which was seen as a sign leading to faith (2:11; 4:54b). This careful parallelism is a Semitic way of indicating the beginning and end of a unified literary cycle.

At the same time, as a transitional unit 4:43–54 also prepares for the next major section in the "book of signs" (cf. 5—10). There, the theme of life which emerges here will be greatly expanded and enriched (e.g., 5:21–29; 6:26–58). Moreover, the motif of conflict, anticipated here by the reference to Jesus as a prophet with "no honor in his own country" (4:44), will be elaborated within the lengthening shadows of Jerusalem. Thus the central paradox of John 5—10, that Jesus provoked death by offering life, is effectively foreshadowed in 4:43–54.

Although this passage functions primarily in relation to the larger units which it links together (chs. 2—4; 5—10), it is instructive to observe the way in which this latter part of John 4 balances the former part of the chapter. In vv. 1–42, the action of Jesus had profound implications for the racial, sexual, and ecumenical issues of his day. But in vv. 43–54, the stress falls on the relevance of Jesus to an individual who may be dying without eternal life. Clearly the gospel is equally concerned to transform the quality both of our outward *fellowship* with others and of our inward *faith*

to God. It is artificial to divide the gospel into its "personal" and its "social" aspects since the saving work of Jesus clearly encompasses both.

(1) The Return to Galilee (4:43–45)

43 After the two days he departed to Galilee. **44** For Jesus himself testified that a prophet has no honor in his own country. **45** So when he came to Galilee, the Galileans welcomed him, having seen all that he had done in Jerusalem at the feast, for they too had gone to the feast.

Having already ministered in Jerusalem (2:13—3:21) and in Judea (3:22–36), Jesus now left Samaria (4:1–42) *after two days* (cf. v. 40) and *departed to Galilee* which, in the eyes of some Jews was like going to the outer boundaries of the Holy Land (cf. Acts 1:8). The very name Galilee was the abbreviation of a Hebrew phrase (*galil-ha-goyim*) meaning the "circle (i.e., region, district) of the Gentiles (i.e., pagans, foreigners)." This northern section of Palestine had been forcibly subdued and reincorporated into Jewish territory only a little over a century earlier (103 B.C.). Even the Jews living in Galilee were looked down on by their Judean countrymen as ignorant of the Law. In returning to this largely secular culture with its concentration of non-Jews, Jesus was fulfilling the role assigned him by the Samaritans as "the Savior of the *world*" (v. 42).

Ironically, the farther Jesus moved from Judaism toward paganism the greater the degree of acceptance he received. In Jerusalem the response had been divided and superficial at best (2:20, 23–25; 3:10); in Judea it was more extensive and enthusiastic though marred by the false issue of competition (3:22,26–30); but in Samaria it eventually became profound even after a difficult beginning (4:39–42). Here, however, *the Galileans welcomed him* as soon as he arrived on the basis of what *he had done in Jerusalem at the feast.* The very deeds that had angered or confused official Judaism had caused their hearts to rejoice. This pattern of response led *Jesus himself* to affirm the bitter truth of the proverb that a prophet has no honor in his own country (cf. Matt. 13:57; Mark 6:4). At the very center of the holy nation in Jerusalem his own received him not (cf. 1:11), whereas on the periphery in Galilee he found an openness among those who were not bound by the tradition of a proud heritage (cf. Matt. 4:12–17).

(2) The Healing of an Official's Son (4:46–54)

46 So he came again to Cana in Galilee, where he had made the water wine. And at Capernaum there was an official whose son was ill. 47 When he heard that Jesus had come from Judea to Galilee, he went and begged him to come down and heal his son, for he was at the point of death. 48 Jesus therefore said to him, "Unless you see signs and wonders you will not believe." 49 The official said to him, "Sir, come down before my child dies." 50 Jesus said to him, "Go; your son will live." The man believed the word that Jesus spoke to him and went his way. 51 As he was going down, his servants met him and told him that his son was living. 52 So he asked them the hour when he began to mend, and they said to him, "Yesterday at the seventh hour the fever left him." 53 The father knew that was the hour when Jesus had said to him, "Your son will live"; and he himself believed, and all his household. 54 This was now the second sign that Jesus did when he had come from Judea to Galilee.

The most striking example of this favorable reception in Galilee was by an official or officer attached to the royal court (basilikos) who was probably a Gentile with limited Jewish sympathies (cf. Matt. 8:5–13; Luke 7:1–10). When he heard that Jesus had come from Judea to Galilee (a recurring refrain for emphasis in 4:3,43,47,54), he went from Capernaum to Cana to beg for the healing of his son who was at the point of death. One indication of his urgency is provided by the likely inference that he made this arduous 15–20 mile journey from the seashore up to the highlands in one day (v. 52b) between sunrise (ca. 6:00 A.M.) and the seventh hour (ca. 1:00 P.M.).

At first glance it may appear cruel for Jesus to have greeted such parental desperation with the abrupt retort, Unless you see signs and wonders you will not believe.

The pronouns (you), however, are plural rather than singular, which means that what Jesus . . . said to him was primarily for the benefit of the curious crowd gathered around. He wished to learn if the troubled official had come with concerns that went deeper than the insatiable desire of these Galileans for spectacular works such as they had already seen in Jerusalem (v. 45). The imploring reply, Sir, come down before my child dies, left no doubt that the officer wanted Jesus himself, not some impressive spectacle which he might perform, and that he wanted Jesus for the sake of his son and not for his own selfish desires.

The response of Jesus would have completely disappointed the seekers after signs and wonders, for he neither went with the official, as requested, nor did he give him any tangible proof that healing would occur. Instead, he sent him away with nothing but a promise, Go; your son will live. It would take sturdy faith indeed for that anxious father to retrace his steps clinging only to a handful of words, but the man believed the word that Jesus spoke to him and went his way. He had come with the fear that his son would die but found in Jesus one so profoundly conscious of his power that he was certain that life would triumph. The officer embraced this conviction and staked his return upon it. His own faith was not simply awakened by Jesus; in a deeper sense, he dared to have faith in Jesus' faith!

Nor was this trust to be disappointed. Unable to depart until sometime after the seventh hour (1:00 P.M.), he could not reach Capernaum before dark and so was forced to spend a long night away from home. The next day, as he was going down, his servants met him with the good news that his son was living. When he realized that on yesterday the fever had left him at the very hour when Jesus had given his assurance, the officer believed as did all his household. The timing of the cure was not a coincidence but provided further confirmation that God had authenticated those words of Jesus which the officer had brought back from Cana in hope.

As *the second sign* done by Jesus in *Galilee,* this story "sign-ified" spiritual truth which could be discerned only by faith. In keeping with an emphasis throughout chapters 2—4, three levels of belief are distinguished within this story, each with its different understanding of the place of signs.

First, in v. 48, belief based only on seeing signs and wonders is summarily rejected. Miracles as such can never be an adequate basis of faith. For example, an incident almost identical to this is recorded in the Babylonian Talmud where the son of Rabbi Gamaliel was healed in exactly the same hour that Rabbi Hanina had prayed for him and sent messengers back with the word that his fever was gone (*Berakoth* 34*b*). If faith were proportionate to the impressiveness of mighty works, one would have to believe in Rabbi Hanina equally with Rabbi Jesus! Realizing the fickleness of human expectations and the ambiguity of human perceptions, Jesus steadfastly refused to substitute some outward prodigy for inward commitment as the foundation of an enduring relationship with God.

Second, in v. 50, belief understood as obedient trust in the word of Jesus is made the basis for going on one's way in the hope that life will triumph over death. Rather than miracle creating faith, a notion rejected in v. 48, faith provides the perspective by which miracle can be properly understood. The officer did not see any signs and wonders, for Jesus worked as a physically absentee Lord who did the miracle from afar. The lack of any visible techniques or audible formulas pointed to God himself as the ultimate source of the healing.

Third, in v. 53, belief is understood in an absolute sense as divine confirmation through the events of history of one's trust in the word of Jesus. In this final stage, miracle is not the basis of hope but the vindication of a hope already awakened by Jesus. To ground one's confidence in the seeing of signs and wonders is folly, for the new age had not finally come (i.e., all death is not now abolished). But to ground one's confidence in the word of Jesus is true faith, for he was the agent of the new age who mediated the realities of the end-time in advance.

Those who find the clue to ultimate reality in Christ will have their faith strengthened by particular "breakthroughs" which effectively foreshadow the life of the age to come. The servants saw the cure but could not discern its deeper meaning (i.e., it was not for them a *sign*) because they had not first been to Jesus. But the officer who had already embraced the *word* of Jesus knew that this healing was no mere coincidence or puzzling exception but was a clear pointer to Jesus as Lord of the age to come when life would be eternal and death would be no more.

II. The Resistance to the Revealer (5:1— 10:42)

In chapters 2—4 six gifts of the new age were described in swift succession. Jesus, however, remained largely in the background, pointing to himself as giver either not at all (2:9; 4:1–3,50) or only in limited fashion (2:19; 3:13–15; 4:26).

Inevitably, however, questions needed to be answered concerning his credentials to function as the agent of divine fulfillment. Thus the focus in chapters 5—10 moves from the gifts to the giver, from a sixfold understanding of the work of the Messiah to a sixfold understanding of his person. Here, Jesus is presented as the authority of life (5:1–47), the bread of life (6:1–71), the water of life (7:1–52), the judge of life (8:12–59), the light of life (9:1–41), and the shepherd of life (10:1–42).

This shift is seen clearly in the increasingly significant use which is made of the phrase "I am" (*egō eimi*).[17] In chapters

17 For details on *egō eimi*, see E. Stauffer and F. Buechsel in Kittel, TDNT, II, 352–54, 399–400; Raymond Brown, *The Gospel According to John,* "The Anchor Bible," (Garden City: Doubleday & Co., Inc., 1966), XXIX, 533–38; C. H. Dodd, *Interpretation,* pp. 93–96.

2—4 the formula was used only once (4:26) in a general, anticipatory fashion, whereas in 5—10 it occurs more than a dozen times in connection with central Christological claims. Most unusual is the absolute form without any predicate (6:20; 8:24,28,58) by which Jesus applied a divine self-designation from the Old Testament to himself, thereby claiming to reveal the eternal being of God in his own earthly life (cf. Ex. 3:14; Isa. 43:10). Against this background, greater meaning attaches to the employment of "I am" with the predicate nominative. In chapters 5—10 Jesus so identified himself as the bread of life (6:35,41,48,51), the light of the world (8:12), the door of the sheep (10:7,9), and the good shepherd (10:11,14).

As we shall see, all of these predicates are basic metaphors used throughout the Old Testament to describe spiritual reality. By coupling them with the *egō eimi*, Jesus thereby identified his person with his work. For example, he both *gave* bread and *was* bread; i.e., he was at once the giver and the gift. Here lies the central conviction of chapters 5—10: because that which Jesus came to offer was *himself*, an evaluation of his work is finally impossible apart from an evaluation of his person. Jesus dared to insist that his innermost being and his divine mission were inseparable!

In dramatic contrast to the transcendent claims of Jesus stands the sinister hostility of the Jews (cf. 5:16,18; 6:41,66; 7:1, 19,25,30; 8:37,40,59; 9:16,29,34; 10:31, 39). In this section the conflict has not yet reached its breaking point but is characterized by those tentative responses of doubt and uncertainty which wavered between acceptance and rejection (e.g., 6:41,52,60–61; 7:12–13,30–32,40–44; 9:16; 10:19–21). Most striking in these passages is the dissonant note that many "murmured" or "muttered" about Jesus (6:41,43,61; 7:12, 32) and the summary refrain, "There was a division (*schisma* or schism) among them over him" (7:43; 9:16; 10:19).

The dynamic at work in this discord was a decisive sifting of Israel in the face of two irreconcilable alternatives posed by Jesus and the Jewish leadership. The judgment given to the Son (5:22–30) had already begun to be executed. The great apostasy was underway, not because some apocalyptic antichrist had appeared in time of cosmic tribulation (cf. 1 John 2:18–22), but because the incarnate Christ had appeared among his people and called them to their God-given destiny.

The dramatic character of this conflict was heightened by placing each controversy in the context of a Jewish religious festival.[18] Chapter 5 is connected with an unidentified "feast of the Jews" (v. 1), chapter 6 with "the Passover, the feast of the Jews" (v. 4), chapters 7—9 with "the Jews' feast of Tabernacles" (7:2), and chapter 10 with "the feast of Dedication at Jerusalem" (v. 22). These national celebrations perpetuated the memory of Israel's greatest redemptive epochs in the past and anticipated her most glorious hopes for the future.

By utilizing this stage on which to press his claims, Jesus related the entire sweep of holy history to his brief mission. Moreover, by identifying himself with the fundamental symbols used in the festal liturgies (e.g., "I am" the bread, water, light), Jesus implied that he was the reality to which ritual pointed. The incredible significance of these claims is fully appreciated only when seen in a worship setting, for there the symbolism is clearly intended to point directly to God.

We are now in a position to understand the central issue between Jesus and the Jews in John 5—10. On the one hand, Jesus claimed to fulfill the Scriptures and to usher in the new age. He applied to himself those biblical symbols used in worship which had been reserved exclusively for God. He insisted on exercising divine prerogatives as the unique Son of his Father. On the other hand, the Jews saw him as one who broke the sabbath law (5:18),

---

[18] On the festival background of John 5–10, see T. C. Smith, *Jesus in the Gospel of John* (Nashville: Broadman Press, 1959), pp. 144–183.

who was untrained in rabbinic studies (7:15), and whose origin was obscure (7:27,41,52) or even questionable (8: 19,41). The crucial problem posed by this conflicting evidence was that of legitimacy. How could the divine claims of Jesus be verified in the light of his complete absence of human credentials? That is the question with which all of these chapters will struggle and to which they will give the profoundest answer in the New Testament.

1. The Authority of Life (5:1–47)

John 5 is admirably suited to serve as an introduction to the large unit comprising chapters 5—10. Not only does it effectively develop the paradoxical themes of conflict and life-giving introduced in the immediately preceding section (4:43–54), but its opening miracle (5:1–9a) carries forward the motif of the limited power of earthly water which recurred throughout chapters 2—4 (cf. 2:6–8; 3:5; 4:1–3; 4:12–15). More important, the basic discussion of the authority of Jesus in chapter 5 prepares for the debate over the authentication of Jesus' ministry which dominates chapters 5—10. The Christological principles enunciated here provide the foundation on which to understand his claims to be bread, water, judge, light, and shepherd.

Scholars have long recognized that it would improve the topographical sequence of the Gospel narrative to place chapter 6 before chapter 5. On the present arrangement, Jesus traveled from "Cana in Galilee" (4:46) "up to Jerusalem" (5:1), thence "to the other side of the Sea of Galilee" (6:1) and, "after this Jesus went about in Galilee" (7:1). Needless to say, this is hardly a connected itinerary! The proposed rearrangement would connect the two miracles which occurred on opposite sides of the Sea of Galilee (4:46; 6:1) as well as the obviously related material in 5:1–47 and 7:15–24.

However, this tidy solution—which is also an effort to conform the fourth Gospel more closely to the Synoptics—overlooks the important consideration that John 5 provides the Christological presuppositions for John 6 and so should precede it. Surely the writer was aware of the awkwardness of the geographical references, but he left them in his account because they were a part of the incidents which he recounted. No effort was made to arrange the text in topographical sequence because the primary concern was with an orderly theological development. The Jerusalem arguments of John 5 may have come chronologically later than the Galilean disputes of John 6, but they were logically prior and so have been placed first in order to facilitate the reader's pilgrimage over the terrain of faith.

(1) The Cure of a Lame Man (5:1–9a)

¹ After this there was a feast of the Jews, and Jesus went up to Jerusalem.

² Now there is in Jerusalem by the Sheep Gate a pool, in Hebrew called Beth-zatha, which has five porticoes. ³ In these lay a multitude of invalids, blind, lame, paralyzed. ⁵ One man was there, who had been ill for thirty-eight years. ⁶ When Jesus saw him and knew that he had been lying there a long time, he said to him, "Do you want to be healed?" ⁷ The sick man answered him, "Sir, I have no man to put me into the pool when the water is troubled, and while I am going another steps down before me." ⁸ Jesus said to him, "Rise, take up your pallet, and walk." ⁹ And at once the man was healed, and he took up his pallet and walked.

An unnamed *feast of the Jews* provided the occasion for *Jesus* to leave behind his popularity in Galilee (4:45,54) and go *up to Jerusalem* as a prophet with "no honor in his own country" (4:44). In both places, his word brought life to those as good as dead (4:50; 5:8), but in the pagan north such healing prompted faith (4:53) whereas in the pious south it provoked persecution (5:16)—and that during a sacred season of religious celebration!

The description of the site *in Jerusalem* where this incident occurred is difficult to understand, both because the ancient manuscripts exhibit numerous variations in the wording of v. 2 and because any text chosen still leaves the syntax ambiguous. The

RSV translation assumes that there was a pool with the *Hebrew* name *Beth-zatha* which had five *porticoes* around it, and that this pool was located *by the Sheep Gate.* The NEB translation, however, assumes that "Sheep" was the name of the body of water rather than of a nearby gate (there is no word for gate in Gr.), that it was the building "with five colonnades" rather than the pool which had the Hebrew name, and that this name should be spelled "Bethesda" (as in the RSV marg.) rather than Beth-zatha.

On all three of these differences the more recent NEB translation is probably to be preferred.[19] It seems likely that just north of the Temple area was located a large "Sheep-Pool," so named in folklore either because it lay on the route of the sheep destined for sacrifice at the Temple or because a red coloration of its water suggested the blood of animal slaughter. To this twin basin (one side for men, the other for women), used perhaps by Temple pilgrims for ritual lustrations, Herod had added five elaborate porticoes which surrounded the four sides and divided the two sections across the middle. (In the time of Jesus, this entire structure may well have been the most impressive public bath in Jerusalem.)

Still, not the best Area of town.

??

Because the waters were famous for their curative powers, however, the pool had attracted *a multitude of invalids, blind, lame, paralyzed.* **One man** who *lay* beside the ornate columns near the edge of the pool *had been ill for thirty-eight years*—the length of Israel's wilderness wanderings (Deut. 2:14). With characteristic sensitivity (cf. 2:25), Jesus recognized *that he had been lying there a long time;* and so he sought to engage the will and to quicken hope with the question, **Do you want to be healed?** A sense of need, however acute, is never sufficient as the sole impetus to seeking help; for need coupled with

frustration can quickly lead to futility as a settled way of life. Only when desperation is linked with desire does a person seek help at whatever risk may be involved. Further, illness may allow one to escape from responsibility, or it may give one the attention which he might otherwise miss. It is far from axiomatic that every sick person really wants to be well. *"Enjoying poor health"*

The forlorn answer of the invalid suggested how easily despair could have become second nature. Not only was he physically helpless, but apparently he was bereft of friends as well for he had **no man** to help him *into the pool* when the sudden stirring of the water invited an immediate response.[20] As a result, while he struggled to drag his body into the water someone else not invalid or lame would step down first. It is interesting to observe that none of those who received a cure in this fashion either remained or returned to help those less fortunate companions with whom they had so recently languished.

Despite so many disappointments, at least the man had stayed there and continued to try for a cure. Jesus challenged this spark of hope with the command, **Rise, take up your pallet, and walk** (cf. Mark 2:9–12). Whereas the water about him was only of limited potency (cf. 4:7–15), true restoration could come in obedience to this word of a stranger (cf. 4:50). Nor had Jesus misjudged the intensity of his longings. Lacking any tangible proof that the surge of strength which he now felt would be adequate, and without any favorable omen from the waters which had fascinated him so long, the cripple nevertheless leaped to his feet, **took up his pallet** and walked away.

(2) The Criticism of the Jews (5:9b–18)

Now that day was the sabbath. [10] So the Jews said to the man who was cured, "It is the

---

[19] The NEB, unlike the RSV, was prepared after the important contribution of Joachim Jeremias, *The Rediscovery of Bethesda: John 5:2,* "New Testament Archaeology Monograph," No. 1 (Louisville: Southern Baptist Theological Seminary, 1966), pp. 9–38.

[20] This phenomenon may have been a whirlpool effect caused either by the gushing of an intermittent spring or by the complicated drainage system of the twin pool. A legendary explanation attributing the moving of the water to an angel has been inserted at vv. 3b–4 in many ancient manuscripts but is not a part of the original text.

sabbath, it is not lawful for you to carry your pallet." ¹¹ But he answered them, "The man who healed me said to me, 'Take up your pallet, and walk.' " ¹² They asked him, "Who is the man who said to you, 'Take up your pallet, and walk'?" ¹³ Now the man who had been healed did not know who it was, for Jesus had withdrawn, as there was a crowd in the place. ¹⁴ Afterward, Jesus found him in the temple, and said to him, "See, you are well! Sin no more, that nothing worse befall you." ¹⁵ The man went away and told the Jews that it was Jesus who had healed him. ¹⁶ And this was why the Jews persecuted Jesus, because he did this on the sabbath. ¹⁷ But Jesus answered them, "My Father is working still, and I am working." ¹⁸ This was why the Jews sought all the more to kill him, because he not only broke the sabbath but also called God his Father, making himself equal with God.

For *the Jews*, the healing of a lame man had an entirely different significance because the *day* on which it occurred was *the sabbath*. This observance served both as a weekly remembrance of God's rest on the seventh day of creation (Ex. 20:11) and as a ritual anticipation of the promised rest of the messianic age (cf. Heb. 4:1–10). The Hebrew word *shabbath* meant a cessation of activity or abstinence from labor. Thirty-nine main classes of work were prohibited in the Mishnah, the last of which was "taking out aught from one domain to another" (*Shabbath* 7:2; cf. Jer. 17:19–27). Since these regulations were probably enforced during the New Testament period, it was *not lawful* for the man *to carry* his *pallet* on the sabbath.

So concerned were his accusers with this breach of the Jewish legal tradition that they showed no interest in the reason for the man's behavior or in the good fortune which had suddenly overtaken him (cf. Mark 3:1–6). Obviously intimidated by the threats of the religious leadership, the man quickly shifted responsibility for his actions to Jesus, yet in so doing bore indirect witness to the one who had *healed* him. After 38 years of helplessness he was ill-prepared to argue with trained theologians over the elaborate sabbath regulations which they had developed (contrast 9:24–34). This was especially the case since he *did not* even *know who* had

healed him (cf. 9:12,25,36), Jesus having withdrawn from the excited *crowd* that thronged the porticoes around the pool (cf. v. 41).

Perhaps because the man had been charged with sin as a sabbath lawbreaker, he later made his way to the *temple* where *Jesus* (deliberately? cf. 9:35) *found him* and reminded him of his cure: *See, you are well!* In gratitude for this divine gift the man was enjoined to *sin no more;* i.e., he should not let the bitter memory of 38 tragic years continue to separate him from God. Bad as it had been to lie on a mat for most of his life, it would be even *worse* to be spiritually deformed, for God does not judge sickness, but he does judge sin. Notice that Jesus was just as concerned over whether a person were a cripple on the inside as on the outside. The man, however, apparently was more concerned about the accusation which had been leveled against him by the religious authorities, and so he *went away* in fear or confusion to tell *the Jews that it was Jesus who had healed him.*

Now that the instigator of this sabbath infraction had been identified, *the Jews* began to *persecute Jesus,* not merely for a single offense but because *he* repeatedly (as suggested by the imperfect tense of the Greek verb) *did this* sort of thing *on the sabbath.* How could an unknown and unaccredited "young rebel" be allowed to free men from the restraint of those venerable laws that had shaped the very character of Jewish life for centuries? Since society never knows how far a lawbreaker intends to take his freedom from accepted conventions, the safest course is to suppress him entirely before the fragile system of public order is threatened with collapse.

In responding to this attack, Jesus did not defend himself by contending that he had broken no sabbath laws. Rather, he turned the tables by insisting that he was doing the very things on the sabbath that God himself did and therefore was observing the day better than his antagonists! Jewish theologians realized that God's creative activity had not stopped when he "rested" on the seventh day (Gen. 2:2). The rabbis taught that the works of divine providence continued unabated on the sabbath (e.g., rain, birth, death). Philo advanced a more subtle argument to the effect that God could actually labor while "at rest" since his work did not make him weary (*On the Cherubim*, 86—90). Elsewhere he contended that God, having finished the creation of mortal things, began on the seventh day to shape things "more divine" (*Allegorical Interpretation*, I, 5–6). Jesus may have alluded to such notions in the affirmation, *My Father is working still* (i.e., even on the sabbath).

The distinctive feature in this rebuttal was not some novel view of the sabbath but the linking of his own labors as coordinate and continuous with those of God: *and I am working* (too). By thus identifying himself with the One who had given the sabbath and its laws, Jesus dared to put himself beyond the reach of the established legal system. *The Jews* immediately sensed in this argument an implicit claim to be *equal with God,* a conclusion which seemed confirmed by the way in which he *called God his* own *Father.* Therefore, they *sought all the more to kill him* as one guilty of blasphemy.

(3) The Claims of Jesus (5:19–29)

¹⁹ Jesus said to them, "Truly, truly, I say to you, the Son can do nothing of his own accord, but only what he sees the Father doing; for whatever he does, that the Son does likewise. ²⁰ For the Father loves the Son, and shows him all that he himself is doing; and greater works than these will he show him, that you may marvel. ²¹ For as the Father raises the dead and gives them life, so also the Son gives life to whom he will. ²² The Father judges no one, but has given all judgment to the Son, ²³ that all may honor the Son, even as they honor the Father. He who does not honor the Son does not honor the Father who sent him. ²⁴ Truly, truly, I say to you, he who hears my word and believes him who sent me has eternal life; he does not come into judgment, but has passed from death to life. ²⁵ "Truly, truly, I say to you, the hour is coming, and now is, when the dead will hear the voice of the Son of God, and those who hear will live. ²⁶ For as the Father has life in himself, so he has granted the Son also to have life in himself, ²⁷ and has given him authority to execute judgment, because he is the Son of man. ²⁸ Do not marvel at this; for the hour is coming when all who are in the tombs will hear his voice ²⁹ and come forth, those who have done good, to the resurrection of life, and those who have done evil, to the resurrection of judgment.

Although Jesus claimed to be doing the sabbath work of God, he did not base this identity of function upon an equality of status. On the contrary, as *the Son* he could *do nothing of his own accord.* This relationship of complete dependence was like that of a son learning the family trade from his father. Just as a skilled artisan would work at his craft while the apprentice first watched and then repeated his actions, even so God showed Jesus all that he was doing, and *only* what the Son "saw" the Father doing would he do *likewise.*²¹ God could entrust a divine assignment to Jesus because he was certain that it would be perfectly obeyed. Jesus was not some sort of "second God" with an independent role of his own. His claims did not contradict that classic monotheism which had long been at the center of Israel's faith.

To be specific, two prerogatives which clearly belonged to *the Father* had been delegated to *the Son:* (1) to raise the dead and give them life; and (2) to judge all men. If the Jews really wanted to *marvel,* they should have realized that Jesus was doing far *greater works* than the healing of one lame man. Indeed, he was carrying out in their midst the very eschatological activities that God was expected to perform at the end of the world! For this reason *all* should *honor the Son, even as they honor the Father,* by hearing the Son's word, which meant to believe in the one sending him. Jesus was deserving of the highest honor, not because he had claimed some exalted status but precisely because he had been obedient without any thought of

---

²¹ The view that in 5:19–20a Jesus employed the "simple picture of a son apprenticed to his father's trade" has been developed by C. H. Dodd, *More New Testament Studies* (Grand Rapids: Wm. B. Eerdmans, 1968), pp. 30–40.

honor.

The most urgent thing for the Jews to realize (note the *truly, truly*) was that the *hour* of resurrection which they knew was *coming* in the future had *now* arrived in the ministry of Jesus. Even the spiritually *dead* could *hear the voice of the Son of God* and those who heard would *live,* not with physical life which soon expires but with the eternal *life* which *the Father* has *granted* to *the Son.* It was his possession of God's own life, not his earning of human credentials, that provided the basis for the *authority* which had been *given* Jesus to *execute judgment.* Mercifully, the arbiter of human destiny was no remote cosmic figure but *the Son of man* who knew the frailties of earthly existence.

This advent of realized eschatology did not mean, however, that futuristic eschatology had been abandoned by Jesus. Quite to the contrary, the end of history had become even more significant now that its meaning was being disclosed in the present. Jesus was quite willing to accept the traditional hope of Judaism, regarding which his hearers needed *not marvel* since they already accepted its validity. He readily acknowledged that a final *hour* was *coming* when *all* those *in the tombs* would come forth to a judgment based on works, whether *good* or *evil* (cf. Rom. 2:6-9). But the important point was that this great resurrection would be called forth by the same *voice* which now rang in their ears (cf. the word *hear* in vv. 24,25,28). Thus, even the most remote future hope required an immediate decision regarding Jesus. And the miracle was that a decision of faith would allow that hope to begin to come true here and now.

(4) The Evidence for the Claims (5: 30-47)

30 "I can do nothing on my own authority; as I hear, I judge; and my judgment is just, because I seek not my own will but the will of him who sent me. 31 If I bear witness to myself, my testimony is not true; 32 there is another who bears witness to me, and I know that the testimony which he bears to me is true. 33 You

sent to John, and he has borne witness to the truth. 34 Not that the testimony which I receive is from man; but I say this that you may be saved. 35 He was a burning and shining lamp, and you were willing to rejoice for a while in his light. 36 But the testimony which I have is greater than that of John; for the works which the Father has granted me to accomplish, these very works which I am doing, bear me witness that the Father has sent me. 37 And the Father who sent me has himself borne witness to me. His voice you have never heard, his form you have never seen; 38 and you do not have his word abiding in you, for you do not believe him whom he has sent. 39 You search the scriptures, because you think that in them you have eternal life; and it is they that bear witness to me; 40 yet you refuse to come to me that you may have life. 41 I do not receive glory from men. 42 But I know that you have not the love of God within you. 43 I have come in my Father's name, and you do not receive me; if another comes in his own name, him you will receive. 44 How can you believe, who receive glory from one another and do not seek the glory that comes from the only God? 45 Do not think that I shall accuse you to the Father; it is Moses who accuses you, on whom you set your hope. 46 If you believed Moses, you would believe me, for he wrote of me. 47 But if you do not believe his writings, how will you believe my words?"

The central issue in this chapter is the divine *authority* of Jesus. Having been claimed in vv. 1-9a, controverted in vv. 9b-18, and clarified in vv. 19-29, it is now corroborated in vv. 30-47. The necessity of authenticating the ministry of Jesus was painfully obvious, since he conspicuously lacked the very credentials on which the religious leaders in Judaism were accustomed to depend. He could not derive his power either from family origins, as did the hereditary priesthood, or from advanced training, as did the rabbis. Nor could he appeal to the sanctions of Scripture as interpreted by the weight of religious tradition, for he had clearly violated the letter of the code by "working" on the sabbath. What support, then, could Jesus summon to reinforce his exalted claims?

The answer to that crucial question had both a negative and a positive aspect. Negatively, Jesus insisted that he could *do nothing* on his *own authority.* He was utterly unlike the succession of messianic pretenders in his day who chose impressive titles and advanced inflated claims for themselves. He could not base his authority on self-aggrandizement because he was motivated *not by his own will* but by the *will* of the One who had *sent* him. Therefore, he was willing to follow the rule of Scripture (Deut. 19:15) that *testimony* not rest on a single self-witness but that it be confirmed by *another.* Positively, this other who bore *witness* to Jesus was God himself. Here was ultimate corroboration, for there could be no doubt that *the testimony* which he bore was *true.* So certain was Jesus of divine approval that he dared to call the supreme Ruler of the universe as chief witness for the defense!

But how could other men grasp this transcendent testimony which already lay at the bedrock of Jesus' consciousness? In the hope that earthly evidence would be helpful, Jesus pointed to three subsidiary sources, *not* in order to *receive* testimony *from man* but because these three witnesses were all given by the Father and so pointed both to Jesus and back to God. The manner in which they are introduced suggests a formal debate or trial in which Jesus, the cosmic judge of v. 22, defends himself as the one accused and the readers become the jury.

John the Baptist (vv. 33–35).—The religious leadership had already *sent to John* (1:19,24), and he had *borne witness to the truth* about Jesus (cf. 1:19–34; 3:27–30). Like Elijah of old (cf. Ecclus. 48:1), he was a burning and shining lamp illumining Israel's path to the discovery of the Messiah. To be sure, John was only a vessel that could not give off light of itself (cf. 1:8), but even so the Jews had been *willing to rejoice* for the short *while* that he ministered with the light given him by God. John had been a popular prophetic figure who awakened a great deal of eschatological excitement among the populace.

The mighty works (v. 36).—For all of the significance of a preparatory witness (cf. 3:28), Jesus had a *testimony . . . greater than that of John* which came from his own

ministry of fulfillment. Despite John's likeness to Elijah, it is never recorded that he worked a miracle, whereas *the Father* had *granted* Jesus *to accomplish* many mighty *works.* These were not impressive spectacles that called attention to themselves but were revealing signs pointing to the meaning of the mission on which Jesus had been *sent.* Admittedly, *these very works* were not self-authenticating—note the hostile reaction to the healing of the lame man in this chapter —but at least they were tangible evidence that should not be ignored. Perhaps sabbath scruple had been violated; nevertheless, a helpless invalid for 38 years was now walking about in plain view.

The Scriptures (vv. 37–40).—Once again Jesus insisted that the source of all true witness to himself lay in *the Father* who had *sent* him. At the same time, he acknowledged that God's *voice* had *never* been *heard* and his *form never seen* (cf. 1:18). How, then, could the divine testimony be received on earth? The Jews themselves would have answered that although God was transcendent beyond hearing or seeing, *his word* had been given men in *the scriptures* where they could *search* for it and so find *eternal life.* Accepting this premise of his opponents, Jesus offered the Old Testament as the third source of witness to himself. At the same time, he charged that God's *word* written in holy Scripture was *not abiding* in their hearts because they would *not believe* in him who had been *sent* by the ultimate author of the Scriptures.

In citing this threefold testimony to himself, Jesus showed a willingness to accept tangible support for his transcendent claims. But he was equally convinced that the strength of this support came only from God and thus required an acceptance of God to be valid. Anyone could hear what John had said, and see what Jesus had done, and read what was written in the Scriptures, but all of this would mean nothing apart from an openness to the God who alone confirms his own truth.

Today we still have fearless prophets, impressive works, and inspired Scriptures, and they still point beyond themselves to

God as their source and to Christ as their object. Men are not finally convinced to believe in Jesus by eloquent preaching, or by deeds of mercy, or even by the words of Holy Writ. These witnesses do not somehow make him authoritative; rather, they derive their own authority from him. In the nature of the case, the claim of Christ could be substantiated only by God himself as men came to the Son and discovered that in so doing they received the kind of *life* that had been given him by the Father (cf. v. 26).

Jesus concluded this discussion by turning back on his accusers the charge of religious egotism that had been hurled at him from the outset (v. 18). He needed not to *receive glory from men* because he had the assurance of *the love of God* within (cf. v. 20a), which they did not. Unlike a messianic pretender who would come in *his own name* to make inflated boasts of the role he intended to play, Jesus had come only in his *Father's name* to represent the reality of God by a life of obedience. It was ironic that the Jews would *receive* a man who called attention to himself and reject one who called attention to God.

Nor was the reason difficult to discern. Any religious enthusiast willing to be motivated by his own pride would just as readily pander to the pride of others, with the result that they would all *receive glory from one another.* But because Jesus sought *the glory that comes from the only God,* he could exalt neither himself nor his advocates. Here pride is clearly identified as a barrier, not to religion as such (where it is so easily exploited), but to belief in one who refused to use God to gratify the insatiable appetite of the human ego. The books of *Moses* had long ago taught that glory belongs only to God. Since the Jews *set* their *hope* on this great prophet, he would *accuse* them for a failure to *believe* this truth as enunciated both in *his writings* and in the *words* of Jesus.

2. The Bread of Life (6:1–71)

John 6 is not only the longest chapter in the Gospel but is by far the most extensive treatment devoted to a single theological theme. As such, it is surprising to discover that only a few simple points are made in this elaborate discussion of spiritual bread. At the same time, these rather obvious aspects of the analogy are developed with a subtlety and skill that make this section one of the theological masterpieces of the New Testament.

Several factors help to account for the distinctive character of this chapter. Because bread had long been a basic metaphor for spiritual sustenance in the Old Testament, it was already the object of homiletical treatment by the rabbis at the time when this Gospel was written. The Greeks also had reflected on the idea of heavenly food which nourishes eternal life, prompting apologists such as Philo to allegorize at length on the manna sent by God from heaven. The early church, of course, pondered deeply the meaning of religious meals in the light of the prominence given to the breaking of bread, especially in the celebration of the Lord's Supper. In its present form, John 6 illustrates how these manifold conceptions current in the first century could find new focus when applied to the person and work of Jesus.

Two references near the beginning and the end of this chapter suggest more precise antecedents in the background of Jesus and/or the writer of the Gospel. In v. 4 we learn that the discourse on the Bread of life was delivered at a time when the Passover festival was fast approaching, while v. 59 indicates that the place was in the synagogue at Capernaum. In the first century, the synagogue services followed a regular pattern of Scripture readings (lections) which had been coordinated with the great celebrations of the religious calendar. During the Passover season, paraphrases (targums) of appropriate passages such as Joshua 5 would be read and then expounded (midrash) by the rabbis utilizing the rich fund of homiletical material (haggadah) developed over many years of repeated efforts. John 6 seems to draw upon these Jewish exegetical traditions both to explain Jesus in the light of Scripture and to explain Scripture in the light of Jesus.[22]

Of the various Passover motifs in John 6, clearly the dominant one is that of bread or manna. God's miraculous care of his people during the Exodus and wilderness wanderings was especially remembered at Passover time. Note Psalm 78:12–54, particularly vv. 24–25, for the background of this entire chapter (cf. Neh. 9:9–15; Wisd. Sol. 16:20–21). So significant was the gift of manna in the desert that it became the pattern by which messianic bread was expected to be given in the new age. Because Joshua 5:10–12 stated that the manna had stopped at the time of the first Passover in the Promised Land, rabbinic tradition supposed that it was still being made and kept hidden in heaven (cf. Rev. 2:17), from whence it would again resume at a final Passover with the coming of the Messiah. For Jesus, at the one time of the year when these expectations were most intense, to make bread miraculously and then to claim to give manna greater than Moses was obviously calculated to have the greatest possible impact on those who saw and heard him.

By pointing exclusively to himself both as the giver and as the gift of heavenly bread, Jesus pressed a claim which relentlessly sifted his audience, beginning on the periphery of the crowd and moving to the very center of the disciple band. The superficial enthusiasm provoked by the feeding of the five thousand quickly chilled to be replaced by skeptical questions and taunting demands. As Jesus progressively revealed the implications of his claims, the respondents progressively "murmured," "argued violently," and were "scandalized."

22 On this background see Peder Borgen, Bread from Heaven. "Supplements to Novum Testamentum," Vol. 10 (Leiden: E. J. Brill, 1965); Bertil Gärtner, John 6 and the Jewish Passover. "Coniectanea Neotestamentica," No. 17 (Lund: C.W.K. Gleerup, 1959); Bruce J. Malina, The Palestinian Manna Tradition. "Arbeiten zur Geschichte des späteren Judentums und des Unchristentums," No. 7 (Leiden: E. J. Brill, 1968); Wayne A. Meeks, The Prophet-King: Moses Traditions and the Johannine Christology. "Supplements to Novum Testamentum," Vol. 14 (Leiden: E. J. Brill, 1967).

At first, this opposition came from "the people," i.e., a general crowd; but then it shifted from the multitude to "the Jews," i.e., the religious leadership. Eventually, the discontent spread to "many disciples" who "drew back and no longer went about with him." At last, even the twelve were included as the shocking disclosure was made that one of them was a traitor. No visible boundaries protected the members of any group from that shattering judgment at work in the ministry of Jesus (cf. Matt. 7:21–23).

The general form of the chapter as narrative (miracle) followed by discourse (teaching) is readily apparent and parallels somewhat the sequence in John 5. The precise structure of the discourse, however, is very difficult to determine and expositors widely disagree. The present treatment emphasizes the dialogical character of the discourse by recognizing three main parts, each introduced by a claim of Jesus and concluded by a conflict which that claim provoked. On this pattern, the discourse considers the Bread of life in relation to its source (vv. 25–34), its nature (vv. 35–51), and its reception (vv. 52–65). This discussion is connected to the feeding miracle which anticipates it (vv. 1–15) by a transition which links the two parts both geographically and theologically (vv. 16–24). The entire chapter concludes by recording a crisis in Jesus' relation to his disciples (vv. 66–71) reminiscent of the Caesarea-Philippi watershed in the Synoptics (Mark 8:27–33).

(1) The Feeding of the Five Thousand (6:1–15)

[1] After this Jesus went to the other side of the Sea of Galilee, which is the Sea of Tiberias. [2] And a multitude followed him, because they saw the signs which he did on those who were diseased. [3] Jesus went up into the hills, and there sat down with his disciples. [4] Now the Passover, the feast of the Jews, was at hand. [5] Lifting up his eyes, then, and seeing that a multitude was coming to him, Jesus said to Philip, "How are we to buy bread, so that these people may eat?" [6] This he said to test him, for he himself knew what he would do. [7] Philip answered him, "Two hundred denarii

would not buy enough bread for each of them to get a little." ⁸ One of his disciples, Andrew, Simon Peter's brother, said to him, ⁹ "There is a lad here who has five barley loaves and two fish; but what are they among so many?" ¹⁰ Jesus said, "Make the people sit down." Now there was much grass in the place; so the men sat down, in number about five thousand. ¹¹ Jesus then took the loaves, and when he had given thanks, he distributed them to those who were seated; so also the fish, as much as they wanted. ¹² And when they had eaten their fill, he told his disciples, "Gather up the fragments left over, that nothing may be lost." ¹³ So they gathered them up and filled twelve baskets with fragments from the five barley loaves, left by those who had eaten. ¹⁴ When the people saw the sign which he had done, they said, "This is indeed the prophet who is to come into the world!"

¹⁵ Perceiving then that they were about to come and take him by force to make him king, Jesus withdrew again to the hills by himself.

This is the only miracle of Jesus to be recorded in all four Gospels. Both the Synoptics and John agree that it marked a crossroads in the Galilean ministry of Jesus. The incident continued to be important in the early church because of its ties to similar feeding miracles in the Old Testament (especially 2 Kings 4:42–44) and to the celebration of the Lord's Supper. For every generation the story records in classic fashion the sufficiency of Jesus to meet human need even when the resources of his followers are meagre.

The location of this event is difficult to determine, *the other side of the Sea of Galilee* presumably referring to the eastern shore (across from Capernaum on the western shore as in 4:46–54), which could agree with the Lukan setting at Bethsaida (Luke 9:10, but cf. Mark 6:45). However, some manuscripts of v. 1 take *Tiberias* not as an alternate name for the *Sea of Galilee* (there is no word for sea with Tiberias in the Greek text) but as a reference to the city by that name on the southwest shore of the lake. This reading seems to be confirmed by v. 23, although the import of that verse is not entirely clear either. Obviously, the geographical details have been subordinated to the theological message of the miracle.

Wherever the location, clearly it was near the Sea of Galilee from whence *Jesus went up* "on the mountain" (not *into the hills* as in RSV), *and there sat down with his disciples.* To sit with one's disciples was to function as a rabbi, and to do so on the mountain was to teach the revelation of God. In this instance the time was as significant as the place, since the *Passover,* the great religious *feast of the Jews, was at hand* (cf. 2:13). The paschal celebration, observed annually in the spring, commemorated the deliverance of the nation from Egypt and thereby anticipated similar acts of divine salvation in the future. The placement of a cryptic reference to this festival in v. 4 may be the writer's way of hinting in v. 5 that the *multitude,* by *coming* to Jesus instead of to Jerusalem, could find in him the true Passover sacrifice (cf. 1:29; 19:31a; 1 Cor. 5:7b).

For Jesus, this hungry crowd provided an opportunity to *test* or teach his disciples an important truth about dealing with human need. To *Philip,* who was from Bethsaida (1:44) and may have known the local resources of the region, he raised the characteristic Johannine problem of the source from whence *to buy* adequate *bread* for the *people* to *eat.* His answer that *two hundred denarii* would scarcely provide each mouth with a morsel immediately identified the magnitude of the difficulty at an earthly level (cf. 4:11).

The RSV footnote indicating that "the denarius was worth about twenty cents" is correct but potentially misleading, since for us such an amount is mere pocket change whereas in ancient Palestine it could represent a day's wage (Matt. 20:2,9–10,13). Thus we should not think of *two hundred denarii* as equal to $40.00 but as equivalent to the earnings of a poor laborer for almost a year. The account does not make clear why Philip suggested this amount. If it happened to be the total currently in the disciples' money box (12:6), then his reply might have been a frustrated lament: "We couldn't feed this crowd if we spent all of our available funds!"

To compound the problem further, *Andrew*, another disciple from Bethsaida (1:44), next reported that out of the *many* who by now had arrived he was able to locate one *lad* who had *five barley loaves and two fish.* While Philip may have been hastily counting up the disciples' coins, Andrew presumably had been canvassing the crowd with results that were equally dismal. *Barley* bread was the cheaper food of the poor while pickled *fish* was little more than a spread or relish as topping for the buns. A popular tradition has emphasized the willingness of a small boy to share his lunch with Jesus, but of this praiseworthy motive the account is silent. Instead, the point made by Andrew was the same as that by Philip: *What are they among so many?* This recognition that all the available human resources were hopelessly inadequate provided a backdrop against which to understand the sovereign initiative of Jesus who *himself knew* all along *what he would do.*

Unlike his followers, Jesus did not despair over the meager resources at their disposal. Instructing the disciples to arrange *the people* on the *grass* in orderly fashion (permitting an approximate count of some *five thousand men*), he *took the loaves* and, having *given thanks, he distributed them* to the multitude. To take, bless, and then give was one of the most profound patterns of Jesus' activity by which he symbolized the truth that if men would offer him whatever they might have, however earthly and limited, he could call down God's heavenly grace upon it and thereby return it with a spiritual potential which the giver never dreamed it could convey. These actions, which also characterized the Last Supper (cf. Mark 14: 22–23), are perpetually reinacted in the Supper thereby conveying a central truth of Jesus' ministry in deed rather than in word.

The emphases in this account are on abundance and on abiding. The people were given *as much as they wanted* until *they had eaten their fill.* Furthermore, *the frag-*ments left over* were carefully *gathered* so that *nothing* would *be lost* (lit., "perish," the same word as in v. 27). That *twelve baskets* could be *filled* with the *fragments* that were *left* gave ample evidence that Jesus had more than satisfied *those who had eaten.* In Cana, he had been careful to leave "filled" with water six large jars "for the Jewish rites of purification" (2:6–7); here, he left *filled* with bread *twelve baskets* representing the 12 tribes of Israel. In both cases, he had "ful-filled" the inherited systems of the past but had gone far beyond them in his ability to meet human need.

To *the people,* the sight of 12 baskets filled with bread seemed to be a *sign* that the messianic banquet was ready to be spread. Accordingly, they hailed Jesus as *the prophet who is to come unto the world* (cf. 4:19; 7:40; 9:17), thereby identifying him with the promised "prophet like Moses" (Deut. 18:15,18) whose prototype had provided Israel with manna in the wilderness. Galilee was a hotbed of eschatological enthusiasm in the first century, and it did not require much provocation to launch an abortive messianic movement for national deliverance (Josephus, *Antiq.,* XX, 97–98,167–172). *Perceiving* that this multitude was *about to come and take him by force* (cf. Matt. 11:12) in order *to make him* function as an earthly *king,* Jesus turned his back on an earthly crown and *again* sought the solitude of the mountain (cf. Matt. 4:3–4).

(2) The Crossing of the Sea (6:16–24)

16 When evening came, his disciples went down to the sea, 17 got into a boat, and started across the sea to Capernaum. It was now dark, and Jesus had not yet come to them. 18 The sea rose because a strong wind was blowing. 19 When they had rowed about three or four miles, they saw Jesus walking on the sea and drawing near to the boat. They were frightened, 20 but he said to them, "It is I; do not be afraid." 21 Then they were glad to take him into the boat, and immediately the boat was at the land to which they were going. 22 On the next day the people who remained on the other side of the sea saw that there had

been only one boat there, and that Jesus had not entered the boat with his disciples, but that his disciples had gone away alone. 23 However, boats from Tiberias came near the place where they ate the bread after the Lord had given thanks. 24 So when the people saw that Jesus was not there, nor his disciples, they themselves got into the boats and went to Capernaum, seeking Jesus.

There are hints in the Synoptic accounts of the feeding (Mark 6:30–33,45) to the effect that the disciples may have encouraged the groundswell to draft Jesus as a new Judas Maccabeus leading another revolt in the desert (1 Macc. 1—4; 2 Macc. 8—15). If so, this may explain why they were not welcome to join their Master when he took refuge again on the mountain to pray "by himself" (v. 15; cf. Mark 6:46). As the disappointed crowd / dispersed, this troubled band found themselves halfway up a hill, away from home, temporarily without their leader, and *evening* fast approaching. They knew nothing to do but go *down to the sea,* get *into a boat,* and begin to row for *Capernaum* (from whence they had come? cf. 2:12; 4:46), probably trying to hug the shoreline in the hope that Jesus would soon join them. To add to their woes, it soon became completely *dark* (cf. 3:2; 13:30), *Jesus had not yet come to them,* and the *sea rose because a strong wind was blowing.*

Battling the sudden squall for *three or four miles,* the disciples finally *saw Jesus walking on the sea and drawing near to the boat.* When he reached them *they were frightened,* perhaps because of the raging storm, or because he had suddenly loomed up before them in the dark, or because they anticipated his rebuke of their role at the feeding. On the other hand, their fear may have been a sort of holy awe evoked because of the supernatural character of his coming. In any case, he relieved all of their anxieties with the reassuring words, *It is I* (*egō eimi*); *do not be afraid.* Gladly they took him *into the boat, and immediately the boat was at the land to which they were going.* In the presence of Jesus there was a peace which the disciples had not known during the long hours of the night while he was away.

It is not clear whether this immediate deliverance from the fury of the storm to the safety of the shore was intended to be understood as miraculous or not. The reference may mean only that the disciples were much nearer their destination than they had supposed, having already been blown by the storm for *three or four miles,* which is the approximate distance across the western arc of the lake from Tiberias to Capernaum. If this be the case, then the miraculous character of *walking on the sea* is also left ambiguous in this account (though not in Mark 6:45–54 and especially not in Matthew 14:22–33; the incident is omitted by Luke). The preposition here translated *on* (*epi*) may just as clearly mean "by" or "beside" (cf. 21:1) and is so used both in v. 16 (*to* the sea) and in v. 21 (*at* the land). If this rendering be chosen, the narrative would imply that while the disciples toiled at their oars through the storm, Jesus made his way up the coast toward Capernaum where he was sighted walking along the shore. Some would even suppose that he had waded out into the surf in search of his men, but such conjectures go beyond the evidence in the text.

When interpreting whether a miraculous element was intended in these references it is important to note the Johannine treatment of the entire unit (vv. 16–22). By comparison with Matthew and Mark, the story is told with brevity and a minimum of theological elaboration. There is little or no interest in the storm itself as a threat to the disciples nor in the power of Jesus to overcome its terrors. The test of faith here, if there be such, lies not in whether water will support human feet (either those of Jesus or of some disciple) but in whether Jesus is the great "I am" (*egō eimi*) of God. In actuality, faith does not really seem to be at issue; it is nowhere mentioned and the only response of the disciples is that they "wished" (RSV, *were glad*) to take Jesus aboard. The incident is not called a "sign," nor are we told that it evoked any religious response. Even though there is nothing in the Johannine account which denies the miraculous, this element is not as prominent here as in Matthew and Mark.

Probably, therefore, the Evangelist included the story because it was in his source at this point (as also in the Synoptics), because it did explain how Jesus got across the lake (cf. vv. 22–25), and because its symbolism was appropriate to the Passover context of the entire chapter (v. 4). The exodus from Egypt had involved a crossing of the sea, made possible when a strong wind caused the waters to rise and part (Ex. 14:21–29). Psalm 78 connected this passing through the waters (v. 13) with the giving of manna (v. 24), to which John 6 will turn next in vv. 25–34. Supremely, this Passover deliverance of the people was seen as a testimony to the personal guidance of God himself:

> Thy way was through the sea,
> thy path through the great waters;
> yet thy footprints were unseen.
> Thou didst lead thy people like a flock
> by the hand of Moses and Aaron.
> (Psalm 77:19–20)

Whatever the coming of Jesus to Capernaum meant to the disciples, it certainly mystified some of *the people* who had participated in the feeding *on the other side of the sea.* Realizing that the *disciples* had departed without *Jesus* in the only available *boat,* they supposed that he had remained alone on the mountain overnight. *On the next day,* however, he was nowhere to be found, nor had *his disciples* returned to pick him up. Realizing that he must have somehow made his way to *Capernaum,* those *who* were still *near the place where they ate the bread after the Lord had given thanks* (note the eucharistic overtones in this editorial description) got into *boats from Tiberias . . . and went to Capernaum, seeking Jesus.*

(3) *The Source of the Bread of Life* (6: 25–34)

²⁵ When they found him on the other side of the sea, they said to him, "Rabbi, when did

you come here?" ²⁶ Jesus answered them, "Truly, truly, I say to you, you seek me, not because you saw signs, but because you ate your fill of the loaves. ²⁷ Do not labor for the food which perishes, but for the food which endures to eternal life, which the Son of man will give to you; for on him has God the Father set his seal." ²⁸ Then they said to him, "What must we do, to be doing the works of God?" ²⁹ Jesus answered them, "This is the work of God, that you believe in him whom he has sent." ³⁰ So they said to him, "Then what sign do you do, that we may see, and believe you? What work do you perform? ³¹ Our fathers ate the manna in the wilderness; as it is written, 'He gave them bread from heaven to eat.' " ³² Jesus then said to them, "Truly, truly, I say to you, it was not Moses who gave you the bread from heaven; my Father gives you the true bread from heaven. ³³ For the bread of God is that which comes down from heaven, and gives life to the world." ³⁴ They said to him, "Lord, give us this bread always."

When Jesus was finally located *on the other side of the sea* (an awkward expression if a journey from Tiberias to Capernaum is meant), his seekers made no mention of the spiritually symbolic meal which they had so recently shared together but sought rather to satisfy their curiosity as to *when* and how he had *come.* Sensing the superficiality of such a question, *Jesus answered* with a solemn pronouncement, *Truly, truly,* that cut to the heart of their inward condition (cf. on 2:25; 3:2–3; 4:16–18). They had not sought him because they now *saw* the meaning of the *signs* that pointed to his true significance but because they had eaten their *fill* of bread and were hungry again. He had given them dinner the day before and now, after one night, they were back wanting breakfast!

This accusation by Jesus sharply defines two opposing views of the goal of life: to see or to eat? To some, man is primarily a spiritual being who lives by insights, convictions, and intangible values; to others, he is primarily a physical being engaged in a lifelong struggle for bread. Jesus clearly showed his concern for the material needs of life by feeding a hungry multitude, but he did so in such a way as to signify those realities which may be appropriated only by faith. Although it was obvious that these eager petitioners had not moved beyond the physical level, Jesus did not repudiate their request for a second meal but used it as a springboard to teach them the necessity for a more lasting satisfaction than material realities can offer (cf. 4:31–32). The very fact that all earthly *food* soon *perishes* —even the bread and fish which Jesus had provided—should show the importance of finding *the food which endures to eternal life* (cf. 4:13–14,31–34).

Behind this line of reasoning so central to Johannine theology lies a significant clue to Christian evangelism. Every person is created with unfulfilled physical appetites. But nothing material, however urgently it may be needed, can finally satisfy man because it *perishes;* i.e., being finite, it is not ultimate but points to the Creator behind it. Regardless of a person's religious presuppositions, he eventually discovers that anything tangible—whether food or drink or sex or possessions—furnishes only transient fulfillment. This sense of incompleteness which every man experiences as a result of his efforts to find satisfaction in earthly things provides the basis on which he may be prompted to search for heavenly things that bring lasting satisfaction to life.

One of the fundamental differences between perishing and permanent food is that a person must *labor* constantly for the former, whereas the Son of man will *give* the latter. Jesus reminded the crowd that they had traveled at least three or four miles to Capernaum (v. 19); yet the food which they now sought would last only a few hours, and then they would have to go to work again looking for more. Would it not be better to search for *the Son of man* on whom *God the Father* had *set his seal* of approval, thereby attesting that he had come down from heaven (3:31–36), and let him *give* the kind of *food which endures to eternal life?*

The crowd, however, much like the Samaritan woman (4:14–15), was still more interested in eating a loaf than in finding a person. Picking up only the first part of Jesus' proposal ("Do not labor for the food which perishes, but for the food which endures"), they now asked, *What must we do, to be doing* (lit., "laboring," the same verb used in v. 27a) *the works of God?* Jesus had intended a contrast between men laboring for that which perishes and the Son of man giving that which endures. His hearers, however, assumed that he meant to distinguish between working for man to earn the earthly bread that perishes and working for God to earn the heavenly bread that endures. How hard it is to understand religion as gift instead of chore!

Not to be deterred by this misunderstanding, Jesus adapted his argument to fit the response of the crowd. They had asked about *doing the works* (plural) *of God,* but he answered in terms of the one true *work* (singular) *of God,* which was to *believe in him* whom God had *sent.* This work of faith did not involve compulsive human efforts such as the crowd contemplated but a continuing openness to the work of God in sending his Son into the world. The act of belief is the antithesis of self-seeking religious activism because it involves the acceptance of the divine initiative by which God acted to give men salvation in Christ. This grace-through-faith approach leaves men not less but infinitely more responsible, for now they must respond in obedient love to the Son who bears the *seal* of having been *sent* by God, rather than attempting to conform by anxious striving to a set of regulations ·prescribed in their religious tradition.

Not only had Jesus redefined the relationship of faith to works, but he had pointed again to himself as the source of enduring spiritual sustenance. Unable to sidestep this issue any longer, the crowd now asked, *Then what sign do you do, that we may see, and believe you?* If the true "work" which they should do was to accept *the work of God* in sending Jesus, then what *work* could Jesus *perform* to show that he was God's agent? At first, it may seem incredible for the crowd to have made such a request less than 24 hours after witnessing the feeding of thousands. Surely this miracle should have been sufficient to convince even the most skeptical. Actually, however, they were not only aware of that recent event but were consciously comparing it with the experience of their ancestral *fathers* who had eaten *manna in the wilderness* as a result of the ministry of Moses.

During the Passover season (v. 4), it was customary in the synagogue (v. 59) to make a special study of those Scriptures related to the events of the Exodus. In so doing, the Jews had found *written* there a recurring reference to the effect that *He gave them bread from heaven to eat* (not an exact quotation of any one text; cf. Ex. 16:4,15; Neh. 9:15; Psalms 78:24–25; 105:40). Assuming that this "bread from heaven" mentioned in the Old Testament was the "food which endures" recommended by Jesus, and realizing that the original reference was to the sending of manna, the crowd now challenged Jesus to match Moses by giving them miraculous bread not once—as he had already done —but every day. If he could provide a fresh supply each morning, they would not need continually to "labor for the food which perishes" but would "believe in him" as a new Moses on the basis of this "work" which he performed.

In reply, Jesus willingly made use of the text which they had adapted from the Bible, but he challenged their exegesis at two crucial points: (1) The "he" should not be interpreted as a reference to Moses but to God, which is clear from the context in the Old Testament (e.g., Ex. 16:15). By definition, only someone in heaven could be the source of bread from heaven. (2) The verb to give should be understood as present rather than past, a change of tense based on understanding differently the vowels to be pronounced with the consonants in the Hebrew original. Thus they should not have understood the text to mean that *Moses* gave but that *my Father*

gives the true bread in question.

This exegetical clarification, which is much after the manner of Jewish homiletical midrash, enabled Jesus finally to define *the bread of God* on the basis of its source as *that which comes down from heaven* and, because of its cosmic origin, *gives life to the world*. Moses was not the ultimate source of such bread because, unlike the Son of man, he was not from heaven. In this case, their use of the Scriptures had gone astray because it was not rooted exclusively in the sole sufficiency of God as the giver of every good and perfect gift. Led at last to a dawning recognition of spiritual reality, the crowd exclaimed, much in the half-selfish spirit of the Samaritan woman (4:15), *Lord, give us this bread always*.

(4) The Nature of the Bread of Life (6:35–51)

35 Jesus said to them, "I am the bread of life; he who comes to me shall not hunger, and he who believes in me shall never thirst. 36 But I said to you that you have seen me and yet do not believe. 37 All that the Father gives me will come to me; and him who comes to me I will not cast out. 38 For I have come down from heaven, not to do my own will, but the will of him who sent me; 39 and this is the will of him who sent me, that I should lose nothing of all that he has given me, but raise it up at the last day. 40 For this is the will of my Father, that every one who sees the Son and believes in him should have eternal life; and I will raise him up at the last day."

41 The Jews then murmured at him, because he said, "I am the bread which came down from heaven." 42 They said, "Is not this Jesus, the son of Joseph, whose father and mother we know? How does he now say, 'I have come down from heaven'?" 43 Jesus answered them, "Do not murmur among yourselves. 44 No one can come to me unless the Father who sent me draws him; and I will raise him up at the last day. 45 It is written in the prophets, 'And they shall all be taught by God.' Every one who has heard and learned from the Father comes to me. 46 Not that any one has seen the Father except him who is from God; he has seen the Father. 47 Truly, truly, I say to you, he who believes has eternal life. 48 I am the bread of life. 49 Your fathers ate the manna in the wil-

derness, and they died. ⁵⁰ This is the bread which comes down from heaven, that a man may eat of it and not die. ⁵¹ I am the living bread which came down from heaven; if any one eats of this bread, he will live for ever; and the bread which I shall give for the life of the world is my flesh."

The initial identification of the bread of God (v. 33) had been ambiguous because the word translated "that" (*ho*) could refer either to bread (which is masculine in Greek) or to a person. In the latter case the phrase would be rendered, "The bread of God is *he who* (rather than *that which*) comes down from heaven." Having led the crowd at last beyond their longing for physical bread, Jesus now clarified the personal nature of true spiritual sustenance with the unequivocal declaration, *I am the bread of life.* His crucial role as both giver and gift had been anticipated in vv. 27 and 29, but here it was given ultimate expression by means of the solemn *I am* (*egō eimi*) formula which identified Jesus with the nature of God. The Jews had likened the wisdom of God mediated by the study of the Law to bread (e.g., Prov. 9:5), but Jesus dared to put himself above these realities as the one who could finally nourish and satisfy the needs of man.

Because he had first *come down* from God, every person who comes to him finds the basic needs of life fully met. These twin themes of Jesus "coming down" to men on mission and of believers "coming to" him in faith are central to this chapter and to the entire Gospel. The concept of "coming down from heaven" expresses eschatology in spatial rather than in temporal terms, much like the key phrase of the Lord's Prayer, "on earth as it is in heaven" (Matt. 6:10). The concept of "coming to" Jesus indicates that the human response to the divine initiative involves not some chore to be completed (v. 27) but a vital companionship to be cultivated.

At this point the people were challenged to reach a third and climactic level in their understanding of bread. (1) At first, they wanted physical bread such as they had received at the feeding across the sea (v. 26) with the difference that, like the manna of old, it be given every day (v. 31). (2) Shown that all physical bread perishes, even the daily manna, the crowd then asked for an endless supply of the "true bread" which the Father gives from heaven. (3) But now Jesus explained that one does not need the Bread of life "always" (i.e., over and over again) because he who eats that kind of bread *shall not hunger* any more. Furthermore, since the Exodus had involved the giving of both "bread from heaven for their hunger" and "water from the rock for their thirst" (Neh. 9:15), Jesus added that those who accepted him would *never thirst* again (cf. 4:13–14). Unlike Moses, what Jesus does for men he does once for all (cf. Heb. 7:27; 9:12; 10:10).

Despite this ultimate offer, however, many in the crowd who had traveled for miles in search of another meal would not accept the unexpected gift of a spiritual feast. Even though they had *seen* both his godly life and the sign of his power to give supernatural bread, they would *not believe.* Such rejection did not finally frustrate Jesus, however, for he set human freedom in the context of divine sovereignty. *All* of those who did *come* were gifts from his *Father* (cf. 17:6); i.e., they came because God had validated for them the authenticity of his Son (v. 27; cf. 5:30–47).

Further, however unpromising they seemed to be from a human perspective, Jesus was unwilling ever to *cast* a one of them *out* (cf. Matt. 8:12; 22:13), for he had come not to do his *own will* but *the will* of the one who *sent* him. The Gethsemane spirit characterized his entire ministry, not just one episode near its end (cf. Mark 14:36). Those who trusted themselves to Jesus discovered that he was utterly dependable *to lose nothing* which had been given him (i.e., not allow any to perish; cf. vv. 12,27) but to *raise it up at the last day* (cf. 5:19–29).

This section in vv. 36–40, which summarizes much of the argument in chapter 5, begins with a reference to those who *have seen* (*heōrakate*) and yet do *not believe*, whereas it ends with a mention of every one who *sees* (*theōrōn*) the Son and *believes* in him. It is important to grasp the way in which "seeing" is related both to belief and to unbelief. On the one hand, friend and foe alike were able to see the earthly life of Jesus. Even regarding the miraculous signs there was no argument over what actually happened. God did not play favorites and disclose his truth only to apocalyptic seers or to mystic visionaries. The incarnation was tangible and thereby accessible to sensory experience whether one believed or not.

On the other hand, men assign meaning to what they see in the light of the perspective from which they view life. Some looked at Jesus only with surface sight through the spectacles of tradition, from which frame of reference what they saw was shockingly unconventional. Others, however, looked at the same phenomenon and beheld a glory visible only to eyes of faith. In balanced fashion this Gospel affirms both that men are led to believe on the basis of what they see and that they are enabled better to see because of what they have believed (e.g., cf. 14:7–11; 20:24–29). Man is not merely an earthly being limited to sensory perceptions (empiricism) nor is he merely a spiritual being dependent on faith perceptions (gnosticism). Rather, sight and insight, flesh and spirit, the visible world of creation and the invisible world of redemption, meet in the event of revelation.

The Jews, however, assumed that divine revelation required a more impressive mode of disclosure than a solitary life of humble origins and so they *murmured* at Jesus much as the Israelites had murmured against Moses in the wilderness. Was not this man who claimed to *have come down from heaven* actually a local citizen named *Jesus, the son of Joseph, whose father and mother* were known to some of the Galileans gathered in the Capernaum synagogue (cf. Mark 6:3)? God's deliverer was

expected to arrive either as a Davidic king on the royal highway or as a Son of man on clouds of glory. How could they accept him as having come *down from heaven* when everyone knew that he had grown up in the obscure village of Nazareth?

Dismissing this effort to measure life by earthly origins (cf. 1:13; 3:1–7), Jesus pointed instead to God as the ultimate source who had *sent* him to earth and who now *draws* each one coming to him (cf. Jer. 31:3). Even though God was the prime mover behind everything that happened in Jesus' ministry, this sovereign initiative did not suppress but rather supported human freedom. Precisely because the Father did the "drawing" and the "teaching" (cf. Isa. 54:13), man was given the opportunity to do the "hearing" and the "learning." In this process Jesus could serve as the unique mediator because he alone had *seen* the Father (cf. 5:19–20) and yet was a man seen by others on earth (v. 40).

Verses 47–51 serve both as a conclusion summarizing the main teachings on the nature of the Bread of life in vv. 35–51 and as a transition anticipating the discussion on the reception of the Bread of life in vv. 52–65. The solemn formula, *Truly, truly,* identified as divine revelation the following disclosures clarified up to this point in the dialogue: (1) The *life* which is *eternal* rather than perishing is sustained not by what one eats but by what one believes. (2) Jesus himself is *the bread* which faith appropriates in order to have *life*. (3) As such, Jesus is superior to *the manna* which the Jewish *fathers* were given in *the wilderness* because they *ate* and then *died* (i.e., not only physically but spiritually, in that they failed to inherit the promises of God), whereas whoever *may eat* of Jesus will *not die* (i.e., he may die physically but will not die spiritually).

Mention of eating in vv. 49–50 leads to the introduction of a new theme in v. 51, that of receiving *living bread* when it is a historical person rather than a literal loaf. Now we are told for the first time that *the bread which* Jesus would *give for the life of the world* was his *flesh*. In the next section, the theological implications of this strange assertion will be elaborated.

(5) The Reception of the Bread of Life (6:52–65)

⁵² The Jews then disputed among themselves, saying, "How can this man give us his flesh to eat?" ⁵³ So Jesus said to them, "Truly, truly, I say to you, unless you eat the flesh of the Son of man and drink his blood, you have no life in you; ⁵⁴ he who eats my flesh and drinks my blood has eternal life, and I will raise him up at the last day. ⁵⁵ For my flesh is food indeed, and my blood is drink indeed. ⁵⁶ He who eats my flesh and drinks my blood abides in me, and I in him. ⁵⁷ As the living Father sent me, and I live because of the Father, so he who eats me will live because of me. ⁵⁸ This is the bread which came down from heaven, not such as the fathers ate and died; he who eats this bread will live for ever." ⁵⁹ This he said in the synagogue, as he taught at Capernaum.

⁶⁰ Many of his disciples, when they heard it, said, "This is a hard saying; who can listen to it?" ⁶¹ But Jesus, knowing in himself that his disciples murmured at it, said to them, "Do you take offense at this? ⁶² Then what if you were to see the Son of man ascending where he was before? ⁶³ It is the spirit that gives life, the flesh is of no avail; the words that I have spoken to you are spirit and life. ⁶⁴ But there are some of you that do not believe." For Jesus knew from the first who those were that did not believe, and who it was that should betray him. ⁶⁵ And he said, "This is why I told you that no one can come to me unless it is granted him by the Father."

The first mention by Jesus that he would *give* men *his flesh* to eat immediately provoked violent controversy as the Jews *disputed* (lit., "fought") *among themselves* over such repugnant terminology which on the surface seemed to suggest cannibalism. In response, Jesus did nothing to mitigate their distress but heightened the offense by demanding not only that they *eat the flesh of the Son of man* but that they *drink his blood* as well. Needless to say, the drinking of human blood was especially unthinkable to those whose religion enforced time-honored scruples against partaking even of animal blood (cf. Gen. 9:4; Lev. 3:17; 17:10–14; Deut. 12:23). Despite the of-

fensiveness of the language, however, it was repeated again and again as the exclusive condition for having *eternal life*, for finding true *food* and *drink*, and for the mutual "abiding" of the believer and Jesus.

Although this new direction in the development of the bread analogy was disconcerting to the Jews, it had been prepared for very carefully and in fact was demanded by the two previous claims already advanced in this discourse. In vv. 25–34 Jesus maintained that he gave the true bread of God from heaven, while in vv. 35–51 he further established that he was himself that bread of life. If, therefore, Jesus *gives* the bread that he *is*, and if bread by its very nature is to be eaten, then it follows that one must somehow eat Jesus himself. This is clearly the intent throughout vv. 52–59, where *he who eats my flesh and drinks my blood* is but another way of saying *he who eats me*. The identity of giver and gift means that one cannot take something from Jesus without taking Jesus himself.

But this does not entirely explain the use of such seemingly repulsive phraseology as "eating flesh" and "drinking blood." In Hebrew thought, flesh and blood stood for the physical, earthly corporeality of an individual person or of humanity in general (cf. Matt. 16:17 where "flesh and blood" means man on earth in contrast to God in heaven). By pointing explicitly to his *flesh* and *blood*, Jesus was insisting that the life-giving sustenance which he offered men was conveyed, not by some timeless thought or intangible spirit unrelated to his particular life, but by his incarnate existence as a concrete historical reality living in their midst. Incredible as it may have seemed, the claim is made that he drew his very life from *the living Father* and therefore that those who "ate" him could draw their life from him. His temporal existence was the unique link mediating the eternal life of God to man.

To accept his humanity as the locus of the divine life on earth did not mean, however, that he was limited to what could be conveyed by the flesh. *Hard* as it was to believe that the bread of heaven had come down in one lowly life, how much harder it would be *to see the Son of man ascending where he was before* and so realize that Jesus always had been and always would be the mediator of the world above. *Flesh* itself was *of no avail;* rather, the flesh of Jesus was crucial because it was interpenetrated by the *spirit that gives life.* His *words* were not earthbound utterances conveying only sensory experiences but were the vehicles of that *spirit* and *life* which were his from the heavenly realm (cf. 3:6).

Paradoxically, therefore, two apparently contradictory contentions are equally emphasized in the two paragraphs of this section. In vv. 52–59 the stress falls on the indispensability of appropriating the flesh-and-blood Jesus as the one tangible manifestation of eternal life lived out on earth and so offered to all men. In vv. 60–65, however, the stress falls on the indispensability of appropriating the spirit and life of that heavenly realm where Jesus had been *before* and to which he would ascend again. Both of these perspectives are held in balance because of the conviction that in Jesus flesh and spirit, matter and meaning, the world below and the world above, were perfectly fused. As the Prologue has already declared (1:14), the eternal Word who existed with God before anything was made actually became earthly flesh and blood without thereby ceasing to be heavenly spirit and life.

This central conviction provides the perspective from which to answer the frequently debated question of whether vv. 51*b*–58 also allude to the Lord's Supper. This celebration is not specifically mentioned either in this chapter or anywhere else in the fourth Gospel. Therefore, it is quite legitimate to maintain that the teachings in John 6 have no direct relevance for an understanding of the Lord's Supper. However, it would be strange if so important an observance in the life of the early church were completely ignored in a comprehensive Gospel concerned to root the Christian movement in the ministry of Jesus. Almost inevitably a major discourse on bread would come to be connected with the "breaking of bread," even if this were not its original application.

One way to interpret the silence of John 6 on the Supper is to suppose that its primary concern was not to record the institution of the rite but to establish a theological foundation for the proper understanding of the Supper by pointing to Jesus himself as "sacramental," i.e., as the material means of spiritual grace. In an ontological sense, he is the unique one in whom the invisible has become visible, the heavenly has become earthly, the infinite has become finite. Only as believers eat his flesh and drink his blood do they thereby partake of the life of God.

This does not mean that the elements used in the Lord's Supper should be understood as symbols in the same way as a flag or a ring serve as symbols, for in the history lying behind those representations there is no perfect incarnation of the realities to which they point. Because the eating of eucharistic bread may be accompanied by *the spirit that gives life* and by *the words that* Jesus has *spoken,* such an act done in faith may nurture a personal relationship to him who alone is the Bread of life.

Whether or not John 6 was originally addressed to the question of the Lord's Supper, it nevertheless contains one of the most explicit warnings in the New Testament that unless our observances are in fact a communion with the incarnate Christ they are of no avail. At the same time, the conviction expressed here that "the Word became flesh" and offered himself to be eaten provides our assurance that God is willing to identify himself with the tangible and so provide a particular opportunity to encounter through it the fulness of his presence.

This section concludes by anticipating the crisis of rejection described in vv. 66–71. Just as one can refuse to eat physical bread, so one can choose *not to believe* in the Bread of life. Even though Jesus *knew from the first who those were that did not believe, and who it was that should betray him,* he did not try to coerce faith. Certain that God alone could overcome doubt and denial, he was content to welcome those *granted him by the Father* (cf. vv. 37,44). No experience is more painful than rejection, particularly when one is trying only to be of help. Jesus faced such frustration in the confidence that if he would be true to the One sending him, he would be given those followers who were open to the drawing power of God.

(6) The Testing of the Twelve (6:66–71)

66 After this many of his disciples drew back and no longer went about with him. 67 Jesus said to the twelve, "Will you also go away?" 68 Simon Peter answered him, "Lord, to whom shall we go? You have the words of eternal life; 69 and we have believed, and have come to know, that you are the Holy One of God." 70 Jesus answered them, "Did I not choose you, the twelve, and one of you is a devil?" 71 He spoke of Judas the son of Simon Iscariot, for he, one of the twelve, was to betray him.

Throughout this chapter, the cruciality of decision has been sharpened until it reaches ultimate expression in this concluding paragraph. Positively, what began as superficial adulation (vv. 14–15) ended in the sincere confessions, *You have the words of eternal life* and *You are the Holy One of God* (cf. Mark 1:24). Negatively, what began as theological argument (vv. 41,52,60) ended in personal rejection as *many of his disciples drew back and no longer went about with him.* John 6 opens with 5,000 excited warriors (v. 15) and closes with twelve troubled disciples, one of whom was a traitor!

Jesus clearly realized that men differed so drastically in their attitudes toward him that he would eventually suffer in the crossfire of conflicting reaction. Already the passion motif had been sounded in references to the giving of his flesh for the life of the world (v. 51) and to the ascending of the Son of man (v. 62), but now it was made explicit by the mention of *Judas* who *was to betray him.* From this point on Jesus ministered under the pressure of mortal danger both from without (5:18a) and from within (vv. 70–71).

The theological significance of the sequence in this section has been heightened by conjoining three emphases which were not so closely related in the Synoptic accounts:

First, the confession of Peter was connected to the account of the feeding of the 5,000, as in Luke 9:10–22. (In Matt. 16:13–23 and Mark 8:27–33, the connection is not direct, but the confession accounts are closely related to a theological discussion of the feeding in Matt. 16:5–12 and Mark 8:14–21.) The disciples' confession through their spokesman, Peter, illustrated the central truths of Jesus' miracle and the explanatory discourse which followed. They would not *go away* as did the crowds but would cling to him by faith as the one with *words of eternal life.* If the reader is still confused about what it means to "eat" the flesh and "drink" the blood of Jesus, he has only to study this confession as a paradigm of the proper response.

Second, the confession of Peter was immediately followed by a confession of Jesus announcing his impending passion, as in all the Synoptics (Matt. 16:24–28; Mark 8:34—9:1; Luke 9:23–27). Despite the most loyal attachment of believers, they would not be able to prevent his betrayal unto death. Their faith did not deliver them into a new age of happiness and peace but into conflict and tension from which they could not escape. Hard on the heels of their confident assertion that *we* (the twelve) *have believed, and have come to know,* Jesus announced that one of them was a *devil.* The best possible confession did not make even the innermost circle invulnerable to Satan!

Third, the treachery of Judas was exposed following Jesus' offer of his flesh and blood as food and drink (vv. 52–57). In all of the Synoptics, the sin of Judas was exposed at the Last Supper where Jesus offered the bread and the cup as his body to be eaten and his blood to be drunk (Matt. 26:20–29; Mark 14:17–25; especially Luke 22:14–23). To sup with another was viewed by Oriental hospitality as an intimate experience of fellowship which created a bond even between enemies. For Judas to betray one who offered to eat with him and to provide himself as the food only heightened the shamefulness of his heinous deed. By his betrayal, the *son of Simon Iscariot* both shattered the spiritual solidarity of the twelve and rejected the offer of Jesus to feed him the bread of heaven.

Despite the enormity of Judas' treachery, it is troubling to read that Jesus called him *a devil*. Coupled with the claim that Jesus knew of his betrayal "from the first" (v. 64), some suppose that Judas is pictured in this Gospel as a helpless pawn of Satan, fated to serve as an agent of cosmic evil against his will (cf. 13:2,27; 17:12). A needed corrective to that view is provided by a comparison of this passage with its Synoptic counterpart at the one point where they differ most strikingly. At Caesarea-Philippi, Jesus identified *Peter* as "Satan" (Mark 8:33), whereas here he described *Judas* as "a devil."

Near the close of the Galilean ministry, following a momentous confession of faith by the twelve, two of its number were singled out as emissaries of the evil one. But although they stood together at the outset under that damning indictment, the outcome of their lives could not have been more different: Peter became the chief apostle and Judas died a tragic suicide. Jesus candidly charged two of his chosen leaders with succumbing to satanic temptation, yet he did everything possible to break the tempter's power (cf. Luke 22:31–32; Mark 16:7; John 13:26–30; 17:12). The opposite responses of the two men to the same predicament show that human free will was a crucial factor even in the cosmic struggle between the Christ and the Antichrist.

3. The Water of Life (7:1–52)

John 7 and 8 constitute the central section in the major unit comprising John 5—10. Unlike the surrounding chapters, they consist of small blocks of loosely connected material without any lengthy narrative record of Jesus' works or any continuous discourse setting forth his teachings on a single theme. Major attention is given to the various responses which Jesus elicited as the nature of his person and mission became increasingly clear. The content of these two closely related chapters resembles the summaries of vigorous debates in which Jewish objections to Jesus were forcibly stated and just as forcibly answered.

True to the trend throughout John 5—10, the process of polarization accelerates (cf. 7:1,7,19–20,25,32,44) as three groups grow progressively disenchanted: (1) his brothers (vv. 1–9) because they cannot bask in his public glory; (2) the crowds (vv. 10–44) because they cannot be sure of his theological credentials; and (3) the religious leadership (vv. 45–52) because they fear that his popularity will lead the people astray. In every generation, Christianity may be undermined by subtle family pressures, by the faintheartedness of the fickle masses, and by the jealousies of the ecclesiastical establishment.

The religious background for John 7–9 is provided by the Feast of Tabernacles, the most popular (Josephus, *Antiq.*, VIII, 100) of the three national festivals requiring a pilgrimage to the Temple (Ex. 23:14–17; Deut. 16:16). The name given to this celebration reflects its twofold background as an autumnal agricultural festival of ingathering (Ex. 23:16) and as a religious commemoration of the wilderness wanderings (Lev. 23:39–43). The term tabernacle (booth) suggests the temporary thatched pavilions built in the orchards during harvest season to shelter those guarding the crops overnight. It is also reminiscent of the movable tents in which Israel migrated from Egypt to the promised land.

The observance was held in the month of Tishri (roughly corresponding to our October) for seven days (Deut. 16:13–15; Ezek. 45:25). Later, this period was extended by the addition of an eighth day kept as a sabbath with solemn assembly

(Lev. 23:33–36; Num. 29:35; 2 Chron. 7:9; Neh. 8:18). The first day of the feast, Tishri 15, coincided with the autumnal equinox (Josephus, *Antiq.*, III, 244) and thus signaled the onset of winter when rains were needed to prepare the land for the new crop cycle.

One of the three main rites observed daily during Tabernacles, the morning water libation, provided the direct background to John 7 (cf. Mishnah, *Sukkah* 4:9). A procession of priests brought a golden jar filled with water up from the pool of Siloam to the Temple, where they were greeted by the blowing of the trumpet (*shofar*) and the shouts (*hallel*) of the pilgrim worshipers. The water was poured into a silver bowl on the altar as the symbol of prayer for rain (Zech. 14:16–19) and in remembrance of the gift of water by God to Israel in the desert (Ex. 17:1–7; Num. 20:2–13; 1 Cor. 10:1–4). It was in this highly charged context that Jesus cried out, "If any one thirst, let him come to me and drink" (7:37), thus offering himself as the answer to Israel's deepest needs as defined both by nature and by history.

(1) The Coming of Jesus to Jerusalem (7:1–13)

1 After this Jesus went about in Galilee; he would not go about in Judea, because the Jews sought to kill him. 2 Now the Jews' feast of Tabernacles was at hand. 3 So his brothers said to him, "Leave here and go to Judea, that your disciples may see the works you are doing. 4 For no man works in secret if he seeks to be known openly. If you do these things, show yourself to the world." 5 For even his brothers did not believe in him. 6 Jesus said to them, "My time has not yet come, but your time is always here. 7 The world cannot hate you, but it hates me because I testify of it that its works are evil. 8 Go to the feast yourselves; I am not going up to this feast, for my time has not yet fully come." 9 So saying, he remained in Galilee.

10 But after his brothers had gone up to the feast, then he also went up, not publicly but in private. 11 The Jews were looking for him at the feast, and saying, "Where is he?" 12 And there was much muttering about him among the people. While some said, "He is a good man," others said, "No, he is leading the people astray." 13 Yet for fear of the Jews no one spoke openly of him.

Although Jesus had now alienated many Galileans (6:41,52,60,66), his greatest opposition came from *the Jews* concentrated in *Judea,* where efforts were already underway to *kill* him (5:18). To add to the heartbreak of a rapidly deteriorating situation, the *brothers* of Jesus were insensitive to the hostile pressures under which he was working. Aware only of the glowing reputation which he had brought back from his earlier ministry in Judea (2:23; 3:26; 4:1,45), they urged him to use the popular Feast of Tabernacles now *at hand* as an occasion to *go to Judea* so that his *disciples* there could see the impressive *works* which he was doing, such as the recent feeding of the 5,000. Their logic was self-evident. Assuming that Jesus sought to be *known openly* as a public religious leader, they encouraged him to *show* what he could *do* in the religious center of the *world* rather than to work in the obscurity of Galilee.

Although the brothers seemed ready to acknowledge that Jesus was doing impressive *works* with potential publicity value, the Evangelist was certain that they did *not believe in him* (cf. Mark 3:21,31). In fact, his closest earthly kin may have been taunting him to revive a dying cause and recoup his losses in Galilee (6:66) by cultivating those who had become his disciples during the first trip to Judea (3:22,26; 4:1). The family may have been willing to support his movement as long as it succeeded, and sincerely hoped that it would do so, but they were unprepared to commit themselves to Jesus whatever the outcome might be.

Recognizing that this request of his brothers—much like an earlier prompting of his mother (2:3)—was not motivated by a true understanding of his mission, Jesus replied that the opportune moment for his manifestation to Israel was determined by God's *time* rather than by theirs (cf. 2:4b). Peter had tried to turn him aside from the cross (Mark 8:31–33), whereas here his brothers offered the adulation of the festival crowds in place of the dark designs of

Judas (6:71). But Jesus knew that he could never serve as a popular functionary at religious celebrations because his task was to *testify* of the *world* that its works were *evil* (cf. 3:19–21). He would not confuse the limelight of men with the searchlight of God. Thus, unlike his brothers, he refused to "go along with the crowd" to the feast but *remained* instead *in Galilee*.

A few days later, however, *after his brothers had gone up to the feast*, Jesus *also went up* to Jerusalem, *not publicly* or "openly" as they had proposed but *in private* or "secret" (cf. 10:24). As was the case with his mother at Cana, he refused to be pressured by a human request even from his family, but later he acted independently to carry it out in accordance with his divine mission (cf. comment on 2:3–4). At the practical level, Jesus may have wished to avoid the political enthusiasm which often escalated among the pilgrims as they journeyed to a festival in Jerusalem (cf. 12:12–19). Only a short while earlier he had narrowly escaped the clutches of an excited Galilean crowd at the Passover season (6:15), and he did not want to be caught in a similar ground swell during Tabernacles.

The resolute determination of Jesus to make his every move at the right time and in the right spirit contrasted sharply with the indecision of those awaiting his arrival in Jerusalem. The *Jews* wondered *where* he might be, while the *people* carried on a muted debate over whether he was *a good man* or whether he was *leading the people astray*. Their unwillingness to talk *openly* about Jesus *for fear of the Jews* stands in contrast with Jesus' unwillingness to work "openly" lest he call attention to himself rather than to God.

(2) Conflict over the Authority of Jesus (7:14–24)

¹⁴ About the middle of the feast Jesus went up into the temple and taught. ¹⁵ The Jews marveled at it, saying, "How is it that this man has learning, when he has never studied?"

¹⁶ So Jesus answered them, "My teaching is not mine, but his who sent me; ¹⁷ if any man's will is to do his will, he shall know whether the teaching is from God or whether I am speaking on my own authority. ¹⁸ He who speaks on his own authority seeks his own glory; but he who seeks the glory of him who sent him is true, and in him there is no falsehood. ¹⁹ Did not Moses give you the law? Yet none of you keeps the law. Why do you seek to kill me?" ²⁰ The people answered, "You have a demon! Who is seeking to kill you?" ²¹ Jesus answered them, "I did one deed, and you all marvel at it. ²² Moses gave you circumcision (not that it is from Moses, but from the fathers), and you circumcise a man upon the sabbath. ²³ If on the sabbath a man receives circumcision, so that the law of Moses may not be broken, are you angry with me because on the sabbath I made a man's whole body well? ²⁴ Do not judge by appearances, but judge with right judgment."

Surprising both the crowds who expected him earlier and his brothers who expected him not at all, Jesus suddenly appeared at the *temple* (cf. Mal. 3:1) *about the middle of the feast*, i.e., on the third or fourth day. As he *taught* there, the *Jews marveled* at his *learning* since they knew that he had *never studied*. This did not imply that Jesus was illiterate, but that he had never received formal theological training under an accredited rabbi. The charge was serious since only by such an education could public teachers master the precedents of the past and so maintain the continuity of a normative religious tradition.

In reply, Jesus insisted that the absence of rabbinic credentials did not mean that he was a self-seeking religious "independent" who said whatever he pleased. Rather, his *teaching* was *not* his own but belonged to God who had *sent* him. In turning the tables, Jesus claimed to have studied in the greatest rabbinic academy of all! The weightiness of his words came not from their conformity to a venerable past but from their fidelity to a transcendent source. Because his doctrine was derived from above, it was more authoritative than the accumulated wisdom of the centuries.

Although Jesus could not bolster his teaching by recourse to rabbinic credentials, he did cite three types of evidence to substantiate his position (vv. 17–23): First, he cited the corroboration of an obedient conscience (v. 17). If his hearers would go beyond surface considerations and inwardly *will to do* the *will* of God, then they would *know whether* the *teaching* in question was *from God or whether* Jesus was *speaking on . . .* [his] *own authority.* In the very process of living out the teaching of Jesus, men would discover that it coincided with their deepest commitment to God's will, that it enabled them to fulfill their highest religious aspirations, and that they could thus infer his true intentions as their teacher.

Second, Jesus cited the witness of a selfless ministry. Because he lacked proper ordination, he had been accused of speaking *on his own authority.* But that approach would have involved seeking *his own glory,* whereas his only purpose was to seek *the glory of him who sent him.* The complete absence of self-seeking pride should have convinced his accusers that Jesus was a man of *true* integrity in whom there was no deceptive *falsehood.* Transparent humility is always a key credential that accredits the authentic servant of God.

Third, Jesus cited the fulfillment of scriptural intention. One of the proudest boasts of the Jews was that *Moses* had given them *the law.* But the divine unity of gift and demand meant that the law was not something to cherish as a prized possession but something to keep (lit., "to do") in actual conduct. This they were obviously not doing, since the attempt *to kill* Jesus was a violation of the prohibition against murder at the heart of the law (Ex. 20:13). The incredulous retort, *You have a demon! Who is seeking to kill you?* may have come from Galilean pilgrims unaware of the sinister plots which were common knowledge in Jerusalem (v. 25; cf. 5:18). Or it may have been the protest of a crowd that was not yet ready to do Jesus any physical violence but whose inner hostility was recognized by him as murderous in its design (cf. Matt. 5:21–22).

In contrast to their unconcern for keeping the spirit of the law, Jesus now illustrated how he had fulfilled its deepest intention. As recorded in 5:2–9a, Jesus actually *did* (same verb as "to keep" in v. 19) *one deed* in healing a lame man which continued to impress them (cf. v. 31). They should now compare this miracle with the act of *circumcision* which *Moses gave* in the law. (The writer parenthetically explains that this rite was *not* originated by *Moses* himself, e.g., it was not in the Decalogue, but had come *from the fathers,* such as Abraham in Gen. 17:9–14.) Since circumcision was always to be administered on the eighth day (Lev. 12:3), babies born on the sabbath would also be circumcised *upon the sabbath . . . that the law of Moses may not be broken.* If this symbolic act affecting only a part of the body was permissible on the sabbath, why —arguing from the lesser to the greater— should they be *angry* with Jesus for using a holy day to make a *man's whole body well?* As Moffatt vividly paraphrases, "Are you enraged at me for curing, not cutting, the entire body of a man upon the sabbath?"

Although this argument was drawn from Jewish principles, it clearly went beyond Jewish practice both in spirit and scope. The rabbis permitted religious work on the sabbath, including circumcision, only in accordance with the rule that exceptions are justified when life is in imminent danger. By contrast, in healing an invalid of 38 years Jesus obviously could have waited one more day in order to avoid the sabbath. But he was not interested in overriding its regulations because a person might die. Rather he welcomed the opportunity to fulfill its redemptive purpose in order that men might live (cf. Mark 3:1–6).

The general principle underlying Jesus' approach is summarized in the climactic v. 24: *Do not judge by appearances, but judge with right judgment* (cf. Matt. 7:1–5). Instead of setting up superficial external standards by which to measure religious authenticity, men should evaluate both the teacher and his teachings in terms of those ultimate norms which lie beneath the surface as matters of substance rather than sight.

(3) Conflict over the Origin of Jesus (7:25-31)

25 Some of the people of Jerusalem therefore said, "Is not this the man whom they seek to kill? 26 And here he is, speaking openly, and they say nothing to him! Can it be that the authorities really know that this is the Christ? 27 Yet we know where this man comes from; and when the Christ appears, no one will know where he comes from." 28 So Jesus proclaimed, as he taught in the temple, "You know me, and you know where I come from? But I have not come of my own accord; he who sent me is true, and him you do not know. 29 I know him, for I come from him, and he sent me." 30 So they sought to arrest him; but no one laid hands on him, because his hour had not yet come. 31 Yet many of the people believed in him; they said, "When the Christ appears, will he do more signs than this man has done?"

Unlike the festival crowd in v. 20, *Some of the people of Jerusalem* knew that Jesus was *the man whom* the religious authorities were seeking *to kill* (cf. 5:18). Although he was still *speaking openly* in the Temple, which during the Feast of Tabernacles provided the most effective forum in all Judaism, this could hardly mean that the *authorities really* knew him to be the Christ (the rhetorical question in v. 26 expects a negative answer). Even the untrained populace could advance a convincing reason not to accept his claims. Because *the Christ* was to appear suddenly and supernaturally, *no one* would *know where* he had come from (cf. Mal. 3:1; 2 Esdras 7:26-28; 13:32), whereas they knew that Jesus had come from lowly Galilee (cf. vv. 41-42).

In ancient Palestine, without the use of family names, a man was usually identified primarily by his place or parentage, e.g., "Jesus of Nazareth, the son of Joseph" (1:45). Because the Jerusalemites thought that they knew where Jesus came "from," they thereby supposed that they knew his identity. Having already faced the charge that his parents were known (6:42), Jesus now met the accusation that he was from an obscure village and region without sig-

nificance in messianic prophecy, a particular liability in the eyes of residents from the most famous religious city of the world. In both cases the issue was that of origins, a favorite Johannine theological theme.

In reply, Jesus indirectly asked two related questions with gentle irony, *You know me, and you know where I come from?* At the earthly level each part might be answered affirmatively, but at a deeper level both queries required a negative response. Contrary to customary presuppositions, Jesus could not be understood in terms of heredity (parentage) and/or environment (place) because his life was not lived of his *own accord* but in terms of a transcendent imperative. Despite the basic Jewish claim to know God in a way that the heathen did not, Jesus dared to charge (in the Temple!) that they did *not know* the one who *sent* him and thus were ignorant of the central clue to his very existence. By contrast, Jesus could claim to *know* God in the personal relationship of mission (*I come/he sent*).

As the discussion shifted from the work of Jesus to his person, the reaction of the Jews became increasingly hostile. Stung both by the accusation that they did not truly know God and by the inference that Jesus knew him uniquely, the citizens of Jerusalem decided to wait no longer for the authorities to act but took matters into their own hands and *sought to arrest him.* However, his *hour had not yet come* when all the issues would be clarified and his death seen in its true significance, thus their mob action proved abortive, perhaps because *many of the people* still *believed in him* because of the *signs* which he had *done.*

(4) Conflict over the Destination of Jesus (7:32-36)

32 The Pharisees heard the crowd thus muttering about him, and the chief priests and Pharisees sent officers to arrest him. 33 Jesus then said, "I shall be with you a little longer, and then I go to him who sent me; 34 you will seek me and you will not find me; where I am you cannot come." 35 The Jews said to one another, "Where does this man intend to go

that we shall not find him? Does he intend to go to the Dispersion among the Greeks and teach the Greeks? ³⁶ What does he mean by saying, 'You will seek me and you will not find me,' and, 'Where I am you cannot come'?"

Once *the Pharisees heard* about the impatience of the *crowd* to silence Jesus, they formed an alliance with the *chief priests,* and this fateful coalition *sent officers to arrest him.* The Pharisees were the leaders of popular piety centered in the synagogues, whereas the chief priests belonged to the aristocratic Saducean families who drew their strength from control of the Jerusalem Temple. Together the two groups held a balance of power within the Sanhedrin; thus they could easily arrange for the arrest even of a provocative public figure such as Jesus (cf. 11:47,53,57). Normally, the devout Pharisees had little to do with the more worldly chief priests, but in this instance they were united by opposition to one who seemed to threaten the entire religious establishment.

In the face of such formidable foes Jesus now began to speak of his earthly life as near its end: *I shall be with you a little longer* (cf. 16:16–24), *and then I go to him who sent me.* The natural corollary of being sent was to return; expressed spatially, the descent to earth implied the ascent back to heaven. The "whence" and the "whither" of Jesus belong together as twin aspects essential to an understanding of Johannine Christology.

At this dramatic moment when the arresting party was tracking him down, when some in the divided crowd sought him in curiosity while others reacted in faith, doubt, or derision, Jesus responded with the enigmatic pronouncement, *You will seek me and you will not find me; where I am you cannot come.* At first sight it seemed quite obvious that he could easily be found. After all, was he not at that moment the most notorious person in the city? Thus *the Jews* wondered aloud just *where* he might *go* that they could not *find* him. Since Tabernacles was the pilgrim festival par excellence to which many Jews

from *the Dispersion* journeyed, this suggested the possibility that Jesus might try to escape to the regions beyond Palestine. Since he had already been exposed as a false teacher within Israel, the Jews contemptuously supposed that he would have to flee to *the Greeks* and see if he could *teach* them.

In this answer, of course, the Jews did not reckon with a destination beyond the boundaries of time and space, and so they completely failed to fathom that he would go to the Father with whom he had always been (note the unusual use of *I am* in v. 36). And yet, ironically, they spoke far more truth than they could imagine (cf. 11:49–52) for in going to heaven Jesus did go to the "Dispersion" among the Greeks. By his ascension, Jesus launched the Christian mission enterprise which went quickly beyond both Palestinian and Diaspora Judaism to the other nations of the Hellenistic world.

(5) *The Offer of Living Water* (7:37–39)

³⁷ On the last day of the feast, the great day, Jesus stood up and proclaimed, "If any one thirst, let him come to me and drink. ³⁸ He who believes in me, as the scripture has said, 'Out of his heart shall flow rivers of living water.'" ³⁹ Now this he said about the Spirit, which those who believed in him were to receive; for as yet the Spirit had not been given, because Jesus was not yet glorified.

When the *last day of the feast* of Tabernacles arrived, Jesus decided to make use of its dramatic symbolism to present himself as the Water of life. At this point a very difficult problem of punctuation complicates the interpretation of the words used to assert this claim. At least three different understandings of the passage are possible (cf. the RSV text and footnote and the NEB text and footnote):

First, Jesus may be identified as the source of the living water by paraphrasing: "If any one thirsts, let him come to me; in other words, let the one who believes in me drink (of my water). This would be in accordance with the scripture that said, 'Out of his (i.e., Jesus') heart shall flow rivers of living water.'" In favor of this interpretation is 4:10,14a, where Jesus offers to give living water; 7:39, where water = the Spirit that Jesus will later give (20:22); 19:34, where water flowed from the pierced side of Jesus; and Revelation 22:1, where "the river of the water of life" flowed "from the throne of God and of the Lamb" (Jesus).

Second, the believer becomes the source of living water when the paraphrase is punctuated: "If any one thirst, let him come to me and drink. The one who does so by believing in me is aptly described in the scripture which said, 'Out of his (i.e., the believer's) heart shall flow rivers of living water.'" Supporting this interpretation are the best known commentaries and translations (e.g., the KJV-RSV tradition), although scriptural corroboration is limited. In 4:14b Jesus spoke of a spring of water welling up within the believer (cf. Isa. 58:11), but that reference does not make explicit that the spring will become a source of sustenance for others.

Third, it is possible and even probable that the scriptural citation from the Old Testament was loosely attached to the pronouncement of Jesus which precedes it, either by Jesus at that time or by the Evangelist at a later time (note that v. 39 is clearly an explanatory addition by the Evangelist). As a supplement to the saying of Jesus in vv. 37b–38a, rather than as an integral part, the antecedent of **his heart** would be determined primarily by the original context of this citation in the Old Testament and only secondarily by its acquired context in John. Approached in this fashion, the source of the living water may be taken to be neither Jesus nor the believer but God himself, as will become clear below from our study of the background of the scriptural citation.

To reconstruct: the core of Jesus' proclamation was probably a Hebrew couplet in poetic parallelism which we may translate literally:

"If any one thirst, let him come to me,
And let drink the one who believes
    in me."

This invitation was to be understood, however, not as the proposal of an isolated individual acting on his own authority but as the fulfillment of the scriptural promise that God would give rivers of living water to provide drink and abundance for his people. Worshipers at Tabernacles who had already celebrated God's gift of rain in nature for their crops and had commemorated God's gift of water in history for the Exodus pilgrims were called now to look neither to the skies nor to a rock but to the person of Jesus as the mediator of those divine resources that could quench their own spiritual thirst.

The interpretation of this passage is complicated not only by the problem of punctuation but by the difficulty of identifying *the scripture* cited in v. 38b. As was also true of the text on "bread from heaven" in 6:31, the exact wording, **Out of his heart shall flow rivers of living water,** is not found in the Old Testament but appears to be a summary of many similar passages, particularly in the prophets, which use thirst (i.e., drought, aridity, infertility) and water (i.e., rain, wells, springs) as metaphors for human longings and their fulfillment (e.g., Isa. 12:3; 43:18–21; 55:1; 58:11). Three particular themes recur: water flowed from the rock in the wilderness for the Exodus pilgrims (Psalms 78:15–16; 105:41; Isa. 48:21); water will flow out from the Jerusalem Temple to irrigate the surrounding desert (Ezek. 47:1–12; Joel 3:18; Zech. 14:8); the Spirit will be poured forth like water on a thirsty land (Isa. 44:3; Joel 2:28).

In none of these verses is it actually stated that water shall flow like rivers **out of** someone's **heart** (koilia, lit., belly). However, this expression is a Semitic idiom referring to the seat of one's emotions and so is here equivalent to saying that the water will come from a person's innermost self. All of the passages listed above quite clearly imply that God himself is the ultimate source of "streams in the desert." As Creator he pours water on the thirsty land, while as Redeemer he pours his blessings on the true Israel (Isa. 44:3). This means that Jesus was claiming to function in the same way as God when he offered himself at the Temple as the one from whom believers could drink.

True to his principles of interpretation (cf. 2:22; 12:16), the Evangelist was concerned to present this crucial claim not only in relation to Jesus and to Scripture but to the life of the church as well. Thus he explains that this metaphor of living water was really a way of talking *about the Spirit, which those who believed in him were to receive.* To be sure, *the Spirit had not yet been given* as a separate reality while Jesus was still with his followers in the flesh, for during that time their experience of the Spirit was inseparable from their experience of Jesus (cf. 1:33; 3:5,13,31,34). But after Jesus was *glorified* in the resurrection and ascended to the Father in heaven, the Spirit was given to believers in a way clearly distinguishable in their experience from the incarnate presence of Jesus on earth (cf. 14:25–26; 16:7). Christians reading this Gospel should realize that in their being indwelt of the Holy Spirit they have the living water of which Jesus spoke and thus confirm in their own experience the truth of his claim.

(6) The Reaction of the People (7:40–44)

40 When they heard these words, some of the people said, "This is really the prophet." 41 Others said, "This is the Christ." But some said, "Is the Christ to come from Galilee? 42 Has not the scripture said that the Christ is descended from David, and comes from Bethlehem, the village where David was?" 43 So there was a division among the people over him. 44 Some of them wanted to arrest him, but no one laid hands on him.

In claiming to be the Water of life, Jesus had spoken very simply and directly ("come to me . . . believe in me") without using any impressive titles to call attention to himself. Jewish theology of the day, however, was rife with complex and often fanciful theories as to the identity and credentials of the Messiah. Despite the reluctance of Jesus to indulge in such speculations, *the people* immediately began to measure his *words* in the light of their preconceptions. So concerned were they to analyze the proffered water that they never took time to drink it!

Thinking perhaps of Moses, who brought forth water by striking a rock in the wilderness, some supposed that Jesus might *really* be *the prophet* promised in Deuteronomy 18:15–18, while others were prepared to identify him as *the Christ* (Messiah). This latter verdict, however, clashed with the knowledge that Jesus was *from Galilee* (cf. 6:42; 7:27,52), whereas *the scripture said that the Christ is descended from David* (e.g., 2 Sam. 7:12–13; Psalm 89:3–4; Jer. 23:5) *and comes from Bethlehem, the village where David was* (cf. Mic. 5:2; Matt. 2:4,6).[23]

As is often the case, the result of this speculative theological debate was *a division among the people* over Jesus (cf. 9:16; 10:19). *Some of them wanted to arrest him,* particularly those Jerusalemites who were influenced by the official opposition to Jesus (cf. vv. 25,30), but *no one laid hands on him,* largely because his mighty works (vv. 21,31) and commanding authority (v. 46) had won him support among the pilgrims to the feast. Apparently the people had been polarized into two groups. At one extreme were those so committed to a particular set of inherited messianic expectations that they were not open to the uniqueness of Jesus as an act of God in the present. At the other extreme were those who were completely open to an impressive display of power from the latest religious leader but who, lacking any theological rootage, were fickle in their sudden enthusiasms.

(7) The Reaction of the Leaders (7:45–52)

45 The officers then went back to the chief priests and Pharisees, who said to them, "Why did you not bring him?" 46 The officers answered, "No man ever spoke like this man!" 47 The Pharisees answered them, "Are you led astray, you also? 48 Have any of the authorities or of the Pharisees believed in him? 49 But this crowd, who do not know the law, are ac-

23 On the themes of prophet and Christ, here and in the Jewish background, see Meeks, pp. 32–61.

cursed." 50 Nicodemus, who had gone to him before, and who was one of them, said to them, 51 "Does our law judge a man without first giving him a hearing and learning what he does?" 52 They replied, "Are you from Galilee too? Search and you will see that no prophet is to arise from Galilee."

The crowd was not the only group that shrank back from arresting Jesus (v. 44). Earlier in the feast, *the chief priests and Pharisees* had sent *officers* to accomplish this very task (v. 32), but now they went back to report that their mission had been a failure. When asked in exasperation *why* they had not brought Jesus, these armed constables admitted that they had been paralyzed by the power of his words. Never had they heard a mere *man* speak with such authority, i.e., as rabbi, prophet, and Messiah combined! Although they knew that he had no authorized credentials, they could not gainsay the impact of his teachings.

Incensed by this unsolicited testimony from their own forces, *the Pharisees* accused the Temple police of being *led astray* along with the populace (cf. v. 12). This charge reflects the basic reason for the opposition of the religious leadership to Jesus. They were not merely intolerant of his personal claims but were deeply concerned over the excitement he was arousing among the masses. As members of the Sanhedrin, they were held responsible by the Romans for any messianic movements that threatened to disrupt the peace. Better to silence one disturber than to lose all of their hard-earned privileges granted by Rome (cf. 11:47-50).

In order to coerce conformity to the status quo, the establishment was determined to present a united front: *Have any of the authorities or of the Pharisees believed in him?* How powerfully the pressures of group membership can inhibit individual decision (cf. 12:42–43). Moreover, when that group occupies places of great responsibility, how hard it is for them to be open to radical change (cf. 3:1–15). All too easily an inbred elite can become contemptuous of the masses and suppose that nothing significant is ever initiated at the grassroots level. In the case of the Pharisees, an aristocracy (or meritocracy) of training caused them to dismiss the *crowd* as *accursed* "rabble" (NEB) who did *not know the law* and therefore whose support of Jesus was worthless.

But *one* of their number, *Nicodemus,* had known Jesus at closer range (3:1–15) and was not so easily convinced by this refusal to judge the case on its own merits. To those proud of their knowledge of the law he pointed out that their very procedures were violating the law by judging Jesus *without first giving him a hearing and learning what he does.* Instead of answering this valid protest, the Pharisees turned upon their colleague with the retort, *Are you from Galilee too?*—as if being from a certain region were any basis for supporting Jesus (cf. on v. 27). Although many prophets had come from Galilee in the past (e.g., Jonah; cf. 2 Kings 14:25), Nicodemus was reminded that a *search* of the Scriptures would reveal no passage predicting that the great eschatological *prophet* (v. 40) was *to rise from Galilee.* How easily one may sidestep the self-evident claims of God by a proof-text approach to the Bible!

4. The Judge of Life (8:12–59)

Chapters 7 and 8 are closely connected in historical background, literary form, and theological content, a unity which is seen more clearly when the interpolation in 7:53—8:11 is removed. Both sections are set in the Jerusalem Temple (7:14,28; 8:20,59) during the Feast of Tabernacles (7:2,37; cf. "again" in 8:12). They consist largely of polemical material arranged in brief units which convey to the reader an impression that he is overhearing snatches of a running debate between Jesus and the Jews. John 7 begins and John 8 ends with references to messianic secrecy, this motif clamping the two chapters together in thematic fashion.

The Feast of Tabernacles featured not only the ritual of water libation (lying behind chapter 7) but also the ceremony of lights which provided the background for chapter 8 (Mishnah, *Sukkah*, 5:2–4). On the first night of the festival, and perhaps later, giant golden candlesticks erected in the Court of Women were lit by setting fire to cloth wicks in four golden bowls atop each of them. So radiant was the light that every courtyard in Jerusalem was said to be illumined. At the Temple, pious men sang and danced as they juggled firebrands in a dazzling display of color and pageantry. Falling at the autumnal equinox, the agricultural significance of this rite was a plea for the dark winter months to be followed by sun for crops in the spring (cf. Zech. 14:6–8, where light and water are both closely connected to the seasons). Historically, the drama commemorated the guidance of God in leading Israel through the wilderness with a pillar of fire by night (Ex. 13:21).

In this setting, Jesus identified himself as "the light of the world" (v. 12), parallel to his earlier proclamation as the water of life (7:37). Utilizing these basic agricultural analogies, he announced that he was as indispensable to the development of the human spirit as rain and sun are to the cultivation of earthly crops. Moreover, he offered to lead Israel in a new exodus from spiritual bondage (cf. vv. 32–36), thus declaring himself greater than the rock which provided water and the pillar of fire that furnished light in the wilderness. The time had come to move beyond symbol to reality in worship. Jesus not only became the true temple (cf. 2:19–22) but offered himself as the fulfillment of its most sacred festivals and of the Scriptures which they sought to dramatize.

The initial theme of light is used to describe a dynamic process of sifting precipitated by the ministry of Jesus. Ironically, as the Jews moved toward a negative consensus in their judgment of Jesus (vv. 13,22,41,48,52–3) and the danger to his life steadily mounted (vv. 20,37,40,59), his enemies thereby condemned themselves for their blindness in the face of the Light of the world.

For sheer bitterness, John 8 is unrivaled in this or any other Gospel. The Jews charged Jesus with egotism (v. 13), suicidal tendencies (v. 22), illegitimacy (vv. 19,41), and insanity (vv. 48,52). Jesus, in

Text and Commentary (7:53—8:11)

53 *They went each to his own house,* 1 *but Jesus went to the Mount of Olives.* 2 *Early in the morning he came again to the temple; all the people came to him, and he sat down and taught them.* 3 *The scribes and the Pharisees brought a woman who had been caught in adultery, and placing her in the midst* 4 *they said to him, "Teacher, this woman has been caught in the act of adultery.* 5 *Now in the law Moses commanded us to stone such. What do you say about her?"* 6 *This they said to test him, that they might have some charge to bring against him. Jesus bent down and wrote with his finger on the ground.* 7 *And as they continued to ask him, he stood up and said to them, "Let him who is without sin among you be the first to throw a stone a her."* 8 *And once more he bent down and wrote with his finger on the ground.* 9 *But when they heard it, they went away, one by one, beginning with the eldest, and Jesus was left alone with the woman standing before him.* 10 *Jesus looked up and said to her, "Woman, where are they? Has no one condemned you?"* 11 *She said, "No one, Lord." And Jesus said, "Neither do I condemn you; go, and do not sin again."*

This passage is not printed in the RSV text though it appears in the margin, because the available evidence demonstrates conclusively that it was a later addition to the Gospel of John. The overwhelming majority of the best Greek manuscripts omit this section entirely, while some of the others which include it do so either with a special marking (e.g., asterisk, obelus) or at various locations (e.g., after John 21:24 or Luke 21:38). Almost entirely unknown in the East during the first millennium, the passage is attested primarily in the Western or Latin textual tradition and by the great mass of late medieval Greek manuscripts. From these two sources, however, the passage found its way into both the Vulgate and the KJV, thereby becoming widely known throughout Christendom.

Internal evidence confirms the verdict of external evidence that this passage was not originally a part of the fourth Gospel. The style of the story is more Lukan than Johannine. The setting fits well with Synoptic descriptions of Jesus' last week in Jerusalem (compare the striking similarities between John 8:1–2 and Luke 21:37–38). Perhaps the account was eventually inserted here because it took place in the Temple (8:2; cf. 7:14,28; 8:20,59) and illustrated the way in which Jesus "judged no one" (8:15).

There is no reason to doubt the substantial authenticity of the story. Although it was probably never intended to be a part of any of the four canonical Gospels, the early church found its value to be so great that it was included at various points in the record to ensure its continuing survival. When studying the Gospel of John, however, the reader should move directly from 7:52 to 8:12 and not allow this insertion to obscure the close connection between these two chapters.

turn, accused them of not knowing God (v. 19), of dying in sin (v. 21), and—as children of the devil—of being murderers and liars (vv. 37,40,44). Such polemical language is not limited to this Gospel (cf. Matt. 23:15) but is particularly prominent here because John 8 was written when the clash between synagogue and church was at its fiercest. In an era when Christianity was just beginning to define its independence and Judaism was struggling for its very survival, it was not difficult to remember and to express in the most extreme form those clashes which had produced the irreparable break between Jesus and his contemporaries.

Because of the miscellaneous character of the material, its internal design is difficult to determine. On the whole, 8:12–59 is a succession of five scenarios in each of which controversy is prompted by one or more provocative sayings of Jesus. The unifying theme is that of judgment. After an opening paragraph on the authority and validity of Jesus to judge (vv. 12–20), the argument next considers the urgency (vv. 21–30), the effect (vv. 31–38), and the standards (vv. 39–47) of his judgment. The section then closes with a claim that Jesus' judgment is a matter of life or death because of his unique relationship to God (vv. 48–59).

(1) The Credentials of the Judge (8: 12–20)

12 Again Jesus spoke to them, saying, "I am the light of the world; he who follows me will not walk in darkness, but will have the light of life." 13 The Pharisees then said to him, "You are bearing witness to yourself; your testimony is not true." 14 Jesus answered, "Even if I do bear witness to myself, my testimony is true, for I know whence I have come and whither I am going, but you do not know whence I come or whither I am going. 15 You judge according to the flesh, I judge no one. 16 Yet even if I do judge, my judgment is true, for it is not I alone that judge, but I and he who sent me. 17 In your law it is written that the testimony of two men is true; 18 I bear witness to myself, and the Father who sent me bears witness to me." 19 They said to him therefore, "Where is your Father?" Jesus answered, "You know neither me nor my Father; if you knew me, you would know my Father also." 20 These words he spoke in the treasury, as he taught in the temple; but no one arrested him, because his hour had not yet come.

At an unspecified time during the Feast of Tabernacles, Jesus again challenged his hearers in the Temple with a companion claim to 7:37 by announcing, I am (egō eimi) the light of the world (cf. 9:5; 12:46). Against a backdrop of rejection by the leaders of Israel (7:45–52), Jesus defiantly insisted that he who follows me (cf. 1:43), instead of the Jewish authorities, will not walk in their spiritual darkness (seen so clearly in 7:52), but will have the light of life (cf. 1:4–5).

Choosing to debate his very first words, I am, the Pharisees saw in them not a veiled claim to divinity but an expression of personal egotism, You are bearing witness to yourself. In reply, Jesus argued that even though he did so—certainly not in a self-seeking fashion (cf. 5:30–31)—his testimony was nevertheless true because, unlike them, he knew both whence he had come and whither he was going (twin themes clarified in 7:25–36). Most men make unreliable judgments because they are creatures of the present who can neither reconstruct the past nor anticipate the future. Consequently, they judge according to the flesh, i.e., in the light of what they can see on an earthly level at any given moment (cf. 7:24). By contrast, Jesus evaluated everything in an eternal context, combining hindsight with foresight to achieve insight that transcended the tangible and the transient.

As the light of the world, Jesus was not only a true witness (cf. 1:6–8) but a true judge as well. In vv. 15b–16a, two apparently contradictory statements provide the clue to the dialectical character of this role: I judge no one. Yet . . . I do judge. On the one hand, Jesus had not come to judge (cf. 3:17; 12:47) in the condemnatory sense of evaluating men according to the flesh, i.e., by outward appearances (cf. 7:24). On the other hand, Jesus had come to judge (cf.

5:22; 9:39) in the sense of confronting men with a life and death decision. This judgment sprang from no effort to establish his own superiority but from a complete identity of function with God: *For it is not I alone that judge, but I and he who sent me.*

The coordinate activity of Jesus and God also helped to meet the intent of the Jewish *law* which prescribed that *the testimony* of at least *two men* was needed to establish what was *true* in criminal cases (e.g., Num. 35:30; Deut. 17:6; 19:15). In this instance, Jesus himself bore one veracious witness (vv. 13–14), while his Father bore the other. At the level of faith this argument was completely convincing, for no two witnesses could be more trustworthy than God and his unique Son. At the level of Jewish trial procedure, however, this reasoning was highly suspect because the law normally stipulated two or three witnesses other than the accused. Since Jesus, the accused, was the only witness the Jews could see, this meant that he had no corroborating testimony at all.

In unusual cases, however, the rabbis did permit evidence to be established by the person in question plus one other witness; thus the Jews asked, *Where is your Father?* to see if Jesus could produce this additional support. Although the Galileans had claimed to know his earthly father, Joseph (6:42), the Jerusalemites were either ignorant of parentage or suspicious of its legitimacy (cf. 8:41). More serious, they misunderstood what had been a reference to his heavenly *Father* because they did not truly *know* him. This failure was based on an inability to understand Jesus spiritually, for to know him was to *know* his *Father also.* In Jewish eyes that claim was sheer blasphemy deserving of death, but *no one arrested him* for making it because *his hour had not yet come.*

(2) The Cruciality of His Judgment (8:21–30)

21 Again he said to them, "I go away, and you will seek me and die in your sin; where I am going, you cannot come." 22 Then said the Jews, "Will he kill himself, since he says, 'Where I am going, you cannot come'?" 23 He said to them, "You are from below, I am from above; you are of this world, I am not of this world. 24 I told you that you would die in your sins, for you will die in your sins unless you believe that I am he." 25 They said to him, "Who are you?" Jesus said to them, "Even what I have told you from the beginning. 26 I have much to say about you and much to judge; but he who sent me is true, and I declare to the world what I have heard from him." 27 They did not understand that he spoke to them of the Father. 28 So Jesus said, "When you have lifted up the Son of man, then you will know that I am he, and that I do nothing on my own authority but speak thus as the Father taught me. 29 And he who sent me is with me; he has not left me alone, for I always do what is pleasing to him." 30 As he spoke thus, many believed in him.

A note of urgency is introduced into the Temple debates by the resumption of the departure motif developed in 7:32–36 and by defining its sinister implications for Jesus' hearers. Soon he would *go away* by returning to heaven and they would seek him in vain because they knew not the Father. As one *from above* (i.e., *not of this world*), he was going where those *from below* (i.e., *of this world*) could not come (cf. 3:6,31; 6:63). The first time this theme was introduced, the Jews misunderstood Jesus to mean that he would "go to the Dispersion among the Greeks" (7:35), whereas here they supposed that he would put himself beyond their reach by committing suicide.

This hypothesis represented a tragic distortion of Jesus' efforts to warn his antagonists that the time was short to accept his offer of salvation. If they forced his departure from this world by lifting him up on the cross (cf. v. 28), they would *die* in their *sin* of finally rejecting the redemption which he offered (cf. Mark 3:28–29). Such spiritual death was inevitable if they refused to accept the one who gave "living" water (7:38) and was the light of "life" (8:12). Their only hope was to *believe* that he was the divine "*I am,*" the one in whom the eternal being of the life-giving God had been manifested among men.

Once again, by an even more serious misunderstanding, the Jews failed to recognize in this absolute use of *ego eimi* the Old Testament formula for a theophany of the self-existent God (cf. Ex. 3:14; Isa. 41:4; 48:12). Hearing Jesus say simply "I am" (not *I am he*, RSV), and supposing that he would add some predicate such as "the light of the world" (as in v. 12), they replied, *Who are you?* (or "You are *who?*"). There was no way for Jesus to answer this obtuseness except to stand by what he had *told* them *from the beginning*. Because of their negative response, there was much that he could have said about them of a judgmental nature; but he would refrain both because such matters could be left in the hands of the One sending him, who was *true* (cf. v. 50), and because his mission was to *declare to the world* what he had *heard* from his Father, not what he thought of his enemies.

Even though Jesus continued to magnify God, he knew that the "hour" would soon arrive when as Son of man he would ascend to the place from whence he had come by being *lifted up* on the cross. In that supreme hour of revelation, surely some of his hearers would come to *know* that he was the great *I am* who represented God so completely that he did *nothing on* his *own authority* but spoke only as *the Father* had *taught* him (cf. 7:16). But regardless of the response, the One who *sent* him never *left* him *alone* for Jesus *always* did *what* was *pleasing to him*. Moved by this utterly transparent confession of devotion to God, many were persuaded to believe in Jesus.

(3) The Consequences of His Judgment (8:31–38)

³¹ Jesus then said to the Jews who had believed in him, "If you continue in my word, you are truly my disciples, ³² and you will know the truth, and the truth will make you free." ³³ They answered him, "We are descendants of Abraham, and have never been in bondage to any one. How is it that you say, 'You will be made free'?"

³⁴ Jesus answered them, "Truly, truly, I say to you, every one who commits sin is a slave to sin. ³⁵ The slave does not continue in the house for ever; the son continues for ever. ³⁶ So if the Son makes you free, you will be free indeed. ³⁷ I know that you are descendants of Abraham; yet you seek to kill me, because my word finds no place in you. ³⁸ I speak of what I have seen with my Father, and you do what you have heard from your father."

The opening words of this paragraph present a problem because *the Jews* who are here said to have *believed in* Jesus will soon be called children of the devil who are trying to kill him (vv. 43–44). Three factors may help to explain this puzzling turn in the narrative.

First, the author has made a slight but significant adjustment from v. 30, where many believed "in him" (*eis auton*), to v. 31, where the Jews believed *him* (*auto*). Unfortunately, this shift from the accusative to the dative is not indicated by the RSV translation of both phrases as *believed in him*. Since this distinction is generally meaningful throughout the Gospel, the writer may be suggesting that the Jews of v. 31 had come to give intellectual credence to certain doctrinal propositions about Jesus but that they did not share that higher form of faith which lodged personal trust in him.

Second, Jesus himself accepted the faith of v. 31 as conditional. These believers would *truly* be his disciples only *if they continue in* his *word*. Obviously there were many with the name disciple who failed to do just that (6:66). Jesus clearly recognized the possibility of a halfway house of faith and cherished no illusions regarding its adequacy (cf. on 2:23–25). If one from the innermost circle of the chosen twelve was a devil (6:70), then some from a fickle following in Jerusalem could certainly prove to be the same!

Third, events in the church at the time when this Gospel was written confirmed the possibility that "believers" could turn out to be children of the devil. In 1 John, the author was faced with the need of devising tests to distinguish true faith from false. There were those within the church who continued to commit sin (1 John 3:8; cf. John 8:21,24) and so were "children of the devil" rather than "children of God" (1 John 3:10; cf. John 8:38,41–42,44). Some members "hated" their Christian brethren and so were spiritual "murderers" like Cain, "who was of the evil one and murdered his brother" (1 John 3:11–13; cf. John 8:44). These striking parallels show that the situation which Jesus faced was but the historical archetype of that internal conflict that sifts the people of God in every generation.[24]

Aware that the precarious spiritual position of those *Jews who had believed in him* was much like that of Israel during its wilderness wanderings, Jesus offered them the possibility of true freedom from bondage. If they would "abide" (RSV, *continue*) in his teaching they would thereby come to know God's *truth,* which is not a set of timeless ideas but a dynamic power that can *make* men *free.* Contrary to the frequent use of this verse as an academic slogan, the promise is not made that education as such results in freedom from spiritual bondage. Unwilling to admit even the need for such liberation, which shows that their believing involved a changed view of Jesus without a changed view of themselves, the Jews replied that as the spiritual heirs of Abraham they had *never been in bondage to any one.* In a political sense, of course, they had often been enslaved, and were so by Rome at that very time, but they had never capitulated to the foreign deities of their captors.

In meeting this objection, Jesus developed his teaching on bondage and freedom in relation to the concepts of slavery and sonship. Since evil is not the violation of an abstract rule but submission to a personal tyrant (v. 44), *every one who commits sin is a slave to sin* (cf. Rom. 6:12–18; Gal. 4:3,8–9; 5:1). Such slavery would make it impossible to fulfill the basic condition of discipleship, *If you continue in my word,* because *the slave does not continue in the house for ever; the son continues for ever.* At least two circumstances may have prompted the inclusion of the little parable of slave and son in v. 35 to illustrate the importance of continuing in the house for ever.

First, an Old Testament story of Abraham related how Ishmael, his slave son by Hagar, was driven out while Isaac, his free son by Sarah, retained permanent tenure (Gen. 21:9–14; cf. Paul's treatment of this typology in Gal. 4:21–31). Those who boasted that they were *descendants of Abraham* should ponder whether they were sons of the Ishmael-type or the Isaac-type! In this case, the difference would not be determined by whether their mother happened to be Hagar or Sarah but by whether they were willing for *the Son* to make them sons who would be *free indeed* to dwell in the Father's house. Second, the writer may have known of a parallel situation in the early church in which some had gone "out from us," i.e., left the Christian fellowship. "If they had been of us, they would have *continued* with us," but their departure from the household of God made plain that they were "not of us" (1 John 2:19).

In the case of his Jewish contemporaries, Jesus readily conceded that they were *descendants of Abraham* in a physical sense, but their reaction to him showed that Abraham was not their *father* in a spiritual sense.[25] In Jewish thought, this greatest of the patriarchs was venerated as a model of righteousness (Gen. 18:19; 26:5; Ecclus. 44:19), whereas his offspring now sought to *kill* Jesus. During his own lifetime, Abraham gladly received the Lord when he came to visit in human form (Gen. 18:1–15), but now the *word* of one who spoke only of what he had *seen with God* found *no place in* Abraham's progeny. Old

---

24 On the setting of this section more broadly in the Judaistic struggles of the early church, see C. H. Dodd, *More New Testament Studies,* pp. 41–57.

25 The distinction between true and false descendants of Abraham was also maintained in the rabbinic tradition; cf. Mishnah, *Aboth* 5:19, and *Midrash Rabbah* on Genesis 21:12.

Testament theology represented Abraham as the one through whom Israel would become a worldwide blessing (Gen. 12:1–3; 18:18; 22:17–18), but now his race was on the verge of putting out the "light of the world" (v. 12). Clearly they were doing *what* they had *heard from* a *father* who was neither Abraham nor the *Father* of Jesus.

(4) The Criterion of His Judgment (8: 39–47)

39 They answered him, "Abraham is our father." Jesus said to them, "If you were Abraham's children, you would do what Abraham did, 40 but now you seek to kill me, a man who has told you the truth which I heard from God; this is not what Abraham did. 41 You do what your father did." They said to him, "We were not born of fornication; we have one Father, even God." 42 Jesus said to them, "If God were your Father, you would love me, for I proceeded and came forth from God; I came not of my own accord, but he sent me. 43 Why do you not understand what I say? It is because you cannot bear to hear my word. 44 You are of your father the devil, and your will is to do your father's desires. He was a murderer from the beginning, and has nothing to do with the truth, because there is no truth in him. When he lies, he speaks according to his own nature, for he is a liar and the father of lies. 45 But, because I tell the truth, you do not believe me. 46 Which of you convicts me of sin? If I tell the truth, why do you not believe me? 47 He who is of God hears the words of God; the reason why you do not hear them is that you are not of God."

Faced with the personal alternatives of bondage or freedom, slavery or sonship, the Jews clung tenaciously to that sense of racial solidarity which provided their greatest sense of pride and privilege (cf. Matt. 3:7–10). The implied suggestion that their paternity might be otherwise was met with the firm insistence, *Abraham is our father,* to which Jesus simply repeated the negative argument of v. 37, that he could see no spiritual kinship between *what Abraham did* and their desire to *kill* him, as well as the positive argument of v. 38 that they *do what* their *father did.* The laws of heredity are as consistent in the spiritual sphere as in the physical: "Like father, like son."

Stung to anger that a fellow Jew would

attack their Abrahamic theology (cf. Matt. 8:11–12; Luke 16:19–31), the disputants replied with two arguments of their own. Negatively, they denied that they were *born of fornication.* This may have been a claim much like v. 33 that they had never been apostate in the prophetic sense of spiritual adultery (e.g., Hosea 1:2; 2:4,13; 4:15), or it could have been an oblique defamation of Jesus' own birth as illegitimate (cf. v. 19). Positively, they decided to transcend the whole debate over human antecedents by identifying their *one* spiritual *Father* not as Abraham but as *God.*

Rather than rebutting the ugly implications of their statement about fornication, Jesus used the occasion to clarify his true relation to God. More important than the circumstances of his earthly birth was the fact that he *proceeded and came forth from God,* and that *not of* his *own accord* but as one on a divine mission. So inseparable were sender and sent that *if God* actually *were* the Jews' *Father*—a condition manifestly untrue—they *would love* his Son also. But such an intimate relation to God was beyond their ability to *understand.* They were not able to comprehend what Jesus said because they could not *bear to hear* the divine *word* (Gr. *logos*) which was being articulated by his spoken words (Gr. *lalia*). They were obediently attentive to whatever their own "father" said (v. 38b) but were deaf to the message of the heavenly Father conveyed through Jesus.

The reason for this complete dichotomy was immediately clarified by the identification of their *father* as *the devil* whose *desires* it was their *will . . . to do.* In contrast to Jesus, who "from the beginning" had been the source of divine life (vv. 24–25), this ultimate adversary had *from the beginning* been a *murderer* for he brought death into the Garden of Eden (Gen. 3:1–19) and prompted Cain to slay his brother Abel (cf. 1 John 3:8,12,15). Although Jesus offered men the saving truth (v. 32) which he himself told, the devil had *nothing to do with the truth* but was, by nature, *a liar and the father of lies.*

Here, then, was the deepest reason why

even those who believed Jesus to be a man of incredible spiritual commitment (v. 31) did not themselves *believe* the *truth* of God when he applied it to their lives: because only *he who is of God* really *hears the words of God,* whereas they were *not of God,* but of their father, the devil.

At first reading, this line of argument attributed to Jesus may deeply offend the sensibilities of those who recoil from condemning any man as a pawn in the hands of Satan. The problem lies more with a failure to understand first-century thought forms than with such Faustian theology. Jesus did not deduce that certain men were fated to live evil lives because they were enslaved by the devil; quite the opposite, he induced from their actual conduct that they must serve such a tyrant and that it was their own *will to do* so. That such bondage was voluntary and could be broken by true belief in Jesus was the point of his whole appeal (vv. 31–2,36,46).

Actually, behind all of these sobering accusations lay the merciful recognition that men themselves are not the sole cause of all their problems. The issue is not simply who a man *is* but who he is *of* (i.e., of God or of the devil, v. 47). Jesus recognized that men could be victimized by forces outside their lives: the binding power of religious tradition, of national pride, of racial prejudice. As he moved toward the hour of supreme conflict, increasingly the devil—not some little group of misguided men—became his chief antagonist (12:31–33; 16:33). The good news in this forbiddingly dark passage is that Jesus died to break the grip of cosmic evil on individual lives. The man who thinks that he alone is the cause of his problems usually supposes that he alone can overcome them, whereas the man who discovers that he is a child of the devil is best prepared to discover in Jesus the only one who can break that hideous strength (cf. on 6:70–71).

(5) The Claim of the Judge (8:48–59)

48 The Jews answered him, "Are we not right in saying that you are a Samaritan and have a demon?" 49 Jesus answered, "I have not a demon; but I honor my Father, and you dishonor me. 50 Yet I do not seek my own glory; there is One who seeks it and he will be the judge. 51 Truly, truly, I say to you, if any one keeps my word, he will never see death." 52 The Jews said to him, "Now we know that you have a demon. Abraham died, as did the prophets; and you say, 'If any one keeps my word, he will never taste death.' 53 Are you greater than our father Abraham, who died? And the prophets died! Who do you claim to be?" 54 Jesus answered, "If I glorify myself, my glory is nothing; it is my Father who glorifies me, of whom you say that he is your God. 55 But you have not known him; I know him. If I said, I do not know him, I should be a liar like you; but I do know him and I keep his word. 56 Your father Abraham rejoiced that he was to see my day; he saw it and was glad." 57 The Jews then said to him, "You are not yet fifty years old, and have you seen Abraham?" 58 Jesus said to them, "Truly, truly, I say to you, before Abraham was, I am." 59 So they took up stones to throw at him; but Jesus hid himself, and went out of the temple.

Once Jesus had made explicit that his opponents' spiritual lineage was not of Abraham or of God but of the devil, they replied by accusing him of being *a Samaritan* and having *a demon.* In John 4 Jesus had ignored centuries of prejudice to define a faith not based on racial identity (cf. 4:9,21–23,42); here he may have received a backlash from that breakthrough. In Jewish eyes the Samaritans were half-breed heretics with illegitimate ancestry (cf. 8:41) because of their intermarriage with pagans. As a superstitious people among whom sorcery was rife (cf. Acts 8:9–24), it was easy to suppose that if Jesus were like a Samaritan he would *have a demon* (cf. 7:20). This would mean that his father, not theirs, was the devil. Refusing to be caught in an escalating battle of words, Jesus simply denied the charge, restated the God-centered purpose and spirit by which he lived, and left the issue in the hands of the *One* who would *be the judge* of what was true (cf. v. 26).

Seeking to recover the positive alternative implicit in his initial claim to be the "light of life," Jesus now summarized the issue at stake in the entire discussion: *If any one keeps my word, he will never see death.* For *the Jews,* however, this invitation only confirmed that Jesus had *a demon.* Since the best in Israel including even *Abraham* and the *prophets* had always *died,* because Satan the "murderer" brought death into the world "from the beginning" (an argument advanced by Jesus himself in v. 44!), the offer by Jesus of some magical immunity from death was proof that he was in league with the devil (cf. the parallel line of reasoning in Mark 3:22). Otherwise he would be *greater than* both *Abraham* (cf. 4:12) . . . *and the prophets*—an unthinkable conclusion!

In this exchange (vv. 51–53) two striking differences divided Jesus and the Jews. First, the latter group steadfastly refused to existentialize death as their own spiritual problem but viewed it instead as the physical change which terminates every man's life. Of course, Jesus knew as well as anyone that Abraham and the prophets had died and that each generation would continue to die, but he was concerned to help men discover those realities that survive the dissolution of the body. Further, Jesus showed the proper way to existentialize the spiritual problem of death by making present obedience (i.e., "keeping his word") the basis of future hope. For himself, Jesus was confident of eternal glory not because he had some mystical vision of the beyond but because he was "honoring the Father" then and there.

In answering the thematic question which climaxes the entire chapter, *Who do you claim to be?,* Jesus swiftly recapitulated his main contentions: that his life, unlike theirs, was one that eschewed self-*glory,* that truly knew God, and that kept the *word* of truth. Then, to reinforce the promise that those who kept his word—just as he kept the Father's word—would *never see death,* he returned to the discussion of Abraham in a way that also clarified his own deepest identity. In emphasizing that *Abraham died,* the Jews had overlooked two ways in which their own theology taught that the patriarch transcended *death.* To begin with, even during his

earthly lifetime Abraham was permitted to *see* by faith the *day* of the Messiah and thereby anticipate the triumphant consummation of the promises made to him (cf. Gen. 2:15–18 as interpreted in Gal. 3:16; 2 Esdras 3:14; Rom. 4:16–21; Heb. 11:8–19). Moreover, Abraham survived death to live with God in Paradise (Matt. 8:11; Mark 12:26–27; Luke 16:22–23) from which vantage point he *saw* the incarnation of the Christ *and was glad.*

Still thinking in literalistic terms, *the Jews* reduced this grand spiritual vision to mathematical terms and calculated that Jesus was *not yet fifty years old* (i.e., he was still a young man); and therefore it was preposterous to claim that he had *seen Abraham,* who lived centuries earlier. In reply, Jesus staggered his hearers with the claim, *Before Abraham was, I am.* The contrast between the verbs *was* (Gr. *ginomai*) and *am* (Gr. *eimi*) implied that before Abraham ever came into being by earthly birth Jesus already existed eternally because he shared the nature of God (cf. 1:1). So blasphemous was this assertion to the Jews that they *took up stones* to destroy him on the spot without benefit of formal trial. Instead, the "light of the world" hid himself (cf. Mark 4:22) and *went out of the temple* whose proprietors "received him not" (1:11).

5. The Light of Life (9:1–41)

John 9 is a dramatic interlude set in the midst of the complex controversies of chapters 5—10. The simplicity of the story was insured by developing its structure from a single miracle told with an economy of words (vv. 6–7) and a single saying summarizing its spiritual significance (v. 39). The artistry of the account, which is unsurpassed anywhere in the Gospel, was achieved by alternating the themes of light and darkness so as to portray the dialectic of a judgment already at work.

As an extended illustration of central motifs in John 5—10, this chapter is closely related to its larger context. There are many striking parallels to the healing of the lame man in 5:2–9a and the resulting controversy over working on the sabbath in 5:9b–18. Blindness and lameness are quite naturally connected (cf. Isa. 35:5–6) because sight is needed in order to walk (note 8:12, "He who follows me will not *walk* in darkness but will have the *light* of life"). Further, we have in 9:1–41 a brilliant commentary on the thematic claim of 8:12; for here Jesus, the light of the world, shines into the life of a blind beggar while the Pharisees demonstrate what it means to walk in darkness. Finally, the fact that the healed man was "cast out" by the Jews (v. 34) but "found" by Jesus (v. 35) prepares for the good shepherd motif in John 10 where Jesus "leads out" his own (10:3–4) and protects them from false leaders of the flock (10:1,5,8,12–13).

Dominating the discussion in John 9 is the theme of light conquering darkness (essentially a sermon on the text in 1:5). Skillful use is made of the analogy between physical sight and spiritual insight, a parallelism also found in the Old Testament (e.g., Isa. 29:18; 32:3; 35:5; 42:6–7) and in the Synoptic Gospels (especially in Mark 8 where the gradual restoration of sight to a blind man of Bethsaida in vv. 22–26 parallels the opening of the disciples' "eyes of faith" in vv. 27–30). Here the gift of vision to one born blind prepared for his progressive illumination in coming to "see" (v. 39b) the significance of Jesus in several stages: first as a "man" (v. 11), then as a "prophet" (v. 17), later as one "from God" (v. 33), finally as "Son of man" (v. 35) and even as "Lord" (v. 38).

On the other hand, just as physical light has its counterpart in darkness, so this pilgrimage toward spiritual sight by the healed beggar only exposed the deepening blindness of his detractors, who thought themselves to be the "enlightened" religious leaders of Judaism (v. 39c). At the outset, they seemed prepared to accept the validity of the healing (v. 15), but as its theological implications unfolded (v. 16a) they began both to doubt its validity (v.

18) and to impugn the one who had performed it (vv. 16a; 24b). What started as an open disagreement (v. 16) quickly became dogmatic disapproval (v. 24) which ended in a coercive effort to force someone else to disown his faith (v. 34).

The structure of John 9, unlike the two preceding chapters, is relatively easy to analyze.[26] After the miracle of physical sight was wrought and confirmed (vv. 1–12), its significance was debated in the form of a "trial" narrative (vv. 13–34) featuring the Pharisees as plaintiffs representing the religious establishment and the blind man as defendant representing those changed by the power of Jesus. Three major problems were identified by these interrogations: that the healing violated the law because it was performed on the sabbath (vv. 13–17); that it encouraged personal faith in Jesus and so could lead to exclusion from the synagogue (vv. 18–23); that it was performed by an unaccredited religious worker who could not be depended upon to perpetuate the Mosaic tradition (vv. 24–34). Unwittingly, Pharisaic harassment did not cow the blind man into subjection but emboldened a defense of his healer which became more spirited and skillful as it progressed. The end result was that to his miracle of physical sight was added the deeper miracle of spiritual insight while on the Pharisees was passed the tragic verdict of spiritual blindness and guilt (vv. 35–41).

(1) Sight for a Beggar Born Blind (9: 1–12)

¹ As he passed by, he saw a man blind from his birth. ² And his disciples asked him, "Rabbi, who sinned, this man or his parents, that he was born blind?" ³ Jesus answered, "It was not that this man sinned, or his parents, but that the works of God might be made manifest in him. ⁴ We must work the works of him who sent me, while it is day; night comes, when no one can work. ⁵ As long as I am in the world, I am the light of the world." ⁶ As he said this, he spat on the ground and made clay

26 On the structure and background of John 9, see J. Louis Martyn, *History and Theology in the Fourth Gospel* (New York: Harper & Row, 1968), pp. 3–41.

of the spittle and anointed the man's eyes with the clay, 7 saying to him, "Go, wash in the pool of Siloam" (which means Sent). So he went and washed and came back seeing. 8 The neighbors and those who had seen him before as a beggar, said, "Is not this the man who used to sit and beg?" 9 Some said, "It is he"; others said, "No, but he is like him." He said, "I am the man." 10 They said to him, "Then how were your eyes opened?" 11 He answered, "The man called Jesus made clay and anointed my eyes and said to me, 'Go to Siloam and wash.' so I went and washed and received my sight." 12 They said to him, "Where is he?" He said, "I do not know."

Since chapter 8 concluded with a reference to Jesus' departure from the Temple, 9:1 may imply that in so doing he *passed by* one of the gates where the afflicted were accustomed to beg (cf. Acts 3:2). In such a religious setting, the encounter with *a man blind from his birth* could have prompted the *disciples* to ask their *Rabbi* about the perennial problem of evil. In the case of congenital defects, the basic explanation that sin causes suffering was applied by the rabbis in one of two ways: either a prenatal sin had been committed by the fetus, or the iniquity of the fathers was being visited "upon the children to the third and fourth generation" (Ex. 20:5). The form of the disciples' question reflected that debate: *Who sinned, this man or his parents, that he was born blind?* Today we still argue whether human tragedy is primarily a matter of individual responsibility or the legacy of the past.

In his reply, Jesus refused to grasp either horn of the disciples' dilemma: *It was not that this man sinned, or his parents, but that the works of God might be made manifest in him* (cf. Luke 13:1–5). The disciples approached tragedy in search of someone to blame, whereas Jesus was concerned with what he could change. The disciples were interested in human causes and so viewed the matter from its beginning, but Jesus was interested in divine results and so pointed to its possible ending. To the disciples the blind man was a question mark, an object of detached speculation, while for Jesus he was an opportu-

nity, a subject needing involved compassion.

This does not mean, however, that Jesus cherished any illusions regarding the difficulties of overcoming human misery. His eschatological approach to theodicy was qualified both by a positive imperative and by a negative warning. First, an unusual use of singular and plural pronouns summoned the disciples to share his attitudes: *We must work the works of him who sent me* (cf. 3:11 for a similar use of I/we = Jesus/disciples), a messianic task which was possible because it was then the new *day* of God's deliverance. But remembering those who so recently would have stoned him (8:59), the somber prediction was added, *Night comes, when no one can work* (cf. 3:19; 11:9–10; 1:35–36; 13: 30). Such a fearful eventuality did not paralyze action, however, but heightened Jesus' urgency to labor for *as long as* he was *in the world.* The miracle which followed immediately provided an illustration of his defiance of the looming darkness and a fulfillment of his claim in 8:12 to be "the light of the world."

Typically, the procedures utilized in giving sight to the blind man were suggestively symbolic. The use of spittle involved a substance completely from within Jesus, a spontaneous gift of himself, while its combination with the dust of the earth to make clay was reminiscent of the original creation of man (Gen. 2:7). To smear such a primitive salve on the man's eyes and bid him grope his way to *wash in the pool of Siloam* was a means designed to test his faith—just as Elisha had challenged the leper, Naaman, to wash in the Jordan (2 Kings 5:9–14). Even the name of the pool, which in one etymological derivation could mean *Sent*, appealed to the Evangelist as appropriately symbolic since the blind man was being sent there by the one who had himself been sent from God. The bold initiative of Jesus, coupled with the unquestioning obedience of the blind man, resulted in a cure: he *came back seeing.*

So unexpected and decisive was the

transformation that *the neighbors and those who had seen him before as a beggar* found it difficult at first to accept what had happened. To *some* the man seemed to be himself, but to *others* he appeared only to be *like him*—a combination symbolic of the Christian convert who remains the same and yet becomes like a different person. When the healed man confessed that he was indeed the one they had known as a blind beggar, an explanation of his cure was requested. In rehearsing what had happened, he was able at this stage to identify *Jesus* by name (contrast 5:13) but did *not know* anything significant about him, being ignorant even of where he might be found (cf. vv. 35–36).

(2) The Problem of Sabbath Violation (9:13–17)

[13] They brought to the Pharisees the man who had formerly been blind. [14] Now it was a sabbath day when Jesus made the clay and opened his eyes. [15] The Pharisees again asked him how he had received his sight. And he said to them, "He put clay on my eyes, and I washed, and I see." [16] Some of the Pharisees said, "This man is not from God, for he does not keep the sabbath." But others said, "How can a man who is a sinner do such signs?" There was a division among them. [17] So they again said to the blind man, "What do you say about him, since he has opened your eyes?" He said, "He is a prophet."

No sooner was a born blind beggar enabled to see than *the Pharisees,* who had never done anything for him, began to throw theological sand into his newly opened eyes. As the man recounted his cure, it became clear that Jesus had violated the law on two counts by healing on *a sabbath day* (cf. on 5:1–18): he acted when no emergency endangered human life instead of waiting until a later time; he "kneaded" the dust with spittle to make clay, a class of work forbidden on the day of rest (Mishnah, *Sabbath* 7:2).

Jesus had responded to a pathetic case of human need at his earliest opportunity out of a sense of urgency lest the encircling gloom deepen into darkness "when no one can work." Far from seeing such activity as a violation of the true intention of the sabbath, he had already argued that the day symbolizing messianic rest was the best possible occasion on which to carry forward the divine restoration of creation (cf. 5:16–18).

From the Jewish perspective, the Pharisees were left with a dilemma: if Jesus were good enough to do *such signs,* how could he be bad enough to do them in a way that deliberately did not keep the sabbath (cf. Deut. 13:1–5)? A *division* was created *among them* as they took sides, some insisting that the social fabric of Judaism must be held together by conformity to the law, while others recognized that an individual need had been met even if by unauthorized procedures. Unable to agree among themselves, the Pharisees turned back to the healed man for an opinion of Jesus. Pressured to assign some meaning to this experience, the defendant now allowed that his healer must be a *prophet* (e.g., like Elisha, who healed Naaman by sending him to wash). In the fourth Gospel, "prophet" is never faith's highest designation for Jesus (4:19; 6:14; 7:40), thus the reader knows that more is to come.

(3) The Problem of Synagogue Exclusion (9:18–23)

[18] The Jews did not believe that he had been blind and had received his sight, until they called the parents of the man who had received his sight, [19] and asked them, "Is this your son, who you say was born blind? How then does he now see?" [20] His parents answered, "We know that this is our son, and that he was born blind; [21] but how he now sees we do not know, nor do we know who opened his eyes. Ask him; he is of age, he will speak for himself." [22] His parents said this because they feared the Jews, for the Jews had already agreed that if any one should confess him to be Christ, he was to be put out of the synagogue. [23] Therefore his parents said, "He is of age, ask him."

The primitive level of medicine practiced in the first century, coupled with the widespread gullibility of the masses, made it wise to investigate carefully any reputed claims of miraculous healing, particularly the receiving of *sight* by one who *had been blind.* Since the beggar was said to have been *born* without sight, obviously his parents were the logical ones both to confirm the identity and to explain the transformation of their son.

Thrust suddenly into the glare of an official interrogation, the parents were filled with fear strong enough to stifle the joy that should have been theirs over the good fortune that had suddenly come to the family. After all, for years they had endured the suspicion or even accusation that the boy might have been born blind because of their sin (v. 2)! But an unexpected change—even for the better—could prove as embarrassing in the home as in the synagogue. Thus, even though they were forced to concede that he was their *son* who had been *born blind* they refused to comment on either the healing or the healer. Since he was *of age,* i.e., old enough to be a legal witness, he would have to *speak for himself.*

The parents had volunteered a lack of information because *they feared* the power of the leading Pharisaic *Jews* to *put out of the synagogue* any one who *should confess* that Jesus was the **Christ** (Jewish Messiah). The threat of ostracism from the leading institution of Jewish community life was a shattering prospect during the New Testament era when the danger of racial and religious extinction made loyal cooperation all the more essential. So critical did the situation become following the destruction of the Temple in A.D. 70 that the Sanhedrin (*Beth Din*) instituted formal procedures for the excommunication of Jewish Christians as heretics (*minim*). This fateful rupture between Judaism and Christianity was of great concern to the fourth Evangelist who sought to meet the problem by relating it to the earliest clashes of Jesus and his followers with the Pharisees (cf. 12:42; 16:2).[27]

(4) The Problem of an Unaccredited Healer (9:24–34)

24 So for the second time they called the man who had been blind, and said to him, "Give

[27] On this development, see Smith, pp. 22–36, and Martyn, pp. 17–41, 148–150.

God the praise; we know that this man is a sinner." 25 He answered, "Whether he is a sinner, I do not know; one thing I know, that though I was blind, now I see." 26 They said to him, "What did he do to you? How did he open your eyes?" 27 He answered them, "I have told you already, and you would not listen. Why do you want to hear it again? Do you too want to become his disciples?" 28 And they reviled him, saying, "You are his disciple, but we are disciples of Moses. 29 We know that God has spoken to Moses, but as for this man, we do not know where he comes from." 30 The man answered, "Why, this is a marvel! You do not know where he comes from, and yet he opened my eyes. 31 We know that God does not listen to sinners, but if any one is a worshiper of God and does his will, God listens to him. 32 Never since the world began has it been heard that any one opened the eyes of a man born blind. 33 If this man were not from God, he could do nothing." 34 They answered him, "You were born in utter sin, and would you teach us?" And they cast him out.

Unable any longer to question the fact of the healing, the Jews now tried to conform its meaning to their theological position by commanding the man to swear on oath that Jesus was *a sinner.* The idiom, *Give God the praise* (cf. Josh. 7:19), was much like our courtroom formula, "So help me God" (cf. TEV, "Promise before God that you will tell the truth!"). Having moved beyond their debates of v. 16, the Pharisees now presented a solid front (*We know*) representing the religious leadership of the nation, a formidable consensus calculated to overwhelm a single illiterate beggar. But for a blind man now able to see, an ounce of personal experience was worth a pound of rabbinic theology. He had been allowed to receive his healing before being required to believe certain things about it, thus he would formulate his faith by reflecting on the facts rather than by twisting the facts to fit someone else's traditional faith.

Momentarily checked by this masterful repartee, the Jews tried to make a fresh start by rehashing the facts of the case, only to be castigated for not paying attention when they were recited earlier (v. 15). But the cruelest cut of all was the ironic taunt: *Why do you want to hear it again? Do you too want to become his disci-*

ples? Stung by this slashing counter-offensive, the Jews fell back on their confidence in ancestry and tradition: *We are disciples of Moses,* i.e., faithful interpreters of the Mosaic law. A fundamental premise of Scripture was that *God* had *spoken to Moses,* whereas the origin of Jesus and the source of his inspiration were completely obscure (cf. 7:27,41,52; 8:19,41). The point was not simply that Jesus was an unknown heretic; rather, he was leading the people astray by influencing such as this blind man to be *his disciple.*

For the former blind man, the fact that Jesus had *opened* his *eyes* shed light on the inability of the Jews to determine *where* Jesus had come *from.* As a miracle without precedent *since the world began* (i.e., there is no record of such in the Old Testament), this wondrous work must have been wrought by God. But since God *listens* only to a true *worshiper* who *does his will,* Jesus must be *from God* and not a *sinner* as they had supposed. In turning the tables on his adversaries and using their own theology against them, the beggar committed the ultimate insult of trying to *teach* his official teachers! Infuriated by this affront and unable to answer the logic of his argument, they simply condemned him as totally depraved (cf. v. 2) and *cast him out* of their midst (cf. v. 22). Once again those so proud of their physical and religious birth paid ironic tribute to the Jesus, who gladly accepted men *born in utter sin,* without physical or spiritual sight, and led them to the light.

(5) The Paradox of Judgment (9:35–41)

35 Jesus heard that they had cast him out, and having found him he said, "Do you believe in the Son of man?" 36 He answered, "And who is he, sir, that I may believe in him?" 37 Jesus said to him, "You have seen him, and it is he who speaks to you." 38 He said, "Lord, I believe"; and he worshiped him. 39 Jesus said, "For judgment I came into this world, that those who do not see may see, and that those who see may become blind." 40 Some of the Pharisees near him heard this, and they said to him, "Are we also blind?" 41 Jesus said to them, "If you were blind, you would have no guilt; but now that you say, 'We see,' your guilt remains.

The man healed by Jesus, in gaining the one thing he needed most, seemed to have lost everything else as a result. Gone was his vocation as a professional beggar, since that role in society was based on blindness (v. 8). His neighbors were confused (v. 9), his parents were intimidated (v. 22), and his leaders were enraged (v. 34). Now that he could see for the first time, there was nowhere to go. He was not welcome at work, home, or church (synagogue)—all because of a man he had never seen and knew not where to find (v. 12)!

Having *heard* of this plight, *Jesus* again took the initiative and *found* (cf. 5:14) the man whose eyes he had opened that he might also give him spiritual sight. Characteristically, he began with a question (cf. 5:6) that focused the central issue: Would this lonely Jewish outcast accept the verdict of his people's judges who had just passed such a severe sentence on his life (designed to make him recant and return to the synagogue?), or would he *believe in the Son of man* designated by God as cosmic judge and arbiter of eternal life? When the man asked just *who* that supernatural figure might be, Jesus startled him with the announcement that the future could now be experienced in his own life: *You have* now *seen him, and it is he who speaks to you* (cf. 4:26). In response, the man turned from his Jewish accusers to trust one in whom there is no condemnation: *Lord, I believe.* Having discovered how dangerous it can be to see the world for what it is, he now learned how redemptive it can be to see Jesus for who he is.

The drama concludes with an incisive commentary by Jesus on the significance of what had happened. The polarization prompted by his miracle of mercy reflected a process of *judgment* inherent in the very mission on which he *came into this world.* The blind man represented *those who do not see* that are enabled to *see,* whereas the Pharisees represented *those who see* that become *blind* (cf. a parabolic parallel to this great reversal in Matt. 25:31–46).

Hearing of the part assigned them in this drama by Jesus, *some of the Pharisees* challenged his interpretation by asking rhetorically, "You are not saying that even we are blind, are you?" If anything, the answer of Jesus was even more crushing than his original indictment: "Would to God that you were blind!" If only they could feel the need for light—which obviously they did not—then help would be forthcoming. But to absolutize their blindness as sight represented a deliberate perversity for which they would be held responsible: *Your guilt remains* (cf. Mark 3:28–30).

This process of judgment by which the coming of Jesus caused those who could "see" to "become blind" (v. 39) may be understood best from three perspectives:

The Old Testament.—The prophets, in particular, were profoundly aware that God's own efforts to lay a claim upon his people often provided the occasion for a rejection of that challenge. Although the intent of the divine action may have been redemptive, its effect could become judgmental. Jesus was no harsher on his fellow Jews than Isaiah had been in pointing out that a ministry of the unheeded word actually serves to shut the unseeing eye (note the use of Isa. 6:10 in John 12:37–40).

The ministry of Jesus.—Before this Gospel was written, the Evangelist brooded long over the inescapable conclusion that the religious leadership of Judaism, those with the most light to see the significance of Jesus, were the very ones who had led in rejecting him. Ironically, a mission of mercy which offered new forgiveness, freedom, and fulfillment was the provocation that drove some Jews to a "blind" defense of established traditions. It was impossible to understand the ministry of Jesus without some explanation of why it ended on a cross (cf. 1:11).

The early church.—Finally, by the time this Gospel was written, Gentiles who by birth were "blind" to the revelation of God had accepted the light in Christ more readily than the Jews, most of whom had decided to spurn the Christian invitation. In a sense, Gentile converts recapitulated the spiritual pilgrimage of the man *born* blind (note the emphasis in vv. 1–2, 19–20, 32–34), while the Jews who could not be won were mirrored in the wellborn Pharisees of Jesus' day who deliberately forfeited their spiritual privileges. John 9, like Romans 9, is an attempt to clarify the mystery of Israel's unwillingness to embrace her Messiah.

Unless clearly understood, this judgment of Jesus by which "those who see . . . become blind" could be linked with the "children of the devil" motif in 8:31–59 to support a theology of fatalistic determinism which views the work of Christ as arbitrary or even capricious. Lest any such distortion tempt the reader, we have been presented in 9:1–41 with a clear paradigm of the way in which Jesus actually worked.

Far from condemning the blind to remain in that condition, he took the initiative in giving both physical and spiritual illumination to a helpless victim who could not escape the darkness by his own efforts but who was willing to receive the light (cf. 1:12). To be sure, others sank even deeper into darkness but they did so on the basis of the light which they falsely supposed themselves to possess. From beginning to end, the beggar confessed to an ignorance of Jesus (vv. 12,25,36) and thus could be taught his true significance, while the Pharisees throughout were certain that they understood Jesus (vv. 16,24,29) and so did not even feel the need to learn.

6. The Shepherd of Life (10:1–42)

The absence of a major break at the beginning of this chapter shows its close connection with the preceding section (a new setting is not given until v. 22). The exclusion of a would-be disciple of Jesus from the synagogue (9:34) prepared for a discussion of the fold into which such a one could be received (10:3–4,9,27) and protected (10:11–15,28–29) from the false leaders of God's flock (10:1,5,8,26). Explicit reference in 10:21 to the miracle recorded in 9:6–7 suggests that the healing of the blind man continued to be a factor in the discussions of Jesus with his opponents.

A further connection with the larger context is indicated by the setting of John 10 at "the feast of the Dedication" (v. 22). In accordance with the pattern throughout chapters 5—10 of relating each unit directly to a Jewish religious celebration, John 7—8 took place during the Feast of Tabernacles (7:2,14,37; 8:12,59), while John 9 either came at the same time or shortly thereafter (9:1,5). Although Dedication fell some three months later, it was celebrated in a manner parallel to Tabernacles (2 Macc. 1:9,18; 10:5–6). For example, so much use was made of fire from lampstands and candlesticks (note 2 Macc. 1:18–36) that Dedication was popularly called "the festival of Lights" (Josephus, *Antiq.*, XII, 319, 325), a designation which links the background of John 10 to the theme of Jesus as "the light of the world" in John 8—9.

Like Tabernacles, the Feast of Dedication was also designed to honor the true dwelling place of God with his people, in this case by memorializing the cleansing and rededication of the Temple which Judas Maccabeus accomplished in 164 B.C. following its desecration by the Syrians under Antiochus Epiphanes (1 Macc. 4:36–61; 2 Macc. 10:1–9). The terms used for this renewal of worship (Heb., *Hanukkah;* Gr., *Egkainia*) had also been used to describe the consecration of the tabernacle by Moses (Num. 7:1–11), the first Temple by Solomon (1 Kings 8:62–64), and the second Temple by the returned exiles (Ezra 7:16–18), and so were evocative of the efforts in every generation to prepare a place of purified devotion to God.

Against this background, Jesus identified himself at the climax of the chapter (v. 36) as the one "whom the Father consecrated" (*hagiazō*, a synonym of *egkainizō* used in the LXX of Num. 7:1), i.e., as the one set apart by God to be both the undefiled altar and its unblemished sacrifice (v. 11). His death would come at the hands of those false religious leaders whose purpose was "to kill" (v. 10, *thuō*, lit. to

slaughter a sacrifice). On the very occasion when the Jews were celebrating the cleansing of their Temple after its corruption under false high priests such as Jason and Menelaus, who betrayed their office by contributing to the Syrian desecration, Jesus dedicated himself to lead the people of God even at the cost of dying and so to fulfill the highest intentions of the feast.

The employment of pastoral imagery in John 10 may have been influenced by the practice of using Old Testament texts concerned with sheep and shepherds as synagogue readings on the sabbath nearest the Feast of Dedication. The primary prophetic passage was Ezekiel 34, a chapter which is crucial to the conceptual background of John 10.[28] There, God is presented as the good shepherd (vv. 11–16; cf. Psalms 23:1; 80:1; Isa. 40:11; Jer. 23:3; 31:10) and Israel as the sheep of his pasture (vv. 25–31; cf. Psalms 74:1; 79:13; 95:7; 100:3). Because unfaithful shepherds (rulers) of Israel had betrayed the flock, God would sternly judge them for their dereliction (vv. 2–10; cf. Jer. 10:21; 12:10; 23:1–2; Zech. 11:15–17), just as he would judge between true and false sheep within the flock (vv. 17–22). In place of harassment from false shepherds and false sheep, God promised to set over the flock a messianic shepherd, his servant David (vv. 23–24; cf. Jer. 23:4–6)—this restoration of the Davidic monarch being the only theme in Ezekiel 34 not developed in John 10. The dominant contention both in Ezekiel 34 and in its New Testament counterpart is the same: the care of the flock requires the replacement of a long line of false shepherds with the one true servant shepherd provided by God.

Three characteristics of Jesus' ministry provided the criteria for his claim to replace the Pharisees as God's undershepherd in Israel: First, he *gathered* his sheep into one flock (vv. 3–4,14–16,27),

[28] See Aileen Guilding, *The Fourth Gospel and Jewish Worship* (Oxford: Clarendon, 1960), pp. 127–142; Smith, pp. 166–174.

thus insuring the unity of the church, whereas his enemies allowed the people of God to become scattered (vv. 5,12). Second, he *guarded* his sheep from destruction (vv. 7–8,11–15, 28b–29), thus insuring the security of the church, whereas his opponents fled when the flock was ravaged by foes (vv. 12–13). Third, he *guided* his sheep into good pasture (vv. 3,9–10,28a), thus insuring the vitality of the church, whereas his predecessors came only to steal, rob, kill, and destroy (vv. 1,8,10).

In form, John 10 is divided into two main parts by the fresh start at v. 22. Nevertheless, the entire chapter is a loose literary unity held together by the underlying motifs related to the Feast of Dedication and by the explicit pastoral imagery in both parts (e.g., vv. 26–27 elaborate on vv. 3–5).

(1) The Symbolism of Sheep and Shepherd (10:1–6)

¹ "Truly, truly, I say to you, he who does not enter the sheepfold by the door but climbs in by another way, that man is a thief and a robber; ² but he who enters by the door is the shepherd of the sheep. ³ To him the gatekeeper opens; the sheep hear his voice, and he calls his own sheep by name and leads them out. ⁴ When he has brought out all his own, he goes before them, and the sheep follow him, for they know his voice. ⁵ A stranger they will not follow, but they will flee from him, for they do not know the voice of strangers." ⁶ This figure Jesus used with them, but they did not understand what he was saying to them.

The treatment of the healed blind man by the Jews in the preceding account made Jesus doubly certain (*Truly, truly*) that the people of God were being harassed by false religious leaders, here likened to *a thief and a robber*. These terms may refer to the Pharisees who had just tried to take everything away from the beggar cured by Jesus (cf. Matt. 23:13), including the welcome of his parents, the legitimacy of his miracle, and the fellowship of his synagogue. Or they may refer generally to the Sadducean and priestly authorities who controlled the Temple establishment which

Jesus elsewhere likened to "a den of robbers" (Mark 11:17) because it deprived non-Jews of an equal opportunity to worship God. Or, again, since Judas was called a "thief" (12:6) and Barabbas a "robber" (18:40)—as were the two brigands with whom Jesus was crucified (Mark 15:27)—these terms may point to Zealots who had resorted to deception and violence for religious purposes. Probably, the accusation was intended as a general indictment of any methods that exploit rather than serve the sheep.

In contrast to all of those who make improper approaches to the flock, the true shepherd is one who *enters by the door,* i.e., he is open and direct (cf. 18:19–21, and note especially the way in which Jesus contrasted himself to the "robber" in Mark 14:48–49). Rather than trying to slip in *by another way,* he is willing to be identified and admitted by *the gatekeeper,* i.e., to have his true purposes understood by all. His relation to the sheep is one of reciprocal knowledge: on the one hand, they are able to *hear* (recognize) *his voice* while, on the other hand, he is able to call *his own sheep by name* (cf. 11:43; 20:16). Instead of casting them out on their own (as the Jews did in 9:34), he both brings them *out* as *his own* and *goes before them* as the trusted leader whom they are willing to *follow.* The sheep are blessed not only with a receptive ear to *know his voice* but with a "divine deafness" to *the voice of strangers* from whom they *flee.*

These symbolic sayings in vv. 1–5 are called a *figure* which, like the parables in the Synoptics (cf. Mark 4:13), the hearers of Jesus *did not understand.* While they grasped readily enough what was being said about sheep, they were not ready to be grasped by what was being said *to them.* Strangely enough, the term used here (figure, *paroimia*) never appears in the Synoptics, whereas the familiar term there (parable, *parabolē*) does not occur in John. Both, however, are related to the Hebrew *mashal* which refers to a wide variety of proverbial or figurative language. Other uses of·*paroimia* in the fourth Gospel (16:25,29) suggest a primary connotation here of enigmatic discourse somewhat like the more highly developed Synoptic parables which manifest allegorical traits (e.g., Mark 12:1–9).

(2) Jesus and the Flock of God (10: 7–18)

⁷ So Jesus again said to them, "Truly, truly, I say to you, I am the door of the sheep. ⁸ All who came before me are thieves and robbers; but the sheep did not heed them. ⁹ I am the door; if any one enters by me, he will be saved, and will go in and out and find pasture. ¹⁰ The thief comes only to steal and kill and destroy; I came that they may have life, and have it abundantly. ¹¹ I am the good shepherd. The good shepherd lays down his life for the sheep. ¹² He who is a hireling and not a shepherd, whose own the sheep are not, sees the wolf coming and leaves the sheep and flees; and the wolf snatches them and scatters them. ¹³ He flees because he is a hireling and cares nothing for the sheep. ¹⁴ I am the good shepherd; I know my own and my own know me, ¹⁵ as the Father knows me and I know the Father; and I lay down my life for the sheep. ¹⁶ And I have other sheep, that are not of this fold; I must bring them also, and they will heed my voice. So there shall be one flock, one shepherd. ¹⁷ For this reason the Father loves me, because I lay down my life, that I may take it again. ¹⁸ No one takes it from me, but I lay it down of my own accord. I have power to lay it down, and I have power to take it again; this charge I have received from my Father."

The Hebraic mind liked to take a familiar image borrowed from ordinary life and meditate upon the many ways in which it might be analogous to realities in the spiritual realm. Faced with a stubborn lack of understanding on the part of his hearers, *Jesus again* returned to the pastoral scene pictured in vv. 1–5 and began to identify parallels with the religious situation in which he found himself. Two main aspects were selected for treatment.

a. I Am the Door (vv. 7–10)

The symbolism of the door, introduced in the little parable of the proper approach to the sheep (vv. 1–3a), was highly suggestive because of its widespread use in the Old Testament (e.g., Gen. 28:17; Psalm 78:23), in Jewish apocalypses (e.g., Testament of Levi 5:1; cf. Rev. 4:1), in the Hellenistic world (e.g., Gnostic mythologies), and in the teachings of Jesus (e.g., Matt. 7:13–14; cf. John 1:51; Rev. 3:7–8). Here it is given two applications in which the function of Jesus is likened not to that of the shepherd but to that of the gate and its keeper.

In v. 8 Jesus regulates the access of shepherds to the sheep, whereas in v. 9 he regulates the access of the sheep to fold and pasture. In other words, Christ alone controls both the ministry and the membership of the church. Whereas the rulers of the old Israel were accredited by heredity (priests, kings) and by human ordination (rabbis), the leaders of the new Israel are admitted to service only by Christ. Likewise, whereas one gained entry to the old Israel by circumcision, sacrifice, and faithfulness to the Law, one may enter the new Israel only *by me,* i.e., through personal faith in Christ. In promising that all whom he accepts *will be saved,* Jesus claimed to do the supreme work of God. Such salvation is not a static possession but a dynamic pilgrimage *in and out* to *find* the *pasture* of *life* which he will *abundantly* provide.

However great are the blessings that come to the messianic flock through Jesus, it may at first seem harsh and uncharitable to contrast *all* the religious leaders *who came before* him as *thieves and robbers* whose *only* purpose was *to steal and kill and destroy.* This accusation should be understood in its biblical context by comparing it with the equally fierce denunciations of false leaders in the Old Testament (e.g., Ezek. 34:2–10; Jer. 10:21; 12:10; 23:1–2; Zech. 11:15–17). Just as Jesus in John 9 was no harder on unbelievers than Isaiah had been, so here he was no more severe in condemning ministerial malpractice than Ezekiel had been. Everyone entrusted with the spiritual welfare of others must face the sober truth that "to whom much is given, of him will much be required" (Luke 12:48).

b. I Am the Good Shepherd (vv. 11–18)

Because of the sudden shift of symbolism at this point, some commentators feel obliged to explain how Jesus could be both a door and a shepherd at the same time by pointing out that in ancient Palestine the sheepherder often slept across the threshold of the fold in order to regulate traffic to and fro. Such clarifications are not necessary, however, for here we have a series of reflections on pastoral life in which various aspects of the picture are selected because they illumine the work of Jesus. In other words, the reality being described was greater than its earthly analogy. Men are more than sheep and Jesus was more than a shepherd, thus the pastoral illustration became applicable at whatever points it fit his life rather than those features of his ministry becoming valid which followed pastoral practice.

This is especially clear in the first application of the *good shepherd* symbol to Jesus as one who *lays down his life for the sheep.* It is true that protecting a defenseless flock in open fields may involve extreme danger from wild animals (cf. 1 Sam. 17:34–35). Further, as the little parable of the *hireling* and the *wolf* makes clear, an owner whose entire livelihood is at stake will take risks from which an employee with only a day's wage at stake would run. To this extent the pastoral parallel was relevant: Jesus did "lay his life on the line" in risking danger for his own (e.g., 11:7–16), whereas the paid religionists of his day showed little concern for the common man ravaged by the devouring forces of evil (cf. Matt. 10:16; Acts 20:29; 1 Peter 5:8).

But at this point the analogy breaks down because no shepherd willingly goes to his death for sheep in the way that Jesus did for men. The basic purpose for protecting a flock from danger is that the sheep may be sheared and/or slaughtered. Jesus did not lead men to good pasture in order to fatten them for the kill but in order that they might have *life* and have it **abundantly.**

This repeated picture of a sacrificial shepherd (*I lay down my life* occurs five times in vv. 11–18), comes neither from Palestinian custom nor from Old Testament background but is an original contribution of Jesus to an understanding of the role of the good shepherd for which there is no analogy from the entire field of animal husbandry.

The second application of the *good shepherd* model is at the point of the reciprocal knowledge between shepherd and sheep, here likened to the intimate bond between Jesus and his *Father.* Already Jesus had been calling out his own from the *fold* of Judaism (cf. vv. 3–4), but this was only the beginning of the fulfillment of a future hope that one day the scattered flock of God would be united. Unlike the Old Testament expression of this hope (e.g., Ezek. 34:23–24; Mic. 2:12; Jer. 23:3), however, Jesus would reach out beyond Judaism to *other sheep* that were *not of this fold* and *bring them also* into that *one flock* created by him as the *one shepherd* (cf. 11:52). Since this future unification (*there shall be*) would take place as a result of his death (v. 15*b*; cf. 12:20–32), obviously it would have to be carried out on earth by his followers. Their mission to the Gentiles, however, was viewed as a work of Jesus himself (*I must bring them*), who had already found *other sheep . . . not of this fold* both in Samaria (4:1–42) and in Galilee (4:43–54).

This explanation of pastoral imagery concludes by emphasizing that its most distinctive feature, the death of the shepherd, was rooted in the relationship between Jesus and his Father. Whereas an earthly shepherd might accidentally lose his life in an emergency, Jesus freely decided to *lay down* his *life* of his *own accord.* Far from being suddenly overpowered by some mortal foe, he had the *power* to *lay down* his *life* whenever he chose. Moreover, unlike any human shepherd, Jesus also had the *power* to *take* his life back *again*. He would not lose his life because he was helpless but because he was obedient, and God would honor that obedience in the victory of his resurrection. Paradoxically, then, his self-giving sacrifice was both voluntary (*of my own accord*) and at the same time was a *charge* (command) which he had *received* from his *Father*. Jesus found perfect freedom in yielding to the sovereignty of God.

(3) The Sifting of True and False Sheep (10:19–21)

[19] There was again a division among the Jews because of these words. [20] Many of them said, "He has a demon, and he is mad; why listen to him?" [21] Others said, "These are not the sayings of one who has a demon. Can a demon open the eyes of the blind?"

Ezekiel 34 had recognized that the flock could be imperiled not only by foes from without and by false shepherds from within but also by bad sheep that "push with side and shoulder, and thrust at all the weak with their horns, till they have scattered them abroad" (v. 21; cf. another expression of this same insight in Matt. 7:13–23). Within the fold where Jesus worked, there was a *division among the Jews* between those who reiterated the charge of *demon* possession (cf. 7:20; 8:48,52) and those who remembered that he could *open the eyes of the blind* (cf. 9:16).

It is striking to find here such stereotyped responses which merely perpetuated earlier reactions to Jesus. No matter what he taught, the debate still raged between those scandalized by his intimacy with God and those impressed by his works of power. Neither side seemed moved by the poignant anticipation of his passion just announced more explicitly than ever before. No one seemed ready to reevaluate the religious leadership in Judaism and ask if it was really protecting the people of God from their deadliest foes. How easy it was to sidestep the real issues by limiting debate to the repetition of tired alternatives.

(4) The Work of the Good Shepherd (10:22–30)

[22] It was the feast of the Dedication at Jerusalem; [23] it was winter, and Jesus was walking in the temple, in the portico of Solomon. [24] So the Jews gathered round him and said to him, "How long will you keep us in suspense? If you are the Christ, tell us plainly." [25] Jesus answered them, "I told you, and you do not believe. The works that I do in my Father's name, they bear witness to me; [26] but you do not believe, because you do not belong to my sheep. [27] My sheep hear my voice, and I know them, and they follow me; [28] and I give them eternal life, and they shall never perish, and no one shall snatch them out of my hand. [29] My Father, who has given them to me, is greater than all, and no one is able to snatch them out of the Father's hand. [30] I and the Father are one."

A disclosure of the complete dedication of Jesus to his Father's will provided an appropriate background against which to announce that the Jewish *feast of the Dedication* was being celebrated *at Jerusalem*. The cold weather of *winter* (December) led Jesus to seek shelter *in the portico of Solomon* where *the Jews* with equally cold hearts *gathered round him*. Taking his symbolic discourse on the good shepherd as a veiled or cryptic utterance designed to *keep* them *in suspense*, they demanded to be told *plainly* whether Jesus claimed to be *the Christ* (cf. Luke 22:67).

In response, *Jesus answered* that he had already *told* them of his identity and mission by *the* messianic *works* which he was doing *in* his *Father's name* (cf. 5:36) but that they did *not believe* (cf. 5:16; 7:3–5; 9:16,24). If they could misconstrue such obvious deeds of mercy, how much more would they misunderstand even the most explicit statements—particularly since the concept of *the Christ* in Jewish thought did not include the notion of suffering and death which was central in the thinking of Jesus (vv. 11–18). The root problem in this failure to communicate was a lack of commitment: they did not *believe* because they did not *belong*.

By contrast, Jesus carefully described what it meant to *belong* to his *sheep* and in so doing provided a summary of his *works* in the *Father's name*. Four components were identified in the dynamics of discipleship: (1) The sheep *hear* the voice of the shepherd; i.e., they are open to the message of the gospel. (2) Because they are willing to listen, they learn that Jesus already "knows" them; i.e. he is sensitive to their individual needs. (3) Convinced that he cares and can help, they *follow* him in a personal relationship of trust. (4) In this pilgrimage he "gives" the eternal life that no foe can destroy (cf. Luke 12:32). Notice the beautiful balance achieved here between human and divine initiative: the sheep *hear* and *follow* while the shepherd "knows" and "gives." We listen but he speaks; we ask but he knows; we follow but he leads; we receive but he gives.

Since Jesus worked as God's representative, his flock always enjoys divine protection from false leaders who would snatch them away (as in 9:24–34). Between the flock and all its foes stands the fearless Shepherd as a bulwark of security. To be in his *hand* is also to be in *the Father's hand* because the two *are one*. The unity affirmed here is not primarily a metaphysical oneness of being, a mystical oneness of emotion, or a moral oneness of will. Rather, the reference in this context is to a shared oneness of power and concern on which the followers of Jesus may depend to save them from destruction by their foes (cf. Matt. 16:18). Notice the theological balance reflected in this simple phrase. God and Jesus *are* (plural) two persons and thus not identical, yet they are *one* (singular) and thus inseparable.

(5) The Person of the Good Shepherd (10:31–39)

31 The Jews took up stones again to stone him. 32 Jesus answered them, "I have shown you many good works from the Father; for which of these do you stone me?" 33 The Jews answered him, "We stone you for no good work but for blasphemy; because you, being a man, make yourself God." 34 Jesus answered them, "Is it not written in your law, 'I said, you are gods'? 35 If he called them gods to whom

the word of God came (and scripture cannot be broken), 36 do you say of him whom the Father consecrated and sent into the world, 'You are blaspheming,' because I said, 'I am the Son of God'? 37 If I am not doing the works of my Father, then do not believe me; 38 but if I do them, even though you do not believe me, believe the works, that you may know and understand that the Father is in me and I am in the Father." 39 Again they tried to arrest him, but he escaped from their hands.

Once *again* (cf. 8:59), in reaction to his claim to be "one" with God, *the Jews took up stones* to lynch Jesus because—to them —he was guilty of *blasphemy* (Lev. 24:16). Refusing to understand him in the light of his *many good works* which could only have their source in *the Father*, they instead took his words of v. 30 out of context and interpreted them literally to mean that he, *being a man*, was trying to *make* himself *God*.

If the Jews were interested only in the surface meaning of words without regard to their larger setting, Jesus could meet them at that level with an *ad hominem* argument from their own Scriptures. In the *law* (OT) *it* was *written . . . I said, you are gods* (cf. Psalm 82:6). Since, as his opponents insisted, *scripture cannot be broken* (i.e. every word must stand), this would make it necessary to take at face value the fact that God himself *called* the men in Psalm 82 *gods*, presumably because they were judges *to whom the word of God came* for their use in the administration of justice. If so, why should Jesus be guilty of blasphemy, since he had referred to himself not as one of these "gods" but only as *the Son of God*? After all, he was not an unjust judge like the men called gods in the Psalm (cf. 82:2) but was one *consecrated and sent into the world by God*.

Lurking within this little piece of rabbinic exegesis (which the Jews in 7:15 claimed that Jesus was not trained to do!) lay an implicit *a fortiori* argument to the effect that if divinity could be ascribed to those who were only recipients of the word in the Old Testament, how much more it was appropriate for one who had always *been* the Word (1:1) to be so described. Further, if the Jews were quite happy to perpetuate an annual religious festival in honor of the dedication of their Temple by the warrior Judas Maccabeus, why were they not willing to honor even more a life "dedicated" (*hagiazō*) by God himself?

To be sure, as an *ad hominem* argument the defense of Jesus was designed to show the Jews the folly of taking his words out of their proper setting in relation to his *works*. As anyone who examined the context of Psalm 82 could readily see, the words there did not really imply that men were "gods" (cf. v. 7). Just so, anyone who looked at the entire ministry of Jesus would see that he was not a man trying to *make* himself *God*—or anything else for that matter. Rather, he was one whom God had made man and sent to do his works. If his antagonists could not at first fathom his relation to the Father, at least they could *believe the works* (cf. v. 25) of the Father which he did and in this way begin to know (*gnōte*) and increasingly *understand* (*ginōskēte*) the mutual indwelling of Father and Son. But, alas, there was no willingness even to take this first step and believe what their eyes had seen; hence Jesus was forced to escape *from their hands* (contrast vv. 28–29!) in order to avoid *arrest*.

(6) *Retirement Across Jordan* (10:40–42)

40 He went away again across the Jordan to the place where John at first baptized, and there he remained **41** And many came to him; and they said, "John did no sign, but everything that John said about this man was true." **42** And many believed in him there.

These verses mark a conclusion not only to this chapter but to John 5—10 as well. Now that the mounting resistance of the Jews had reached a breaking point, Jesus *went away* from Jerusalem eastward *across the Jordan to the place* (Bethany?) *where John at first baptized* (cf. 1:28; 3:26). With every effort to reach the Jews of Jerusalem at an end, *he remained* in Transjordan probably during the winter months between the Feast of Dedication in December (10:22) and the onset of the Passover season in March (11:54–55). Perhaps, Jesus sought relief from the crushing failure to reach his own by retracing his spiritual pilgrimage back to the place where he had begun with such success (3:26).

Ironically, the stubborn unbelief which Jesus encountered in the Holy City stood in sharp contrast to the *many* who *came to him* and *believed in him there*. The last word is emphatic: *there* beyond Jordan, not in Jerusalem, Jesus found simple faith (cf. 3:26) among those prepared by John the Baptist (cf. 1:6–8,19–34; 3:25–30; 5:33–35). Unlike Jesus, *John* had not been a miracle worker (*did no sign*) but what he *said about* Jesus had power because it *was true*. (Note the parallels with 4:39–42 where the Samaritans confirmed a secondary testimony to Jesus by a direct experience with him.)

The fact that Jesus had successfully evaded the clutches of his enemies (v. 39) meant that any decision to return to the tensions of Jerusalem was entirely voluntary on his part. No temptation would be stronger than to stay where he was accepted—after all, should not one work where there is the best chance of success? The next two chapters will show why Jesus forsook the sanctuary of the rural countryside to "lay down his life" for his own in the city.

III. *The Rejection of the Revealer* (11:1 —12:50)

The "book of signs" (chs. 2—12) traces the descent of the Redeemer who "came to his own home, and his own people received him not" (1:11). Following initial reception (chs. 2—4) and growing resistance (chs. 5—10), his public ministry now reached the third and final stage of outright rejection (chs. 11—12). This unit functions both as the climax to the first half of the Gospel and as the preparation for the "book of the passion" in the second half. As such, it represents the literary midpoint on which the plot of the entire book pivots.

At least three features reflect the function of these chapters as the conclusion to John 2—12. First, the historical stage is set against the background of the Jewish Passover (11:55; 12:1), as was the case near the outset of the two preceding units (cf. 2:13; 6:4). This threefold Passover cycle is not intended to indicate the length of the public ministry of Jesus but serves as a literary device designed to give unity and symmetry to the arrangement of the material in John 2—12. Further, growing Jewish opposition in the form of somewhat spontaneous attempts to suppress Jesus (e.g., 5:18; 7:25, 32; 8:59; 10:31,39) here eventuates in a more formal decision by the ruling establishment to put him to death (11:53). Finally, the counter theme of Jesus as "life" which was anticipated in the Prologue (1:4), illustrated in John 2—4 (especially 4:46–54), and explained in John 5—10 (especially 5:19–29), is here given definitive expression in both word and deed through the raising of Lazarus (11:1–44).

These same three features in John 11—12 also effectively introduce the reader to the remaining chapters of the Gospel in 13—20. The Passover celebration (11:55; 12:1) provided normative categories out of Israel's history by which to understand the death of Jesus (13:1) at the same time that the sacrificial lambs were being slaughtered in the Temple on the day of preparation for the Passover (19:14,31; cf. 1 Cor. 5:7). Again, the determination of the Sanhedrin to destroy Jesus (11:53) signals the end of his "public trial" in the preceding chapters (cf. comment on 1:19–28) and results in his departure to the Father (chs. 13—17) by being lifted up on the cross (chs. 18—19). Supremely, the raising of Lazarus anticipates the resurrection of Jesus (chs. 20—21) with which the Gospel ends. Heretofore, the "hour" of Jesus' ascent through crucifixion and resurrection had not yet come (2:4; 7:30; 8:20), but now it was arriving (12:23,27).

Because John 11—12 is at once a summary of Jesus' life and a foreshadowing of his death, the theological perspective in the material is highly paradoxical. Again and again, two apparently contradictory convictions are affirmed: (1) that from an historical perspective, men destined Jesus to die tragically because of the way in which he lived for God; (2) that from an eternal perspective, God destined Jesus to live triumphantly because of the way in which he died for men. The reader is invited to appropriate this paradox by faith and learn in his own experience that if historically the Christian is called to die by truly living, then eternally he is called to live by truly dying.

Parallel to this paradox of life-through-death in chapters 11—12 is the related paradox of acceptance-through-rejection. On the one hand, many of the Jews refused to believe even in the face of a return from the dead (11:45–54). The treachery of Judas surfaced in open protest (12:4–6). Jesus likened his life to a single seed buried in the soil (12:24). At last he "hid himself" (12:36) and faced the darkness of rejection alone (12:39–43). On the other hand, however, his death would gather the scattered children of God (11:52). The raising of Lazarus not only triggered his condemnation but caused the "whole world" to go after him (12:19), including the Greeks (12:20–21). The seed that died would bear "much fruit" (12:24). The cross of shame would draw "all men" to Jesus (12:32). In short, rejection by Israel would provide the occasion of acceptance by the Gentiles (cf. Rom. 11:11–32). God reduced his people to a remnant not in order that his cause might fail in the world but in order that from the few might come the many. This is why hope for the inclusion of other nations increased as disappointment over the self-exclusion of the Jews also increased.

1. Jesus the Resurrection and Life (11:1–54)

The raising of Lazarus, far from being an isolated incident, has close parallels with similar occurrences reported in the biblical period.[29] In most of these accounts, however, the healer was not personally involved in the tragedies but functioned somewhat as a passive channel of divine power in bringing life to one who was often a complete stranger; thus little or nothing was made of his person as a result of his work. By contrast, John 11 emphasizes the profound concern of Jesus for his dear friend Lazarus (vv. 3,5,11,36), the way in which his own destiny was at stake in the healing (vv. 33,35,38,45–53), and the implications of the miracle for an understanding of his nature and mission (vv. 4,15,25–27).

A comparative study of John 11 with its biblical and extra-biblical parallels suggests that in raising Lazarus the uniqueness of Jesus lay not in what he did but in what he claimed it meant (v. 25). The miracle itself is hardly mentioned (vv. 43–44), having been abruptly dropped as soon as it was introduced. Nevertheless, despite a complete absence of embellishment or sensationalism, some have suggested that the Lazarus story is a nonhistorical narrative created either out of the parable of the rich man and Lazarus in Luke 16:19–31 or out of the theological imagination of the Evangelist.

It may be granted that the Gospel of John contains symbolic stories such as the "figure" (10:6) of the sheep and shepherd in 10:1–5. This account need not be a literal description of some historical event for the spiritual claims of 10:7–18 to be true, but 11:1–44 is of a different character. For example, it contains faithful portrayals of persons known from other sources

(e.g., compare vv. 1–2,5,20,28–29,32 and 12:1–3 with Luke 10:38–42), as well as specific place names (vv. 1,18) and the presence of numerous witnesses (vv. 45–46; cf. 12:1–2,17). Clearly, it was understood by the writer to be a record not only of eternal truths but of the historical causation that led to the death of Jesus (note the connection of vv. 1–44 with vv. 45–54). The Lazarus narrative is neither more theological nor less historical than other miracle stories in the fourth Gospel.

But if the Gospel intends us to understand that Lazarus literally came out of the tomb, how can it emphasize the negative reaction to such an event (vv. 45–54)? Hard as it is to suppose that Lazarus conquered death, it seems even harder to conceive of anyone who saw such an event not being overwhelmed with wonder. Yet the record explicitly states that the miracle divided even the eyewitnesses into believers and unbelievers (vv. 45–46). Straightway the enemies of Jesus plotted his demise, not in spite of what he had done but because of it (vv. 47–48). Many today have problems because they are certain that Lazarus could not have come out of the tomb, but many who were there had problems because they were certain that he did do so!

At least four factors explain how such an incredible event could have left men free to believe or disbelieve. (1) This was only a temporary return to earthly existence; eventually Lazarus died again. (2) This was an isolated instance affecting only one man; no one else came out of the tombs that day. (3) This was the return of one who had very recently died; no one dead for several months or years had ever been raised. (4) This led to the resumption of a former way of life; nothing else was changed in order to create a new heaven or a new earth for his enjoyment.

Thus, even if the historicity of this event be accepted at face value, its meaning can obviously be interpreted in a way hardly calculated to inspire faith. The enemies of Jesus could have argued that even if he

---

29 Note references in the Old Testament (1 Kings 17:17–24; 2 Kings 4:18–37; 13:20–21), in rabbinic literature (*Midrash Rabbah* on Leviticus, X, 4; '*Abodah Zarah* 10ᵇ and *Megillah* 7ᵇ in the Babylonian Talmud), in Hellenistic writings (Philostratus, *Life of Apollonius*, IV, 45; Lucian, *Philopseudes*, 25; Pliny, *Natural History*, VII, 37), in the Synoptic Gospels (Mark 5:22–43; Luke 7:11–17; cf. Matt. 11:5), and in the history of the early church (Acts 9:36–43; 20:9–12). For further details see H. van der Loos, *The Miracles of Jesus*, "Supplements to *Novum Testamentum*", VIII (Leiden: E. J. Brill, 1965), 559–566.

were able to provide a temporary reprieve from death, did this not merely postpone its inevitable triumph? Since the dead usually stay buried in their tombs, would the emergence of a solitary exception encourage most men to believe that they might be so fortunate? It was recognized that the spark of life might remain for a few days deep within one who gave every appearance of being dead, but what hope was there after decay had reduced the body to dust? Finally, was it really such a promising prospect to return to the same old set of problems which one had faced in a former life?

These considerations suggest that the Lazarus episode was intended as a sign (v. 47) designed to strengthen belief (v. 15) rather than as incontrovertible proof whose meaning would be self-evident to all who beheld it. As a sign, this event did not directly disclose the reality of the resurrection but only provided an earthly analogy to it in what may more accurately be called the physical restoration of Lazarus. The fourth Gospel itself was concerned to establish this distinction by contrasting the raising of Lazarus with that of Jesus: (1) Lazarus came forth only after men rolled away the stone from the door of his tomb (vv. 39,41) whereas Jesus needed no such human help (20:1); (2) Lazarus came forth still bound with his grave cloths (v. 44) whereas Jesus passed through these cloths and left them behind (20:6-7); (3) Lazarus returned to his earthly relations (12:1-2) whereas Jesus ascended to his Father in heaven (20:17).

In other words, Lazarus was only a sign of the resurrection whereas Jesus was the reality itself. The first man to be truly raised from the dead was not Lazarus but Jesus (1 Cor. 15:20). Lazarus went back for a time to the limitations of earthly existence where he immediately faced death again (12:10), whereas Jesus went beyond death to transcend forever its dominion over life (Rom. 6:9). This is why Jesus, not Lazarus, claimed to be the "resurrection and the life" (v. 25). When the latter

came forth from the grave, he had no more to offer the world than when he went in except the witness of a new lease on life which pointed away from himself to Jesus as its source. It took faith to see in Lazarus more than a medical marvel, to believe that he signified the possibility of eternal life in the midst of time. Only Jesus, not Lazarus, could awaken such faith.

(1) The Death of Lazarus (11:1-16)

¹ Now a certain man was ill, Lazarus of Bethany, the village of Mary and her sister Martha. ² It was Mary who anointed the Lord with ointment and wiped his feet with her hair, whose brother Lazarus was ill. ³ So the sisters sent to him, saying, "Lord, he whom you love is ill." ⁴ But when Jesus heard it he said, "This illness is not unto death; it is for the glory of God, so that the Son of God may be glorified by means of it."

⁵ Now Jesus loved Martha and her sister and Lazarus. ⁶ So when he heard that he was ill, he stayed two days longer in the place where he was. ⁷ Then after this he said to the disciples, "Let us go into Judea again." ⁸ The disciples said to him, "Rabbi, the Jews were but now seeking to stone you, and you are going there again?" ⁹ Jesus answered, "Are there not twelve hours in the day? If any one walks in the day, he does not stumble, because he sees the light of this world. ¹⁰ But if any one walks in the night, he stumbles, because the light is not in him." ¹¹ Thus he spoke, and then he said to them, "Our friend Lazarus has fallen asleep, but I go to awake him out of sleep." ¹² The disciples said to him, "Lord, if he has fallen asleep, he will recover." ¹³ Now Jesus had spoken of his death, but they thought that he meant taking rest in sleep. ¹⁴ Then Jesus told them plainly, "Lazarus is dead; ¹⁵ and for your sake I am glad that I was not there, so that you may believe. But let us go to him." ¹⁶ Thomas, called the Twin, said to his fellow disciples, "Let us also go, that we may die with him."

Lazarus of Bethany is unknown in the Synoptic Gospels but not his sisters *Mary* and *Martha* (see Luke 10:38-42). The picture in both places is that of a family devoted to Jesus and he to them. The *sisters* assume that the *Lord* will recognize a reference to their brother—without mention of name—as *he whom you love* (*phileō*), while the Evangelist states that *Jesus loved* (*agapaō*) *Martha and her sister and Lazarus* (cf. vv. 11,36). This emphasis has given rise to the identification of Lazarus with the "beloved disciple" (13:23; 18:15?; 19:26–27; 19:35?; 20: 2–8; 21:7; 21:20–23; 21:24?) since he is the only follower whom Jesus is said to have loved (the rich man in Mark 10:21 did not become a disciple).

The message *sent* to Jesus (in seclusion across Jordan? cf. 10:40) that *Lazarus was ill* was probably an indirect request for help from his *sisters* (note the similar use of statement as petition in 2:3). As in the case of the man born blind (9:3), Jesus viewed bodily infirmity not as a tragedy which would end in *death* but as an opportunity for *the glory of God* to be manifest through *the Son*. But since his personal affection for Lazarus was so strong, any effort to carry out the divine purpose could be misinterpreted as an expression only of human concern. Moreover, Jesus could not have reached Lazarus before death even if he had left immediately, as vv. 6 and 17 make clear. Once he fully realized this, either from the report of his friend's symptoms or by supernatural insight, he lingered in isolation *two days longer,* probably to struggle with his burden of grief and to discover the response which would meet the needs of his friends and also be true to the will of God (cf. 2:3–5; 7:3–10).

Unlike Jesus, who sought only the glory of God, the disciples shrank back from the summons to save another man's life because they feared that it might cost them their own. Therefore, when Jesus bade them join him (*Let us go*) in a return to *Judea,* the *disciples* incredulously retorted that the Jews were *seeking to stone* him (cf. 8:59; 10:31–33) and, if he contemplated going there again, they would not be with him (note the singular *you* in v. 8). In reply, Jesus compared his ministry to the *twelve hours in* a Jewish day (cf. 9:4–5 and the use of "my day" in 8:56). Just as God controlled sunrise and sunset, so he controlled every moment of Jesus' life. Even if his day had almost run its course, he would make the most of the sunset hours and not *stumble* in his course as men

do when the *night* has overtaken the *light.* Thus he would risk helping Lazarus whether they accompanied him or not (note the resolute *I go* in v. 11).

As long as Jesus had life, he also had light by which to walk (v. 9), but Lazarus, being dead, was *asleep* in the night and needed Jesus *to awake him out of sleep* (cf. Mark 5:39). The *disciples* misunderstood Jesus to mean that Lazarus was *taking rest in sleep* and therefore supposed that he could *recover* without their help. Ironically, they spoke more truth than they realized; for, in the presence of Jesus, death is but a refreshing interlude from whose terrors one may be delivered (the word here translated *will recover* also means "will be saved"). Since the disciples were not yet able to grasp the deeper meaning of their own words, they were told plainly that *Lazarus* was *dead* and that Jesus' response to this development would strengthen their faith more than if he had been there before Lazarus' decease.

On the basis of this clarification, Jesus again (cf. vv. 7,15) issued an appeal for shepherds who would lay down their lives for the sheep (cf. 10:11–18): *Let us* (all) *go to him.* This time a disciple named *Thomas*—who is important only in this Gospel (cf. 14:5; 20:24–29)—voiced the fearful willingness of the band to follow (cf. Mark 10:32). Given a choice, they had rather *die with him* than to live without him. Obviously Thomas spoke more out of loyal despair than mature faith, but his tenacious attachment to Jesus represented a more authentic expression of discipleship than did the superficial enthusiasm of those who were impressed by the signs which he did.

(2) Jesus and Martha (11:17–27)

17 Now when Jesus came, he found that Lazarus had already been in the tomb four days. 18 Bethany was near Jerusalem, about two miles off, 19 and many of the Jews had come to Martha and Mary to console them concerning their brother. 20 When Martha heard that Jesus was coming, she went and met him, while Mary sat in the house. 21 Martha said to Jesus,

"Lord, if you had been here, my brother would not have died. ²² And even now I know that whatever you ask from God, God will give you." ²³ Jesus said to her, "Your brother will rise again." ²⁴ Martha said to him, "I know that he will rise again in the resurrection at the last day." ²⁵ Jesus said to her, "I am the resurrection and the life; he who believes in me, though he die, yet shall he live, ²⁶ and whoever lives and believes in me shall never die. Do you believe this?" ²⁷ She said to him, "Yes, Lord; I believe that you are the Christ, the Son of God, he who is coming into the world."

Arriving at *Bethany*, Jesus immediately encountered three problems: First, *Lazarus had already been in the tomb four days.* In popular Jewish belief the human spirit hovered near the body for three days, then departed as the color of the corpse began to change. Normally death would be irrevocable and all hope abandoned for one buried four days. Second, *many of the Jews* from nearby Jerusalem had come to *console* the family, suggesting perhaps the prominence of the deceased. Although these mourners were not particularly hostile under such delicate circumstances (cf. vv. 36–37), they obviously had close ties with the leadership intent on destroying Jesus (vv. 45–46). Third, *Martha* was not only in the midst of the week of deep mourning that followed Jewish funerals (there was no time to mourn before the funeral since burial was on the day of death), but she was doubtless frustrated and perplexed over the failure of Jesus to be there soon enough so that her *brother would not have died.*

Not to be daunted by her disappointments, however, Martha put the past behind her in an expression of continuing confidence in Jesus that seemed to express a half-hope that *even now* he might be of help. Perhaps she knew his claim that the Father had given him authority to raise the dead (5:21) and so hinted that he *ask* such *from God* on her behalf. This interpretation is reinforced by the reply of Jesus that her *brother* would *rise again.* Such a general assurance was inadequate for Martha, however, since it might mean only that Lazarus would *rise again in the resurrection at the*

last day, a teaching which any good Pharisee could embrace. She knew only too well the doctrine of a final resurrection, for many comforters had doubtless been giving her assurances on this point, but she was not certain what difference Jesus made in the realization of this hope.

The answer to that uncertainty was compressed in the climactic formula, *I am* (*egō eimi*). Jesus himself embodied the reality of the *last day* already come in the midst of time. To *believe* in him meant to appropriate in advance, as it were, the fulfillment awaited in the future and so to anticipate decisively the verdict of eternity. To be sure, men—like Lazarus—would continue to *die* a physical death; but Jesus, as *the resurrection*, would enable them to *live* beyond the grave. Moreover, because Jesus is *the life*, the one who *lives* spiritually because he *believes in* Jesus *shall never die* spiritually whether in this age or in the age to come.

Jesus realized that this ultimate claim would not be self-evident even to a close friend; thus he hung the issues of all eternity on an existential question, *Do you believe this?* At first Martha had confessed, *I know* (v. 24), but now she began, *You are* (v. 27), thus recognizing that eternal life was not a proposition but a person. Drawing again on her Jewish background she summarized his significance in three phrases: (1) *the Christ* (cf. 1:41; 4:29; 7:41); (2) *the Son of God* (cf. 1:34; 1:49); (3) the one *coming into the world* (cf. 6:14). Previous confessions in the fourth Gospel employing these titles suggest that Martha had truly shifted her hopes from the Pharisees to Jesus but that her understanding of him had not yet gone beyond inherited Jewish categories.

(3) Jesus and Mary (11:28–37)

²⁸ When she had said this, she went and called her sister Mary, saying quietly, "The Teacher is here and is calling for you." ²⁹ And when she heard it, she rose quickly and went to him. ³⁰ Now Jesus had not yet come to the village, but was still in the place where Martha had met him. ³¹ When the Jews who were with

her in the house, consoling her, saw Mary rise quickly and go out, they followed her, supposing that she was going to the tomb to weep there. 32 Then Mary, when she came where Jesus was and saw him, fell at his feet, saying to him, "Lord, if you had been here, my brother would not have died." 33 When Jesus saw her weeping, and the Jews who came with her also weeping, he was deeply moved in spirit and troubled; 34 and he said, "Where have you laid him?" They said to him, "Lord, come and see." 35 Jesus wept. 36 So the Jews said, "See how he loved him!" 37 But some of them said, "Could not he who opened the eyes of the blind man have kept this man from dying?"

The scene now shifts from Martha to *her sister Mary* (vv. 1–2) who had remained behind at home (v. 20) as a courtesy to her grieving guests. *Quietly,* Martha summoned Mary to meet Jesus outside the *village* while she took her place with the mourners. But no sooner did Mary try to slip away than she was *followed* by the waiting *Jews* who supposed *that she was going to the tomb to weep there,* a custom during the first days after death. Unperturbed by this discovery of her mission and the intrusion of a potentially hostile audience into her private rendezvous with Jesus, *Mary* immediately *fell at his feet* and repeated the lament of her sister (v. 21) that he had been an absentee *Lord* in their moment of extreme crisis.

No sooner had this plaint been voiced than the situation seemed to go from bad to worse. Upon surveying the scene *Jesus* became more upset than the sisters had been. Several factors explain why he was so *deeply moved . . . and troubled* (lit. why he "groaned violently" and "was shaken" to the depths of his being). In the *weeping* of Mary, Jesus felt the irresistible claim of helpless love compelling him to act then and there (unlike Martha, Mary made no request but simply left everything in his hands). At the same time, he saw in *the Jews who came with her* a return of all his difficulties with Israel (chs. 5—10) and realized afresh the costliness of that conflict and its infinite painfulness to his spirit. In one awful moment of indescribable an-

guish, grief caused by the loss of a loved one mingled with wrath caused by the stubborn skepticism of his own spiritual kinsmen, and *Jesus wept* Gethsemane tears of pathos and frustration, pity and indignation.

It is important to note that those who witnessed the raising of Lazarus were already divided in their attitudes toward Jesus even before the drama began to unfold. Some responded to his tears with tender affection (v. 36), others with cruel cynicism (v. 37—the question expects an affirmative answer; i.e., he could have done something but did not). The revelation about to be given in the sign did not dissolve this dialectic of belief and unbelief but only intensified it (note the role of faith in v. 40). Thus Jesus made his way to Lazarus' grave as if it were his own because he knew that some would not be convinced even if "one should rise from the dead" (Luke 16:31).

(4) The Raising of Lazarus (11:38–44)

38 Then Jesus, deeply moved again, came to the tomb; it was a cave, and a stone lay upon it. 39 Jesus said, "Take away the stone." Martha, the sister of the dead man, said to him, "Lord, by this time there will be an odor, for he has been dead four days." 40 Jesus said to her, "Did I not tell you that if you would believe you would see the glory of God?" 41 So they took away the stone. And Jesus lifted up his eyes and said, "Father, I thank thee that thou hast heard me. 42 I knew that thou hearest me always, but I have said this on account of the people standing by, that they may believe that thou didst send me." 43 When he had said this, he cried with a loud voice, "Lazarus, come out." 44 The dead man came out, his hands and feet bound with bandages, and his face wrapped with a cloth. Jesus said to them, "Unbind him, and let him go."

One reason why the raising of Lazarus left men free to believe or disbelieve was that the approach of Jesus combined divine sovereignty and human dependence.

On the one hand, Jesus *came to the tomb* only when he was ready (v. 6), without yielding to earthly pressures (vv. 3,21,32,37). He dared to challenge death even after *four days* had given opportunity for decay. He was certain that believers *would see the glory of God* (cf. comment on 6:36–40) because the Father had *always* heard his prayers. He made use of no medical techniques but felt it sufficient to arouse Lazarus by crying out *with a loud voice* (cf. 5:25,28). In all of these ways, Jesus showed himself to be the Lord of life and death.

On the other hand, he was *deeply moved again* at the sight of the *tomb*. Not only had he asked where the grave site was (v. 34), but upon arrival he asked someone to take *away the stone* that covered the entrance to the burial *cave*. Finally, when *the dead man came out* he requested others to *unbind him, and let him go.* In one sense, these features show that ultimate power was not wasted on trivial tasks that bystanders could perform; thus this pattern becomes a parable of the little ways in which we can cooperate with the life-giving ministry of Christ. At the same time, however, these very human traits also suggest that Jesus deliberately avoided the role of a spectacular wonder-worker. Obviously anyone with enough power to raise the dead could miraculously move tombstones or snap the strips of linen in which corpses were wrapped, but Jesus characteristically avoided any such ostentation. Rather than dazzle the onlookers by what he had done, Jesus forced them to reflect on the miraculous gift of life "hidden" within the humble circumstances under which Lazarus appeared.

(5) The Response of the Jews (11:45–54)

45 Many of the Jews therefore, who had come with Mary and had seen what he did, believed in him; 46 but some of them went to the Pharisees and told them what Jesus had done. 47 So the chief priests and the Pharisees gathered the council, and said, "What are we to do? For this man performs many signs. 48 If we let him go on thus, every one will believe in him, and the Romans will come and destroy both our holy place and our nation." 49 But one of them, Caiaphas, who was high priest that year, said to them, "You know nothing at all; 50 you do not understand that it is expedient for you that one man should die for the people,

and that the whole nation should not perish." 51 He did not say this of his own accord, but being high priest that year he prophesied that Jesus should die for the nation, 52 and not for the nation only, but to gather into one the children of God who are scattered abroad. 53 So from that day on they took counsel how to put him to death.
54 Jesus therefore no longer went about openly among the Jews, but went from there to the country near the wilderness, to a town called Ephraim; and there he stayed with the disciples.

No sooner had Lazarus come forth than attention shifted from him and focused on the response of the onlookers to Jesus. Even before the miracle was wrought, Jesus had made clear that its basic purpose was not to convince people that Lazarus had come back from the beyond (there is no hint that he was ever asked to describe the afterlife) but that Jesus had come from God. *Many of the Jews* from the Jerusalem area *who had come with Mary* to the tomb *believed in him,* probably somewhat in the spirit of Martha (v. 27). Others, however, *went to the Pharisees,* presumably because they did not believe, and *told them what Jesus had done.* Apparently these witnesses entertained no doubts that Lazarus had come back from the world beyond, but they were unwilling to accept the greater miracle that Jesus had come from God in a way that even Lazarus could never do.

Upon hearing their report, *the Pharisees* enlisted the support of the Sadducean *chief priests,* and together they convened an informal session of the supreme Jewish *council,* called the Sanhedrin. Thus far, this body had done nothing effective to suppress Jesus (cf. 7:25–26,32,45–48), but now decisive action was imperative. The problem was not that Jesus was a fraud—even this hostile group conceded in private that he performed *many signs.* Rather, the danger was that an increasing number of the people would *believe in him* (e.g., v. 45) and thereby transfer their loyalty from the leadership approved by *the Romans* (cf. 12:11, TEV). Jesus had excited the people to believe that a new day was dawning, and a procurator such as Pontius

Pilate would take a dim view of the officials who tolerated such a disturber of the status quo. Any threat of revolution would bring destruction *both* to the *holy place* (i.e., the Temple) and to the *nation.* The dilemma of the council was that they could hardly punish a man for doing *many signs,* yet they could hardly allow him to continue agitating the people.

The solution to this problem was forthcoming from *Caiaphas, who was high priest in that* fateful *year* of all years when Jesus was exalted (actually he served A.D. 18–36). In Jewish thought the high priest, by virtue of his office, was believed to have special powers of divination (Josephus, *Antiq.,* XI, 327; XIII, 299–300); and here, ironically, Caiaphas exercised that prerogative in a profounder way than he could realize. Consciously seeking only to be *expedient,* he proposed that *one man* (Jesus) *should die for the people* if that would prevent *the whole nation* from perishing. But the Evangelist realized that, in a redemptive sense, Jesus did *die* not only *for the* Jewish *nation* but *to gather* as a shepherd *into one* flock *the children of God* then *scattered* throughout the world (cf. 10:16). Thus, in deciding to *put* Jesus *to death,* the Sanhedrin was unwittingly carrying out the deepest purposes of God.

Jesus, realizing both this moral threat and the way in which God could override it, again withdrew from ministering *openly among the* Jerusalem *Jews* and went about a dozen miles out into the hill *country* to *Ephraim,* a *town* so small that today its location is uncertain.

This passage is fundamental for the Johannine understanding of Jesus' death. Historically, he died as a threat to the Temple and nation (cf. Mark 14:58; Acts 6:13–14), i.e., as the disturber of the establishment's control of the status quo. Jesus was an advocate, in the name of God, of drastic change at a time when any change was politically explosive. The Jewish leadership may have regretted deeply the suppression of Jesus (cf. 3:2; 7:50–51; 12:42–43) but, faced with Roman reprisals, accepted it as the lesser of two evils. Theologically, the supreme revelation of Jesus as life was the occasion of his death; i.e., it cost Jesus his life to give us eternal life. But his death provided the basis on which Jew and Gentile alike could be saved and united in one church.

2. Preparation for the Passover (11:55—12:36a)

This section is closely tied to the preceding by the continuation of the Lazarus motif (12:1–2,9–11,17–18). Already in 11:45–54, the Sanhedrin had decided to kill Jesus because he raised Lazarus from the dead. Then, for the same reason (12:2–3), Mary responded to this sentence of death by anointing him for burial (12:1–8). The next day an excited festival crowd tried to draft Jesus as a nationalistic deliverer (12:12–15), again because of his power in raising Lazarus (vv. 8,17–18). How striking that this one miracle should elicit such divergent reactions of hostility, gratitude, and possessiveness.

In form, 11:55—12:36a is a series of rather loosely connected units intended to illumine various aspects of the impending passion. Noticeable here are numerous direct parallels and indirect allusions to incidents and teachings scattered throughout the Synoptic Gospels (e.g., transfiguration, Gethsemane, anointings, seed parables, and sayings on life and death). Although both the Johannine and Synoptic frameworks are more theological than chronological, a comparison suggests that in John the sequence is primarily topical rather than temporal, pulling together for the reader those materials from all periods of Jesus' ministry which expressed most profoundly the meaning of his cross.

(1) The Plot Against Jesus (11:55–57)

55 Now the Passover of the Jews was at hand, and many went up from the country to Jerusalem before the Passover, to purify themselves. 56 They were looking for Jesus and saying to one another as they stood in the temple, "What do you think? That he will not come to the feast?" 57 Now the chief priests and the

Pharisees had given orders that if any one knew where he was, he should let them know, so that they might arrest him.

With this third explicit reference to *the Passover of the Jews* (cf. 2:13; 6:4) we come to the final cycle in the ministry of Jesus. Since the Passover was one of the three great pilgrim festivals in Judaism, as *many* as 100,000 *went up* each year from the outlying *country* to celebrate its observance in *Jerusalem.*[30] Before entering the Temple, those who had become religiously unclean (e.g., by contact with Gentiles in their travels) would spend as much as one week *to purify themselves* (cf. Num. 9:9–14; 2 Chron. 30:17–19).

A lifelike touch is added to this transitional paragraph with the description of curious throngs debating whether Jesus would flaunt the ecclesiastical edict against his life by coming out of seclusion to appear publicly at the *feast.* The decision of the Sanhedrin to destroy him (11:53) was now common knowledge because *orders* had gone out from *the chief priests and the Pharisees* (cf. 11:47) that *any one* who *knew where* Jesus *was* in hiding *should let them know, so that they might arrest him.* What irony that religious pilgrims who had come to *purify themselves* for Israel's most sacred season were directed to serve as informers in a sinister plot against one who had done them no harm!

(2) The Anointing in Bethany (12:1–8)

[1] Six days before the Passover, Jesus came to Bethany, where Lazarus was, whom Jesus had raised from the dead. [2] There they made him a supper; Martha served, and Lazarus was one of those at table with him. [3] Mary took a pound of costly ointment of pure nard and anointed the feet of Jesus and wiped his feet with her hair; and the house was filled with the fragrance of the ointment. [4] But Judas Iscariot, one of his disciples (he who was to betray him), said, [5] "Why was this ointment not sold for three hundred denarii and given to the poor?" [6] This he said, not that he cared for the poor but because he was a thief, and as he had the

---

[30] On calculating the number of Passover pilgrims, see Joachim Jeremias, *Jerusalem in the Time of Jesus,* trans., F. H. and C. H. Cave (London: SCM Press, 1969), pp. 77–84.

money box he used to take what was put into it. [7] Jesus said, "Let her alone, let her keep it for the day of my burial. [8] The poor you always have with you, but you do not always have me."

Since the fourth Gospel appears to date this Passover (Nisan 15) on a sabbath (i.e., from 6:00 P.M. on Friday to 6:00 P.M. on Saturday; cf. 18:28; 19:14,31,42), *six days before* would place the *supper* held in *Bethany* for *Jesus* on the previous Saturday evening. Although *Martha served* (cf. Luke 10:40) *and Lazarus was one of those at table,* it is not certain in whose home the meal was held (cf. Mark 14:3). Attention focuses on *Mary* (cf. 11:2), who *took a pound* (around 12 ounces; we might say a pint) of expensive *ointment* and *anointed the feet of Jesus* with such profusion that *the house was filled with . . . fragrance.* The lavishness of her act was obvious both from the costliness of the perfume and from its use in such quantity that is was necessary to wipe the surplus off *his feet with her hair.*

The shocking originality of Mary's method is immediately apparent from a comparison with the two anointings described in the Synoptic Gospels. In Mark 14:3 an unnamed woman poured this same pure nard on Jesus' head, which was the customary way to anoint a king (e.g., 1 Sam. 10:1), but did not use her hair. Again, in Luke 7:38 a sinful woman used her hair to wipe away tears that had fallen on Jesus' feet so that she could anoint them with ointment, an understandable procedure for one so disreputable. But it was unthinkable for a Jewish woman of Mary's reputation to anoint someone by applying *pure nard* to the humblest part of his body, his unshod *feet* (cf. Luke 10:39), and then wipe off the perfume with the most "glorious" part of her body, her unbound *hair* (cf. 1 Cor. 11:15).

To compound the problem, *Judas Iscariot* voiced a protest that the *ointment* could have served *the poor* by being *sold for three hundred denarii* (the denarius was a silver piece equivalent to a day's wage; cf. comment on 6:7). It seemed incredible to his "practical" mentality that Mary should have been allowed to waste in a moment what a laboring man would earn in a year. The Evangelist hastens to add parenthetically that Judas could hardly have *cared for the poor* but coveted Mary's contribution for the disciples' common treasury because he was in charge of *the money box* (cf. 13:29) and could pilfer from it as he pleased. That Judas *was a thief* may be understood as yet another explanation of his betrayal of Jesus (cf. 6:70–71; 13:2,26–30).

Jesus met every objection to Mary's strange ritual by explaining that it was valid as a symbolic anticipation of his *burial*. Not only was she grateful that her brother had been restored, but she was sensitive to the terrible price Jesus would pay for his part in that miracle. According to Jewish burial practice, a great quantity of spices would cover even his feet (cf. 19:39–40), as she now foreshadowed in token fashion. This strong defense by Jesus (*Let her alone*) reflected not only his preoccupation with the passion but his gratitude that someone else understood and honored his ordeal at a time when even the closest *disciples* seemed heedless of the crisis through which he was passing.

Jesus' closing comment, that although the disciples would *not always have* him with them they would *always* have the *poor,* was not intended as a cynical rebuff of efforts to alleviate poverty by means of charity; nor was it an attempt to assert the primacy of personal devotion to himself over social concern for others. Rather, it was a warning to his followers that they should be struggling with the great sickness in mankind that was dragging him to his death rather than trying to cover a corner of the symptoms by glibly volunteering to spend somebody else's money.

(3) *The Plot Against Lazarus* (12:9–11)

⁹ When the great crowd of the Jews learned that he was there, they came, not only on account of Jesus but also to see Lazarus, whom he had raised from the dead. ¹⁰ So the chief priests planned to put Lazarus also to death, ¹¹ because on account of him many of the Jews were going away and believing in Jesus.

One reason why Jesus appreciated so deeply what Mary had done was its contrast not only to the thoughtlessness of his disciples but also to the superficial enthusiasm of the crowds. One such group of *Jews,* probably Judeans from the vicinity of Jerusalem, upon learning that *Jesus* was at Bethany (12:1) *came* there *not only* to see this famous fugitive (11:56–57) *but also* to gawk at *Lazarus, whom he had raised from the dead.* The silence of the record as to their reaction suggests that they wanted to *see* that *Lazarus* was biologically alive but not to "perceive" that Jesus was the source of eternal life for all who believe.

As Lazarus began to gain increasing notoriety, the chief priests realized that the death of Jesus would not stamp out the movement which he started because his life had been shared with others. Already they must have resented Lazarus for upsetting their Sadducean theology (since it had no doctrine of resurrection); and now this mounting popularity meant that they would have *to put Lazarus also to death,* "because on his account many Jews were leaving their leaders and believing in Jesus" (v. 11, TEV). Just as the blind man in gaining sight lost all else (9:34), so Lazarus in gaining new life in Christ was marked for murder. Here was the ultimate perversity of Jesus' enemies—to condemn a man to death simply because he was alive!

The literary purpose of this transitional paragraph is to connect the anointing at Bethany (vv. 1–8) with the triumphal entry into Jerusalem (vv. 12–19). Neither this sequence of the two events nor their close juxtaposition are found in the Synoptic Gospels (cf. Mark 11:1–10; 14:3–9 and parallels). The Johannine arrangement of anointing followed immediately by entry was designed to emphasize the paradox of a "buried king" (vv. 7,13) whose victory was in his defeat, whose glory was in his shame, whose crown was in his cross.

(4) The Triumphal Entry (12:12–19)

12 The next day a great crowd who had come to the feast heard that Jesus was coming to Jerusalem. 13 So they took branches of palm trees and went out to meet him, crying, "Hosanna! Blessed is he who comes in the name of the Lord, even the King of Israel!" 14 And Jesus found a young ass and sat upon it; as it is written,
15 "Fear not, daughter of Zion;
   behold, your king is coming,
     sitting on an ass's colt!"
16 His disciples did not understand this at first; but when Jesus was glorified, then they remembered that this had been written of him and had been done to him. 17 The crowd that had been with him when he called Lazarus out of the tomb and raised him from the dead bore witness. 18 The reason why the crowd went to meet him was that they heard he had done this sign. 19 The Pharisees then said to one another, "You see that you can do nothing; look, the world has gone after him."

Whereas in the Synoptics the entry took place three days before the anointing (Mark 11:1–20; 14:1–3 and parallels), here it followed that event on *the next day.* This careful chronological reference conveys the impression of a countdown as Jesus approached the "hour" of his ultimate destiny. When rumor reached *Jerusalem* that he *was coming* in from the outlying suburb of Bethany, *a great crowd who had come to the feast . . . went out to meet him.* Presumably, many of these pilgrims were Galileans with the same nationalistic enthusiasms which Jesus had rebuffed at Passover time just one year earlier (6:4,15).

One clue to the crowd's intention was provided by their deliberate strategy of utilizing *branches of palm trees* as the Maccabees had done when celebrating the deliverance of the Temple and city from Syrian conquerors (2 Macc. 10:7; 1 Macc. 13:51). Since the palm branch had come to be used on coins and in Temple feasts as a perpetual reminder of these Maccabean exploits, to wave such fronds in the face of Jesus was a symbolic way of encouraging him to do the same against the Romans. A further indication of their mood was reflected in the cry *Hosanna!*—a chant

which meant "Save (deliver) us now!"— and in their blessing of Jesus as *he who comes in the name of the Lord* (cf. Psalm 118:26). In the original context this phrase referred to the Temple pilgrim on his way to worship, but here it was reinterpreted by the crowd to mean *the King of Israel* on his way to conquest.

In the midst of this demonstration Jesus carried out a demonstration of his own by finding a young ass on which he *sat* to symbolize his mission as a man of peace. This action was reminiscent of Zechariah 9:9 where Israel's *king* was indeed to come, not on a warrior's stallion but *sitting on an ass's colt* both "triumphant" and "humble" at the same time. Even *his disciples* could *not understand* this paradox *at first,* but later *when Jesus was glorified* (i.e., ascended), the threefold interaction of the indwelling Spirit, historical memory, and written Scripture yielded the missing insight (cf. 2:22; 7:37–39).

The inability of the disciples to comprehend the strange symbolism of their Master did not leave Jesus without a *witness.* The smaller Judean *crowd* that had seen him raise Lazarus (11:45) reported that *he had done this sign,* prompting the larger Galilean crowd visiting in Jerusalem to go out and hail this conqueror of death as their new-found King. This convergence of enthusiasm by those from north and south convinced *the Pharisees* that all their efforts (11:57) had come to *nothing. Look,* they lamented in ironic understatement, *the world has gone after him.*

(5) The Request of the Greeks (12: 20–26)

20 Now among those who went up to worship at the feast were some Greeks. 21 So these came to Philip, who was from Bethsaida in Galilee, and said to him, "Sir, we wish to see Jesus." 22 Philip went and told Andrew; Andrew went with Philip and they told Jesus. 23 And Jesus answered them, "The hour has come for the Son of man to be glorified. 24 Truly, truly, I say to you, unless a grain of wheat falls into the earth and dies, it remains alone; but if it dies, it bears much fruit. 25 He who loves his life loses it, and he who hates his life in this world

will keep it for eternal life. 26 If any one serves me, he must follow me; and where I am, there shall my servant be also; if any one serves me, the Father will honor him.

Symbolic of the cryptic truth uttered by the Pharisees (v. 19), some Greeks (i.e., non-Jews) *among* the Passover pilgrims *came* saying, *We wish to see Jesus.* On the surface, this may have been no more than the request for an interview with one to whom they were attracted (e.g., because he had cleansed the Court of the Gentiles in the Temple for their use). The Evangelist, however, undoubtedly viewed these Greeks as the Gentile mission field in microcosm now ready to *see* (i.e., believe in) *Jesus* as the Saviour of the world.

Appropriately enough their petition was directed first to *Philip* and then, through him, to *Andrew*, the two disciples with Greek names who were both from the Hellenistic city of Bethsaida (1:44). Even though *they* immediately *told Jesus* of this enticing opportunity to escape from the frustration and dangers of ministering to the Jews, there is no hint that the Greeks got to *see* him at this time. Such silence is deliberate, for the *hour* had *come* (cf. Mark 14:41) when Jesus as *Son of man* would *be glorified*, not by the adulation of a wider audience but by the loneliness of rejection from his own people. Rather than the Greeks "seeing" him save himself by an escape to the Hellensitic world, the reader will see him in the agony of choice (v. 27) as he decides by his death to save others instead.

He would not remain *alone*, however, for his death on the cross would be like *a grain of wheat* which, because it *falls into the earth and dies*, thereby *bears much fruit*. Just as one cannot "see" wheat by looking at a tiny seed, so the Greeks could not truly "see" the meaning of Jesus until the world mission of the church had been launched by his death and resurrection. These Greeks, who had come to Jerusalem for the Passover because they were inquirers or proselytes interested in Judaism, needed to learn that Jesus would go to the cross in order to provide the basis on which the whole world might be saved. To this day, there is no reason to go to the "Greeks" (i.e., to the mission field) unless we are prepared to take the universal message of the cross.

Jesus not only taught the necessity of his death for a redemptive world mission, but he sought to apply its meaning to the nature of discipleship (cf. Mark 8:34–37). To horde seed is to ruin it while to sow seed is to free it for multiplied usefulness. Just so, one who possessively *loves his life* will thereby destroy it while one who *hates his life in this world* (cf. Luke 14:26), i.e., who is willing to lose it for the sake of others, will thereby gain eternal life which can never be taken from him.

This central paradox is further clarified and balanced in two ways by v. 26. First, the "hating of one's life" is no passive renunciation of self, for the disciple is also actively to *follow* (cf. comment on 1:43). Second, one may give himself away to others and still be serving Christ (note the repetition of *I . . . me . . . my* in v. 26). There is no cleavage between mission action to the Greeks and personal attachment to the Messiah (cf. Matt. 25:40).

(6) *The Commitment to the Passion* (12:27–36a)

27 "Now is my soul troubled. And what shall I say? 'Father, save me from this hour'? No, for this purpose I have come to this hour. 28 Father, glorify thy name." Then a voice came from heaven, "I have glorified it, and I will glorify it again." 29 The crowd standing by heard it and said that it had thundered. Others said, "An angel has spoken to him." 30 Jesus answered, "This voice has come for your sake, not for mine. 31 Now is the judgment of this world, now shall the ruler of this world be cast out; 32 and I, when I am lifted up from the earth, will draw all men to myself." 33 He said this to show by what death he was to die. 34 The crowd answered him, "We have heard from the law that the Christ remains for ever. How can you say that the Son of man must be lifted up? Who is this Son of man?" 35 Jesus said to them, "The light is with you for a little longer. Walk while you have the light, lest the darkness overtake you; he who walks in the darkness does not know where he goes.

[36] While you have the light, believe in the light, that you may become sons of light."

It was easy for Jesus to realize that the vocation of a seed is to die so that the fruit hidden within it may multiply (v. 24) but much harder for him to accept the same vocation at the hands of his countrymen. In a moment of Gethsemane anguish he counted the cost of his commitment to the cross: *Now is my soul troubled* (cf. Mark 14:33–34). It would have been only human to say, *Father, save me from this hour* (cf. Mark 14:35), but such a petition was incompatible with his divine *purpose.* Instead, Jesus prayed, *Father, glorify thy name* (i.e., "allow me to manifest to men thy true character").

Immediately *a voice* of direct revelation *from heaven* confirmed that God had been *glorified* by the work of Jesus in the past (e.g., by the signs) and that he would continue to be glorified *again* in the future (e.g., by the death and resurrection). Apparently, this communication was accompanied by thunder (as, e.g., at Sinai), which some of *the crowd standing by* interpreted as a natural phenomenon, while *others,* more attentive to the reassurance which Jesus had just received, claimed that *an angel* had *spoken* (cf. Luke 22:43). Because of his intimate relation to God, Jesus himself needed no outward authentication, whether by thunder or by angel. The audible manifestation of the *voice* had *come* not for his sake but for theirs (cf. 11:42); thus they were to make of it what they could.

Fortified by an overwhelming sense of heavenly approval, Jesus triumphantly cried, *Now* (cf. v. 23) *is the judgment of this world* (cf. 5:22–24; 8:15–16). These words were not a vindictive threat against his human enemies but a testimony that the power of God had repulsed the efforts of *the ruler of this world* (i.e., Satan) to reign in his life (cf. on 6:70–71). Because Jesus would never compromise with evil, even when *lifted up from the earth* in cruel crucifixion, his victory of obedience would *draw all men* to himself. The emphasis is not on the totality of the response, for that

would depend upon faith, but on the universality of the appeal. Judaism offered men a national shrine, a racial circumcision, and a sectarian religious law. By contrast, there was nothing partisan or provincial about the obedience, love, and power demonstrated at the cross. Jesus did not die because he had lost the battle but rather because he had won it against every force that enslaves the human spirit and estranges man from God.

With customary callousness the *crowd* ignored the liberating courage of Jesus and sought instead to measure his claims by their messianic preconceptions (cf. 7:40–43; 10:19–21). Whereas he had spoken paradoxically of the *death* he *was to die* by being "lifted up," they inferred *from the law* (i.e., Scriptures) that *the Christ remains forever,* probably a reference to the permanence of the Davidic kingship (Psalm 89:36; Ezek. 37:25). Ironically, they envisioned a messiah who would live to perpetuate Jewish nationalism forever while Jesus by his death sought to transcend that vision and become a magnet drawing *all men* to a kingdom not of this world.

So irreconcilable were these opposing viewpoints that the questions of the crowd could not be answered. Instead, in the little parable of the traveller at sunset, Jesus sharpened the urgency of availing oneself of the *light* before the *darkness* falls (cf. 9:4–5; 11:9–10). Although many in the crowd already were walking in spiritual *darkness* and did *not know where* they were going, as long as Jesus was with them there was an opportunity to *believe in the light* and so *become sons of light.* With this vivid summary of the alternatives confronting Israel, Jesus concluded his public ministry in their midst.

3. Conclusion to the Book of Signs (12: 36b–50)

Further proof that chapters 2—12 comprise a major unit within the Gospel is provided by this elaborate conclusion which clearly divides the Gospel into two parts. Chapter 12 prepares for this formal postscript with several preliminary "conclusions" which express with finality the termination of the public ministry (12:7–8,23,31,35–36). This last section differs, however, both in the retrospective summation by the Evangelist (vv. 36b–43) and in the soliloquy by Jesus (vv. 44–50). Here the second person plural of direct discourse to the Jews is dropped, and these paragraphs are directed primarily to the reader.

(1) The Final Rejection of Jesus (12: 36b–43)

When Jesus had said this, he departed and hid himself from them. ³⁷ Though he had done so many signs before them, yet they did not believe in him; ³⁸ it was that the word spoken by the prophet Isaiah might be fulfilled:
"Lord, who has believed our report,
and to whom has the arm of the Lord been revealed?"
³⁹ Therefore they could not believe. For Isaiah again said,
⁴⁰ "He has blinded their eyes and hardened their heart,
lest they should see with their eyes and perceive with their heart,
and turn for me to heal them."
⁴¹ Isaiah said this because he saw his glory and spoke of him. ⁴² Nevertheless many even of the authorities believed in him, but for fear of the Pharisees they did not confess it, lest they should be put out of the synagogue: ⁴³ for they loved the praise of men more than the praise of God.

His ministry to Israel at an end, Jesus *departed and hid himself*, the third withdrawal from Jerusalem in the final months before the passion (cf. 10:40–42; 11:54). During the public ministry *he had done* a great *many signs* (cf. 7:31; 11:47; 20:30; 21:25), although chapters 2—12 record only a few. The purpose of these signs, to lead men to *believe in him* (cf. 20:31), had been realized in such limited fashion that the resulting situation abundantly fulfilled the descriptions of Israel's unbelief (cf. Isa. 53:1; 6:10). Jesus was not the first messenger of God to encounter opposition. In searching for an explanation, the early church soon discovered that the Old Testament had deep insight into the dynamics of rejection, particularly in the prophets and Psalms.

These verses do not reflect anti-Semitic prejudices directed against Israel by frustrated Christians but represent a judgment on the Jews by their own Scriptures (see comment on 9:41). The primary concern here is not to damn any individual but to explain the consistency of God in achieving his purposes throughout the history of his people. For centuries, the fearful words of Isaiah had stood in Scripture as a warning of Israel to itself. The whole appeal of Jesus' ministry—lamentably unheeded—was, "Don't let this prophecy come true for you!" In fact, it was the vision of Jesus in his preexistent *glory* with God that prompted Isaiah to utter his warning in the first place (the antecedent of *his* and *him* in v. 41 seems to refer to Jesus, not God).

Proof that vv. 37–41 are not meant to condemn the Jews collectively is provided by vv. 42–43, which report that *many even of the authorities believed in him*. Surely it took a double measure of mercy to count this group as believers since for *fear of the Pharisees they did not confess it, lest they should be put out of the synagogue* (cf. 9:22). In a more popular period, Jesus had encountered superficial faith based on the impressiveness of his signs (e.g., 2:23–25; 7:31), whereas here faith was half-formed because it had been repressed by intimidation from the power structure. In the former case faith was defective because it did not put God above the love of self, whereas in the latter case it was flawed because it did not put God above the love of *others*. Nevertheless Jesus honored such faith, however feeble, in the hope that it would flower into courageous and self-forgetful discipleship.

(2) The Final Claim of Jesus (12:44–50)

⁴⁴ And Jesus cried out and said, "He who believes in me, believes not in me but in him who sent me. ⁴⁵ And he who sees me sees him who sent me. ⁴⁶ I have come as light into the world, that whoever believes in me may not remain in darkness. ⁴⁷ If any one hears my

sayings and does not keep them, I do not judge him; for I did not come to judge the world but to save the world. ⁴⁸ He who rejects me and does not receive my sayings has a judge; the word that I have spoken will be his judge on the last day. ⁴⁹ For I have not spoken on my own authority; the Father who sent me has himself given me commandment what to say and what to speak. ⁵⁰ And I know that his commandment is eternal life. What I say, therefore, I say as the Father has bidden me."

This final paragraph in the "book of signs" provides a formal résumé of the public message of Jesus to Israel, summarizing theological themes developed in 3:16-21; 5:19-29; and 8:12-26. Since Jesus had already gone into hiding (v. 36b), the passage has no historical setting and thus is given a timeless quality. The utter solemnity of style reinforces the gravity of the issues which must be pondered by the reader.

The connection with the preceding paragraph, especially vv. 39-40, is crucial. There the emphasis was on the sovereignty of God in dealing with hardened hearts and blinded eyes. But lest this appear to abrogate human freedom, here is an explicit appeal to "believe" in the heart and to "see" with the eyes. Man is judged because he does not "keep" or "receive" the sayings of Jesus, not because God desires his destruction. Clearly acceptance or rejection of Jesus are ultimate options open to every man.

The chief concern of the passage is to assert the primacy of God in the mission of Jesus. As the one who *sent* Jesus into the world, God is both the beginning and the end of faith, of sight, of judgment, of authority, and of revelation. Far from posing as a "second God" or in any way calling attention away from God—the basic charge levelled by the Jews in the name of monotheism—Jesus worked only to confront men with the reality of God in the totality of life. Paradoxically, in claiming no human status for himself—whether priestly, rabbinic, or kingly—he differed uniquely from all religious leaders and thereby demanded

some verdict as to his person. Chapters 13—21 tell how he should be "glorified" in the light of his "humiliation" in chapters 1—12.

Part Two: The Book of the Passion (13:1—20:31)

Now that the "book of signs" (chs. 2—12) has traced in successive stages the descent or humiliation of the Son of God, the "book of the passion" (chs. 13—20) will complete the "parabola of redemption" (see p. 210) by describing his ascent or exaltation to the Father. This great reversal of earthly rejection also takes place in three stages: (1) the preparation of the disciples for the cross and the coming of the Spirit (chs. 13—17); (2) the crucifixion of Jesus as the lifting up of obedient love (chs. 18—19); (3) the resurrection of Jesus which strengthens the faith of his followers and empowers them for mission (ch. 20).

It is highly significant that this turning point in the plot of the Johannine drama is located before rather than after the crucifixion. As a result, the cross is presented not as the final indignity suffered by a defeated martyr but, paradoxically, as the coronation of a triumphant King who reigns from a tree of shame. In the resurrection God did not somehow rescue Jesus from the disgrace of a scandalous death; rather, he confirmed that the crucifixion was itself the victory that had finished the work of redemption (cf. 19:30).

Such a perspective helps to explain the poise of Jesus throughout his passion. There was no fear, agony, or despair. Jesus anticipated every move of his adversaries and alone remained in complete control of the situation (cf. 13:11,18–19,26–27; 16:33; 18:4–6,33–37; 19:26–27,30). This does not mean, however, that the Evangelist has given us a falsified account free of suffering in order to present Jesus as a self-sufficient Stoic. Quite to the contrary, he has conceived of the whole Gospel as an extended passion story (note such introductory references as 1:10–11,29,36; 2:4,13–22). Already in 5:16–18 Jesus was facing persons bent on killing him. His entire public ministry was in one sense a "trial" characterized by bitter controversy.

Thus the very design of the Gospel shows that Jesus faced the ordeal of the cross, as it were, in advance of the event (e.g., 10:11; 12:27). Unlike the Synoptics where Gethsemane came later, by the time chapter 13 opened his struggle was over, the desolating despair of Israel's rejection was past, and he moved forward in the joy of perfect obedience and in the certainty of future glory.

This transition in the Gospel marks a major shift not only in the ministry of Jesus but in the role of the disciples. To this point, after a brief introduction in 1:35–51 the closest followers of Jesus had played a strikingly small part. Throughout the great debates of chapters 5—10, when the Jewish authorities demanded witnesses who could testify on Jesus' behalf, the disciples were neither summoned nor did they volunteer any defense of their leader. When occasionally they played a modest role, it was invariably marred by lack of insight (e.g., 6:5–9,15–19,66–71; 9:1–4; 11:8,12–16; 12:4–6,16,20–23). The strong impression is given in John 1—12 that Jesus ministered alone and that his primary concern was with Judaism and its religious leadership.

By contrast, the disciples occupy a prominent place in John 13—21. If the first half of the Gospel is a commentary on how the old Israel "received him not" (1:11), the second half is a commentary on how those of the new Israel "who received him" were enabled to become the true children of God (1:12). In chapters 1—12, the emphasis was on the dialectic of light and darkness that judged Israel's response to the offer of life (*phōs/phōtizō* and *skotia/skotos* occur in this sense 32 times in 1—12 but never in 13—21). In chapters 13—21, however, the emphasis is on the love between Father and Son that is to be reproduced in the lives of believers (*agapē/*

agapaō and *philos/phileō* occur in this sense 12 times in 1—12 but 48 times in 13—21). This shift gives a strongly personal and ethical character to the fellowship of the church depicted in John 13—21 which contrasts strongly with the schism which rent the Jewish fellowship in John 1—12 (Dodd, *Interpretation*, pp. 398–399).

I. Jesus Prepares His Disciples (13:1—17:26)

In all four Gospels considerable private discourse involving Jesus and his disciples comes between the close of the public ministry and the beginning of the passion. The most extensive one of these interludes is John 13—17, partly because it presents in one unified section the Johannine equivalent of material which the Synoptics present separately as sayings of Jesus delivered on the Mount of Olives (Matt. 24:1—25:46; Mark 13:1–37; Luke 21:5–36), in the upper room (Matt. 26:20–30; Mark 14:17–26; Luke 22:14–38), and at Gethsemane (Matt. 26:36–46; Mark 14:32–42; Luke 22:40–46). By combining these teachings on the future, on the death of Jesus, and on the importance of prayer, the fourth Gospel has carried to climactic expression an emphasis only partially developed in the other Gospels.

The fusion of this esoteric material into a homogeneous unit represents the most original literary contribution of the Evangelist to the structure of his Gospel. Nowhere else in early Christian literature is discipleship more comprehensively linked to the historical ministry of Jesus in the past, to the indwelling of the Spirit in the present, and to the struggle of the church with the world in the future. By placing this section at the midpoint of the Gospel rather than at its end, the Evangelist thereby insisted that the church is not an idea which men conceived in the aftermath of tragedy but is the ongoing life of the people of God which Jesus transformed as an integral part of his task on earth. The disciples were not caught unprepared by the sudden departure of their leader, for he had already defined for them the post-resurrection nature of their existence. Just so, the reader is helped to grasp the "glory of the cross" in chapters 18—19 because in chapters 13—17 he has already been introduced to the kind of community which it will bring into being.

The great concern of Jesus for the fate of his followers—even though he was the one about to die!—is reflected in the three ways by which he prepared them for the ordeal soon to unfold. First, utilizing the simplest method of all, he provided a personal example in the foot-washing as an acted parable of the meaning of the cross (13:1–30). Next, he followed this object lesson with detailed instruction in a farewell discourse on Christian existence in the era after his death (13:31—16:33). Finally, as a spiritual climax, he employed the most exalted method of all, divine intercession, to set the destiny of the disciples in an eternal context through his prayer of consecration (17:1–26). No follower of Jesus is asked to embrace the cross of chapters 18—19 until he has first been shown what it meant to the Master, has been taught what it will involve for himself, and has been offered to God in prayer by the one who conquered its every terror.

The most distinctive subject matter in chapters 13—17 concerns the counselor (RSV) or Paraclete (from the Gr. *parakletos*), a concept referred to in five passages here (14:15–17, 25–26; 15:26–27; 16:7–15) and in 1 John 2:1, but nowhere else in the New Testament.[31] This title for the Holy Spirit (cf. 14:17,26; 15:26; 16:13) cannot be translated adequately by a single English term because it has connotations of advocate or witness, of intercessor or spokesman, of comforter or consoler, and of teacher or guide. Although the word had not been used earlier in either Hebrew or Greek to designate a religious

office, its meaning was anticipated both in the Old Testament pattern of a tandem relationship between departing leaders and the successors who carried on their work (e.g., Moses/Joshua, Elijah/Elisha) and in the late Jewish view of angelic spirits as defenders of God's people and mediators of divine truth. The fundamental difference, of course, is that in the fourth Gospel the role of the Paraclete is linked exclusively to Jesus. Because everything to be done by the Paraclete was also said to have been done by Jesus, the former functions as the continuing reality of the latter in the world after his ascension.

The primary mission of the Paraclete is described as twofold: (1) to indwell the disciples as that source of strength and insight which formerly was theirs in Jesus; (2) to judge the world by the victory which Jesus won in his earthly trials with Satan. An understanding of these roles was especially relevant to the church at the time when this Gospel was written. As apostolic eyewitnesses began to die out, some must have supposed that the last living link with the earthly Jesus would be severed.

John countered with the assurance that through the ministry of the Paraclete the Christian community not only had a permanent connection with the incarnate Lord but that this Spirit would guide later generations to understand Jesus just as he had enabled the earliest disciples to do so. Furthermore, the church need not lose hope over the failure of an early return by Jesus to end this evil age. Jesus had already come back in the Comforter to fill with meaning the interval before the final consummation. The world might suppose that the cross had destroyed everything for which Jesus stood because death seemed to banish him from the earth, but the church knew that his Spirit was alive and triumphant in its midst.

1. The Last Supper (13:1–30)

This opening scene in the upper room is as surprising for what it omits as for what it includes. The dominant feature in the Synoptics—the institution of the Lord's Supper

---

[31] On the Paraclete in the Gospel of John, see Raymond E. Brown, "The Paraclete in the Fourth Gospel," *New Testament Studies*, 13 (1967), pp. 113–132, and the literature cited there, especially Hans Windisch, *The Spirit-Paraclete in the Fourth Gospel*, trans. James W. Cox; "Facet Books, Biblical Series," 20 (Philadelphia: Fortress, 1968).

—goes unmentioned here, while in its place stands an incident—the foot washing —which is not referred to in the Synoptics. The basic reason for this silence seems to be a desire to guard the Supper from misunderstanding on two fronts.

First, the distinctive Johannine dating by which the last meal is eaten on Nisan 14, the night *before* the Passover (rather than on Nisan 15, the night *of* the Passover, as in the Synoptics) suggests a concern to distinguish the Christian rite from its Jewish counterpart. While the Passover may have provided certain historical antecedents to the Supper, the two observances could never have had the same significance because the latter was based on the death of Jesus at the hands of those who were preparing to celebrate the former. Thus the institution of the Supper was omitted here lest it be wrongly inferred that Jesus was thereby perpetuating a Jewish custom.

Again, in the Christian world at the time of the fourth Gospel, there were tendencies toward the extreme sacramentalizing of the Supper as the "medicine of immortality" or "antidote against death" (Ignatius, *Ephesians* 20:2) and as itself "the flesh of our Saviour Jesus Christ" (Ignatius, *Smyrnaeans* 7:1). John may have feared that the Supper would become a substitute for the historical uniqueness of Jesus, and so he suppressed any suggestion that the founder of Christianity inaugurated an act of worship designed to perpetuate his incarnation through tangible symbols. In place of this hypersacramentalism, John insisted that the life of Jesus was fixed in the past but that its meaning could become present to each new generation primarily as the Spirit contemporized his unrepeatable words and deeds (cf. on 6:52–65).[32]

(1) The Washing of the Disciples' Feet (13:1–11)

¹ Now before the feast of the Passover, when Jesus knew that his hour had come to depart

---

32 This view is developed by Helmut Koester, "History and Cult in the Gospel of John and in Ignatius of Antioch," *Journal for Theology and the Church,* 1 (1965), pp. 111–123.

out of this world to the Father, having loved his own who were in the world, he loved them to the end. ² And during supper, when the devil had already put it into the heart of Judas Iscariot, Simon's son, to betray him, ³ Jesus, knowing that the Father had given all things into his hands, and that he had come from God and was going to God, ⁴ rose from supper, laid aside his garments, and girded himself with a towel. ⁵ Then he poured water into a basin, and began to wash the disciples' feet, and to wipe them with the towel with which he was girded. ⁶ He came to Simon Peter; and Peter said to him, "Lord, do you wash my feet?" ⁷ Jesus answered him, "What I am doing you do not know now, but afterward you will understand." ⁸ Peter said to him, "You shall never wash my feet." Jesus answered him, "If I do not wash you, you have no part in me." ⁹ Simon Peter said to him, "Lord, not my feet only but also my hands and my head!" ¹⁰ Jesus said to him, "He who has bathed does not need to wash, except for his feet, but he is clean all over; and you are clean, but not all of you." ¹¹ For he knew who was to betray him; that was why he said, "You are not all clean."

Just as the "book of signs" (chs. 2—12) was introduced with an impressive theological affirmation (1:50–51) which depicted the arrival on earth of the Man from heaven, so the "book of the passion" (chs. 13—20) begins with an equally exalted preface (13:1–3) which provides the theological basis on which he would *depart out of this world to the Father.* Two sweeping summaries each provide a threefold interpretation of the events about to unfold.

First, in v. 1: (1) Since the passion of Jesus came just *before the* Jewish *feast of the Passover* (cf. 18:28; 19:14,31,42), the drama of the true paschal Lamb (1:29,36) was to be played out against the backdrop of Israel's holy history. (2) Unlike earlier occasions when premature human pressure was applied (2:4; 7:30; 8:20), Jesus' *hour* of voluntary self-sacrifice *had* now *come* on the divine timetable (cf. 12:23,27; 17:1). (3) This climactic act of obedience involved the loving of *his own . . . to the end* (cf. 1:11–12) both in a quantitative sense (i.e., to the bitter end of his life) and in a qualitative sense (i.e., to the *n*th degree; cf. 15:13).

Second, in vv. 2–3: (1) The limitless love of Jesus for his followers was a deliberate response to the initiative of *the devil* that *Judas Iscariot, Simon's son,* should *betray him* (cf. 6:70-71; 13:27). (2) Such sacrificial devotion unto death on the part of Jesus was not a sign of weakness, however, but of omnipotence on the part of one who knew *that the Father had given all things into his hands* (cf. Matt. 28:18). (3) This sense of sovereign authority in a moment of mortal peril sprang from the certainty that both his origin and his destination—his "whence" and his "whither"—were rooted in *God.*

In order to initiate his disciples into the mystery of his impending passion, Jesus symbolically acted out those transcendent truths at the bedrock of his self-consciousness. First, he *laid aside his garments,* suggestive of the laying aside of his life for his own (cf. the same verb, *tithēmi,* in 10:17-18). Then he *girded himself with a towel* (cf. 1 Peter 5:5), *poured water into a basin, and began to wash the disciples' feet.* This strange behavior was completely unprecedented both because it took place *during supper* (cf. vv. 2a, 4a), whereas it was customary to bathe the feet before a meal, and because even Jewish slaves were not required to perform tasks so menial. In the opening scene of the passion drama, Jesus demonstrated that his earthly career had now reached its nadir. Having descended to the depths of abject humiliation, he now began his ascent to the heights from the lowest point imaginable.

The circumstances which prompted this shocking strategy are perhaps described in Luke 22:24-27. As the disciples squabbled over who among them was greatest, the one who knew that God *had given all things into his hands* took into those hands the implements of the lowliest slave (cf. Phil. 2:7)—no crown or sceptre but a pitcher and basin!—in order to show that true greatness consists not in where one sits but in how one serves (Luke 22:27). The use of water for washing may suggest that the servant work of Jesus was to cleanse his followers from sin by his approaching death (cf. 1 John 1:7).

As was the case also in the Synoptics (cf. Mark 8:31-33), Peter sought to repudiate this paradox of a slave-king because he did *not know* then *what* Jesus was *doing,* although *afterward*—in the light of the crucifixion and resurrection—he would come to *understand* (cf. 16:12-13). But Jesus just as firmly insisted that if he did *not wash* Peter's feet—i.e., if Peter refused to learn this lesson—then the follower could *have no part in* the destiny of his Master. Faced with this terrible alternative, Peter impulsively swung to the opposite extreme and now asked for more instead of less than he had been offered: *Lord, not my feet only but also my hands and my head!*

To correct both extremes Jesus told the little parable of the bathtub and basin: *He who has bathed* completely before going out to dinner *does not need to wash* his entire body again when he arrives at the home of the host, for he is already *clean all over.* However, he may need to *wash . . . his feet* which have become dusty on the road. Just so Peter and the others were already *clean* from their earlier commitment to Jesus (cf. 15:3)—except, of course, for Judas *who was to betray him*—but they still needed to have their understanding cleansed, as it were, from "travel stains" on the pilgrimage of discipleship. The conversion that conquers sin involves a decisive beginning that becomes the basis for a daily renewal of grace.

This exchange between Jesus and Peter brilliantly illumines the dynamics of a growing faith. At first, Peter refused to learn the hard lesson of the cross on the assumption that his commitment was already complete, only to be told that deeper discoveries were essential to a relationship with Jesus. Overreacting to this rebuke, he then embraced the opposite error of supposing that all of his earlier commitments were now invalid. But Jesus assured him that one does not have to start over again in order to outgrow previous limitations. A young person, for example, is not asked to renounce a baptism based on childhood faith as the price for becoming a mature believer. Jesus both honors our beginnings in the past and demands our openness to the future.

(2) The Example of Jesus (13:12–20)

12 When he had washed their feet, and taken his garments, and resumed his place, he said to them, "Do you know what I have done to you? 13 You call me Teacher and Lord; and you are right, for so I am. 14 If I then, your Lord and Teacher, have washed your feet, you also ought to wash one another's feet. 15 For I have given you an example, that you also should do as I have done to you. 16 Truly, truly, I say to you, a servant is not greater than his master; nor is he who is sent greater than he who sent him. 17 If you know these things, blessed are you if you do them. 18 I am not speaking of you all; I know whom I have chosen; it is that the scripture may be fulfilled, 'He who ate my bread has lifted his heel against me.' 19 I tell you this now, before it takes place, that when it does take place you may believe that I am he. 20 Truly, truly, I say to you, he who receives any one whom I send receives me; and he who receives me receives him who sent me."

Having "laid aside his garments" (v. 4) as a symbol of the way in which he would lay aside his life, Jesus now took *his garments* again as a symbol of the way in which he would take back his life (cf. the same verb, *lambanō*, in 10:17), thus resuming the rightful *place* that was his as *Teacher and Lord. If* he, *then*, whose servanthood would be validated by God in the resurrection, had willingly *washed* the disciples' *feet*, they *also ought to wash one another's feet.* After all, he was the *master* and they were the *servant;* he was the sender and they were the *sent.* The pattern of Jesus' passion not only provided abstract truths which they should *know* but a concrete *example* which they should *do,* thereby uniting theology and ethics. In the first century humility was despised as no virtue at all, but Jesus made it the badge of discipleship. The priorities set in this passage eventually altered the moral landscape of mankind.

A problem is raised because the practice which Jesus utilized to provide an example of humility is nonexistent in our culture. For the first disciples nothing could have

dramatized the role of a servant more forcefully than the washing of their feet (cf. 1 Tim. 5:10); whereas for contemporary western man this act would have no self-evident significance at all. This means that to carry out the intention of Jesus we must search for new servant forms which have the same equivalent impact in our society as footwashing did in ancient Palestine.

As was true in the preceding paragraph (vv. 10–11), this unit also closes with a somber reference to the treachery of Judas. Perhaps Jesus realized that his insistence on lowly service was the emphasis to which Judas most violently objected. In any case, Jesus was not taken by surprise that rejection could come from within the disciple band for *scripture* itself recorded how even a "bosom friend" might spurn the hospitality proffered him, like an animal kicking the hand that feeds it (Psalm 41:9). Jesus had *chosen* to take that risk in seeking to reach men of widely varying persuasions, and now he was realistically aware that Judas had not responded to his lavish love (vv. 1–2).

Therefore, he warned his disciples in advance so that when the betrayal did *take place* they would know that he was no helpless victim but rather the great *I am* (*egō eimi*); i.e., that he represented the divine presence of God whose providence would not be overruled even by the most terrible choices which it permitted men to make. Typically, this warning was coupled with the promise that anyone willing for Jesus to *send* him on mission as a servant apostle would be united not only with Jesus but with the God who had *sent* him.

(3) The Betrayal of Jesus (13:21–30)

21 When Jesus had thus spoken, he was troubled in spirit, and testified, "Truly, truly, I say to you, one of you will betray me." 22 The disciples looked at one another, uncertain of whom he spoke. 23 One of his disciples, whom Jesus loved, was lying close to the breast of Jesus; 24 so Simon Peter beckoned to him and said, "Tell us who it is of whom he speaks."

25 So lying thus, close to the breast of Jesus, he said to him, "Lord, who is it?" 26 Jesus answered, "It is he to whom I shall give this morsel when I have dipped it." So when he had dipped the morsel, he gave it to Judas, the son of Simon Iscariot. 27 Then after the morsel, Satan entered into him. Jesus said to him, "What you are going to do, do quickly." 28 Now no one at the table knew why he said this to him. 29 Some thought that, because Judas had the money box, Jesus was telling him, "Buy what we need for the feast"; or, that he should give something to the poor. 30 So, after receiving the morsel, he immediately went out; and it was night.

The very mention of a traitor in their midst *troubled* the *spirit* of *Jesus* (cf. 11:33; 12:27). This is the last time that such inner turmoil is mentioned in this Gospel, suggesting that in the defection of an intimate disciple Jesus anticipated the agony of the cross. Although the betrayal was a matter of the utmost importance (*Truly, truly*) which the group needed to know in advance (cf. v. 19), Jesus graciously veiled the identity of the culprit (*one of you*) so as to shield him from the rage of his companions, to leave open the freedom of choice to change, and to confront each one present with the necessity of self-examination (cf. Mark 14:19 where all of the disciples began to ask, "Is it I?").

Thrown into confusion by this announcement, the disciples signaled through *Simon Peter* to the *one . . . whom Jesus loved* to find out for them *who it* was *of whom he* spoke. In this first explicit reference to the "beloved disciple" (cf. on 11:3) it is not clear whether he was considered one of the twelve or not. Located to the right of Jesus at the table, his head was *close to the breast of Jesus* (cf. 1:18) as they reclined on their left sides during the meal, thus facilitating a whispered consultation. Upon relaying Peter's query, *Who is it?*, he was told, *It is he to whom I shall give this morsel when I have dipped it.* In the social custom of that day it was a mark of special favor for the host to dip bread in the sauce and personally serve a guest.

This suggests that the identification of *Judas* in such fashion was more of a private

unmasking than a public exposé. To Jesus this simple act represented love's last appeal to one on the verge of perdition (cf. 17:12). To *Judas* it may have seemed like a final invitation to accept Jesus' strategy of suffering love, an offer which he rebuffed as *Satan* was allowed to enter *into him*. To the disciples, however, it may have been merely a thoughtful gesture on the part of Jesus as he dispatched Judas on a hasty errand because he *had the money box* containing the group's funds (cf. 12:6). Apparently *no one at the table* (unless it be the beloved disciple) could fathom that Jesus had utilized a tender act of affection to designate his traitor. This would explain their failure to stop Judas as he set out on his sinister business.

As Judas *went out,* the door opened revealing that *night* had fallen outside. The darkness was a fit habitat to envelop Judas as he carried out his dark designs (3:19). But on the inside, with the traitor gone, Jesus was *now* able to share with his disciples the glory of the Son of man (v. 31). Thus the stage was set for the final act in the drama of the light that "shines in the darkness" (cf. 1:5a). The farewell discourse about to begin (13:31—16:33) will explain how "the darkness has not overcome it" (cf. 1:5b; 16:33).

2. The Departure and Return of Jesus (13:31—14:31)

The first cycle of material in the farewell discourse is demarcated by the departure of the devil's emissary, Judas, in 13:30 and by the coming of the satanic ruler himself in 14:30–31. Between these points, Jesus countered this sinister development by discussing with the disciples his own departure to the Father and his coming again to abide with them. This theme is dominant throughout 13:31—14:31, verbs for "going" and "coming" (*akoloutheō, erchomai, poreuomai, hupagō*) being used at least 20 times in a spiritual rather than a spatial sense.

The internal structure of this somewhat miscellaneous collection of sayings has been built around questions from four identified disciples (Peter, Thomas, Philip, Judas) whose questions are distributed throughout the section to carry the dialogue forward (13:36; 14:5,8,22). Taken together, these queries reflect not only the uneasiness of Jesus' followers during the hours before his death but also the problems troubling the early church at the time when this Gospel was written. The basic issue was: Where is Jesus? How are his followers now related to him and to each other? The basic answer here developed was: The risen Jesus is related to Christians on earth as the Father was related to him while he was on earth. The closeness of the man Jesus to his unseen heavenly Father has been made the model for the bond which should now exist between the church and its ascended Lord (14:20). Just as the presence of the Spirit given by God to Jesus (1:32–33; 3:34) was not other than or less than the presence of the Father with him (5:19–20; 10:30,38), so the presence of the Paraclete given by Jesus to the church (14:16–17, 25–26) is also to be understood as the presence of the Lord with his own (14:3,18,23).

The thematic motif of troubled hearts near the beginning (14:1) and the end (14:27) of this section suggests that its primary purpose was to provide reassurance for a community that was fearful because it had been cut loose by the inexorable movement of time from its ties with the original Christian generation. As death dissolved the last links with those who had been eyewitnesses of the incarnation, the ongoing church was reminded that Jesus had promised his followers a better situation after his departure than before (14:28–29).

Note the advantages of the post-resurrection era which are described in this section: (1) the support of a loving fellowship (13:34–35); (2) the preparation of a place in the Father's house (14:2–3); (3) the knowledge of the way of salvation (14:4–6); (4) the power to do greater works than Jesus had done (14:12);

(5) the privilege of petitionary prayer (14:13–14); (6) the help of the Paraclete or Spirit of truth (14:16–17,25–26); (7) the personal return of both Jesus and his Father to make a home with their loved ones (14:18–23); and (8) the provision of a peace that the world does not know (14:27).

Obviously, the fourth Gospel has not minimized the significance either of the first coming of Jesus in the midst of history (e.g., 1:14; 6:53–58) or of his final coming at the end of history (e.g., 5:28–29; 6:39–40,44,54; 12:48), but equal emphasis has also been given to his spiritual coming during the interval between the two. The type of apocalyptic material contained in the great eschatological discourse which stands at this point in the Synoptics (Matt. 24–25; Mark 13; Luke 21) is nowhere to be found here, perhaps because it had been widely misunderstood by early Christians to mean that the end of the world would take place in their generation (cf. Matt. 24:29,34; Mark 13:29–30; Luke 21:31–32).

Instead, in the theology of Christian existence developed throughout John 13—17, and especially in 13:31—14:31, we have the most daring reinterpretation of the relationship between time and eternity attempted anywhere in the New Testament. Now that the eschatological Redeemer had entered the historical process, the two realms were no longer related spatially as in Greek thought (the world above and the world below), or temporally as in Hebrew thought (the present age and the age to come), but paradoxically; i.e., by faith one lives where the two worlds interpenetrate and the two ages overlap.

(1) The Discussion with Peter (13:31–38)

31 When he had gone out, Jesus said, "Now is the Son of man glorified, and in him God is glorified; 32 if God is glorified in him, God will also glorify him in himself, and glorify him at once. 33 Little children, yet a little while I am with you. You will seek me; and as I said to the Jews so now I say to you, 'Where I am going you cannot come.' 34 A new command-

ment I give to you, that you love one another; even as I have loved you, that you also love one another. ³⁵ By this all men will know that you are my disciples, if you have love for one another."

³⁶ Simon Peter said to him, "Lord, where are you going?" Jesus answered, "Where I am going you cannot follow me now; but you shall follow afterward." ³⁷ Peter said to him, "Lord, why cannot I follow you now? I will lay down my life for you." ³⁸ Jesus answered, "Will you lay down your life for me? Truly, truly, I say to you, the cock will not crow, till you have denied me three times.

Once Judas had *gone out* from the disciples for the final time (cf. 1 John 2:18–19), those events were *now* set in motion by which Jesus as *Son of man* would be *glorified* (cf. 17:1). But because Jesus did not seek glory for himself, *God* would also be glorified by the obedient love shown at the cross, as he had been by the entire ministry which led up to this climax. Note that God himself gave the glory that he then received back in return; i.e., the work of Jesus was a divine act from start to finish. All that any man can do to enhance the "reputation" or "prestige" of God on earth is to let God be God in his life as Jesus did in his.[33]

Note also that this glorification of Jesus was a thing both of the past (*is glorified*) and of the future (*will glorify*), in that the commitment to suffer had already been made but was yet to be carried out. God is not honored either by a momentary decision that never leads to courageous actions or by an impulsive action not based on deep and abiding decisions, but by a consistent life in which the word and the deed, the inward and the outward, the past and the future are all one.

Since his glorification in death lay immediately ahead (*at once*), Jesus would be *with* his *little children* (cf. *orphanos*, Gr. in 14:18) only for *a little while* (cf. 16:16–24) and then would be *going* where they could not *come* until later (contrast 7:33–36, where the Jews were given no

---

[33] On the meaning of "glory," see A. M. Ramsey, *The Glory of God and the Transfiguration of Christ* (London: Longmans, Green and Co., 1949), and on its use in John 13—17, see pp. 69–81.

---

hope of ever coming). Meanwhile, to fill the void created by his physical absence, the disciples were commanded to *love one another even as* he had *loved* them (cf. 13:1). This *commandment* was *new* in that it made love the central ethical reality of life and defined that love by the historical example of Jesus. The Israelite was enjoined by the Old Testament to love his neighbor as himself (Lev. 19:18), whereas the disciple was to emulate one who loved his neighbor more than himself (cf. 15:13).

Obviously, a love based on the unique revelation given in Jesus could not be required of everyone; but even though limited to his *disciples* it was intended as a witness to *all men*. Since Jesus was going away, his followers would no longer be identified by their attachment to his physical presence but by their perpetuation of his kind of love in the life of a visible community.

Proof that Christian morality must be based on the example of Jesus rather than on the inner impulses or even the sincere convictions of the disciples was immediately provided by *Simon Peter*. Even though Jesus had plainly stated that they could not come where he was going but that they could love as he was loving, Peter sought to sidestep this responsibility by questioning what Jesus was to do (cf. 21: 18–22). When told that he could not *follow* Jesus *now* (i.e., that he could not share his unique cross) but that there would be abundant opportunities to *follow* Jesus *afterward* (i.e., that new possibilities for discipleship would be opened up by his death), Peter ignored this promise of a brighter future and in his impatience to do something *now* offered to *lay down* his *life* for Jesus.

In response, Jesus shattered the courageous boast of Peter by solemnly assuring him that the *cock* would *not crow* until he had *denied* him at least *three times*. "Cockcrow" was the name given to the third watch of the night (12:00—3:00 A.M.), hence Jesus predicted that Peter's loyalty would not last until the next morning! There is no reason to doubt the good intentions of Peter, but they were not adequate for the ordeal which Jesus was facing. The dramatic contrast in the two parts of this passage between the "I have loved you" of Jesus and the "I will lay down my life for you" of Peter highlights the truth that discipleship cannot be based on how we lay down our life for him but on how he lays down his life for us.

(2) The Discussion with Thomas (14:1–7)

¹ "Let not your hearts be troubled; believe in God, believe also in me. ² In my Father's house are many rooms; if it were not so, would I have told you that I go to prepare a place for you? ³ And when I go and prepare a place for you, I will come again and will take you to myself, that where I am you may be also. ⁴ And you know the way where I am going." ⁵ Thomas said to him, "Lord, we do not know where you are going; how can we know the way?" ⁶ Jesus said to him, "I am the way, and the truth, and the life; no one comes to the Father, but by me. ⁷ If you had known me, you would have known my Father also; henceforth you know him and have seen him."

There were many reasons for the *hearts* of the disciples to be *troubled:* one of them would betray Jesus (13:10–11,18,21); another would deny him thrice (13:38); most disturbing, Jesus was going where none of them could follow (13:33,36). As an antidote for despair Jesus bade them *believe* both *in God* and *in* himself. By faith their world that seemed so empty without him would become not a haunted house but a spiritual home with *many rooms* that included a *place* prepared for them by the "going" (i.e., the death and resurrection) of Jesus.

The KJV has translated *rooms* in this passage as "mansions." This term was taken over by Tyndale directly from the Latin *mansiones* which meant an "abode, dwelling place, habitation, rest camp, or way station," as did the Greek *monai.* The emphasis in the original word itself was on a place to stay rather than on the impressiveness of the place.[34]

Two possible circumstances may have

prompted Jesus to describe his future relations with the disciples as life together in a *house* with *many rooms.* First, these words were uttered almost in the shadow of the Temple, which was commonly called the *Father's house* (cf. 2:16). Outside the sanctuary proper (Gr. *naos*) were many shelters where the weary pilgrim might rest. Jesus may have alluded to this familiar arrangement when teaching that he would *go and prepare a place* (Gr. *topos*, a regular term for the Temple, as in 11:48); i.e., by his death and resurrection he would become the true spiritual temple (2: 19–21) filling the universe with the presence of God (4:21–24; cf. Isa. 66:1), leaving no corner vacant, no room empty. It would have been particularly relevant to Jews after A.D. 70 who had been driven from Jerusalem when their physical Temple was destroyed to learn that the "body" of Christ (2:21)—i.e., the church—was like a sanctuary where one might find both the reality of God and a resting place for the weary pilgrim.

A second basis of comparison is suggested by the Synoptic account of how Jesus, on the preceding day, had sent two of his disciples ahead to "prepare" a guest "room" for the Passover meal (Mark 14:12–16). They had not known the way but followed a man who led them to "a large upper room" where everything had been "prepared." This incident may have been utilized as an analogy in which the disciples' relationship to Jesus after his departure was likened to the intimate fellowship which they then enjoyed with him in the prepared place of a house with many rooms.

It has been traditional for many to interpret vv. 1–3 as a promise that either at death or at his second advent Christ *will come again and will take* the believer to be with himself in heaven. Particularly in the KJV translation, with its use of "mansions," the passage has provided great comfort and hope as a favorite funeral text. Several considerations suggest, however, that this passage may refer primarily to a coming of the risen Christ to the believer during this

---

[34] For details both on the meaning of *monai* and on the interpretation of this passage, see Smith, pp. 118–122.

earthly life in order to strengthen and reassure his troubled heart:

(1) The central concern of the disciples in the larger context is not with where they will go after death but with whether they will be left alone on earth after Jesus departs to the Father (13:33,36–37). (2) The answer of Jesus is that the disciples will not be abandoned but that both he and the Father will come to abide with them in the presence of the Paraclete (14:16–17,18,21,23,28). (3) The key word *rooms* (Gr. *monai*) in v. 2 is found elsewhere in the New Testament only in v. 23 where it is translated "home." There the reference is to the way in which Christians can learn to live "at home" in this world after the incarnation because the exalted Christ and his Father *will come again* to abide with them in spiritual fellowship.

If this be the main thrust of the passage, then its teaching serves not to weaken but rather to strengthen the Christian hope of heaven. Our experiences with Christ during the earthly pilgrimage furnish evidence that he has conquered death, and this in turn becomes the basis for our assurance that in him we may one day do likewise. If anything, John 14 promises not just that we shall one day go to heaven (for which see passages such as 17:24) but that Jesus has already brought heaven to us. Perhaps the best commentary on *that where I am you may be also* is from the Great Commission, "and lo, I am with you always, to the close of the age" (Matt. 28:20).

Up to this point, the destination of Jesus' journey had not been identified (13:33,36; 14:2–3); and yet he now told the disciples that they knew *the way where* he was *going;* i.e., they knew the road but not where it would lead. Immediately, *Thomas* objected that a knowledge of the destination was needed in order to *know the way.* To this Jesus replied that he himself was the true and living *way* and this was all that they needed to know. In other words they could begin to follow in the right direction (13:36) before seeing the ultimate destination. Unlike either the apoca-

lyptist or the Gnostic, the Christian does not need some special esoteric knowledge of the beyond in order to journey on the way of salvation below. Although he must live as does everyone in a world of sin and darkness, there is no reason to doubt the reality of a better world just because it has not yet been reached.

Two reasons are given why following Jesus as *the way* should be sufficient for the disciples. First, he is the only way by which *one comes to the Father.* Even though the disciples had not reached their final destination, they could be sure that God was the one waiting for them at the end of the pilgrimage. Second, to know Jesus was to know his *Father also,* so inseparable were the two (cf. 10:30). In a sense, the end had been anticipated from the beginning as God permitted himself to be *seen* in the earthly life of his Son.

(3) The Discussion with Philip (14:8–14)

⁸ Philip said to him, "Lord, show us the Father, and we shall be satisfied." ⁹ Jesus said to him, "Have I been with you so long, and yet you do not know me, Philip? He who has seen me has seen the Father; how can you say, 'show us the Father'? ¹⁰ Do you not believe that I am in the Father and the Father in me? The words that I say to you I do not speak on my own authority; but the Father who dwells in me does his works. ¹¹ Believe me that I am in the Father and the Father in me; or else believe me for the sake of the works themselves.

¹² "Truly, truly, I say to you, he who believes in me will also do the works that I do; and greater works than these will he do, because I go to the Father. ¹³ Whatever you ask in my name, I will do it, that the Father may be glorified in the Son; ¹⁴ if you ask anything in my name, I will do it.

Despite the clarifications offered by Jesus in vv. 1–7, the disciples were still confused. He had claimed to be "the way," yet his path led straight to a cross; to be "the truth," yet he could convince none of the religious leaders to embrace his cause; to be "the life," yet he would be dead in less than twenty-four hours!

Philip gave voice to the desire of the disciples for less ambiguous evidence in which to believe (cf. v. 1): *Lord, show us the Father, and we shall be satisfied.* Once again Jesus explained that Christian faith does not rest on impressive epiphanies such as those claimed by other religions, for God had come not in dazzling splendor but in human flesh: *He who has seen me has seen* all that human eyes are permitted to see of *the Father* (cf. 1 John 1:1). This is not a claim that the eternal God limited himself to the brief earthly life of Jesus but that he chose to be uniquely present there.

So complete was the mutual indwelling of Father and Son that the *words* and *works* of Jesus actually were the words and works of God. Philip would find the answer to his request by believing Jesus when he said, *I am in the Father and the Father in me.* If that ultimate assertion seemed difficult to accept, he could begin by believing him *for the sake of* those *works* which even the Jews had recognized that "no one can do . . . unless God is with him" (3:2). To be sure, miracle-faith is never as mature as personal faith, but better to believe on a superficial level than not to believe at all (cf. on 2:23–25; 5:36). At least the works were signs pointing to realities greater than *themselves.* While it is better to have the reality than the sign, it is also better to have the sign than to be lost!

If the disciples would *truly* believe *in* Jesus and not just give assent to his claims, then they *also* would *do the works* which he did. In fact, because his going *to the Father* by death and resurrection was to usher in an era of fulfillment, at that time the disciples would be able to do even *greater works than these.* Since works were intended to produce faith, this promise was abundantly fulfilled by the early Christian mission to the Gentiles that resulted in far more believers than Jesus ever won on earth. If the readers of this Gospel were discouraged because they had seen the departure of the earthly Jesus but not his return in glory, they should have realized that the spread of the Christian movement as men were converted by faith was a mightier work than some spectacular de-

nouement in history that would shut off that possibility forever.

Because of the complete oneness of God and Jesus (vv. 9–11), the latter was a proper object not only of faith (v. 12) but of prayer (v. 13). Once his work of redemption was finished and he was exalted to the Father, he would *do* for his own *whatever* they asked in his *name,* i.e., consistent with his character as it had been revealed by his earthly life (cf. 16:23–24). Everything that Jesus did in the flesh had *glorified the Father* (cf. 13:31–32). Now he would help his followers to continue that mission through the power of answered prayer.

(3) The Discussion with Judas (14:15–24)

15 "If you love me, you will keep my commandments. 16 And I will pray the Father, and he will give you another Counselor, to be with you for ever, 17 even the Spirit of truth, whom the world cannot receive, because it neither sees him nor knows him; you know him, for he dwells with you, and will be in you.

18 "I will not leave you desolate; I will come to you. 19 Yet a little while, and the world will see me no more, but you will see me; because I live, you will live also. 20 In that day you will know that I am in my Father, and you in me, and I in you. 21 He who has my commandments and keeps them, he it is who loves me; and he who loves me will be loved by my Father, and I will love him and manifest myself to him." 22 Judas (not Iscariot) said to him, "Lord, how is it that you will manifest yourself to us, and not to the world?" 23 Jesus answered him, "If a man loves me, he will keep my word, and my Father will love him, and we will come to him and make our home with him. 24 He who does not love me does not keep my words; and the word which you hear is not mine but the Father's who sent me.

The tremendous promises of vv. 12–14 were not made unconditionally. *If you love me* (cf. v. 21) controls the entire context in which Christ offered help to those who *keep* his *commandments* (cf. 13:34). Not only may they pray to him (vv. 13–14), but he *will pray the Father* who *will give* the disciples *another Counselor* (Gr. *paraklētos*). For the limited time that he was with them Jesus had been their source of strength, but now they would have a comforter, defender, and instructor who would *be with* them *for ever.* To be sure, *the world* could not *receive* the Paraclete *because it neither sees him nor knows him,* but this would not present any new problem since Jesus himself had been treated no better. He, too, had not been received (1:11; 3:11,32; 5:43; 12:48) by a world that "knew him not" (1:10,26; 8:14,19) and could not see the Father working in his life (6:36). Even the disciples had found it hard to know and see Jesus aright (vv. 8–9) but they would truly *know* the Paraclete because *he dwells* (abides) *with you, and will be in you.*

In the same breath that Jesus announced the coming of *another Counselor,* he assured the disciples, *I will come to you* (as in v. 3). This meant that the Paraclete would not be a different presence from that of Jesus but would be the same reality which they had known during his incarnate life. His "little children" (13:33) would not be left *desolate* or "orphaned" (Gr. *orphanos*) when, after *a little while,* he would disappear in death, because *in that* new *day* following his resurrection they would know that he had been made to *live* again *in* the *Father.* But they would *live also* because of a three-way mutual indwelling that now included the disciples within the kind of relationship that Jesus had shared with the Father during his days on earth (cf. 1 Cor. 3:23).

Throughout this section, the disciples had repeatedly expressed their desire for a clear revelation of those eschatological realities to which the life of Jesus was leading (cf. the questions in 13:36; 14:5,8). Now Jesus made explicit that he would become *manifest* not in cataclysmic portents but in the reality of reciprocal love. Still thinking in terms of a cosmic epiphany, *Judas (not Iscariot)* inquired how an effective manifestation could go unseen by *the world.* Elaborating on the promise in vv. 2–3, *Jesus answered* that both he and his *Father* would *come* in *love* to the one who *loves* him and keeps his *word* (13:34). Notice that in v. 3 the be-

liever is received into a room prepared by Christ in his Father's house, whereas here Christ and the Father occupy a room in the human heart which the disciple has prepared by love.

In this passage we have one of the profoundest answers in the New Testament to the delay of the Parousia. Prior to the end of time, Christ had already *come* to the church in the interim following his resurrection. Nor was this presence some inferior substitute for the apocalyptic splendor of which the disciples dreamed. Rather, they were here taught that until Christ is seen in heavenly glory (17:24) he may be seen on earth in deeds of love by which men *keep* his *word,* just as he also lived by love in obedience to his Father's word (14:31). It was as hard for the early church as it is for us to realize that love is a truly ultimate reality and that when men love one another they reveal the ultimate power that will transform the universe.

(5) Summary: the Legacy of Jesus (14:25–31)

25 "These things I have spoken to you, while I am still with you. 26 But the Counselor, the Holy Spirit, whom the Father will send in my name, he will teach you all things, and bring to your remembrance all that I have said to you. 27 Peace I leave with you; my peace I give to you; not as the world gives do I give to you. Let not your hearts be troubled, neither let them be afraid. 28 You heard me say to you, 'I go away, and I will come to you.' If you loved me, you would have rejoiced, because I go to the Father; for the Father is greater than I. 29 And now I have told you before it takes place, so that when it does take place, you may believe. 30 I will no longer talk much with you, for the ruler of this world is coming. He has no power over me; 31 but I do as the Father has commanded me, so that the world may know that I love the Father. Rise, let us go hence.

As this section of the farewell discourse draws to a close, Jesus is pictured delivering his valedictory, much like a man making a will *while* he is *still with* his loved ones. First, he promised that the Father who sent him would also *send* the Paraclete in his *name* (cf. vv. 16–17)—i.e., as his representative, on his authority, with his spirit. Thus, although his followers would have to adjust to a nonphysical form of his presence, they would not need to transfer their loyalties to a new leader, for the Paraclete would teach by bringing to *remembrance all that* Jesus had *said* to them (cf. on 16:12–15). Under the tutelage of the Holy Spirit, the church would enjoy the freedom to grow in its understanding of Jesus but not to outgrow the truth uniquely revealed by his life. The fourth Gospel itself is a magnificent illustration of the fulfillment of this promise since it reflects the creative fusion of historical memory with spiritual insight.

Another valuable legacy of Jesus was the *peace* that he would *leave with* them. His poise throughout the turbulent events of the passion is perhaps the most remarkable feature of that record (cf. 16:33). *The world* claimed to provide the peace of Rome (*Pax Romana*), but Jesus did *not give* an uneasy truce won with might and maintained by fear. Rather, his peace could relieve and assure *hearts* that were *troubled* because he would *go away* by a death of obedient love and then *come to* them in the victory of his resurrection. Rather than *be afraid*, they should *have rejoiced* over his departure *to the Father*, for God was *greater than* Jesus as the ultimate source of all that he had done for them.

The time for talking was at its end as Jesus turned his attention to the *ruler of this world*, who even then was *coming* to challenge him. It took supreme confidence to say, *He has no power over me*, for events would soon make Jesus appear to be utterly helpless. But he knew that if only he would *do* as the Father had *commanded* him, the *world* would come to *know* a kind of *love* for *the Father* that evil could never overcome. Bracing himself for this supreme conflict, Jesus, in words reminiscent of Gethsemane, bade the disciples share his readiness: *Rise, let us go hence* (cf. Mark 14:41–2). Since chapters 15—17 show that Jesus was not yet ready to depart literally, this cry must have summoned the disciples to an inner preparation which would interiorize in advance the ordeal that they soon would face in the garden.

3. The Responsibility of the Disciples (15:1—16:33)

Jesus now described in 15:1—16:33 the nature of discipleship during the era ushered in by his departure and return. The many parallels between chapters 13—14 and chapters 15—16 suggest that these two cycles of material may have served originally as alternative forms of a farewell discourse, but in this present form the latter chapters clearly presuppose the former and elaborate on the concepts introduced there. Despite the abrupt break at 14:31, the material in John 13—16 stands in a convincing theological sequence, making unnecessary the ingenious rearrangements which have been proposed to improve its order.

The central theme in 15:1—16:33 is that of the church in the world after the going away and the coming again of its Founder. This new situation is viewed from two perspectives. First, the inner life of the Christian community is described in fellowship with the risen Lord and the Paraclete (15:1–17; 16:12–15). Second, with the help of this indwelling divine presence, the disciples are pictured in victorious conflict with a hostile world (15:18—16:11). Following the longest monologue in the Gospel, this section concludes with a dramatic dialogue (16:16–33) which recapitulates the argument of the entire farewell discourse in chapters 13—16.

A dominant concern in 15:1—16:33 is to prove who is a true disciple (15:8). Positively, authentic Christianity is demonstrated by loving one another (15:9–10,12–13,17) and, negatively, by enduring the hatred of the world (15:18–20; 16:2–3). Otherwise, one is taken away (15:2) and cast forth (15:6) from within or else one falls away due to pressure from without (16:1). This recurring emphasis suggests that the present section was particularly relevant for the kind of church described in 1 John whose very existence was being tested (2:26; 4:1) by the same demonic forces with which Jesus grappled at the cross (2:18; 4:3). From this kindred writing, 1 John, we learn that there were those who did not love the brethren (2:9,11; 3:10,15; 4:8,20) but loved the world instead (2:5; 4:5). Some even "stumbled" (2:10) and "went out" from the fellowship (2:19) to "walk in darkness" (1:6; 2:11), guilty of mortal sin (5:16). One can almost read between the lines of this Johannine epistle the struggle of the (Ephesian?) church to be faithful to the legacy of the upper room.

(1) Abiding in Love Bears Fruit (15: 1-17)

[1] "I am the true vine, and my Father is the vinedresser. [2] Every branch of mine that bears no fruit, he takes away, and every branch that does bear fruit he prunes, that it may bear more fruit. [3] You are already made clean by the word which I have spoken to you. [4] Abide in me, and I in you. As the branch cannot bear fruit by itself, unless it abides in the vine, neither can you, unless you abide in me. [5] I am the vine, you are the branches. He who abides in me, and I in him, he it is that bears much fruit, for apart from me you can do nothing. [6] If a man does not abide in me, he is cast forth as a branch and withers; and the branches are gathered, thrown into the fire and burned. [7] If you abide in me, and my words abide in you, ask whatever you will, and it shall be done for you. [8] By this my Father is glorified, that you bear much fruit, and so prove to be my disciples. [9] As the Father has loved me, so have I loved you; abide in my love. [10] If you keep my commandments, you will abide in my love, just as I have kept my Father's commandments and abide in his love. [11] These things I have spoken to you, that my joy may be in you, and that your joy may be full.

[12] "This is my commandment, that you love one another as I have loved you. [13] Greater love has no man than this, that a man lay down his life for his friends. [14] You are my friends if you do what I command you. [15] No longer do I call you servants, for the servant does not know what his master is doing; but I have called you friends, for all that I have heard from my Father I have made known to you. [16] You did not choose me, but I chose you and appointed you that you should go and bear

fruit and that your fruit should abide; so that whatever you ask the Father in my name, he may give it to you. [17] This I command you, to love one another.

The vine was a favorite designation for Israel in the Old Testament (Isa. 5:1; Jer. 2:21a; Hos. 10:1; Ezek. 15:1-5; 19:10-11; Psalm 80:8-11). Thus, in claiming to be the *true vine*, Jesus thereby claimed to constitute the true Israel. Since his *Father* was likened to the *vinedresser*, Jesus' use of the divine self-designation, *I am* (*egō eimi*) aptly suggested both his identity with and subordination to the God of Israel. The basic purpose of the vine-branch analogy was to describe an abiding relationship between Christ and the believer which, like that earlier between Israel and Yahweh, was intended to *bear more fruit* (cf. Isa. 5:2; Hos. 10:1).

The warning that *every branch of mine* (i.e., any disciple) *that bears no fruit* is taken *away* and *cast forth* to wither and be *burned* in *the fire* is reminiscent of the Old Testament where every major vine passage ends on a similar note of judgment (cf. Isa. 5:5-7; Jer. 2:21b; Hosea 10:2; Ezek. 15:6-8; 19:12-14; Psalm 80:12-16). It also recalls Jesus' rejection of the fig tree for displaying foliage without fruit (Mark 11:12-14; cf. Matt. 21:33-41; Luke 13:6-9). More directly it alludes to the sifting of those who drank unworthily of "the fruit of the vine" (cf. Didache 9:2) both at the Last Supper (Mark 14:18-19) and at the eucharistic meals of the early church (1 Cor. 11:27-32). In the historical context of this Gospel the reference may be primarily to Judas (cf. 13:2,18,21-30 and especially compare 13:10-11 with 15:3), while for the later readers it may identify those who had gone out of the church because "they were not of us" (e.g., 1 John 2:19).

The development of the concept of "abiding" to describe the relationship between *the vine* and its *branches* (*menō*, to abide, is used 10 times in vv. 4-10) significantly clarified the nature of Christian mysticism. Note the following distinctive characteristics: (1) Rather than being absorptionistic, the identity of both parties is preserved—"abide in *me* and I in *you*." (2) The content of the relationship is not ecstasy but love—to *abide in me* means to *abide in my love*. (3) The attachment of the two parties is not an end in itself, for the purpose is to *bear fruit* (*karpos*, fruit, appears six times in vv. 2–8, twice more in v. 16; cf. Matt. 3:8–10; 7:16–20; Rom. 7:4; Gal. 5:22). (4) The bond between Christ and the believer is not maintained by the immediacy of an emotional experience but by the abiding of his *words* given in history and mediated through the life of a human community. (5) Finally, the entire relationship stands under both judgment (v. 6) and grace (v. 3), thereby balancing responsibility and privilege (v. 7). On the one hand there are *commandments* to *keep*, while on the other there is a *joy* that *may be full* (cf. 16:24; 17:13).

The one *commandment* which had both its source and its standard in Jesus was that they *love one another* as he had *loved* them (cf. 13:34). Here, such love is likened to that shown by one who in self-sacrifice would voluntarily *lay down his life for his friends* (cf. 10:11,15,17–18). In 13:16 Jesus had referred to his disciples as *servants* and, as would often be true of such persons, they did *not know what* their *master* was *doing* (cf. 13:36; 14:5,8,22). Now, however, he had *made known* to them *all* that he had *heard* from the *Father* (cf. 13:19; 14:4,6–7,9–10) and thus he *called* them *friends*. There was nothing cliquish about this circle of friends, however. For one thing, they had not chosen each other (i.e., the Christian is not free to pick his own spiritual friends) but had been chosen by Jesus. For another, they were to *go and bear fruit* by winning others, and this new fruit was to *abide* (i.e., the mutual abiding of disciple and Lord was to extend to all who would be won through the *love* which they were commanded to have for *one another*). The church is to be exclusive in its loyalty to Christ but not *excluding* in its outreach to others.

(2) The Hatred of the World (15:18—16:4a)

18 "If the world hates you, know that it has hated me before it hated you. 19 If you were of the world, the world would love its own; but because you are not of the world, but I chose you out of the world, therefore the world hates you. 20 Remember the word that I said to you, 'A servant is not greater than his master.' If they persecuted me, they will persecute you; if they kept my word, they will keep yours also. 21 But all this they will do to you on my account, because they do not know him who sent me. 22 If I had not come and spoken to them, they would not have sin; but now they have no excuse for their sin. 23 He who hates me hates my Father also. 24 If I had not done among them the works which no one else did, they would not have sin; but now they have seen and hated both me and my Father. 25 It is to fulfil the word that is written in their law, 'They hated me without a cause.' 26 But when the Counselor comes, whom I shall send to you from the Father, even the Spirit of truth, who proceeds from the Father, he will bear witness to me; 27 and you also are witnesses, because you have been with me from the beginning.

1 "I have said all this to you to keep you from falling away. 2 They will put you out of the synagogues; indeed, the hour is coming when whoever kills you will think he is offering service to God. 3 And they will do this because they have not known the Father, nor me. 4 But I have said these things to you, that when their hour comes you may remember that I told you of them.

Throughout the farewell discourse, the basic advance in thought defines how the disciples, after the departure of Jesus, were to reproduce in their corporate life and thereby extend throughout history those realities central to the earthly life of their Lord. Having drawn his followers into the circle of love which he shared with the Father (15:1–17), Jesus now invited them into that arena of conflict which he shared with the world. Ironically, they would be privileged to identify with Jesus not only by bearing much fruit but also by bearing up under much persecution (this may have been anticipated by the reference to pruning in 15:2).

The pattern of persecution for which the disciples were being prepared first unfolded in the ministry of Jesus. As one *sent* by the God whom the world did *not know,* he *had . . . come* not to tell men what they wanted to hear, or to be a spokesman for the prevailing religious tradition, or even to call attention to himself, but to lay the totality of the divine claim upon humanity. This meant that he was rejected as an alien intruder whom the *world . . . hated* and eventually *persecuted.*

Such hostility could not be dismissed as a thoughtless misunderstanding, however, for Jesus had clearly *spoken to them* of the will of God and had *done among them the works which no one else did* (e.g., 9:32). Although the world did not truly know Jesus, they knew enough to *have no excuse for their sin* (i.e., there is a level of understanding that may leave a man responsible but not committed). No, the willful rebellion which Jesus encountered came from those who had *seen* enough to believe but instead *hated both him* and his *Father,* as a phrase in Scripture put it, *without a cause* (cf. Psalms 35:19; 69:4).

In like manner to their Lord, the disciples were *not of the world* because Jesus had chosen them *out of the world* (cf. v. 16). Since they proclaimed the same message (*word*) as their *master* (cf. 13:16), they would suffer the same fate of hatred and persecution because *the world* loves only *its own* who are *of the world* (cf. 17:14–18). So fierce was this antagonism that they would need to be kept from *falling away* (cf. 15:6). As subsequent events bitterly confirmed, they would be put *out of the synagogues* (cf. 9:22,34; 12:42; Acts 14:1–6; 17:1–15; 18:4–7; 19:8–9; on Asia Minor, note Rev. 2:9; 3:9) and even be killed by those who thought thereby to offer *service to God* (cf. Acts 9:1–2; 22:19; 26:9–11; Gal. 1:13–14; Phil. 3:6). Just as the Christian is drawn into a three-way reciprocal love relationship involving the Father, Son, and fellow believers (15:9–10,12), so he also shares with these same three a reaction of hatred from the world (15:18–19,23–24).

In the face of such bleak prospects, Jesus identified three bases of hope for the disciples. First, there would be not only a parallel of persecution between his ministry and theirs but also one of acceptance: *if they kept my word, they will keep yours also.* In spite of massive opposition, Jesus had been able to recruit a remnant and they would, too. Further, they would not be caught off guard by the onslaught of evil. When the hour of conflict came, they would be able to *remember* that Jesus had predicted as much (cf. 13: 19; 14:29). To be forewarned was to be forearmed! Finally, just as Jesus had been *sent* from the Father to *come* and speak to the world (15:21–22), so now he would *send* them *from the Father* the *Counselor* or *Spirit of truth* who, when he *comes,* would *bear witness* to Jesus. In this persecution context, the Paraclete was to function primarily as a defender not of the disciples but of Jesus, thereby bolstering the work of those *witnesses* who spoke not of themselves but of what it was like to be *with* him *from the beginning* (cf. Acts 1:21–22).

(3) *The Help of the Holy Spirit* (16: 4b–15)

"I did not say these things to you from the beginning, because I was with you. [5] But now I am going to him who sent me; yet none of you asks me, 'Where are you going?' [6] But because I have said these things to you, sorrow has filled your hearts. [7] Nevertheless I tell you the truth: it is to your advantage that I go away, for if I do not go away, the Counselor will not come to you; but if I go, I will send him to you. [8] And when he comes, he will convince the world of sin and of righteousness and of judgment: [9] of sin, because they do not believe in me; [10] of righteousness, because I go to the Father, and you will see me no more; [11] of judgment, because the ruler of this world is judged.

[12] "I have yet many things to say to you, but you cannot bear them now. [13] When the Spirit of truth comes, he will guide you into all the truth; for he will not speak on his own authority, but whatever he hears he will speak, and he will declare to you the things that are to come. [14] He will glorify me, for he will take what is mine and declare it to you. [15] All that the Father has is mine; therefore I said that he will take what is mine and declare it to you.

Passing reference to the Paraclete in 15:26 leads now to a fuller exposition of his role in the era after the earthly Jesus had gone *away*. This explanation was *not* needed *from the beginning* of Jesus' relation to the disciples (cf. 15:27) because at that time the ministry of the Spirit was inseparable from Jesus' physical presence *with* them. So satisfied were the disciples with this tangible association that *none* of them had asked *where* he was eventually *going*. Their failure to ponder his ultimate destination—which parallels a contemporary preoccupation with the "Jesus of history"—resulted in an inadequate understanding of his person and work, leaving them ill prepared to face his departure via the cross. They should have realized the *advantage* of his ascension but instead *sorrow* now *filled* their *hearts*.

To counter the notion that they would be abandoned to serve an absentee Lord, Jesus again promised to *send* the Paraclete (cf. 15:26) to fill his own place in their lives. Previously the Spirit had been pictured as a defender or witness as Jesus continued "on trial" whenever the disciples presented his claims to others. Now, however, the tables are turned and *the Counselor* is seen as a prosecutor or judge whose role is defined by a single Greek verb (*elegchō*) with multiple meanings. The basic notion of "expose" may connote (1) "to clarify" in the sense of to bring to light; (2) "to convince" in the sense of to bring to conviction; (3) "to confute" in the sense of to correct or confound (cf. the NEB paraphrase). The general implication is that the Paraclete would prove the world wrong at those points where it had rejected both Jesus and his followers.

Three specific tasks illustrate the range of this ministry of reproof. (1) The Spirit would show up the *sin* of the *world* for what it is by establishing that it had resulted in a refusal to *believe in* Jesus. (2) He would further correct the mistaken notion that *righteousness* could not be seen in the cross by which Jesus returned *to*

his *Father* and was seen *no more* on earth. (3) Finally, he would clarify that *judgment* was no longer to be viewed as a far-off cosmic event but as a present historical process *because* already, in trying to destroy Jesus, *the ruler of this world* had been *judged* in advance of the end of time (cf. 14:30). Through the preaching (in Greek often called *paraklēsis*) of the church, the Paraclete confronted the world with the necessity of a drastic change in its notions *of sin and of righteousness and of judgment* as a result of the coming of Jesus.

In addition to this outward ministry to the world (vv. 8–11), the Counselor would also have an inward ministry to the church (vv. 12–15). As the disciples struggled to frame the unchanging message of Christ for changing times, *he* would *guide* them *into all the truth*. Ultimate reality was not to be sought in a set of timeless facts which may be mastered at any moment but in companionship with the *Spirit of truth* who leads one on a pilgrimage of discovery (cf. 14:4–7). Because all truth about God lays a transcendent claim upon man, it is something one must not only believe but also *bear* (i.e., take responsibility for in actual conduct). Jesus, with a sound instinct for the timing of truth, realized that during his brief ministry the disciples had not developed the depths of commitment necessary to implement all of the *things* which he longed to *say* to them. He was confident, however, that those seeds of truth which lay latent in his words could one day be harvested after cultivation by the community under the guidance of the Spirit.

This conception of eschatological truth (i.e., of truth that has a future) was based on a careful balance between continuity and change. On the one hand, there would be no rigidly fixed dogma once-for-all delivered from the past, for the task of the Paraclete was to prepare God's people to face those new *things* that were sure *to come* along life's way. On the other hand, he would *declare* a relevant word based not *on his own authority* but on a contemporizing of what Jesus had already revealed of the Father. The Spirit would not be the source of innovative fads that victimize the church with the tyranny of the temporary; rather he is the source of insight to understand and of courage to apply those truths which the church has received. Most of us have more truth (e.g., in the Bible) than we are able to *bear*. Our need is for a skillful guide (cf. Acts 8:31) who can help us take responsibility for the deeper implications of the gospel which we have not been willing either to understand or to apply.

(4) The Paradox of Discipleship (16: 16-24)

16 "A little while, and you will see me no more; again a little while, and you will see me." 17 Some of his disciples said to one another, "What is this that he says to us, 'A little while, and you will not see me, and again a little while, and you will see me'; and, 'because I go to the Father'?" 18 They said, "What does he mean by 'a little while'? We do not know what he means." 19 Jesus knew that they wanted to ask him; so he said to them, "Is this what you are asking yourselves, what I meant by saying, 'A little while, and you will not see me, and again a little while, and you will see me'? 20 Truly, truly, I say to you, you will weep and lament, but the world will rejoice; you will be sorrowful, but your sorrow will turn into joy. 21 When a woman is in travail she has sorrow, because her hour has come; but when she is delivered of the child, she no longer remembers the anguish, for joy that a child is born into the world. 22 So you have sorrow now, but I will see you again and your hearts will rejoice, and no one will take your joy from you. 23 In that day you will ask nothing of me. Truly, truly, I say to you, if you ask anything of the Father, he will give it to you in my name. 24 Hitherto you have asked nothing in my name; ask, and you will receive, that your joy may be full.

Throughout John 13—16 Jesus gave splendid reassurances to the disciples in order that they might have abounding joy (cf. 15:11; 16:24; 17:13). One promise not made, however, was the absence of conflict. In fact, side by side with tender comfort came stern warnings of inevitable persecution. The coexistence of these apparently contradictory themes in the

same section creates the paradox of sorrowful joy which is clarified in vv. 16-24.

At the outset, the two sides of the paradox are summarized in symmetrical formulae (vv. 16-17,19): (1) *A little while, and you will see me no more* refers to the departure of Jesus through the dark tunnel of tragedy (e.g., 13:33), while (2) *a little while, and you will see me* refers to the triumphant return of the risen Lord in his living Spirit (e.g., 14:19). The use of the same phrase, *a little while,* in both instances was designed to heighten the paradox by juxtaposing two convictions. On the one hand, Jesus' future in the flesh was utterly defenseless and vulnerable to disaster; almost before the disciples could realize it, his life would be snuffed out. On the other hand, hard on the heels of unmitigated tragedy would come unqualified triumph.

Such profound use of the phrase "a little while" is reminiscent of the exilic ordeal of Israel in the Old Testament (Isa. 26:16-21), of the "three day" predictions of Jesus in the Synoptics (Matt. 12:40; Mark 8:31; 14:58; cf. John 2:19), and of the dilemma of the martyr church eager to see the judgment of God (Rev. 6:9-11). As such, it reflects a tension central to the biblical dynamics of hope.

Because of the disciples' difficulty in grasping this terse summary which had compressed the Master's destiny into a single paradox, Jesus illustrated its implications by comparing their situation to that of a *woman . . . in travail* (cf. Isa. 66:7-9). Just as an expectant mother has *sorrow* (i.e., physical suffering) when *her hour* of delivery *has come,* but *no longer remembers* that brief *anguish* when she is filled with *joy that a child is born,* so the disciples would have *sorrow* in the nightmare of evil's hour; but their *hearts* would *rejoice* "a little while" later when he returned and saw them *again. In that day* (v. 23) when God turned their *sorrow . . . into joy* (v. 20), *no one* would be able to take it *from* them (v. 22). Just as a woman has no desire to question the pain of the birth process, once the arrival of her baby has made it all supremely worthwhile, so the disciples would *ask* Jesus *nothing* when all that they had hoped for from God became available.

(5) Faith in Conflict (16:25–33)

25 "I have said this to you in figures; the hour is coming when I shall no longer speak to you in figures but tell you plainly of the Father. 26 In that day you will ask in my name; and I do not say to you that I shall pray the Father for you; 27 for the Father himself loves you, because you have loved me and have believed that I came from the Father. 28 I came from the Father and have come into the world; again, I am leaving the world and going to the Father."

29 His disciples said, "Ah, now you are speaking plainly, not in any figure! 30 Now we know that you know all things, and need none to question you; by this we believe that you came from God." 31 Jesus answered them, "Do you now believe? 32 The hour is coming, indeed it has come, when you will be scattered, every man to his home, and will leave me alone; yet I am not alone, for the Father is with me. 33 I have said this to you, that in me you may have peace. In the world you have tribulation; but be of good cheer, I have overcome the world."

Up to this point in his efforts to instruct the disciples, Jesus had often taught *in figures* (cf. 16:5), e.g., in the symbolic discourse on the vine and branches (15:1–11) and in the analogy of the woman in travail (16:21). In the new era ushered in by the resurrection, however, he would be able to *tell* them *plainly of the Father*. The difference would not be based on a change in God, as if he had deliberately concealed himself in the past. God did not need any promptings from Jesus in order to disclose himself (v. 26*b*) for he had already loved the disciples and sent his Son in order that they might know him better. Rather, the change would come in the disciples as the interpreting Spirit enabled them to understand what God had disclosed through the ministry of Jesus (aptly summarized in v. 28).

The disciples, however, unwilling to wait "a little while" for this new era of insight, mistakenly supposed that *the hour* had already come when Jesus would be *speaking plainly* to them. No sooner had they prematurely claimed to *know* enough so that there was no further *need . . . to question* Jesus than he shattered their overconfidence with a sober appraisal of their true prospects. Rather than the *hour* now having come when they would *believe* all things, the hour had *come* when they would all *be scattered, every man to his home.* This realistic response to an inflated confession was a characteristic strategy of Jesus (cf. 6:68–70; 13:38) which showed that the church owed its existence not to the courage of its charter members but to the founder *alone.*

The disciples were rebuked for supposing that one could possess the understanding that faith needs without first experiencing the cross and resurrection (cf. Mark 8:31–33). The Gospel of John is often singled out for its emphasis on "realized eschatology"; but here, as elsewhere in chapter 16, the opposite concern was uppermost. The end of the journey had not been reached. What Jesus had put "a little while" in the future the disciples tried to realize prematurely in the present (note the key word "now" in vv. 29,31). What they needed to understand was that they had not reached this goal but that Jesus had! Because the *Father* was *with* him, he —and he *alone*—had *overcome the world.* As a result of his conquest, they could take courage (i.e., *be of good cheer*) in the midst of continuing conflict. Their poise in tribulation would come not because they had finally arrived (cf. 14:4–5) but because of the gift of his *peace* and because of the prayer which he now offered on their behalf (17:1–26).

4. The Prayer of Consecration (17:1–26)

John 17 is widely acclaimed as the loftiest spiritual passage in the fourth Gospel. The illustration in chapter 13 and the instruction in chapters 14–16 are climaxed and transfigured in the intercession of chapter 17. Only Jesus could pray such a prayer, combining as it does complete submission to God and complete sovereignty over man. With all the world shouting that he was a failure, with death staring him in the face, Jesus was sublimely confident that he had done exactly the right thing. The so-called Lord's Prayer (Matt. 6:9–13)— which might better be labeled the "Disciples' Prayer"—discloses the depths of our human helplessness, whereas this prayer opens a window on the heights of his divine sufficiency. Here is the historical basis for the profoundest teaching on prayer in the New Testament—that Christ ever lives to make intercession for his own (cf. Luke 22:31–32; Rom. 8:26–27; Heb. 7:25). The last thing for the disciples to learn before facing the cross (chs. 18–19) was that its terrors could be conquered (16:33) not because they had prayed for him but because he had prayed for them!

The unusual time perspective indicated by the verb tenses provides a significant clue to the character of the prayer. At the outset of the "book of the passion," the hour of glorification on the cross which had previously been future (2:4; 7:30; 8:20) now shifted into the present (12:23,27,31; 13:1,31; 16:32). Here, however, the departure from the world is viewed as already accomplished in the past (vv. 4,11–12a,13a,24). How could Jesus claim that he had finished all his work and ascended to the Father when he had not even gone to the cross? The answer is that through prayer he was projected in advance, as it were, into the heavenly realm (cf. Luke 9:28–31). The disciples thereby were permitted a glimpse of the eternal relationship which existed between Jesus and his Father. Here, in a more mystical Johannine idiom, is an equivalent of the Synoptic conviction that prayer is eschatological—i.e., that it enables us to experience "on earth" things as they are "in heaven" (Matt. 6:10). Prayer provides an eternal vantage point from which to accept temporary defeats for "a little while" (16:16) because we have seen the end from the beginning.

The structure of the prayer is clearly separated in three parts in order to indicate the theological priorities for which it contends. Unlike the Lord's Prayer, which bids us pray for ourselves last, Jesus here prayed for himself first (vv. 1–5) because he had already overcome the world (16:33) and thus would glorify the Father in all that he did. The self-consecration of Jesus was crucial because everything which follows in the prayer depended upon his finished work. Next, Jesus turned to pray for his disciples (vv. 6–19) rather than for the unbelieving world because their work was necessary as a mediating link of living witnesses. Finally, Jesus prayed for the unity of all who would believe through them (vv. 20–26), in order that the world might know the love which is the deepest reality of the Godhead. The careful sequence of the prayer suggests that the glorified Christ is the only hope of the church, that the church witnessing to truth is the only hope of new converts, and that the loving fellowship of all converts is the only hope of an unbelieving world.[35]

(1) Jesus Prays for Himself (17:1–5)

[1] When Jesus had spoken these words, he lifted up his eyes to heaven and said, "Father, the hour has come; glorify thy Son that the Son may glorify thee, [2] since thou hast given him power over all flesh, to give eternal life to all whom thou hast given him. [3] And this is eternal life, that they know thee the only true God, and Jesus Christ whom thou hast sent. [4] I glorified thee on earth, having accomplished the work which thou gavest me to do; [5] and now, Father, glorify thou me in thy own presence with the glory which I had with thee before the world was made.

Unlike the sinner who "would not even lift up his eyes to heaven" (Luke 18:13), Jesus *lifted up his eyes to heaven* in the sublime confidence that God had *given him power over all flesh* (i.e., mankind). Now that the climactic *hour* of his destiny had *come*, the complete unity of the human and the divine would be seen in two ways.

[35] For an effort to sketch the historical setting of John 17 in the life of the early church, see Ernst Kaesemann, *The Testament of Jesus*, trans. Gerhard Krodel (Philadelphia: Fortress, 1968).

First, the *Father* would *glorify* the *Son* and *the Son* in turn would *glorify* the Father; i.e., Jesus was a perfect mirror of the divine majesty reflecting the radiance of God rather than calling attention to himself. Second, Jesus would *give* eternal life to those whom God had *given him;* i.e., Jesus claimed no credit for his converts apart from the working of God in their lives. Some men pray for what they think they can get from God; Jesus prayed for what he could give back to God in a life of obedient service.

Mention of *eternal life* in v. 2 caused the Evangelist to pause and insert parenthetically in v. 3 a description of this central reality in terms of "knowing" the *only true God* and *Jesus Christ whom* he had *sent.* Here is one of the clearest indications in the New Testament that faith and knowledge may be equivalent rather than antithetical. To know God in the Johannine sense is to have an existential commitment to him as a living subject rather than to accept certain facts about him as a contemplated object. Further, this personal relation to God had become a present reality (cf. 14:7*b*) whereas in the Old Testament the prophets spoke of the direct knowledge of God as a future hope (Hos. 6:3; Jer. 9:3,6,24; 31:34). Now, man's awareness of the *only true God* was inseparable from a knowledge of the one whom he had *sent.* Notice how classic monotheism was not compromised by an affirmation of the unique role which *Jesus Christ* played in the history of divine revelation.

One reason why Jesus deserved to stand beside God as a subject of saving knowledge was that he had *glorified* the Father *on earth.* Rather than posing as a second God, Jesus did only the *work* which he had been given *to do* (cf. 4:34; 5:17) and thereby pointed away from himself to the one who had sent him. Without a trace of conceit he now looked back on a task *accomplished,* having reached a point of spiritual fulfillment that even the greatest saints dare not claim to have attained (cf. Phil. 3:12–14). The deepest audacity of his

prayer is seen, however, in his unwillingness to be satisfied with an earthly pilgrimage that had reached its goal. Longing to enlarge the significance of his historical ministry, Jesus now prayed that his *glory* might once again become cosmic as had been the case when he was preexistent *with* God *before the world was made* (1:1–2; Phil. 2:6,11). By the ascension, the redemptive work that was finished at one time and place would become valid for all times and places.

(2) *Jesus Prays for His Disciples* (17: 6–19)

⁶ "I have manifested thy name to the men whom thou gavest me out of the world; thine they were, and thou gavest them to me, and they have kept thy word. ⁷ Now they know that everything that thou hast given me is from thee; ⁸ for I have given them the words which thou gavest me, and they have received them and know in truth that I came from thee; and they have believed that thou didst send me. ⁹ I am praying for them; I am not praying for the world but for those whom thou hast given me, for they are thine; ¹⁰ all mine are thine, and thine are mine, and I am glorified in them. ¹¹ And now I am no more in the world, but they are in the world, and I am coming to thee. Holy Father, keep them in thy name, which thou hast given me, that they may be one, even as we are one. ¹² While I was with them, I kept them in thy name, which thou hast given me; I have guarded them, and none of them is lost but the son of perdition, that the scripture might be fulfilled. ¹³ But now I am coming to thee; and these things I speak in the world, that they may have my joy fulfilled in themselves. ¹⁴ I have given them thy word; and the world has hated them because they are not of the world, even as I am not of the world. ¹⁵ I do not pray that thou shouldst take them out of the world, but that thou shouldst keep them from the evil one. ¹⁶ They are not of the world, even as I am not of the world. ¹⁷ Sanctify them in the truth; thy word is truth. ¹⁸ As thou didst send me into the world, so I have sent them into the world. ¹⁹ And for their sake I consecrate myself, that they also may be consecrated in truth.

Turning from himself to the disciples, Jesus now rendered an account of his stewardship during the days when his eternal glory was laid aside for a season (vv. 6–8). A little earlier the thousands had thronged to him (6:10; 11:48; 12:19), but now many of these no longer stood beside him in his hour of supreme trial (cf. 6:66; 12:42; 13:21). Instead of bitterly resenting these heartbreaking results, Jesus rejoiced over his modest remnant as a manifestation of divine generosity (cf. 3:27). God first gave *them to* Jesus (vv. 6a, c) and he in turn had *given* them *everything* that God had *given* him (cf. 3:35; 5:21–22). There is no way to explain a church fellowship except as the embodiment of grace, for here men come together not because they are attracted to each other but because they are summoned by a word not of their own devising.

This does not mean, however, that there was no response for the disciples to make. Even a gift has to be *kept* in order to be effective. In the case of God's "inexpressible gift" (2 Cor. 9:15), this response involved three things (v. 8): (1) openness to receive the words which God had given Jesus to speak in history; (2) understanding to *know in truth* (cf. v. 7) that God was the source of his life; (3) commitment to the mission on which God had sent him. Note again, as in v. 3, the central role of knowledge as the foundation for an enduring faith.

Now that Jesus was to be *no more in the world,* the disciples would need the same protection from the Father that he had provided them on earth (vv. 9–12). Only in this way could they *be one* and not be fragmented by their foes. The basis of this spiritual security was not organizational, for Jesus had *kept them* in the *name* which God had *given* him (i.e., the bond between the disciples was a shared revelation of the nature of God). The need for unity was not simply that they might strengthen each other, but primarily that they might give visible expression to the way in which Jesus and God *are one* (cf. v. 10). This, in fact, explains why Jesus was *praying for* the disciples instead of *for the world*—not because the world was "past praying for" (cf. v. 20) but because the oneness of believers is the necessary link between one

God and one world (cf. 13:34). If a band without the common ties of race or nation could stay together in a day when the world was dividing into warring camps, this would furnish tangible proof of the reconciling power of God.

So concerned was Jesus to guard his flock from fragmentation (cf. 10:11–16) that none *of them* had been *lost* except Judas, *the son of perdition.* This defection, however, only brought to fullest expression a sad fact referred to earlier in *scripture,* that those with least cause are often the ones that rebel (cf. 13:18). In 2 Thessalonians 2:3–4, the "son of perdition" represents the ultimate antagonist who precedes the Parousia by opposing God in the name of God. Here Judas, in preceding the glory of the cross with a dastardly betrayal of the one whom he followed, incarnated that "realized apostasy" characteristic of the antichrists that always rise up in the last hour (1 John 2:18).

To shatter the solidarity of the disciple band compromises both its separation from the world and its witness to the world, for the revolutionary oneness of the church in a broken world is the best proof that what Christ has done for it was of God and not of man. In this sense, to oppose or even to weaken the unity of the church is to play the role of Judas!

The proper relationship of the church to the world is carefully delineated in vv. 14–19 as paralleling the earlier relationship of Jesus to the world. Two points are made in paradoxical fashion. To begin with, the church is *not* to be *of the world even as* Jesus was *not of the world.* This does not mean, however, that God should *take them out of the world;* rather, they should be *sent . . . into the world* just as Jesus was sent *into the world* (cf. 20:21). The tension created by this twofold emphasis is designed to maintain a balance between separation and penetration as the church fulfills its calling both to holiness and to mission.

This dialectic—*not of . . . but into*—which was to be distinctive of the church's life in the world, characterized those who had been "sanctified" or "consecrated" (same Gr. verb, *hagiazō*, is used for both terms). This setting apart was not an exercise in self-help, however, but resulted from the cleansing *word* (cf. 15:3) which Jesus had *given* his own that they might know *the truth* (cf. 8:31–32). Not only did Jesus deliver this divine revelation but he obeyed it himself, thus giving his followers an unforgettable example of what it means for one man to *consecrate* himself. In the Old Testament it was common to view the sacrificial system and everything associated with it as sanctified, but here Jesus focused entirely on a holy people without reference to holy times or places. As had been the case with Jesus, the disciples became the true temple of God's dwelling wherever they extended his body throughout the world (cf. 2:19–21).

(3) *Jesus Prays for Future Believers* (17:20–26)

20 "I do not pray for these only, but also for those who believe in me through their word, 21 that they may all be one; even as thou, Father, art in me, and I in thee, that they also may be in us, so that the world may believe that thou hast sent me. 22 The glory which thou hast given me I have given to them, that they may be one even as we are one, 23 I in them and thou in me, that they may become perfectly one, so that the world may know that thou hast sent me and hast loved them even as thou hast loved me. 24 Father, I desire that they also, whom thou hast given me, may be with me where I am, to behold my glory which thou hast given me in thy love for me before the foundation of the world. 25 O righteous Father, the world has not known thee, but I have known thee; and these know that thou hast sent me. 26 I made known to them thy name, and I will make it known, that the love with which thou hast loved me may be in them, and I in them."

Jesus' determination to send his disciples into the world despite its hatred and evil reflected a universal concern which is now given a climactic place in the prayer (vv. 20–23). As his followers bore witness to the word of truth which he had given them, the ultimate ground of their confi-

dence would be the realization that everyone led *to believe . . . through* that *word* had already been prayed for by Christ. The purpose of this prayer was that the expansion of the church not threaten its original unity. The basis of that unity was again defined as a shared belief in the unity of God and Christ as sender and sent. When the Christian fellowship reflects in its corporate life the same kind of spiritual harmony that existed between Jesus and the *Father,* the *world* will realize that Jesus did not merely teach men how to be cooperative; rather, he mediated to them the oneness of the Godhead itself. Jesus did not compromise the monotheism of God, for the Father was *in* him and he was *in* the Father so completely that they were *one* in purpose and spirit. As Jesus shared this relationship with his followers by sending them as he had been sent, they could experience the divine unity-in-diversity and so *become perfectly one* in their sense of mission to the *world.*

In vv. 20–23 the unity of the church is described in terms of mission (*sent*), whereas in vv. 24–26 it is considered in terms of motive (*love*). Although a common purpose helps to hold the church together, this is never enough, for even the most despotic movement (e.g., naziism) can unite around a burning sense of mission. Jesus protected the church's unity of mission against corruption by praying also that the *love with which* God had *loved* him might be *in them* as it had been in him. Once again, nothing less than the reality that holds the Godhead together was made the basis for the oneness of the church. In a theological sense, true ecumenism rests on a trinitarian foundation. There is no reason to hope that a human community on earth may be many and yet one unless it is ontologically true that the divine community in heaven is many and yet one.

The ultimate reason for the church to *become perfectly one* is *that the world may* thereby *know* the true nature of God as one (i.e., may understand that monotheism is not a philosophical or ethical principle but a shared determination to love). When the nature of God is truly grasped, his glory is said to be seen. This manifestation is here traced in three stages: (1) God gave his *glory* to the historical Jesus (cf. 1:14); i.e., the oneness of Father and Son was revealed in the incarnation. (2) Jesus, in turn, gave this same glory to his disciples, so that they might exhibit in the life of a growing and diverse community those realities which had perfectly united Jesus to God. (3) But Jesus knew that this oneness could never be complete on earth (cf. v. 12), so he prayed that those *given* him as believers (cf. v. 6) might be *with* him in heaven *to behold* his eternal *glory* and so share the ultimate harmony of the community of heaven. The unity of the church is not only an evangelistic imperative if the world is to know the meaning of Christ; it is also an eschatological hope which believes that the oneness to which we witness on earth best anticipates the life of the world beyond.

II. Jesus Dies for His Disciples (18:1— 19:42)

Following the most original section in the fourth Gospel (chs. 13—17), the passion narrative in chapters 18—19 parallels more closely than elsewhere the treatment in the Synoptic Gospels. In both cases we have a description of the arrest of Jesus, his appearance before judicial authorities of the Jews and Romans, the threefold denial of one of his leading disciples, the crowd's choice of Barabbas, the mockery, crucifixion with two others, death, and burial before sundown on Friday.

At the same time, many Synoptic features do not appear in John: the agony in Gethsemane, the kiss of betrayal by Judas, the condemnation by the Sanhedrin for blasphemy, the carrying of the cross by Simon of Cyrene, the reviling by the crowd around the cross, the cry of desolation, the darkness at noonday, and the tearing of the Temple veil. Likewise, the Johannine presentation contains a number of details not found elsewhere: Jesus' voluntary arrest to protect the disciples, his interrogation by Annas, the dialogue with Pilate regarding his kingship, the role of the beloved disciple, the cry of completion, the spear thrust producing an effusion of blood and water, and the lavish anointing of his body for burial by Joseph and Nicodemus.

The effect of these striking differences is to heighten the royal divinity of Jesus precisely in the hour of greatest shame. His foreknowledge of these tragic events enabled him to be in complete control when they arrived. Rather than taking him by surprise, they were accepted as the fulfillment of Scripture. Throughout the turmoil Jesus never collapsed under stress but moved calmly and confidently according to a divine plan. Hints of victory anticipated throughout chapters 13—17 now began to be realized. The crucifixion was not simply the casting down of a helpless victim. It was also the "lifting up" or exaltation of a triumphant victor. His death was viewed by the Evangelist not as a humiliating prelude to the ascension but as an integral part of it. For Jesus did not simply die; he chose to die in a way that introduced profound spiritual influences into the lives of his followers.[36]

1. Jesus Accepts His Passion (18:1–18)

This introductory section sets the stage for all that follows in chapters 18—19. The sovereign initiative of Jesus in going forth to meet his destiny dominates the unit and stands in dramatic contrast to the impetuousness and vacillation of his disciple, Peter. The strong impression is created that only Jesus really understood what was happening and that the outcome depended entirely upon him.

(1) The Arrest in the Garden (18:1–11)

¹ When Jesus had spoken these words, he went forth with his disciples across the Kidron valley, where there was a garden, which he

---

[36] On the royalty of Jesus in his passion see E. C. Colwell and E. L. Titus, *The Gospel of the Spirit* (New York: Harper and Brothers, 1953), pp. 71–106.

and his disciples entered. ² Now Judas, who betrayed him, also knew the place; for Jesus often met there with his disciples. ³ So Judas, procuring a band of soldiers and some officers from the chief priests and the Pharisees, went there with lanterns and torches and weapons. ⁴ Then Jesus, knowing all that was to befall him, came forward and said to them, "Whom do you seek?" ⁵ They answered him, "Jesus of Nazareth." Jesus said to them, "I am he." Judas, who betrayed him, was standing with them. ⁶ When he said to them, "I am he," they drew back and fell to the ground. ⁷ Again he asked them, "Whom do you seek?" And they said, "Jesus of Nazareth." ⁸ Jesus answered, "I told you that I am he; so, if you seek me, let these men go." ⁹ This was to fulfil the word which he had spoken, "Of those whom thou gavest me I lost not one." ¹⁰ Then Simon Peter, having a sword, drew it and struck the high priest's slave and cut off his right ear. The slave's name was Malchus. ¹¹ Jesus said to Peter, "Put your sword into its sheath; shall I not drink the cup which the Father has given me?"

Only after *Jesus had spoken* the *words* recorded in John 13—17 was he ready to go *forth with his disciples* to meet the enemy. The route led from the place of the last supper in Jerusalem eastward *across the Kidron valley* to *a garden* or orchard where he *often met . . . with his disciples* (further proof of an extended ministry in Jerusalem). Apparently *Judas* not only *knew the place* but assumed that Jesus would go there after the meal. Thus, in carrying out his plan to betray Jesus (13:21–30), Judas *went there* with a large *band* of Roman *soldiers* together with *some* Jewish *officers* (Temple guard) *from the chief priests and the Pharisees.* Obviously, a delegation numbering several hundred (a Roman cohort normally had 600 soldiers) was not needed with *lanterns and torches and weapons* to arrest one unarmed man during the Passover full moon. One possibility is that the public leadership may have suspected Jesus of having concealed a small private army on the outskirts of the city.

Jesus, knowing all that was to befall him (cf. 13:18–19), did not flee from this coalition of foes but voluntarily *came forward* to identify himself as the one whom they

sought. *Judas was* left *standing* among his conspirators with no role to play. Properly speaking, Jesus was not arrested by this mighty host but gave himself up. So sovereign was his response, *I am he* (*egō eimi*), that hardened soldiers recoiled before its impact *and fell to the ground* (cf. 7:45–47). Men trained to track down craven criminals were completely unprepared for this ultimate theological affirmation. So completely was Jesus in control of the situation that he named the conditions of his self-surrender: *let these men go.* Already he had prayed for the protection of his flock and the preservation of its unity (17:12; cf. 10:11–18); now he moved to *fulfil* that *word* in a situation of grave danger.

This acceptance of responsibility for those who had committed themselves to his keeping was based on no worthiness of their own, as is vividly illustrated by the foolish reaction of *Simon Peter.* In contrast to Jesus, who had shielded the disciples with the sheer strength of his inner poise, Peter *drew* a sword, *struck the high priest's slave and*—in an effort, no doubt, to cleave his head asunder—*cut off his right ear.* The presence of weapons among the disciples is surprising and may reflect their covert preparation for the ordeal which Jesus had intimated (cf. 13:37). In any case, because Peter forgot that vengeance belongs only to God (Rom. 12:19), his best intentions were not good enough. Jesus bade him *put* the *sword into its sheath* and depend instead upon his own strategy, which was to *drink the cup which the Father* had given him (cf. Mark 14:36). Peter had thought that he was willing to die for Jesus, but his courage would soon collapse (vv. 17, 25,27). He needed, instead, to be willing for Jesus to die for him.

(2) The Arraignment Before Annas (18: 12–14)

¹² So the band of soldiers and their captain and the officers of the Jews seized Jesus and bound him. ¹³ First they led him to Annas; for he was the father-in-law of Caiaphas, who was high priest that year. ¹⁴ It was Caiaphas who had given counsel to the Jews that it was

expedient that one man should die for the people.

Captivity has long been the lot of the people of God. Here Jesus stood in representative bondage for all who through him would become free. The fact that those who had *seized Jesus . . . first . . . led him to Annas* shows that the arrest had been engineered primarily by the Jews, else he would have been taken first rather than last to the Roman governor, Pilate.

Annas had been installed as high priest in A.D. 6 by Quirinius but was deposed in A.D. 15 by Valerius Gratus (Josephus, *Antiq.*, 18:26,34). Apparently he remained the "power behind the altar," however, for all five of his sons eventually succeeded him as high priest (Josephus, *Antiq.*, 20:198) as did his son-in-law, Joseph, who was called *Caiaphas* (cf. Luke 3:2). Although Caiaphas served in office A.D. 18–36 (Josephus, *Antiq.*, 18:35,95), John identified him as *high priest* in *that* one fateful *year* when he counseled *the Jews* that it would be *expedient* for Jesus to *die for the people* (cf. 11:49–52).

(3) The Arrival of Peter and Another Disciple (18:15–18)

[15] Simon Peter followed Jesus, and so did another disciple. As this disciple was known to the high priest, he entered the court of the high priest along with Jesus, [16] while Peter stood outside at the door. So the other disciple, who was known to the high priest, went out and spoke to the maid who kept the door, and brought Peter in. [17] The maid who kept the door said to Peter, "Are not you also one of this man's disciples?" He said, "I am not." [18] Now the servants and officers had made a charcoal fire, because it was cold, and they were standing and warming themselves; Peter also was with them, standing and warming himself.

At least two disciples *followed Jesus* to the priestly quarters where he was being interrogated, *Simon Peter* and *another* unidentified *disciple*. The remarkable statement is made that this latter disciple *was known to the high priest*, on which basis he not only *entered the court of the high priest along with Jesus* but soon arranged to have Peter brought in also. Such familiarity and

influence with the priestly retinue suggest a citizen of Jerusalem or the surrounding Judean environs, perhaps even a person of some prominence. It is uncertain whether an identification with the beloved disciple is intended (cf. 13:23; 19:26–27; 20:2–9; 21:7,20–23). John, son of Zebedee, may have been but likely was not a personal acquaintance of Caiaphas, but Lazarus may have been (cf. 11:18–19,45–47); although it is hard to imagine that he would have been welcome and could have remained inconspicuous under these circumstances (cf. 12:9–11). Probably this account illustrates that Jesus had many Judean followers from whose memories the Johannine passion narrative was first drawn (Dodd, *Historical Tradition*, pp. 86–88).

Although the unnamed disciple remained unobtrusively in the background, attention focused immediately upon Peter. *The maid* who let him in the door asked if he were not one of Jesus' disciples to which the unequivocable answer was given, *I am not*. The defenses of this "rock-man" (cf. comment on 1:42) who had boasted of his willingness to fight to the death (13:37) crumbled before the accusing chatter of a servant girl! This first of three denials (cf. vv. 25,27) stands in dramatic juxtaposition to the stalwart witness of his Master (vv. 19–23). Peter stood before the *charcoal fire* warming himself in silence while Jesus stood before his tormentors insisting that he had always "spoken openly to the world" (v. 20). How ironic that Peter seemed to be free when actually he was bound by fear to silence, while Jesus seemed to be bound when actually he was free from fear to speak.

2. Jesus Defends His Passion (18:19— 19:16)

Three characteristics of the Johannine trial narrative are particularly distinctive in comparison with their Synoptic counterparts:[37]

[37] For these and other distinctives of the Johannine trial narrative see Dodd, *Historical Tradition*, pp. 32–120. Dodd's careful study of the entire passion narrative (pp. 21–151) is of great value.

(1) The Jewish phase of the trial is strongly subordinated to the Roman. An informal appearance before Annas is included in John alone (18:19–23), but the judicial proceedings before Caiaphas which are so crucial in the Synoptics (cf. Mark 14:53–65 and parallels) are not described at all (vv. 24,28). By contrast, the dealings with Pilate which are only briefly mentioned in the Synoptics (cf. Mark 15:1–15 and parallels) here occupy a dominant position (18:28—19:16). By devoting 6 verses to Jesus before the Jewish tribunal but 29 verses to his confrontation with Rome, the fourth Gospel has made the latter encounter decisive, indicating thereby that nothing less than the judgment of the world was taking place and not just an internal religious squabble among the Jews.

(2) Throughout the Roman trial in John, the issue of kingship is uppermost (18:33–38; 19:2–5,12–16), a theme which is mentioned but not developed in the Synoptics (cf. Mark 15:2,9,12 and parallels). Here everything turns upon the title "king" (*basileus*). Against a political interpretation of his ministry, Jesus defined his kingship in terms not of supporters who would fight but of the sovereignty of truth, thereby demonstrating that both he and his followers were not guilty of sedition against Rome (18:33–37). The Jews, however, shrewdly used their hated subjugation to compel Pilate to act by insisting that any friend of Caesar must suppress even a harmless pretender to the throne (19:12,15). Goaded into action despite his reservations, Pilate determined to have the last word by condemning Jesus to the cross as a political rival, thereby insinuating to those who had taunted him that this was the only king the Jews deserved to have (19:19–22). Thus, though neither side intended it, Jesus ended his life under a sign proclaiming in three languages his rival kingship to Caesar.

(3) Finally, the central encounter between Jesus and Pilate is arranged by John with a dramatic artistry unrivaled elsewhere in the Gospels. The basic literary device is to present seven scenes that alternate between the Jews outside the praetorium and Pilate on the inside: [38]

I (outside)—Jewish accusation (18:28–32)

II (inside)—Roman interrogation (18:33–38a)

III (outside)—Jewish rejection (18:38b–40)

IV (inside)—Roman castigation (19:1–3)

V (outside)—Jewish repudiation (19:4–7)

VI (inside)—Roman reexamination (19:8–11)

VII (outside)—Jewish condemnation (19:12–16)

The effect of this arrangement is to highlight the hostile pressure which the Jews exerted on Pilate. Four times (18:40; 19:6, 12,15) they are said to have "cried out" ("yelled," Moffatt), a strong Greek verb (*kraugazō*) suggesting a demonic fury which even Rome could not withstand.[39] Again and again the mob overrode his impulse to justice and countered his efforts to release Jesus. Here was a case where church and state should have remained separate— but for the sake of the state. (What a conceit to assume that priests are always right and politicians are always wrong!) In this case both Jew and Gentile stood guilty for their complicity (cf. Rom. 1:18—3:20) but, if anything, the former more so (cf. comment on 19:11).

(1) The Interrogation by the High Priest (18:19–24)

[19] The high priest then questioned Jesus about his disciples and his teaching. [20] Jesus answered him, "I have spoken openly to the world; I have always taught in synagogues and in the temple, where all Jews come together; I have said nothing secretly. [21] Why do you ask me? Ask those who have heard me, what I said to them; they know what I said." [22] When he had said this, one of the officers standing by struck Jesus with his hand, saying, "Is that how you answer the high priest?" [23] Jesus answered him, "If I have spoken wrongly, bear witness

[38] R. H. Strachan, *The Fourth Gospel* (3d ed.; London: SCM Press, 1941), pp. 310–318.
[39] R. H. Lightfoot, *St. John's Gospel*, ed., C. F. Evans (Oxford: Clarendon, 1956), p. 325.

to the wrong; but if I have spoken rightly, why do you strike me?" 24 Annas then sent him bound to Caiaphas the high priest.

It is not clear just which *high priest* now *questioned Jesus*. In v. 13 Jesus had been taken to Annas, while in v. 24 he would be sent to Caiaphas, thus presumably the interrogator here was Annas. However, since Caiaphas was actually high priest at that time (v. 13), the reference could mean that he had come to his father-in-law's quarters for an informal investigation of Jesus before convening a more formal session of the Sanhedrin nearby in his own official residence. The term *high priest* does not decide the issue since it could refer either to the single head of the priestly order or to those members of the select families from which high priests were chosen.

In any case, Annas and Caiaphas were probably working together to lay the foundation for a political charge which Pilate would hear. The line of questioning suggests that an effort was made to extort from Jesus the admission that he had been training secretly a band of seditious rebels. If so, this would not be the first effort to discredit a renewal group by identifying it as a political action movement. Jesus answered the implied charge forthrightly by insisting that he had always *spoken openly to the world* and had utilized the approved institutions of *synagogues* and *temple* for this purpose. Since *all Jews* came together in these places, Jesus invited the high priest to *ask those who* had *heard* him about *what* he had *said to them*. Since he had *said nothing secretly*, there were plenty of witnesses who might be subpoenaed, thus he should not be forced to convict himself.

In challenging the very basis on which he was being questioned, Jesus was not, so to speak, "taking the Fifth Amendment" by refusing to answer, for his life was already an open book for all to read. Rather, in exposing the failure of the Jewish chief justice to gather evidence from several witnesses according to established procedures

(cf. comment on 5:31–32) he made plain that the case was prejudiced from the start. This protest was immediately met by *one of the officers standing by* who *struck Jesus with his hand* for the effrontery of answering the high priest in such fashion. Always there are those who suppose that fundamental questions of justice can be swept aside with a show of brute force.

It is interesting to observe that in this situation Jesus did not respond to the blow by literally "turning the other cheek" (cf. Matt. 5:39), but rather by replying in such a courageous fashion that it invited a further blow. Jesus' teachings as a whole do not enjoin passive silence in the face of every injustice. Here, for example, Jesus himself insisted upon settling the matter by due process: *If I have spoken wrongly, bear witness to the wrong; but if I have spoken rightly, why do you strike me?*

With this show of courage it became clear that Jesus could not be intimidated by verbal harassment, thus *Annas then sent him bound to Caiaphas the high priest,* perhaps in the hope that more formal proceedings would yield better results. A full scale trial could not have been held in the middle of the night, however, nor is any session of the Sanhedrin recorded here (vv. 24,28). From the perspective of the fourth Evangelist the Jews had already had their chance to judge Jesus and, in reaching a negative verdict, had been judged by him (cf. comment on 1:19–28; introduction to 5:1—10:42; and 12:36*b*–50).

(2) The Denial by Peter (18:25–27)

25 Now Simon Peter was standing and warming himself. They said to him, "Are not you also one of his disciples?" He denied it and said, "I am not." 26 One of the servants of the high priest, a kinsman of the man whose ear Peter had cut off, asked, "Did I not see you in the garden with him?" 27 Peter again denied it; and at once the cock crowed.

Since the reader already knows from 13:38 of Jesus' prediction that Peter would deny him three times, the suspense has mounted since 18:17–18 where the scene suddenly shifted after Peter had issued only one denial. Now, against the backdrop of Jesus' courage, we return to *Simon Peter* as he warmed himself before the fire. By now the group had taken up the challenge of the maid, *Are not you also one of his disciples?* No sooner did a second denial escape his lips than *one of the servants* (or slaves) *of the high priest* forced the issue again, this time because, as *a kinsman of the man whose ear Peter had cut off,* he was confident that he had seen him *in the garden* with Jesus. A shift in the Greek construction (from *mē* to *ouk*) suggests that the questions in vv. 17 and 25 expect a negative answer (i.e., "You are not one of his disciples are you?"), while the one in v. 27 expects an affirmative answer (i.e., "I *did* see you with him, didn't I?"), in which case the pressure was mounting on Peter to show his hand.

With the third denial Peter had not a moment to wait for the fulfillment of Jesus' prediction (13:38): *at once the cock crowed.* Since the third watch of the night (12:00—3:00 A.M.) was called "cockcrow," the sound which Peter heard may have been that of a literal fowl or it may have been the bugle note which sounded from the Tower of Antonio at the close of the third watch to announce the changing of the guard. In either case Jesus had been correct: that disciple who had claimed the most courage could not make it through one night without denying the deepest commitment of his life.

(3) The Accusation Against Jesus (18: 28–32)

28 Then they led Jesus from the house of Caiaphas to the praetorium. It was early. They themselves did not enter the praetorium, so that they might not be defiled, but might eat the passover. 29 So Pilate went out to them and said, "What accusation do you bring against this man?" 30 They answered him, "If this man were not an evildoer, we would not have handed him over." 31 Pilate said to them, "Take him yourselves and judge him by your own law." The Jews said to him, "It is not lawful for us to put any man to death." 32 This was to fulfil the word which Jesus had spoken to show by what death he was to die.

The scene now shifts to the Roman *praetorium,* a complex which seems to have included the governor's residence, military barracks, and a judgment hall. Its location in the city is uncertain; probably it was either a part of the Tower of Antonio just beyond the Temple area or it was connected with Herod's palace farther to the northwest. It was here that the trial proper began, for earlier Jewish efforts had broken off abruptly with indecisive results (v. 24). The time was *early* (*prōi*), which may refer to the last watch of the night (3:00—6:00 A.M.). The date was Nisan 14, on the eve of the Jewish Passover. Because the Jews desired to *eat the passover* on the next evening they refused to *enter the praetorium* of the pagan governor lest they *be defiled* (even though the defilement could have been removed by ritual lustration before the new day began at 6:00 o'clock that night). What irony to suppose that the outward spot where they stood could somehow insure religious purity when their inward thoughts were dominated by the desire to secure Jesus' death!

As a concession to their scruples during this holy season, *Pilate went out to them* to inquire of the *accusation* against Jesus. When told only that he was an *evildoer,* the prefect [40] assumed that some Jewish code had been transgressed and so bade them to *judge him by* their *own law.* The reply that they did not wish to exercise jurisdiction because it was *not lawful* for them *to put any man to death* is very difficult to interpret. Historians have been unable to determine with confidence from the available evidence whether or not the Romans at this time allowed the Jews to

---

40 Traditionally, Pilate has been called a procurator, although the title is not so used in the New Testament but comes from Tacitus, *Annals,* 15:44. At the time of Jesus, it may have been anachronistic since a provincial governor of the equestrian order seems to have been designated as *procurator* from the reign of Claudius (A.D. 41–54), before which time he would have been called *praefectus* or *pro legato.* Perhaps Pilate carried both titles at various stages of his career. See Jerry Vardaman, "A New Inscription which Mentions Pilate as 'Perfect'," *Journal of Biblical Literature,* 81 (1962), pp. 70–71.

practice capital punishment.[41] If they did not, then this verse may mean that the Jews deemed Jesus worthy of death and wanted Pilate to intervene because only he could pass such a sentence. If they did, then the verse may mean that, whereas the Jews could execute one of their number for religious offenses by stoning (cf. 10:31–33; 11:53; Acts 7:58–60), in this case they wanted to shift the charge from blasphemy to treason and have Jesus executed by crucifixion, which only Rome could administer (cf. 19:10).

Apparently the Evangelist understood the matter in the latter sense for he commented that the Jewish strategy served to *fulfil the word which Jesus had spoken* (cf. 12:32–33) *to show by what death* (i.e., "lifting up" = crucifixion) *he was to die.*

(4) The Appearance Before Pilate (18: 33–38a)

[33] Pilate entered the praetorium again and called Jesus, and said to him, "Are you the King of the Jews?" [34] Jesus answered, "Do you say this of your own accord, or did others say it to you about me?" [35] Pilate answered, "Am I a Jew? Your own nation and the chief priests have handed you over to me; what have you done?" [36] Jesus answered, "My kingship is not of this world; if my kingship were of this world, my servants would fight, that I might not be handed over to the Jews; but my kingship is not from the world." [37] Pilate said to him, "So you are a king?" Jesus answered, "You say that I am a king. For this I was born, and for this I have come into the world, to bear witness to the truth. Every one who is of the truth hears my voice." [38] Pilate said to him, "What is truth?"

In turning Jesus over to Pilate, the Jewish authorities must have reported not only that he was an "evildoer" (v. 30) but that he claimed to be a king (cf. 19:12; Luke 23:2). Obviously this was a charge with which a representative of Caesar would have to reckon and so *Pilate entered the praetorium again* and began to interrogate Jesus on this point. No sooner had he

started, however, than Jesus recognized in his words the contemptuous charge trumped up by the Jews and therefore recalled Pilate to his judicial responsibility with a question, *Do you say this of your own accord, or did others say it to you about me?* In so doing he forced Pilate to face whether he would be a willing pawn in a sinister plot or a man of independent judgment worthy of his office. Stung by this unexpected answer—which was really a question that reversed their roles and made Jesus the judge—Pilate retorted that he was not *a Jew,* i.e., that the indictments of the Sanhedrin meant nothing to him, but that since Jesus was a Jew he would have to answer to the charges lodged against him by his *own nation and the chief priests.*

In this opening exchange Jesus had succeeded in shifting the method of Pilate. No longer did he ask leading questions insinuated by others but now sought to discover Jesus' side of the matter: *what have you done?* This gave Jesus opportunity to seize upon the charge of *kingship* and redefine it as *not of this world,* which was the point of greatest concern to Pilate. Proof that Jesus was not a Zealot seeking to overthrow Rome could be seen in the fact that his *servants* did not *fight* to prevent his arrest by *the Jews* (18:11; cf. Matt. 26:52–55). This did not mean that the world was excluded from his royal domain but only that his *kingship* was not *from the world* (i.e., the source of his sovereignty was not the power which men confer on their earthly leaders), nor was his cause served by the weapons of darkness.

Now Pilate supposed that he had heard from the lips of Jesus as well as from the Jews an admission that he claimed to be *a king.* But once again he was brought up short with the warning that the way he understood kingship did not necessarily coincide with the way Jesus understood it: *You say that I am a king.* Meaning is not adequately conveyed just because a speaker has said a certain thing; it is also necessary for the listener to hear what he intended. This was particularly difficult for

---

[41] The literature on this question is extensive. For a recent study see A. N. Sherwin-White, *Roman Society and Roman Law in the New Testament* (Oxford: Clarendon, 1963), pp. 1–47.

Pilate because he had been conditioned for a lifetime to understand kingship in terms of military might. Thus Jesus moved swiftly to redefine the concept in positive fashion: *For this I was born, and for this I have come into the world* (i.e., this is where my kingship is "from"—v. 36), *to bear witness to the truth.* Pilate or anyone else would hear his voice with understanding only if he was *of the truth.*

This climactic confession of Jesus represents a significant testimony to the unity of power and truth. Most civilizations have been built on the assumption that the two are incompatible—i.e., that power is irrational and that truth is impotent. The tensions between rulers and thinkers are too well known to need comment. Against this disastrous alienation Jesus affirmed both that he who witnesses to the truth exercises a power that will prevail and, conversely, that he who would reign must submit his power to the test of truth. Pilate had been schooled to believe that kings ruled by might and not by truth, i.e., that truth was on the side of the biggest battalions. Looking at this young Jewish "king" in fetters before him he was moved to ask (in cynical contempt or in wistful surmise?), *What is truth?* Little could he dream that when his Caesar had been long forgotten, this Man's truth would reign over a vaster domain than Rome had ever known.

(5) The Offer of Barabbas (18:38b–40)

After he had said this, he went out to the Jews again, and told them, "I find no crime in him. 39 But you have a custom that I should release one man for you at the Passover; will you have me release for you the King of the Jews?" 40 They cried out again, "Not this man, but Barabbas!" Now Barabbas was a robber.

In raising the ultimate question of truth Pilate had tried to evade responsibility for a decision regarding Jesus by a retreat into relativity (i.e., our conceptions of truth differ so greatly that it is impossible to decide finally between them). Now he tried to avoid the necessity of choice by an act of clemency. Going back *out to the Jews again*, he first assured them that Jesus was

guilty of *no crime;* i.e., his conception of kingship was not political and therefore not seditious. Then, referring to a *custom* (for which we have no evidence outside the Gospels) that he *release one man . . . at the Passover,* Pilate offered to *release* for them the so-called *King of the Jews.*

Even this effort quickly boomeranged, however, as the frenzied crowd expressed a preference for *not this man, but Barabbas!* John alone adds that *Barabbas was a robber* (Gr. *lēistēs*), a term often used for those rebels who took to the hills and by marauding banditry sought to harass the occupation forces of Rome. If this had been Barabbas' role, the crowd may have urged his release not as a petty thief but as a hero of the national resistance movement. To his grief Pilate learned that a leader who will not face the question of truth and judge a case on its own merits (v. 38a) may soon face instead the cries of an angry mob. The search for truth may be difficult, but it is preferable to the whims of a crowd that so readily would choose a gangster who had robbed under the cloak of patriotism instead of the "king" who would not cater to their nationalistic aspirations.

(6) The Effort to Release Jesus (19:1–11)

1 Then Pilate took Jesus and scourged him. 2 And the soldiers plaited a crown of thorns, and put it on his head, and arrayed him in a purple robe; 3 they came up to him, saying, "Hail, King of the Jews!" and struck him with their hands. 4 Pilate went out again, and said to them, "Behold, I am bringing him out to you, that you may know that I find no crime in him." 5 So Jesus came out, wearing the crown of thorns and the purple robe. Pilate said to them, "Here is the man!" 6 When the chief priests and the officers saw him, they cried out, "Crucify him, crucify him!" Pilate said to them, "Take him yourselves and crucify him, for I find no crime in him." 7 The Jews answered him, "We have a law, and by that law he ought to die, because he has made himself the Son of God." 8 When Pilate heard these words, he was the more afraid; 9 he entered the praetorium again and said to Jesus, "Where are you from?" But Jesus gave no answer. 10 Pilate therefore said to him, "You will not speak to me? Do you not know that I have power to release you, and power to crucify you?"

11 Jesus answered him, "You would have no power over me unless it had been given you from above; therefore he who delivered me to you has the greater sin."

Stymied by his well-meaning but ineffectual efforts at acquittal through subterfuge, Pilate now sought to pacify the howling crowd with cruelty. First Jesus was *scourged,* which involved flogging the victim with a whip of leather straps to which pieces of metal or bone were often attached to aggravate the torture. Then he suffered the indignity of a mock coronation as *soldiers* placed a *crown of thorns* (briar wreath) *on his head, . . . a purple robe* around his body, and then jeered him as *King of the Jews* while striking him *with their hands.* Normally such punishment was administered just before crucifixion in order to hasten death (cf. Mark 15:15-20 and parallels), or it could come earlier in an effort to extract a full confession, but in the Johannine sequence the purpose was rather to satisfy the lust of the crowd for blood.

To this end Pilate *went out again* to the Jews and once more affirmed the innocence of Jesus. Coupled with this announcement, however, he paraded Jesus wearing the *crown of thorns and the purple robe* and *said to them, Here is the man!* This is perhaps the supreme example of irony in the entire Gospel. Pilate meant, "Look, I have reduced your royal pretender to a pitiful parody of kingship; is not that enough to satisfy your hostilities?" But the reader hears in his words a deeper reality, "Behold the true (Son of) man in his hour of perfect obedience; is not that enough to see and be saved?"

Roused afresh to fury by this stratagem, *the chief priests and the officers* screamed for vengeance, identifying for the first time their deepest desire, *Crucify him, crucify him.* Goaded to exasperation by their chants, Pilate dared them to take the law into their own hands: *Take him yourselves and crucify him, for I find no crime in him.* This was now the third time that Pilate had sought to acquit Jesus (18:38; 19:4,6) but

the Jews were adamant: *We have a law* (against blasphemy), *and by that law he ought to die* (Lev. 24:16), *because he has made himself the Son of God* (cf. 5:18; 10:33). In this instance, the Jews rather than Pilate paid unconscious tribute to the true significance of Jesus by identifying him, even in derision, as the Son of God (cf. 1:34,49; 3:18,35; 5:19-23; 11:27).

These words of ironic confession also had their impact on Pilate, for he *entered the praetorium again* and, perhaps with a growing sense of awe which could not be stifled, resumed the discussion with Jesus (cf. 18:36b) by asking *where* he was *from.* Realizing that the question had already been answered for those who could "hear" his voice (18:37), Jesus made no further response. Slighted by this "imperial silence" which quietly assumed an authority that needed no earthly proof, Pilate began to bluster by reminding Jesus of his *power* either *to release* or *to crucify* him.

In the face of this blatant assertion of authority Jesus simply *answered* that Pilate could perform his judicial functions only by virtue of an office which had been *given* by God for the maintenance of public order (cf. Rom. 13:1). Although Pilate would be accountable to a greater power *from above* for whatever he did, it was not Pilate but the one *who delivered* Jesus to him that was guilty of the *greater sin* before God, for that person had acted out of deliberate treachery whereas Pilate was only trying to do the job assigned him. The person indicated by this reference is not identified. Although Satan himself might have been intended, the specific allusion is more probably either to Judas or to the high priest. Perhaps the singular *he* was meant to cover anyone who had contributed to the unwarranted arrest of Jesus.

(7) The Condemnation of Jesus (19: 12-16)

12 Upon this Pilate sought to release him, but the Jews cried out, "If you release this man, you are not Caesar's friend; every one who makes himself a king sets himself against Caesar." 13 When Pilate heard these words, he

brought Jesus out and sat down on the judgment seat at a place called The Pavement, and
in Hebrew, Gabbatha. 14 Now it was the day of
Preparation of the Passover; it was about the
sixth hour. He said to the Jews, "Here is your
King!" 15 They cried out, "Away with him,
away with him, crucify him!" Pilate said to
them, "Shall I crucify your King?" The chief
priests answered, "We have no king but Caesar." 16 Then he handed him over to them to be
crucified.

With the admission from Jesus in v. 11
that far from wishing to overthrow the governor's office by rebellion he honored it as
a gift from God, Pilate once again *sought to
release* him, only to be shouted down by
the Jews with the insinuation, *If you release this man, you are not Caesar's friend;
every one who makes himself a king sets
himself against Caesar.* Undoubtedly, this
was the most compelling argument which
the Jews could advance against acquittal.
"Friend of the Emperor" was a coveted
title which Pilate may have held or to
which he may have aspired; thus he dared
not compromise his reputation for loyalty to
Caesar by failing to take seriously the
charges against Jesus. The fact that Pilate
was later removed from office as the result
of a local protest illustrates the potential
jeopardy in which he was now being
placed by the Jews (cf. Josephus, *Antiq.*,
18:85–89).

For the third and last time *Pilate . . .
brought Jesus out* and one of them—the
Greek is not clear which—*sat down on the
judgment seat.* If it was Pilate, he was
preparing to render a verdict; if it was
Jesus, a further effort was being made to
heighten the mockery. Now that the climax
of the trial had been reached, careful mention is made of the historical circumstances
as if the smallest details of this moment are
worth remembering. The *place* was *called
The Pavement,* presumably because it had
been constructed out of carefully laid
stones. Because this courtyard was connected with the praetorium, it may have
been either at the Tower of Antonio or at
Herod's palace (cf. on 18:28); both locations had a rocky elevation which could

have been called *Gabbatha* ("projecting
ridge") *in Hebrew* (Aramaic). The date
was Nisan 14, the *day of Preparation for
the Passover* (contrast Mark 14:1,12,42).
The time was near noon (12:00), *about
the sixth hour* (contrast Mark 15:25,33),
when the paschal lambs were being prepared for sacrifice. As Synoptic comparisons
show, all of this information is distinctive to
the fourth Gospel and suggests its utilization of an independent source.

In a final effort to have the case laughed
out of court, Pilate *said to the Jews* in
mocking sarcasm, *Here is your King;* i.e.,
"This poor wretch is the only king that I
will let you have." Even this attempt at
cruel jest backfired as the Jews were emboldened by ridicule to cry again and again
for his crucifixion. Unable to secure Jesus'
release through pity, Pilate appealed to
national pride: *Shall I crucify your King?*
The challenge was subtle: "I am unwilling
to follow your wishes and execute him as a
criminal. Would you still want to go
through with it if I publicly humiliated him
as your king; i.e., if I nailed your highest
hopes to a tree of shame?" Faced with this
terrible alternative the Jews were driven to
repudiate their theocratic heritage in order
to force the hand of Pilate: *We have no
king but Caesar.* Realizing that they were
prepared to pay any price to claim their
victim, *he handed him over to them to be
crucified.*

The account does not record that Pilate
actually passed a sentence of death upon
Jesus for, in one sense, he did not reach his
own verdict of guilty but only yielded to a
Jewish verdict which was thrust upon him.
In the Johannine drama Pilate is presented
primarily as an uncomprehending Roman
suddenly caught in a Jewish struggle which
he neither understood nor approved. With
biting irony the Evangelist suggests that
there was more insight in Pilate's naive
pagan impulses than in all the careful calculations of the Jewish priesthood. At
every turning point Pilate's instinct was for
acquittal. Finding that this option was completely unacceptable to the local power

structure, he resorted to devious ploys in an effort to suspend judgment. But Jesus' foes were relentless. When at last Pilate capitulated to their pressure, the full force of the demonic operating in the frenzied crowd stood fully revealed. It would be hard to find anywhere a more damning indictment of the depravity into which even religion may sink.

3. Jesus Fulfills His Passion (19:17–42)

The preceding section made clear how Jesus was tried as King; this section now shows how he died as King. While there is no effort to hide the hideous shame and suffering of a public crucifixion, even the most obscene details are given a new dignity either because they paid unconscious tribute to the royalty of Jesus or because they represented the fulfillment of scriptural prophecy or because they illustrated the perfect obedience of Jesus to his Father's will. The fact that the account combines straightforward historical narration with profound theological reflection shows once again that the Gospel did not derive its faith from esoteric speculation but from Spirit-led meditation upon the ministry of Jesus. The great paradox of this passage is that instead of finding it difficult or even impossible to see God at work in this apparent catastrophe it was possible to see his glory revealed here more clearly than anywhere else.

(1) The Crucifixion and Inscription (19:17–22)

17 So they took Jesus, and he went out, bearing his own cross, to the place called the place of a skull, which is called in Hebrew Golgotha. 18 There they crucified him, and with him two others, one on either side, and Jesus between them. 19 Pilate also wrote a title and put it on the cross; it read, "Jesus of Nazareth, the King of the Jews." 20 Many of the Jews read this title, for the place where Jesus was crucified was near the city; and it was written in Hebrew, in Latin, and in Greek. 21 The chief priests of the Jews then said to Pilate, "Do not write, 'The King of the Jews,' but, 'This man said, I am King of the Jews.'" 22 Pilate answered, "What I have written I have written."

Since public ridicule was one purpose of crucifixion, it was customary for the condemned victim to carry the transverse part of his own cross along a prominent route to the place of execution. No mention is made here of the conscripted role played by Simon of Cyrene (Mark 15:21 and parallels), perhaps in order to emphasize the theological truth that Jesus completed his saving work without human assistance. Like Isaac of old (Gen. 22:6), he carried the materials for his own sacrifice.

The destination was a site near the city —i.e., just outside its wall (cf. Heb. 13:12). Later we are also told that it was close to a garden (vv. 41–42). The name of the place in Hebrew (Aramaic) was Golgotha, which meant a skull. The Latin form of this word in the Vulgate is Calvaria, which explains why Golgotha and Calvary have become interchangeable today. No explanation is given of why the place was so named. A likely conjecture is that it was the scene of regular executions, thus the epithet became appropriate because the skull symbolizes death. The exact location of the site is uncertain, largely because Christians showed no interest in the question before the fourth century. Today the two main competing locations are the Church of the Holy Sepulcher and Gordon's Calvary, but neither has strong claims to authenticity.

Crucifixion was designed not only to expose the naked victim to public shame but to induce death by slow physical torture. Since no vital organs were damaged when the body was nailed or tied to the tree, death usually came only after several days as the result of excruciating hunger, thirst, muscle cramping, and shock. So repulsive was the ordeal that Rome reserved it only for slaves and foreigners. In Palestine it was commonly used to punish robbery and sedition. Therefore, when they crucified Jesus and with him two others, this was to all outward appearances just another grim reminder of the power of Rome. No description is given in John of the *two others* (cf. Luke 23:39–43), attention focusing entirely on *Jesus* in the middle *between them.*

As already indicated in v. 15, Pilate was determined to retaliate for the untenable position in which the Jews had placed him by coercing his concurrence to crucify Jesus. Thus over this gruesome scene he placed a *title . . . on the cross* which read, *Jesus of Nazareth, the King of the Jews.* To add injury to insult Pilate had the inscription *written in Hebrew, in Latin, and in Greek* that all the world might know the kind of king the Jews deserved for their recent efforts. All the protests of *the chief priests* could not persuade Pilate to change what he had *written.* For the Evangelist, the irony of it all was that Pilate had unwittingly proclaimed the universal authority of Jesus to rule the world from a cross!

(2) The Distribution of Jesus' Clothing (19:23–24)

23 When the soldiers had crucified Jesus they took his garments and made four parts, one for each soldier; also his tunic. But the tunic was without seam, woven from top to bottom; 24 so they said to one another, "Let us not tear it, but cast lots for it to see whose it shall be." This was to fulfil the scripture,
  "They parted my garments among them,
  and for my clothing they cast lots."

In a crucifixion the victim was stripped of all his clothing which greatly increased both the public shame of the occasion as he became unable to cope with his bodily functions and his physical torture as the result of exposure to the elements and to insects. His garments were considered a perquisite of the executioners, in this case a squad of four soldiers. First they *made four parts* and each took *one,* perhaps the headdress, sandals, outer cloak, and girdle. This left the *tunic* or undergarment which could not be divided because it was of one piece *without seam, woven from top to bottom.* The decision was made *not* to *tear it* into four parts but to *cast lots for it* that

one of their number might have it undamaged.

From a Christian perspective, this somewhat callous proceeding was seen to fulfill *the scripture* found in Psalm 22:18. This psalm was one of the central passages in the Bible of the early Christians to which they turned in an effort to understand the passion of Jesus. Beginning with the familiar, "My God, my God, why hast thou forsaken me?" (cf. Mark 15:34), it describes the lament of one in the grip of a mortal peril. Just before the verse quoted here the psalmist cried, "A company of evildoers encircle me; they have pierced my hands and feet" (v. 16). As the psalmist became so emaciated that he could count all his bones, his neighbors and relatives stared and gloated over his predicament (v. 17) and even began to divide his personal belongings among themselves before he was dead (v. 18). As the same thing happened to Jesus, the sense of apparent helplessness by the righteous sufferer in the face of his tormentors found expression in fullest measure.

It is interesting to note that in the psalm the two lines about dividing garments and casting lots are in Hebrew parallelism and refer to one act, whereas in John these lines are made to refer to the two successive acts described in v. 23 and in v. 24a (cf. a partially similar adaptation of Zech. 9:9 in Matt. 21:5–7). While this use of the Old Testament may reflect an inadequate understanding of Semitic poetry, it also shows that the original meaning of the Scripture has been modified to fit the actualities of history rather than that the facts of history have been twisted to fit some prior view of Scripture. In other words, the fulfillment was greater than the prediction and so controlled its use.

(3) The Mother of Jesus and the Beloved Disciple (19:25–27)

25 So the soldiers did this. But standing by the cross of Jesus were his mother, and his mother's sister, Mary the wife of Clopas, and

Mary Magdalene. 26 When Jesus saw his mother, and the disciple whom he loved standing near, he said to his mother, "Woman, behold, your son!" 27 Then he said to the disciple, "Behold, your mother!" And from that hour the disciple took her to his own home.

John gives more prominence to women in connection with the crucifixion than any other Gospel. In the Synoptics, a group of women are mentioned at the end of the account as "looking on from afar" (Mark 15:40–41 and parallels), whereas here they are introduced almost from the outset as *standing by the cross of Jesus*. Problems of punctuation make it difficult to determine how many were listed. Probably four were enumerated, perhaps to represent believing counterparts to the four soldiers referred to in v. 23: (1) *his mother*, known outside this Gospel as Mary; (2) *his mother's sister*, otherwise unknown unless she be identified with Salome on the basis of Mark 15:40 and Matthew 27:56 (which would make the sons of Zebedee first cousins of Jesus); (3) *Mary the wife of Clopas*, who may have been the mother of James the younger and of Joses, as in Mark 15:40; and (4) *Mary Magdalene*, mentioned here for the first time in this Gospel but destined to play a unique role in its climactic chapter (20:1–18).

These women are introduced to provide the setting in which *Jesus saw his mother, and the disciple whom he loved standing near*. Although Jesus had now taken upon himself the cares of the world, he was no less concerned about the cares of his mother. In the same spirit of concern which he had shown for the protection of his disciples (17:11–12; 18:8–9), he refused to let personal agony distract him from the practical duties of a son. To his mother (here called *woman* as in 2:4) he commended the beloved disciple as her *son* (i.e., as the one who would take his place in her life), while *to the disciple* he presented Mary in her new role as his *mother*. *From that hour* this ideal *disciple* accepted the responsibility laid upon him and *took her to his own home* which, it seems logical

to infer, was in the Jerusalem area. Elsewhere Jesus had promised that his followers would receive "spiritual mothers" (e.g., Mark 3:33–35; 10:30), and here this teaching was literally fulfilled.[42]

(4) The Death of Jesus (19:28–30)

28 After this Jesus, knowing that all was now finished, said (to fulfil the scripture), "I thirst." 29 A bowl full of vinegar stood there; so they put a sponge full of the vinegar on hyssop and held it to his mouth. 30 When Jesus had received the vinegar, he said, "It is finished"; and he bowed his head and gave up his spirit.

Only after Jesus *finished* all of his work which he had been sent to do and faced the fact that death was near did he think of himself enough to say, *I thirst,* thereby reflecting his full involvement in one of the most agonizing accompaniments of crucifixion. Even this admission was not a sign of weakness, however, but was to *fulfil the scripture* in Psalm 69:21 which depicted the plight of the righteous sufferer who was given only cheap sour wine to quench his thirst. It is not surprising that a bowl full of this same *vinegar* wine *stood* at the cross, since it was a popular drink of soldiers. From this supply *a sponge full* was *held* to Jesus' *mouth* in an effort to slake his thirst. It is not certain whether the sponge was lifted to his lips *on hyssop* (Gr. *hussōpos*), a small bushy plant used in connection with the Passover (Ex. 12:22; cf. Heb. 9:19), or on a soldier's javelin (Gr. *hussōi*). The latter would obviously function much better for this purpose, but its reading here requires a conjectural emendation of the Greek word found in our best manuscripts. In either case, because this drink was not drugged (as in Mark 15:23; Matt. 27:34) but actually produced a refreshing effect, *Jesus* willingly *received* it.

This done, the lips that a moment earlier were so parched with thirst that they cried out in agony now shouted in triumph, *It is finished.* This exclamation (Gr. *tetelestai*)

---

42 Some expositors find elaborate symbolism in vv. 25–27. See E. C. Hoskyns, *The Fourth Gospel*, F. N. Davey, ed. (2d rev. ed.; London: Faber and Faber, 1947), p. 530.

may have been heard by the bystanders as a sigh of resignation, an acknowledgment that his cause was finished. The believing reader, however, cannot help but hear an exclamation that the epoch of redemption had reached its climax, that Jesus had truly "loved his own . . . to the end" (13:1). Now every man can take hope not on the basis of his frustrated sense of incompleteness but on the basis of the finished work of Christ.

Having been in control of his passion from the outset, Jesus now voluntarily *gave up his spirit* and died. This may mean only that he yielded back the animating force of his physical life to the creator God who had breathed it into him (cf. Mark 15:37). Some, however, think that a deeper theological truth is being hinted, i.e., that by his death the Holy Spirit was now being "given over" (Gr. *paredōken*) to his followers (cf. 7:39). This seems unlikely in view of the explicit gift of the Holy Spirit to the church which will be described in 20:22.

(5) *The Witness of Blood and Water (19:31-37)*

31 Since it was the day of Preparation, in order to prevent the bodies from remaining on the cross on the sabbath (for that sabbath was a high day), the Jews asked Pilate that their legs might be broken, and that they might be taken away. 32 So the soldiers came and broke the legs of the first, and of the other who had been crucified with him; 33 but when they came to Jesus and saw that he was already dead, they did not break his legs. 34 But one of the soldiers pierced his side with a spear, and at once there came out blood and water. 35 He who saw it has borne witness—his testimony is true, and he knows that he tells the truth—that you also may believe. 36 For these things took place that the scripture might be fulfilled, "Not a bone of him shall be broken." 37 And again another scripture says, "They shall look on him whom they have pierced."

Two problems had been created for the Jews by the timing of Jesus' crucifixion. First, it came on a Friday, *the day of Preparation* for the sabbath which would begin at sunset. Further, since it was Nisan 14 (cf. v. 14), *that sabbath* would also be *a high day* because it coincided with the

opening of the great Passover festival on Nisan 15. Since Deuteronomy 21:22-23 prescribed that a dead body "shall not remain all night upon the tree, but you shall bury him the same day," it was particularly urgent that this regulation be observed on so holy an occasion. Thus *the Jews asked Pilate that their legs might be broken,* a customary way to hasten death during the long ordeal of crucifixion. How ironic to suppose that inflicting further trauma on helpless victims would somehow "prepare" for a better celebration of that day designed to remember the liberation of Israel from Egyptian oppression (cf. comment on 18:28).

As *the soldiers* carried out this grim assignment on *the first* and then on *the other who had been crucified with him,* they discovered that Jesus *was already dead* and so *they did not break his legs.* Instead, *one of the soldiers pierced his side with a spear,* either to assure himself that death was final or to engage in a last act of casual cruelty. When the lance thrust produced an effusion of *blood and water* from the abdominal cavity there could be no doubt that a real body had actually died. Although the establishment of this fact may have been important in the early Christian struggle with Gnostics who claimed otherwise, the Evangelist was concerned to clarify its true significance in two other directions.

First, he strongly emphasized that the effusion of blood and water was seen by one who *has borne witness* to its meaning on the basis of a *testimony* that *he* insisted was *true,* in order that the readers who now have his contribution as a part of this Gospel *also may believe.* It seems clear that this eyewitness was not the final author of the Gospel, since all references to him here are in the third person implying that *he* was a source on which the book has drawn (cf. comment on 21:24-25). A plausible case can be made for identifying this witness with the beloved disciple, both because he has just been mentioned as "standing near" (v. 26) and because a claim similar to v. 35 is repeated in 21:24

where the context clearly connects the two. That the beloved disciple was uniquely suited to grasp the meaning of the blood and water fits the emphasis on his spiritual sensitivity elsewhere in the Gospel (e.g., 20:8; 21:7).

The content of his testimony is not recorded, however, and we are left to infer its essential thrust from the undoubted assumption that the Evangelist wholeheartedly embraced it as well as from the enigmatic passage in 1 John 5:6–8.[43] A basic premise of this Gospel is that physical realities may incarnate and therefore effectively symbolize their spiritual counterparts. Biologically, the body of Jesus must have yielded an emission of *blood* and a clear fluid like *water*. But the Gospel has already given both of these terms rich spiritual significance relating to the quickening and sustaining of eternal life (e.g., 2:7–9; 3:5; 4:14; 6:53–56; 7:38–39; 13:5–10). Therefore, the literal *blood* and *water* which came from the crucified Christ symbolize that he alone is the source of those realities that redeem and nourish whoever *may believe.*

Second, the work of the soldiers also received significance from the fact that once more the Scripture was thereby *fulfilled.* On the one hand, the decision not to break the legs of Jesus meant that in this respect he was like both the righteous sufferer and the Passover lambs of whom it could be said, *Not a bone of him shall be broken* (cf. Ex. 12:46; Num. 9:12; Psalm 34:20). On the other hand, the spear thrust meant that the enemies of Jesus were in the same position as those Jerusalemites of old who would one day *look on him whom they have pierced* (Zech. 12:10) and mourn for their martyred leader. The agelong drama of rejection had now reached its last act.

(6) *The Burial of Jesus* (19:38–42)

38 **After this Joseph of Arimathea, who was a disciple of Jesus, but secretly, for fear of the**

Jews, **asked Pilate that he might take away the body of Jesus, and Pilate gave him leave. So he came and took away his body.** 39 **Nicodemus also, who had at first come to him by night, came bringing a mixture of myrrh and aloes, about a hundred pounds' weight.** 40 **They took the body of Jesus, and bound it in linen cloths with the spices, as is the burial custom of the Jews.** 41 **Now in the place where he was crucified there was a garden, and in the garden a new tomb where no one had ever been laid.** 42 **So because of the Jewish day of Preparation, as the tomb was close at hand, they laid Jesus there.**

Following the death of Jesus, a certain *Joseph* from the town of *Arimathea* in the hill country near Jerusalem requested *Pilate* to let him *take away the body of Jesus* from the cross for burial. It is likely that Joseph was a Jewish leader of some prominence since he had direct access to the Roman governor, his petition was favorably received, and his collaborator in this venture was Nicodemus *who had at first come to* Jesus *by night* (3:1–2). The Synoptics tell us that, like Nicodemus, Joseph was "a respected member of the council" (Mark 15:43) who opposed its action in condemning Jesus (Luke 23:51). John agrees with Matthew 27:57 that Joseph was *a disciple of Jesus* but adds that this was *secretly, for fear of the Jews* (cf. 12:42–43). It is not made clear whether such a characterization would also fit Nicodemus.

Apparently, both men were wealthy in the light of the contribution which each made to the burial of Jesus. Joseph furnished *a new tomb* which he owned (Matt. 27:60) in a *garden* near *the place* of the crucifixion. The fact that *no one had ever been laid* in this rock-hewn tomb made it especially suitable for use by Jesus since Jewish law prohibited the burying of executed criminals in family tombs. Nicodemus, for his part, *came bringing a mixture of myrrh and aloes, about a hundred pounds' weight.* Use of these expensive spices in such great quantity suggested burial honors fit for a king (cf. 2 Chron. 16:14). The royalty of Jesus seen throughout his passion was acknowledged even in death.

The Synoptics indicate that the body of

---

43 On the interpretation of 19:34–35 and 1 John 5:6–8 in relation to the Lord's Supper, see Oscar S. Brooks, "The Johannine Eucharist," *Journal of Biblical Literature,* 82 (1963), pp. 293–300.

Jesus was wrapped in a single linen shroud (Mark 15:46 and parallels), but here the men are said to have **bound it in linen cloths with the spices;** i.e., they wound bandage strips around it with perfumes sprinkled between the folds to combat the odors of decay. Since **the burial custom of the Jews** was being followed, the body itself was left intact and neither cremated (Roman) nor embalmed (Egyptian). With the anointing of Jesus' body completed before the sabbath began, John will not need to record that women came to the tomb after the sabbath in hopes of rendering that final act of devotion (Mark 16:1 and parallels).

III. Jesus Lives for His Disciples (20:1–31)

Reaching the most profound level of paradox in the fourth Gospel, the crucifixion of Jesus has been presented in a historical sense as the lowest point in the humiliation of the Son of man, while at the same time in a theological sense it is the highest point of his "lifting up" or exaltation. From a human perspective the cross was an ultimate indignity, but from a divine perspective it was the triumph of obedient love. Although it appeared to Jesus' enemies that he had died in ignominy and shame, the reader has been shown that in actuality he died like a king.

This brilliant clarification by the Evangelist prepares us to understand the resurrection of Jesus not as the reversal of an apparent tragedy but as the confirmation of a completed victory (19:30). No need was felt to magnify the supernatural glory of the risen Lord (as in Matt. 28:16–20), for that glory had already been manifest so impressively from the cross. In John 20, Jesus moves quietly, almost unobtrusively, among his own. To be sure, he had now transcended the limitations of the physical body and so was free to come and go through closed doors (20:19), but he did not thereby become any less a part of the disciples' earthly existence. If anything, the resurrection appearances were designed to show the true humanity of the divine Jesus

just as the crucifixion scenes showed the true divinity of the human Jesus. (See Dodd, *Interpretation,* pp. 439–442.)

1. The Appearance to Mary Magdalene (20:1–18)

The sudden prominence of Mary Magdalene at this point represents a surprising development in the Johannine narrative. Whereas the Synoptics introduce her early (Luke 8:2–3), in John she has not been mentioned previously except in a list of women at the cross (19:25). Now, however, she is singled out both as the first witness to the empty tomb (20:1–10) and as the first person to whom the risen Lord appeared (20:11–18), in contrast to the Synoptics where she shared these experiences with several other women (Matt. 28:1–10; Mark 16:1–8; Luke 24:1–11; the reference in Mark 16:9 is from a later addition not originally a part of that Gospel).

There are several reasons why it is startling to find Mary playing this crucial role at the climax of the fourth Gospel. In the Jewish world of the first century, the testimony of a woman was not always highly trusted, being considered inferior to that of a man (cf. Luke 24:11). In either case, at least two or more witnesses would be needed to establish the authenticity of so incredible a report (cf. 5:31–32; Deut. 19:15; Mark 14:55–56). The fact that Mary was a Galilean from Magdala, a town so notoriously wicked that the rabbis later attributed its fall to licentiousness, would not enhance the credibility of her testimony in Jerusalem. Most damaging of all, perhaps, was her history of possession by seven demons (Luke 8:2), a psychophysical malady of such severity that, even though she seemed to be cured, her sanity could easily be called into question by the excited report that she had seen a dead man alive again.

Taken together, these considerations suggest that the most momentous news in the spiritual history of mankind was first entrusted to one who by human standards was least qualified to proclaim it. An implied contrast may be intended with the preceding chapter where the ranking power structure of Judaism and Rome contemptuously derided Jesus as "Son of God" (19:7) and "King of the Jews" (19:19). What neither a high priest nor a governor could understand by means of their elaborate procedures of jurisprudence, God permitted a lone woman to discover when even the leading disciples were immobilized by grief and despair. The story of Mary Magdalene beckons the humblest witness to become a harbinger of hope in a world weary with the brutal decisions of its prestigious leaders.

(1) The Discovery of the Empty Tomb (20:1-10)

¹ Now on the first day of the week Mary Magdalene came to the tomb early, while it was still dark, and saw that the stone had been taken away from the tomb. ² So she ran, and went to Simon Peter and the other disciple, the one whom Jesus loved, and said to them, "They have taken the Lord out of the tomb, and we do not know where they have laid him." ³ Peter then came out with the other disciple, and they went toward the tomb. ⁴ They both ran, but the other disciple outran Peter and reached the tomb first; ⁵ and stooping to look in, he saw the linen cloths lying there, but he did not go in. ⁶ Then Simon Peter came, following him, and went into the tomb; he saw the linen cloths lying, ⁷ and the napkin, which had been on his head, not lying with the linen cloths but rolled up in a place by itself. ⁸ Then the other disciple, who reached the tomb first, also went in, and he saw and believed; ⁹ for as yet they did not know the scripture, that he must rise from the dead. ¹⁰ Then the disciples went back to their homes.

According to John, Jesus died on a Friday afternoon, Nisan 14, just before the beginning of that sabbath which was called "a high day" (19:31) because it coincided with the start of the Passover festival on Nisan 15. This Saturday observance was hardly a day of rest or rejoicing for Jesus' followers, however, because his body lay in the tomb. As soon as it became permissible to travel *on the first day of the week,* one of those who had been at the cross (19:25), *Mary Magdalene, came to the tomb early*

on Sunday morning, *while it was still dark* (i.e., during the fourth watch of the night, 3:00—6:00 A.M.). From the Synoptics we would infer that she and other women may not have known that his body had been anointed (19:40) and so came to bestow their final affections on his lifeless form (Mark 16:1).

Imagine Mary's consternation when she *saw that the stone had been taken away from the tomb.* Grave robbery was particularly common in Palestine where the tombs were above ground; in this case such a ghoulish crime could be doubly expected since Jesus had been buried in the borrowed grave of a wealthy donor. Apparently, Mary feared that someone (*they*)— whether thoughtless vandals or enemies who engineered his death—had taken the body itself *out of the tomb* and *laid* it in an unknown place. Instinctively she sought out the leaders of the disciples, *Simon Peter* and *the . . . disciple . . . whom Jesus loved,* and reported this further indignity perpetrated against their murdered Master. Nothing in Mary's report at this initial stage contained a ray of hope. The fact that the tomb was empty seemed proof of further tragedy rather than of final triumph.

In the face of this unexpected development there was nothing for the disciples to do but go to the tomb and see for themselves. As they *both ran, the other* (beloved) *disciple . . . reached the tomb first* but after surveying its contents *did not go in. Peter,* however, who may have held back at first (because of a guilty conscience for his threefold denial?), allowed his impetuousness to conquer the caution shown by his companion in the face of ultimate mystery; and upon arrival he *went into the tomb.* There he *saw the linen cloths* in which the body of Jesus had been bound (19:40) and *the napkin, which had been on his head.* These wrappings were not in disarray as would have been expected if the body had been molested; rather, the bandage strips were *lying* neatly in one place, and the headpiece was *rolled up in a place by itself* (i.e., still twirled turbanlike as it had been wound around his head).

This careful description of the grave-clothes was obviously of great significance as an indication that Jesus had risen in a "spiritual body" (1 Cor. 15:44) that transcended the limitations of the natural order and so could pass through any physical fetters. The uniqueness of such a resurrection contrasts vividly with Lazarus, who was physically resuscitated, and so came forth from the tomb "his hands and feet bound with bandages, and his face wrapped with a cloth" (see comment on 11:44). Here the contents of Jesus' tomb offered the first clue that Easter is not a return to the finitude of earthly existence but a breakthrough to its permanent transformation.

The beloved disciple, who had been stopped short by a first glimpse of the grave, now *also went in.* Once *he saw* the scene he grasped its significance and so *believed* in the risen Christ to which it pointed. The Evangelist adds that this insight was dependent neither on sight nor on Scripture. Later, the church would come to *know the scripture, that he must rise from the dead* (cf. 1 Cor. 15:4), but this deeper appreciation of the Old Testament would be based on the experience of faith called forth by Christ himself. Here is another example of the Johannine conviction that the historical actuality of God's revelation in Christ should control our understanding of Scripture rather than our prior understanding of the Bible determining the way we think God should act in this world (cf. comment on 2:22; 5:39,46; 12:16; 19:24).

(2) The Discovery of the Risen Lord (20:11-18)

11 But Mary stood weeping outside the tomb, and as she wept she stooped to look into the tomb; 12 and she saw two angels in white, sitting where the body of Jesus had lain, one at the head and one at the feet. 13 They said to her, "Woman, why are you weeping?" She said to them, "Because they have taken away my Lord, and I do not know where they have laid

him." 14 Saying this, she turned round and saw Jesus standing, but she did not know that it was Jesus. 15 Jesus said to her, "Woman, why are you weeping? Whom do you seek?" Supposing him to be the gardener, she said to him, "Sir, if you have carried him away, tell me where you have laid him, and I will take him away." 16 Jesus said to her, "Mary." She turned and said to him in Hebrew, "Rabboni!" (which means Teacher). 17 Jesus said to her, "Do not hold me, for I have not yet ascended to the Father; but go to my brethren and say to them, I am ascending to my Father and your Father, to my God and your God." 18 Mary Magdalene went and said to the disciples, "I have seen the Lord"; and she told them that he had said these things to her.

After Peter and the beloved disciple received the anguished report of Mary Magdalene regarding the empty tomb, they raced off to investigate, leaving her far behind. Although she had told the two of her discovery, apparently they "went back to their homes" (v. 10) before having an opportunity to share with her what they had found. Since Mary assumed that the open grave bespoke foul play, there seemed nothing for her to do but retrace her steps and stand guard *weeping outside the tomb.* Unlike the beloved disciple, she had not yet learned the lesson of the upper room, "It is to your advantage that I go away" (16:7).

On her first trip to the garden "it was still dark" and she had seen only "that the stone had been taken away from the tomb" (v. 1). This time, perhaps because it was getting light, *she stooped to look into the tomb.* There *she saw two angels* or divine messengers appareled *in white, sitting where the body of Jesus had lain, one at the head and one at the feet.* When they inquired as to the cause of her distress, Mary reiterated the concern which she had recently shared with the disciples (v. 2), but she made no effort to identify either her Lord or those who had removed his body. Since these two angels now sat where Jesus' body had been laid, she assumed that they might know its whereabouts.

Receiving no answer from the angels,

Mary *turned round* to discover that someone was *standing* nearby in the garden. At this early twilight hour, her eyes brimming with tears, her mind numb with grief, *she did not know* who it was. As the stranger spoke, *Woman, why are you weeping? Whom do you seek?* she could only suppose *him to be the gardener.* Suddenly a new explanation for Jesus' disappearance presented itself. Perhaps the caretaker disapproved of the presence of a criminal's corpse in his garden and so had removed it to another place. Therefore, brushing aside his two questions, Mary blurted out her deepest desire, *Sir, if you have carried him away, tell me where you have laid him, and I will take him away.* Again Mary did not pause to identify Jesus (*him*) or to ponder how she alone might manage to *take* his body *away.* Here is one of the most amazing cases of mistaken identity ever recorded. Because Mary sought a lifeless body instead of a living Lord she mistook the Saviour for a servant!

Only one word was needed to correct this incredible confusion: *Mary.* Perhaps he had spoken in such fashion when banishing the demons and calling her to a true sense of identity (Luke 8:2), or when he looked down from the cross upon her faithful devotion (19:25). In any case she now heard the Good Shepherd calling his sheep by name as he said he would (10:3). In an instant she became convinced of the resurrection not by the eye but by the ear. Whirling in amazement, a single cry escaped her lips, *Rabboni!* a *Hebrew* word meaning *Teacher.* As an intensified form of "Rabbi," this term had come increasingly to be used of God and so here may have been a spontaneous confession equivalent to that of Thomas in v. 28.

Appropriate to such an acknowledgement, Mary fell before him in awe and began to cling to him, probably by grasping his feet. In so doing she made the second major mistake. At first, she had misunderstood his identity, but now she failed to grasp his divinity. Because of her overriding concern to locate the body of Jesus (vv.

2,13,15), she had not realized that his exaltation would involve a transcending of all earthly limitations. *Jesus* gently corrected this error by giving her something better to do: *Do not* continue to (Gr. *haptou*) *hold me, for I have not yet ascended to the Father* (i.e., let go of me as a limited physical presence so that you may soon receive me back as a universal spiritual presence); *but go to my brethren* (i.e., do not clutch me selfishly but share the reality of my resurrection with others). Heretofore, the disciples had been designated as "servants" (13:16) and as "friends" (15:15), but now they were called his brothers, despite their sorry performance during the previous week! When he was taken captive, their courage had collapsed and they were all scattered, but now that he was *ascending* (i.e., transcending time and space) they could all have equal and immediate access to his power.

Further proof of the unique role that Jesus would play after the resurrection is provided by the careful distinction here maintained between *my Father and your Father . . . my God and your God.* Two affirmations are held in balance. First, the Father's direct relationship to Jesus was fundamentally different from his mediated relationship to the disciples. We could say that God was the Father of Jesus by nature but the Father of the disciples by grace. At the same time, the fact that there was only one Father meant that the disciples could share in the victory of Jesus. The same God that brought Jesus from the dead and enabled him to ascend would quicken the disciples and cause them to dwell in heavenly places. What an astonishing message *Mary Magdalene* had to report *to the disciples.* Not only had she *seen the Lord* but she had been given an inkling of what the resurrection meant both to Jesus and to his followers.

2. The Appearances to the Disciples (20:19–31)

In the resurrection appearances to his disciples, Jesus began to fulfill the promises of chapters 13—17. At least five parallels are readily apparent: [44] (1) "I will come to you" (14:18) = "Jesus came and stood among them" (20:19a); (2) "Peace I leave with you; my peace I give to you" (14:27) = "Jesus . . . said to them, 'Peace be with you'" (20:19b); (3) "I will see you again and your hearts will rejoice, and no one will take your joy from you" (16:22) = "Then the disciples were glad when they saw the Lord" (20:20b); (4) "As thou didst send me into the world, so I have sent them into the world" (17:18) = "As the Father has sent me, even so I send you" (20:21); (5) "If I do not go away, the Counselor [Holy Spirit] will not come to you; but if I go, I will send him to you" (16:7) = "He breathed on them, and said to them, 'Receive the Holy Spirit'" (20:22).

The primary purpose of the appearances was to establish the identity and continuity of the earthly Jesus with the risen Lord while at the same time defining the tremendous differences that resulted for the disciples in the shift from the former to the latter. Fundamentally, the appearances were intended to effect a transition: from the seen to the unseen, from the temporal to the eternal, from the limited to the universal, from the physical to the spiritual. In this boundary situation, the church was also being transformed: from fearful to peaceful, from spectators to witnesses, from powerless to Spirit-filled, from vacillating to authoritative.

(1) The Appearance to the Group (20:19–23)

19 On the evening of that day, the first day of the week, the doors being shut where the disciples were, for fear of the Jews, Jesus came and stood among them and said to them, "Peace be with you." 20 When he had said this, he showed them his hands and his side. Then the disciples were glad when they saw the Lord. 21 Jesus said to them again, "Peace be with you. As the Father has sent me, even so I send you." 22 And when he had said this, he breathed on them, and said to them, "Receive

44 A. M. Hunter, The Gospel According to John ("The Cambridge Bible Commentary" [Cambridge: University Press, 1965]), pp. 187–188.

the Holy Spirit. 23 If you forgive the sins of any, they are forgiven; if you retain the sins of any, they are retained."

The fourth Gospel has repeatedly emphasized that a human witness to the significance of Jesus is finally validated by Jesus himself (cf. 1:41–42,45–46; 3:29–30; 4:39–42; 10:40–42). In this instance, both Mary Magdalene (20:18) and presumably the beloved disciple (20:8) had already testified to the reality of the resurrection; but the disciples were still closeted behind locked doors for fear of the Jews. Neither the report of an empty tomb nor the confession of a personal appearance proved convincing, since the former might be attributed to grave robbers and the latter to hallucinations. A decisive change did not take place until Jesus himself came and stood among them, thus corroborating objective information with subjective experience.

Clearly this encounter was similar to and yet different from their last meeting in the upper room. In both cases he had bestowed peace (cf. 16:33), but this time he showed them his hands and his side as proof of the victory that made true peace possible. He was still Jesus, a man with a historical name, but he was also the Lord, a divine figure worthy of worship. Even though those assembled saw one whose wounds were still visible, he could nevertheless appear and disappear at will. These phenomena suggest that they were encountering none other than the one who had been the earthly Jesus but that they were learning to live with him as an abiding spiritual presence.

Now that he no longer functioned as the incarnate one sent into the world by the Father, he would send them as the visible continuation of his earthly ministry (cf. 17:18). Earlier, the disciples had been commanded to love one another as he had loved them (13:34; 15:12); now they were commissioned to be sent to others as he had been sent to them. Just as Jesus began this ministry by receiving the Holy Spirit (1:32–33), so now he breathed on them, *and said to them, Receive the Holy Spirit.* In the power of the Spirit, Jesus had exercised a ministry of mercy and judgment (cf. 12:44–50); likewise the disciples would proclaim his word that sifts men for all eternity: *If you forgive the sins of any, they are forgiven; if you retain the sins of any, they are retained* (cf. Matt. 16:19; 18:18).

Just as God breathed life into the dust and so created man, here the Son of God *breathed* the *Holy Spirit* into his disciples and so created a new manhood. In a sense, vv. 21–23 depict the equipping of the church (i.e., the renewal of the people of God) and the empowering of its ministry. Both the scope and the sequence of the actions summarized here are most significant. First, Christ provided comfort (*peace*) based on his conquest of evil. But lest this gift from the nail-scarred hand be confused with mere contentment, the comforted ones were immediately commissioned to minister in a hostile world. They were not asked to serve in their own strength, however, but were consecrated and empowered by the Holy Spirit. Finally, only those thus filled with the presence of Christ were authorized to arbitrate the ultimate issues of life by pronouncing forgiveness and judgment. Here are the central insights which determine the Johannine understanding of the church.

A problem is created for some because in this passage the Holy Spirit is said to be given *on the evening of the first day of the week* (i.e., less than 24 hours after the resurrection) whereas in Acts 2:4 the Holy Spirit seems to have been given at Pentecost some fifty days after the resurrection. In actuality, of course, the Holy Spirit had been a reality in the world since the time of creation (Gen. 1:2), but from now on his presence would be inseparably connected with the ministry of Jesus. John depicts the first infusion of the Spirit into the disciple band while Acts describes its climactic overflowing after weeks of fellowship together permeated by the power of prayer (Acts 1:14). At this initial stage in

John, the presence of the Spirit was not yet sufficiently strong to launch a world mission; indeed, as the next section will show (20:24–29), the disciples could not even convince one of their own number that they had seen the Lord (v. 25)! In Acts 2, however, what had begun as a gentle "breath" now became "like the rush of a mighty wind" impelling the disciples to a fearless public witness. A comparison of the two accounts suggests that all Christians "receive the Holy Spirit" (John 20:22), but all do not cultivate that Spirit until they are given "utterance" to speak with boldness (Acts 2:4).

(2) The Appearance to Thomas (20:24–29)

24 Now Thomas, one of the twelve, called the Twin, was not with them when Jesus came. 25 So the other disciples told him, "We have seen the Lord." But he said to them, "Unless I see in his hands the print of the nails, and place my finger in the mark of the nails, and place my hand in his side, I will not believe."

26 Eight days later, his disciples were again in the house, and Thomas was with them. The doors were shut, but Jesus came and stood among them, and said, "Peace be with you." 27 Then he said to Thomas, "Put your finger here, and see my hands; and put out your hand, and place it in my side; do not be faithless, but believing." 28 Thomas answered him, "My Lord and my God!" 29 Jesus said to him, "Have you believed because you have seen me? Blessed are those who have not seen and yet believe."

The Gospel of John is singular in showing a special interest in *Thomas, one of the twelve, called the Twin* (Gr. *Didymus*). Other than in listings of the apostles (Matt. 10:3; Mark 3:18; Luke 6:15; Acts 1:13), he does not appear elsewhere, while in the fourth Gospel his character is rather clearly delineated in three passages (11:16; 14:5; 20:25). Thomas was doggedly loyal but spiritually obtuse, a literal-minded disciple who demanded tangible proof of intangible truths. His role as the original Christian empiricist is well illustrated here: *Unless I see . . . , and place my finger . . . , I will not believe.*

It has been said that the trouble with Thomas was not so much skepticism as absenteeism—he simply *was not with them when Jesus came.* A reality had been disclosed in the corporate life of the disciples which they were unable to communicate to him on an individual basis. Note, however, that his inability to accept their testimony did not exclude him from their fellowship for, on the next Sunday (*eight days later* follows ancient practice by reckoning both Sundays in the enumeration), *his disciples were again in the house, and Thomas was with them.* Once more, in this worship setting, even though *the doors were shut, Jesus came and stood among them, and said, Peace be with you* (cf. v. 19).

On this occasion Jesus concentrated so completely on Thomas that the appearance seemed to be a special visitation made entirely for his benefit. It was as if the exalted Christ, having finished the process of exaltation, now came back once more so that one of his own would not be lost (cf. 17:12). During the intervening week, however, Jesus had not been spiritually absent from their midst. Obviously, he had overheard the demand of Thomas enunciated in v. 25, for immediately he bade him fulfill those self-imposed conditions for belief. Thomas needed to be careful about what he was saying, for the walls between heaven and earth are thin to one who has inhabited both realms!

This offer of Jesus in v. 27 stands in dramatic tension with his request in v. 17. There, he had advised Mary Magdalene not to touch him, while here he instructed Thomas to do just the opposite.[45] In the former case a follower needed to learn that the reality of Jesus was not just physical (i.e., that his earthly life was transcended in the resurrection); whereas, in the latter case another disciple needed to learn that the reality of Jesus was not just spiritual (i.e., that the risen Lord was none other than the one who had lived among them). In the balance established by these two

passages the gospel of the resurrection is protected from the two extremes of historicism and gnosticism. Faith cannot be based entirely on the tangible or on the intangible. Rather, it arises at the point where the tension between the two is reconciled and thereby transcended (i.e., faith perceives and embraces the true continuities between time and eternity).

This perspective explains why we are not told whether Thomas actually touched Jesus on this occasion. Confronted with one who was tangible enough to bear the marks of his passion yet intangible enough to appear and disappear at will, Thomas realized that he was dealing not just with an earthly man who had been his *Lord* and Master, nor only with a spiritual being who was now his *God*, but rather with one who united both the temporal and the eternal, the seen and the unseen, the human and the divine, in his own person. In confessing Jesus to be *my Lord and my God*, Thomas brought the Gospel story full circle to the point at which it had begun (1:1)—with this difference, that now even the most stubborn skeptic might come to know that which "in the beginning" had been a cosmic secret.

The response of Jesus to the confession of Thomas served to clarify both the nature of faith and the purpose of this Gospel. As a member of the original apostolic generation, Thomas *believed* because he had *seen* Jesus. But the resurrection appearances necessarily came to an end as the gospel spread to those who had never known the incarnate Jesus. Gentile converts were in no position to recognize the risen Jesus even if he appeared to them in physical form. But this did not put them at a disadvantage vis-a-vis the first followers of Jesus. On the contrary, *those who have not seen and yet believe* are just as *blessed* as Thomas who *believed because* he had *seen* Jesus. At the same time, this does not mean that later generations of believers had nothing to "see" and so were expected to embrace Christianity as a spiritual religion without any anchor in history. The distinc-

---

45 Thomas K. Hearn, Jr., "Reach Hither—Touch Me Not," *Review and Expositor,* 59 (1962), pp. 200–204.

tion here is that later Christians *have not seen* in the same sense that Thomas did. What they are permitted to "see" will now be clarified as the Evangelist interprets the meaning of his Gospel.

(3) The Significance of the Signs (20:30–31)

³⁰ Now Jesus did many other signs in the presence of the disciples, which are not written in this book; ³¹ but these are written that you may believe that Jesus is the Christ, the Son of God, and that believing you may have life in his name.

This summary reads very much like a conclusion to the "book of signs" (chs. 2—12), but in the present context it clearly functions as a climax to the entire Gospel. Reference to *signs* which have been *written* suggests that the appearance to Thomas just recorded (vv. 24–29) was considered in this category (i.e., as a visible pointer to the reality of God in Jesus designed to foster belief). *Many other signs* which *Jesus did . . . in the presence of his disciples* were *not written in this book,* however, lest faith appear to be based only on sight, as, e.g., in the many wonder stories of the apocryphal gospels. No, instead of assuming either that faith may be compelled by overwhelming the senses or that faith is corrupted by an appeal to the senses, the Evangelist included just enough signs to let the reader "see" God at work in the life of Jesus but not so many signs that they became an end in themselves, tempting the reader not to "see" beyond them to the spiritual realities which they signify.

It is here that we come to the Evangelist's deepest conception of his own task. The epoch of the earthly Jesus was now over. He was no longer to be "seen" by his followers either in a pre- or a post-resurrection form. How, then, could the church root its ongoing movement in the unique history of its Lord? The answer lies in what was *written in this book.* Just as the earthly works and words of Jesus were intended as "signs" (i.e., visible propaedeutics to belief), so *this book* was *written* to mediate

those same works and words to the contemporary reader who stood at an ever-increasing distance from that unrepeatable past, in order that he, like the first disciples, *may* also *believe.*[46] The reader who makes a Spirit-inspired use of this Gospel is led to the same point that Thomas was led by an appearance of the risen Lord—i.e., he is shown an earthly *Jesus* and asked to affirm that this man *is* at the same time *the Christ, the Son of God.* When, by faith in Jesus as human and divine, one enters the realm where this world and the world beyond overlap, then *in his name* (i.e., in the reality of the God-man) one may both live in this age and at the same time *have* also the eternal *life* of the age to come.

Conclusion (21:1–25)

There are many reasons to understand chapter 21 as a supplementary appendix added to the Gospel of John in the final stages of composition. (1) An effective climax to the book is reached in 20:30–31, giving 21:1–25 the character of an afterthought. (2) The several resurrection appearances in John 20 do not seem to be presupposed in John 21, suggesting that the two chapters originally circulated independently. (3) Several features of vocabulary and style in chapter 21 point to the possibility of a different hand from the author of the more Semitic sections in chapters 1—20. (4) References to authorship in 21:24–25 make it plausible to suppose that this chapter was added by the final editor who redacted the entire Gospel whereas the preceding chapters rest, by his own admission, on earlier sources.

From the content we may infer that several purposes were served by the addition of chapter 21 to the final draft of this

---

[46] The Greek verb form here translated *may believe* appears in important manuscripts both as an aorist ("may come to believe") and as a present ("may continue to believe"). The evidence is so evenly divided that it is difficult to determine the preferred reading. While the choice affects an understanding of the purpose of the Gospel, it need not modify the understanding of its character as set forth here. (See Smith, pp. 3–4.)

Gospel. (1) Judean and Galilean appearances of the risen Lord, separated in the Synoptics, were thereby unified. (2) The nature of the church's ministry, particularly the respective roles of Peter and the beloved disciple, were clarified. (3) Misconceptions regarding the delay of the Parousia and the resulting deaths of these apostolic leaders were corrected. (4) The authority of the Gospel and its trustworthy foundations were reinforced and defended. In general, John 21 is designed to meet the questions and objections which may well have arisen during the period when an earlier draft of the Gospel (chs. 1—20?) was being used in the church.

I. The Revelation of Jesus in Galilee (21:1-23)

In Matthew 28:16-20 (but see 28:9-10) and in Mark 16:7 (cf. 14:28) the resurrection appearances of Jesus are limited to Galilee, while in Luke 24:13-51 they are restricted to Judea. By describing appearances of the risen Lord only in Jerusalem, John 20 agrees on this point with the distinctive material in Luke, as is frequently the case elsewhere. John 21, however, has close affinities with the approach in Matthew and Mark by virtue of recording an appearance in Galilee beside the Sea of Tiberias, a locale given very little attention elsewhere in John. It may be that by the time this chapter was added, both of the Synoptic approaches were known in the Johannine church and a need was felt to enlarge the fourth Gospel to include their differing emphases.

The vague transitional phrase ("after this") with which the section begins, unlike the many specific chronological references in chapters 18—20 (e.g., 19:14,31; 20:1,19,26), suggests a loose connection with preceding events. It seems strange, for example, that if most or all of the seven disciples mentioned here (including Thomas!) had already seen the risen Lord twice as described in 20:19-29, they would have had so much difficulty in recognizing him again (vv. 4,7,12). Further, in the

shift of scene from Jerusalem to Galilee no indication is given that Peter and the beloved disciple had their homes in Jerusalem (20:10; cf. 19:27) from which, according to Acts 1:4, they were not to depart before Pentecost. Such considerations as these do not call into question the basic reliability of the narrative as much as they imply that the material was not fully integrated into the framework of the fourth Gospel.

1. An Appearance by the Sea of Tiberias (21:1-14)

¹ After this Jesus revealed himself again to the disciples by the Sea of Tiberias; and he revealed himself in this way. ² Simon Peter, Thomas called the Twin, Nathanael of Cana in Galilee, the sons of Zebedee, and two others of his disciples were together. ³ Simon Peter said to them, "I am going fishing." They said to him, "We will go with you." They went out and got into the boat; but that night they caught nothing.
⁴ Just as day was breaking, Jesus stood on the beach; yet the disciples did not know that it was Jesus. ⁵ Jesus said to them, "Children, have you any fish?" They answered him, "No." ⁶ He said to them, "Cast the net on the right side of the boat, and you will find some." So they cast it, and now they were not able to haul it in, for the quantity of fish. ⁷ That disciple whom Jesus loved said to Peter, "It is the Lord!" When Simon Peter heard that it was the Lord, he put on his clothes, for he was stripped for work, and sprang into the sea. ⁸ But the other disciples came in the boat, dragging the net full of fish, for they were not far from the land, but about a hundred yards off.
⁹ When they got out on land, they saw a charcoal fire there, with fish lying on it, and bread. ¹⁰ Jesus said to them, "Bring some of the fish that you have just caught." ¹¹ So Simon Peter went aboard and hauled the net ashore, full of large fish, a hundred and fifty-three of them; and although there were so many, the net was not torn. ¹² Jesus said to them, "Come and have breakfast." Now none of the disciples dared ask him, "Who are you?" They knew it was the Lord. ¹³ Jesus came and took the bread and gave it to them, and so with the fish. ¹⁴ This was now the third time that Jesus was revealed to the disciples after he was raised from the dead.

The *Sea of Tiberias* is clearly referred to in this fashion only here in John (cf. on

6:1,23). The name is taken from a town on its southwest shore built by Herod ca. A.D. 25 in honor of Tiberius Caesar. The fourth Gospel alone in the New Testament uses this designation for the Sea of Galilee or Lake of Gennesaret in the Synoptics. In both accounts *Simon Peter* is the main character in a story which pivots on the fact that he and his associates had toiled all *night* but *caught nothing*. In Luke, only two of "all that were with him" are named, "James and John, sons of Zebedee" (5:9–10); here, these two are mentioned in a party of seven which, in addition to *Simon Peter* and *the sons of Zebedee*, include *Thomas . . . Nathanael . . . and two* others, one of whom is later identified as the beloved disciple (v. 7).

It is not clear in what spirit this fishing party was organized. Hoskyns (p. 552) sees the scene as "one of complete apostasy" which fulfills 16:32, thus reading dejection and the return to a former vocation into the words, *I am going fishing*. Strachan (p. 335), however, rejects this suggestion and takes the fishing as symbolic of the mission of the apostles to be "fishers of men" (cf. Luke 5:10) in which they discover both a continuing need for Christ (without whom *they caught nothing*) and his power to fill their nets with new converts. The choice between these approaches will be determined primarily by the relation of this chapter to John 20. If 21:1–14 is an independent account of an initial resurrection appearance, then Hoskyns may be right. If, however, the mission charge of 20:21 and the gift of the Holy Spirit in 20:22 are clearly presupposed, Strachan may be more nearly correct.

In Palestine, *night* was considered the best time to fish, but even the efforts of trained fishermen proved unsuccessful until Jesus intervened. *Just as day was breaking* he *stood on the beach* unrecognized by *the disciples*, despite the fact that he asked, *Children, have you any fish?* Their failure to *know* either his form or his voice may be understood spiritually as the absence of resurrection faith, or it may be attributed

quite naturally to the twilight hour and/or to their distance from the shore. (It is usually very bright at sunrise in Palestine, although a haze sometimes settles over portions of the Sea of Galilee; note in v. 8 that *they were not far from the land, but about a hundred yards off*.) Again the issue turns on the extent of their transformation since the crucifixion, a fact which must be gauged by determining the relation of this chapter to John 20.

The instructions of Jesus to these forlorn fishermen, *Cast the net on the right side of the boat, and you will find some*, led to immediate success: *they were not able to haul it in for the quantity of fish*. No indication is given whether the catch was viewed as miraculous or whether Jesus happened to notice that the disciples had their backs turned to a large school of fish not far from the shore. The freedom of the story from dramatic embellishment highlights the true miracle which was first perceived by *that disciple whom Jesus loved: It is the Lord!* No sooner had *Simon Peter heard* this than he *put on his clothes, for he was stripped for work*. Probably he had been wearing only a waistcloth wrapped tightly around his loins so that he could dive into the water whenever necessary to free the net from rocks as it moved along the bottom of the lake. Now he grabbed an outer garment and swam to shore while the others *came in the boat, dragging the net full of fish* with them. Here, as in 20:5–8, the beloved disciple was the first with insight, Simon Peter the first with action.

Upon joining Jesus they found that he had already prepared *a charcoal fire there, with fish lying on it, and bread*. To this beginning they were invited to add *some of the fish that* they had *just caught*. Again taking the initiative, *Simon Peter went aboard and hauled the net ashore, full of large fish*. At this point the story seems to make creative use of symbolism—at least from one exegetical viewpoint—in an effort to teach three things about fishing for men.

First, the number of fish, *a hundred and fifty-three of them*, represented a complete catch. Some Greek zoologists held that there were 153 kinds of fish, thus this catch fulfilled Ezekiel 47:10. Further, 153 represented the sum of the first seventeen numbers (1 + 2 + 3 . . . + 17), and so may be represented by an equilateral triangle with 17 units in the base and on each side (see Hoskyns, p. 553). This ideal figure, therefore, could stand for "the full number of the Gentiles" (Rom. 11:25) to be brought in by the apostolic mission. From the outset of their evangelistic efforts, Christ saw the final "catch" and promised that it would be abundant.

Second, the fact that *although there were so many, the net was not torn,* may suggest that the unity of the church, like that of a seamless robe (19:23), would not be rent by the inclusion of the Gentiles (cf. comment on 17:20–21). Addressing a situation in which the church was being threatened by schism (cf. John 10; 17; 1 John 2:19), John 21 offered an assurance that the nets may bulge with all sorts of men but they need not break under the strain of such diversity.

Third, the invitation to *come and have breakfast* could have suggested to the disciples that the expected converts of the world mission would be brought to a meal which Jesus himself had prepared. Without his help the disciples labored in vain, but at his bidding they brought in a perfect catch. Here the analogy begins to break down, as it did in 10:11–18, for fish are meant to be fried just as sheep are meant to be slaughtered. To Jesus, however, men were more than sheep or fish. To fish for fish is to take them from life into death, whereas to fish for men is to take them from death into life (cf. Mark 1:17).

The editorial conclusion indicating that *this was now the third time that Jesus was revealed to the disciples after he was raised from the dead* probably was not an original part of vv. 1–13. As we have noticed at several points, there is really no hint in the story itself that this was the *third* such encounter with the risen Lord. In fact, even this specific number only partially connects 21:1–13 with 20:1–29 since in the preceding chapter there were three rather than two appearances (to Mary Magdalene, to the group, and to Thomas), which would make this the fourth rather than the third revelation. Presumably this enumeration omits the appearance to Mary Magdalene since she was not one of *the disciples* in the same sense as the men.

2. The Responsibility of Simon Peter (21: 15–19)

15 When they had finished breakfast, Jesus said to Simon Peter, "Simon, son of John, do you love me more than these?" He said to him, "Yes, Lord; you know that I love you." He said to him, "Feed my lambs." 16 A second time he said to him, "Simon, son of John, do you love me?" He said to him, "Yes, Lord; you know that I love you." He said to him, "Tend my sheep." 17 He said to him the third time, "Simon, son of John, do you love me?" Peter was grieved because he said to him the third time, "Do you love me?" And he said to him, "Lord, you know everything; you know that I love you." Jesus said to him, "Feed my sheep. 18 Truly, truly, I say to you, when you were young, you girded yourself and walked where you would; but when you are old, you will stretch out your hands, and another will gird you and carry you where you do not wish to go." 19 (This he said to show by what death he was to glorify God.) And after this he said to him, "Follow me."

In the symbolism of the fish (vv. 11–13) the disciples had learned of their opportunities and responsibilities to those outside the church. Now, in the symbolism of the sheep, one of the leaders of the disciples learned of his obligations to those within the Christian fellowship. John 20 had left the status of *Simon Peter* somewhat uncertain following his threefold denial in 18:15–18,25–27. This section provides an account of his full restoration to apostolic service by Jesus himself.

The use of a formal address, *Simon, son of John,* suggests the solemnity of the occasion. The threefold repetition of the question, *do you love me?* (vv. 15,16,17), corresponds to the threefold denial which prompted it. Peter was asked to reaffirm his loyalty to Jesus as emphatically as he had earlier rejected it. Because of a variation in the Greek verbs used for *love* in Jesus' questions and in Peter's answers, there is the strong possibility that in vv. 15 and 16 Jesus was asking for a higher spiritual devotion (*agapaō*) than Peter was ready to give (*phileō*), thus he **grieved** Peter in v. 17 by asking if he loved him even on a human level (*phileō*). In the fourth Gospel, however, these two Greek verbs for *love* sometimes appear to be synonymous; thus it may be that the basic issue is not the kind of love involved but the willingness of Peter to translate personal affection for Jesus into a ministry of concern for the flock. Probably, *Peter was grieved* when Jesus *said to him the third time, Do you love me?* because it reminded him of his third and final failure in the time of testing as signaled by the cockcrow (18:27).

The context does not pinpoint the basis of comparison intended by the reference to loving Jesus *more than these*. Since Peter had returned to his earlier vocation of fishing (v. 3), Jesus may have asked if he loved him more than the boats and nets about the shore. Or, if they conversed near the breakfast fire, Jesus may have inquired whether Simon cared for him more than the other disciples gathered there, as he had implicitly claimed in the upper room (13:37; cf. Mark 14:29). More generally, Jesus may have challenged Peter to decide whether he loved him more than all of those old broken promises which were now only bitter memories.

Whatever the reference, Peter determined to let nothing rival his love for Jesus. Not only was he willing to confess complete loyalty with his lips, a relatively easy thing to do; he was also confident that his Lord, who knew *everything,* would *know* that he loved him. Peter finally realized that the crux of a commitment to Christ lay not in what he said was true, for that could quickly prove to be false (e.g., 13:37), but in what Jesus knew was true in the depths of Peter's being (cf. 2:25; 10:27).

Notice that each time Peter confessed his love, Jesus channeled it with a command to *feed* and *tend* the flock of God (cf. 10:1–5). Despite Peter's miserable performance during the passion, he was not only forgiven but reinstated to service. We sometimes make the distinction that a glaring default of duty may permanently disqualify a minister from further service even though his sin be forgiven by God. Jesus, however, was willing to entrust even his little *lambs* to one who had completely violated his most sacred oaths only a few days before. Not only does one become a disciple through an act of sheer grace, but one also ministers to other disciples because of Christ's willingness to trust those who, despite their love, have failed him so tragically.

Peter's reinstatement provided no easy escape, however, from those sufferings which he had sought to avoid by his denials. As he became *old,* Peter could look forward to the day when he no longer had the freedom that was his when *young* to dress himself and go where he pleased. Instead, he would **stretch out** his **hands** preparatory to being crucified and *another* would *gird* him and carry him out to a place of execution where he did *not wish to go.* But Peter need not concern himself with that future prospect, however bleak. Rather, his present responsibility was to *follow* Jesus to the end, even if that end meant death (cf. on 1:43). As the context emphasizes, this obedience was no private or momentary matter but involved the constant care of the flock.

The Evangelist inserted a parenthetical comment explaining that the reference to Peter's crucifixion as a helpless old man was *said to show by what death he was to glorify God.* This presumably means that the prophecy of martyrdom had been fulfilled and was known to the editor of this final chapter. If so, then the earliest date for the fourth Gospel would be after the execution of Peter. There is no certain information on this point, although it is likely that Peter perished in the Neronian persecution ca. A.D. 64.[47]

[47] For a detailed study of Peter's martyrdom see Oscar Cullmann, *Peter: Disciple—Apostle—Martyr*

3. The Death of the Beloved Disciple (21:20–23)

20 Peter turned and saw following them the disciple whom Jesus loved, who had lain close to his breast at the supper and had said, "Lord, who is it that is going to betray you?" 21 When Peter saw him, he said to Jesus, "Lord, what about this man?" 22 Jesus said to him, "If it is my will that he remain until I come, what is that to you? Follow me!" 23 The saying spread abroad among the brethren that this disciple was not to die; yet Jesus did not say to him that he was not to die, but, "If it is my will that he remain until I come, what is that to you?"

No sooner was Peter bidden to *follow* Jesus even unto martyrdom than he tried to shift the conversation to a consideration of the fate of *the disciple whom Jesus loved,* pictured earlier in 13:23–25. As this description suggests, the primary role of the beloved disciple was to serve as a crucial link between the early church and the historical Jesus. Even though Peter was also a witness to the earthly life of Jesus, he could not carry out this function as well as the beloved disciple because he lacked his insight into the deeper meaning of historical events (e.g., 20:6–8; 21:7). Thus, Peter was to serve primarily to provide courageous leadership, the beloved disciple to provide theological clarification. Then, as now, both roles are needed if the church is to fulfill its responsibilities effectively.

When Peter saw the beloved disciple *he said to Jesus, Lord, what about this man?* It is not clear whether the question may have been prompted by some dissatisfaction with his own assignment (e.g., because it involved martyrdom) or by some reservations regarding the role of the beloved disciple (e.g., because it did not). It may be too farfetched to see in this question the tensions in the early church between supporters of the Gospel of Mark, which had Peter as its authority, and supporters of the Gospel of John, which had the beloved disciple as its authority, but the suggestion is intriguing. Whatever the cause of Peter's query, Jesus was unwilling for it to create a

("The Library of History and Doctrine" [2d rev. and expanded ed.; Philadelphia: Westminster Press, 1962]), pp. 71–157.

false issue. *If it is my will that he remain until I come, what is that to you? Follow me!* Since every disciple is to live by the *will* of Jesus for his life, he is free from the responsibility of planning either his own destiny or that of others. From the beginning of the Christian pilgrimage to its end, it is enough to *follow* Jesus. That was the first word of discipleship which Peter heard (e.g., Mark 1:17), and here it is the last.

The Evangelist was aware that this *saying* had *spread abroad among the brethren* and was being interpreted as a promise *that* the beloved *disciple was not to die.* Concerned to correct this widespread misunderstanding, the writer explained that *Jesus did not say to him that he was not to die,* but only used a hypothetical case for the sake of emphasis in saying to Peter, *If it is my will that he remain until I come, what is that to you?* From this passage it is possible to infer that the beloved disciple, like Peter, had already died, and that the final editor felt the need to explain his death to those who wrongly supposed that he would survive until the Parousia. It may be that some among those addressed by this Gospel still clung to a view that the world would come to an end before all the original apostolic generation had died.

II. Conclusion to the Gospel (21:24–25)

We have already observed that 20:30–31 serves admirably as a conclusion both to the "book of signs" and to the entire Gospel as well, leaving the possibility that 21:24–25 should be understood as a final comment only on chapter 21. The scope of these verses is much wider, however, suggesting that they were intended to supply an alternate conclusion to the whole book.

Two objections seem to have been raised against the Gospel with sufficient force to require an answer. First, for reasons not given, detractors were impugning the reliability of the eyewitness source on which it depended. A plausible guess is that the problem became acute when other Gospels began to circulate and their champions claimed superiority because they rested on the witness of original apostles such as Peter (see comment on 21:21). By contrast, the beloved disciple was not mentioned as one of the twelve and did not appear in the Gospel story until 13:23.

Second, someone seemed to be accusing the fourth Gospel of omitting "many other things which Jesus did"—i.e., of an excessive selectivity which rendered it incomplete. The occasion for this protest may have been prompted by a comparison with the recently circulated Synoptics, all of which included many matters on which the Gospel of John was silent. The remarkable similarity of the other three Gospels may have sharpened the need for an explanation of the differences in the fourth.

1. The Authenticity of the Gospel (21:24)

24 This is the disciple who is bearing witness to these things, and who has written these things; and we know that his testimony is true.

Without further identification in this verse, the reference intended by *this is the disciple* is surely the beloved disciple of vv. 20–23. Although he may have then been dead, he was still *bearing witness* through the pages of this Gospel (cf. comment on 1:15). The extent of that witness, indicated by the vague expression *these things*, doubtless included more than the incident in vv. 20–23 or even the whole of chapter 21. Probably, the reference is to a *written* source which was utilized by the final editor as the basis for the fourth Gospel, somewhat as the preaching of Peter preserved by Mark may have been the nucleus of the second Gospel.

Although the beloved disciple had *written these things* down in order to perpetuate his memories for future generations, he was not himself the editor of this Gospel in its final form. This is shown by the way in which the editor and his church together looked back on his contribution and affirmed: *we know that his testimony is true* (cf. 19:35). The Gospel was more than a repository of historical information. Its initial impetus was the witness of an original participant in the life of Jesus whose testimony was later confirmed and enriched in the life of a believing community. (On this apostolic *we*, cf. 1:14 and see Hoskyns, pp. 86–95.)

2. The Selectivity of the Gospel (21:25)

25 But there are also many other things which Jesus did; were every one of them to be written, I suppose that the world itself could not contain the books that would be written.

Having referred to the "he" of eyewitness testimony and the "we" of corporate confirmation, the writer in the final verse of the Gospel referred directly to himself as *I*. (On these references to "he—me—I" see treatment of authorship in Introduction.") Forthrightly, he acknowledged an awareness that *there are also many other things which Jesus did* which had not been recorded in his Gospel. Like the third Evangelist, he had followed closely the many efforts to compile narratives of the life of Jesus (Luke 1:1–4). But he was not apologetic that his record had been so selective. If *every one* of the things which Jesus did were *to be written,* we might well *suppose that the world itself could not contain the books that would be written.*

With this closing thought the writer connects the conclusion in chapter 21 with the one in chapter 20. In 21:25 he gives a literary reason for his selectivity: so vast is his subject that otherwise the book would never end! The earlier conclusion in 20:30–31 gave a theological reason for the same decision: faith needs only a limited number of signs in order to be pointed in the direction of true belief. No Gospel should give the impression that from its pages one may see enough (i.e., read enough) to be saved. Finally, the time comes to conclude a Gospel about Jesus Christ in order that the reader may leave behind the written word and discover for himself the living Word, who is greater than all the books about him. So may it be for those in every generation who reach this point in the Gospel of John.